COLONIAL ART IN MEXICO

THE TEXAS PAN AMERICAN SERIES

Anonymous. St. Francis. Oil on wood. Behrens Collection, Mexico City.

COLONIAL ART
IN MEXICO

By MANUEL TOUSSAINT

Translated and Edited by

Elizabeth Wilder Weismann

UNIVERSITY OF TEXAS PRESS, AUSTIN & LONDON

The Texas Pan American Series is published with the assistance of a revolving publication fund established by the Pan-American Sulphur Company and other friends of Latin America in Texas. Publication of this book was also assisted by a grant from the Rockefeller Foundation through the Latin American translation program of the Association of American University Presses. Publication was also assisted by the Institute of Latin American Studies of The University of Texas.

Type set by G&S Typesetters, Austin
Printed by the Steck Company, Austin
Bound by Universal Bookbindery, Inc., San Antonio

TRANSLATOR'S FOREWORD

Este libro representa el esfuerzo realizado durante toda una vida. When a book begins with such a sentence, and when the life was that of the pioneer figure in his field—and when, moreover, this man has been not only an example and a teacher but a friend—the translator's task may well include a comment on the author and his life. That this book is the testament and legacy of the man who, more than any other, created the study and the appreciation of the colonial art of Mexico is our reason for translating it. Other authors may treat the subject with more glamor, may give fuller and more precise treatment of certain parts of it, or may have discovered in the intervening twenty years documentation which would have changed his opinions. The work of Manuel Toussaint is still the cornerstone.

Scholars accustomed to the well-cultivated fields of European art can have no notion of what it was like in the early 1920's in Mexico. Don Manuel had come back from Spain where, as he told me, the realization had come to him that in his own country also there were monasteries and churches and palaces like these, paintings like these, altarpieces which it would be fascinating to compare to those of Burgos and Seville. When he was back in Mexico, he set out, with a handful of companions, usually on horseback, to visit places that no one had noticed for centuries. There were no secondary texts to use, no photographs, no paved roads, no maps; you used the account of a sixteenth-century friar like Father Ponce for a guidebook, and travelled much as he had. Nowadays, when a highway leads your car easily to the door in a few hours, it is difficult to imagine the adventure of reaching Yanhuitlán after a two-day ride from the railroad, of finding the monastery there at the bottom of the valley, immense and noble, crammed with riches, in its decimated village. One thinks of the rough and almost invisible trails, of potluck in Indian villages and straw mats to

sleep on. It was a young man's pilgrimage, rich with discovery and surmise. Accounts of many of these early journeys, first printed in newspapers and periodicals, have been republished in the memorial edition of Toussaint's *Paseos coloniales,* and very delightful reading they are.

But Toussaint did not stop with the graceful and evocative essay. He was not trained as an historian of art; he was an autodidact, and yet he created, as it were, the discipline of art history in Mexico. He observed that there was such a thing, and that it rested on two cornerstones—knowing the monuments, and finding out all one could about them—and that the structure of attribution and generalization would be flimsy and personal without this solid base. He set about finding the artifacts (in a literal sense) and recording them, getting photographic documentation, studying contemporary literature and documents, and watching how they fell together into a significant whole. It would be easy to scoff when he apologizes for misplacing a bibliographical reference (though many of his Latin contemporaries would have disdained to offer one), but the fact is that one can trust his honesty. He had a remarkable modesty, indistinguishable from his dignity; I remember his saying, "Why should I invent these things? The truth is far more interesting."

If this text appears inadequate by the standards of the great art historians, let us credit it with avoiding certain faults common to lesser writers. Toussaint accepts the idea that elements of style are the suitable categories for putting a series of artifacts in order, and for revealing their significant relationships; but he avoids the mistake common in half-baked criticism of applying the ready-made formulæ of European art history (Wölfflinian and otherwise) to America. He is truly a New World historian in his willingness to let the categories of description emerge from the monuments themselves—or to leave them uncatalogued, like a haphazard gathering of wild fruits, if that seems to be their nature.

It was in 1925 that Manuel Toussaint published an astonishing final volume, entitled *1525–1925,* in the series *Iglesias de México,* which he was editing with Dr. Atl and José Benítez. Before this nothing of either comprehensive scope or just appraisal had been published on the colonial period in Mexican art, and until this present text nothing has taken its place. In 1930 Toussaint organized a Seminario de Investigaciones del Arte en México to instruct the personnel of the Secretaría de Hacienda in their task of cataloguing the religious monuments which were now government property. Although they succeeded in publishing their material for only two states, the *Catálogo de construcciones religiosas del estado de Hidalgo* (1940) and the *Catálogo de construcciones religiosas del estado de Yucatán* (1943), these monumental volumes are unrivalled in Latin American art history. In 1934 Toussaint was one of the group who organized the Laboratorio de Arte in the Universidad Nacional, which in 1936 became the Instituto de Investigaciones Estéticas, of which he served as director until his death. In the same year he initiated, in the Facultad de Filosofía y Letras of the University, the chair of the Historia del Arte de la Nueva España, which he held for many years. From 1944 to 1954, as head of the official Dirección de Monumentos Coloniales y de la República, he worked indefatigably for the preservation and recording of the colonial and nineteenth-century monuments of Mexico. There he began to build up a photographic archive which would demonstrate the reality and the wealth of the art he loved.

It is hard to realize now how fresh the field was, and indeed, how revolutionary. In the 1920's, when Toussaint and his friends began to publish, an interest in the colonial period was not merely unfashionable, it required something like courage. Mexico was coming of age, in the full tide of anti-Spanish reaction. They knew they had got to see and value and absorb their Indian inheritance, and it seemed that this could be done only by building up contempt for the other side of the house. "Colonial" was a bad word. But Toussaint argued enthusiastically that the eighteenth-century Baroque, rather than a provincial imitation of Spanish style, was a true expression of the Mexican spirit, just as he saw sixteenth-century sculpture not as a crude

failure to duplicate imported style, but as the first integration of Indian and European. It is owing to the integrity of thinkers like Toussaint that we have come to appreciate the formative colonial period as a key to the American cultures.

The mood in which Don Manuel came to colonial art, the young man's mood of excitement and discovery, stayed with him to the end. That is why it was such a pleasure to travel with him in the later years; that is why we were all his pupils. It was his world, that back country where the great market towns with their noble monastery buildings lay so untouched by the twentieth century, so much like the Colony still. He had a wonderful gift for talking to parish priests—not of directing them, but of encouraging them to value the old churchyard cross. He could speak to the country woman in her little restaurant so eloquently in the morning that when we sat down that evening after a hard day in the jeep, there would be a chicken unreasonably delicious in the *cazuela.* And while, witty and urbane, he presided over this feast by candlelight, one realized that he could do this because he belonged there, in that little room in that wide mysterious country, which was still emerging, still realizing the destiny spelled out in its art.

A word about the Spanish text and its documentation. It was actually finished in 1945, although some additions and changes were made before publication in 1949; at the time of Toussaint's death in 1955 he was engaged in revising it for a new edition. This new edition was issued by the Instituto de Investigaciones Estéticas in 1961, with some changes and some additional material, mainly in the notes. There are consequently a number of differences between the two editions, usually trivial, but in a few cases extended and significant. It has been my intention to follow the second edition, both in arrangement and in the slight emendations which usually represent a bringing up to date of the material. In the few instances where I found a conflict, I have had to make my own choice, according to the information I have, and influenced by corrections Don Manuel had noted in the copy he gave me in 1949.

When we planned this translation, it was a temptation to consider a thorough editing of the text, with the addition of all new material in footnotes, and an opportunity for the translator to register disagreement with certain conclusions of the author's. In the end, however, we decided to follow the decision of Justino Fernández in preparing the second edition, and to present this book, now almost twenty years old, as an historic text: the first essay at a full statement on colonial art in Mexico.

In the notes also we follow the second edition of the *Arte Colonial en México*. Nevertheless, we have tried to indicate new and additional material as far as possible within the existing bibliographical framework. Our changes consist in (1) citing fully the sources indicated in the text, and (2) adding relevant new titles. A new Bibliography, more than double the list of authors cited in the second edition, is augmented not only by titles published since 1961, but also by other useful titles, especially in English. There is further a more

specific effort at up-dating: the indication of new information pertinent to specific points in the text. These titles have been added to the footnotes, without editorial comment, for readers who may wish to pursue them. Thus newly found documentation which would obviously have changed Toussaint's opinion is indicated at the point where the discussion occurs, as are general studies more detailed than the scope of this book allows. We have not always been successful in identifying and emending Toussaint's bibliographical references; where we could not do so, we have left the notes as he gave them, in the hope that others may be more agile.

Elizabeth Wilder Weismann

Austin, Texas

ACKNOWLEDGMENTS

Our heartiest thanks go to the Instituto de Investigaciones Estéticas of the Universidad Nacional Autónoma de México, for their full and unreserved cooperation in the preparation of this volume. From the time when Manuel Toussaint himself welcomed the first suggestion of a translation, through the final preparation, the personnel of the Institute, and particularly its present director, Dr. Justino Fernández, have done everything possible to further the project. We are indebted to them above all for their generosity in making available photographs used in the second Mexican edition, which have provided the bulk of our illustrations.

We must also acknowledge with gratitude the assistance of Jorge Enciso, director of the Archivo de Monumentos Coloniales y de la República of the Instituto Nacional de Antropología e Historia, in providing photographs from their negatives, of Antonio Arriaga, director of the Museo Nacional de Historia, and of Miguel Celorio, director of the Museo Nacional del Virreinato. A number of scholars in the field have generously contributed further illustrations: John McAndrew, Pal Kelemen, Loren Mozley, and the late Martin Soria. Miss Nettie Lee Benson, librarian of the Latin American Collections of The University of Texas, has been, as always, cooperative at every turn. A quantity of friends here and in Mexico have helped with the worrying out of Mexican idiom and antique technical terms, especially Max Cetto, of Mexico City, and Luis Eades, of Boulder, Colorado. Special thanks go to Veronica Cetto for her indefatigable pursuit of the illustrative material and for other on-the-spot chores in Mexico.

We note appreciatively that it was Lewis Hanke, then director of the Institute of Latin American Studies at The University of Texas, who originally proposed and encouraged this publication, and that John P. Harrison, the present director, has continued to give us his enthusiastic encouragement. Without the continuous personal interest of the staff of The University of Texas Press the whole project might have failed. The translator must note a personal debt to Press personnel, also, for infinite care in preparing for publication this long text, with its unregenerate inconsistencies, ancient and modern.

FOREWORD TO THE SECOND EDITION

In the year 1955 the Instituto de Investigaciones Estéticas suffered the loss of its director, Dr. Manuel Toussaint, who had founded it twenty years before as the Laboratorio de Arte. Those of us who have enjoyed the privilege of working with him and who have profited by his teaching feel deeply the loss of our master. He was the greatest authority on our colonial art, and he knew how to communicate his knowledge and enthusiasm to students, collaborators, and friends.

The scholars of the Institute, wishing to pay just homage to the memory of Manuel Toussaint, resolved to publish three of his works: first, his *Arte colonial en México,* which had appeared in 1948 and had been for some time out of print; next, his *Paseos coloniales,* of which only a part had been published in 1939; and finally, an unpublished manuscript on colonial painting. The plan for these publications received frank and enthusiastic support from the authorities of the University and, naturally, from Señora Margarita Latapí de Toussaint, his widow, who made available whatever materials were in her possession to assist the project. For this we thank her.

We wish also to note that at the outset the Institute received the cooperation of Dr. Nabor Carrillo and Dr. Efrén C. del Pozo, respectively rector and secretary general of the University, and also of the then director general of publications, Professor Henrique González Casanova. Since then the present rector, Dr. Ignacio Chávez, has given every sort of help, and the director general of publications, Lic. Rubén Bonifaz Nuño, has collaborated effectively, as have the director of the Imprenta Universitaria, Sr. Manuel T. Moreno, and Sr. Ramón Luna, Jefe del Departamento de Corrección.

Thanks are due to various members of the Institute for their efforts and advice, especially Lic. José Rojas Garcidueñas and Dr. Francisco de la Maza. Others have helped in various ways, and the color photographs are the work of Professor Pedro Rojas. Professor Xavier Moyssén Echevería has been directly responsible for the present edition, in close collaboration with the writer; he collected the illustrative material, of which we had less than half, he added to the text certain notes and corrections which Dr. Toussaint had left in manuscript, he was responsible for the proofreading and for supervising the printing, and, in short, we owe this second edition of the *Arte colonial en México* in great part to him.

Except for the notes mentioned above, the text is actually the same as in the original edition. It seemed to us proper to respect the master's work, and to leave it just as he wrote it, in its historical relationship to the study of colonial art.

We decided to present his volume, and the other two which are to follow, in a new format easier to handle than the first edition. It has been designed with a more compact text, in order to increase the number of illustrations by more than a hundred, as well as to improve their quality by avoiding small cuts. It seemed that to separate the illustrations from the text would facilitate consulting them; the reader will find in the margins of the text numbers which refer to the illustrations, easily located by this device. All the notes referring to the various chapters have been placed, with the Bibliography and the Index, at the end of the volume. A special bibliography of studies published after the first edition of the *Arte colonial* has been added to complete that of Don Manuel Toussaint, covering the period 1950–1962.

For the present edition it has been necessary to make new indexes, of artists and of places, for which Srta. Luz Gorráez Arcaute has been responsible, assisted by Srta. Guadalupe Hernández Álvarez and Sr. Danilo Ongay M.

This edition has been enriched by ten color plates

scattered through the text, in order to give a better idea of some monuments and works of art referred to by the author.

For all these reasons we hope that students will find this edition a better presentation of this work which has been unobtainable because it was out of print. And we trust also that the fruit of Manuel Toussaint's knowledge and experience will continue to inspire the study of our colonial art in the future. In any case, whatever is done in this field must build on what the master accomplished. Thus this tribute to his memory may mean also the living continuation of his teaching.

El Director del Instituto de Investigaciones Estéticas

Dr. Justino Fernández

PREFACE

This book represents the effort and achievement of a whole life. Here I offer as a whole, synthesized and ordered, the material which has been partially presented in essays, travel notes, articles, and lectures. It appears as the second volume of the *History of Art in Mexico* projected by the Instituto de Investigaciones Estéticas of the National University of Mexico. The first volume was the *Arte precolumbina de México y de la América Central* by Salvador Toscano, which has been so well received by the critics. Although sponsored and published by the Institute, both of these books are the result of the private research of their authors. We hope soon to have from Justino Fernández a third volume dealing with *Arte Moderno en México,* from 1821 to the present, to complete the series. The realization of this project would in itself justify the existence of the Instituto de Investigaciones Estéticas, without their long history of other publications and activities acclaimed by universities, museums, and scholars in Mexico and abroad.

I am attempting, then, to make a complete history of what is known as colonial art. It is true that no one man can achieve this; essential historical documentation is still lacking, as well as illustrative material necessary to the task. All we can do is to present, quite boldly, what we do know and what we surmise about this complicated material. My interest is not in merely cataloguing it, but in realizing its significance as a whole. If generalizations are often followed by the inevitable lists of works or of artists, it is for the purpose of documenting my statements, and of providing the concrete visual evidence to demonstrate the validity of my assertions.

Now that it is done, I myself am conscious of many doubts and criticisms. It would be a grave fault, certainly, to have left out any important example in the various categories of colonial art. The interested reader or the scholar in search of documentation should not be disappointed by finding no mention of it in this history. And yet, although I trust that no really important monument has been left out, it is almost inevitable that many which I do not know about, or have forgotten, must have been omitted. But this is perhaps not so serious a fault, since I have formulated categories and distinguished styles by which the monuments which are not included, and even those which are still to be discovered, can be classified. It is a fact indeed that in this field new and unknown treasures are found every day. Another problem has to do with my ideas about the divisions of the colonial period; especially in dealing with the Baroque style this has resulted in a certain confusion in the grouping of the monuments. But this could hardly be avoided: indeed the explanation is to be found in the subject itself. Surely it would be absurd to expect a systematic and orderly study of an art which is characterized precisely by disorder.

So I recognize in advance all the defects of this work, not only those I admit to, but also those which will be pointed out by the people who habitually criticize other people's books instead of writing their own. Even so, I believe that this work will serve as a foundation for others which will enlarge it and carry it further.

The Bibliography differs from those which ornament books nowadays; I prefer the old method, which is more trouble but which I find more efficient. That is, I give a general bibliography to begin with, and for each chapter I cite the references supporting my statements there, and the relevant special texts. The scope of the work has meant that in some cases I have lost page references, or even the citations for documents. I can give you the fullest assurance, however, that I have invented nothing; I am heartily sorry for these involuntary omissions, for which I can only offer my sincerest apologies.

Since the original intention, to have this volume as well as its two companions published by a commercial press, has failed, we three authors must express our gratitude to the University for their ready support, acknowledging the cradle, the source, the noble house from which we have all sprung. It is for this reason that my book is dedicated to the Universidad Nacional Autónoma de México. I should like to note that it was the support of Don Alfonso Caso, Don Genaro Fernández MacGregor, and Don Salvador Zubirán, in their position as rectors, and of Don Eduardo García Máynez and Don Francisco González Castro, as secretaries of the University, which made possible this publication. With all the defects natural in a period when any cultural undertaking meets with difficulties, it represents a great achievement.

Finally I wish to express my thanks for the help and collaboration of those who have provided data, photographs, and information. I thank Dr. Don Gabriel Méndez Plancarte for the beautiful Latin translation of the dedication, Señorita María Josefina Sánchez, my faithful assistant, for transcribing the text and for the arduous task of the alphabetical index, my comrades in the Imprenta Universitaria for their careful work, and all who have encouraged me to carry out this work.

CONTENTS

Translator's Foreword vii
Acknowledgments xi
Foreword to the Second Edition xiii
Preface xv
List of Plates xix
Introduction 3

Part One
Art in New Spain at the Time of the Conquest
The Middle Ages in Mexico, 1519–1550

1. Medieval Architecture 9
2. Medieval Painting 38
3. Medieval Sculpture 48
4. The Minor Arts of the Middle Ages 63

Part Two
Art during the Colonization of New Spain
The Renaissance in Mexico, 1550–1630

5. Renaissance Architecture 77
6. Renaissance Painting 129
7. Renaissance Sculpture 153
8. The Minor Arts of the Renaissance Period 162

Part Three
Art in New Spain during the Formation of the Nation
The Baroque Style in Mexico, 1630–1730

9. Baroque Architecture 179
10. Baroque Sculpture 213
11. Baroque Painting in Mexico City 225
12. Provincial Painting 249
13. The Minor Arts during the Early Baroque Period 258

Part Four
Pride and Wealth
The Climax of the Baroque in Mexico, 1730–1781

14. The Great Religious Architecture 275
15. Civil Architecture of the Eighteenth Century 303
16. Painting in Mexico City during the Eighteenth Century . . . 333

17. Painting in the Provinces of New Spain in the Eighteenth Century . . 342
18. Sculpture in the Eighteenth Century 347
19. The Minor Arts of the Churrigueresque Period 358
20. Popular Art in Mexico 382

Part Five
*Art and the Independence of Mexico
Neoclassic Art, 1781–1821*

21. The Royal Academy of San Carlos of New Spain 401
22. Neoclassic Architecture in New Spain 405
23. Neoclassic Sculpture 430
24. Academic Painting in New Spain 440
25. Minor and Graphic Arts 449

Conclusion 457
Sources of Illustrations 459
Bibliography 461
Index 477

LIST OF PLATES

COLOR PLATES   *Facing page*

1. Anonymous. St. Francis. Oil on wood. . . v
2. Anonymous. Pietà (detail). Mural, cloister of the Augustinian monastery, Epazoyucan, Hidalgo. 132
3. Sebastián López de Arteaga. Doubting Thomas (detail). Oil on canvas. 148
4. House of the Conde del Valle de Orizaba (Casa de los Azulejos), Mexico City. . . . 316
5. Angel from a retable. Polychrome and gilded wood. 348
6. Side altar, convent church of La Enseñanza, Mexico City. 356
7. Ignacio María Barreda. Doña Juana María Romero. Oil on canvas. 388
8. Francisco Eduardo Tresguerras. Portrait of his Wife, María Guadalupe Ramírez. Oil on canvas. 420
9. Rafael Jimeno y Planes. Portrait of Jerónimo Antonio Gil. Oil on canvas. 444

BLACK-AND-WHITE PLATES   *Page*

1. City wall, Campeche. 10
2. Fort of San Juan de Ulua and Veracruz in the nineteenth century. 11
3. Map of Mexico City by Alonso de Santa Cruz. 1550–1562. 12
4. Map of Teutenango (Tenango del Valle). 1582. 13
5. Palace of Cortés, Cuernavaca, Morelos. . . 15
6. Las Monjas, Mérida, Yucatán. 15
7. The Plaza Mayor of Veracruz. C. 1830. Oil. . 17
8. Patio of the Hospital de Jesús, Mexico City. . 18
9. Portal of the hospital chapel, Acámbaro, Guanajuato. 19
10. The Plaza Mayor of Mexico City. C. 1565. . 22
11. The Plaza Mayor of Mexico City. 1596. . . 22
12. Nave, church of the Dominican monastery (before 1935), Coyoacán, Distrito Federal. . 24

13. Nave, church of the Franciscan monastery, Zacatlán (de las Manzanas), Puebla. . . . 25
14. Church and open chapel, Franciscan monastery, Tlahuelilpa, Hidalgo. 26
15. Open chapel, Franciscan monastery, Tlalmanalco, México. 27
16. Open chapel, Dominican monastery, Teposcolula, Oaxaca. 28
17. Plan of the open chapel, Dominican monastery, Teposcolula, Oaxaca. 28
18. Plan of the Capilla Real, Franciscan monastery, Cholula, Puebla. 29
19. Façade, Capilla Real, Franciscan monastery, Cholula, Puebla. 30
20. Interior, Capilla Real, Franciscan monastery, Cholula, Puebla. 30
21. Nave, unfinished basilica, Dominican monastery, Cuilapan, Oaxaca. 31
22. Cloister, Franciscan monastery, Huexotla, México. 32
23. Aqueduct of Cempoala. State of Hidalgo. . 33
24. Town fountain, Chiapa de Corzo, Chiapas. . 34
25. Town fountain, Tochimilco, Puebla. . . . 35
26. Town fountain (before 1942), Texcoco, México. 35
27. El Rollo, Tepeaca, Puebla. 36
28. Diego de Valadés. Allegorical Churchyard. . 39
29. Anonymous. Fray Diego de Betanzos. Mural, Franciscan monastery, Tepetlaóztoc, México. . 39
30. Wall decoration, patio of the Hospital de Jesús, Mexico City. 40
31. Anonymous. St. Francis Renouncing His Worldly Goods. Mural, cloister of the Franciscan monastery, Cholula, Puebla. . . 41
32. Anonymous. The Crucifixion. Mural, cloister of the Franciscan monastery, Huejotzingo, Puebla. 42
33. Monogram of Jesus. Mural, Franciscan monastery, Huejotzingo, Puebla. 43
34. Title-Page, *Confesionario breve de Fray Alonso de Molina*. 1569. 43

35. Wall Decoration, cloister of the Augustinian monastery, Culhuacán, Distrito Federal. . . 43
36. Cortés Meets Moctezuma in Tenochtitlán (Mexico City). From the "Lienzo de Tlaxcala" (copy made by Juan Manuel de Illanes). . . 45
37. Making feather work. From the Florentine Codex. 46
38. Date stone, church of the Franciscan monastery, Tecamachalco, Puebla. . . . 49
39. Eagle Knight, portal of a house, Cholula, Puebla. 49
40. Cristo del Pareo. Corn pith, painted. . . 50
41. La Conquistadora. Painted wood. Cathedral of Puebla. 50
42. Descent from the Cross. Wood. Church of El Calvario, Chiapa de Corzo, Chiapas. . . 51
43. The Last Judgment. Posa III, Franciscan monastery, Calpan, Puebla. 52
44. The Last Judgment. Engraving, from Flos Sanctorum. 53
45. Portal, church of Santiago, Angahua, Michoacán. 54
46. Portal, La Guatapera (chapel of the hospital), Uruapan, Michoacán. 55
47. Churchyard cross. Stone. Franciscan monastery, Cuauhtitlán, México. 56
48. Churchyard cross. Stone. Franciscan monastery, Huichapan, Hidalgo. 57
49. Churchyard cross. Stone. Augustinian monastery, Acolman, México. 58
50. Churchyard cross. Stone. Franciscan monastery, Ciudad Hidalgo, Michoacán. 58
51. Baptismal font. Stone. Church of the Franciscan monastery, Zinacantepec, México. . 59
52. Stoup. Stone. Church of the Franciscan monastery, Tlalnepantla, México. . . . 59
53. Pulpit. Stone. Church of the Franciscan monastery, Huaquechula, Puebla. . . . 60
54. Pulpit. Stone. Church of the Franciscan monastery, Huejotzingo, Puebla. . . . 60
55. Dog. Stone. From the fountain of Tepeaca. . 61
56. Lion. Stone. 61
57. Silver crozier; mitre. Embroidered in silver, gold, and pearls. 64
58. Processional cross. Silver. 65
59. Chalice. Silver. 66
60. Stirrups (known as Cortés'). Iron. . . . 68
61. Chest. Wood with wrought iron. . . . 70
62. Gremial of Archbishop Zumárraga (detail). Silk and metal embroidery on velvet. . . . 71
63. Christ as Pantocrator. Feather mosaic. . . 73
64. Plan of the Augustinian monastery, Acolman, México. 78
65. Plan of the Dominican Monastery, Oaxtepec, Morelos. 78
66. Plan of the Franciscan monastery, Huejotzingo, Puebla. 78
67. Churchyard, with church and open chapel, Franciscan monastery, Cholula, Puebla. . . 79
68. Gate to the churchyard, Franciscan monastery, Huejotzingo, Puebla. 79
69. Church, through the churchyard gate, Franciscan monastery, Tula, Hidalgo. . . . 80
70. Posa I, Franciscan monastery, Huejotzingo, Puebla. 80
71. Façade of church and portería, Franciscan monastery, Huejotzingo, Puebla. 80
72. Nave and chancel, church of the Franciscan monastery, Huejotzingo, Puebla. 81
73. Vaulting of the nave, church of the Franciscan monastery, Atlixco, Puebla. 81
74. Exterior, church of the Franciscan monastery, Tepeaca, Puebla. 81
75. Cloister, Franciscan monastery, Huejotzingo, Puebla. 82
76. Refectory, Augustinian monastery, Actopan, Hidalgo. 83
77. View of the Franciscan monastery, Huejotzingo, Puebla. 83
78. West portal, church of the Franciscan monastery, Huejotzingo, Puebla. 84
79. Nave, church of the Franciscan monastery, Tlaxcala. 85
80. Cloister, Franciscan monastery, Tula, Hidalgo. 85
81. North portal, church of the Franciscan monastery, Huaquechula, Puebla. 86
82. St. Peter. North portal, church of the Franciscan monastery, Huaquechula, Puebla. . 86
83. Date stone, Franciscan monastery, Huaquechula, Puebla. 87
84. Façade, church of the Franciscan monastery, Tecali, Puebla. 87
85. Posa II, Franciscan monastery, Calpan, Puebla. 88
86. Posa III, Franciscan monastery, Calpan, Puebla. 88
87. Façade, church of the Augustinian monastery, Yecapixtla, Morelos. 91
88. Façade, Augustinian church and monastery, Epazoyucan, Hidalgo. 92
89. Façade, Augustinian church and monastery, Acolman, México. 93
90. Façade, church of the Augustinian monastery, Yuriria, Guanajuato. 94

91. Facade, church of the Augustinian monastery, Acolman, México. 95

92. Cloister, Augustinian monastery, Acolman, México. 96

93. Nave and chancel, church of the Augustinian monastery, Metztitlán, Hidalgo. . . . 96

94. Façade, church and portería of the Augustinian monastery, Actopan, Hidalgo. 97

95. Baptistry, church of the Augustinian monastery, Actopan, Hidalgo. 98

96. Façade, church of the Augustinian monastery, Yuriria, Guanajuato. 98

97. Cloister, Augustinian monastery, Yuriria, Guanajuato. 99

98. Cloister walk, Augustinian monastery, Yuriria, Guanajuato. 99

99. Portal, church of the Augustinian monastery, Cuitzeo, Michoacán. 100

100. Portal (detail), church of the Augustinian monastery, Cuitzeo, Michoacán. 100

101. Cloister, Augustinian monastery, Cuitzeo, Michoacán. 101

102. Portal, church of the Dominican monastery, Tepoztlán, Morelos. 103

103. Upper cloister, Dominican monastery, Tepoztlán, Morelos. 104

104. Merlons on the roof, Dominican monastery, Tepoztlán, Morelos. 104

105. Portal, church of the Dominican monastery, Chimalhuacán-Chalco, México. . . . 105

106. Facade, church of the Dominican monastery, Coixtlahuaca, Oaxaca. 105

107. Façade, church of the Dominican monastery, Oaxaca. 106

108. Cloister, Dominican monastery, Oaxaca. . . 107

109. Main Altarpiece (detail). Church of the Dominican monastery, Yanhuitlán, Oaxaca. . 108

110. Cathedral of Oaxaca. 110

111. Scheme of the Cathedral of Michoacán. . . 111

112. Façade, Cathedral of Mérida, Yucatán. . . 112

113. Nave, Cathedral of Mérida, Yucatán. . . 112

114. Cathedral of Guadalajara, Jalisco. . . . 113

115. Nave, Cathedral of Guadalajara, Jalisco. . . 114

116. Exterior, church of the Franciscan monastery, Xochimilco, Distrito Federal. 117

117. North portal, church of the Franciscan monastery, Huejotzingo, Puebla. . . . 119

118. Doorway to the chapter room, Cathedral of Mexico, Mexico City. 120

119. Project for remodelling the Palace of the Viceroys. 121

120. Portal, Cabildo (Palacio de Gobierno), Tlaxcala. 121

121. Façade, House of Montejo, Mérida, Yucatán. . . 122

122. Portal of a house, Puebla. 123

123. Portal of a house, Puebla. 124

124. Façade, house of Luis de Mazariegos, San Cristóbal de las Casas, Chiapas. . . . 125

125. Corner of a house (Argentina and Guatemala Streets), Mexico City. 126

126. Façade, chapel of El Rosario, Xochimilco, Distrito Federal. 127

127. Augustinian Fathers. Mural in the stairwell, Augustinian monastery, Actopan, Hidalgo. . 130

128. Anonymous. Pietà. Mural in the cloister, Augustinian monastery, Epazoyucan, Hidalgo. 131

129. Vault under the choir loft, church of the Franciscan monastery, Tecamachalco, Puebla. . 131

130. Juan Gersón. Scene from the Apocalypse. Choir vault, church of the Franciscan monastery, Tecamachalco, Puebla. . . . 132

131. Simón Pereyns. La Virgen del Perdón (detail). Oil. 133

132. Simón Pereyns. Adoration of the Shepherds. Oil. 135

133. Francisco de Zumaya. St. Sebastian. Oil. . . 136

134. Alonso Vásquez. St. Michael. Oil. . . . 138

135. Alonso López de Herrera. Assumption of the Virgin. Oil. 140

136. Baltasar de Echave Orio (the Elder). The Porciuncula. Oil. 142

137. Baltasar de Echave Ibía. Portrait of a Lady. Oil. 144

138. Baltasar de Echave Ibía. Virgin of the Apocalypse. Oil. 145

139. Luis Juárez. Communion of St. Stanislaus of Kostka. Oil. 146

140. Sebastián López de Arteaga. Marriage of the Virgin. Oil. 147

141. Sebastián López de Arteaga. Doubting Thomas. Oil. 148

142. Martin de Vos. St. John the Evangelist. Oil. . 151

143. Main altarpiece (detail). Church of the Franciscan monastery, Xochimilco, Distrito Federal. 154

144. Saint. Main altarpiece, church of the Franciscan monastery, Xochimilco, Distrito Federal. 154

145. Virgin Mary. Main altarpiece, church of the Franciscan monastery, Xochimilco, Distrito Federal. 155

146. Main altarpiece, church of the Franciscan monastery, Huejotzingo, Puebla. . . . 156

147. Saint. Main altarpiece, church of the Franciscan monastery, Huejotzingo, Puebla. . . . 156

148. Main altarpiece, church of the Franciscan monastery, Cuautinchán, Puebla. 157
149. Retable. Church of the Franciscan monastery, Maní, Yucatán. 157
150. Assumption of the Virgin. Main altarpiece, Franciscan monastery, Milpa Alta, Distrito Federal. 158
151. Virgin and Child. Stone. 160
152. Adoration of the Magi (detail). Stone. . . 161
153. Virgin and Child with St. Anne. Painted and gilded wood. 161
154. Platter. Silver. 165
155. Thurible. Silver. 165
156. Marcos Maestre. Capa Pluvial (detail). Silk and metal embroidery. 169
157. Grille and gate. Wrought iron. Chapel of El Santo Cristo, Tlacolula, Oaxaca. . . . 171
158. Chest. Inlaid wood with wrought iron. . . 172
159. Font. Ceramic. Church of the Franciscan monastery, Tepepan, Distrito Federal. . . . 174
160. Talavera vase, Mudejar type. 175
161. Façade, convent church of Las Monjas (Santa Catarina), Morelia, Michoacán. 180
162. Façade, convent church of La Concepción, Mexico City. 181
163. Cathedral of Mexico and Sagrario Metropolitano, Mexico City. 182
164. Nave and choir, Cathedral of Mexico, Mexico City. 183
165. Cathedral of Puebla. 184
166. Nave and choir, Cathedral of Puebla. . . 184
167. Cathedral of Morelia, Michoacán. . . . 185
168. Façade, Cathedral of Morelia, Michoacán. . 185
169. Cathedral of San Cristóbal de las Casas, Chiapas. 186
170. National Palace, Mexico City. Lithograph. . 187
171. National Palace (after 1927), Mexico City. . 187
172. Patio, Colegio de San Ignacio (Universidad de Puebla), Puebla. 188
173. Casa Sola, Avenida Uruguay, Mexico City. . 188
174. Casa de Vecindad. Lithograph. . . . 189
175. Façade, monastery church of San Lorenzo, Mexico City. 191
176. Façade, church and monastery of San Diego (Museo de Churubusco), Churubusco, Distrito Federal. 192
177. House, Avenida 16 de Septiembre, Puebla. . 193
178. Portal, church of La Profesa (San José el Real), Mexico City. 194
179. Façade, convent church of Corpus Christi, Mexico City. 195
180. Façade, church of San Cristóbal, Puebla. . . 196
181. Façade, church of La Soledad, Oaxaca. . . 197

182. Virgen de la Soledad. Façade, church of La Soledad. Oaxaca. 198
183. Portal, convent church of Santa Mónica, Guadalajara, Jalisco. 199
184. St. Christopher. Convent church of Santa Mónica, Guadalajara, Jalisco. 199
185. Façade, church of Santa Cruz de las Flores, Santa Cruz, Jalisco. 200
186. Façade, chapel of San Antonio, Texcoco, México. 201
187. Cloister, monastery of La Merced, Mexico City. 202
188. Façade (detail), monastery church of La Merced, Atlixco, Puebla. 203
189. Rosary chapel, monastery church of Santo Domingo, Puebla. 204
190. Tree of Jesse (detail). Painted stucco. Choir vault, monastery church of Santo Domingo, Oaxaca. 205
191. Chapel of El Santo Cristo, Dominican monastery, Tlacolula, Oaxaca. 206
192. Façade, Church of San Francisco, Acatepec, Puebla. 207
193. Chancel, Church of San Francisco, Acatepec, Puebla. 208
194. Charity. Painted stucco. Nave, church of San Francisco, Acatepec, Puebla. 208
195. Chancel and dome, church of Santa María, Tonantzintla, Puebla. 209
196. Decoration on pendentive (detail). Nave, church of Santa María, Tonantzintla, Puebla. . 209
197. Camarín of the Virgin, Sanctuary of Ocotlán, Tlaxcala. 210
198. Camarín of the Virgin of Loreto, church of San Martín (Museo Nacional del Virreinato), Tepotzotlán, México. 211
199. Retable. Camarín of the Virgin of Loreto, church of San Felipe Neri, San Miguel Allende, Guanajuato. 210
200. Upper facade, Cathedral of Zacatecas, Zacatecas. 212
201. Main altarpiece (detail). Gilded and painted wood. Church of the Augustinian monastery, Metztitlán, Hidalgo. 214
202. Main altarpiece. Monastery church of Santo Domingo, Puebla. 215
203. Main altarpiece. Church of the Franciscan monastery, Ozumba, Mexico. 216
204. Archangel Gabriel. Capilla de los Ángeles, Cathedral of Mexico. 216
205. St. Augustine as Protector. Façade, monastery church of San Agustín (Biblioteca Nacional), Mexico City. 217

206. Assumption of the Virgin. Façade, Cathedral of Mexico. 218
207. Annunciation. Stone. Monastery church of San Lorenzo, Mexico City. 219
208. Descent from the Cross. Painted wood. Sacristy, church of the Dominican monastery, Yanhuitlán, Oaxaca. 219
209. Don Pedro Ruiz de Ahumada. Painted wood. Seminario de San Martín (Museo Nacional del Virreinato), Tepotzotlán, Mexico. . . . 219
210. Choir stalls from the monastery church of San Agustín. Wood. 220
211. God Creating the Sun and Moon. Choir stall from San Agustín. 220
212. Choir of the Cathedral of Mexico. Wood. . 221
213. Choir of the Cathedral of Mexico (detail). Wood. 221
214. Caryatid on a retable. Church of the Franciscan monastery, Quecholac, Puebla. . . . 222
215. St. Clare, from a retable. Painted and gilded wood. Chapel of the Virgen de Aranzazu, Guadalajara, Jalisco. 223
216. José Juárez. The Sainted Children Justus and Pastor. Oil. 226
217. José Juárez. Martyrdom of St. Lawrence. Oil. 227
218. Pedro Ramírez. Christ Waited upon by Angels (detail). Oil. 228
219. Pedro Ramírez. Liberation of St. Peter. Oil. . 229
220. Baltasar de Echave y Rioja (the Younger). Martyrdom of St. Peter Arbués. Oil. . . . 230
221. Antonio Rodríguez. St. Augustine. Oil. . . 232
222. Juan Sánchez Salmerón. Annunciation to Joachim. Oil. 234
223. Juan Correa. Assumption of the Virgin. Oil. . 236
224. Juan Correa. The Apocalypse. Oil (burned, 1967). 237
225. Cristóbal de Villalpando. The Immaculate Conception. Oil. 238
226. Cristóbal de Villalpando. An Allegory of the Church (detail). Oil. 239
227. Cristóbal de Villalpando. The Triumph of the Eucharist (detail). Oil. 240
228. Nicolás Rodríguez Juárez. Marqués de Santa Cruz. Oil. 242
229. Juan Rodríguez Juárez. St. John of God. Oil. . 244
230. Juan Rodríguez Juárez. Duque de Linares, Viceroy of Mexico. Oil. 245
231. Miguel de Herrera. María Josefa de Aldaco y Fragoaga. Oil. 246
232. Luis Lagarto. Illumination from a choir book. Watercolor on parchment. 250
233. Luis Lagarto. Nativity. Parchment. . . . 251

234. Diego de Borgraf. St. Francis. Oil. . . . 252
235. Juan Tinoco. St. James. Oil. 253
236. Monstrance. Silver. 259
237. Brooch. Silver and jewels. 260
238. Brooch, reverse. Silver. 260
239. Chair from the Old Cabildo of Mexico City. Wood with embroidered leather. 262
240. Chair. Wood with embroidered velvet. . . 262
241. Grille and gate. Wrought iron and sheet iron. Church of El Santo Ángel, Analco, Puebla. . 263
242. Lock and hinges. Wrought iron. 264
243. Talavera flowerpot, Chinese type. 265
244. Screen and gallery of the choir. Cathedral of Mexico. 267
245. Main altarpiece. Gilded and painted wood. Church of Santa Prisca, Taxco, Guerrero. . 276
246. Convent church of Santa Brígida (destroyed, 1933), Mexico City. 279
247. Chapel of El Pocito, Villa Madero, Distrito Federal. 280
248. Plan, chapel of El Pocito, Villa Madero, Distrito Federal. 280
249. Sagrario Metropolitano, Mexico City. . . . 281
250. South portal, Sagrario Metropolitano, Mexico City. 283
251. Church of the Santísima Trinidad, Mexico City. 284
252. Balvanera chapel, monastery of San Francisco, Mexico City. Lithograph. 285
253. Nave, convent church of La Enseñanza, Mexico City. 285
254. Nave, convent church of Santa Clara, Querétaro. 286
255. Grille, convent church of Santa Clara, Querétaro. 287
256. Choir, convent church of Santa Rosa de Viterbo, Querétaro. 288
257. Retable of the Virgin. Convent church of Santa Rosa de Viterbo, Querétaro. 288
258. Cloister, monastery of San Agustín (Palacio Municipal), Querétaro. 289
259. Façade, monastery church of San Francisco, Puebla. 289
260. Façade, church of La Valenciana, Guanajuato. 290
261. Dome and chancel, church of La Valenciana, Guanajuato. 291
262. Retable of St. Joseph. Monastery church of San Agustín, Salamanca, Guanajuato. . . . 292
263. Church of La Salud, San Miguel de Allende, Guanajuato. 293
264. Retable. Monastery church of El Carmen, San Luis Potosí. 294

265. Church of Santa Prisca and San Sebastián, Taxco, Guerrero. 295
266. Nave and choir, church of Santa Prisca, Taxco, Guerrero. 296
267. Retable. Capilla de Jesús Nazareno, church of Santa Prisca, Taxco, Guerrero. 297
268. Sacristy, church of Santa Prisca, Taxco, Guerrero. 298
269. Façade, sanctuary of Nuestra Señora de Ocotlán, Tlaxcala. 298
270. Façade (detail), sanctuary of Nuestra Señora de Ocotlán, Tlaxcala. 299
271. Capilla de San José, church of the Seminary of San Martín (Museo Nacional del Virreinato), Tepotzotlán, México. 299
272. Nave, church of the Seminary of San Martín (Museo Nacional del Virreinato), Tepotzotlán, México. 300
273. Façade, church of the Seminary of San Martín (Museo Nacional del Virreinato), Tepotzotlán, México. 301
274. Palace of the Ayuntamiento (Cabildo), Mexico City. 304
275. Palace of the Audiencia de Nueva Galicia (Palacio de Gobierno), Guadalajara, Jalisco. . 305
276. Royal Customs House, Mexico City. . . . 306
277. Seminary (Palacio de Gobierno), Morelia, Michoacán. 306
278. Patio, Holy Office of the Inquisition, Mexico City. 307
279. Façade, College of San Ildefonso (National Preparatory School), Mexico City. . . . 308
280. Patio, College of San Ildefonso, Mexico City. . 308
281. Portal, College of San Ildefonso, Mexico City. 309
282. Façade, College of San Ignacio (Las Vizcaínas), Mexico City. 310
283. Chapel portal, College of San Ignacio (Las Vizcaínas), Mexico City. 311
284. Patio, College of San Ignacio (Las Vizcaínas), Mexico City. 312
285. Patio, Hospital de San Juan de Dios, Atlixco, Puebla. 313
286. Plan of the Hospital Real de San Miguel (Hospital de Belén), Guadalajara, Jalisco. . 313
287. Biblioteca Palafoxiana (Biblioteca del Estado), Puebla. 314
288. The Plaza de Guardiola: House of the Marqués de Santa Fe de Guardiola, house of the Conde del Valle de Orizaba, and monastery of San Francisco, Mexico City. Lithograph. . 316
289. House of the Conde del Valle de Orizaba (Casa de los Azulejos), Mexico City. . . 317
290. House of the Marqués de Jaral de Berrio (of the Conde de San Mateo de Valparaíso of Iturbide), Mexico City. 318
291. Portal, house of the Marqués de Jaral de Berrio, Mexico City. 319
292. Patio, house of the Marqués de Jaral de Berrio, Mexico City. 320
293. House of the Conde de Santiago de Calimaya, Mexico City. 320
294. Portal, house of the Conde de Santiago de Calimaya, Mexico City. 321
295. Patio, house of the Conde de Santiago de Calimaya, Mexico City. 322
296. House of the Marqueses de San Mateo de Valparaíso (Banco Nacional), Mexico City. . 322
297. Portal, house of the Conde de Heras Soto, Mexico City. 323
298. Corner decoration, house of the Conde de Heras Soto, Mexico City. 323
299. House of the Conde de la Cortina, Mexico City. 324
300. Houses of the Mayorazgo de Guerrero (Academia Nacional de Música), Mexico City. 325
301. Country house of the Conde del Valle de Orizaba (Casa de los Mascarones), Mexico City. 326
302. Detail of two houses, Puebla. 327
303. Casa de los Muñecos, Puebla. 328
304. Casa del Alfeñique (Museo de la Ciudad), Puebla. 328
305. Patio of a house, Querétaro. 329
306. House of the Marqués de la Villa del Villar del Águila, Querétaro. 330
307. Noble house, Oaxaca. 331
308. José de Ibarra. Self-Portrait. Oil. 334
309. Miguel Cabrera. Assumption of the Virgin. Oil. 335
310. Miguel Cabrera. Doña María de la Luz Padilla y Cervantes. Oil. 335
311. Miguel Cabrera. Sor Juana Inés de la Cruz. Oil. 336
312. Miguel Cabrera. Sor María Josepha Augustina Dolores. Oil. 337
313. Juan Patricio Morlete Ruiz. St. Louis Gonzaga. Oil. 338
314. José de Alcibar. Sor María Ignacia de la Sangre de Cristo (detail). Oil. 339
315. Antonio Pérez de Aguilar. The Cupboard. Oil. 340
316. Luis Berrueco. St. Catherine. Oil. 343
317. Joseph Joaquín Magón. Doña María Manuela de Ovando. Oil. 343

318. Miguel Jerónimo Zendejas. Death of St. Joseph. Oil. 344
319. St. Joachim with the Virgin Mary, from the retable of St. Joachim. Church of San Cosmé, Mexico City. 348
320. Virgin of the Immaculate Conception (La Purísima). Polychrome and gilded wood. . . 349
321. St. Francis (detail). Polychrome and gilded wood. 349
322. Virgin of Loreto. Painted wood. . . . 350
323. Altar de los Reyes. Cathedral of Mexico. . . 351
324. Altar de los Reyes (detail). Cathedral of Mexico. 352
325. The Coronation of Iturbide (detail). Oil. . . 353
326. Cupboard. Wood. 359
327. Wardrobes, table, and chairs. Wood with leather. 359
328. Chair. Painted wood with reed seat. . . . 360
329. Chair. Wood with damask seat. . . . 360
330. Wardrobe. Inlaid wood. 361
331. Chest of drawers, mirrors. 361
332. Sacristy table. Wood. 362
333. Confessional (Confesionario del Penitenciario), Cathedral of Mexico. . . 363
334. Choir lectern. Wood. 364
335. Choir lectern. Wood and ivory. . . . 364
336. Altar text (palabrero). Silver. 366
337. Door pull and studs. Wrought iron. . . . 370
338. Dalmatic. Embroidered in silk, silver, and gold. 372
339. Chasuble. Embroidered in silk, silver, and gold. 373
340. Fluting angels (detail of chasuble). Embroidered in silk, silver, and gold. . . 373
341. Kitchen, convent of Santa Rosa, Puebla. . . 375
342. Patio of the Casa de Ejercicios, Church of La Concordia, Puebla. 376
343. Gardener. Glazed tile panel. 377
344. Holy Family. Ivory. 379
345. Santiago Matamoros (St. James the Moor-Killer). Painted wood. 383
346. Mask of a Christian, from the dance "Moros y Cristianos." Painted wood. 385
347. Anonymous. Ex-voto of Joseph Patricio Polo. Oil. 387
348. Painted chest. Wood. 390
349. Anonymous. Painted screen: Country Pleasures. 391
350. Anonymous. A Mexican Kitchen. Oil. . . 392
351. Anonymous. The Plaza Mayor of Mexico City. Oil. 393
352. Anonymous. St. Marina. Oil. 394

353. Blas Bisente. Archangel Raphael with Donor. Oil. 394
354. Ignacio María Barreda. María Manuela Esquivel y Serruto. Oil. 395
355. Our Lord of Patience (Cristo del Cacao). Corn pith, painted. 396
356. Crucifix. Church of the Franciscan monastery, Tlaxcala. 396
357. Crucifix. Corn pith, painted. 397
358. Retable from the Castrense chapel. Painted stone. Church of Cristo Rey, Santa Fe, New Mexico. 397
359. Rafael Jimeno y Planes and José Joaquín Fabregat. The Plaza Mayor of Mexico City in 1797. 403
360. José Damián Ortiz de Castro. Commemorative monument. Church of San Hipólito, Mexico City. 408
361. Cupola of the Cathedral of Mexico. . . . 410
362. Façade, College of Mines, Mexico City. . . 411
363. Side door, main façade, College of Mines, Mexico City. 412
364. Stairway and patios, College of Mines, Mexico City. 413
365. House of Pérez Gálvez, Mexico City. . . . 414
366. Hospicio Cabañas, Guadalajara, Jalisco. . . 415
367. Façade, church of Loreto, Mexico City. . . 417
368. Interior, church of Loreto, Mexico City. . . 418
369. Portal, convent church of Jesús María, Mexico City. 420
370. Fountain, Salto del Agua, Mexico City. Lithograph. 421
371. Fountain of San Miguel, Puebla. . . . 421
372. Francisco Eduardo Tresguerras. Self-Portrait. Oil. 422
373. Church of El Carmen, Celaya, Guanajuato. . 423
374. Portal, church of El Carmen, Celaya, Guanajuato. 424
375. Side portal, church of El Carmen, Celaya, Guanajuato. 424
376. House of the Conde de Casa Rul, Guanajuato. 425
377. Caja de Agua, San Luis Potosí. . . . 426
378. José Manzo. Self-Portrait. Pastel. . . . 427
379. Altar de los Reyes, Cathedral of Puebla. . . 427
380. Alhóndiga de Granaditas, Guanajuato. . . 428
381. Rafael Jimeno y Planes. Portrait of Manuel Tolsá. Oil. 431
382. Manuel Tolsá. Virgin of the Immaculate Conception. Polychrome and gilded wood. . 432
383. Manuel Tolsá. Charles IV. Bronze. . . . 433
384. Manuel Tolsá. Charles IV (detail of horse). Bronze. 433

xxv

385. Mariano Arce. Pietà. Polychrome wood. . . 438

386. Rafael Jimeno y Planes. Miracle of the Well. Oil. 442

387. Rafael Jimeno y Planes. Assumption of the Virgin (detail). Oil. 442

388. José María Vásquez. Doña María Luisa Gonzaga Foncerrada y Labarrieta. Oil. . . 444

389. José Luis Rodríguez de Alconedo. Doña Teresa Hernández Moro. Pastel. . . . 447

390. José Luis Rodríguez de Alconedo. Self-Portait. Pastel. 448

391. Monstrance. Silver. 450

392. José Luis Rodríguez de Alconedo. Charles IV. Silver. 451

393. Juan Ortiz. Virgin of the Rosary. Woodcut. . 452

394. Alejo Infante. Our Lady of Refuge. Engraving. 453

395. Jerónimo Antonio Gil. Medal Commemorating the Founding of the Academia de San Carlos. Silver. 455

MEXICEAE · UNIVERSITATI ·

PALLADIS · SEDI ·

PULCHRARUM · ARTIUM · NUTRICI ·

IN · ADVERSIS · COLUMINI ·

IN · PROSPERIS · DECORI ·

IN · LABORIBUS · PRAEMIO ·

IN · OMNIBUS · MATRI ·

EMMANUEL · TOUSSAINT ·

MINIMUS · FILIUS ·

OFFERT · DICAT · CONSECRAT ·

A. D. MCMXLVIII

COLONIAL ART IN MEXICO

INTRODUCTION

The conquest of Mexico occurred at a stirring moment in the history of Europe. Perhaps never before had a period been so charged with momentous events—social, political and artistic. The Middle Ages were over; men were changing the steel cuirass for silken garments, and for the first time in their lives, so harsh and wandering, they began to know the delights of art, which up to then had been reserved for the Church. The classics were resurrected from the dust of the monasteries, copied and read and loaded with erudite commentaries. Printing, recently invented, multiplied the texts to put them within reach of all. So the Renaissance, which had begun long before in Italy, gradually spread about and became the common attitude.

The philosophical and literary phase of the Renaissance, Humanism, gave the intellectuals a position of importance. Latin continued the language preferred by scholars, and ignorant people were looked down upon; the illustrious leader of the movement, Erasmus of Rotterdam, in a frankly eclectic spirit, assumed that he could govern and improve the world from his ivory tower. As someone has put it, Humanism seems to be essentially an externalization of the spiritual world, in order to capture, through the resources of philosophical experience, the essence of the knowable world.

Politically, Europe was witnessing the rise of the modern nations. With the marriage of Ferdinand and Isabel, the reconquest of Granada which expelled the Moors from Spanish territory, and the discovery of America, Spain in turn achieved her national unity.

National culture in Spain was represented by an art not precisely original, and yet distinguishable from the art of other countries; it was Gothic, already under Renaissance influence, the so-called Isabelline Gothic, the style of Los Reyes Católicos. This was to provide the models when the time came to build great churches in America. The Mudejar style was also to be pro-

longed in the countries newly discovered and conquered. Painting in the New World was affected by the same influences as in the Old: Flanders, Italy, and the Spanish primitives. The minor arts reached America saturated with Moorish style; as if the conquistadors could not free themselves from the soft Oriental ways which had represented refinement in their rough life.

Such, in general terms, was the conquistadors' artistic baggage, which was to suffer the shock of aboriginal art, and later the fusion with it to produce, in good time, the art we call colonial.

Let us see then what sort of art the Europeans found in Mexico, the country they had added to the kingdom of Spain. The Indians we call Aztecs, the last branch of the Nahuatl ethnic group, were not the most cultured of the aborigines. They were a group of warring peoples, bent on conquest; and their art, their learning, and their customs revolved around their mysterious and recondite theogonies. In architecture their most important building was the temple, the *teocali*; we can read in the accounts of the conquistadors their ingenuous amazement at the sight of these structures. In general, the temple precinct was an enormous open area surrounded by walls within which, overshadowing everything, rose the great pyramid on whose summit stood the sanctuary of the sanguinary deity who received their sacrifices. There were also other, lower buildings, some of them circular, which served various purposes, such as maintaining the sacred fire. The whole country was covered with temples; it has been stated that there were more than forty thousand of them.

The houses of the humble people were simple huts, *jacalli,* of reeds and mud; their open-air life reduced domestic architecture to a minimum, since like the ancient Spartans they used their hovels only for sleeping. The nobles, the lords, like their ruler, inhabited palaces of a grandeur appropriate to their rank. Cortés and

3

all his men were lodged in a single palace, that of Atzayácatl. What were these palaces like? According to the chroniclers they were composed of great patios surrounded by rooms; some were of more than one story, and had towers.

Sculpture was the most vigorous art of these peoples, as if their strength had to be embodied in basalt to be transmitted to the future. All the sculpture is symbolic; every relief, every ornament carries a hidden meaning. We find a few portraits of surprising realism, but these were perhaps at the periphery of art. Beauty for these peoples was ancillary to religion; the gods, the only beautiful beings, were in appearance monstrous, and the more divine they were, the more monstrous.

Indigenous painting was first of all didactic. Only the learned, the historians or the astronomers, knew how to use painted signs to transmit the secrets of their science, their history, and their mysterious cosmogony. Mural painting flourished; it was usually decorative in character, although there are some Maya murals, and some at Teotihuacán, which show almost naturalistic scenes from daily life, drawn with a childlike and affecting ingenuousness. The books of these people, the prehispanic codices, are almost all masterpieces of painting, sometimes of extraordinary plastic value.

The minor arts flourished with unexampled splendor among the indigenous peoples. Gold was worked in unbelievable filigree, and objects were cast in various metals by techniques which mystified the Spanish silversmiths. They carved the precious stones, *chalchihuite* and jade; they made mosaics of turquoise; they worked rock crystal so that the objects seem cut in diamond. They wove fabrics of cotton and of rabbit hair. Most astonishing of all, they contrived those marvelous feather mosaics which were to astonish Europe—and which they continued to make after the Conquest for religious images and ecclesiastical ornaments, and even maps of whole regions. The descriptions and inventories of the objects sent back to the Old World sound like the fabulous treasure of an Oriental romance.

When we consider the wealth of art which the Spaniards found in the land they conquered, we face the question which has inevitably challenged all historians of art in America. What influence did indigenous art have on European art? Was "colonial art" simply an outpost of Spanish art? Did the Indians leave a decided mark on the new style, which could be compared, for example, with the influence of the Moors in Europe?

All such questions have either been left unanswered, or else been answered in the most arbitrary ways. Some Spanish critics, and even the Europeanizing Mexican writers, assume that the Indians left not the slightest trace on the art imported from Europe: the country accepted Western European culture, and all its art is clearly Spanish. For the indigenists, on the contrary, the only positive value in colonial art is the persistence of the native hand throughout the three centuries of the Viceroyalty: the Spaniards and their art remained foreigners in the land.

It seems hardly necessary to say that neither of these extreme positions is acceptable. If the Indians could not influence European style definitively, because of the great disparity between the two kinds of art, as well as between the social systems they expressed, it is still impossible to avoid seeing, especially in sculpture, the Indian hand which remembers its technical habits and at times follows the ancient models. A certain number of pieces have been found which show, on the one hand, that the Spaniards were not intolerantly determined to snuff out the culture of the conquered people and, on the other, that the Indians were not unwilling to collaborate as far as they could in the new style. One of the cardinal aims of this book—in which we trust we may be successful—is to show at every step this persistence of the indigenous spirit, casting a soft tinge of melancholy over the works of the proud conqueror. Actually, at the present time no one except a few self-styled historians any longer argues this question; one hardly knows whether to be more amazed at their Jacobin anachronism or at their ignorance.

When new social groups formed by the fusion of the Spanish people with the native races appear in the land, we witness the culmination of this process: their art, the Baroque, is already individual; deeply influenced by the old Indian spirit, it has already been transformed into the hybrid, the mestizo.

In studies of colonial art it has always been the custom to divide the material by centuries—the three centuries of the Spanish Viceroyalty and the short period of twenty-one years in the nineteenth century. This division is absurd; artistic styles do not interrupt their development abruptly at the turn of a century in order to begin a new style with the new century. Thus it is essential to develop a system of historical divisions corresponding to the changes in style, and related to the sociological changes from which those styles sprang.

When we consider the panorama of the viceregal period carefully it is clear that there is a logical basis for such divisions, and that these do indeed reveal themselves in terms of stylistic change. Thus the first period is naturally that of *The Conquest,* which did not end in 1521 with the fall of the Aztec capital, but continued through all the first half of the century in various expeditions to subjugate the rest of the country. This period of conquest and military life expresses itself in art in the survival of medieval style, such as the rich development of Gothic architecture at that time. Don Antonio de Mendoza is the "medieval" viceroy. After 1550 there was less danger of uprisings. Encomiendas (land grants to the Spaniards including the inhabiting Indians) continued in spite of the New Laws, which abolished the usage. The conquistador began to turn into a colonist; the mines produced fabulous riches. This period we call *The Colonization;* it covers the second half of the sixteenth and a good part of the following century. Here examples of Renaissance style are found, not only in architecture, with its Plateresque buildings, but in painting, sculpture, and the minor arts of the time. Don Luis de Velasco is the first Renaissance viceroy. A special element in this period is the Mudejar style, which, represented by some examples in the sixteenth century, flourishes exceptionally in the early part of the seventeenth, as if it were related to the expulsion of the Moors from Granada, that unfortunate achievement of Philip III.

The seventeenth century is already quite different. The colonists have taken root in the new country; their families multiply, and they begin to distinguish, slowly but clearly, between the European and the American Spaniard. The *criollo* is acquiring a notion of his nationality different from that of the *gachupín,* who already arouses the hatred of the old colonists because he has come to exploit a country that he did not help to conquer. In those days a new style was taking form: the *Baroque.* After a brief flowering of the style of Herrera at the beginning of the century, Mexican Baroque began to imitate the Baroque of Spain, still moderate in form. But little by little it changed, until at the end of this century and in the early part of the eighteenth, it was entirely different from its archetype: it was already Mexican Baroque, a living and lasting demonstration that the new country had achieved its own personality. The quality of this Baroque is ascendant complication, with its twisting of forms and exuberance of ornamentation. This style was at its height in Mexico around 1690. It was the product of a society in which everything—culture, manners, art, literature, and even science—was colored by the same mood, at once of inquiry and of luxury. Never has a society found an art more appropriate. Mexican Baroque reached a point where it even influenced the art of Spain, like a son who has come of age and proudly condescends to advise his father.

After 1730 the Baroque began to evidence a special character in Mexico, different from what it had been: this is the style we know as the *Churrigueresque.* The adoption of the estípite—the inverted obelisk—in place of the twisted column characteristic of earlier Baroque gives Mexican Churrigueresque its individual quality. If one can find antecedents for this in Spain—and there are many—Mexican Churrigueresque is still unique in the world in the specific style of the monuments and their great number. Sacheverell Sitwell is right to devote an important chapter of his book *The Spanish Baroque* to Mexico; although his information is inadequate, as he himself admits, it is one of the most interesting parts of the work, and shows that a complete study of Baroque architecture is impossible without considering the monuments of Mexico. Less richly, though more accurately, Bevan in his excellent book, *History of Spanish Architecture,* refers to a good many Mexican buildings, as does the Marqués de Lozoya in his comprehensive *Historia del arte hispánico.*

The final period covers the time from the founding of the Academia de San Carlos (1781) to the achieving of independence. From the sociological point of view, an artistic *oeuvre* of lower quality expresses the breaking up of society, as the ideas of the French Encyclopedists were gaining ground and thus preparing the way for political independence. To the rationalism they invoked, the Academy replied by fixing rules and standards for the art which had once moved in an atmosphere of perfect liberty, but which had degenerated into license. It was a time of crisis, and was saved only by a few glorious names. These artists were able to create monuments of the first rank within the style we call *Neoclassicism,* a style which seems to echo the scepticism which had taken possession of the world. The road was mapped, the ideas of liberty reached the boiling point in 1810, and, after a decade of struggle, political autonomy was achieved. But art was in decadence; war has never been propitious for anything but bloodshed; art needs peace. When Mexico found itself free, it did not know where to go. Various European countries were attractive, but France, which had given the germ of the ideas of independence, seemed to the Mexicans (as to all the world at that time) the center of culture and of art. Independent Mexico turned its back on Spain, which had created it and given it personality, and dedicated itself to copying France blindly. For better or for worse, the nineteenth century is a century of imitation of France.

PART ONE

Art in New Spain at the Time of the Conquest

The Middle Ages in Mexico, 1519–1550

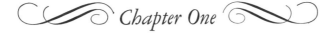

Chapter One

MEDIEVAL ARCHITECTURE

Military Architecture

HE FIRST NEED of the conquistadors, in architecture, was to build fortresses. Although these were of a temporary character in the beginning, and certainly lacked any architectonic quality, later they were constructed according to the rules. Fortifications should properly be considered in a chapter on engineering, but we shall discuss them here to simplify the plan of our work, since it will be interesting to get this scattered information together.

The first fortress was built in the Villa Rica de la Veracruz the same year the conquistadors landed, 1519. Bernal Díaz del Castillo tells of it with his usual detail:

And we made a fort, from the foundations, and in building it up to the height for laying the beams and making embrasures and square towers and barbacans, we were in such a hurry that Cortés himself was the first to carry earth on his back, and stones, and to dig the foundations, and all the captains and soldiers likewise; we kept on working without stopping to finish it quickly.[1]

Later, with the soldiers of Camargo, Alonso García Bravo arrived. He knew something about architecture, and it is said that in Pánuco he decided that a palisade should be built around the Spanish garrison, and that

he went to direct the fortress of the second city of Villa Rica.[2]

But the most important fortress built by the conquistadors was *Las Atarazanas* (a name derived from the Arabic *dar as saana,* meaning an arsenal) which was situated east of the city of Mexico on the site where later (after 1572) the hospital of San Lázaro was built. Hernán Cortés himself describes his fortress:

on the side exposed to the lake there are two very strong towers with embrasures in the necessary places; and one of these towers extends beyond the wall in one direction, with embrasures, to overlook one wall, and the other in the other direction in the same way; between these two towers extends a building of three vaults, where the brigantines are kept, with a door to go in and out to the lake between the towers, and this building also has its embrasure; and at the end of this building toward the city there is another very big tower, with many rooms below and above, with defensive and offensive fortifications toward the city.[3]

[1] Bernal Díaz del Castillo, *The True History of the Conquest of New Spain,* Vol. 23, Ch. XLVIII, pp. 174–175.
[2] Francisco A. de Icaza, *Conquistadores y pobladores de Nueva España,* No. 92. See also Manuel Toussaint, Federico Gómez de Orozco, and Justino Fernández, *Planos de la ciudad de México.*
[3] Hernando Cortés, *Five Letters,* p. 272.

9

1. City wall, Campeche.

The Conquistador shows pride in his work: "It is so made," he continues, "that although I have seen a good many arsenals and fortresses, I have never seen its equal, and many who have seen more than I agree with me."

This fort was begun in 1521 and finished in 1524, since the documents say that the Ayuntamiento (the municipal council) was moved from Coyoacán to Mexico City when the Atarazanas was finished. We do not know who directed the work, but probably not Alonso García Bravo, since he would certainly have boasted of it. Perhaps it was in the hands of one of the architects of Hernán Cortés, of whom we shall speak below.

Las Atarazanas ceased to function as a fort after the lake began drying up, and was used only as a prison for political criminals in the conflicts which began at once to disturb the government of the emerging country.

In the instructions given Don Antonio de Mendoza in 1535, he was ordered to report whether it would be wise to fortify Mexico City, surrounding it with walls, as Nuño de Guzmán had been ordered to do in 1528.[4] That tyrannical head of the First Audiencia had built only the first story of one fortress. Nothing was done, and the project of walling Mexico City was never carried out; it would have been practically impossible anyway, because the Spanish city was surrounded by water, and the native huts were crowded around the outskirts without plan or order.

Various fortifications were undertaken in New Spain during the sixteenth century. Some were to protect the ports against the frequent attacks of pirates, as in Campeche (1), where they began to fortify the port in 1557,[5] and in Acapulco, from which they sent in 1582 a plan of the fort to be built. Others were to protect towns against natives who were still unsubdued. However, by mid-century the necessity of building forts in the towns had passed, because the monastery churches

[4] Real Cédula, abril 5, 1528. Vasco de Puga, *Cedulario*, I, 66.
[5] Cresencio Carrillo y Ancona, *El obispado de Yucatán*, I, 156.

2. Fort of San Juan de Ulua and Veracruz in the nineteenth century. Engraving.

were built so strongly as to be real fortresses, and in fact served as such when necessary. We must not neglect, however, the efforts to defend the port which was then the most important in the country, San Juan de Ulúa. In 1537 the viceroy, Don Antonio de Mendoza, wrote to the court of Spain that they had begun the work, but "at present," he says, "all we are doing is getting great rocks for the foundations, and waiting for some able *maestro* to come from Spain to take charge of it."[6] The master must have come, for the work was done, and already between 1566 and 1568 Bernal Díaz writes: "This port is now renowned, and there have been built great bulkheads so that the ships are sheltered from the northers, and here they come to unload the merchandise from Castile for Mexico and New Spain."[7] Bernal Díaz speaks only of defenses against the sea,. not a fortress, but that was built later. In the *Descripción de San Juan de Ulúa,* written in 1571, it is described in this way:

What one sees of the island is rock laid by hand; from this rises a mortared wall of cut stone, north of the south end, leaving almost all the island.to the north; behind this wall the ships take shelter from the northers. At the land end of the wall there is a tower of masonry, with artillery, where there is a governor representing the Viceroy.[8]

This fortification proved inadequate, however, and when the famous military architect of Philip II, Bautista Antonelli, came to New Spain, he did not neglect to report what ought to be built on Ulúa. He had been directing the construction of the Morro Castle in Havana, when he received orders, on December 18, 1589, to go to Honduras, and on February 18, 1590, he came through San Juan de Ulúa. He drew up a plan for the port and left instructions for its fortification, to give at least temporary protection to the shipping that arrived there (2). He also inspected the new road which Dr. Palacios had laid out from San Juan de Ulúa to Mexico City, and made his report to the King from the capital

[6] *Documentos inéditos del Archivo de Indias,* II, 186–190.
[7] Díaz del Castillo, *True History,* Vol. 23, Ch. XIV, p. 56.
[8] *Papeles de Nueva España,* V, 200.

11

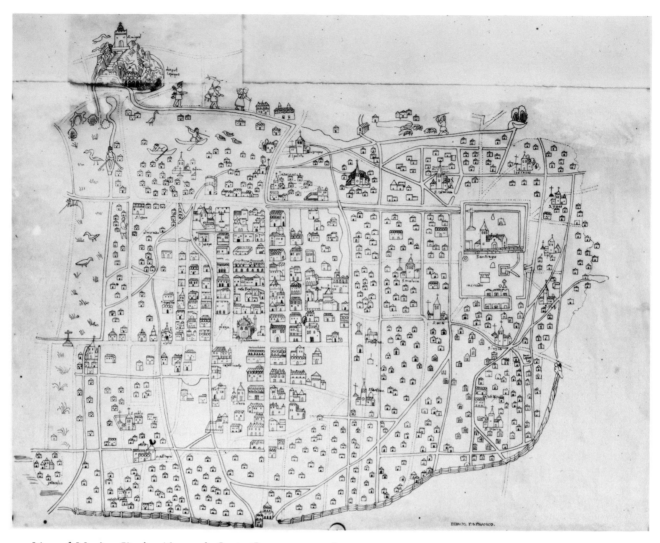

3. Map of Mexico City by Alonso de Santa Cruz. 1550–1562.
Museo Nacional de Antropología e Historia, Mexico City.

on March 1 of that year.[9] The construction at Ulúa seems to have been directed by Juan Sánchez Talaya, for the *fiscal de su majestad* brought legal action against his heir, his brother Ginés, concerning the building accounts.[10]

Civil Architecture

City Planning

In laying out the first cities of America the conquistadors followed the systems used in the Old World, especially in Andalusia, which always had a strong influence on colonial art. There were two basic types: the gridiron plan used in flat country, and the irregular plan of mountainous sites. The first, which has been attributed to Hippodamos of Miletus, was used by the Romans, who brought it to Spain. The idea of an irregular plan came from the Moors.[11]

We know who laid out the city of Mexico: it was

[9] Eugenio Llaguno y Amírola, *Noticias de los arquitectos y arquitectura de España*, III, 61. See also the excellent study of Diego Angulo Íñiguez on Bautista Antonelli.

[10] Ginés was also an architect, since he is found directing the work of Santo Domingo in 1563. *Epistolario de Nueva España*, XV, 76. See also on this subject José Antonio Calderón Quijano, *Historia de las fortificaciones en Nueva España*.

[11] See Manuel Terán, "Baja Andalucía," *Revista de Occidente*, No. 157.

the same Alonso García Bravo we have mentioned (3). He himself states in his record of *Méritos y Servicios:* ". . . because he was an able mathematician, Cortés appointed him to draw up the plan for the city of Mexico, with all the streets and squares as they now are."[12] He was not, as it has been claimed, the first *alarife* of the city, that is, the supervisor of public works. Later he lived in Oaxaca, which he also laid out, as he did Veracruz. In the middle of the century, between 1540 and 1550, Juan Ponce wrote that "he has served and is now serving Your Majesty in directing the building and planning of the said City" of Mexico.[13]

We also know who laid out the city of Querétaro. "The town of Querétaro is most elegantly laid out in the form of a checkerboard, as the said Juan Sánchez de Alanís planned it, with very large and spacious streets, well arranged and orderly."[14] The city of Valladolid, now called Morelia, was mapped in 1542 and 1543 by the same Juan Ponce, who seems to have had the confidence of Don Antonio de Mendoza.[15] Puebla de los Ángeles was built after a plan by Alonso Martín Pérez, called Partidor (the Divider), in the year 1531;[16] other writers state, however, that it was the work of the *corregidor* Hernando de Saavedra.[17]

We cannot actually give details of the theory of city planning which the conquistadors followed. We can only repeat that, as a general rule, on level sites they mapped their settlements in squares, like a checkerboard, while in mountainous places such as the mining towns the plan followed the terrain, with steep and winding streets. A good example of the way a town was laid out in 1582, when the Colony was well established, can be seen in a drawing of Teutenanco found by Don Francisco del Paso y Troncoso, which we reproduce here (4). In the center is the plaza, with the gallows and the *rollo* or pillory. At one side is the church, its large yard surrounded by a crenellated wall, and with an open chapel beside it, and behind, an enor-

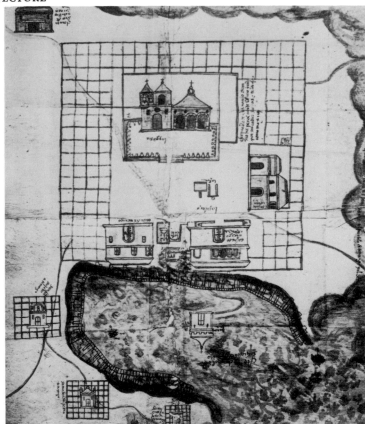

4. Map of Teutenanco (Tenango del Valle). 1582. Archivo de Indias, Sevilla.

mous walled cemetery. Across from the church stands a building with an upstairs loggia, identified as Casas Reales, that is, the government building. On the same side of the plaza one finds the Casa del Clérigo, the priest's house, which is smaller and has a corner window. Between these two buildings there are a public fountain and a shrine. On the third side of the plaza, at the corner of the Casas Reales, is the Casa del Común, which would be the meeting hall of the Indians. The town lies around the plaza, its streets laid out with perfect regularity like a checkerboard. With insignificant variations, this was the plan of the majority of towns under the Viceroyalty.[18]

---

[12] Alonso García Bravo's report, which is to be found in the Archivo de Indias, was generously provided me by Rafael García Granados. See *Información de méritos y servicios de Alonso García Bravo, alarife que trazó la ciudad de México,* ed. Manuel Toussaint; José R. Benítez, *Alonso García Bravo, planeador de la ciudad de México.*

[13] Icaza, *Conquistadores,* No. 689.

[14] See the "Relación de Querétaro, 1582," in Valentín F. Frías, *La conquista de Querétaro,* p. 39.

[15] Icaza, *Conquistadores,* No. 689.

[16] *Boletín del Archivo General de la Nación.*

[17] Mariano Veytia, *Historia de la fundación de la ciudad de la Puebla de los Ángeles,* I, 211.

[18] See Guerrero, *Las plazas de las ciudades de Nueva España en relación con las ordenanzas de Felipe II.* See also Zelia Nuttall, "Ordinances Concerning the Laying Out of New Towns," *Hispanic American Historical Review,* 5 (1922), 249–254; F. Chueca Goitia and L. Torres Balbás, *Planos de ciudades iberoamericanas y filipinas;* George Kubler, "Mexican Urbanism in the Sixteenth

Houses of the Conquistadors

We know a good deal about the conquistadors' houses, both from contemporary accounts and from their representation in the Indian books known as codices. At first the conquistadors lived in the palaces of the Indian rulers of Mexico, but after the capital was conquered they began to build their houses on the *solares,* the plots of land which the Ayuntamiento was passing out generously for that purpose. About 1554 the dwellings presented this appearance: At first glance they seemed like fortresses because of the heaviness of the walls; they were not very high, the lintels and jambs were of cut stone, and over the doors the coats of arms of the owners were displayed; the roofs were flat, of adobe—which around 1581 they began to cover with tiles[19]—and they were drained by gutters of wood or terra cotta; the interior arrangement seems to have consisted of a central courtyard surrounded by galleries.[20] At first it was the custom to build projecting towers; then the Ayuntamiento absolutely prohibited this. Nevertheless they continued to build towers, and this architectural element persisted in a purely decorative form throughout colonial times, as one can see in houses of the eighteenth century (307, 303).

We have quite a few drawings of these early houses, such as those in the so-called Kingsborough Codex, representing the houses built in Mexico City in 1550 by the Indians of the town of Tepetlaóztoc for its violent *encomendero,* Gonzalo de Salazar.

Houses of the Leaders

If the houses of the conquistadors looked like for-tresses, those of their leaders were still larger and more sumptuous. Bernal Díaz says in reference to the establishment of Cortés that when Garay arrived, "Cortés was building his houses and palaces and they were as great and as big and of as many patios as the Labyrinth of Crete."[21]

In fact Don Hernán Cortés chose for himself the finest houses of the Aztec capital, the Casas Viejas and the Casas Nuevas (the Old Palace and the New Palace) of Moctezuma, which were granted to him in a decree dated June 9, 1529.[22] Before this the Conquistador had lived in Coyoacán, undoubtedly in the house of the principal *cacique* (Indian chief, or nobleman) of the community. It was ðn the white walls of this house that the captains of the conquering army and their chief wrote satirical exchanges. It is not clear whether Cortés built a house in Coyoacán at that time. It seems likely that he did, and that it was precisely on the site of the building they now designate as the Casa de Cortés. Furthermore, the Indians of Coyoacán complained because Cortés had not paid them for the work they did in building his house; as we know that other Indians built his houses in Mexico City, it seems clear that here they are talking about a house in Coyoacán. However that may be, the present building dates from the seventeenth century and was later ceded by the Marquesado del Valle (the heirs of Cortés) to the community of Indians of Coyoacán, according to interesting documents published by Zelia Nuttall.[23]

The Casas Viejas were built by Indians from Chalco, Huejotzingo, Tepeapulco, and Otumba, between 1522 and 1529. It seems that the architect was Juan Rodríguez, who was given his *solar* on November 15, 1525.[24] In 1528 Cortés gave orders that shops should be built on the lower floor of his buildings, so that they could be rented.[25]

The site of these buildings occupied the area between the modern streets Avenida Madero, Calle de Tacuba, Calle de Isabel la Católica, and Monte de Piedad. Towers stood at the four corners; one can still see vestiges of them on some of the corners, though as purely decorative elements. On the upper floor of the principal façade there was an arcaded loggia with a stone balustrade, as well as large windows (10).

The Casas Nuevas stood where the Palacio Nacional now is, and were constructed somewhat later. In 1528 only the lower floor had been built; it consisted of three patios surrounded by galleries, and was all of masonry, richly roofed with cedar. The architects of this building

Century," *Art Bulletin,* 34 (1942), 160–171; George Kubler, *Mexican Architecture of the Sixteenth Century,* pp. 68–102; Dan Stanislawski, "The Origin and Spread of the Grid-Pattern Town," *Geographical Review,* 36 (1946), 105–120; Dan Stanislawski, "Early Town Planning in the New World," *Geographical Review,* 37 (1947), 95–105; George M. Foster, *Culture and Conquest. America's Spanish Heritage,* 34–49.

[19] Letter of the Conde de la Coruña to Philip II, *Cartas de Indias,* I, 341–342.

[20] This plan derives from the plan of the Sevillian house, which in turn goes back to the ancient Roman dwelling, but is influenced also by the Arabs.

[21] Díaz del Castillo, *True History,* Vol. 30, p. 256.

[22] Vasco de Puga, *Cedulario,* I, 258.

[23] In the *Memorias de la Sociedad Científica "Antonio Alzate,"* if I remember correctly. See also Nuttall, *Datos históricos relativos a la llamada "Casa de Cortés" o Casa Municipal en Coyoacán.*

[24] Mexico City, *Actas de Cabildo de la ciudad de México.*

[25] Mariano Cuevas, *Cartas y otros documentos de Hernán Cortés,* p. 45.

5. Palace of Cortés, Cuernavaca, Morelos.

seem to have been the same Juan Rodríguez and Rodrigo de Pontecillas. When the viceregal government wanted a building of its own, these houses were bought from the descendants of the Conquistador, as we shall see in considering civic architecture.

Cortés built a palace in Cuernavaca also, of which something still remains.[26] It is said to have been started in 1523 and completed in 1528. The present building has been modernized, and disagreeable windows and balconies have been added, but undoubtedly the shell of the building dates from the earliest times, as do the arched loggias in front and in back (5). My reason for affirming this is its similarity to the ruins of the palace of Don Diego Colón in Santo Domingo, which was built some years earlier.[27]

Oaxaca became the capital of Cortés' feudal domain, and the Conquistador built another house there. It was located on a *cu,* a pre-Conquest temple platform, according to the *Instructions* which the first viceroy, Don Antonio de Mendoza, wrote to his successor. Because

6. Las Monjas, Mérida, Yucatán.

[26] See Valentín López González, *El palacio de Cortés en Cuernavaca.*
[27] Erwin Walter Palm, *Los monumentos arquitectónicos de la Española,* pl. LXI–LXVII.

15

of this, among other reasons, the Spanish community moved into the area intended for the Indians, which was called Huayacac, and from which the present name Oaxaca comes.[28]

In the town of Coyoacán two houses are said to have belonged to the conquistadors Pedro de Alvarado and Diego de Ordaz. Neither of these houses is documented, and their construction seems rather to date from mid-seventeenth century.

In fact no properly documented example of this type of house exists. Perhaps the one that most nearly approaches it (at least its exterior) is the so-called Casa de las Monjas (the Nuns' House) of Mérida in Yucatán. It has that high stone façade crowned by an arcaded tower, exactly like the houses we see drawn on the codices and maps (6).

Government Buildings

The first local authority in New Spain was the Ayuntamiento of the Villa Rica de la Veracruz. There is no record of any special building constructed for this body; probably they used some temporary construction, abandoned when the Villa Rica was moved to the location it occupied later. The second Ayuntamiento was that of the city of Mexico, instituted as soon as the Aztec capital fell to the conquistadors. While the city was being rebuilt the Ayuntamiento met in Coyoacán, probably in the same building where Don Hernán Cortés was living. Their records have been lost, so that it is hard to be specific about the place where they worked or their activities in that period. In 1524 the Ayuntamiento moved to Mexico City and began to meet in the house of Cortés, according to the *Actas de Cabildo*.

In the allotment of grants of land (the *solares*), six were designated for municipal buildings, meat market, and prison. The city began to construct a small building; the rest of the land, however, was seized by the treasurer, Alonso de Estrada, who only in 1527, by a decree dated December 13, was made to give it back to the city. At that time the Casa del Ayuntamiento was begun; it was finished in 1532. On the tenth of May the Cabildo was installed in its new building. (Cabildo, Consistoria and Ayuntamiento are here used interchangeably.) As the building was not large enough,

they bought for 12,000 pesos a piece of land which extended to the corner of the Calle de San Agustín, and enlarged the Casas Consistoriales; this occurred in 1564. In 1582 the prison was built, and the first public granary.[29]

Always in need of money—with their funds continually used up in ceremonies to celebrate events such as the arrivals of viceroys, the royal successions, the birth of royal children, and so on, the first concern of the Ayuntamiento was to build shops on the first floor of their buildings, just as Cortés had in his; in the Actas de Cabildo one finds repeated discussion of the construction and renting of these shops. We do not know what this first Palacio del Ayuntamiento was like, but presumably it was not very different in style from the other buildings of the period we have been describing.

All over America special buildings were constructed to house the Cabildos. We still have that of Veracruz, which is one of the most common types (7), that of Antigua Guatemala, those of Jujuy, Salta, and Buenos Aires (recently reconstructed) in the Argentine Republic, among the most important. In all of these buildings we note the great arcade which in Mexico is called a *portal,* and one or several towers, which may serve for a clock or for the lighthouse in a coastal city like Veracruz. Although all these buildings are evidently of a later period, one can feel confident that they follow an earlier type which quite likely took shape in the period we are considering.

Two buildings of the greatest historical importance were conserved from this period until relatively recent times, one in fact, and the other at least in memory, in the name of a square. I refer to the buildings which were called *tecpans,* apparently a reminiscence of the ancient palaces of the Indian rulers.

The Tecpan de la Parcialidad de San Juan, which was sometimes called the Tecpan de México, was finished in the year 1566. It had been decorated with a painting representing the genealogy of the Indian nobles who had governed Mexico, and bore the Emperor's coat of arms. The building disappeared, but its memory continued in the name of a small square which still in mid-nineteenth century was called the Plazuela del Tecpan de San Juan.

The Tecpan de Tlatelolco survived almost to our time, and some columns of the original building still remain. In a document narrating the remodelling of the building in the last third of the sixteenth century there is a plan which, in spite of the conventions of Indian

---

[28] *Instrucciones que los virreyes de Nueva España dejaron a sus sucesores,* p. 238.

[29] See the Actas de Cabildo for the relevant years.

7. The Plaza Mayor of Veracruz. c. 1830. Oil on canvas.
Museo del Estado, Guadalajara, Jalisco.

drawing, gives us an idea of its arrangement.[30] In the façade was a great portal with a cross; one entered a large patio surrounded by galleries; at the left, in a separate building with its arched doorway, the caciques assembled to give audience to the natives; near the back was a fountain, and occupying the whole rear part was a great hall which opened in three round arches and certainly must have been used as the meeting place of the *macehuales,* the common people. A wall seems to cut off the right-hand side of the great patio: this was the garden, shaded by leafy plants. At either side of the main structure were apartments: the one on the right seems to have been for the reception of the viceroys on their visits to the Tecpan; the one on the left may have served in the same way for the archbishop. At the left the building was completed by a wing which held the prison, and at the back were the steam baths, the famous *temascales,* which the Indians enjoyed so much.

The columns of the galleries surrounding the patio

resemble those we see in the cloisters of the oldest monasteries of the sixteenth century. They are low; the bases and capitals are alike, and typical in form. The columns at the left-hand side seem to have had plain shafts, while those at the right are ornamented. Such is the building as the drawing describes it.

Buildings of Charitable Foundations

Hardly was the land conquered when hospitals were needed, for both the Spaniards and the Indians. Hernán Cortés was the founder of the first hospital of Mexico. Near Tlaxcala he established a hospital for lepers which was called the Hospital de San Lázaro; this did not last long because Nuño de Guzmán destroyed it, on the pretext that they were contaminating the city's water. Another institution founded by the Conquistador himself, which still exists, is the Hospital de la Purísima Concepción, which since the seventeenth century has been called the Hospital de Jesús Nazareno (8). As early as 1524 it is mentioned; it was apparently founded right after the Conquest, on a site called Huitzilan.

[30] Justino Fernández, "El códice del Tecpan de Tlaltelolco," *Investigación histórica,* 3.

17

8. Patio of the Hospital de Jesús, Mexico City.

Two of the artisans who worked on this hospital are known. Pedro Vázquez, who settled in Mexico on September 2, 1530, did the wooden retable in the Capilla Mayor of the church.[31] Diego Díaz, a Portuguese stonecutter and sculptor, carved a corner window which was destroyed only in 1800; the inscription, which lasted thirty-three years more, read:

Diego Díaz de Lisbona de nación portugués
hizo esta ventana. Año de 1535[32]

"Diego Díaz, Portuguese, made this window. The year 1535"

The building has undergone constant reconstruction, so that it would seem to have little significance as architecture of this period. The present church is of the seventeenth century.

Another hospital of great importance in the early

days of the Colony was that of the Amor de Dios, which the first Bishop of Mexico, Don Fray Juan de Zumárraga, established for treatment of venereal diseases. It stood on the site of the present Escuela de Artes Plasticas. Don Fray Juan de Zumárraga endowed the hospital as best he could, going so far as to give it the archepiscopal buildings themselves, a donation which naturally was withdrawn later.

The doctors Cosimo and Damian were patron saints of this hospital, and until the nineteenth century medallions representing them were preserved on either side of the doorway, which suggests that the portal was Plateresque in design. The hospital was receiving the sick at the beginning of 1540. It survived, with the ups and downs of all charity institutions, until July 6, 1788, when it was closed.

Another of the oldest hospitals is that of Santa Fe near Mexico City. It was founded at the end of 1531 or the beginning of the following year by Don Vasco de Quiroga. Construction seems to have begun at once, since on the map attributed to Alonso de Santa Cruz,

---

[31] Lucas Alamán, *Disertaciones sobre la historia de la República Megicana*, Appendix I.
[32] *Ibid.*

drawn by Indians around 1555, it already appears with a very good building. Don Vasco de Quiroga administered the hospital of Santa Fe as an appendage of his bishopric of Michoacán.

Of the hospitals founded in this period by the Venerable Bernardino Álvarez under the protection of San Hipólito, only the ruins of the one in Oaxtepec can still be seen. We shall speak of the one in Mexico City later, when we come to discuss the eighteenth century.

But the most famous hospitals in the early days of the Colony are certainly those founded by Don Vasco de Quiroga and the Franciscan friars in his bishopric of Michoacán. Of these the most important were in Uruapan, Pátzcuaro, Acámbaro, Santa Fe de la Laguna, Tzintzuntzan, and Cuitzeo. The hospitals were composed of a great rectangular patio with an open chapel in the center; two of the sides were used for men and for women, respectively, and there were administrative offices on the other sides. But the importance of these hospitals derives less, perhaps, from the architectural structure than from the social organization which they embodied and which made them significant institutions. It is impossible to imagine a cooperative system for all the Indians of a village with more practical wisdom and justice than the one which ruled in these hospitals, where everyone had his allotted work and received his fair pay. The hospital was the central office of the organization, for which all the members of the community had to contribute their labor; around it were grouped their houses, which were called *familias* because each one housed a family. There was community land, where everyone was required to work in turn; the produce went to support the hospital and to pay wages to the Indians. Furthermore, Don Vasco invented a plan to encourage local industry, namely that each village should specialize in one craft. In our time such an idea would be unwise, but in that period, when the Indians were just beginning to enter into the European way of life, it was most beneficial. There was no ruinous competition, the inhabitants of each village were able to perfect themselves in their special craft, and this system developed trade throughout the region to satisfy their needs. The organization of these hospitals founded by Don Vasco de Quiroga was inspired by the famous *Utopia* of St. Thomas More, as the scholars have shown.[33] A splendid thing, that what was utopian for cultured Renaissance Europe could be practised, as a reality, among the Indians of New Spain!

We have remains only of the hospitals of Uruapan,

9. Portal of the hospital chapel, Acámbaro, Guanajuato.

Acámbaro, and Santa Fe de la Laguna. At Uruapan, where the hospital was called La Guatapera by the Tarascan Indians and much venerated as the place where their apostle died, nothing of interest remains but the portal of an exterior chapel, richly ornamented and with an image of the founder, Fray Juan de San Miguel, in a niche over the door (46). The style is Mudejar Plateresque, with an *alfiz* and shields on either side.

[33] Silvio Zavala, La "Utopia" de Tomás Moro en la Nueva España. See also Justino Fernández, Santo Tomás Moro y "La Utopia de Tomás Moro en la Nueva España," with an essay by Edmundo O'Gorman.

19

There are also vestiges of the original structure inside, the most notable being a small stone window with Mudejar carving.

The hospital at Acámbaro shows a chapel portal like that at Uruapan, in the same style and similarly disposed (9). The work at Uruapan has a certain indigenous flavor, while that at Acámbaro shows a definitely European hand.

The hospital of Santa Fe de la Laguna still exists, though without importance as architecture. Before this village construction, with its wooden posts and thatched roofs, we are moved not so much by aesthetic emotion as by the memory of that holy man, Don Vasco de Quiroga.

Educational Buildings

One of the first undertakings of the friars was the education of the Indians. The worthy Franciscans can claim credit for being the first educators of America. Their educational establishments included every level of learning which could be imparted to the Indians. The very first classes, what we now call kindergarten, were held in the monasteries, for the little ones who had been gathered there. The establishment offering primary and secondary education was the Colegio de San Juan de Letrán, so famous in the history of Mexican education. It was founded by the Franciscans near their main house in Mexico City. The request for land was made on July 12, 1529, and the first teacher was the worthy Fray Pedro de Gante. His original purpose was to teach the Indians to read and write. In 1548 a royal decree directed that the college should be considered in the new *repartimiento*—the fiduciary assignment of laborers—to provide them an income. In 1585 the University tried to take over the college, even offering to construct a building for them, which implies that by then the original building was in bad condition. The friars defended their school, which continued independent, although precariously so for lack of funds. Much later they resorted to the expedient of allowing their students, dressed in their long robes, to attend funerals in a body as paid mourners. The college continued to exist up to the beginning of the nineteenth century.

Near the monastery of San Francisco was another school, attached to the famous chapel of San José de los Naturales (St. Joseph's of the Natives). Padre Gante founded and supported this also, and its purpose was to teach arts and crafts to the Indians. From this school

came painters, sculptors, carpenters, masons, stonecutters, and other craftsmen and artists. From the descriptions the chroniclers have left us, it seems that this school had no building of its own, but that the work was carried on in some of the church buildings.

The institution of higher learning was the Imperial Colegio de Santa Cruz de Tlaltelolco. Although it is said to have been established earlier, its official foundation dates from 1537, when Don Antonio de Mendoza, the first viceroy, allotted an annual income to support it, donating also an hacienda of his own in the Cazadero. Don Luis de Velasco, by order of the Emperor, added two thousand ducats a year from the Real Erario to this income; it was actually at this time that the college added the title "Imperial" to its name. The curriculum consisted of Latin, logic, and philosophy, and the faculty included the most illustrious Franciscans in Mexico: Fray Maturino Guiberti, Fray Andrés de Olmos, Fray Bernardino de Sahagún, Fray Arnaldo de Basacio, Fray Juan de Gaona, Fray Juan de Focher, and so on. The students led a monastic life. This splendid college did not last for long; at Velasco's death in 1564 the funds were cut off. The building remained for many years, and it was still shown in 1605 as the ruin of something marvellous which had been lost. A little after this the Colegio de San Buenaventura was established in the same place, with the same purpose as the old Colegio de Santa Cruz.

The Royal and Pontifical University of Mexico. The documentation concerning the foundation of the University has been discussed by Don Joaquín García Icazbalceta.[34] The chronicler Herrera had stated that the initial order to found the institution was given to the first viceroy, Don Antonio de Mendoza, in 1539, in response to a petition of the distinguished Fray Bartolomé de las Casas; but Don Joaquín, for impressive reasons, rejected this statement. Recently the document concerned has been discovered in the Archive of the old Ayuntamiento by Professor Luis Chávez Orozco.[35] It is dated October 3, 1539, in Madrid. At the petition of the Ayuntamiento of the Capital that he found a university *"de todas las ciencias"* ("with all the subjects") Don Antonio de Mendoza appointed teachers in the subjects most esteemed at that time, and this foundation was like a seed of the new university which

---

[34] See Joaquín García Icazbalceta's Introduction to the first dialogue in Francisco Cervantes de Salazar, *México en 1554.*
[35] Luis Chávez Orozco in *Excelsior,* agosto 11, 1947.

the Viceroy had promised the professors to organize definitively later. We are entirely ignorant of any details about this school, either the professors or the courses they taught.

To fulfill his agreement and give his foundation legal status, the Viceroy, supported by the Ayuntamiento and the prelates of the various orders, then solicited the Court of Spain to establish a university in Mexico. Since the Viceroy left in 1550 for Peru, he did not receive the answer to his request.

The decrees which founded the University of Mexico were sent on September 21, 1551. An annual endowment of 1000 pesos of gold from the mines was assigned to it, plus the income from the cattle ranches which Don Antonio de Mendoza had granted his earlier foundation. It was given all the privileges and exemptions enjoyed by the University of Salamanca, except for certain limitations which were later removed by a decree of October 17, 1562. The Holy See confirmed the foundation, recognizing the kings of Spain as patrons and founders, and later authorized the title "Pontifical" to be added to the designation "Royal" which it carried.

Don Luis de Velasco, in obedience to these mandates, founded the Real y Pontificia Universidad de México. The first building in which the University began its work was located at the corner of the Calle de la Moneda and the Calle del Seminario, in the house of Doña Catalina de Montejo, according to the chronicler Grijalva, or in that of Juan Martínez Guerrero, according to Sigüenza y Góngora. The foundation ceremony took place on January 25, 1553, in San Pablo, probably in the place where the Augustinians later established their college. There was a High Mass and a procession of all the personages in attendance to the building mentioned. On the third of the following June studies were inaugurated with a Latin oration by Francisco Cervantes de Salazar, one of the masters. On the fifth, the first course began, and each of the others on succeeding days, since the Viceroy and the Audiencia wished to be present for the inauguration of each course. The first faculty of this institution, whose names should be recorded with respect, was made up of the following men: rector, Dr. Don Antonio Rodríguez de Quesada, *oidor* of the Real Audiencia; chancellor (*maestrescuela*), Don Gómez de Santillana, also an *oidor*; professors: theology, Fray Pedro de la Peña, Dominican; Holy Scripture, Fray Alonso de la Veracruz, Augustinian; canon law (called *Decretales*), Dr. Pedro Mo-

rones; civil law (*Leyes e Instituta*), Fray Bartolomé de Frías; arts, Presbítero Juan García (priest); rhetoric, Mæstro Francisco Cervantes de Salazar; grammar, Bachiller Blas de Bustamante. The first meeting of the full faculty was held on July 21, 1553.

Since we are interested in the University from the architectural point of view, we should mention the various localities it occupied. After this first building, which was inadequate, they moved elsewhere. In 1561 the University was said to be occupying a house belonging to the Hospital de Jesús, but Don Joaquín García Icazbalceta observes that there is no historical proof of this. If our learned historian had known the plan of the Plaza de México preserved in the Archivo de Indias, which can be dated between 1562 and 1566 (10), his opinion about the second location of the University would have been definite. In fact, an ample building facing on the street now called Guatemala (formerly, Calle de las Escalerillas) bears the legend *"Estas son las escuelas"* ("These are the schools"). This building stood on land which belonged to the Cathedral, and it was pulled down later to build the Seminary there. We see a large portal with decoration in relief on its lintel, and on the upper story three rectangular windows. Although one cannot entirely credit the drawing, which in such maps was generally conventional, at least it suggests what the University was like in that period.

On June 1, 1574, the King gave the University the *solar* on which the house of the Ávila family had stood; this had been entirely demolished after the famous conspiracy of the Marqués del Valle. This land was at the corner of the present Calle de Guatemala and Calle de Argentina; the University could not build there, however, because the lot was so small.

On May 24, 1584, the rector of the University appeared before the Audiencia requesting that four *solares* in the Plaza del Volador be sold to the University from the property of the Marqués del Valle. The Marqués' representative opposed the request, but in spite of his argument, the Audiencia agreed to the petition and the pieces of land were evaluated at five hundred pesos each. The Marqués' estate brought suit against this decision, but they could not prevent the buildings' being started.

The cornerstone was laid on the first of June of the same year. The architect was Capitán Melchor Dávila, but he could not have done much because he died that same year, after a fall from the scaffolding while he was working at the restoration of the Old Cathedral.

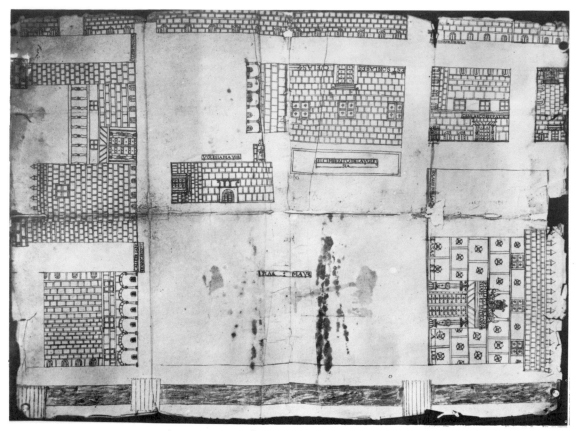

10. The Plaza Mayor of Mexico City. c. 1565. Archivo de Indias, Sevilla.

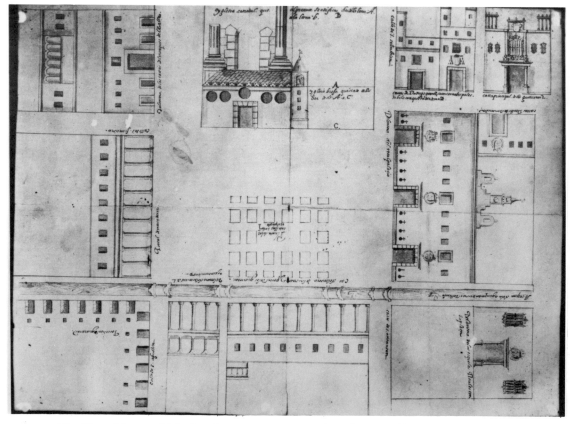

11. The Plaza Mayor of Mexico City. 1596. Archivo de Indias, Sevilla.

The work was continued, possibly by Rodrigo Dávila, nephew of Melchor, who took his place in the work on the Cathedral, or by Claudio de Arciniega, a famous architect who had built many important buildings.

The suit brought by the Marqués del Valle stopped the work in 1585, and so it remained until June 9, 1589, when a part of the building then occupied by the University collapsed, endangering the students and interrupting their studies. The University moved into the house of the Marqués del Valle, but the authorities ordered that work on their new building should be resumed, and in that same year, 1589, the University occupied it, although it was not completely finished.

On another map of the Plaza de México, dated 1596, we can see the first building which the University had on its permanent site (11). It is a simple façade; the portal is framed by columns, with a flat lintel, and over this portal is a large royal coat of arms; at either side are Renaissance grills. We repeat our warning as to the accuracy of such drawings: it is hardly possible, for instance, that such a large building would have had so few openings. But in any case we can get some idea of what the building was like, and identify its architecture as characteristic of the Plateresque style.

Religious Architecture

Churches and Monasteries

At the time of the conquest of New Spain the first churches were makeshift, simple shelters to protect the priest and the worshippers from the weather. Very soon, however, the need to build permanent churches was felt, and then by a natural coincidence the solution of the early Christians, the basilica, was adopted. Probably the untrained architects also remembered the numerous churches of basilica type in Andalusia, which according to Angulo Íñiguez indicate a Moorish influence.[36] The basilica offered obvious advantages, especially in its simplicity of construction; with plenty of wood, it was easy to roof the nave and two aisles with beams and trusses. Since material, almost in excess, and plenty of labor were available, they could build churches of considerable capacity in this way. The Old Cathedral in Mexico City was such a basilica built in the early period. The Franciscans had used this church before they built their own; later it was elevated to cathedral rank. It was built before 1532, and the bases of the octagonal columns—which surely represent a Mudejar influence—were made from pre-Hispanic materi-

als.[37] It had a nave and two aisles, the nave had a gabled timber roof, and the aisles, flat ceilings on beams. The architect was Martín de Sepúlveda. This church lasted for a good many years; in 1585 it was thoroughly restored for the convening of the Third Council, and from the accounts of this rebuilding it has been possible to reconstruct the whole thing.[38] It was demolished in 1628.

A similar building in basilica plan with two aisles and a timber roof was the first cathedral of Puebla de los Ángeles, which was begun in 1536 and finished in 1539. Its completion, among other things, determined the moving of the archepiscopal see from Tlaxcala to the new community.

We know that the early churches of the three mendicant orders in Mexico were also in basilica form. The Franciscans had first arrived in 1523, followed the next year by the boatload of twelve friars who are considered the founders of their order in New Spain. At first, as we have said, they occupied the church which later became the Cathedral, and then in 1525 they moved to their own church, on the site where they later built the Convento Grande de México. We know that this church, too, was a basilica.

The Augustinians reached the country in 1533, and soon after were able to build their church, also in basilica form.

The Dominicans had arrived earlier, in 1526, but had been haunted by bad luck, and it was not until 1534 that they could be considered established. Their first church, like the others, was a basilica in plan.

As we have said, all of these churches had timber roofs. The first vault constructed in New Spain was on the old church of San Francisco in Mexico City, and the chronicler Fray Gerónimo de Mendieta gives the following paragraph about it, which is interesting also in describing the Indians' part in church building:

The stonecutters, who were very skillful (as we have said), made their sculpture without iron, using only stone tools, and very fine to see. After they had chisels and mallets and other instruments of iron, and saw the work our sculptors did, they improved wonderfully, and they make and decorate round, segmental and terciate arches, rich

---

[36] Diego Angulo Íñiguez, *Arquitectura mudéjar en Andalucía durante los siglos XIII, XIV, XV.*

[37] Some of these stones can still be seen in a corner of the churchyard of the Cathedral of Mexico.

[38] Toussaint, "La primitiva catedral de México," in *Paseos coloniales,* pp. 1-5.

12. Nave, church of the Dominican monastery (before 1935), Coyoacán, Distrito Federal.

doorways and windows; and whatever arabesque and grotesque decoration they have seen, they make all of it, and they have made many very nice churches and houses for the Spaniards. What they had not mastered, and admired when they saw it, was the making of vaults; and when the first one was made (which was the chapel of the old church of San Francisco de México, built by a stonecutter from Castile) the Indians marvelled to see a thing vaulted, and they could not believe but that when the scaffolding and centering was removed the whole thing must come down. So when they were to remove the scaffolding, none of them dared to pass below. But when they saw that the vault stayed in place, then they lost their fear. And before long the Indians by themselves made two little vaulted chapels which are still standing in the patio of the principal church of Tlaxcala, and since then they have built and vaulted very fine churches and also houses in the hot country.[39]

Characteristics of the basilicas constructed in those early days survive in the church of San Sebastián in Mexico City, with its single nave and flat beamed roof.

[39] Gerónimo de Mendieta, *Historia eclesiástica indiana*, pp. 409–410.

The parish church of Coyoacán, before the reconstruction which it has recently suffered, presented the ancient look of these earliest churches (12). It was constructed by the Dominicans, to whom the friars of San Francisco had ceded the mission; the date 1587 on the front refers to the Renaissance façade which was added later to the old church. This church, for all it had been repaired at various times, remained an example of the primitive church of the first half of the sixteenth century, perhaps the most archaic in Mexico. Since the work of renovation, one can fairly say that the interior has lost practically all artistic interest.

Another basilica which is still intact and is perhaps the most elegant example of the group is the Franciscan church of Zacatlán de las Manzanas, whose portal is dated 1564 (13). The basilica form is perfect: two lines of columns with semicircular arches separate the aisles from the nave; the roofs are of flat beams, but over the nave there must have been a framed or carved ceiling. Obviously this church, with its elegant forms and delicate arches, does not date from the primitive period; but we can think of it as a survival of the form of the early basilica churches built in New Spain.

The same basilica plan, elegant and fine, appears in

24

13. Nave, church of the Franciscan monastery, Zacatlán (de las Manzanas), Puebla.

14. Church and open chapel, Franciscan monastery, Tlahuelilpa, Hidalgo.

the church of the Franciscan convent of Tecali in the state of Puebla (84). Although in ruins, it still repays study.

We should note also the basilica of Quecholac, which is very like that of Tecali, although it has been extensively modified in rebuilding.[40]

Of later date, but no less interesting, is the ruined basilica of the Dominicans at Cuilapan, Oaxaca, of which we shall speak below (21).

Open Chapels

At first the Indians were stubborn about accepting the Catholic religion; they were too deeply involved with their own religion, too shocked by the disaster of their defeat, to accept the foreign ways easily. It took five years, the friars say, for the Indians to become convinced that the men of God offered them the only protection possible against the *encomenderos.* Then they gave themselves fervently to the new religion, even

though to their childlike mentality it was merely a change of gods. For them the new faith seemed to offer much that was pagan and even idolatrous; contemporary accounts relate that many Indians continued to worship the old idols, and it may be that they thought of the saints of the new religion also as idols who had vanquished the old ones.

With the real conversion of the Indians the numbers of the faithful grew so rapidly that the churches, large as they were, proved quite inadequate for the multitude of converts. The friars therefore found a special solution to meet this problem: their solution was the "open chapel" or *capilla de indias,* the chapel of the Indians.[41]

40 On these two basilicas, see the article by John McAndrew and Manuel Toussaint, "Tecali, Zacatlán, and the *Renacimiento Purista* in Mexico," *Art Bulletin,* 34 (1942), 311–325.

41 On the open chapels, see Robert Ricard, *La "conquête spirituelle" du Mexique,* and the article "Capillas de Indias en Nueva España," by Rafael García Granados in *Archivo español de arte y arqueología,* 11 (1935), 3–29. See also John McAndrew, *The*

26

15. Open chapel, Franciscan monastery, Tlalmanalco, México.

16. Open chapel, Dominican monastery, Teposcolula, Oaxaca.

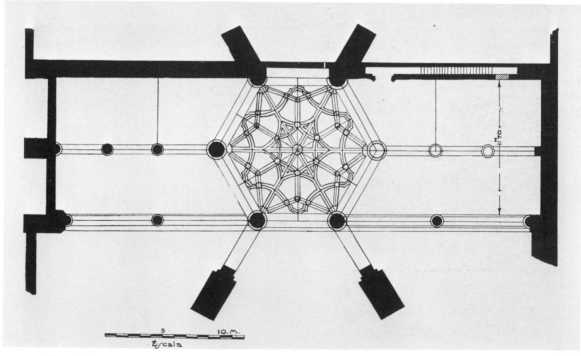

17. Plan of the open chapel, Dominican monastery, Teposcolula, Oaxaca.

The open chapels constituted perhaps the unique analogy possible between the Christian church and the indigenous *teocali,* the small temple building. In both cases, the ceremony took place in the open air: the priests alone were in a covered enclosure, while the congregation stood in a great churchyard, exactly as they had in the sacred precinct of the Indians. These chapels, moreover, were the most original religious architecture of the colonial period, since the basic conception was different from anything in Europe, even the mosque.

The open chapels which were built in New Spain can be classified in four types. First, the simplest type consisted of a presbytery under a single arch, opening to the great churchyard, or *atrio.* The size of the chapel depended on the dimensions and visibility of the arch, and on the size of the church yard. Many such chapels are in existence. Among the most notable are that of the Augustinian monastery of Actopan, whose opening is a single hemispherical vault of great audacity, that of Yautepec, which also consists of a single daring arch, and that of Coixtlahuaca in the Mixteca Alta, notable for its Renaissance ornament. The chapel of Tlahuelilpa (14), in the state of Hidalgo, whose decorative carving suggests a Portuguese Mudejar influence, is on the second story and not very big—for we should note that these chapels are sometimes on the ground, and sometimes upstairs.

The second type of chapel consists of one or more bays, usually perpendicular to the axis of the church, with a presbytery opening from the middle. In these chapels it seems that not only the officiating priest but part of the congregation, certainly those of importance, were accommodated within the building. There are many examples of these more complicated chapels. Among the most important is the one at Tlalmanalco (15), which seems never to have been completed, and whose relief decoration will be discussed in the chapter on sculpture; it dates from 1560, if we are correct in

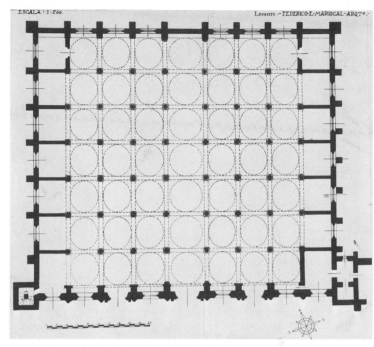

18. Plan of the Capilla Real, Franciscan monastery, Cholula, Puebla.

interpreting one of the reliefs as the year-sign "3 *pedernal"* (3 flint), which corresponds to that year.[42] The chapel at Teposcolula (16, 17), in the Mixteca Alta of Oaxaca, is a sophisticated structure with refined Renaissance detail.[43] The chapel of Cuernavaca, with its three large arches, is exceptional in standing parallel to the axis of the church; that of Otumba has a series of arches. The chapel of the Hospital de Indias at Tzintzuntzan, with its pure Renaissance ornament, is dated 1619, which demonstrates the survival and extension of this architectural type into the seventeenth century.[44] At Tepoztlán, Morelos, the chapel is in ruins, but can be reconstructed from the remains.

Thirdly, open chapels were also built with multiple parallel bays. This type recalls the structure of the Mohammedan mosque, and it was built in this way to care for a similar situation. The two most important chapels in the style of mosques were the Capilla de San José de los Naturales, which was part of the Franciscan establishment in Mexico City, and the so-called Capilla Real, the "Royal Chapel" of the Franciscan monastery at Cholula in the state of Puebla. San José de los Naturales had seven parallel bays, open all across the front; the interior was so large that it was chosen for display-

Open-Air Churches of Sixteenth-Century Mexico; Erwin Walter Palm, "Las capillas abiertas americanas y sus antecedentes en el Occidente cristiano," *Anales del Instituto de Arte Americano y Investigaciones Estéticas,* 6 (1953), 45–64.

[42] McAndrew, *Open-Air Churches,* pp. 535–543.

[43] See Angulo Iñiguez, "La capilla de indios de Teposcolula y la catedral de Siena." McAndrew (*Open-Air Churches,* pp. 543–555) comments: "It was the unanticipated first sight of this chapel, which he was the first to rediscover, that animated Manuel Toussaint to devote the rest of his life to the study of the colonial art of his country."

[44] McAndrew, *Open-Air Churches,* pp. 507–508.

19. Façade, Capilla Real, Franciscan monastery, Cholula, Puebla.

20. Interior, Capilla Real, Franciscan monastery, Cholula, Puebla.

ing the catafalque for the funeral services for Charles V.[45] The Capilla Real in Cholula still exists, though considerably altered (18, 19, 20, 67); in plan and general appearance it recalls the famous mosque of Córdoba. The original chapel collapsed soon after it was built, but the present building, though a later restoration, retains the character of the original.[46] A similar chapel may have been attached to the Franciscan hospital of Etzatlán, in Jalisco, whose parallel colonnades of low arches were later closed to form a church. These open chapels in mosque form did not fulfill their purpose ideally: it is fairly clear that the Indians crowding outside would have difficulty seeing, because the congregation filled the chapel and because the great number of columns interfered, especially considering the distance to the presbytery. This may be partly why open chapels in the form of mosques are so scarce.

The same could be said of the fourth type, the open chapel in the form of a basilica, of which we have found only one example, at Cuilapan, near Oaxaca (21). It is a perfect basilica with nave and two aisles, but at both sides, instead of walls, are arches which must have been open from the beginning and which would permit participation in the ceremony from outside the building. Studying the building with care, one finds it in fact difficult to believe that it was an open chapel. Burgoa, the Dominican chronicler of Oaxaca, says that many doorways opened into this church so that the Indians could pass in and out easily.[47]

Open chapels were used practically throughout the colonial period. It is amusing to observe that nowadays the open chapel, instead of helping the faithful to attend the ceremonies of the church, goes in search of them, so that they can be present without effort. Thus we see an open chapel built on the Plaza Mayor in Puebla so that the vendors can hear Mass without bothering to go to church.

It is not certain but that other American countries may have used open chapels. A few examples which have been claimed in Peru are not clear enough to prove that such chapels were ever so numerous or so general as in New Spain and its outposts, such as New Mexico, where they are abundant. Actually, I think the situation is quite plain: the number of converts was never so immense in the other American countries as it

21. Nave, unfinished basilica, Dominican monastery, Cuilapan, Oaxaca.

was in Mexico, and where you do not have the cause, you will hardly expect the result. This is not to say that it is impossible that open chapels may have been built in other places.

Monastic Architecture

We do not know what the earliest monastic buildings in New Spain were like. From the reports of the friars and the complaints of the viceroys we do know that in the beginning monasteries were built without any system, and that the friars, taking advantage of the great supply of Indian labor and the abundance of materials, often built excessively. Others, however, made very humble buildings, especially the Franciscans. Mendieta, in his *Historia eclesiastica Indiana,* even gives the measurements proper for a cloister:

[45] *Ibid.,* pp. 368–399.
[46] *Ibid.,* pp. 400–411.
[47] *Ibid.,* pp. 598–620.

31

22. Cloister, Franciscan monastery, Huexotla, México.

The buildings which are made for the friars' dwellings should be very humble and in accordance with the wish of our Father St. Francis; thus convents should be laid out to contain no more than six cells in the dormitory, eight feet wide and nine feet long, and the corridor to be at the most five feet wide, and the cloister should not be of two stories, and should be seven feet in width. The house where I am writing this was built according to this rule.[48]

The cloister of the monastery at Huexotla, where Father Mendieta wrote his magnificent history, still exists (22). It is indeed a tiny cloister, of heavy columns hardly taller than a man, with segmental arches, only three to a side. A later, forbidden, second story added to the cloister is roofed with wood. All of Huexotla has an air of the primitive and austere; only the flowers, exuberant in color and luxuriance, bring gaiety to this little work of art.

Another of the early monasteries which preserves its

48 Mendieta, *Historia,* pp. 255–256.

small cloister is at Tecómitl—cruder, less artistic and less evocative than that of Huexotla.

It was not until after the middle of the sixteenth century that monastic architecture, now systematized with the approval of viceregal and ecclesiastical authority, produced the great series of conventual buildings. This will be studied in the following section.

Hydraulic Architecture

Aqueducts

One of the first necessities of the new settlements in New Spain was to secure an abundant water supply. The Indians knew all about the art of building aqueducts; their aqueduct from Chapultepec carried water to the ancient city of Tenochtitlán for many years. There was also another aqueduct which brought water from Churubusco when the supply from Chapultepec was no longer adequate for the Indian capital.

In the colonial period the needs of the new city increased. They not only improved the aqueducts from

23. Aqueduct of Cempoala. State of Hidalgo.

Chapultepec and Churubusco, but brought in water from other sources. Thus a big project was carried through to build an aqueduct from the Lomas de Santa Fe. Later the aqueduct of Churubusco deteriorated, so that during the whole colonial epoch Mexico City was supplied by the springs of Chapultepec, whose aqueduct went all the way to the fountain known as the *Salto del Agua* (370), and by those of Santa Fe, whose waters were carried by an aqueduct called the Arcos de la Tlaxpana up to the Puente de la Mariscala.[49]

Probably the most impressive colonial monument of hydraulic architecure was the aqueduct called the Arcos de Cempoala, which can still be seen near the village of Otumba (23). This was the work of a Franciscan, Fray Francisco de Tembleque, whose name has come down to us wreathed in legend as the friar who almost miraculously executed this extraordinary construction, between 1553 and 1570.[50]

In a discussion of hydraulic engineering, the great task known as the "Desagüe de México"—the draining of Mexico City—deserves a special chapter. Because of the situation of the city in relation to the mountains, the Lake of Texcoco would flood it every year in the rainy season, sometimes to a depth of more than eight

feet. This terrible situation had tormented all city governments since the earliest Indian settlements. Beginning in the sixteenth century they began to work at drainage projects to carry off the excess water; but it was only in recent times, under General Díaz, that the problem was solved scientifically. As this is really a matter of engineering, and has been thoroughly studied elsewhere, we will not go into it here, but refer readers to the book published in 1901, *Las Obras del Desagüe de México*.

Fountains

Among the most important monuments decorating the colonial plazas were the fountains where the people got their water. Among the oldest documents we have is a reference to the stonecutter who made the fountain, basin and column, of the main Plaza of Mexico City; he was called Juan de Entrambas Aguas, and received fifty pesos for his work.[51]

---

[49] See Manuel Romero de Terreros, *Los acueductos de México en la historia y en el arte.*
[50] L. Salazar, "Arquería de Zempoala," *Anales del Ministerio de Fomento,* 2 (1877), 141.
[51] *Actas de Cabildo de la ciudad de México.*

24. Town fountain, Chiapa de Corzo, Chiapas.

The most important of the early Colonial fountains still in existence is in Chiapa de Corzo, in the state of Chiapas (24). It is in the form of a circular temple, made of brick like Mudejar constructions, and was finished in 1569 under Fray Rodrigo de León.[52]

Another early fountain is still in use in the town of Tochimilco in the state of Puebla (25). It has several spouts, and on the center post a coat of arms of the town with an inscription in Nahuatl.

A fountain of Gothic design, whose elegant arches carried the water to a number of outlets, used to stand in Texcoco (26). It was one of the oldest in the country, but was barbarously demolished in 1942.

All the monasteries had fountains in the center of their cloisters, and some in dry countries also had reservoirs to collect rain water for time of drought. These buildings had a perfect system of drainage; not a single drop of water was lost as it ran down through perfectly

[52] See José R. Benítez, *La fuente monumental de Chiapa de Corzo.*

constructed pipes to fill the large underground tank, from which it could be drawn when it was needed.

Bridges

A country as mountainous as New Spain, furrowed by ravines and rivers, required the immediate construction of bridges. The conquistadors put up temporary bridges; it is said that vestiges of the wooden bridges which Cortés had to build on his fantastic expedition to Honduras still remain, and that they are called *puentes de Cortés*. But wooden bridges deteriorated rapidly, and so it was necessary to construct bridges of stone. It is difficult to prove that any bridge of the first half of the sixteenth century still exists in Mexico, but it is indisputable that many were built. In Mexico City itself a great number of small bridges were needed to cross the canals; these had to be rebuilt from time to time until in the end the channels were filled in and the bridges became only a memory in the street names. So, until the vulgar taste for modernizing wiped away this last trace of colonial times, we had the Calle del Puente

34

25. Town fountain, Tochimilco, Puebla.

26. Town fountain (before 1942), Texcoco, México.

27. El Rollo, Tepeaca, Puebla.

their enthusiasm for viceroys or archbishops when they arrived to govern the country. The Ayuntamiento, though always out of funds, never missed a chance to set up showy arches for welcoming the viceroys, to erect stages more or less rich for the ceremony of swearing allegiance to the kings, or to build the most costly catafalques possible for the funerary honors of princes and monarchs.

Other constructions which might be called monuments of civic display are the *rollos*. A *rollo,* generally speaking, means a pillory, where sentences were read and justice executed near the gallows (4). In some cases, however, the *rollo* is more than a simple column; the most striking example is in the city of Tepeaca (27), which was originally called Segura de la Frontera. The *rollo* of Tepeaca is an octagonal tower which has Mudejar windows, double-arched with a column in the center, and with Gothic detail; it immediately recalls the Torre del Oro in Seville. According to the codex *Introducción de la justicia en Tlaxcala,* the *rollo* in Tlaxcala seems to have been similar. There is also a cylindrical tower with an interior staircase in Tlaquiltenango, Morelos, which is called *el rollo de Cortés,* but from its position at the edge of the town and its more military character, we suspect that it was a watchtower for defense, and not a true *rollo.*

Just as human servility raised monuments to flatter the governors, human vanity led the potentates to construct magnificent tombs for their mortal remains and those of their descendants. The funerary sculpture of Spain forms an unbroken line of splendid monuments; in the service of the grandees art outdid itself to provide dwellings for the afterlife. The Spaniards in Mexico were not exempt from this ambition, and although unfortunately we have not one single tomb from this early period, we know that the conquistadors did build them in the churches of which they were patrons. In the church of San Agustín there was the tomb of Martín de Ircio and his family, in Santo Domingo were those of many of the nobility, beginning with the first viceroy, Don Luis de Velasco. In the Dominican church at Yanhuitlán there can be seen on either side of the presbytery two little chapels, now closed up, which undoubtedly contained the tomb of the *encomenderos* who built the church, Francisco and Gonzalo de las Casas. At Tepoztlán, in the state of Morelos, small chapels of magnificent Renaissance design can be seen at the left of the vaulted space which serves as an

de Monzón, Calle del Puente de Palacio, Calle del Puente de la Leña, Calle del Puente del Espíritu Santo, and so on.

The Architecture of Display

In the early years not much building was done purely for show, of the sort which appears when cities have reached a certain prosperity. Two attitudes, however, prompted the governors and the inhabitants of Mexico City to erect monuments. The first was the obsequious attitude of the officials, which led them to celebrate everything that happened at the Spanish court with temporary monuments, or to display in the same way entry into the monastery, and these undoubtedly served as tombs. Only the praying statues of the gentlemen are missing; otherwise they might be tombs in Spain.[53]

What were these Mexican tombs like? Undoubtedly they were like those in Spain, which can be reduced to two types: the tomb on the floor, with a sarcophagus and a reclining portrait or simple inscription, or the wall tomb enclosed in an arch or frame where one sees the praying or reclining portrait of the defunct, with coat of arms and inscriptions. It seems certain that the first tombs were at least partly Gothic, but very soon they must have been carved in the splendid Plateresque style.[54]

[53] According to a note written in his personal copy of this book, Don Manuel Toussaint had changed his opinion about these chapels, in agreement with the elucidation of Francisco de la Maza, in his review of this volume, "Arte colonial de México," *Cuadernos americanos,* 8 (1949), 232–236.

[54] See Toussaint, "La escultura funeraria en la Nueva España," *Anales del Instituto de Investigaciones Estéticas,* 11 (1944), 41–58.

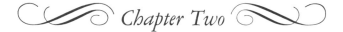

Chapter Two

MEDIEVAL PAINTING

Christian-Indigenous Painting

PAINTING IN Mexico after the European conquest can by no means be considered a mixture or fusion of Indian art with that of the Spanish Renaissance. Things so different in character cannot interchange and merge together; as we have said, it was only the materials of painting and the Indian workmen that were made use of in the new style.

Painting was used to decorate the churches and monasteries. At first, it seems, they tried ornamenting the churches with mosaics of flower petals incrusted on the straw-mats called *pétatl*, but that form of decoration was extremely fragile and evanescent. Another possibility was to make images and even decorations in feather mosaic (63). But featherwork also was perishable by its very nature, and especially susceptible to the attack of insects. So they came back to painting. The friars organized real art centers, such as the famous school of arts and crafts founded by Fray Pedro de Gante as an annex to the chapel of San José de los Naturales in the Convento Grande de San Francisco in Mexico City. In this first school of painting they used engravings as models for the painters, and the images they had brought with them were reproduced in great

numbers. There is no other type of painting in which we find so intimate a relationship between the Indian and the European mode, and this is why we call it "Christian-Indigenous." It is Christian because the purpose is essentially religious, but it is Indian inasmuch as we still feel in it the indigenous hand, and sometimes the poverty of means of the untrained artist. The chroniclers state that it was Fray Pedro de Gante himself who taught the Indians painting, but it is doubtful that this worthy friar had a technical knowledge of art. Rather we must suppose that there were other friars, among them some trained artists, who devoted themselves to teaching painting. Fray Diego de Valadés should be mentioned here; it is on record that he was an artist, or at least drew well enough, since in his book *Rhetorica Christiana,* which was later published in Europe, there are adequate illustrations and engravings signed *Valadés fecit* (28).[1]

The indigenous chronicles, which afford us valuable information on the history of Mexico in this period,

[1] Diego de Valadés, *Rhetorica Christiana* (Perusiae: apud Petrumiacobum Petrutium, 1579). See also Francisco de la Maza, "Fray Diego Valadés," *Anales del Instituto de Investigaciones Estéticas,* 13 (1945), 15–44.

28. Diego de Valadés. Allegorical Churchyard. Engraving. From *Rhetorica Christiana* (Perusiae, 1575).

29. Anonymous. Fray Diego de Betanzos. Mural, Dominican monastery, Tepetlaóztoc, México.

are also full of drawings. Although the artists trained in this school continue to work in the second half of the century, it is merely an extension of this early style, and hence is noted here.

Miscellaneous Paintings

Among the pictures preserved from this period is a panel representing *St. Francis* which belonged to Señor Federico Gómez de Orozco (color, facing p. v). In this painting, which belongs to the category of the "primitives," one recognizes both the ingenuousness of the naive artist and the elementary technique of the student. It is painted in oils, and well preserved.

A picture which undoubtedly dates from the middle of the century is the portrait of *Fray Domingo de Betanzos* preserved in his hermitage attached to the Dominican monastery of Tepetlaóztoc in the state of Mexico (29). Perhaps it is a copy of a mural painting made when the Friar was still living, but in any case it has the same quality of the primitive and the ingenuous.[2]

2 Manuel Toussaint, *Paseos coloniales*, pp. 11–14.

30. Wall decoration, patio of the Hospital de Jesús, Mexico City.

From the Indian chronicles we can cite the following historical notes: in the year 1556 the painters Pedro Quauhtli, Miguel Toxoxhícuic, Luis Xochitótotl, and Miguel Yohualahuach completed a painting representing *Señores que habían gobernado el país azteca* ("Noblemen who have ruled the land of the Aztecs"). Two other native painters, Fernando Colli and Pedro Xóchmitl, painted in 1569 a picture of *The Fourteen Acts of Mercy* for the prison in Mexico City.

Don Francisco del Paso y Troncoso and some other American historians state that the Indian painter Marcos de Aquino or Marcos Cipac mentioned by Bernal Díaz del Castillo was active around 1555. They say that he painted many pictures, in collaboration with Pedro Chachalaca, Francisco Xinmámal, and Pedro de San Nicolás. The most important was the altarpiece of the chapel of San José de los Naturales. It was composed of seven paintings: above, *The Crucifixion* in the center, with *St. Bonaventure* and *St. Louis the Bishop* on either side; below, *St. Joseph*, patron of the chapel, between *St. Francis* and *St. Anthony of Padua*, and *The Last Supper* as predella. This retable is represented in one of the drawings for the year 1564 in the Aubin Codex.

Mural Painting

The most interesting work of this school is undoubtedly the mural decoration of churches and monasteries. From the earliest days a fresco technique was used, and this made the work quite permanent. As early as 1539 we hear of the religious festivities of the Indians in Tlaxcala from Fray Toribio de Benevente, who was known as Motolinía, in his *Historia de los indios:*

For Easter they had the chapel in the churchyard finished, a very impressive work which they call *Bethlehem*. The outside was then painted in four days in fresco, so that the rain would never wash it off. In one panel they painted the first three days of the creation of the world, and in another panel, the other three days; in two more panels they put the Tree of Jesse with the genealogy of the Mother of God, who is at the top, very beautiful, and in the other, our Father St. Francis; another part shows the Church, His Holiness the Pope, cardinals, bishops, etc; and on the other side, the Emperor, kings, and knights. The Spaniards who have seen the chapel say that it is one of the most delightful things of its kind in the kingdom of Spain.[3]

[3] Motolinía (Toribio de Benevente), *Motolinía's History of the Indians of New Spain*. Trans. Francis Borgia Steck, p. 156.

The decoration which the Indians painted on churches and monasteries is called *de romano,* grotesque, or arabesque decoration (30). It consists of friezes and borders of foliate motifs, with medallions or niches showing scenes such as the Crucifixion, or the figures of saints. There are cases where the whole building is decorated in this way; in other places the painting is concentrated in certain areas, especially the cloister.[4]

We can cite even older mural decoration in fresco, that in the cloister of the Franciscan monastery in Cholula, which bears the date 1530.[5] It shows a scene from the *Life of St. Francis* (31), and constitutes, with other pictures of the same type there, one of the oldest documents in the history of Mexican art.

Another picture at Cholula, the *Mass of St. Gregory,* is interesting not only for the history of art, but for that of religion, since we can see in it what the ecclesiastical ornaments and utensils were like in those early days. The way all the objects are arranged, and the very vestments of the priests, are reminiscent of the Indian codices.

Another monastery which has a great deal of fresco decoration is Huejotzingo (32). These paintings are from several periods, but some of them are among the earliest, such as the representation of *The First Twelve Franciscans.* Their Christian names are written so absurdly, most of them all wrong, that this in itself would prove them the work of Indians.

In the Franciscan monastery of Tlalmanalco considerable painted decoration has survived. In the lower cloister there is a portrait of *Fray Martín de Valencia* and a *St. Clare,* besides the purely decorative painting.

In the monastery of Cuernavaca, which is also Franciscan, a valuable painting can be seen in the cloister, unfortunately in bad condition. It represents *The Spiritual Lineage of St. Francis,* that is, all the male and female saints of the Franciscan Order, arranged in a procession with their names. In the center, in three little panels, are scenes from the life of St. Francis, and the whole thing is framed in the Franciscan cord. This painting, like many which were in the various

31. Anonymous. St. Francis Renouncing His Worldly Goods. Mural, cloister of the Franciscan monastery, Cholula, Puebla.

Franciscan establishments, recalls, on the one hand, the engravings in early European books showing the lineage of saints, but also, on the other, the Indian genealogies drawn in the codices. There is also a good deal of arabesque decoration at Cuernavaca.

The Augustinian monasteries also were decorated magnificently with fresco painting. Even the earliest, like that of Ocuituco, in the state of Morelos, show the typical ornamentation of the cloister with friezes, and the vaults painted to imitate coffers with rosettes.

In the monastery at Acolman one can still see such paintings in the cloisters, most of them with very little color, principally in black and white. The influence of wood engraving is extraordinarily plain in them; the *Crucifixion* recalls sixteenth-century woodcuts, even Dürer's. Certain purely decorative motifs document the theory that woodcuts provided models for these mural decorations. Here we find, for example, a monogram of Jesus wreathed in fruits and flowers (33) which comes

---

[4] See Toussaint, *La pintura en México durante el siglo XVI*; Toussaint, *Pinturas murales en los conventos mexicanos del siglo XVI*; Toussaint, "La pintura mural en Nueva España," *Artes de México,* 4 (1954), 8–30; Martin Soria, "Notes on Early Murals in Mexico," in *Studies in the Renaissance,* 6.

[5] This date is doubtful, in reference to the construction of the building, but accords with the spirit of the painting. (The date has now been removed from the painting.) Cf. George Kubler, *Mexican Architecture of the Sixteenth Century,* pp. 361 ff.

32. Anonymous. The Crucifixion. Mural, cloister of the
Franciscan monastery, Huejotzingo, Puebla.

from the title page of the *Confesionario breve en
lengua Mexicana y Castellana* by Fray Alonso de
Molina, printed in Mexico by Antonio de Espinosa in
1569 (34).

A group of Augustinian monasteries in the state of
Morelos are notable for the great abundance of painting
preserved in them. The richest is at Atlatláuhcan. The
lower cloister looks like a Moorish building, its vaults
painted in coffers, with strapwork and foliate motifs of
great beauty at the corners. The chapels of the churchyard also have painted vaults; the open chapel has one
of the richest and most elegant of these frescoed decorations. In the monastery of Yecapixtla few remains
of painting can be seen, but there is little doubt that
careful investigation would uncover more. At Totolapan various painted areas can be seen; on the stairway
the principal decoration is a frieze in which the design,
pierced through a glossy red plaster, leaves part of the
stone uncovered. In the monastery of Tlayacapan the

paintings which have been revealed by removing a
heavy coat of plaster make a disagreeable impression
because they have been pocked to make the new plaster
adhere better. In the monastery of Zacualpan de Amilpas one can see in the lower cloister interesting scenes
from the history of the Augustinian saints. It is a pity
that these murals were repainted in the nineteenth
century, for they have lost their original character and
look now like popular painting. There are also some
portraits in this monastery.

Fresco painting is to be found in many other Augustinian monasteries, Malinalco, for instance, and Yuririapúndaro and Culhuacán. Most interesting, at Culhuacán, are decorations using indigenous motifs, borders
in stepped-fret designs (35). One might call them archaistic; they seem to show that Indian artists alone
worked there. It is difficult to evalute the artistic quality
of these paintings because of their deterioration.

The convent of Actopan, in the state of Hidalgo,

33. *(Above)* Monogram of Jesus. Mural, Franciscan monastery, Huejotzingo, Puebla.

34. *(Above, right)* Title Page, *Confesionario breve de Fray Alonso de Molina.* México: Antonio de Espinosa, 1569.

35. Wall decoration, cloister of the Augustinian monastery, Culhuacán, Distrito Federal.

offers a great deal of painting, dating from many periods, but since the most important work is in full Renaissance style, we shall study it in a later chapter.

The Dominican monasteries were no exception in the matter of fresco painting. In the monastery of Atzcapotzalco, near the capital, it can be seen in the usual forms: at the entrance, portraits of the Dominican friars who first reached New Spain, and in the cloister decorative friezes, angels, and strapwork.

In the monastery of Tepetlaóztoc there are large circular paintings with scenes of the Passion in the cloister. Also in the splendid monastery of Tepoztlán, in the state of Morelos, considerable remains of painting may be seen in the cloister.

The monastery of Oaxtepec, also in Morelos, is especially important; the figures of friars and of saints which decorate the lower cloister achieve at times an emotional validity which, however ingenuous, suggests the self-conscious artist rather than the indigenous craftsman.

Of the three great Dominican monasteries in the Mixteca Alta, painted decoration has survived only in that of Yanhuitlán. On the wall of the stair well is a huge *St. Christopher,* especially interesting because his cloak is drawn in the parallel folds typical of Byzantine painting.

Many circumstances have contributed to the preservation of these fresco paintings. In the first place, their technique made them indelible, and secondly, they were often covered with heavy coats of plaster when they had deteriorated, or when the new taste for oil painting made the friars prefer to cover their cloister walls with great series of paintings on canvas. One might say that the skill of the fresco painters combined with the ignorance of the eighteenth-century friars to conserve this early art. At present, investigations are being made in many of the buildings, with the idea of restoring their original decoration, at least in part. It should be noted that the Indians themselves had developed an elementary fresco technique before the Conquest, though it cannot be compared by any means to the art of the great Renaissance muralists. In these sixteenth-century murals nothing like a full palette was used, but simply two or three colors and rudimentary shading. But it was undoubtedly a true fresco technique, as we know not only from the testimony of the chroniclers and from the guild ordinances, but from the preservation of the paintings.

Post-Hispanic Codices

This designation refers to the documents written in hieroglyphic form after the conquest of New Spain. The Indians could not change their method of writing instantly; any complaint presented to the Crown or the viceregal authorities could only be written out in their own way—in their ideographs or in the phonetic glyphs which they were beginning to develop.

From the great number of codices made after the Conquest we shall mention only some which have real aesthetic value. Many of them are quite without artistic interest.[6]

Perhaps the most valuable codex of this period was the Lienzo de Tlaxcala (the Tlaxcala Cloth), of which the original has unhappily disappeared.[7] It was seven meters long and two and a half meters wide, and it was painted in mid-century by the Tlaxcalans, to request privileges from the Crown in return for the help given to Spain during the Conquest. A copy, now preserved in the Museo Nacional, was made in the middle of the eighteenth century by a painter of Tlaxcala, Juan Manuel de Illanes (36). The quality of the *lienzo* is clear. The artist knows how to draw the movements of his models; he is still bound by certain conventions of indigenous art, and his figures have not a trace of expression, but these little scenes show imaginative insight and a true decorative sense in the arranging of the figures.

Tira de Tlatelolco (Tlatelolco Roll).[8] This codex represents the principal events in Mexico in the sixteenth century, up to the funeral of Don Luis de Velasco. It is valuable for the detail of the figures, the exactitude of the costumes, and the pleasant effect of the painting on vellum.

Códice Mendocino (Codex of Mendoza).[9] It is sup-

[6] See Donald Robertson, *Mexican Manuscript Painting of the Early Colonial Period: The Metropolitan Schools*; George Kubler and Charles Gibson, *The Tovar Calendar*, pp. 37–41; Federico Gómez de Orozco, "La decoración en los manuscritos hispano-mexicanos primitivos," *Anales del Instituto de Investigaciones Estéticas*, 3 (1938), 48–52.

[7] *Homenaje a Cristóbal Colón; antigüedades mexicanas.* This publication has been reprinted as "Lienzo de Tlaxcalla: la conquista de México; explicación de Alfredo Chavero," in *Artes de México*, 51–52 (1964), 1–80.

[8] *Anales de Tlaltelolco*, ed. Heinrich Berlin and Robert H. Barlow.

[9] *The Mexican Manuscript Known as the Collection of Mendoza*, trans. James C. Clark.

Tenochtitlan.

36. Cortés Meets Moctezuma in Tenochtitlán (Mexico City). From the Lienzo de Tlaxcala (copy made by Juan Manuel de Illanes). Museo Nacional de Antropología e Historia, Mexico City.

posed that the first viceroy, Don Antonio de Mendoza, had this book painted to send to the Emperor Charles V. The ship which was carrying the codex in 1549 was captured by French privateers, and the book was taken to Paris. The manuscript is in three parts: a chronology of Indian history from the founding of the city of Mexico up to the reign of Moctezuma II, a tax register, and a report on customs of the ancient Mexicans. The most notable illustration is the one representing the founding of Mexico City, which is excellent in design.

Relación de Michoacán (Chronicle of Michoacán).[10] This book is a mixture of Indian and European, that is, it contains a narrative in Spanish illustrated with drawings in the indigenous tradition. The Relación is the most valuable document we have for the history of the Tarascan Indians, and it has real value also as a work of art. The exactitude with which the personages are drawn, the exuberant fantasy of their costumes, the complete difference between these figures and those of the other codices, and the consequent exotic quality it assumes—everything serves to demonstrate clearly that

10 *Crónicas de Michoacán,* ed. Federico Gómez de Orozco. See also Nicolás León, "La relación de Michoacán," *Revista mexicana de estudios históricos,* 1 (1927), 197–213.

37. Making feather work. From the Florentine Codex.

the world of Michoacán was different from the Aztec world. Consequently this codex, besides the artistic value of its illustrations, is valuable as introduction to an extremely interesting region.

Introducción de la justicia española en Tlaxcala (The Introduction of Spanish Law into Tlaxcala). This beautiful codex records the moment when the corregidor of Puebla, Hernando de Saavedra, convinced the Indians of Tlaxcala to accept the authority of the Spanish courts. Its artistic value lies in the stylization of forms and the rendering of movement, and in important iconographical detail. We see a tower like the *rollo* of Tepeaca; the *corregidor's* chair and the table of the clerk are also interesting.

Códice de Tepetlaóztoc (Kingsborough Codex).[11] This was designated the Kingsborough Codex by Don Francisco del Paso y Troncoso; actually it is a petition from the Indians of Tepetlaóztoc complaining about their *encomenderos*, especially Gonzalo de Salazar. In his study of the codex Troncoso points out its artistic quality; the artist not only paints the figures, but knows how to express the feelings of each individual.

Códice Sierra (Sierra Codex).[12] This is made up of fragments of an expense book of the church of Santa Catalina Texupan in the Mixteca Alta of Oaxaca, and was published by Dr. León in 1903. It is valuable principally for illustrating the objects used in the cult in the sixteenth century, and has no great artistic merit.

Códice Osuna (Osuna Codex).[13] This record of the complaints of the Indians of Mexico City was presented to the Visitador (Inspector) Valderrama in 1565; it

was published in Madrid in 1878. It is interesting because it shows architectural projects, like the foundations of the Cathedral and the construction of the big dike to the east of the city. The finest things in it are the symbols of Mexico City and of its four divisions, called *barrios*.

Códice Florentino (Florentine Codex).[14] A beautiful set of illustrations to the *Historia de las cosas de Nueva España* by Fray Bernardino de Sahagún (37). The plants and flowers of Mexico are represented, as are the customs of the Indians. It shows the work of various hands and also the influence of woodcuts.

Códice Durán (Durán Codex).[15] This codex illustrates the history written by Fray Diego Durán; its plates are of uneven quality.

Lienzo de Jucutácato (the Cloth of Jucutácato).[16] According to some authorities, this also illustrates the peregrinations of the Tarascan Indians to settle in Michoacán. The great number of religious symbols indicates, according to others, that it deals rather with the establishment of religion in the country which was later known as Michoacán. It has no great artistic worth.

[11] *Códice Kingsborough; memorial de los indios de Tepetlaóztoc al monarca español,* ed. Francisco del Paso y Troncoso.
[12] *Códice Sierra; fragmento de una nómina de gastos del pueblo de Santa Caterina Texupan,* ed. N. León.
[13] *Códice Osuna.* See also Lucas Alamán, *Disertaciones sobre la historia de la República Megicana.*
[14] Bernardino de Sahagún, *Historia general de las cosas de Nueva España* (Florentine Codex).
[15] Diego Durán, *Historia de las Indias de Nueva España.*
[16] *Lienzo de Jucutácato.*

Códice de Yanhuitlán (Codex of Yanhuitlán).[17] The remains of this fine codex are preserved in the Academia de Bellas Artes in Puebla. It is a Mixtec manuscript which consists of records of this very old town and its monuments. The figures of colonial personages represented in it show its high artistic level.

There are a great many more codices of secondary importance, since almost every village had one to describe its boundaries, and things like this turn up quite frequently. However, this fact has also created a situation in which there has been extensive forgery of codices dealing with landholdings.

The First European Painters in New Spain

All the historians of Mexican art, with rare exceptions, have accepted the figure of Rodrigo de Cifuentes as the first Spanish painter to work in New Spain. His biography, rich in interesting detail, was written for the *Diccionario universal* by the Conde de la Cortina.[18] Modern writers, however, are in agreement that the biography published in the *Diccionario* is simply a fraud, or a joke of the Conde de la Cortina, since the documents which he cites do not exist, or rather the references he gives for the documents are apocryphal. Don Bernardo Couto has the honor of having been the first to doubt the existence of this artist.[19] It is curious to see how writers persist in accepting the figure of Cifuentes; the only explanation is that, for want of any other information about early artists, they cannot give up his name without leaving a great gap in their texts.

Apparently the first actual artist for whom we have documentation was Cristóbal de Quesada. His existence is based on his own statement in the middle of the sixteenth century, published among those of his contemporaries in the *Conquistadores y pobladores de Nueva España* by Don Francisco A. de Icaza. Quesada says that the first viceroy of New Spain ordered him to accompany Francisco Vásquez de Coronado in his expedition to Cíbola and Quivira, to make a pictorial record of the new land.[20] He had reached Mexico in 1538, and if he is the man of the same name whom Gestoso records in Seville in 1534, he can be presumed an Andalusian.

We do not know of any work of his resulting from the expedition into New Mexico, but considering its disastrous end and the poverty of the villages discovered, we can assume that instead of painting "the things found in the land" what he did was to hunt for his dinner and defend himself against the terrible Indians.

Nevertheless, it is likely that he did some painting during his stay in New Spain, although he drops out of sight after giving this information, and we do not even know whether he died in Mexico or went back to Spain.[21]

---

[17] See *Códice de Yanhuitlán,* ed. Wigberto Jiménez Moreno and Salvador Mateos Huiguera.

[18] *Diccionario universal de historia y geografía,* II, 314–315.

[19] José Bernardo Couto, *Diálogo sobre la historia de la pintura en México,* p. 42. See also Francisco Pérez Salazar, *Historia de la pintura en Puebla,* pp. 62–65.

[20] No. 1298.

[21] On the whole period see Toussaint, *Pintura colonial en México*; George Kubler and Martin Soria, *Art and Architecture in Spain and Portugal and their American Dominions*; Emily Edwards, *Painted Walls of Mexico.*

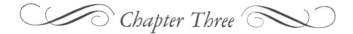

MEDIEVAL SCULPTURE

Indigenous Sculpture

OF ALL THE ARTS flourishing in Mexico when the Spaniards arrived, sculpture was the most highly developed. In their stone figures the indigenous religions had given eternal form to the mysterious concepts of their rites and their theogenies. Basalt was perhaps the appropriate medium for the expression of the Aztec soul; and because they lacked iron tools to work their sculpture, one sees the Indian spirit even more directly impressed on it, as Paul Morand has so finely observed. Indian sculpture is essentially symbolic and decorative; each figure has its meaning, every relief is a symbol, religious or chronological. But even within these limitations, the indigenous culture succeeded in creating magnificent sculpture, powerful, expressive, and splendidly stylized. The stupendous monoliths, which are certainly the masterpieces of Aztec art, are themselves the proof: the *Coatlicue,* the *Cuauhxicalli de Tizoc,* and the piece popularly known as the *Aztec Calendar.*

Along with this great sculpture, symbolic and recondite, there was also a realistic mood in which the human figure was represented, its form interpreted quite naturalistically. So we have a certain number of heads which are almost portraits, like the *Head of the Dead Man,* the *Eagle-Knight, The Sad Indian,* etc. Yet it may be that these portraits, which seem to us excellent works of art, were at the periphery of what the Indians meant by art. For them the concept of beauty was inextricably involved with that of divinity, which was the more beautiful the more monstrous, the more recondite, and indeed, the less humane it was.

Beside this sculpture, with its strange power, the Europeans set their Isabelline Gothic and Renaissance sculpture. What could they do for each other? It was certainly in sculpture that Indian elements had the best chance of surviving, because of the medium, the identity of materials, and the technical skill of the Indian craftsmen.[1]

A certain amount of sculpture has survived from this time, in which, regardless of the subject matter, not only the workmanship but even the spirit of Indian art continues. Such is a coat of arms which came from the little church of the Sanctorum to the Museo Nacional in Mexico City. This extremely interesting stone

[1] See George Kubler, "On the Colonial Extinction of the Motifs of Pre-Columbian Art," in Samuel K. Lathrop, *Essays in Pre-Columbian Art and Archaeology,* pp. 14–34; Elizabeth Wilder Weismann, *Mexico in Sculpture.*

is a European heraldic shield, designed in the usual manner; but the frame is composed of vegetable motifs which clearly follow the indigenous conventions. We have not succeeded in identifying the family represented by this device, but its antiquity is obvious, and it shows how the Indians interpreted a European subject in their own way.

There is another coat of arms, on a tombstone in the town of Tilantongo in the Mixteca Alta. Here not only the motifs are Indian—weapons and shields (*chimales*)—but the very manner in which the carving is executed. The division into quarters and the sculptural technique are absolutely Indian.

On the church of Tecamachalco, in the state of Puebla, there is a commemorative stone (38). Its appearance is so indigenous that if we did not see the Roman letters of the inscription, we should take it for a pre-Hispanic relief. The Roman letters spell out a Nahuatl inscription: "Begun in 1589, completed in 1591." Above this, on a rock pierced by arrows, stands a crowned eagle, from whose beak issue the glyphs of blood and of fire.

Architectural details may also be found where, if

38. Date stone, church of the Franciscan monastery, Tecamachalco, Puebla.

39. Eagle Knight, portal of a house, Cholula, Puebla.

49

40. Cristo del Pareo. Corn pith, painted. Museo Regional, Pátzcuaro, Michoacán.

41. La Conquistadora. Painted wood.
Cathedral of Puebla.

the form itself is European, the technique and even the motifs of the ornament are Indian. Such are the capitals of the Renaissance cloister at Acolman, in the state of México (92). The design of the whole thing is entirely European, but motifs from indigenous flora have been adapted to create decoration quite outside European conventions. The same thing occurs on the impost blocks of the doorway of a house in Cholula, in the state of Puebla (39). They are ordinary Plateresque imposts, with a pearl moulding of the

Gothic type; but the bird which forms the capital is in fact an Eagle-Knight, and the plumes are stylized exactly as in pre-Hispanic sculpture. We can see this also in a little monolithic window from Teotihuacán now in the Museo Nacional. The arch is the typical Plateresque ogee arch, but the frame is decorated with indigenous floral motifs, and at the bottom is a series of stylized rosettes which we shall see persisting in many portals of the sixteenth century.

Another documented indigenous survival of some

42. Descent from the Cross. Wood. Church of El Calvario, Chiapa de Corzo, Chiapas.

43. The Last Judgment. Posa III, Franciscan monastery, Calpan, Puebla.

importance is a matter not of the style, but of the material of sculpture. This is the sculpture made of *tzompantle*. The *tzompantle* is a native tree which the Europeans called *colorín* because of the red color of its small seeds. The pith of this tree offers a soft material for sculpture, which is then painted like wooden sculpture. And from the earliest days after the Conquest images were also made from *caña de maíz,* the pith of corn stalk. The biographers of Don Vasco de Quiroga relate that he had the image known as *Nuestra Señora de la Salud* (Our Lady of Good Health), which is venerated in Pátzcuaro, modelled in this material by the Indians. Churches and museums still have figures of Christ made of corn pith (40, 355, 357), and a well-known story relates that the documents denouncing the crimes of the First Audiencia reached Spain hidden inside one of these images.[2]

[2] See Abelardo Carrillo y Gariel, *El Cristo de Mexicaltzingo; técnica de las esculturas en caña*; Julián Bonavit, "Esculturas tarascas de caña de maíz y orquídeas," *Anales del Museo Michoacana*, Ep. 2, No. 3 (1944), 65–68.

European Sculpture

In contrast to this sculpture of indigenous tendency, some European sculpture brought over by the conquistadors should be noted. A very few images of this sort have come down to us. Probably the most venerable is the image of *Nuestra Señora de los Remedios,* which is still preserved in the sanctuary at Los Remedios. According to the legend, this image of the Virgin was abandoned by a Spanish soldier on the Noche Triste (the "Sad Night" of Cortés' flight from Tenochtitlán), and found by a chief who took it home; later, as a result of miracles wrought by the image in a place called Otoncalpulco, the sanctuary was built there. It is not a figure of great artistic value; it is small, and since it is dressed in cloth—the classic hoop skirt of Spanish images—we are speaking only of a bust.

In the Cathedral of Puebla is another such image, known as *La Conquistadora* (41), but it too is of slight artistic importance.

In the church of the Hospital de San Lázaro in Mexico City there was another image, known as *Nuestra*

Señora de la Bala, so named because it saved from death a soldier who had been shot.

Another little image from the early days of the Colony is the one preserved in the church of Santa Fe, undoubtedly brought there by that excellent man Don Vasco de Quiroga when he built his famous hospital of that name for the Indians. This is a polychrome high relief representing the Virgin with the Child Jesus and St. John the Baptist, which certainly dates from the period of the Italian Renaissance. It too is called *Nuestra Señora de la Salud,* the advocacy of all the hospitals established by Don Vasco in New Spain.

Also from this period, it is said, are the so-called *Cristos de los Conquistadores.* There are four of these in Mexico City: two in the Cathedral, one in the Capilla de la Expiración of the monastery of Santo Domingo, and the other in the church of La Profesa. Legend has it that Charles V gave them to Mexico, but there is no proof of this at all. What one can say is that they are sculptures of some merit, perhaps from the middle of the century, and apparently Andalusian.

A sculpture of medieval flavor, clearly European in character though possibly executed in Mexico, is the wood relief in the church of Guadalupe in Chiapa de Corzo, Chiapas. It represents *The Descent from the Cross,* and its style takes us back to the fifteenth century in Europe (42). The delicately painted wood is very hard; it seems to be what is called *quiebrahacha* (hatchet-breaker) in that region.

Decorative Sculpture

For a methodical study of our sculpture in this early period, it is convenient to classify it according to its purpose, as the guilds classified it, when they were later set up. So we divide it into decorative sculpture and statuary, and subdivide each of these into stone and wood. These subdivisions correspond to the different crafts: the *cantero* works in stone; the *escultor* or *imaginero* carves human figures of wood, with or without clothing; and the *entallador* does all the decorative carving in wood which the great retables require. To these we must add the *ensamblador,* or joiner, whose work it is, as the name implies, to assemble the multitudinous parts of the retable.

Beginning with the study of decorative sculpture in stone, we discover three interesting topics: decorative sculpture based on engravings (just as we found in painting), sculpture in which medieval reminiscences,

44. The Last Judgment. From *Flos Sanctorum* (Saragosa, 1521).

especially Gothic, are to be found, and finally, sculpture which shows a strong indigenous influence.

Some examples of decorative sculpture based on engravings have been identified. In the old Franciscan monastery of the city of Tlaxcala are reliefs in stone which appear to have been copied from woodcuts. Such are the two reliefs of *The Annunciation,* at either side of the door of the chapel called the Tercer Orden: the Virgin is like an Italian Madonna, and yet the Angel, in the stylization of the wings and the strongly constructed head, and most of all in the indigenous glyphs representing speech which appear by his head (quite apart from the phylactery issuing from his mouth) betrays the indigenous craftsman. Two similar reliefs, representing St. Peter and St. Paul, can be seen on the only surviving posa, or churchyard shrine there.

45. Portal, church of Santiago, Angahua, Michoacán.

Also from prints, though with strong indigenous flavor, are the reliefs of the posas of the monastery of Calpan, in the state of Puebla. The relief of *The Last Judgment* (43) was taken from a woodcut which appears in a Latin grammar of the fifteenth century (44), although at first glance it appears, like all of them, to be purely Indian work.[3]

The classical example of decorative sculpture copied from an engraving is afforded by the door jambs of the side portal of the Franciscan church in Texcoco, in the state of México, which undoubtedly came from the earlier church there. At first glance we have the impression of an inscription in large capital letters; more careful observation shows that they are nothing but the letters of the alphabet in order. Apparently the Indians, observing how the friars put inscriptions in Roman letters about their monuments, thought they were doing likewise by simply copying the letters from a printed handbook. The letters are actually Renaissance in style; we consider them here because they were copied from a print. Such decoration was used also in Europe.

Decorative sculpture with Medieval reminiscences is quite plentiful, and the catalog will be larger when a systematic study of the matter has been made. Let us cite for the time being the great amount of Gothic detail in the church of Yecapixtla, Morelos (87): the great rose window over the main door, the pulpit (which has some Renaissance detail), the framing of the cloister doors, with their characteristic crockets, the pedestals and canopies of the main portal.

On the façade of the Franciscan church at Cholula also is Gothic ornament—the same crockets on the main doorway—and although the rose window is already Renaissance in style, the whole feeling of the façade remains Gothic (67). Many of the colonial buildings of this period have windows with stone tracery exactly as in the Gothic buildings of Europe; at Totolapan, in the state of Morelos, for example, at Yecapixtla, and at Yanhuitlán in the Mixteca Alta. In many other places tracery has been replaced by plain windows; some fragments of Gothic tracery are still lying about the Franciscan monastery at Texcoco.

Decorative sculpture which shows indigenous in-

46. Portal, La Guatapera (chapel of the hospital), Uruapan, Michoacán.

fluence is quite common.[4] As in all the art of the colonial period, influences of various sorts intermingle. In some cases, like the great open chapel of Tlalmanalco (15), one feels a kind of Romanesque survival in the ingenuous placing of the figures around the triumphal arch, and plenty of Gothic reminiscences in the clustered columns of the arcade, while the total effect is Plateresque, and the character of the sculpture itself is absolutely Indian. Perhaps the most interesting part of the sculpture is the series of portraits which appear on the capitals of the pilasters; strongly personal, they may represent the chiefs of the town or the

[3] See Kubler, *Mexican Architecture in the Sixteenth Century*, pp. 375–377, nn. 50–53; 391–394.
[4] On this subject, see José Moreno Villa, *La escultura colonial mexicana*; Weismann, *Mexico in Sculpture*; Alfred Neumeyer, "The Indian Contribution to Architectural Decoration in Spanish Colonial America," *Art Bulletin*, 30 (1948), 104–121.

47. Churchyard cross. Stone. Franciscan monastery, Cuautitlán, México.

sculptors who worked there.[5] In Coyoacán, now standing beside the façade of the church, is a doorway whose round arch is vigorously carved with vegetable motifs. This doorway resembles nothing in Europe; if extending the ornament the whole width of the archivolt makes us think of Romanesque work, the detail of the ornament is entirely indigenous. The portal of the recently discovered church of Angahua is one of the most important examples in this category (45). It recalls the beautiful portal of the Hospital Chapel in Uruapan (46), the famous "Guatapera" founded by Fray Juan de San Miguel, but it is more ornate. Here, wonderfully mixed, we have the Renaissance Plateresque flavor of the total design, the Mudejar exaggeration of the *alfices,* superimposed in an extraordinary series, and the pure Indian taste in the technique of the modest reliefs. Inside the church are more Moorish elements, and the date 1577, probably referring to its construction.[6] On the Dominican church of Coixtlahuaca, in the Mixteca Alta of Oaxaca, the indigenous influence is again manifest: at either side of the side door are reliefs of the Symbols of the Passion, with a head on each one, and from these heads come Nahuatl speech glyphs. Certainly it must have been an Indian who carved this sculpture.

Among the important monuments of decorative sculpture in stone are the great crosses which were raised in the monastery churchyards. At first very tall crosses were made from tree trunks; they could be seen from a great distance, but they were a terrible hazard as lightning conductors, since the Indians always gathered around them. In the year 1539 it was decreed that the crosses should be made of stone, and not so high as the wooden ones, to avoid this danger.[7] A considerable number of stone crosses can still be seen. The most remarkable is undoubtedly the cross of Cuautitlán, in the state of México, which bears the date 1555 (47). Its sculpture is interesting: there are two portraits on it, which are said to represent the friar who was Prior of the monastery at that time, and the *encomendero,* Alonso de Ávila. Another very beautiful cross is that of the Franciscan monastery of Huichapan, in

48. Churchyard cross. Stone. Franciscan monastery, Huichapan, Hidalgo.

the state of Hidalgo; its fine low reliefs are completely Plateresque in character (48). Another interesting cross is at Jilótepec, also in Hidalgo: it rises from a great square base decorated with a frieze of shields which is reminiscent of the top stage of a pyramid. At Santa Cruz Atoyac and Huipulco there are crosses with fleur-de-lis finials, like that of Cuautitlán. The cross of

[5] See John McAndrew, *Open-Air Churches,* pp. 535–539; Weismann, *Mexico in Sculpture,* pp. 54–55, 197–198.

[6] F. H. Rhode, "Angahuan," *Anales del Instituto de Investigaciones Estéticas,* 14 (1946), 5–18; Manuel Toussaint, "Angahua," *Journal of the Society of Architectural Historians,* 5 (1945–1946).

[7] Joaquín García Icazbalceta, *Don Fray Juan de Zumárraga.*

49. Churchyard cross. Stone. Augustinian monastery, Acolman, México.

50. Churchyard cross. Stone. Franciscan monastery, Ciudad Hidalgo, Michoacán.

the Augustinian monastery at Acolman presents a curious contrast (49). A relief of the Virgin is carved on the block of stone which serves as a base for the cross, and this sculpture is so primitive that it seems rather an idol than a Christian image. The cross, however, is covered with delicate reliefs which do not impair its cylindrical profile, and at the crossing a beautiful head

of Christ recalls Renaissance sculpture, especially in contrast to the figure below. The cross of El Cardonal, in the state of Hidalgo, is a mixture of Indian style, in the primitive symbols of the Passion, with the European character of the fine inscription above. Recently some crosses have been discovered with an indentation at the crossing, as if to hold a disk of some precious stone, exactly as the Indians did with their mysterious idols (50). This has been interpreted as a proof of indigenous survival in Christian art.[8]

Other examples of this sort are the baptismal fonts, the holy-water fonts, and some pulpits. The most impressive of all the baptismal fonts is that of Zinacantepec, which is covered with reliefs and dates from 1581 (51), but there are many others which might be mentioned. The font of Chimalhuacán Chalco, with its profuse floral ornament, is dated 1542; that of the Franciscan monastery of Acatzingo, with its strong in-

[8] Rafael García Granados, "Reminiscencias idolátricas en monumentos coloniales," *Anales del Instituto de Investigaciones Estéticas,* 5 (1940), 54–56.

51. Baptismal font. Stone. Church of the Franciscan monastery, Zinacantepec, México.

52. Stoup. Stone. Church of the Franciscan monastery, Tlalnepantla, México.

digenous flavor, is dated by a Nahuatl glyph, "four rabbit," which corresponds to 1574; that of Yecapixtla is ornamented with four mermaids. Holy-water stoups of indigenous style are numerous, from the richest, like that of Cholula, to the most simple, where the use of the Franciscan cord makes us think of the pre-Conquest *cuauhxicallis,* the vessels to receive the blood of sacrificial victims (52).

Some remarkable pulpits also have been preserved. Almost all of them are polychrome and gilded. To cite a few of the most important, there is one at Huaque-

chula, very rich and Indian in its decoration (53), one at Yecapixtla reminiscent of Isabelline Gothic, a very simple one at Huexotla, with only the Franciscan cord as ornament, others at Huejotzingo (54) and at Acolman.

We do not know what the retables were like in this earliest period. Perhaps there were retables in a Gothic style; some were simply painted; some were made in feather mosaic. No sculptured retables from this time have been preserved; the earliest we have are already in the Renaissance style.

53. Pulpit. Stone. Church of the Franciscan monastery, Huaquechula, Puebla.

54. Pulpit. Stone. Church of the Franciscan monastery, Huejotzingo, Puebla.

56. Lion. Stone. Museo de Chiapas,
Tuxtla Gutiérrez, Chiapas.

55. Dog. From the fountain of Tepeaca. Stone.
Museo Nacional del Virreinato, Tepotzotlán, México.

Figure Sculpture

In the category of sculpture in the round we do have some pieces which can be assumed to date from the earliest days of New Spain. Among these, the most ingenuous in form and most impressive in size are the great saints on the façade of the Dominican church of Teposcolula in the Mixteca. They undoubtedly came from the earlier church and were preserved because of their high quality, and set in niches on pedestals which seem to be large capitals built into the wall.

Equally primitive is the Crucifix which breaks the pediment of the church at Yecapixtla, in Morelos; it is a squat figure, almost Asiatic (87).

Another archaic Crucifix stands in the center of the cloister at Maní, in Yucatán; this, too, is heavy in proportions, and ingenuous in feeling.

At Pátzcuaro, in the chapel at the edge of town known as El Humilladero, is a stone crucifix which was made for Don Vasco de Quiroga and bears the date 1552. Later, in the seventeenth century, the cross was covered by this chapel which took its name; but the sculpture itself is very primitive. Unfortunately it has been painted, and the paint prevents one's seeing its real character.[9]

Rude but vigorous early sculpture are four doglike figures which, with eight others, originally decorated the fountain of the Franciscan monastery of Tepeaca, in the state of Puebla (55). Until recently they stood on one of the streets leading into the main plaza of the town, and they are now in the museum at Chapultepec. Their vigorous form makes them seem like pre-Conquest animals, and they must have been some of the first sculpture made in New Spain. The large lion preserved in the Museo de Chiapas, in Tuxtla Gutiérrez, has the same quality (56). If we did not know that there were no lions of this African type in America, we would take this for pre-Conquest sculpture; the technique is identical, in the treatment of the mane and in the teeth of inlaid bone, and so is the stylization of the body.

These works of art which are authentic survivals of indigenous style have been given the designation

9 See also Toussaint, *Pátzcuaro*.

tequitqui by José Moreno Villa. This is an accurate and useful term, but only if it is limited to real survivals, and is not extended to what we call popular art, or to popular imitations of European art, which require different consideration, as we shall see in due time.[10]

The Artists

There are some notices of the sculptors who worked in this early period, although it is hard to distinguish the sculptor, properly speaking, from the stonecutter working on architecture. In any case it is interesting to give what documentation we have, as a core to which other students in the future can add new facts and information. We have already mentioned Juan de Entrambas Aguas, *cantero,* who worked in the Plaza Mayor of Mexico City. We should note Pedro Vázquez, also a *cantero,* who settled in the city on September 2, 1530, and seems to have been the architect of the first church of the Hospital de Jesús. Diego Díaz de Lisboa, a Portuguese *cantero,* was living in Mexico City on July 18, 1530; he was *maestro de obras* (building supervisor) of the Real Audiencia, and at mid-century, when the report on *Conquistadores y Pobladores* was drawn up, he was mentioned twice.[11] The report states that he taught the art of stonecutting to all the Indians. He must have worked steadily to earn his living, but the only thing we know by him is a corner window, double-arched with a little column in the middle, which was in the Hospital de Jesús. Don Lucas Alamán has handed down the record of this window, which was in existence until 1833; it had an inscription which read: *Diego Díaz de Lisbona, de nación portugués, hizo esta ventana año de 1535* ("Diego Díaz of Lisbon, of Portuguese nationality, made this window in the year 1535"). Alamán incorrectly read *Deusbona.*[12] Another

cantero of this early period was Bartolomé Coronado, who on August 31, 1536, signed a contract with Licenciado Juan Altamirano, cousin and friend of Hernán Cortés, to execute various carving for his residence, on the Calle del Hospital on the way to Ixtapalapa, that is to say, the buildings which are now known as the house of the Condes de Santiago de Calimaya.[13] In 1549 Juan de Arrúe, *entallador,* arrived in New Spain; he had worked on the cathedral of Seville two years before, according to Gestosa.[14] Arrúe must have worked in various places in New Spain, but we know nothing more of him except that a little before 1565 he married Marta Calzontzin in Pueblos de Ávalos, in the present state of Colima. In that year the colonial painter, also called Juan de Arrúe after his father, was born of this marriage; probably the sculptor Arrúe died quite early, for there is a good deal of documentation about his son's work, while he is never mentioned again.[15]

Such is the information, certainly rather slight, which we can offer about this first period of colonial sculpture. It shows, nonetheless, that there was already intensive work in this field which was in time to produce such remarkable works of art.

[10] Moreno Villa, *Escultura colonial,* pp. 16–18; Weismann, *Mexico in Sculpture,* pp. 11, 190.

[11] Francisco A. de Icaza, *Conquistadores y pobladores de Nueva España,* Nos. 890, 1272.

[12] Lucas Alamán, *Disertaciones sobre la historia de la República Megicana,* p. 85.

[13] I am indebted for this information to my esteemed friend, Don Agustín Millares Carlo.

[14] José Gestoso y Pérez, *Ensayo de un diccionario de los artífices que florecieron en Sevilla,* p. 74.

[15] Francisco Pérez Salazar, *Historia de la pintura en Puebla.*

Chapter Four

THE MINOR ARTS
OF THE MIDDLE AGES

Silversmiths, Goldsmiths, and Lapidaries

OTHING AMAZED the Europeans more in the conquest of New Spain than the great quantity of splendid jewels which they found there. The Indians indeed were masters in the art of working precious metals. The lists of valuable pieces which the Spaniards dispatched to the crown have been published, as well as the tribute lists of the *caciques* and the *encomenderos*. From these documents we can see that it was not simply the intrinsic value of the metal which attracted the conquistadors, but that they were overwhelmed by the beauty of the objects. They even commissioned some to be made, as we shall see.[1] It was in Europe that these Indian artifacts were considered merely in terms of the value of the metal; everything was melted down when it arrived from New Spain, so that while there are numerous examples of feather work in European museums, there is not a single piece of gold work.

That the Indian silversmiths continued to work and that the Spaniards made use of their skill is obvious. On the other hand, we know for certain that European craftsmen also came to the colony immediately. Among the oldest pieces recorded which are already European in character, we should mention first the golden lizard,

an ex-voto which Hernán Cortés sent to Guadalupe in Extremadura in gratitude for his recovery from the poisonous bite of such a creature. Until a few years ago it remained in the monastery, and then went to the Instituto de Valencia de Don Juan in Madrid. In recent times there has been some question about this jewel, since it is ornamented with enamel, which the Indians had not yet learned to use, and its form, as well as the technique of setting the pearls, seems entirely European.[2] There is also a medal which Cortés is supposed to have carried, which, even if it was not actually made in New Spain, is in the style of that period. It shows Nuestra Señora de la Candelaria wearing a rich robe and the imperial crown, holding her Son in her arms. The embroidered velvet case in which Cortés carried the medal has also survived.[3]

We do know about a jewel commissioned by Cortés himself as a gift for Charles V. It was a culverin, or little cannon, completely covered with relief and cast

---

[1] Marshall H. Saville, *The Goldsmith's Art in Ancient Mexico.*
[2] Federico Gómez de Orozco, "El ex-voto de Hernán Cortés?" *Anales del Instituto de Investigaciones Estéticas,* 8 (1942), 51–54.
[3] *México a través de los siglos,* II, 142–143.

57. Silver crozier, mitre. Embroidered in silver, gold, and pearls. Museo Nacional del Virreinato, Tepotzotlán, México.

they had in their pagan days can be found in the illustrations of the Codex of Tepatlaóztoc,[6] where we see a piece of gold work among "those given to Luis Baca." It is a cross on a three-stepped base; each arm of the cross has a ring with three bells on each side, and nine bells hang from the base. This sort of work must have been made expressly to pay the tribute, since it is unlikely that it existed in such quantity as the taxes demanded. Among the treasure of the chapel of Cortés' palace in Cuernavaca there was, according to the inventory of 1544, "a gilded cross with its figure and base of silver, all gilded, which they say was made by Indians."[7]

Fray Bernardino de Sahagún, always so precise in his detail, describes the difference between the technique of the Indian craftsmen and that of the Europeans.[8] The Indian goldsmiths made their mould by mixing clay and ground charcoal, and this mould was carved with a copper scraper. The colonial silversmiths made the mould of a mixture of clay and sand; the sculpture was carved in wax. Both methods are lost-wax processes, but the Indians carved the mould, according to Sahagún, while the Europeans carved the core. The Indians mixed their wax with white copal, an innovation which the Spaniards willingly appropriated, since it gave the wax an excellent consistency.

In 1526 the Spanish court prohibited silversmiths in New Spain. We do not know the reason for this prohibition, but perhaps it was their intention that the raw metal should be sent to Spain, to give work to the Spanish silversmiths, and that the precious objects for the Colony should come from there. But it is hardly credible, when they had worked precious metals so exquisitely and were still doing so, that the craft could have been immediately suppressed—especially when the mines of the new colony were beginning to pour out metal. This prohibition was softened by the edict of August 21, 1528, which merely prohibited silversmiths from having in their houses or shops bellows, forges, or crucibles, that is to say, the apparatus for smelting and refining metals. However, they could carry out these operations in the Casa de Fundición (the

in an alloy of silver with gold. It was made by Francisco de Mesa, a gunner, and Rodrigo Martínez, a smelter.[4] It would appear to be untrue, therefore, that this was the work of Indians, unless they made the wax model and the Spaniards only cast it. It cost 27,500 gold pesos, and was engraved with this legend:

Aquesta nació sin par;
yo en serviros sin segundo;
Vos sin igual en el mundo.[5]

which might be translated freely: "This is unique; I am first in your service; you are without equal in the world." They say that when Charles V received this jewel he gave it to his secretary, Francisco de los Cobos, who lost no time in melting it down for jingling coins.

Proof that the Indians continued working in gold as

[4] Epistolario de Nueva España, III, 170.
[5] Manuel Romero de Terreros, Las artes industriales en la Nueva España, p. 18.
[6] Códice Kingsborough; memorial de los indios de Tepetlaóztoc, fol. 232.
[7] Documentos inéditos relativos a Hernán Cortés y su familia.
[8] Bernardino de Sahagún, Historia general de las cosas de Nueva España, Lib. 9, Ch. 16.

official foundry) under the eye of the inspectors, and then work the metal in their shops. In this way the silversmiths kept on working; the Ayuntamiento of Mexico City appointed alcaldes and *veedores* (directors and overseers) in 1532, but it was not until 1559 that the prohibition was entirely removed.[9]

Metal craftsmen were divided into three groups: the *platero de oro,* who worked only in gold, the *platero de plata,* or silversmith, and the *platero de mazonería,* the silversmith in relief, which seems to have meant an engraver. (Note that the word *platero,* silversmith, is used for working both silver and gold.) Besides these three types of craftsmen, there was the goldbeater (*batihoja*), who made gold leaf and silver leaf, and the wiredrawer (*tirador d'oro*), whose craft it was to convert silver and gold into delicate thread for embroidery. These crafts were not organized in guilds until later, however; and we shall study them at that time. For now we must be content to consider some artifacts of the period.

Our documentation comes from paintings; it is not certain that these objects were made in New Spain, or that they actually existed at all, but they still give some idea of what fine metal work was like in Mexico in those early days. Work for the church was the most important, and we can study several pieces in the fresco representing *The Mass of St. Gregory* at Cholula, which we have already referred to. Here then is a crozier, Gothic in design and ornament; the crook, ornamented with little balls, rises from a hexagonal prism, while the shaft is twisted like a Franciscan cord (57). There is a chalice of common form; a pyx which has a certain Renaissance look already, with its two columns and curved pediment bearing a shield with the device of the Five Wounds; a lavabo with its simple pitcher, and candleholders which resemble the crozier, their large cups decorated with foliage. We can find religious artifacts also in the Sierra Codex, under the years from 1551 to 1558. The candleholders date from 1551; one is still completely Gothic, with a large

58. Processional cross. Silver. Museo Nacional de Historia, Mexico City.

socket pan and the typical ball ornament, the other somewhat Renaissance. The chalice, of 1553, is still Gothic, with its large eight-sided base and a dove carved on the cup; the candelabra are turned on a lathe, and seem to be the kind in which the candle is stuck onto a sharp spike. The processional cross appears under the year 1558 (58); its fringed hanging of rich cloth is patterned with arches and columns.[10] On this

---

[9] José Torre Revello, in his interesting study *El gremio de plateros en las Indias Occidentales,* states that the *cédula* of August 21, 1528, was not enforced in Mexico (p. 12). This would appear very strange to me, and unreasonable. In fact this *cédula* was in force, as is shown by a reference to it in the guild regulations of 1746, under Ordinance 22. Here it is stated that the provisions of this *cédula* are in force, with the modification that equipment for founding can be used in their shops, though not in their houses.

[10] *Códice Sierra: fragmento de una nómina de gastos del pueblo de Santa Catarina Texupan.*

59. Chalice. Silver. Museo Nacional del Virreinato, Tepotzotlán, México.

subject Fray Toribio de Benevente (Motolinía) tells us in his *Historia de los indios* that in the beginning the trappings of these processional crosses were made of gold and feathers, with images worked in the same way.[11]

About jewelry we have little information, since there are no inventories dating from this early period. We know something about rings, because Don Vasco de Quiroga, in that way of his which was the essence of loving-kindness, left two rings in the town of Santa

Fe, so that the Indians could marry properly, as well as twelve coins to use for the dowry. These have all disappeared, but Dr. León in his biography of Don Vasco gives a picture of one ring which still survived at that time. It seems to have been heart-shaped, with a stone crudely set.[12]

We have some information about the treasure of the Cathedral of Mexico in those early days, thanks to an inventory of the sacristy made in 1541. There were five silver chalices (59); the most valuable was large, with twelve little bells hanging from it, and a paten. Probably it was of a Gothic type. They had also the following: a large censer of silver, with its chain and cover; a silver vessel for incense, with its spoon; a large cross of silver with its Christ, and its base; two silver verges with their knobs at the top, and a plainer one for the verger; two silver candle-holders; two cruets of the same material, with their stoppers; eight small candlesticks; a gilded crucifix, given by the Canon Juan Bravo; and "two great candlesticks of silver which belong to the church, with their bases, and on them, lions."

The prize piece of this period was a pyx which may have been made in Mexico, or else brought back by Bishop Zumárraga from his trip to Spain. It was of silver gilt, covered with engraved figures; the most important was St. Helena with the True Cross, but there were also the Annunciation, St. Peter, St. Elizabeth, the Virgin and Child, and the Crucifixion, without mentioning an infinity of angels and cherubs. On the base were two enamelled coats of arms, and the handle was in the shape of a griffon. This valuable piece survived for long years, until finally, because it seemed old and unfashionable, it was melted up with other things to replace a silver lectern which had been stolen.

To conclude, we give the names of silversmiths of this period which we have come upon. We must repeat again that without further research it is difficult to form any dependable opinion about them. Pedro de Fuentes, 1524; Héctor Méndez, 1527; Diego Martín, 1527; Pedro de Espina, 1528 (Ac. Cab., 1535); Diego Martínez and Juan de Celada, 1526; Francisco Esteban, 1532; Francisco Hernández, 1534; Antonio Hernández, 1536; Gaspar Pérez, 1532; Bartolomé Ruiz, 1536; Francisco Ruiz, 1537; Pedro de Salcedo, 1534–1537;

11 Motolinía (Fray Toribio de Benevente), *Motolinía's History of the Indians of New Spain.*
12 Nicolás León, *El Ilmo. Señor Don Vasco de Quiroga, obispo de Michoacán.*

Alonso de Padilla, 1538; Gómez de Luque, 1539; Gonzalo Rodríguez (Portuguese), 1536; Pedro Hernández, 1540; Gentil Melchor, 1542; Cristóbal Sánchez de Herrera, 1541; Luis Rodríguez, 1541; Báez Enrique and Ramón de Cardona, 1546.

Very early there were lapidaries in New Spain, that is, men who knew how to cut precious stones. As far as we know the Indians did not have diamonds, sapphires, rubies, or emeralds. The conquistadors called all green stones "emeralds," but they were really only jade, that is, jadeite, which was called *chalchihuite,* and was the stone most prized by the Indians. They also used turquoise—with which they made beautiful mosaics—obsidian, and rock crystal. Precious stones evidently reached Mexico very quickly, as everything does go where there is gold. Proof of this is afforded by the references to gem cutters in the documents. There are not many, but enough to indicate that precious stones were being cut in Mexico. We shall give here all that we have found on this subject, and not return to it again.

In 1536 the Inquisition tried Juan Franco, native of Seville, lapidary, for witchcraft.[13] Just a little later we find Andrés Morales, otherwise known as Juan Alemán, a lapidary by trade. He was tried in the time of Bishop Zumárraga, for what crime we do not know. His *sambenito* (a placard with the name of penitents convicted by the Inquisition) was kept in the Cathedral in Mexico City.[14]

Later we find "Joseph de la Aya, lapidary, a native of Zeeland, resident in Mexico, a Calvinist heretic. Reconciled in the year 1601."[15]

This scant documentation, found by chance, allows us to assume that, like the other sumptuary crafts such as the weaving of rich cloth, the art of cutting precious stones was pursued in Mexico.

Wrought Iron in the Early Colony

Some blacksmiths came with the conquistadors, since war requires the working of iron, for repairing ships, making weapons, and many other things. As we all know, the Mexican Indians did not have iron until the Spaniards brought it from Europe and later began to mine it in the new country. It is interesting therefore that the first controlling legislation over any craft was the set of ordinances for blacksmiths and locksmiths, enacted by the Ayuntamiento on March 15, 1524, that is, in the second session of the Cabildo in Mexico City. In fact this was simply a price list: since the iron

objects which are so indispensable to daily life were not available, the ironworkers were charging exorbitant prices, and so the Ayuntamiento established a fair price for the most common objects. In these ordinances the distinction which later seemed advisable between blacksmiths and locksmiths was not made.

In the lists of the conquistadors made by Orozco y Berra, the following blacksmiths appear: Lázaro Alonso Hernando, Bartolomé González, Francisco Gutiérrez, and Juan García. Hernando Martín, whose name appears in 1524, should be added.

The Marqués de San Francisco observes that this is perhaps the only craft in New Spain which was not liable to indigenous influence, since the Indians had not known the use of iron. All the same, since indigenous influence works not only through the material but also in the decoration of the object, it is quite possible that some of the earliest wrought iron may have shown indigenous elements in its design, as it did later.

In any case, the technique of working iron was exactly that employed in Spain. There were two types, namely cast iron, made in sand molds, and wrought iron, where the metal was heated in a forge and hammered out, taking advantage of the ductility of the hot metal.

Since at first they did not mine iron in Mexico, it had to be brought from Spain; the Basque mines especially supplied the metal for many years to all the blacksmiths in New Spain.

It is most unlikely that any piece of wrought iron dating from this early period exists today. We can assume that the wrought iron made in Mexico before 1550 was influenced by Gothic ironwork, and that perhaps already they were beginning to make grilles of a more Renaissance character such as later, at the end of the century, are an essential part of the houses in Plateresque style.

The Gothic character persists in some much later wrought iron. Many of the large nailheads which cover the doors of our sixteenth-century churches are Gothic in design: a rose with four heart-shaped petals at the corners. Gothic ironwork also continued in domestic use, like the door knockers in the form of animals, more or less stylized, and the balconies, brackets, and supports which were sometimes decorated, especially in the city of Oaxaca, with wrought-iron foliage very Gothic in flavor.

[13] *Los judios en la Nueva España,* p. 100.
[14] *Ibid.,* pp. 19, 35.   [15] *Ibid.,* p. 62.

60. Stirrups (known as Cortés'). Iron. c. 45 m. Museo Nacional del Virreinato, Tepotzotlán, México.

There is one unsolved problem in the minor arts which might be stated here so that future scholars can resolve it. In the Museo de Historia in Mexico City, and in some private collections, large cruciform stirrups are preserved (60). From the style of the ornament on these stirrups, sometimes Mudejar and sometimes Renaissance, it has been assumed with good reason that they come from the sixteenth century and that some of them may have been brought over by the conquistadors themselves. They seem to be Arabic in origin, but no one has found any documentation about them. Don Antonio Cortés, in his interesting book on wrought iron,[16] advances the theory that these stirrups were used only in the eighteenth century. He founds his opinion on the fact that riders with cruciform stirrups

[16] Antonio Cortés, *Hierros forjados*.

appear in the painting representing the Plaza of Mexico City about 1767 (351). Cortés denies that these stirrups were used in Mexico in the sixteenth century, pointing out that in post-Conquest codices the stirrups used by the conquistadors are shown as small simple supports for the foot, and not the large cruciform type. It is undeniable that these stirrups continued to be used in the eighteenth century; this is demonstrated by the obviously Rococo decoration of some examples. But this does not mean that such stirrups were not used earlier, and if Cortés admits that they were used by the Arabs from the twelfth century on, there is no reason to believe that they would not have appeared in Mexico before the eighteenth century. They are in fact a Mudejar survival.

I have no documentation on which to base a definitive conclusion on these interesting archeological objects, but an idea occurs to me which might help to clarify the question. Could it be that such bulky stirrups are actually meant to increase the weight which the horse is carrying, a sort of ballast to prevent very spirited horses from throwing their riders? There seems no other motive for making them so big and cumbersome. It is my suggestion that the conquistadors brought some of these stirrups with their horses and that they used them for a time near the coast—many of the surviving stirrups seem to come from the state of Veracruz. But I believe that once Cortés and his band had come up to the central plateau the stirrups proved too heavy, considering that the riders were also clothed in iron, and that furthermore the altitude of the new land made the horses less powerful than at sea level. Consequently they had to lighten the load they were carrying, and it is for this reason that in all the pictures of battles the Spaniards are shown using light stirrups.

If they continued to be used throughout the colonial period, it was because the rider no longer wore armor, and when he crossed the Plaza Mayor, among the crowds attending the fiesta, he thought it advisable to use these stirrups so that, carrying more weight, his horse would be less lively.

I repeat that I don't consider this question settled; but I thought it would be interesting to note these ideas, so that in time it can be resolved.

Carpentry and Wood Carving

The Mexican Indians were skilled carpenters, but they did not use wood as widely and extensively as the Europeans. Their furniture cannot be compared to that of Europe, the Renaissance Europe which in Italy produced the most sumptuous of furniture, and in a Spain still under Arabic influence gave us the excellent work we call Mudejar.

Straw mats and leather were the basis of Indian furniture. The chairs we know as *equipales* are a colonial survival of indigenous furniture; the name is simply the Indian word *icpalli,* meaning a chair. Another indigenous survival of this kind is the Mexicanism *petaca* for a suitcase; this is obviously derived from *petlacalli,* which means a box (or a house) of reeds.

We can see what Indian furniture was like in the illustrated codices: everything was low, the Indians did not sit as we do on a high chair, but seem to have squatted instead. As one of the chroniclers said, his heels were the Indian's best chair.

The furniture used in the early Colony was far from the rich Renaissance furniture which later ornamented the palaces of the nobility. From the codices, again, we extract the illustrations for this chapter. The table was simply a board laid over two benches, and so was the bed, except that then the benches were lower. In the Florentine Codex we can see a stool made simply of a round top supported by three rounded legs. Perhaps the chest was the most important piece of furniture at that time; we suppose that they had no wardrobes, for even at the end of the sixteenth century none are listed in the inventories of houses in Mexico City. Chests of every size were used to keep everything, from the largest objects down to jewelry and insignificant things (61). The hierarchy of the chests seems to have been as follows. The largest kind was called an *arcón,* and was a large box of wood with little feet at the corners and wrought-iron locks. The chests which held the funds of a community had three locks, so that three different people had to be present to open them, and misusing the money or removing it had to be done with at least two accomplices. Clothes were kept in *arcas,* stockings and other small objects in *arquetas,* and jewelry or other valuable things in *arquillas.* Chests for travelling were not of wood but of leather reinforced with iron, and sometimes embroidered with maguey fiber in fantastic patterns—some of them quite Moorish—or at other times decorated with embossed designs.

The most interesting subject in the furniture of this period is the chair. In all the post-Conquest codices we see these chairs represented so clearly that there is no doubt what they were (36): we can be just about sure that they were the chairs the conquistadors brought with them in their ships. It is the old Florentine folding chair, with double curves to form the legs and seat. It is curious to see how the Indians, unskilled in perspective drawing, represent the chair from the front but attach the arms as if it were in profile. These chairs continued in use throughout the sixteenth century.

Ecclesiastical furniture seems to have been very humble in the early years; the fixed furniture, such as choir stalls, altars, pulpits, and grilles, will be considered in treating decorative sculpture. The few examples of church furniture from this period show a Gothic ornament typical of the fifteenth century, linen-fold panels. This may be seen on the lectern for choir books in the church at Yecapixtla, on a cupboard in the sacristy at Tula, and others. Doors and windows

61. Chest. Wood with wrought iron. Museo de Churubusco, Distrito Federal.

were also decorated in this way (35), for instance the reverse of the wooden doors of the Franciscan church in Huejotzingo and the small window shutters in the church of Coixtlahuaca.

Textiles

The culture which the conquistadors brought with them was that of the full Renaissance, but profoundly influenced by the Moors of Spain. This helps to explain the scarcity of furniture which we have noted: the rooms were hung with tapestries and embossed leather, the floors richly carpeted; the ladies and gentlemen sat on cushions, and furniture was very scarce.

It is known that Hernán Cortés established the cultivation of silk in New Spain, and it is reasonable to suppose that if they produced silk thread they would have also used it for weaving and embroidery. Silk workers were at first subject to the ordinances laid down by Charles V for the silk weavers of Granada

(on December 22, 1526), but later they were given their own ordinances.

We have very little documentation about the crafts of weaving and embroidering, but there is evidence to indicate that in those distant times there existed a considerable group of weavers, of velvet as well as damask and brocade, and of embroiderers, too—perhaps even more of these, as embroidery is naturally a home industry. Mendieta tells us that it was a very virtuous Italian lay brother, called Fray Daniel, who taught the Indians the art of embroidery. After having trained the Indians of Mexico City, he did the same in Michoacán and Jalisco.[17]

So we can be reasonably sure that the gremial of Fray Juan de Zumárraga in the treasure of the Cathedral of Mexico (62) was embroidered in that city before his death in 1548. Also the Actas de Cabildo of

[17] Gerónimo de Mendieta, *Historia Eclesiástica Indiana*, p. 379.

1528 informs us that in that year a banner was made for the fiesta of St. Hippolitus, giving the names of the merchants and the artisan, Pedro Jiménez, who were concerned in it.[18]

In 1540 Esteban de Porras was received into the guild as a weaver of velvet; in 1543 Pablo de Tapia, himself a weaver of velvet, was named inspector for that material, and Martín Díaz, inspector for satin, taffeta, velvet, and damask; Francisco Durán Cornejo is also mentioned as weaving all these types of silk; Alonso Múñoz, also a weaver, was made clerk (*escribano*) of the guild, and Hernando de Robles, a velvet-weaver, named as *mayordomo*. In regard to embroidery, ordinances were issued by the Ayuntamiento on September 20, 1546, and confirmed by Don Antonio de Mendoza on June 7 following. According to these, elections of the inspectors were to be held in the Hospital de las Bubas, where a Virgen de las Angustias was patron of the guild.[19] Spaniards, for their examination, were to embroider an image of many-hued gold, with its face, hands, and feet embroidered in flesh colors, and another image in silk. The Indians were examined in *"obras de corte,"* in arabesque patterns, in the making of cord, in silks of different hues, and whatever else they knew.[20] So it is clear that the arts of weaving and embroidering in silk flourished in the period we are discussing.

What we still do not know, for lack of documentation, is whether they wove tapestry in Mexico. We do now have evidence that tapestries were used in New Spain just as in the homeland, that is, in great abundance. From the inventories of the house of Hernán Cortés in Cuernavaca, which were made in 1549, we learn that practically all the walls were covered with tapestry or leather hangings.[21]

There were twenty-one tapestries in Cortés' house, among them some which must have been remarkable, for both their subjects and their quality. One of the most valuable was a "tapestry cloth with figures, new, with much silk, with a King at the top of the cloth, a branch in his right hand and a scepter in the other, and at his feet, the god Cupid, front view, which was five *varas* minus a quarter in height, and eight *varas* and a

62. Gremial of Archbishop Zumárraga (detail). Silk and metal embroidery on velvet. Museo Nacional del Virreinato, Tepotzotlán, México.

quarter wide." Other important tapestries were a series of three with figures of elephants; another with a griffon, a lion and various birds; a new tapestry with the Golden Fleece; another, also new, showing a nude man with a blue cape over the right shoulder; one with St. George, another with two white horses; and another with a king and an angel, which perhaps made a pair with the first one we quoted. They had also eight figured portieres, or curtains. There were fourteen rugs of various sizes, probably enough to carpet all the rooms.

The *guadameciles,* those leather hangings made in

[18] Romero de Terreros, *Artes industriales,* p. 182.

[19] J. M. Marroquí, *La ciudad de México,* p. 329.

[20] Juan Francisco de Barrio Lorenzot, "Compendio de las Ordenanzas de la Muy Noble, Insigne y Muy Leal e Imperial Ciudad de México," MS, fol. 145.

[21] *Documentos inéditas relativos a Hernán Cortés,* pp. 225–241.

Córdoba, tanned, gilded, and painted, were equally numerous in the house of Cortés. They seem to have been all of one type, for they are described as worked in gold and silver, with medallions; they were very large, some as big as four by three *varas*. There were fifteen of them, and it may be that they were used in hot weather in place of tapestry, which holds the heat more.

The first Cathedral of Mexico City, whose poverty was always remarked by visitors, had nevertheless its small treasure. When we come to consider Renaissance crafts we shall speak of the magnificent custodias, and it might be more suitable to discuss their tapestries at that time. But since we shall not return to this craft, and since many of the tapestries must have been old, we shall discuss them all here, admitting that some may have been actually of Renaissance design, like those in the house of the Marques del Valle. The Cathedral owned a set of eight tapestries representing the history of King Saul, six telling the story of Judith and Holofernes, another set of eight panels with the acts of Solomon, and a single tapestry of silk representing the Incarnation.[22] These tapestries, like the great collections which still exist in the cathedrals of Europe, were used to decorate the walls of the church on the feast of Corpus Christi.

Feather Work

We have mentioned, in speaking of early painting in Mexico, that the need for images and decoration in the churches was temporarily filled by pictures and decorations in feather mosaic. This feather work is one of the most extraordinary manifestations of Indian skill and artistic feeling. That the friars very early made use of feather mosaic is shown by the following quotation from Fray Toribio de Benevente, written around 1540; he is speaking of the sacristes of the churches:

They place the Holy Sacrament reverently and devoutly in *custodias* of silver, and beside this they adorn their reliquaries very beautifully, inside and out, with rich and brilliant work in gold and feathers; there are in this country very able artists engaged in such work, which in Spain and in Italy they would prize highly and admire with open mouths, as everyone does who has just arrived. And if the examples of this work which have reached Spain appear imperfect, with ugly figures and images, this imperfection is the fault of the painters who first make the sketch and drawing. After them comes the *amantécatl* (for so they call the artist who applies the feathers, and from this the Spaniards call all the craftsmen *amantecas*, although this

name applies only to the feather-workers, and all the other craftsmen have their own special names). And when they give a good drawing to these *amantecas*, they make a good picture in feathers. Since the painters have become skillful and give good drawings, they now make very beautiful pictures and arabesque mosaics of feathers and gold . . .[23]

Fray Bernardino de Sahagún, who studied the Indians' activities so carefully, gives in his great work every sort of detail about the making of feather mosaics, and in the plates of the Florentine Codex (37) one can see the drawings illustrative of his information.[24] From what the venerable Franciscan says, it appears that the *amanteca* used two methods. The first consisted in sticking the feathers with paste to form a mosaic. The layers underneath were made with ordinary feathers from common birds, while for the upper layers, which stood out from this uniform background, they used the feathers of birds which were much prized. The second method consisted of sewing the feathers with thread and twine. The matter is not entirely clear, but one might suppose that the first method served for making feather mosaics, images, and shields, while the second was used for cloth and for the headdresses, where it was necessary to sew the long plumes of the quetzal, which either hung behind or stood up from the headdress.

The most impressive testimonial to this industry, passionate like everything from his pen, is given by Fray Bartolomé de las Casas. Here is what the worthy Apostle to the Indians says:

What seems certainly to exceed all human ingenuity, and inasmuch as it will be no less new than rare to the other nations of the world, so much the more should be admired and esteemed, is the craft and art which those Mexican people know so well and perfectly, of making out of natural feathers with their own natural colors all that they and any other excellent and skillful painters whatsoever can paint with their brushes. They were accustomed to make many things of feathers, such as animals and birds and men, capes and shawls to cover themselves, vestments for the priests and crowns or miters, shields and *moscadores* and a thousand other sorts of things that they fancied. These feathers were green, red or ruby, purple, flesh color, yellow, blue or blue-green, black and white, and all the other colors, mixed or pure, not dyed by any human effort—but all natural, taken and had from different birds

[22] Toussaint, "La primitiva catedral de México," in *Paseos coloniales*, pp. 1–5.

[23] Motolinía, *Memoriales*, p. 91.

[24] Sahagún, *Historia*, Libs. 60–64.

. . . They placed these feathers on a cotton cloth, and on a board, and from this, just as they might take with a brush the colors which they had prepared in their shells and saucers, so they took the feathers of all colors which they had prepared in their boxes or cups, all different and separate . . . and stuck them with a certain paste very delicately, so that for the eyes, in the face of a man or an animal, where it is required to put black and white and the pupil of the eye, with the subtlety of a great painter who might make the different parts of the eye with a small and very delicate brush, so they did the same, and made it all in feathers, and this is surely a marvelous thing.

He goes on to speak of the work which the Indians did after the Europeans had come:

After our images and our things came with the Spaniards, they had a wide field and effective occasion to demonstrate the liveliness of their understanding, the freshness and freedom of their capacities, or perception and understanding, and their great capability, since as our pictures and altarpieces are large and well painted, in many colors, they had occasion to extend their talents and exert themselves more and better . . . Finally, pictures and retables and many other things of ours they have made and make every day of feathers, introducing also gold in suitable places, which makes the work more beautiful and precious, so that it may well arouse great admiration anywhere in the world.[25]

The art of feathers served as a substitute for two things, painting and embroidery. For the first, they made images, and for the other all sorts of ornaments, miters, altar fronts, and everything the ritual required. We do not know for sure where this art flourished especially, but the old reports seem to indicate that Michoacán was the best region for feather mosaic. There is a reference which suggests that in mid-century, precisely the period we are considering, feather mosaics of extraordinary quality were being made in Pátzcuaro. When Don Vasco de Quiroga was in Mexico City about the affairs of his bishopric, he needed a map of Pátzcuaro and the surrounding country, and wrote to his vicar-general, Juan García, to send him a painting showing the episcopal see and its environs. The vicar-general replied, on March 12, 1549, that it was not possible to send the picture because Fray Diego de Chávez had all the painters working in the monastery of Tiripitío, but, he says, "meanwhile until it can be

63. Christ as Pantocrator. Feather mosaic. Museo Nacional del Virreinato, Tepotzotlán, México.

painted, I have procured a cloth which I have sent, with the picture in feathers of everything Your Lordship asked for, and even some more; I don't know if it will serve; the other will be painted and sent when we can."[26] For anyone who knows the region of Pátzcuaro, the beauty of the lake and all the landscape, it would be hard to conceive anything more marvellous than a mosaic of feathers representing it all.

That the Indians continued to work with feathers as they had before the Conquest is also shown in the Kingsborough Codex,[27] which illustrates the feather capes which the Indians of the town of Tepetlaóztoc gave the commissioner, Gonzalo de Salazar, when he returned to Spain. They are exactly the same as those which were made before the Spaniards had conquered Mexico.

It would take too long and be inappropriate to give

[25] Bartolomé de las Casas, *Historia de las Indias,* Ch. 61.
[26] León, *Don Vasco de Quiroga,* p. 232.
[27] *Códice Kingsborough,* fol. 228.

73

a detailed list of the examples of Mexican feather work preserved in different museums, but we must mention the most important. In the Museo Nacional de México there is a *Christ as Pantocrator* of the sixteenth century (63); also two little *Saints* and a *St. John the Baptist,* the saints from the seventeenth century and the Baptist from the eighteenth. In the Museo Michoacana in Morelia there is a *Virgin of Guadalupe,* and in the Franciscan church at Calpan, a picture of *St. Andrew.* Two other valuable pieces are in the Museo de Guadalupe outside Zacatecas. There are also feather mosaics in various private collections.

The most important examples of this art, however, are preserved in European museums. One cannot omit the miter, with its mulitude of saints and scenes from the Passion, which is in the Escorial,[28] or the similar miter in the Pitti Palace in Florence. There are various examples in the Museo Arqueológico in Madrid, and in the Armería Real a magnificent leather shield, of which a reproduction can be seen in the *Enciclopedia* published by Espasa-Calpe.[29] In Vienna also are several objects assumed to be from the gift sent to Charles V by Cortés, among them a headdress which is said to have belonged to Moctezuma.[30]

The art of working with feathers degenerated steadily as time passed. Perhaps the ascendancy of painting and of such popular arts as lacquer and ceramics diminished the need for working these mosaics which needed such great skill and great patience. Perhaps the Indians were not properly recompensed. In any case, feather mosaics of quality soon disappeared, and if the genre has indeed been carried on even up to our time, especially with pictures of birds and flowers, it is quite without interest. It can be considered only from the point of view of popular art, a thing which has been uprooted from its ancient lineage and traditions.[31]

---

[28] See Francisco de la Maza, "La mitra mexicana de plumas de El Escorial," in *Homenaje a Rafael García Granados.*

[29] *Enciclopedia universal ilustrada europeo-americana,* II, 859.

[30] Cf. G. Maler, "Un primoroso ropaje de plumas," *Anales del Museo Nacional,* Eps. 1, 3 (1886), 1–3.

[31] Rafael García Granados is preparing a scholarly monograph on feather work, where all the examples now preserved will be illustrated.

PART TWO

Art during the Colonization of New Spain

The Renaissance in Mexico, 1550–1630

Chapter Five

RENAISSANCE ARCHITECTURE

Monastic Architecture

THE MEDIEVAL SURVIVALS which we have noted in the first half persisted almost to the end of the sixteenth century, but the mood was changing, shifting its emphasis to art as the necessities of military defense grew less urgent.

The great conventual architecture of mid-century might indeed be classified as a medieval survival; these large churches and fortified monasteries stand as the final expression in the world of the Middle Ages. While Europe was developing in a free atmosphere of culture and of art, in America a new feudalism was emerging, as the Indians were divided up among *encomenderos*. But these great monuments, for all their appearance of medieval fortresses, were already feeling the effect of the Renaissance, like something borne on the wind. And since they continued to be built in the same way up to the end of the century, it is more systematic to include them all in this second part, even when they still appear more like fortresses than churches.

It was the first viceroy, Don Antonio de Mendoza, who, working with the provincials of the mendicant orders, systematized the form which these monasteries were to follow, as he reports in the instructions which, like all the viceroys, he had to write for his successor. This interesting document is worth studying.[1]

The Viceroy says that great errors had been made in the building of monasteries and public works; and that what was needed had not been built, for lack of architects and proper planning. To remedy this evil, he says, he had drawn up with the Franciscan and Augustinian friars a reasonable plan according to which all the monasteries should be built, and he recommends to his successor that the Dominicans also should build according to the same plan, in the future. He further suggests that they should employ, among others, Toribio de Alcaraz, "who has built very well many times, monasteries and bridges, as well as other buildings."

The reasonable plan to which the Viceroy refers can be generalized from the innumerable conventual buildings of the three religious orders dating from the second half of the sixteenth century. They follow a pre-

[1] *Instrucciones que los virreyes de Nueva España dejaron a sus sucesores*, I, 46–48.

77

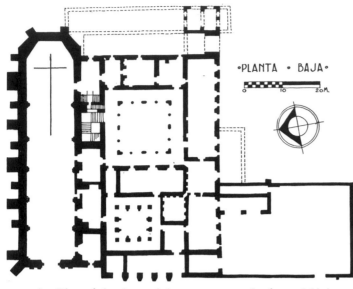

64. Plan of the Augustinian monastery, Acolman, México.

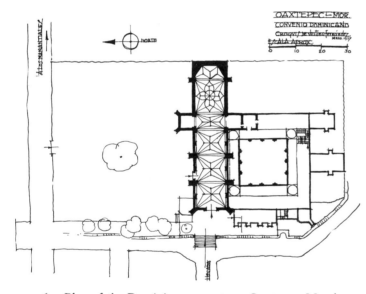

65. Plan of the Dominican monastery, Oaxtepec, Morelos.

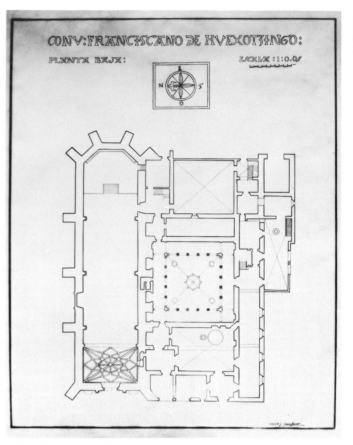

66. Plan of the Franciscan monastery, Huejotzingo, Puebla.

scribed model, and are undoubtedly those of which Don Antonio de Mendoza wrote (64, 65, 66).

The establishment was made up of three parts: the great yard in front, the church, and the monastery. The churchyard, which is today called the *atrio,* the *cementerio,* or the *campo santo,* is a large open space enclosed by crenellated walls (65), with three gateways at the axes, the principal one opposite the church (68); these

gateways are occasionally fortified (69). Where the axes meet stands a cross which in the early days was of wood but after 1539 was made of stone, as we have noted (50). In the four corners are shrines, which are called *posas* (70), because the procession paused there, *posaban,* when the custodia containing the sacrament reached them.[2]

At the back of the churchyard stand the buildings of the monastery (71): the elevated façade of the great church with its rich portal, the open chapel if there is one, and the *portería,* the arcaded entrance to the monastery, which sometimes served also as an open chapel. The churchyard was in the early days as important as the church itself (28), and we cannot help thinking of the great courtyards which were an essential part of the

[2] On *posas* see John McAndrew, *The Open-Air Churches of Sixteenth-Century Mexico*; George Kubler, *Mexican Architecture of the Sixteenth Century*; Raul Flores Guerrero, *Las capillas posas de México.*

67. Churchyard, with church and open chapel, Franciscan monastery, Cholula, Puebla.

indigenous temple complex. It is perhaps the last ves-
tige, the unique aspect, in which we can remark a
subtle indigenous survival in the religious architecture
of the Viceroyalty—a survival not in decoration, but in
a basic element of the plan.

The most important part of the establishment is the
church, which consists of a great nave, the principal
door facing west, and the high altar at the east end.
Over the portal is a choir supported by a vault (73);
there is also another portal which almost always faces
north (117), and doors communicating with the convent. In the beginning the great nave was covered by a
barrel vault; later they built Gothic vaults, first simple
and later complicated with ribs and tracery until they
seem like stone lace. The apse of the church is rectangular or polygonal, rarely semicircular (72, 74), and is
filled with a great retable of carved and gilded wood,
with polychrome sculpture, oil paintings, and polychrome ornament.

This type of church is exactly what Emile Bertaux
classifies as Isabelline Gothic, that is, the style of the

68. Gate to the churchyard, Franciscan monastery,
Huejotzingo, Puebla.

79

69. Church, through the churchyard gate,
Franciscan monastery, Tula, Hidalgo.

70. Posa I, Franciscan monastery, Huejotzingo, Puebla.

71. Façade of church and portería,
Franciscan monastery, Huejotzingo, Puebla.

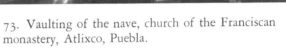

72. Nave and chancel, church of the Franciscan monastery, Huejotzingo, Puebla.

73. Vaulting of the nave, church of the Franciscan monastery, Atlixco, Puebla.

74. Exterior, church of the Franciscan monastery, Tepeaca, Puebla.

75. Cloister, Franciscan monastery, Huejotzingo, Puebla.

churches built at the moment of transition from Gothic to Plateresque.[3]

Beside the church is the monastery, usually to the south, although occasionally one finds it on the north. The monastery is built around the cloister, the pleasantest and most evocative part of the building (75). These are no longer the tiny cloisters we saw in the beginning; they are of two stories, almost always vaulted on the ground floor (98) and beamed on the upper story, although some more sumptuous establishments have vaults on both levels. There is not a standard type of cloister; they develop from primitive simplicity to more complicated forms, while the pointed arches of the Middle Ages give way to the full Renaissance. Around the lower cloister lie the rooms devoted to the life of the monastery: the *sala de profundis,* where the

community met, the refectory (76), decorated with a large painting of the Last Supper, the kitchen, the storerooms, and the stables. Some of the large vaulted rooms must have served for the schools where the friars taught the language and doctrine to the Indian boys.

Around the upper cloister are the dormitories, opening off the spacious corridor, with a larger cell, sometimes formed of two rooms, for the prior. The library also is upstairs.

Such in general is the type of monastery which was built in Mexico after 1550, or a few years earlier. It would be absurd to imagine that these structures were all alike; each one offers variations, special regional details, which add interest and make them more appealing to the discerning visitor.

Now we shall review the principal monasteries of this period which have survived. It should be understood, however, that we do not offer this as a complete catalogue; we are not undertaking to draw up an inventory of colonial art, but simply to show the general characteristics of the monuments, and to refer to those which seem to us the most important.

Franciscan Monasteries

The Province of the Santo Evangelio de México[4]

Tepeaca. The monastery of Tepeaca is indubitably the prototype of the Franciscan monastery of this period. It was founded in 1530 by Fray Juan de Rivas, but the present monastery and church were not built until 1580. Regardless of the date, the church seems more archaic. There is no hint here of Renaissance style; it is still the Middle Ages, crude and vigorous, which we feel in the extraordinary fortifications that compose this building (74). For it is a true fortress, in which the strategic details seem to have been worked out before the requirements of the church itself.[5] The

---

[3] See Toussaint's "Supervivencias góticas en la arquitectura mexicana del siglo XVI," *Archivo español de arte y arqueología,* 11 (1935), 47–66.

[4] For Franciscan foundations in general, see Alonso Ponce, *Relación breve y verdadera;* Gerónimo de Mendieta, *Historia Eclesiástica Indiana;* Juan de Torquemada, *Monarquía Indiana;* Agustín de Vetancurt, *Chrónica de la provincia del Santo Evangelio de México;* Kubler, *Mexican Architecture;* Diego Angulo Íñiguez, *Historia del arte hispanoamericano,* I; Kubler and Martin Soria, *Art and Architecture in Spain and Portugal and Their American Dominions;* McAndrew, *Open-Air Churches;* Robert Ricard, *La "conquête spirituelle" du Mexique.*

[5] Cf. John McAndrew, "Fortress Monasteries," *Anales del Ins-*

76. Refectory, Augustinian monastery, Actopan, Hidalgo.

monastic building is rude, and of less interest than the church.

Convento Grande de México. We have already spoken of the original church of the Franciscans in Mexico City. The building, which dated from mid-century, seems not to have been very important; it was remodelled by Fray Francisco de Gamboa, who reached Mexico in 1568, took orders before 1570, and died in 1604. It had a carved wooden roof, covered with lead, and its principal retable had paintings by Basilio Salazar. The apse, or *capilla mayor*, was divided from the nave by a great screen of wrought iron made in Cantabria, which cost more than ten thousand ducats.[6]

We have discussed above the chapel of San José de los Naturales, a dependency of this monastery. There is

tituto de Investigaciones Estéticas, 23 (1955), 31–38; Toussaint, *Paseos coloniales,* pp. 39–43.

[6] Vetancurt, *Chrónica,* p. 43. See also Manuel Romero de Terreros, "La iglesia de San Francisco de México," *Anales del Instituto de Investigaciones Estéticas,* 20 (1952), 41–43; Fidel de Jesús Chauvet, "The Church of San Francisco in Mexico City," *The Americas,* 7 (1950–1951), 13–30.

77. View of the Franciscan monastery, Huejotzingo, Puebla.

78. West portal, church of the Franciscan monastery, Huejotzingo, Puebla.

nothing now remaining of the sixteenth-century buildings. The present church was rebuilt in the seventeenth century; so were the cloisters, of which portions still exist, although now used for other purposes.[7]

Tlalmanalco. It cannot be assumed that this monastery is among the oldest, in spite of its primitive vaulting. According to the *Relación del Obispado de México* it was three-quarters finished in 1582, and in 1585, when Father Ponce visited it, they were just building the cloister. The church, for all its primitive vaulting,

is not mentioned by Father Ponce at all, so that its construction must be dated between his visit and 1591, the date which appears on its two portals. We have mentioned the extraordinary open chapel here, notable for the diverse influences that show in its remarkable decorative sculpture (15). It carries an indigenous year-sign which can be interpreted as 1560.

Huejotzingo. The original monastery of Huejotzingo was built by Fray Juan de Alameda, but that was certainly not the building we see today (66, 68, 70, 71, 72, 75, 77, 78, 117). This church was unfinished in 1562. It dates from mid-century, according to the inscription on one of the posas (70). Considering the technical perfection of the whole establishment, we might well attribute it to that Toribio de Alcaraz who, according to the Viceroy, had made excellent monastery buildings. Huejotzingo is a veritable museum, with its paintings (32, 33), its magnificent retable by Simón Pereyns, dated 1586 (132, 146, 147), and its wealth of artistic detail.[8]

Puebla. The immense Franciscan church, finished between 1567 and 1570, goes back to the building period of the mid-sixteenth century. The choir was the work of Francisco Becerra, a famous Spanish architect who had a part in many buildings, as we shall see. The side door dates from the sixteenth century; its decoration still displays the coat-of-arms of Tlaxcala, the original see. Other parts of the building, such as the façade and the tower, are of later date (259).

Texcoco. The present church dates from the seventeenth century, as the cloister and portals apparently do. Relics of the earlier church are the decorative sculpture we have described.

Tlaxcala. This is not the original foundation, since the city was moved; but the existing monastery is of great interest. It was almost all constructed of archeological stone, as one can see on the exterior. Its most remarkable feature is the roof of carved and inlaid wood which covers the church, the most splendid example of *alfarje* which has been preserved (79); it shows how fully this magnificent Mudejar technique was carried on in New Spain. In Tlaxcala they show the font in which the Indian "senators" were baptized, and the pulpit from which the faith was preached for

[7] See McAndrew, *Open-Air Churches,* pp. 399 ff.
[8] See the excellent monograph by Rafael García Granados and Luis MacGregor, *Huejotzingo.* See also George Kubler, "Architects and Builders in Mexico, 1521–1550," *Journal of the Warburg and Courtauld Institutes,* VII, No. 1–2 (1944), 7–19.

79. Nave, church of the Franciscan monastery, Tlaxcala.

80. Cloister, Franciscan monastery, Tula, Hidalgo.

the first time. There are no documents to support these assertions, but only the primitive character of the objects.[9]

Cholula. The immense church of this monastery was built between February 7, 1549, when the cornerstone was laid by the Bishop of Tlaxcala, and April 30, 1552, when it was dedicated, according to the inscription, now effaced, which could formerly be read on the choir vault. Given these dates, it is almost certain to have been the work of Toribio de Alcaraz. Of its two portals, the main doorway still retains some Gothic characteristics, like the crockets and the large rose window, although with Renaissance ornament (67). The side portal is already frankly Renaissance. A remarkable feature of this monastery is the open chapel in the form of a mosque (18, 19, 20) which we have already discussed.[10]

Cuernavaca. The establishment was made in 1529. The date 1552 appears on the side portal of the church, but it has been so much rebuilt that practically nothing but the shell remains of the original building. Francisco Becerra worked on it. The tower dates from 1713. At the end of the church can be seen the open chapel of which we have spoken.[11]

Tula. The first monastery of Tula was built in 1529 under Fray Alonso Rangel. The present one may be dated between 1550 and 1553. The church is a real

[9] See Fidel de Jesús Chauvet, *Los franciscanos y sus construcciones en Tlaxcala*; Charles Gibson, *Tlaxcala in the Sixteenth Century*, pp. 43–46.

[10] See Francisco de la Maza, *La ciudad de Cholula y sus iglesias.*

[11] See Federico Gómez de Orozco, *El convento franciscano de Cuernavaca.*

85

82. St. Peter. North portal, church of the Franciscan monastery, Huaquechula, Puebla.

81. North portal, church of the Franciscan monastery, Huaquechula, Puebla.

crenellated fortress completely faced with cut stone (69). The portal is Renaissance in style, while the columns of the cloister retain that sixteenth-century Gothic survival of suppressing the capital, so that the moldings of the arch pass directly into the shaft (80). According to Mendieta, the architect of Tula was Fray Antonio de San Juan.

Tochimilco. A magnificent monastery on the slopes of Popocateptl. The arches of the ribbed vaulting in the church are still pointed. The portal is Renaissance in style, Italian in mood.

Zacatlán de las Manzanas. We have already described the basilica church of this monastery (13). The cloister is extraordinarily primitive; its lower gallery has arches no taller than a man, while the upper cloister recalls Spanish wooden architecture.[12]

Tlalnepantla. This church has suffered so many changes that one can hardly find anything of the original structure. Perhaps the side door, dated 1587, is the

[12] Toussaint, *Paseos coloniales,* pp. 16–18.

oldest part. Francisco Becerra says he worked at this monastery, but it is not easy to determine what he may have done.

Huaquechula. A beautiful monastery with much fine work. The church is of the usual form; corner buttresses support the façade. Its rich portal is one of the treasures of Mexican Plateresque sculpture, although it retains some characteristics of Isabelline Gothic. The round arch of its doorway opens between engaged columns, around which the moldings of the jambs are extended at base and springing; the edge of the arch is plain, but all the rest is covered with rich foliated ornament in relief. In the spandrels—an Isabelline motif—angels are holding coats of arms, like the eagles of San Juan de los Reyes in Toledo. The cornice is unusual, formed of a double row of corbels; higher up a relief is enclosed in an apocopated *alfiz.* Above this is a round window.

The side door is even more interesting, for it is undoubtedly related to the posas at Calpan (81). The basket-handle arch, whose corners describe a quarter

83. Date stone, Franciscan monastery,
Huaquechula, Puebla.

84. Façade, church of the Franciscan monastery,
Tecali, Puebla.

circle, is fluted. On the jambs are reliefs of St. Peter
(82) and St. Paul, affectingly naive, and the whole
doorway is crowned by another relief, full of medieval
feeling, representing the Last Judgment.

At the right of the church is the open chapel, consisting of a large arch in an *alfiz,* whose interior vault is
the richest example of a Gothic ceiling in New Spain.
The cloister is in the usual form, though one can see
that originally it consisted of a single story, with heavy
piers and buttresses which come to a pointed profile.
The upper cloister, lighter and timber-roofed, already
speaks of the seventeenth century.

One cannot doubt that this monument was the work
of Indians. If the character of the ornament on the two
façades were not enough to prove this, we have the
date on the exterior of the apse (83): beside the
Christian date, *1569 años,* is a Nahuatl inscription.[13]

Tecali. This monastery, once beautiful, is in ruins.
Of its great basilica church we have only the façade,
whose portal is a unique example of pure Renaissance

design (84), and the elegant colonnades of the nave.
In the apse are traces of painted Mudejar decoration.
Its splendid retables have been preserved in the parish
church nearby, a building of no importance.[14]

Cuautinchán. This famous monastery stands sad and
abandoned. In the entrance arcade there used to be a
fresco of the Indian *tonalámatl,* or sacred calendar.
Decorations of the same sort may still be seen in the
cloister, and in the church are two retables of the greatest interest: one by Arrúe, which we shall study in detail (148), and another dedicated to San Diego de
Alcalá, which is perhaps the work of Pereyns.

Quecholac. This must have been an interesting monastery, with a basilica church like those of Tecali and
Zacatlán. Today we can see how it was rebuilt as a parish church, where the retables and other relics from the
earlier church are preserved.

13 *Ibid.,* pp. 96–99.
14 *Ibid.,* pp. 87–89.

85. Posa II, Franciscan monastery, Calpan, Puebla.

86. Posa III, Franciscan monastery, Calpan, Puebla.

Tepeyanco. The ancient monastery is in ruins. Its rich retables are now in the parish church, a pleasant Baroque building of the eighteenth century.[15]

Atlihuetzía. A ruined church. One can see the principal portal, with an *alfiz* very like that of the Franciscan church in Tlaxcala. The open chapel has three arches and a vaulted sanctuary.[16]

Calpan. Few sixteenth-century monuments make such an impression on the visitor as the very ancient monastery of Calpan, near Huejotzingo in the state of Puebla. One's first impression on stepping into the enormous churchyard is of some exotic country of the Orient, not Mexico. In the extraordinary sculpture of the posas, which we have treated in detail above (43, 44, 85, 86), in the magnificent portal of the church (which suffers from a stupid renovation that enlarged the window disproportionately), it is all splendid, both for the indigenous flavor of its sculpture and for an authentic primitive quality which we rarely find. The date should be set between 1540 and 1550, the date of the posas at Huejotzingo (70), which are more uni-

form, more restrained, more architectonic, and consequently, later.[17]

Totimehuacán. Near the city of Puebla, at the foot of the very ancient volcano called Malinche, lies the picturesque town of this name. There are still ruins of the old Franciscan building. We know that Francisco Becerra, the famous architect, built "a chapel" there. I assume this refers to the apsidal chapel which still exists, covered by ribbed vaulting. The rest is wreckage of the past, affecting but dead. The retables are now in the parish church, an interesting example of the popular Baroque of Puebla in the eighteenth century.[18]

Tepeji del Rio. Very ancient is this lovely monastery.

15 See Romero de Terreros, "El antiguo convento franciscano de Topoyanco," *Memorias de la Academia Mexicana de Historia,* 12 (1953), 299–305; Gibson, *Tlaxcala,* pp. 46–47.
16 See Gibson, *Tlaxcala,* pp. 47–57.
17 See Rafael García Granados, "Calpan," *Universidad de México,* 1 (1930–1931); Elizabeth Wilder Weismann, *Mexico in Sculpture,* pp. 198–199.
18 See José Rivero Carvallo, *Totimehuacán, convento y templo franciscanos.*

One feels sure of this, for the merlons of its crenellated churchyard are ornamented with disks like the earplugs of the Indians. The church, the open chapel, and the cloister are all well preserved.

Xochimilco. Situated in the most picturesque town near the capital, with its landscape of canals and *chinampas* (floating gardens) perhaps unique in the world, this monastery is consequently less visited than it deserves. Nature absorbs all our curiosity for herself, leaving the works of man, no less valuable, abandoned and forgotten. Nonetheless, the monastery of Xochimilco—what still remains of it—is admirable (116). It was founded in 1535, and the original church was built between 1543 and 1546. It had at first a wooden roof in the Mudejar style, which was later replaced by vaults and a dome. The most valuable thing here is the magnificent Renaissance retable (143, 144, 145), which we shall study later.[19]

Atlixco. A monastery situated on a hill above the town, which gives it even more the effect of a fortress. A church of ribbed vaults, with a narrower apse (73). A cloister with only three arches on a side, as in the earliest monasteries.

Huichapan. According to the *Relación* of Padre Ponce, this monastery was all finished in 1585, with its church, cloister, dormitory, and garden. The present church dates from the eighteenth century, 1753 to 1763, and was the work of an *alarife,* a municipal supervisor of works, called Antonio Simón, apparently an Indian. The chapel of the Third Order is interesting, and there is a magnificent stone cross which can compare with the finest we have (48).

Tepeapulco. The interesting portal of this church comes from the earlier building. The rich relief ornament of the jambs continues around the arch. On either side pilasters equally covered with magnificent relief are carried up to form a large *alfiz* which frames a relief panel; this is crowned by a little niche which may be of later date. The church has been rebuilt in high Baroque style, but the cloister seems to date from the sixteenth century.[20]

The Province of San Pedro y San Pablo de Michoacán[21]

Tzintzuntzan. It is very difficult to determine what parts of the present buildings at Tzintzuntzan date from the sixteenth century. The first tiny monastery provided the church where Don Vasco de Quiroga took possession of his bishopric in 1538. This was replaced by one built by Fray Pedro de Pila, which in the time of Padre Larea was one of the largest buildings in the country, according to his *Cronica.* No detailed study has been made to determine the history of these buildings. There are two open chapels: the one beside the hospital, of 1619, is nonetheless still Plateresque in feeling; the other, more archaic, seems to date from the sixteenth century.[22]

Valladolid, now called Morelia. One can still find the cloister and the outer walls of the monastery, with their traditional ogee windows. The present church apparently dates from the seventeenth century.

Pátzcuaro. The Franciscan monastery of Pátzcuaro is in ruins; on the walls can be read the date 1576. The church, although it may not be the original one, looks so archaic that it recalls the most ancient Romanesque churches of Spain; perhaps no other church in Mexico is so like them. The ingenuous cloister, its arcades supported on Mudejar pillars, is very charming. Its little Plateresque portal is a jewel.[23]

Uruapan. The Franciscan monastery of Uruapan was founded by Fray Juan de San Miguel. Parts of the hospital which was attached to this ancient building still exist. The chapel, called La Guatapera, has an interesting Plateresque façade, its round arch enclosed in an *alfiz,* and a niche with the figure of the founder, all covered with fine reliefs which show evidence of the Indian hand through the Mudejar motif (46).

Zacapu. The most interesting feature is the portal, at once rich and sober, with a double window over the arch of the doorway. Perhaps all the portals of the same type which we find in the region derive from this portal.

Erongaricuaro. In this picturesque town, on the shores of Lake Pátzcuaro, there are remains of the old Franciscan monastery. The most important detail is the portal, of sober Plateresque design with an *alfiz* ornamented with cockleshells.

Acámbaro. The monastery at Acámbaro is not the original building; that was constructed sometime after 1532, the date when its foundations were completed.

[19] See Rafael García Granados, *Xochimilco.*

[20] See José Gorbea Trueba, *Tepeapulco*; "Ciudad Sahagún y sus alrededores," *Artes de México,* (1964), 56–57.

[21] On Franciscan building in Michoacán, see especially Mendieta, *Historia*; Alonso de la Rea, *Crónica de la orden de N. Seráfico P. S. Francisco*; Pablo de la Purísima Concepción Beaumont, *Crónica de Michoacán.*

[22] McAndrew, *Open-Air Churches,* pp. 507–508.

[23] Toussaint, *Pátzcuaro.*

The church had been built by Diego de Guzmán, but later was rebuilt and completely changed. The hospital, with its admirable chapel, is all that remains from the sixteenth century (9).

The Province of San José de Yucatán[24]

The religious architecture of Yucatán has a special characteristic which distinguishes it from other parts of the country: the churches are generally crowned by a large *espadaña,* a wall belfry, lifting its serrated silhouette above the façade.

Campeche. This was the first Franciscan establishment of the province, founded in 1546. By the seventeenth century the church was almost in ruins and divine service was being held in the open chapel, according to Cogolludo. Furthermore, since the monastery was left outside when the city was walled, another one was being built at that time inside the city. There is a little church preserved on the edge of town where according to tradition the first Mass was celebrated.

Mérida. The monastery was founded in 1547 on one of the hills which Montejo had chosen for his fortress. The church, though not very big, was built of masonry and vaulted; the cloister, also small and primitive, was decorated in the seventeenth century with large pictures representing the life of St. Francis. According to Padre Lizana, the architect of this establishment was Fray Antonio de Tarancón. It no longer exists.

Maní. This house was founded a little after that of Mérida. Cogolludo describes the church in this way: ". . . its church is of a single nave, vaulted, joined to another for the Indians, and both dedicated to San Miguel Arcángel." The cloister at Maní is of a rude architecture comparable to that of the more solid Dominican buildings of the central plateau, such as Tepoztlán in Morelos. There is a remarkable stone crucifix in this cloister, which we mentioned in treating the early sculpture.

Conkal. Founded in 1549 by Fray Francisco de Villalpando, but repaired through the activity of Fray Francisco Navarro.

Izamal. This monastery was the work of the worthy father Fray Diego de Landa, who founded it in 1549. In 1552 it was still not finished, since Father Landa was ordered to complete it. It was Fray Francisco de la Torre who did so, in 1561. The architect, according to Lizana, was Fray Juan de Mérida. The church is the sanctuary of the image called Nuestra Señora de Izamal. The enormous churchyard is enclosed by arcades between the posas, and ramps connect the different levels. The effect of the ensemble is admirable.

Valladolid. A work by the same architect, Fray Juan de Mérida, according to Lizana. The church is of masonry, with a vaulted roof, and there is a retable with paintings. It had a tabernacle which seemed "modern" to the chronicler Cogolludo; that is to say, one can assume that the retable was of the sixteenth century, while the tabernacle was already Baroque.

Motul. A vaulted church built in the seventeenth century, with a transept and cupola. The monastery dates from 1567, according to Cogolludo, but a mission had been established there as early as 1555 according to Padre Lizana.

Calkiní. Founded by Fray Luis de Villalpando, according to Lizana; Cogolludo gives 1561 as the date of the establishment.

Zizantum. This monastery was established in 1567. Padre Lizana says the church was the best that the Indians had in Yucatán; according to him it was built by Fray Lorenzo de Bienvenida. Cogolludo in speaking of it says that "it is one of the largest naves in this Realm." Its vault has collapsed.

Tizimín. A house founded, according to Cogolludo, in 1563. Padre Lizana says that Fray Lorenzo di Bienvenida built it.

Ticul. Founded in 1591. The church seems to be of the seventeenth century. Cogolludo describes it as a "modern" building with a nave and two aisles, large enough to be a cathedral, and this kind of church was typical after 1600.

Augustinian Monasteries[25]

The establishments of the Order of St. Augustine rank among the most sumptuous built in New Spain. They provide the finest examples of the Plateresque style. The Augustinians were not constrained like the Franciscans by a vow of poverty, and as the Court as-

---

24 On ecclesiastical monuments in Yucatán, see the *Catálogo de construcciones religiosas del Estado de Yucatán.* See also Bernardo de Lizana, *Historia y conquista espiritual de Yucatán;* Diego López de Cogolludo, *Historia de Yucatán.*

25 For Augustinian buildings in general, see Juan de Grijalva, *Crónica de la orden de n. p. S. Agustín en las provincias de la Nueva España;* Matías Escobar, *Americana Thebaida;* Federico Gómez de Orozco, "Monasterios de la orden de San Agustín en Nueva España, siglo XVI," *Revista mexicana de estudios históricos,* 1 (1927), 40–54; Kubler, *Mexican Architecture;* McAndrew, *Open-Air Churches;* Angulo Íñiguez, *Historia,* I; Ricard, *La "conquête spirituelle";* Catálogo de construcciones religiosas del Estado de Hidalgo.*

sisted them amply in their work, they were able to achieve superb buildings. Certain provincials indeed dedicated themselves to making them as rich as possible; thus Grijalva remarks that Padre Vertavillo would like to have used for his churches and monasteries "only stones weighed in carats"—that is, precious stones.

The Province of the Dulce Nombre de Jesús de México

Mexico City. The cornerstone of the second building of the Augustinian foundation in the capital was laid on August 28, 1541, by Don Antonio de Mendoza. The Indians of Texcoco worked on it, and by royal order their tribute was used to finance it. Later the King took over the expense of the work, which was finished in 1587. We know from the *Diálogos* of Cervantes de Salazar that in 1554 the church was still not finished, that it had a Mudejar ceiling of coffered wood which rested on stone arches, and lateral chapels which were used by the nobility for burial. The cloister was roofed by coffered vaulting, and there were two dormitories with many cells, also vaulted. That church suffered a terrible fire on the eleventh of December, 1676. The present church was built at the end of the seventeenth century.[26]

Ocuituco. The first monastery which the Augustinians founded outside Mexico City, in the year 1534. The town was an encomienda of Bishop Zumárraga until 1544, when in compliance with the New Laws it was taken away from him. Of its great church nothing is left; the cloister remains, primitive enough, decorated with painting on walls and vaults. The fountain has been reconstructed, with its original sculpture.

Totolapan. Founded in 1534 by Fray Jorge de Ávila. A heterogeneous building in which it is not easy to determine the old parts. The cloister, a rude construction of popular flavor, seems to date from the second half of the sixteenth century. The church is perhaps later.

Yecapixtla. Founded in 1535. Apparently begun between that date and 1540 and finished a little later. Although Yecapixtla, as we have said, is the monument retaining the greatest number of Gothic details, the Renaissance seems to be taking over there in visible form (87). Thus the north portal of the church is a good example of Plateresque decoration, including fauns and satyrs in a frankly pagan spirit.[27]

Zacualpan de Amilpas. Of the great variety of buildings which make up this monastery, the oldest is the

87. Façade, church of the Augustinian monastery, Yecapixtla, Morelos.

cloister. One cannnot call it Renaissance work, but rather medieval, although its technical perfection indicates that it dates from this period. It stands like an invincible fortress; instead of arches it could be said to have doorways on the ground floor; and on the upper level, windows. Built all of cut stone, it makes as singular an impression as anything in our colonial architecture.

Ocuilan. Nothing remains of the monastery of Ocuilan except the four walls of the cloister and two great fragments of the outer wall of the church. From what

26 See Romero de Terreros, *La iglesia y convento de San Agustín.*

27 Toussaint, *Paseos coloniales,* pp. 33–38.

88. Façade, Augustinian church and monastery, Epazoyucan, Hidalgo.

Grijalva says in his *Crónica,* the church was very sumptuous, and we know that there were paintings by the celebrated Simón Pereyns on its principal retable.

Epazoyucan. The Franciscans brought the Gospel to this town, as early as 1528; in 1540 the Augustinians established themselves there. The monastery must have been built by 1556, since in that year Archbishop Montúfar complained that a costly retable was being made for the church (88). In the cloister of this monastery there are frescoes which are perhaps the most important in all of New Spain (128; color, facing p. 132). I assume that they were painted by Juan Gersón, an Italianate Fleming who in 1562 decorated the choir vault at Tecamachalco.[28]

Malinalco. The monastery was founded in 1540. The present building cannot be considered a work of art of

[28] See Xavier Moyssen, "Tecamachalco y el pintor indígena Juan Gersón," *Anales del Instituto de Investigaciones Estéticas,* 33 (1964), 23–40.

the first order; it is a rude monument which seems intended for permanence ‎rather than beauty. In the church was a retable painted by Pereyns in 1568, which has since disappeared. In the cloister remains of fresco painting can be seen.

Acolman. According to the chroniclers this monastery was founded in 1539, but Padre Román gives the following year. We do not know what the original church was like; the present one gives evidence of various changes (64). First there was a great nave, which seems to have had a carved wooden ceiling, and a rib-vaulted apse. In the seventeenth century heavy pilasters were added to the interior walls, a barrel vault with lunettes was built, and buttresses were erected against the outside to carry the thrust. To the original structure was added in 1560 a portal which is one of the purest examples of Plateresque design in Mexico (89). Technically it indicates an absolute command of decorative carving. Acolman's Plateresque so perfectly represents the requirements and characteristics of the style that one can assert, without any reservations, that it was the work of a European craftsman. The cloister at Acolman, although it cannot be classified as Plateresque, and even offers such traits of Isabelline Gothic as the ball moldings that encircle the capitals of the lower arcade, is still a splendid example of Renaissance architecture (92). Its probity of line is such that one might indeed call the architect a "purist." For all this, the capitals of the upper arcade are plainly Indian, to such a degree that if we were to come upon one of them isolated, we should never imagine it part of a building in the European tradition, but suppose it some exotic sculpture.

Metztitlán. The monastic buildings here were constructed after 1541, when it was made a priory (93). Its church presents a Plateresque façade with Romanesque reminiscences, namely a kind of splayed arch over the portal. Crowning the church is one of the wall belfries typical of Augustinian buildings of this period, although it may in fact be a later addition.

Actopan. Founded in 1550. The architect of this imposing monastery is said to have been Padre Fray Andrés de Mata, although we do not have any reliable document to prove it. The monastery of Actopan is one of the most impressive of our colonial monuments; we see in it at once both the rudeness and the tremendous size of the early buildings, with a Renaissance spirit superimposed to mitigate its primitive severity (76, 94, 95). The design of the portal is in that special Plater-

89. Façade, Augustinian church and monastery, Acolman, México.

esque mode which recalls Romanesque façades, both in the tympanum raised above the doorway, and in the large splayed arch which encloses it. The interior of the church is roofed by ribbed Gothic vaults, and the cloister is also Gothic, with pointed arches on the ground floor. The upper cloister, however, is built in round Renaissance arches, which do not correspond with the arches of the lower cloister. One of the most important features of this monastery is its painted decoration (127), which we shall discuss in the proper place.[29]

Ixmiquilpan. This monastery seems a replica of that of Actopan, and is said to have been built by the same

friar, Andrés de Mata. Actopan is superior, however, in both the quality of its detail and the grandeur of the total effect.[30]

Tlayacapan. A monastery founded in 1554 at the place where the Indians made their great stand against the army of the conquistadors, at the foot of the last spur of the mountains of Tepoztlán. We do not know exactly when it was built, but only that in 1572 it was already finished. At Tlayacapan the monastery is not on

[29] See Luis MacGregor, *Actopan.*
[30] See Abelardo Carrillo y Gariel, *Ixmiquilpan.*

93

90. Façade, church of the Augustinian monastery, Yuriria, Guanajuato.

91. Façade, church of the Augustinian monastery, Acolman, México.

92. Cloister, Augustinian
monastery, Acolman, México.

93. Nave and chancel, church of
the Augustinian monastery,
Metztitlán, Hidalgo.

94. Façade, church and portería of the Augustinian monastery, Actopan, Hidalgo.

95. Baptistry, church of the Augustinian monastery, Actopan, Hidalgo.

96. Façade, church of the Augustinian monastery, Yuriria, Guanajuato.

the south side of the church, but on the north. The most important building is the church, of enormous proportions, with its wall belfry at the top of the façade. The cloister employs a form dear to the Augustinians: the exterior pilasters come to a pointed profile like the prow of a ship or the cutwater one sees on the buttresses of old bridges.

Jonacatepec. Its cloister seems to be a copy of that of Zacualpan de Amilpas, which is near by. The church is of later date.

Atlatláuhcan. One of the last monasteries to be built in the sixteenth century by the Order of St. Augustine, since it was founded in 1570. In the church vertical lines predominate. The most interesting thing about this monument is the painted decoration, of which there is a great quantity; the painting of the cloister vault imitates Mudejar coffering.[31]

The Province of San Nicolás de Tolentino de Michoacán[32]

Tiripitío. Of the original monastery of Tiripitío, finished in 1548, with its magnificent Mudejar ceiling of carved wood, practically nothing has survived. The re-

mains of vaulted rooms which we can still see seem to date from the seventeenth century. In 1540 in this monastery the first Casa de Estudios Superiores (House of Advanced Studies) in Mexico was established. In recent times it has been rebuilt in fairly adequate form.

Valladolid (Morelia). The monastery of San Agustín in Morelia seems to have been founded in 1550, according to Padre Román; but only vestiges of the original fabric remain. The cloister, with a fine fountain in the middle, is now a tenement; inside, some little windows dating from this early period can be seen. Everything else seems to have been rebuilt later.

Yuririapúndaro. According to Román the foundation dates from 1550, and the monastery was con-

[31] See Romero de Terreros, *Atlatláuhcan*.
[32] On Augustinian building in Michoacán, see also Diego Basalenque, *Historia de la provincia de San Nicolás de Tolentino de Michoacán*.

97. Cloister, Augustinian monastery,
Yuriria, Guanajuato.

98. Cloister walk, Augustinian monastery,
Yuriria, Guanajuato.

structed between 1566 and 1567 under Fray Diego de
Chávez. The architect was Pedro del Toro, who left his
portrait, with that of his wife, sculptured on the *portería* of the building.[33] The church of Yuriria is extraordinarily like a fortress, and in fact we know that several
times it served as a refuge not only for the friars but
for all the people of the town against attack by hostile
Indians (96). In plan it does not have the usual single
nave, although one cannot say it has a transept either;

rather there are two naves which intersect, forming almost a Greek cross. The two portals of the church at
Yuriria are interpretations of the façade of the church
at Acolman (89, 90, 91); one can call them popular
Plateresque, and they were probably made at the end of
the sixteenth century. The cloister shows the form we
have mentioned, with buttresses of pointed profile, and
its arcade is a good example of the Renaissance cloister
with medieval reminiscences (97, 98).

Cuitzeo. This town was first converted by the Franciscans and the secular clergy, until in 1550 Don Vasco
de Quiroga gave it to the Augustinians. The monastery

[33] Escobar, *Americana Thebaida*. See also José Gorbea Trueba,
Yuriria; Toussaint, *Paseos coloniales*, pp. 92–95; Kubler, "Architects and Builders," pp. 7–19.

99. Portal, church of the Augustinian monastery, Cuitzeo, Michoacán.

100. Portal (detail), church of the Augustinian monastery, Cuitzeo, Michoacán.

of Cuitzeo is one of the most interesting monuments in Mexico. Church and monastery alike are well preserved, so that they can be easily studied. The most interesting thing about the church is its portal; it is an excellent example of Plateresque design, with every characteristic of the type (99). However, when one studies this portal in detail, he realizes that it is the work of Indian hands—just the opposite of Acolman, where one feels only the European chisel. All the motifs that appear on the portal at Cuitzeo have the unmistakable stamp of the indigenous (100); it seems self-evident that this work was done after a drawing by a Spanish sculptor, but by Indian stonecutters. This idea seems to be confirmed by the inscription which can be read over the doorway: *Fr. Io metl me fecit*, which Angulo translates as "Francisco Juan Metl made me."[34] The cloister at Cuitzeo is not so powerful as that at Yuriria, but it is more elegant (101); over the upper arcade there is a series of gargoyles, each one a fantastic monster, all different, and markedly Gothic in character. The fine construction of this monastery can be seen even in the cistern which collects rain water; it is still used by the people of the town, since the water of the lake is brackish.

Ucareo. Founded in 1554 and built in 1555 by Padre Juan de Utrera, who was the first prior and an excellent architect. The chroniclers say that when the Viceroy learned that they were constructing a sumptuous monastery in the wilderness he ordered the building stopped. The architect obeyed, but he had the Indians keep working, cutting the stone at the quarry and working the wood in the forest. When everything was ready, he asked permission to build a monastery which would be finished in one year, and when this was authorized, he built, with the prefabricated material, the monastery he had planned.[35] It was all roofed with wood, and still well preserved in Basalenque's time. At present it is in ruins.

Charo. Founded in 1550, it was constructed during the second half of the sixteenth and part of the following century. The cloister has slender columns and flat arches, with some Renaissance doorways. The church is covered by a barrel vault, the apse by a spherical cloistered vault, as it were a proto-cupola.[36]

Dominican Monasteries[37]

Although the friars of St. Dominic were the second order to reach Mexico, they began to build later than the Augustinians, and for that reason we consider them in this order. And it is proper to do so, for we find in their churches at an early date variations from the plan

101. Cloister, Augustinian monastery, Cuitzeo, Michoacán.

agreed to by the friars and the Viceroy. They were the first to construct chapels along the nave, and the first to build transepts and to elevate the vaulting over the crossing. These churches actually announce the cruciform plan typical of the seventeenth century. The Dominicans are less sumptuous than the Augustinians, but more so than the Franciscans, and they have a certain eclecticism which gives their buildings greater variety.

The Province of Santiago de México

Mexico City. The Dominicans in Mexico City built their second monastery in the latter half of the sixteenth century. According to Padre Ojea the church of Santo Domingo had the following appearance.[38] It was built like the church of Atocha in Madrid, inside of white stone, and outside of *tezontle,* a porous red volcanic stone; the portal resembled that on the church of the Escorial. The church had a single nave with a transept and side chapels, many of them faced with tile. It had an *alfarje,* a carved and inlaid roof of cedar, cof-

34 Angulo Íñiguez, *Historia*, I, 359. See also Toussaint, "El convento de Cuitzeo," *Arquitectura*, 6 (jul. 1940), 17–22; Toussaint, *Paseos coloniales*, pp. 92–95.

35 Kubler, "Ucareo and the Escorial," *Anales del Instituto de Investigaciones Estéticas*, 8 (1942), 5–12.

36 See Raul Flores Guerrero, "El convento de Charo y sus murales," *Anales del Instituto de Investigaciones Estéticas*, 22 (1954), 123–132.

37 On Dominican buildings, see Agustín Davila Padilla, *Historia de la fundación y discurso de la provincia de Santiago de México*; Hernando de Ojea, *Libro tercero de la historia religiosa de la provincia de México de la orden de Santo Domingo*; Alonso Franco y Ortega, *Segunda parte de la historia de la provincia de Santiago de México*; Ricard, *La "conquête spirituelle"*; Kubler, *Mexican Architecture*; Angulo Íñiguez, *Historia*; McAndrew, *Open-Air Churches*.

38 Ojea, *Historia religiosa*, pp. 9–20.

fered in gold and blue, with nine double joists decorated in knotwork. The wooden *cimborio* was octagonal, also with knot ornament, but richer; outside, the roof was covered with lead. We have already said that there were many tombs of the noble families of New Spain in this church. Perhaps because of the weight of the church and the undependable terrain, the building began to sink, so that it was necessary to build a new one.

Oaxtepec. This was the first monastery the Dominicans established after their house in Mexico City; into its foundations they built the idol Ometochtli which had been worshipped at Tepoztlán. This monument is well preserved, in a picturesque village with delightful springs. The church is a simple nave with ribbed vaults and pointed arches, and a barrel-vaulted transept, which seems earlier in date. The cloister is constructed of cut stone like that of Zacualpan, but it is more elegant. The upper cloister is later in date; it covered the windows of the church and an opening had to be made to give them light. The buttresses are of pointed profile; both stories are roofed by half-barrel vaults. The vault of the lower cloister is painted with Mudejar ornament, and on the walls are important frescoes, including paintings in niches at the corners.

Yautepec. The church is roofed with a barrel vault, divided into five sections by large pilasters and protruding arches; over the apse is a higher barrel vault. The cloister, covered with a barrel vault resting on the heavy square piers, is decorated with Mudejar painting. The pointed buttresses of the upper cloister rest on the projections of the piers.

Puebla. The original monastery in Puebla must have been a temporary building; Francisco Becerra built the second church, which is said to have been begun in 1571. We do not know what it was like; the present church dates from the middle of the seventeenth century.

Tepoztlán. The Dominican monastery of Tepoztlán is one of the most important monuments of the sixteenth century remaining in Mexico. The town is given extraordinary beauty by the fantastic background of the mountains on all sides; high on one of the ridges stands an interesting temple dedicated to the god Ometochtli. The friars reached Tepoztlán between 1551 and 1559, and the first conversion was the work of Fray Domingo de la Anunciación, who threw down the idol of Ometochtli from its high temple and then, breaking it to pieces, set them into the foundation of the church at

Oaxtepec. The church here seems to have been begun between 1560 and 1570; Francisco Becerra was in some way concerned with it. In all the churches he worked on we find a portal finished by a sort of triangular pediment, although the general style of the portals varies a good deal. And in fact we cannot be sure of the part this architect played in any of the buildings which Llaguno y Amírola attributes to him in New Spain.[39]

What is interesting about Tepoztlán is the effect of the whole ensemble, and the Renaissance details which were added to the original building. The sanctuary is covered by a ribbed groin vault. The principal portal is extraordinarily interesting, Plateresque in design, with sculpture of medieval character (102). It is composed of little columns whose entablature is a frieze from which rises a triangular pediment; the whole portal is decorated with circular medallions, some showing the Dominican cross, some the monogram of the Virgin. In the triangle of the pediment there are figures in relief, the Virgin of the Rosary between St. Dominic and St. Catherine, and these figures have a primitive crudity out of keeping with the rest. Above the pediment two angels, very primitive in flavor, support a large slab for an inscription. The inscription has disappeared; if we knew what it had said certain problems which Tepoztlán still presents might be cleared up. The monastery is rough in construction; its cloister, built with heavy buttresses, seems meant to defy the centuries, but is undeniably picturesque (103). The whole thing is battlemented, and at the corners of the roof the merlons are grouped to form finials of great originality (104).

Coyoacán. The Franciscans first evangelized Coyoacán, but as early as 1528 the town was given over to the Dominican friars. Various historical elements are discernible in the building. The early church was a great basilica, extremely strong, which we have already discussed (12). To that building, which must date from mid-sixteenth century, was added the present façade, dated 1582. This portal is not Plateresque, but Renaissance, even Purist, in style. The cloister dates from the second half of the sixteenth century; its most interesting feature is the decorated ceiling at the four corners

[39] Eugenio Llaguno y Amírola, *Noticias de los arquitectos y arquitectura de España,* III, 57. See also Efraín Castro Morales, "Francisco Becerra en el valle de Puebla," *Anales del Instituto del Arte Americano e Investigaciones Estéticas,* 13 (1960), 11–26; Enrique Marco Dorta, "Arquitectura colonial; Francisco Becerra," *Archivo español de arte,* 16 (1943); Toussaint, *Paseos coloniales,* pp. 106–110.

102. Portal, church of the Dominican monastery, Tepoztlán, Morelos.

103. Upper cloister, Dominican monastery, Tepoztlán, Morelos.

104. Merlons on the roof, Dominican monastery, Tepoztlán, Morelos.

of the lower cloister, divided into square coffers with painted figures. We have already spoken of the portal now standing at the left of the church façade. Equally interesting is the double-arched portal which was originally the main entrance to the churchyard; on axis with the main doorway of the church, it stands in its original place, but isolated now across the plaza. Its proportions are Plateresque, but the angels sculptured on the jambs are completely indigenous in execution.

Atzcapotzalco. Parts of this building are very ancient. The wall of the apse of the church perhaps dates from 1565, when we know the original church was finished. The body of the church appears to be later; the cloister certainly dates from the end of the sixteenth century and retains vestiges of fresco painting.

Chimalhuacán. The monastery of Chimalhuacán Chalco dates from the sixteenth century, and the façade of the church has one of the most interesting portals we know (105). There is a really fantastic mixture of styles here. An *alfiz* frames it, and all the area within the *alfiz* is covered by a diaper of straps and stars very Mudejar in mood. Above are two medallions with the Dominican fleur-de-lis cross, two coats of arms of Charles V, and in the center a niche with an image.

The basket-handle arch, with its vigorously ornamented archivolt, gives the whole thing a Plateresque quality; but the mouldings of the *alfiz* are Gothic. Furthermore it is certainly the work of Indian sculptors; the various items in the design are all interpreted differently, as each stonecutter understood them. In the baptistry at Chimalhuacán there is a very interesting stone baptismal font, which we have mentioned above.[40]

Tlaquiltenango. A monastery rudely built of irregular stone. It was built by the Franciscans and later transferred to the Dominicans. The side portal, of cut stone, is identical with that of the church at Cuernavaca, while the main portal is very plain. Over the door leading to the cloister there is an interesting fresco with portraits of Dominican friars. The posas, almost in ruins, are also very archaic.

Coixtlahuaca. The church of Coixtlahuaca is twin brother to that at Yanhuitlán, though it has certain peculiarities which give it a different character. There are the two portals, for instance. The principal façade could be described as Plateresque *sui generis*; it is deco-

[40] See Romero de Terreros, "El convento dominicano de Chimalhuacán-Chalco," *Anales del Instituto de Investigaciones Estéticas,* 30 (1961), 91–96.

105. Portal, church of the Dominican monastery, Chimalhuacán Chalco, México.

106. Façade, church of the Dominican monastery, Coixtlahuaca, Oaxaca.

rated by niches, and in the center appears a great rose window, whose petals, formed of coffers and rosettes, seem the stylization of some native flower (106). The side portal follows the same theme, with another large rose window, but is flanked by the two reliefs, with the Symbols of the Passion sculptured by Indians, of which we have spoken. The monastery is better preserved than that of Yanhuitlán, but the open chapel is a ruin.[41]

Teposcolula. The original monastery of San Pedro y San Pablo has disappeared. Of the old church, only the statues of saints placed on the new façade remain. The chapel of Santa Gertrudis, a piece of popular architecture reminiscent of Romanesque building, which re-

calls the Panteon de San Isidro in León, Spain, no less, is said to date from the eighteenth century. The open chapel of Teposcolula still stands, although in ruinous state (16, 17); we have described it above.[42]

The Province of San Hipólito de Oaxaca[43]

Oaxaca. The great Dominican monastery of Oaxaca is undoubtedly the most important building in the city (107, 108). Two Dominican houses are recorded in the old Antequera: the original one built by a friar of

[41] Toussaint, *Paseos coloniales,* pp. 28–32.
[42] *Ibid.,* pp. 25–27.
[43] On Dominican monasteries in Oaxaca, see Francisco de Burgoa's two books, *Palestra historial* and *Geográfica descripción.*

107. Façade, church of the Dominican monastery, Oaxaca.

San Diego named Minaya, and the one we see now. This was begun in 1570 and finished in the early years of the seventeenth century; the friars moved into it in 1608, although the building was not finished. This church has a weighty nave and transept of rather low vaults with lateral chapels all along the nave. It is in fact an excellent example of the type of church the Dominicans introduced. The decoration inside the church is magnificent; there are no recorded dates, but this polychrome gilded relief in stucco was probably made in the seventeenth century (190). We can postulate the presence here of artists from Puebla, like those who decorated the Capilla del Rosario.[44]

Yanhuitlán. The four most important monuments built by the Dominicans in Mexico are all in the region of Oaxaca called the Mixteca Alta, at Yanhuitlán,

[44] See Antonio Arroyo, *El monumental convento de Santo Domingo de Oaxaca.*

Teposcolula, Coixtlahuaca, and Tlaxiaco. These four monuments show such similarities that we should undoubtedly attribute them to the same architect, although their variations indicate that the Indian workmen who built them were different. The first church at Yanhuitlán was begun in 1541, but the *encomendero,* Francisco de las Casas, was poor and stingy, so that the church and convent were not worthy of the important town that Yanhuitlán then was. When his son Gonzalo inherited the encomienda, he threw his efforts into building a great monastery, and succeeded; this seems to have been between 1555 and 1575. The church of Yanhuitlán is a monument of the first rank, which would not be out of place in any European city. Its isolated situation, in a town which was rapidly depopulated in the colonial period, the lack of care which it has suffered, especially when it was used as a fortress in the civil wars, and the earthquakes which frequently scourge the region have resulted in great damage, so

108. Cloister, Dominican monastery, Oaxaca.

that it is destined to disappear before long, if it is not properly cared for. The great nave is covered with ribbed vaulting and richly furnished with retables in the Plateresque, Baroque, and Churrigueresque styles; the main retable contains paintings by Andrés de la Concha (109) and there is much other valuable art in this building (208). The monastery is in ruins, but from what remains one can imagine the magnificence of the cloister and the rooms it must have had long ago. At present the Dirección de Monumentos Coloniales is beginning the restoration of this building.[45]

Cuilapan. The great monastery of Cuilapan, near Oaxaca, must have been also a monument of the first rank, although, according to Martínez Gracida, neither

monastery nor church was ever finished. The cloister at Cuilapan differs in construction from all the other cloisters we know: the lower story has polygonal buttresses, on which rest the semicylindrical engaged columns of the upper story, and the semicircular arches of the upper story, with their sharply cut mouldings, also spring from engaged columns. The large basilica church appears to have served as an open chapel, as we have said already (21). The monastery is said to have been built by the Portuguese legate, Antonio de Barbosa.

The Province of San Vicente de Chiapas y Guatemala[46]

The first Dominican friars to come directly from Spain to Chiapas arrived with Fray Bartolomé de las Casas, although the Dominican Fray Domingo de Betanzos had evangelized the region. Chiapas was a center of intense artistic activity, and fortunately mag-

[45] Toussaint, *Paseos coloniales,* pp. 18–24; José Gorbea Trueba, *Yanhuitlán.*

[46] See Salvador Toscano, "Chiapas: su arte y su historia coloniales," *Anales del Instituto de Investigaciones Estéticas,* 8 (1942), 27–43.

109. Main altarpiece (detail). Gilded wood; oil on canvas. Church of the Dominican monastery, Yanhuitlán, Oaxaca.

nificent monasteries and churches still exist there. Dating from this period are the monastery of Chiapa de Corzo, the ruins at Tecpatán,[47] and certain parts of the monastery of San Cristóbal las Casas, although the greater part of it, and especially the magnificent church, dates from the seventeenth century.

The Beginning of the Great Cathedrals

No buildings of the other religious orders, either of friars or of nuns, have survived from this period. It is obvious that they existed, but either because time has ruined them, or because the orders were relatively rich and could rebuild them, the fact is that we cannot show any appreciable remains of any monuments built by the Carmelites, the friars of San Diego, the Jesuits, the Mercedarians, or any order of nuns in the sixteenth century.

The establishment of the secular clergy slowly but surely reduced the importance of the regular clergy. The bishops went on secularizing the monasteries little by little, that is, they brought them under the episcopal authority and removed the autonomy which they had enjoyed in the early days by special concessions of the Holy See and the Spanish Crown. But it was not until the following century that the parish church became important from the architectural point of view. In the period we are now considering the cathedrals, which were begun at this time, were the highest expression of religious architecture.

Seven cathedrals were established during the sixteenth century. Tlaxcala, the first, had been named in 1518 as the Obispado Carolense on the island of Cozumel, and was later moved to Tlaxcala. Its first Bishop, Fray Julián Garcés, presented his credentials to the Ayuntamiento of Mexico City on October 19, 1527. The see was moved to Puebla in 1539, still retaining the official title of the Bishopric of Tlaxcala. The Cathedral of Mexico was established in the capital in 1530, that of Oaxaca in 1535, of Michoacán in 1536, of Yucatán in 1561, of Chiapas in 1538, and finally of Guadalajara, with its seat in Compostela, in 1548.[48]

Cathedral of Puebla

We have seen that the first Cathedral of Puebla, like that of Mexico, was a basilica, a nave with aisles, roofed with wood. In 1587 it was repaired by Juan de Alcántara, who added vaulted chapels on either side, and a large one for the apse.

The facts about the beginning of the present cathe-

dral are not clear. The order for its construction has not been found. What is certain is that it was begun in 1575 by Francisco Becerra, who planned both exterior and interior of the church. It was to be a rectangular plan, with nave and two aisles of the same height, a *capilla mayor* at the end, with the sacristy on one side and the chapter on the other, and vaulted chapels. It was to have four towers but no dome. In 1634 Juan Gómez de Trasmonte, architect of the Cathedral of Mexico, modified Becerra's plan and adopted one similar to the metropolitan cathedral.[49] Soon after, work was suspended, not to be resumed until the period of Bishop Palafox, who finished the interior, as we shall see in Chapter 9 (166).

Cathedral of Mexico

The first cathedral in Mexico City, which we have discussed above, was pulled down in 1626 (10, 11). They had thought that the new church would be ready for use by that time; actually the work was not very far along, and they were to wish many times for their old parish church. The building of the present cathedral church of Mexico had been ordered by a royal decree of October 7, 1536, although for the time being nothing was done. On the eighth of August, 1544, a new decree ordered the Viceroy to proceed with the planning of the church. The Viceroy delivered his plan two years later; it was to be a fortified church with a tower at each corner. The Court rejected the project. On March 21, 1551, a new decree directed that the dean and chapter (since there was at the time no archbishop) should have a plan drawn. It seems that this was not done. The decree which we assume to have been the order for the present church is dated August 28, 1552. It directs that the cost of the work should be divided in three parts, between the Crown, the Indians, and the Spaniards, including both *encomenderos* and those without estates. In 1554 Archbishop Montúfar wrote to the Court that he and the Viceroy wished to begin building the church: it should be like the Cathedral of Seville,

[47] Heinrich Berlin, "El convento de Tecpatán," *Anales del Instituto de Investigaciones Estéticas,* 9 (1942), 5–13.

[48] See Angulo Íñiguez' study *Las catedrales mejicanas del siglo XVI*—interesting, like all his work. See also José R. Benítez, *Las catedrales de Oaxaca, Morelia, y Zacatecas.*

[49] See Efraín Castro Morales, "La catedral de Puebla y Juan Gómez de Trasmonte," *Anales del Instituto de Investigaciones Estéticas,* 32 (1963), 21–36; Efraín Castro Morales, "Luis de Arciniega, mæstro mayor de la catedral de Puebla," *Anales del Instituto de Investigaciones Estéticas,* 27 (1958), 17–32.

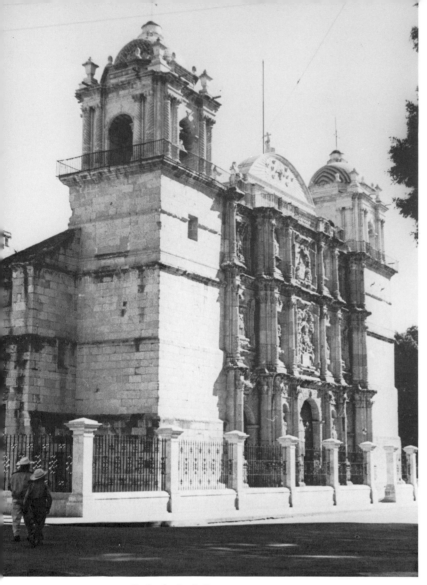

110. Cathedral of Oaxaca.

and it would be oriented east to west. They began laying these foundations, as shown in the Codex Osuna of 1564.[50]

The project was too ambitious, however, and Montúfar himself wrote in 1558 that they should be satisfied with a church like that of Segovia, or the new Cathedral of Salamanca. A plan for this new church was drawn up by Claudio de Arciniega, who had arrived in Mexico that same year; it was carried to Spain for official approval in 1567 by the *maestrescuela* Don Sancho Sánchez de Muñón. Two years later new decrees were sent, and in accordance with these the viceroy, Don Martín Enríquez, called a meeting in the Casas Reales on February 15, 1572, with the archbishop, the archdeacon, the treasurer and the precentor of the Cathe-

dral. The result of their deliberation fixed the definitive character of the Cathedral:

It was agreed that it be located and built on the site where the arcade called Lerma stands, using part of the small plaza which is in front of the houses of the Marqués del Valle . . . oriented north-south, with the Puerta del Perdón toward the Plaza Mayor and the bell tower at the front of the said church, and that it should be built with three well-lighted naves, and lateral chapels, and all roofed with wood.

The cornerstone was laid in 1573, and work went ahead eagerly. In the early seventeenth century the architect Juan Miguel de Agüero, who had built the Cathedral of Mérida, was in Mexico City, and constructed a model with certain modifications of Arciniega's project: roofing the building with vaults instead of timber, in particular. Then work was interrupted, and when it was resumed, they considered a new plan sent by Philip III, the work of Juan Gómez de Mora. In a meeting of May 19, 1616, the Commission decided to reject this new project, and to continue following the plan of Claudio de Arciniega and the model of Miguel de Agüero. So they did, and the present Cathedral is the result, with some modifications made in the seventeenth century.[51]

The Cathedral of Mexico is in the lineage of the magnificent Hispanic cathedrals (163). In plan it is intimately related to all of them; in style it seems to have inclined toward a Renaissance Purism, which at the beginning of the seventeenth century turned into Herrerian. It is curious, considering the time when it was begun, that it retains no Plateresque quality. Perhaps it was the influence of the Escorial at the end of the sixteenth and the beginning of the following century which made the monument—which may be considered the official expression of architecture in New Spain—adopt the style of Juan de Herrera. The plan

[50] *Códice Osuna.*
[51] On the Cathedral of Mexico see three studies by Toussaint: *La catedral de México, Iglesias de México, II*; "La catedral de México; sus cronistas mas recientes," *Anales del Instituto de Investigaciones Estéticas,* 3 (1939), 5–19; *La Catedral de México y el Sagrario Metropolitano.* This last monumental monograph includes much new documentation which has completely changed our interpretation of the great building. See also Heinrich Berlin, "Artífices de la Catedral de México," *Anales del Instituto de Investigaciones Estéticas,* 11 (1944), 19–39; Leopoldo Martínez de Cossío, "Documentos para la historia de la Catedral de México," *Anales del Instituto de Investigaciones Estéticas,* 33 (1964), 93–102; Jorge Olvera, "La catedral metropolitana de México, I," *Artes de México,* 32 (1960), 3–76.

followed that of the new Cathedral of Salamanca; its exterior seems influenced by that of Jaén. Baroque contributions were to sweeten the severity which characterized it in the beginning; but that is matter for another chapter.

Cathedral of Oaxaca

The first church here, which dated from 1535, and seems to have been finished by 1544, must have been provisional, like the original cathedrals in México and Puebla. One cannot doubt that a more important church followed the earliest one, although the recurrent earthquakes that scourge the region may well have prevented a large building. However it may have been, we know nothing of this church. The present Cathedral dates only from the eighteenth century (110).

Cathedral of Michoacán

Don Vasco de Quiroga, appointed as first bishop of Michoacán when Fray Luis de Fuensalida resigned the office, was installed in Tzintzuntzan, the then capital of Michoacán, on August 6, 1538. A little church, which the Franciscans had abandoned on building their new one, served for the ceremony of installation. On the following day, August 7, 1538, he took possession of the site on which he was to build his cathedral in Pátzcuaro, to which he had already determined to move the see. From the context of this document it is clear that he neither built nor thought of building a cathedral in Tzintzuntzan.[52] The cathedral which he then built in Pátzcuaro, dedicated to San Salvador, was later ceded to the Jesuits when they arrived in the city. We don't know what it was like; consideration of other cathedrals of the period suggests that it probably would have been a basilica, so useful and easy to build.

But Don Vasco de Quiroga, that great apostle, in his divine fervor dreamed of creating a cathedral worthy of the most splendid diocese imaginable. We have the plan for it, a radiating church, not polygonal like the old Byzantine churches, but with five distinct naves meeting at a central sanctuary (111). The author of this plan and first architect of the building seems to have been Toribio de Alcaraz.[53] Of this imposing edifice only a single nave was built; it survives, after many reconstructions and additions, as the church called Nuestra Señora de la Salud, but one can tell nothing about its original style. When the see was again moved, to Valladolid, a new cathedral was begun, which was finally completed after a thousand vicissitudes as the

111. Scheme of the Cathedral of Michoacán. Archivo de Indias, Sevilla.

present Cathedral of Morelia. It belongs entirely to the seventeenth and eighteenth centuries.

Cathedral of Mérida, Yucatán

The first cathedral of Mérida was a temporary building, just like the others. After this primitive church a more imposing one was begun; the cost, like that of all the cathedrals in New Spain, was divided three ways, between the Crown, the *encomenderos,* and the Indians. We do not know who drew the plans, but we know that Bishop Toral began the construction, which was later carried on by Don Diego de Santillán, who had been instructed to push the completion of the church. At this time the architect was Pedro de Aulestia. The work continued under the next bishop, but it was not until 1585 that the real architect, who was to finish the church in its definitive form, appeared. This architect was Juan Miguel de Agüero, who was working on the fortifications of Havana in Cuba when he was ordered by the Crown to go to Mérida.[54] Juan Mi-

[52] Toussaint, "La primitiva catedral de Michoacán," in *Paseos coloniales,* pp. 145–150.

[53] See the biography by Nicolas León, *El Ilmo. Señor Don Vasco de Quiroga, primer obispo de Michoacán,* and the monograph *Pátzcuaro* by Toussaint. See also John McAndrew, *Open-Air Churches,* pp. 629–649.

[54] Llaguno y Amírola, *Noticias de los arquitectos,* III, 67.

112. Façade, Cathedral of Mérida, Yucatán.

113. Nave, Cathedral of Mérida, Yucatán.

guel de Agüero finished the cathedral in 1598, so that this church is the oldest of the cathedrals built in Mexico, or indeed on this continent.[55]

The façade of the Cathedral of Mérida is strange (112): it consists of a great central section which indicates a higher nave than there really is, and two towers joined to it by very high walls. Two small portals open in these walls, and in the middle a large arch frames

55 On the Cathedral of Mérida, see José García Preciat, "La catedral de Mérida," *Archivo español de arte y arqueología*, 11 (1935), 73–93. It is strange that García Preciat was apparently not familiar with Llaguno's work.

the main portal. The church has a nave and two aisles, and a transept; heavy columns, which appear to be of the Tuscan order, support the arches of the hemispherical vaults (113). Over the crossing is a dome on pendentives. The interior of the vaults and the dome is decorated with a curious coffering which makes an unusual effect. As for its style, the church cannot be called Plateresque, but seems to be groping for the pure Renaissance style. The towers were not finished until later, and most unhappily, since there is no proportion between the heavy bases and the insignificant second and third stories.

114. Cathedral of Guadalajara, Jalisco.

115. Nave, Cathedral of Guadalajara, Jalisco.

Cathedral of Chiapas

Like the other bishoprics of New Spain, Chiapas had a primitive cathedral which Fray Bartolomé de las Casas found when he reached his see at the beginning of 1545, ". . . a small building, poor, and without ornaments." The Apostle of the Indians stayed there so short a time that he could do little about it. It seems probable that in time a new church was built, unless they used the same one, reconstructing it when necessary from time to time. The present church apparently dates from the seventeenth century.[56]

Cathedral of Nueva Galicia

The first cathedral of this bishopric, whose seat was originally in Compostela, was a thatched chapel. In 1561 the see was moved to Guadalajara, and in a decree of May 18 of the same year, Philip II ordered the construction of a new cathedral whose cost was to be divided as usual between the Crown, the *encomenderos,* and the Indians. It is said that Bishop Ayala laid the cornerstone on July 31, 1571. We know that the supervisor of the work was the architect Martín Casillas, but his activity on this cathedral must have been after 1585, when he was still working on the new Cathedral of Mexico. In fact, work was still going on in Guadalajara in 1602, and the dedication of the church took place on February 19, 1618.[57]

There is an enormous contrast between the exterior of the Cathedral of Guadalajara and its interior. Outside, perhaps because of the towers rebuilt at the beginning of the nineteenth century in really bad taste, and the various other additions to the structure, the Cathedral does not make much impression (114). But its interior is astonishing: it is the only cathedral in Mexico which looks like a Gothic church; from the columns spring ribs which sustain the vaulting and carry us straight into the epoch of Gothic architecture (115).

Purism

Just as in Spain, there flourished in Mexico a type of Renaissance architecture which followed the classical canons and kept itself pure of Plateresque exuberance. This was nothing like an independent development; obviously the Spanish architects who went to Mexico must have brought these ideas of Renaissance architecture, inspired by the classical architectural treatises, especially Serlio's. The first monument in this "Purist" style, as the Marqués de Lozoya has observed,[58] is the "Túmulo

Imperial," the catafalque for the death of Charles V. The date of this monument was 1559, and it was the work of the famous architect Claudio de Arciniega. It had two stories, the first a Greek cross in plan, and the second, a square, both with Tuscan columns and triangular pediments; pyramidal obelisks topped by balls stood on the columns of the first story, and the friezes of both entablatures were ornamented *a la romana.* This monument seems a distant antecedent of the architecture which was later to flourish in Spain. The Dominican monasteries of the Mixteca region may also be considered examples of Purist style, especially the open chapel of Teposcolula (16), which can by no means be classified as Plateresque, and the façade of the church at Tecali (84), which we must surely attribute to Arciniega, considering its resemblance to the Túmulo Imperial.

Some of the cloisters, for example those of Acolman (92), Cuilapan, and Molango, should be classed as true Renaissance and not Plateresque. Various other isolated details, such as the old portal of the monastery of San Agustín in Pátzcuaro (now pulled down to build a theatre), even the *portería* of the monastery at Actopan (94)—where only the candlesticks are Plateresque—are examples of Purist style.

Genuine evidence of Purist architecture may be found in the large basilicas of the sixteenth century: Zacatlán de las Manzanas, which has survived complete (13), Tecali—only walls and colonnades—(84) and Quecholac, later converted into the parish church.[59]

Among the houses built in the second half of the century, many must have been in this style; it was not always easy to build a house with a sumptuous Plateresque portal. Thus the house in Puebla known as the Casa del Deán, the residence of the dean, De la Plaza, which is dated 1580, is a splendid example of a Renaissance house, not a Plateresque.[60]

There are many doorways in this severe style: the cloister entrance of Santo Domingo in Oaxaca, dated

---

[56] See Toscano, "Chiapas."

[57] Luis del Refugio de Palacio y Basave, *La catedral de Guadalajara.*

[58] Juan Contreras y López de Ayala, Marqués de Lozoya, *Historia del arte hispánico,* III, 57. See also Francisco Cervantes de Salazar, *Túmulo imperial de la gran ciudad de México.*

[59] See McAndrew and Toussaint, "Tecali, Zacatlán and the *Renacimiento Purista* in Mexico," *Art Bulletin,* 24 (1942), 311–325.

[60] See also Francisco de la Maza, "Las pinturas de la Casa del Deán," *Artes de México,* 2 (1954), 17–24.

1575; the side door of the Augustinian church at Metztitlán, with its elegant lines, and above all, the principal portal of the basilica at Tecali (84), a superb piece of design, which would be an ornament to the most sophisticated church anywhere in the world.

But it was certainly in the great cathedrals that pure Renaissance style found its fullest expression. All of them, in their oldest parts, show a sober Renaissance mood which is sometimes so extreme as to become really Herrerian (118), metamorphosed with the passing of time, as we can see in the Cathedral of Puebla.

Obviously the pure Renaissance style coexisted with the Plateresque, but we must distinguish the differences between the two styles.

The Plateresque Style

The oldest church where we find evidence of Plateresque design is the ancient monastery of San Agustín Acolman (89, 91). The large portal is like a great decorative shield placed over the old medieval structure; there is a stimulating contrast between the rudeness of the building and the suavity and elegance of the sculpture which forms the portal. There is no doubt that the sculptor-architect of this portal came directly from Spain; nothing about it indicates an indigenous hand, and the technique of the carving is so perfect that the portal might be part of any Spanish church. The only difference one might note is the double archivolt, which seems like a Romanesque reminiscence. In the opinion of the Marqués de Lozoya, the design of the portal recalls that of the church of Santa María de Calatayud, but the technique of the sculpture is related to the school of Riaño de Sevilla.[61] This façade is dated 1560.

We find a popular interpretation of the Acolman façade in the two portals of the Augustinian church at Yuririapúndaro (90, 96). It is easy to see, comparing photographs of the two monuments, how the sculptor of Yuriria has created a popular Plateresque design, adding picturesque details to the purity of Acolman, so that one can call this a genuine example of popular Plateresque style in the hands of mestizo sculptors.

The façade of the church of Cuitzeo in Michoacán is the most unusual and extraordinary example of Spanish Plateresque (99, 100). None of the characteristics of the style are lacking. But if we study the motifs in some detail, we are convinced that it is the work of indigenous sculptors. Everything bears the unmistakable stamp of the Indian hand—the carving of the feathers in the eagles' wings, the way the shields are made, the very method of carving the stone—it is all absolutely different from the façade of Acolman. One can predicate that the façade of the church at Cuitzeo was planned by a Spanish architect who gave a general drawing for the portal, but that it was worked out entirely by Indian stonecutters. The inscription over the door leads us to believe that the author of this work of art has a Nahuatl name. Angulo is of this opinion, as we have said: Francisco Juan Metl.

We have already spoken of the open chapel at Tlalmanalco (15). We might repeat here our comments on this monument, which is so much like the portal at Cuitzeo: that is, it too is a Plateresque building executed entirely by indigenous workmen, and we have noted the importance of the portraits which appear on it. Among the multitude of detail in these reliefs is one which can be interpreted as "three flint," a date corresponding to 1560.

The portal of the Dominican church at Chimalhuacán Chalco is an excellent example of Plateresque design, even though it retains considerable Mudejar feeling (105). The space enclosed in the *alfiz* is covered by interlacing fillets and stars, over which are medallions with Dominican crosses characteristic of the Plateresque style, two coats of arms of Charles V, and a niche with an image. The arch is flat and richly carved, with a quarter-circle bend. We can also be certain that this portal was carved by Indian sculptors.

A good many portals follow the type of Chimalhuacán, with its *alfiz*. The design and the form of the arch vary, but the use of the *alfiz*—that Mudejar element which consists of framing the archway in a rectangular panel, and which the Plateresque designers found so much to their taste—is characteristic.

We find a portal in this style on the chapel of the Franciscan hospital at Acámbaro (9). The great *alfiz* is divided horizontally by a moulding in the center and the space is all covered with stars; the doorway is a round arch, with medallions on the jambs; and the archivolt, which oddly enough is narrower than the jambs, is profusely carved. Two engaged obelisks frame the portal, reaching up to the horizontal moulding which divides the *alfiz*.

Another portal of the same type is that of the Augustinian church at Tlamaco, in the state of Hidalgo. A big *alfiz* rests on two heavy buttresses, something like Chimalhuacán Chalco. A sort of pediment formed

116. Exterior, church of the Franciscan monastery, Xochimilco, Distrito Federal.

by heavy mouldings and topped by a medallion and a cross is enclosed by the *alfiz*.

An interesting example of this group of portals decorates the Franciscan church at Erongarícuaro. It seems at first a Romanesque doorway, with its semicircular arch and heavy voussoirs. The *alfiz* is decorated with five large cockleshells in high relief; contrary to the shells of Spanish decoration, their concave surface is presented to the spectator. Over the doorway is a double arched window enclosed not in an *alfiz* but in a complete quadrangular frame, and crowned by a still larger shell.

Perhaps the oldest portal of this type is the one still to be seen at the side door of the Franciscan church in Puebla. It is so old that it still uses the coat of arms of Tlaxcala, which was originally the seat of the bishopric. The *alfiz* is unusually high for its width; within this frame heavy mouldings make a pronounced triangular pediment. The arch is flat, its corners curved in quarter circles, and is covered with sculpture so flat that it reminds us inevitably of pre-Hispanic relief.

A portal similar in composition, though simpler, is that of the Hospital of Uruapan (46): it is just a great *alfiz* with a niche above it for the statue of the founder, Fray Juan de San Miguel, and shields on either side, one bearing the Franciscan symbol of the Five Wounds and the other meant for the royal coat of arms, although that has disappeared.

There is a simple Plateresque portal, with an *alfiz*, on the church of Santa Cruz Atoyac in the Distrito Federal. It is dated December 29, 1563, and shows us what the portals of these humble country churches must have been like.[62]

Perhaps we should designate a special category of the Plateresque to include some church portals which are eccentric in design and must therefore be described individually. The main portal of the church at Xochimilco is one of these (116). It is dated 1590, and has Corinthian columns of somewhat popular character, a round arch which pushes up the architrave, and, above a little frieze, a window with strongly cut mouldings, and angels in relief carved by a rude Indian hand.

Another of this group is the portal of the Franciscan church at Calpan, a curious example mingling all sorts of styles. There are strange columns and an ornamented arch; two angels in relief, indigenous in style like those of the posas we have already studied, hold up a Franciscan shield with the Five Wounds. Candleholders, stylized like an indigenous plant form (the flower stalks of the maguey) frame a double window of Italian flavor, which is crowned by a large shell; this has been stupidly enlarged out of proportion with the rest.

The portals of the Augustinian monasteries of Actopan (94) and Ixmiquilpan are also a special type of Plateresque. The one at Actopan has Romanesque traits, such as the large splayed arch of the tympanum; between the columns is a series of niches, and above the entablature an elegant Plateresque window with baluster columns.

Among these examples of Plateresque design should be noted also the side doors of many of the churches. In some places where the main portal is still Gothic or Renaissance the side door is frankly Plateresque. This is true at Cholula, where there is a north portal of extraordinary grace and elegance.

The side door of the Franciscan church at Huejotzingo is also in marked contrast to the sober Mudejar portal of the main façade (117). It is wildly Plateresque; the archivolt, decorated with a fantastic stylization of the chain of the Order of the Golden Fleece, recalls the Manueline sculpture of Portugal.[63]

The same thing can be said of the Franciscan church at Xochimilco. While the Plateresque main portal is relatively severe, as we have seen, this north portal is very ornate, with rather ridiculous detail, like the very slender columns resting on rectangular bases three times their width. A flat arch with a heavy moulding in the form of the Franciscan cord continues down the jambs, and over this is another, round, arch marked by a heavy rolled fillet. In the center there is a fantastic coat of arms, and over this first story there is a second, with a niche flanked by angels, and over that another niche with eagles on either side, all crowned by the Hapsburg eagle.

The side door of the church at Yecapixtla is completely Plateresque. Here is the classic round arch framed in columns, the portrait medallions in the spandrels, the cornice, and urns as finials to the columns. The full Renaissance has arrived; even satyrs appear in the low reliefs decorating the jambs.

There are many other side doors so peculiar in design that they cannot be classified. One of these is the north portal of the Franciscan church of Tecamachalco,

---

[62] Toussaint, "La iglesia de Santa Cruz Atoyac," in *Paseos coloniales*, pp. 9–11.

[63] Florentino Pérez Embid, *El mudejarismo en la arquitectura portuguesa de la época manuelina*.

which shows a curious mixture of styles. There is a little *alfiz* with a moulding and Gothic balls, and within this a trilobate arch worked with a vigorous Indian relief. And to give this portal a still more particular flavor, the *alfiz* is filled in with dark *tezontle,* making an effect not to be found elsewhere.

In the region of Michoacán the Plateresque style, which had produced such magnificent examples as the 1577 portal to the cloister of San Francisco in Pátzcuaro, survived in churches and monasteries well into the seventeenth century. Examples of this are the portal of San Agustín in Morelia, which seems to date from that period, and the portal of San Francisco in the same city, which is dated 1610. A group of portals, of which the oldest seems to be the rich and well-proportioned example at Zacapu, all follow the same pattern, with a twin-arched window over the arched doorway. The portals of the parish churches of Uruapan and Jacona are like this. The same arrangement appears on the church at Tzintzuntzan. This is not the original church, and it does not have the proper orientation. The façade is an example of mestizo Plateresque; it should perhaps be assigned to the seventeenth century, from the period when the town recovered some importance as Pátzcuaro declined after the moving of the episcopal see to Valladolid. In the same town of Tzintzuntzan are three other churches related in style to the Plateresque. First, there is the large church of the Tercer Orden, where the handsome curves of the gable seem to point to the eighteenth century. Second, the open chapel of the hospital, dated 1619, is soberly Plateresque. A third example is the open chapel beside the present Franciscan church, which although enclosed in a later structure, is plainly a Plateresque building from the end of the sixteenth century, related in certain motifs to the portal of the great church at Cuitzeo. Indeed, this style managed to survive in some parts of New Spain for many years.

The Herrerian Style in Mexico

The bare and severe architectural style developed by Juan de Herrera in the Escorial never enjoyed great popularity in America. The reason for this can be found in the social climate of the period. On the one hand, there was still no homogeneous cultural group in Mexico, and for the rest, the qualities of austerity and renunciation expressed by the Herrerian style were far from congenial to a young country, where making money and spending it ostentatiously were the principal preoccupations. Furthermore, for the newly converted

117. North portal, church of the Franciscan monastery, Huejotzingo, Puebla.

Indians richer and more attractive churches were wanted, churches such as were built first in the Plateresque, and later in the Baroque style.

We should review, however, the monuments of New Spain in which a Herrerian influence appears. We ought not to forget that according to Padre Ojea the façade of the second church of Santo Domingo in Mexico City was an "imitation" of the Escorial. In surviving buildings the oldest examples of this style seem to be the north doors of the Cathedral in Mexico City, finished around the end of the sixteenth century. They are quite characteristic. The two doorways inside the Cathedral which lead to the chapter room (118) and the sacristy—the latter dated 1623—are also very sober, though with a certain grace. As if they had not enough strength and severity, a wrought-iron gate, heavy and very high, completes the prisonlike effect.

118. Doorway to the chapter room, Cathedral of Mexico, Mexico City.

The church of the Jesuit college of San Pedro y San Pablo was built between 1576 and 1603 by the Jesuit architect Diego López de Arbaiza. He is said to have built there the first cupola in New Spain. In any case, the façade, which must date from about the end of the construction, is very severe and a good example of Herrerian design.

The Herrerian influence continued into the seventeenth century, as for example in the portal of the church of Santa Clara in Mexico City, which dates from 1661. The coats of arms which decorate it are a pleasant survival of Plateresque design.

In Puebla also we find evidence of this style. First of all there is the Cathedral, which uses those pilastered forms on the towers, and the pyramidal pinnacles so dear to the Herrerian (165). San Ildefonso, a church built by Bishop Mota y Escobar and finished in 1621, also presents a façade extremely austere, although its design has an Italian quality. The style continued up to the middle of the seventeenth century in the sober and rigid façade of Santo Domingo.

Civil Buildings

The Palace of the Viceroys

The representatives of the King did not have their own building in New Spain until 1562. In the beginning the Audiencia and the viceroy lived and worked in the house of Hernán Cortés, which was called Casas Viejas de Moctezuma. The viceregal authorities, convinced of the unsuitability of the Royal Government's functioning in the house of a private citizen, proposed to the Crown that the Old Houses of Moctezuma should be purchased; this was arranged, and Cortés was given an advance of 9,000 pesos. We do not know why the sale did not go through; it was not until much later that the Spanish government bought the New Houses of Moctezuma—now the National Palace of Mexico—for 34,000 *castellanos,* which included the 9,000 pesos already advanced to Cortés. The deed was signed on January 19, 1562, and the royal officials took possession of the building on August 19 following. It is reasonable to suppose that they quickly made the changes necessary for its use as the Royal Palace (10).

Various representations of this old Palace have been preserved on screens painted before 1692, when it was destroyed. From these we see that it was irregular in form, as if it had been rebuilt in various stages after its purchase in 1562 (11). One of the first to work on it was Claudio de Arciniega, who probably made the principal portals, dated 1563 and 1564. Don Lucas Alamán, in his *Disertaciones,* reproduces a drawing by the Jesuit Simón de Castro, with the ridiculous statement that it records the appearance of the Palace.[64] Actually it is a project for its remodelling which, as Alamán himself informs us, was not accepted. This was a pity, since it projects a Renaissance palace markedly Italianate in style, while the project which was chosen

[64] Lucas Alamán, *Disertaciones sobre la historia de la República Megicana,* II, Appendix, p. 9.

was already Baroque, and without special architectural merit (119).

Other Civil Architecture

The Plateresque decoration of houses and civic buildings is clearly a manifestation of luxury. Sometimes it was the Indians who carved these Plateresque portals for the European buildings. Among the most valuable of these is the very ancient Palacio de Gobierno in the city of Tlaxcala, which unfortunately has been altered recently in a most deplorable way. This venerable building had two portals. One is decorated by a composite arch, where a heavy band of sculpture between strong mouldings continues to form a sort of *alfiz* above (120). The other portal is more sober, but with the same indigenous decoration, and in the center a little arcade and loggia, both ornamented in the same style. We have no documentation on this building, but one can be sure that it goes back to at least the middle of the sixteenth century. The ornamented arch of convex curves seems to be a motif from Portuguese Mudejar design, here transplanted to New Spain.[65]

Other civil architecture with Plateresque ornament appears on the plan of the center of Mexico City (1596) in the Archivo de Indias (11), which was published for the first time in my book on the Cathedral of Mexico.[66]

On that map there are three buildings in this style; the most important is the Palacio de los Virreyes of which we have just spoken. The conventional drawing hardly tells us what the building was really like. It appears simply as a large structure with three portals on the ground floor, each topped by a royal coat of arms, and with embrasures immediately above the foundations. The upper floor has small windows, with larger ones only over the three portals, and from the roof rises a sort of little temple which holds the clock, and above it, the bell. The Palacio del Ayuntamiento, or Cabildo—the municipal authority—is also conventionally represented on the plan; we see a low trabeated portico above which is another with round arches (11). The lack of proportion in the drawing is evident, and it should not be taken as more than a suggestive representation of the elevations of the buildings.

The third building is the Real y Pontífica Universi-

[65] See Pérez Embid, *El mudejarismo*; Gibson, *Tlaxcala,* p. 128.
[66] See Toussaint, "La primitiva catedral de Mexico," in *Paseos coloniales,* pp. 1–5.

119. Project for remodelling the Palace of the Viceroys, Mexico City. 1692. Archivo de Indias, Sevilla.

120. Portal, Cabildo (Palacio de Gobierno), Tlaxcala.

121. Façade, House of Montejo, Mérida, Yucatán.

dad, on its permanent site after the various moves (11). Anyone who knows the extent of that site will be surprised at the small building shown on this plan. Nevertheless the Plateresque style of the façade is clear: a lintelled portal, with the coat of arms of Charles V over it, and at the sides two rich grilles of the sort so dear to Plateresque craftsmen. From the date of the plan, this must be the building whose cornerstone was laid on June 29, 1584. Its architect was Captain Melchor Dávila, although not for long, since in that same year he died of a fall from the scaffolding in repairing the Old Cathedral of Mexico.[67] Perhaps his nephew,

67 Berlin, "Artífices," p. 24.

122

Rodrigo Dávila, who carried on his work at the Cathedral, succeeded him here too, or perhaps it was Claudio de Arciniega, the most famous architect of the period, who was also working on the Cathedral.

We can also see in this same plan what the archbishop's palace was like: it too is Plateresque in style (11). Although its proportions appear very strange, in fact only two stories are indicated, with two small towers. On the ground floor is a doorway with the archepiscopal coat of arms, and over this an iron grille and windows at the sides; the second floor has plain windows, and at the corners of the roof are the towers.

One cannot get much impression, in this plan, of the façade of the *casas viejas de Moctezuma,* the Old Houses which belonged, as we know, to Hernán Cortés, or rather to his heirs (11). The drawing indicates simply a large building with an enormous portal, smaller doors at either side for shops, and, on the upper story, a loggia of round arches. The towers at the corners are so stylized that we can interpret them only because we know they existed.

The house which is most carefully drawn is that of the Mayorazgo de los Guerrero, because they had initiated the lawsuit for which this plan was an exhibit (11). The same building has existed for many years, and now forms the corner of the Calle de la Moneda and the Correo Mayor. It is a perfect example of the Plateresque house: its portal is sumptuous, framed by columns with complete entablature, and over this a great window of wrought iron with Renaissance detail, also flanked by columns. The family coat of arms is raised above the roof. On the lower floor there are no windows, while on the upper floor there are windows with Renaissance grilles, like those on the Casa de las Conchas in Salamanca; at the corners rise little towers, formed by columns, and battlemented. Undoubtedly this was the appearance of the houses of Mexico City at the end of the sixteenth century, and from it we can reconstruct them in imagination.[68]

We do still have a few examples of the civil architecture of this period; the most important is the Casa de Montejo in Mérida, Yucatán, built by the Indians of Maní in the middle of the sixteenth century (121). It carries the date 1549. The portal of this house is of two stories, and studying its sculpture carefully, we get the impression that it represents two distinct periods of

122. Portal of a house, Puebla.

work—the ground floor is earlier, the second story, later. On the ground floor there are free-standing columns on each side, projecting to give variety to the architecture, with pilasters behind them. Over the entablature a richly decorated frieze follows the profile of the structure in and out, protruding in the center over the keystone to form an ample bracket. The upper story is like an heraldic tapestry or an enormous embroidered hanging. The doorway of the balcony opens in it, with its lintel on brackets; the pilasters framing this section are cut back to accommodate the sculptured figures of warriors in armor, standing on the heads of vanquished demons. In the center is the coat of arms, topped by a helmet whose lambrequin is a foliate decoration branching richly to fill the whole space with or-

68 Toussaint, "Una casa de México en el siglo XVI," in *Paseos coloniales,* pp. 6–8.

123. Portal of a house, Puebla.

nament. This second story also is completed by an entablature with its frieze, simpler than the one below, and is in turn topped by a shield between rampant lions, crowned by the bust of a bearded man. Standing above the cornice of the first story, as if supported by the columns, are two figures of Wild Men, carrying clubs, with curious garments of sheepskin, whose rudely sculptured matted fur makes a curious effect.

The whole portal is noteworthy as an example of decorative sculpture, but we want to stress here one interesting thing about it—the number of portraits it includes. One would like to imagine that the two heads, of an old man and a young woman, at the top of the door panels are portraits of the *adelantado* and his wife, if this same face of a bearded man were not found in many other places. The keystone is a grotesque figure, another bearded man, who supports the central part of the bracket on his shoulders in a position which suggests that the whole work rests upon him. Could it be the architect who wanted himself portrayed in this position? Obviously it recalls the famous Master Mateo, on the Pórtico de la Gloria at Santiago. The Casa de Montejo is the most important example of civil architecture in the Plateresque style which we now have in Mexico.[69]

Another building from this period in a special Plateresque style is a house in Puebla, of which unhappily only the portal remains (122). The house was traditionally known as *La casa del que mató el animal* (The House of the Animal Killer), and is associated with a legend which recounts that a monster, a kind of dragon, appeared every afternoon on the plaza in Puebla, and no one dared to kill it until a certain knight undertook the task and succeeded. The portal is simple, like those of Ávila; it is composed of two jambs and a lintel. The jambs have simple bases and capitals formed of heavy mouldings and horizontal bands; on the bases there are three rosettes of the Indian type, and on the capitals, interlaced plant forms with pecking birds. The decorations of the jambs are framed in flat mouldings, and are hunting scenes, with men holding the leashes of dogs. The general composition of the panels and the dress of the hunters suggest that these reliefs were very likely copied from French or Flemish tapestries of the second half of the fifteenth century. The wide lintel over the door is carved with a frieze of pomegranates and scrolls of foliage. This little monument is a real jewel which deserves better care.[70]

Also in the city of Puebla is another house with a Plateresque portal, known as La Casa de las Cabecitas (The House of the Little Heads) (123). This is not

[69] Jorge Ignacio Rubio Mané and Manuel Toussaint, *La casa de Montejo en Mérida de Yucatán*.

[70] At present this house is the Hotel Italia; its proprietors demonstrate their lack of culture in the signs with which they have defaced this work of art. See Weismann, *Mexico in Sculpture*, pp. 33, 48–49, 197.

the rich Plateresque we have been talking about, but a sober Plateresque which simply offers the typical ornament: a flat arch with medallions bearing portrait heads in the corners.

The most elaborate portal in this style in Puebla was that of the Alhóndiga; one can see what is left of it on the modern building of that name. Its workmanship is so fine that in spite of the reconstruction it still repays attention.

Very similar is another portal, in the city of Oaxaca, with the same arrangement of a flat arch and medallions bearing human heads—a good example of Renaissance design.

In the city of Guadalajara, in the state of Jalisco, is a portal which might be designated an intermediate type. It too has a flat arch with the voussoirs vigorously decorated, and the pilasters forming the jambs are carved in high relief. Over the little entablature is a sort of frieze, richly carved, with the portrait medallions at each end just over the pilasters, and at the top a wide cornice. It has been moved to the Museo del Estado, where it can be admired even though not in its original position.

In Mérida are two other portals of this type, besides that of the Casa de Montejo. One is quite similar to the one in Guadalajara; it has an archaistic heavy Gothic moulding defining the interior of the doorway. The other, which is known as the house of Rivero Traba, has a lintelled portal, and a sort of shallow niche over the lintel with the coat of arms of the owner.[71]

Another portal, more severe but no less attractive, can be seen in San Cristóbal Las Casas, the most noble city of Chiapas (124). It has a coat of arms on the architrave, columns at either side, and lions curiously posed on top of the columns. It was the house of Don Luis de Mazariegos.

Mudejar Survivals

There is no building in Mexico that is completely Mudejar in form, structure, and decoration. The Mudejar art of Mexico was an adaptation of Moorish motifs to the uses of the Colony. In structure, the first basilicas and the open chapels in the form of mosques

124. Façade, house of Luis de Mazariegos, San Cristóbal de las Casas, Chiapas.

were Mudejar, as were the dwellings built like Andalusian houses, which were in turn variations on the Arabic house. Certain architectural elements were also Mudejar, such as the octagonal columns used in early colonial architecture, and, above all, the famous wooden roofs called *alfarjes*.

I have treated this element in Mexican architecture in detail elsewhere;[72] here it must suffice merely to outline the Mudejar influences which appear in the art of the Colony.

The use of *alfarjes*—roofs and ceilings of carved and inlaid wood—was general, and for a simple reason.

[71] See these two houses in Luis MacGregor's "Cien ejemplares de plateresco mexicano," *Archivo español de arte y arqueología*, 11, No. 35 (enero–abril, 1935), 31–45.

[72] Toussaint, *Arte mudéjar en América*. See also Toussaint, "Fray Andrés de San Miguel, arquitecto de la Nueva España," *Anales del Instituto de Investigaciones Estéticas*, 13 (1945), 5–14.

125. Corner of a house (Argentina and Guatemala Streets), Mexico City.

126. Façade, chapel of El Rosario, Xochimilco, Distrito Federal.

It was easier to put up wooden roofs, where there was abundant timber, than stone roofs, which were more difficult to build, and more costly. Thus practically all the early churches in Mexico City had roofs of *alfarje*. Very few of these ceilings have been preserved in Mexico, in comparison with South America, where in such cities as Sucre, Tunja, Bogotá, or Quito are many churches which still retain their Mudejar *alfarjes* intact. The most important *alfarje* roof still existing in Mexico is the one covering the church of San Francisco in Tlaxcala (79), a magnificent work, perhaps from the end of the sixteenth century, which urgently needs skillful and prudent restoration. The ceiling over the sacristy of San Diego in Huejotzingo may be older, since it was part of a building older than the present church. Other examples are a sober ceiling in the chapel of the Tercer Orden in Tulancingo, the corners of the Franciscan church of Tzintzuntzan in Michoacán, and the remains of an *alfarje* now to be seen in the church of La Profesa in Mexico City, which seems to have come from the Jesuit church. There are also many popular versions of *alfarje* ceilings all over the Republic. Another type of roof of Moorish origin is a vault on four crossing arches, used in the *camarines* of Tepotzotlán (198) and of San Miguel de Allende.[73]

Mudejar influence in decoration is to be looked for in the revetment of houses in Mexico City. The use of such surfaces of plaster worked in geometric patterns seems to have begun early in the seventeenth century and persisted almost to the end of the colonial period.

The most impressive building in this style was probably the one known as the Casa del Judio (The House of the Jew), which stood in the Barrio del Cacahuatl, now the district of San Pablo, in Mexico City. The façade was decorated not precisely with an *alfiz,* but with what seems like a sort of tapestry of stucco relief hang-

73 Angulo Íñiguez, "The Mudejar Style in Mexican Architecture," *Ars Islamica,* 2 (1935), 225–230. See also Leopoldo Torres Balbás, "El estilo mudéjar en la arquitectura mejicana," *Al-Andalus,* 6 (1941).

ing with its scalloped fringe and tassels; over this were two angels, three medallions, and a little Baroque structure composed of three niches with their saints; above, a frieze and a kind of pediment. The portal imposed on this decoration, in full seventeenth-century taste, may be of later date. At the corner there was a loggia of mixtilinear arches, very characteristic of Mexican colonial architecture, which was decorated, like the whole wall above, with stucco relief. It appears that the arcade was later closed in with more stucco work, leaving small windows. The doorway below the loggia was also in typical seventeenth-century style, later than the building itself. Hence we assume that the building dated from the late sixteenth or early seventeenth century, and was later altered. This beautiful house no longer exists; we know of it only from a lithograph published in a novel called *Los misterios de México*.[74]

This decoration in stucco relief is to be found on a great number of houses in Mexico City; it is characterized by geometrical designs and by its resemblance to tapestry hung on the walls. Among the most important examples are the following: the house at the corner of Argentina and Guatemala Streets, with a beautiful niche at the corner (125) (it has unfortunately been altered by adding a story); the house of Jerónimo López, at the corner of Avenida Uruguay and Cinco de Febrero Street, now a hotel, whose decoration was completely destroyed and then remade in cement, following the original patterns on the first two floors but somewhat modified on the third.

[74] Niceto de Zamaçois, *Los misterios de México*.

This decoration was also used on churches, some of which are remarkably Mudejar in appearance—like the Capilla del Rosario in Xochimilco, where the combination of stucco relief with glazed tiles looks absolutely Oriental (126). The Capilla de la Concepción in Coyoacán, in the Federal District, also has a façade covered with this relief. The church of the Seminario de San Martín in Tepotzotlán, whose walls date from mid-seventeenth century, is still edged by a broad band of stucco arabesque, like a hanging with tassels. The walls of the church of Tlahuac are similarly covered. Many other churches, which would make an interminable list, were decorated in this style.

It should be noted, furthermore, that the Indians appropriated this method of finishing buildings, and that local types can be distinguished. There are, for example, so many churches of this kind around Texcoco, in the state of Mexico, that it can be called a distinct school of decoration (186). Here the geometrical pattern is often forgotten, and we find ornamental motifs taken from the flora but repeated excessively, over and over, just as in Moorish plaster work. The masterpiece of this type is in the village of Papalotla, near Texcoco. The so-called *arcadas reales,* which is simply the arched entrance to the churchyard, is completely covered with stucco reliefs in the most fantastic and exuberant motifs imaginable, and crowned, moreover, by figures at the top in vigorous silhouette. The date 1733 can be read on this, showing how the Mudejar influence extended even into the eighteenth century; indeed the ornament already falls within the Baroque style.

Chapter Six

RENAISSANCE PAINTING

First Evidences of the Renaissance

HE RENAISSANCE STYLE is already evident in Mexico in some of the wall paintings of the monasteries. Thus the monumental stairway of the Augustinian monastery at Actopan, in the state of Hidalgo, is an example of full Renaissance decoration, reminiscent of certain Florentine palaces (127). This stairwell is decorated by great horizontal bands of Renaissance friezes; above these are arcades of fantastic columns, and in each archway the figure of a saint, richly clothed, is writing or reading in an imposing chair. Although these paintings, like the earlier murals, are still derived from woodcuts, the effect of the whole is so rich and imposing that we cannot but recognize with emotion that the Renaissance has invaded Mexico.

In the Augustinian monastery at Epazoyucan, in the state of Hidalgo, the four corners of the cloister are decorated with fresco paintings; they are still somewhat primitive in mood, but with an undeniable flavor of the Renaissance (128; color, facing p. 132). These paintings were discovered in 1922 by the architect Don Federico Mariscal, and should be dated around 1556. In the paintings at Epazoyucan the three influences which constantly appear in Mexican painting of this period are mingled. They are partly Flemish, as in the *Crucifixion,* with its elongated and hieratic figures—it was never finished, and two white silhouettes indicate missing figures—or in the *Ecce Homo,* with its Christ and Rabbi. But the Italian influence also makes itself felt in this work: the *Death of the Virgin* (over the doorway) is entirely Italianate, and so are various other details. The third influence is that of the Spanish primitives; one picture, the *Road to Calvary,* inevitably recalls an artist like Fernán Gallegos, although in fact they both seem to derive from an engraving by Schongauer. These paintings at Epazoyucan can be attributed, on style, to Juan Gersón.

Other paintings of this same period, which are in contrast to the mural work of the Indians because they are deeply influenced by Renaissance art, are those decorating the vault under the choir of the Franciscan church of Tecamachalco, in the state of Puebla (129). They are not signed, only dated 1562; but in the Anales de Tecamachalco—the Chronicle kept in the town of Tecamachalco—we read that in that year the painter Juan Gersón was at work decorating the church. These paintings by Gersón show both Flemish and Italian influences (130). The Flemish appears in the elongated

127. Augustinian Fathers. Mural in the stairwell,
Augustinian monastery, Actopan, Hidalgo.

129. Vault under the choir loft, church of the Franciscan monastery, Tecamachalco, Puebla.

128. Anonymous. Pietà. Mural in the cloister, Augustinian monastery, Epazoyucan, Hidalgo.

figures, the meticulous realism of detail, and even the types, while the figures of the angels, the rich palette, and the general softness of tone are Italian.[1]

Another example of Renaissance painting in this period is found in the entrance way to the convent at Ozumba. Here we see the *Arrival of the First Twelve Franciscans,* as they are received by Hernán Cortés, and the *Martyrdom of the Boys of Tlaxcala.* The scene of the "niños Tlaxcaltecos," especially, achieves real plastic quality through the unstudied composition, which seems to anticipate modern Mexican murals. There is no doubt that these paintings date from the middle of the sixteenth century, but have been repainted later.[2]

The Guild

European painting was well established in Mexico by the middle of the sixteenth century. The Indians continued their work, but because of the great quantity of painting needed, the quality suffered. The ecclesiastical authorities, assembled in their First Council in

[1] It has recently been discovered that Juan Gersón was an Indian, native of Tecamachalco; see Xavier Moyssen, "Tecamachalco y el pintor indígena Juan Gersón," *Anales del Instituto de Investigaciones Estéticas,* 33 (1964), 23–40.

[2] See Manuel Romero de Terreros, "El convento de San Francisco de Ozumba y las pinturas de su portería," *Anales del Instituto de Investigaciones Estéticas,* 24 (1956), 9, 9–21.

130. Juan Gerson. Scene from the Apocalypse. Oil. Choir vault, church of the Franciscan monastery, Tecamachalco, Puebla.

1555, declared that no painter, Spanish or Indian, could paint images or altarpieces without examination by the church.[3] Before this time Don Luis de Velasco had decreed that Indian painters should be subject to examination; but with this new provision all painting was given into the hands of the church. Certainly the church had the right to scrutinize the propriety of its images, but a control so broad as this decreed by the First Council subjugated painting to the ecclesiastical authorities. The European painters did not agree to any such submission. Renouncing the special privileges they had traditionally held (which in Spain had led to that famous controversy in which they demanded exemption

from taxes, quoting famous men, including Lope de Vega, in support of their position) they requested that a guild of painters should be established, with its own rules, like any craft guild.

The first ordinances for painters and gilders were published in Mexico City on August 9, 1557, and constitute an important document for the history of art in New Spain.

Besides those administrative and religious stipulations which appear in the ordinances of all guilds, there are technical directives which indicate an enormous advance in painting, since there were at least artists capable of setting these requirements. It was required that a painter know how to paint in fresco and in oils, that he know how to draw from a nude or clothed model, that he know perspective, that he know how to paint drapery, and that he should have mastered the decoration known as *grotesque* in Europe, which in New Spain was called *pintura de romano.*

The ordinances divide the members of the guild into four categories: *imagineros*—the painters who know how to make sacred images, the highest category of painting at that time—gilders, fresco painters, and *sargueros,* or cloth painters. *Sargas* were unstretched painted cloths, which were used like tapestry.[4]

The names of a few contemporary artists have been preserved, among them some of the *veedores,* supervisors or overseers of the guild. On May 8, 1556, Juan de Illescas and Bartolomé Sánchez were named; later Pedro Rodríguez and Pedro de Robles filled the same positions, appointed by the viceroy, Don Luis de Velasco. Only in 1590 did special overseers for painting appear, Nicolás de Tejeda and Nuño Vázquez. The last mention of overseers was on March 6, 1595, when we find Francisco de los Reyes and Gaspar Pérez de Rivera. Nicolás de Tejeda appears in Puebla after 1558. Nuño Vázquez seems to come later in Puebla, since he was dead in 1603: his widow, Elena de Rivadeneira, appeared before the notary Juan de Santa Cruz, to make a claim against Bartolomé de Torquemada, to pay what was owing for the work on "the monument in the Cathedral of Mexico"; she got only one hundred pesos.[5] To the names of these craftsmen we should add

[3] *Constituciones sinodales.*
[4] See Francisco Santiago Cruz, *Las artes y los gremios en la Nueva España*; Francisco del Barrio Lorenzot, *Ordenanzas de gremios de la Nueva España*; Manuel Carrera Stampa, *Los gremios mexicanos.*
[5] Archivo de la Catedral de México.

Anonymous. Pietà (detail). Mural, cloister of the Augustinian
monastery, Epazoyucan, Hidalgo.

131. Simón Peréyns. La Virgen del Perdón (detail; destroyed by fire, 1967).
Oil. Cathedral of Mexico.

that of Juan Gersón, author of the paintings at Tecamachalco and perhaps at Epazoyucan. At present these are all the names we know of the group of artists who first represent Renaissance painting in Mexico. Soon the real actors would appear on the stage.

The First Phase of Mexican Colonial Painting

Simón Pereyns and His Group

Renaissance painting in New Spain, whose beginnings we have just sketched, first crystallized in a group of artists gathered around a notable figure, the Fleming, Simón Pereyns.

Pereyns, who was called Perines in New Spain and himself adopted this form even in signing his pictures, came to Mexico with Viceroy Gastón de Peralta in 1566. According to the information given at his trial,[6] he was born in Antwerp, and went in 1558 to Lisbon, where he lived for nine months with a Portuguese painter. From there he went to Toledo, where he found the Spanish court, and worked among the most famous painters of his time who were gathered around Philip II: Antonio Moro, Juan Fernández de Navarrete *el mudo,* the "divine" Morales, and Alonso Sánchez Coello. Pereyns was, then, a court painter who made various portraits of the King and of the royal family.[7] It is obvious that he must have known Gastón de Peralta there, and decided, in a spirit of adventure, to accompany him when he went to New Spain as viceroy. We know that immediately after he arrived the Viceroy ordered the decoration of the Real Palacio with battle scenes in fresco, and that a sinister interpretation was put on this: it was said that the Viceroy intended to lead a Mexican revolt, and had ready an army of thirty thousand soldiers. It is reasonable to assume that these paintings were the work of Pereyns, commissioned by the man who had brought him from Europe. Soon after this, Don Gastón de Peralta returned to Spain because of the unrest in Mexico, and although the painter wanted to go with him, the contracts he had made for paintings prevented him.

Six months after Don Gastón de Peralta left, Pereyns was arrested by the Holy Office of the Inquisition. His crimes consisted in having said that it was more sinful to have a love affair with a married woman than with an unmarried one, that he preferred to paint portraits rather than saints, that he was a Lutheran, and that in confessing you didn't have to tell all your sins. The trial shows Pereyns as enormously ingenuous and simple, but at the same time strong and obstinate, since he resisted the torture. On December 4, 1568, he received his sentence: to paint at his own cost the retable of Our Lady of Mercy for the Old Cathedral of Mexico.

We assume that the painting known as *La Virgen del Perdón,* now on the altar of Our Lady of Pardon in the Cathedral of Mexico, is this work; it seems to be painted on a door covered with canvas (131). Doubtless because of the difference in advocacy, it has been claimed that this painting is signed by Francisco de Zumaya; this signature does not exist. Other people claim that Pereyns' name appears on the back of the panel.

Pereyns' waywardness led him constantly to express unsuitable opinions, and he was denounced to the Inquisition three more times, but the Holy Office paid no attention. In Mexico he married Francisca de Medina, who seems to have been a sister to the wife of Juan de Arrúe, a painter we shall speak of later. We do not know when he died, presumably at the end of the century, either in the capital or in some other important city of Mexico. His *oeuvre* was large: he painted retables for the Franciscan churches of Tepeaca, Huejotzingo, and Tula, and for the Augustinians in Mixquic, Ocuila, and Malinalco; he worked with Concha on the retable of Teposcolula, and painted the pictures of the altarpiece of the Old Cathedral in Mexico City. Of all this—aside from the *Virgen del Perdón,* if it is his— we have only a *St. Christopher,* signed and dated 1588, in the Cathedral of Mexico; the paintings of the retable of Huejotzingo (132, 146), which are dated 1586;[8] and three paintings in the Galerías de Pintura which have recently been attributed to him on style: *St. Cecilia, The Holy Family,* and *St. Lawrence.*

Pereyns' work is uneven, for his output was enormous; but his characteristics stand out at the first glance. From Flanders he retains a taste for a bluish tonality,

[6] Manuel Toussaint, "Proceso y denuncias contra Simón Pereyns en la Inquisición de México," *Anales del Instituto de Investigaciones Estéticas,* 2 (1938), Supplement.

[7] José Moreno Villa has informed me that he has seen in the Archivos del Palacio Real in Madrid receipts signed by Pereyns for work done at Court. It would be desirable to have these documents published so that our information on this important artist might be more complete.

[8] See Heinrich Berlin, "The High Altar of Huejotzingo," *The Americas,* 15 (July 1958), 63–73. See also Enrique Ríos, "Una obra ignorada de Simón Pereyns," *Anales del Instituto de Investigaciones Estéticas,* 9 (1942), 61–65; Diego Angulo Íñiguez, "Pereyns and Martín de Vos," *Anales del Instituto de Arte Americano e Investigaciones Estéticas,* 2 (1949), 25–27.

certain types, the persistence of gilding in his painting, and a certain inherent dryness. Italy gives him the rich palette, the harmonious composition, the unconcern for detail, and the delight in sensuous forms. For another thing, Pereyns likes to paint in dabs; some of his paintings are like enamel, large areas with dashes of color, almost like lacquer.

Pereyns collected a group of artists around him: Francisco de Morales, Francisco de Zumaya, Andrés de la Concha, and Juan de Arrúe.[9] The remodelling of the Old Cathedral in Mexico City in 1585 for the convening of the Third Church Council brought together the most important artists of New Spain, and among them were Pereyns and his group.

Andrés de la Concha

The altarpiece and the gilding of the remodelled nave of the Old Cathedral were the work of Andrés de la Concha, one of the most famous painters of his time. We have only a few works by him. The most important are the paintings still to be seen on the retable of the Dominican church at Yanhuitlán (109); its date is probably about 1575, and the paintings give us a significant artist, in whom Italian influence is struggling with the Spanish style which is already visible in the realism of the figures. Concha was active between 1575 and 1612, and among other work recorded by him were paintings of *Fame* and *Victory* made for the catafalque of Philip II, erected in Mexico City in 1600, and the triumphal arch which he made with Alonso Franco, for the arrival of the new archbishop, Fray García de Santa María, in 1604.

Francisco de Zumaya

Along with Andrés de la Concha appears Francisco de Zumaya. His real name was Francisco de Ibía; he was a native of Zumaya in Guipúzcoa, from which he took his name, and he was a descendant of the noble house of Zumaya, also called Gamboa. He was born in 1532; he reached Mexico a little before 1565, when, on the nineteenth of January, he was granted a plot of land. By 1577 he was married to Catalina de Sandoval, and one of his daughters, Isabel de Ibía, was the wife

[9] See Toussaint, "Tres pintores del siglo XVI; nuevos datos sobre Andrés de la Concha, Francisco de Zumaya y Simón Pereyns," *Anales del Instituto de Investigaciones Estéticas*, 9 (1942), 59–61; Toussaint, "Pintura colonial; notas sobre Andrés de la Concha," *Revista mexicana de estudios históricos*, 1 (1927), 26–39.

132. Simón Peréyns. Adoration of the Shepherds. Oil on canvas. On the main altarpiece, church of the Franciscan monastery, Huejotzingo, Puebla.

of the painter Baltasar de Echave Orio, his countryman. For this reason it is tempting to assume that Zumaya was the teacher of Echave.

We know little about Zumaya's work in Mexico. In 1574 he made the hoods for an Auto de Fe; in the redecorating of the Cathedral he gilded the pulpits of the Capilla del Crucifijo, assisted Concha in the gilding of the ceiling, and painted four waxed windows for the Capilla del Sacramento. Perhaps the only work of Zumaya's we have, now that it is certain that he did not paint the *Virgen del Perdón*, is the *St. Sebastian* which hangs on the upper part of the same Altar del Perdón (133). The legend goes that this St. Sebastian was

133. Francisco de Zumaya. St. Sebastian (destroyed by fire, 1967). Oil. Cathedral of Mexico.

painted by a woman, "la Zumaya," who was the teacher of Echave. There is no historical evidence that Zumaya's daughter was a painter, so that we can interpret the legend as indicating that the painting is by Francisco de Zumaya, who was himself Echave's teacher. Examined carefully, the painting shows an undeniable connection with the work of Echave Orio, especially in the legs and feet, although the head is much weaker.

Francisco de Morales

Francisco de Morales was Pereyns' most determined enemy, and is certainly the most mediocre painter of the group. Morales took advantage of Pereyns; they worked together, and although the Fleming was a much more gifted painter than the Spaniard, they divided the pay equally. Pereyns realized this and tried to free himself; so then Morales arranged that Pereyns should be denounced to the Holy Office. In his own words, what he wanted to do was "throw him out of the country." Francisco Morales was born in 1528; we find him in Mexico after 1566, and it was his wife, Francisca Ortiz, who egged him on to make trouble. In 1572 he made a *palabrero* and lectern for the chapel of the Inquisition, and two years later the catafalque and eight shields for the funeral ceremony held by the Holy Office for Cardinal Don Diego. In 1595 he contracted, with the sculptor Luis de Arciniega, to make a retable for the Franciscan church of Cuautinchán, a work which was not carried out. He collaborated with Pereyns on the retables for the churches of Tepeaca, Mixquic, Malinalco, and Ocuilan. At the end of the century, on March 13, 1597, we find him in Puebla, signing an agreement with Juan de Arrúe. He perhaps died there, since at that time he was seventy years old.

Juan de Arrúe

The most famous painter of this period was Juan de Arrúe, whom the chroniclers, in their zeal to make all names Castilian, call Juan de la Rúa.[10] Arrúe was born in *"los pueblos de Ávalos,"* now Colima, in 1565. He was the son of Juan de Arrúe, a Sevillan sculptor whom we have already mentioned, and his mother was named Marta Calzontzin, though she had no connection with the last ruler of Michoacán. Arrúe was active in Mexico City after 1587, when he married Ana de

[10] The documentation on Arrúe comes largely from the research of Francisco Pérez Salazar, the distinguished historian of Puebla. See his *Historia de la pintura en Puebla.*

Medina. Simón Pereyns was one of the witnesses at his wedding, from which we deduce that the Fleming was his master. Later, after this first wife died, he married again, and had several children. Juan de Arrúe produced a great deal of painting, of which we list the more important. In 1593 he made nine *sambenitos* for the Cathedral of Mexico. In 1599 he painted two altarpieces in Puebla, one for the Hospital de San Pedro, and another for the choir of the old Cathedral. In 1597 he made a large retable for the church of the Franciscan monastery in Tehuacán,[11] which was placed instead in the church of the Franciscans in Cuautinchán, where it still stands (148). In 1607 we know he was in Oaxaca, since he had Diego Martín denounced for arguing about theology, and in 1611 he made there a copy of the figure of the Virgin which had appeared on the trunk of a burned pine tree—this little painting still exists in the Archivo General de la Nación. While he was in Oaxaca he did various work for the Dominican monasteries of Etla and Huitzo, and for Tlacochahuaya he painted a retable of St. Jerome. Later, between 1621 and 1630, Arrúe was working in Mexico City. In 1621 he did the paintings for the catafalque erected to honor Margaret of Austria in the monastery of Santo Domingo, and he also made the triumphal arch for the arrival of the new viceroy, the Marqués de Gálvez. In 1630 he was working in Puebla, from which he was not to return. In 1637 he painted a picture for the monastery of San Bernardo, and in the same year he wrote his will, from which we have taken this information.

Arrúe proves to be a good Renaissance painter. His retable for Cuautinchán is not so rich as those of Huejotzingo or Xochimilco, but has the virtue of a greater simplicity; there is no sculpture, but simply eight principal pictures with six additional ones at the sides. The oil paint has become so opaque with time that it looks like tempera; its tonality is high, with blue hues prevailing. Arrúe's art seems uncomplicated, more simple and straightforward than the painting of Pereyns or Concha.

Alonso de Villasana

The last painter of this period is Alonso de Villasana, about whom we know only one simple fact: that he decorated the church of Nuestra Señora de los Remedios in 1595. This building, which was under the patronage of the Ayuntamiento, had been repaired, and Villasana was the artist commissioned to decorate it. We have a detailed description of these paintings by

Fray Luis de Cisneros, in his book about the Virgen de los Remedios, which was published in Mexico in 1621.[12] This decoration represents the most complete triumph of the Renaissance. There were frescoes, and ten oil paintings: probably the whole church was decorated in fresco, while the oil paintings depicted the history and miracles of the holy image. Among the frescoes were some so completely pagan in inspiration that one wonders how it was possible in that period. There were Old Testament subjects—Judith with the head of Holofernes, Esther and Ahasuerus, Noah's Ark, Rebecca and Eleazer, Solomon and Moses—there were symbolic motifs—such as sibyls, and there were others frankly mythological and pagan—Juno, Neptune, Saturn, Vulcan, Venus, Mercury, and Mars—and to climax the Renaissance mood, the Three Graces.[13]

The Renaissance had taken over painting in Mexico. This period can be thought of as a prelude to the great painting which was to come, and which was inspired by that very mood, sensual and lucid, full of color and of grace—neglecting the spiritual a little, but bringing a vivid sense of life—which we call the Renaissance.

The Precursors

There is a group of painters who constitute a sort of bridge between the artists we have been studying and those who formed the nucleus of the great painting of the early seventeenth century. These are Alonso Vásquez, Alonso López de Herrera, and Alonso Franco.

Alonso Vásquez

Alonso Vásquez is a painter whose work in Spain has been thoroughly studied. Mayer gives us the documentation of his work in Seville, from the *Resurrection* in the parish church of Santa Ana in Triana, signed and dated 1590, through *The Death of St. Hermenegild*, which he left unfinished in 1603, to be completed by Juan de Uceda. Mayer wonders what happened to Alonso Vásquez after 1603, and supposes that he must have died.[14] Actually, Alonso Vásquez had crossed to New Spain, perhaps in the cortege of the Viceroy Mar-

---

[11] The contract for moving this retable was found by Francisco del Paso y Troncoso.

[12] Luis de Cisneros, *Historia de . . . la Santa Ymagen de Nuestra Señora de los Remedios*.

[13] See Federico Gómez de Orozco, "Las pinturas de Alonso de Villasana en el Santuario de los Remedios," *Anales del Instituto de Investigaciones Estéticas*, 14 (1946), 65–80.

[14] August Mayer, *Historia de la pintura española*, p. 194.

134. Alonso Vásquez. St. Michael. Oil. 1.74 x 1.49 m.
Pinacoteca Virreinal, Mexico City.

qués de Montes Claros, who took over his duties precisely in the year 1603. There is no documentary proof of this, but the coincidence is suggestive, and the fact that Vásquez' work in Mexico was intimately connected with Montes Claros tends to confirm it. Alonso Vásquez did considerable work in New Spain. The most important seems to have been the decoration of the chapel of the Palace, where there was a canvas eight *varas* high and four and a half *varas* wide, with *The Martyrdom of St. Margaret,* in honor of Margaret of Austria, the wife of Philip III. Another important work by Alonso Vásquez was the retable of the chapel of the University. These paintings, according to Don Carlos de Sigüenza y Góngora,[15] were Vásquez' favorite work, and represented *St. Catherine,* to whom Viceroy Montes Claros had dedicated the chapel. When the Viceroy went to Peru in 1607, Alonso Vásquez stayed in Mexico, and by the following year was dead. He was married to Doña Inés de Mendoza and had four children: Diego, María, Alonso, and Antonio.[16]

By comparing the paintings of Alonso Vásquez in Seville, we have attributed to him two large paintings in the Galerías de Pintura. These are a *St. Michael* (134) and the *Portrait of a Boy* between two allegorical figures, one apparently an Indian woman, and the other a devil. These paintings were attributed at one time to Echave Orio and earlier to Luis Juárez, both very weak attributions. The vigorous silhouette of the St. Michael recalls the flying angel behind the holy martyr in the Cathedral of Seville. There is the same silhouetting of the figure, and the same position of flight in both. Another picture which seems to be by Alonso Vásquez is a small one in my collection representing *The Conversion of St. Paul.* The vigorous foreshortening of the face, the strong treatment of the musculature, and the similarities in color, convince me that it is another work of this painter from Seville.

Alonso Vásquez, besides the paintings he left in New Spain, contributed much as a teacher; thus the painter José de Ibarra says that he should be given much credit for having introduced "*muy buena doctrina.*" The chroniclers say that Arrúe was his pupil, and although it is more likely that he was originally the pupil of Pereyns, this would not prevent his having received instruction and advice from Vásquez as well.

Alonso López de Herrera

Another artist who flourished at the end of the sixteenth century and the beginning of the seventeenth,

and who has recently been rescued from the mystery surrounding him, is Alonso López de Herrera, who in his own day was called *el divino Herrera.* Two large panels had always been attributed to Alonso Vásquez, one, in the Galerías de Pintura, representing *The Assumption of the Virgin,* and the other, in a private collection, *The Resurrection.* Later two more pictures appeared which were undoubtedly by the same hand: *The Ecstasy of St. Theresa* and a *St. Thomas Aquinas.* With the nucleus of these four paintings, an individual artist emerged, and the attribution to Alonso Vásquez was discarded. Then Señor Romero de Terreros found in the museum's storage a portrait of *Fray García Guerra,* dated 1609, by Alonso López de Herrera, which obviously belonged in the group. So the mystery was cleared up: López de Herrera was the painter of these pictures, and also of others which it was now possible to attribute to him. These are a *Divine Countenance,* signed, in the Galerías de Arte, and another on the Altar del Perdón of the Cathedral of Mexico; a *St. Dominic* in the church at Churubusco, and perhaps another in Santo Domingo; two paintings in the gallery of Don José Luis Bello in Puebla, and a *St. Augustine* in the collection of Don Salvador Ugarte in Mexico City. We know that López de Herrera was a friar of the Order of St. Dominic, and presume that he may have been dead by 1654. In that year, according to documents in the Archivo General de la Nación, Diego de Becerra did a painting for the church of Santo Domingo, which would seem to indicate that the official artist of the Order, Alonso López de Herrera, was no longer alive.[17]

López de Herrera is a great artist, quite worthy of the epithet "divine," which he was given in his own time. His paintings of *St. Theresa* and *St. Thomas Aquinas* are executed with a sensitivity of drawing and delicacy of touch that reveal a man of great gifts. The large panel of *The Assumption* (135), his most important work, seems to combine two different styles: the lower part, the group of Apostles who are present at the miracle, recalls the Italian Assumptions after Titian, both in the brilliance of the coloring and in the vigorous foreshortening of the figures. The upper part, on the other hand, is absolutely Flemish; the Virgin is

---

[15] Carlos de Sigüenza y Góngora, *Triumpho parthénico,* fol. 30.

[16] This information was kindly given me by Don Diego Angulo Íñiguez.

[17] See Romero de Terreros, *El pintor Alonso López de Herrera*; Toussaint, "Cuadros desconocidos de Alonso López de Herrera," *Anales del Instituto de Investigaciones Estéticas,* 12 (1945), 9–14.

135. Alonso López de Herrera. Assumption of the Virgin. Oil. 3.40 x 2.28 m.
Pinacoteca Virreinal, Mexico City.

surrounded by a group of angels who are cut out in silhouette against the background, and in the angularity of their wings and the difference in scale from the rest of the picture a quite different mood is created: it is like a great tapestry hung up as a decoration above the real scene below.

Another artist of this period, though a rather mediocre one, is Alonso Franco. He was active at the beginning of the seventeenth century, when he collaborated with Andrés de la Concha in painting the arch set up to welcome the Archbishop Fray García de Santa María in 1602. Later, in 1604, he signed the portrait of Arias de Villalobos which appears in a book commemorating the Oath of Allegiance to Philip IV, which took place in 1621.[18] The allegorical engraving in the same book, which Don Genaro García did not reproduce in his reprint, must be also by Alonso Franco. He had a certain prestige in his own time; Bernardo de Balbuena praises him in his *Grandeza mexicana*,[19] and Arias de Villalobos speaks of "The vivacity of the celebrated Franco." Unfortunately these are the only references we now have to this painter.

Other artists mentioned by Arias de Villalobos are Tomás de Prado and Vicente Requena. Pesquera seems to have been the only sculptor among all the names he gives. Also active in this period was Martín de Zumaya, who made a side altarpiece for the church of Jocotitlán, for which he was demanding payment between 1613 and 1626.[20] From the dates, this may well be a son of Francisco de Zumaya, perhaps the one Señor Pérez Salazar refers to when he says that Juan de Arrúe III married the daughter of Martín de Zumaya and Leonor de Molina, Micaela de Zumaya, in Puebla in 1632.[21]

The Great Period

All of this seems only to set the scene for the great painting which was now to come. Here the most important name is Baltasar de Echave Orio, whom the historians call "the Elder" to distinguish him from "the Younger," whom they presume to be his son. To avoid confusion, I have preferred to refer to them by their complete names. The first problem about the elder Echave is precisely that of distinguishing him from his family. In fact, my investigations lead me to believe, in agreement with Don Carlos de Sigüenza y Góngora, that there were three artists called Baltasar de Echave. This hypothesis is based on the following considerations: the date when Echave reached America, his first marriage in 1582, a second marriage in 1623, and the

differences which can be noted among the pictures loosely attributed to this name. I distinguish then, three Echaves: Baltasar de Echave Orio (the Elder), Baltasar de Echave Ibía, and Baltasar de Echave y Rioja (the Younger). Baltasar de Echave the Younger appears to be the grandson, and not the son, of Echave the Elder, as everyone has supposed.

In addition there is Manuel de Echave, apparently another son of Baltasar de Echave the Elder, and hence a brother of Echave Ibía. We know only two pictures by this Echave: *The Virgin Investing St. Ildephonsus* (a favorite subject of the period) now in the Museo de Churubusco, and another of *The Holy Family* listed in the catalogue of the Barron Collection. From the scarcity of information one presumes that Manuel de Echave died young.

Baltasar de Echave the Elder

Baltasar de Echave Orio was born in Zumaya, in his family's mansion in Aizarnazábal near Oiquina, where it still stands.[22] He had an older brother, Juan Martínez de Echave Orio, who was born in 1546, and a younger sister, María Juanes de Echave Orio, who married Pedro de Arvide and died in 1596. Echave must have been born a little before 1548 since he made a will in 1573, for which he had to be of age, that is to say, at least twenty-five. In that year he went to the West Indies with his brother, who made frequent trips to America. Contrary to the assumption of Conde Urquijo that Echave's artistic character was already formed when he came to Mexico, the documents show that in 1582 he married Isabel de Ibía in Mexico City; she was the daughter of Francisco de Zumaya, who was surely Echave's teacher, just as Pacheco was Velásquez'. His earliest work dates from 1596, and we may be sure that in 1585 he was not yet an important painter, since he does not appear in the work on the Old Cathedral, which brought together, as we have seen, the most important artists then living in Mexico.

Echave was also a writer, and published a remarkable

18 *Obediencia que México, cabeza de la Nueva España, dió a la Majestad Católica del rey D. Felipe . . . con un discurso en verso del estado de la misma ciudad.* It was misleading of Don Genaro García to entitle his reprint *México en 1623*, since the poem describing the city dates from twenty years earlier.

19 *Capítulo IV.*

20 Document in the Archivo de la Catedral de México.

21 Pérez Salazar, *Historia,* p. 112.

22 Conde de Urquijo, *Casas y Linajas de Echave y Laurcain.*

136. Baltasar de Echave Orio (the Elder). The Porciuncula. Oil. 2.52 x 1.6 m.
Pinacoteca Virreinal, Mexico City.

book in 1607, dedicated to the Conde de Lemos, whose purpose was to praise the antiquity of the Basque language. In this book appears a self-portrait of the artist, and the coat of arms of his noble family.[23]

The paintings of Echave in Mexico are very numerous, but not quite so many as the critics have claimed. The documented works are the following. In 1596 he made ten statues, twenty *sambenitos,* and twenty-one *corozas* (the foolscap worn by those condemned) for the Auto de Fe celebrated in the main plaza of Mexico City on the eighth of December; the materials cost fifty-five pesos, and he was paid ten for his work.[24] In 1601 he painted a gigantic *St. Christopher* for the church of San Francisco. In 1609 he made fourteen paintings for the retable of Santiago Tlatelolco, which still existed in 1860–1861; of these we have now only the two panels of *The Visitation* and *The Porziuncula* (136) in the Galerías de Pintura, to which an *Annunciation* might perhaps be added on the basis of style. Couto says that in the cloister of La Profesa there was a *St. Ignatius in Glory* dated 1610, and from the same place comes *The Martyrdom of St. Apronianus* of 1612. The retable of the Jesuit church was also Echave's work, and from this we still have *The Adoration of the Kings* and *The Agony in the Garden.* To these should be added *The Martyrdom of St. Pontian,* dated early in the century, and the magnificent picture of *The Flagellation* in the Cathedral of Mexico.

Of the twenty-seven paintings attributed to Echave Orio in the Galerías de Pintura, only these which are documented can be assigned to him with assurance. *The Martyrdom of St. Ursula, The Presentation in the Temple,* and another *Visitation* seem to be from his workshop.

The art of Baltasar de Echave Orio truly partakes of the sublimity of the *Siglo de Oro.* He is still a Renaissance painter deriving from Italy, from that happy Italy of brilliant coloring and incomparably elegant forms. He is a Renaissance painter, but of a peculiarly ingenuous nature. His martyrs do not move us; they seem the richly costumed characters of a sumptuous ballet. Their martyrdom is depicted as a child would tell it, without rhetoric or emphasis, simply and humbly. But his technical gifts are immense, both in the

composition of the pictures and in the loving rendering of the forms. One can see certain influences in his work, especially that of the Italianate Fleming, Martín de Vos, in the types, and that of Alonso Vásquez in a certain tendency to a chromatic palette. But little by little Echave frees himself from this pronounced Italianate style and turns his eyes toward Spain and a more realistic concept. Indeed, such a painting as his *St. Apronianus* might be the work of any Spanish artist of his time. Contemporary with Pacheco and Ribalta, but perhaps even stronger than they, it is not absurd to suggest that Echave the Elder might be considered the foremost Hispanic painter of his generation.

Baltasar and Manuel de Echave Ibía

The sons of Echave Orio, Baltasar and Manuel de Echave Ibía, were obscured by his dazzling prestige. Baltasar must have been born between 1583 and 1584, and his career was so closely linked with his father's that we often sense an intimate collaboration between the two artists. But study of Echave Ibía's own paintings reveals a questing personal insight that modestly protests the domination of the master. From his fondness for a blue tonality in the background, I have allowed myself to call him *el Echave de los azules,* the "blue" Echave. Indeed in his paintings the taste for a bluish landscape is developed through extraordinary tonal variety. If this is indeed a convention of color, it still springs from contemplation of nature; for one cannot believe that Echave Ibía simply invented this tonality which is so characteristic of the Mexican dusk.

Echave Ibía married Doña Ana de Rioja in the year 1623, and he must have died in the middle of the century. This short life, far less productive than that of a father who always eclipsed him, derives a certain interest from its very mystery.

Among the pictures in the Galería attributed to Baltasar de Echave Orio is a group which without any doubt should be restored to his son. These are: a *Portrait of a Lady* (137); *St. John the Evangelist; The Virgin of the Apocalypse I* (1620) (138); *The Virgin of the Apocalypse II* (1622); *St. John the Baptist; The Repentant Magdalen;* three small Evangelists (the fourth is to be found in the Museum at Querétaro); *St. Anthony and St. Paul the Hermits.* In Xochimilco is a *Baptism of Christ,* dated 1628, and in the collection of Don Salvador Ugarte, some scenes from the *Stations of the Cross,* with a crowding group of figures. Also attributed to him are a *St. Francis of Paul* of 1625, cited

23 Baltasar de Echave Orio, *Discursos de la antigüedad de la lengua cántabra bascongada.*

24 Archivo General de la Nación. *Inquisición, 1539–1601* (Pasta Nueva).

137. Baltasar de Echave Ibía. Portrait of a Lady. Oil. .62 x .46 m.
Pinacoteca Virreinal, Mexico City.

by Couto, and a *Martyrdom of St. Catherine,* dated 1640, which Couto says was in the cloister of Santo Domingo in Mexico City; a *St. Michael,* dated 1641, belonging to the Arguinzonis family of Durango; and the *Life of St. Francis,* painted in the middle of the seventeenth century, which decorated the cloister of the Franciscan monastery in Mexico City. A further question which must be left to future scholars concerns which of these paintings may be the work of Manuel de Echave Ibía, a figure even more elusive than his brother.

Beside Echave Orio, the son appears less vigorous. These are not any longer the simply constructed figures of the elder painter; one feels a certain rhetorical quality, a preciosity which suggests the Baroque. Nevertheless, Baltasar de Echave Ibía still constructs solidly, nor does he free himself from the spell of the Renaissance.

Luis Juárez

The dearest pupil of Baltasar de Echave Orio, after his sons, was Luis Juárez, who like his master died young. His *oeuvre* extends from 1600 to 1635; but he must surely have been painting before the end of the sixteenth century. He married Doña Elena de Vergara, and had three children: Doña Inés de Vergara, the great painter José Juárez, and Doña Ana de Vergara. He died some time before 1639 and was buried in the monastery of San Agustín, where his family had their tomb.

The list of Luis Juárez' paintings includes a *St. Theresa,* signed, and dated 160–, in the Museo de Guadalajara, and a *Child Jesus appearing to St. Anthony,* dated 1610, which used to be in the Academia. In 1611 he made the paintings for the arch erected to greet the viceroy, Fray García Guerra, which Mateo Alemán describes in his book on the viceroy.[25] In 1620 he made the altarpiece for the church of Jesús María in Mexico City, and between 1631 and 1633 he painted many pictures for the Convento Grande de la Merced in Mexico City.[26]

In Morelia there are some paintings in the Carmelite monastery which represent *St. Michael,* and several in the Cathedral, of which the best is *The Investing of St. Ildephonsus*; this was a favorite subject of Juárez, and

[25] Mateo Alemán, *Sucesos de frai García Gera* (México, 1612); *The Sucesos of Mateo Alemán,* ed. Alice H. Bushee.

[26] Francisco de Pareja, *Crónica de la Provincia de la Visitación de Ntra. Sra. de la Merced.*

138. Baltasar de Echave Ibía. Virgin of the Apocalypse. Oil. 2.50 x 1.70 m. Pinacoteca Virreinal, Mexico City.

139. Luis Juárez. Communion of St. Stanislaus of Kostka. Oil. Salvador Ugarte Collection, Mexico City.

of the Carmelite church at San Ángel, in the Distrito Federal, were several pictures by him, badly repainted, which were destroyed in the fire. In the former Carmelite church—now the parish church—at Atlixco, is a large canvas representing *The Confirmation of the Order of St. Theresa,* and in the collection of Don Salvador Ugarte in Mexico City, one of his finest works, *The Communion of St. Stanislaus of Kostka* (139).

The art of Luis Juárez is unambiguous: it is a mystical art, but this mysticism has a small range of devices: the blank eyes, the ecstatic face, the imploring hands outstretched. He had the most homogeneous style of any artist of his period, to the point almost of monotony. Once you have seen a picture by him, you can identify all of them without reading the *Ludovicus Xuarez,* with which he so complacently signs them. He is a very winning artist, although his gifts do not equal those of Echave Orio, or even of his son. Driven by the demands of his time, he neglects his color, struggles with the difficulties of constructing his aerial figures, and falls back on uncertain formulas to turn out cardboard scenes. His positive qualities are ingenuousness and religious feeling, so that sometimes, as in the *St. Stanislaus,* he achieves a quality of rapture which lets us glimpse for the first time in Mexican painting the ecstasy of Glory. Luis Juárez was an unrealized artist; in the short span of his artistic life he was not able to achieve what he certainly dreamed of. And yet, with all his weakness, he is a painter for whom one feels a deep sympathy.

Sebastián López de Arteaga

This Italianate painting, which had developed without apparent contradiction, now met a sharp, if short-lived opposition in Sebastián López de Arteaga. He had been born in Seville, where he was baptized in the parish of San Salvador on March 15, 1610. His father was a silversmith; his older brother, an engraver; he grew up in an artistic environment. On April 19, 1630, he was admitted to the guild, examined in image painting by Miguel Guelles and Blas Martín Silvestre, masters and examiners of the guild, accompanied by Francisco de Barelo and Jacinto de Samora,[27] masters in the said art; his sponsor was Amaro Vázquez, painter of images. Around 1633 he was still living in Seville, where his difficult character was already evident: an apprentice he had taken in 1632 compelled his guardian

there are two other versions of it in the Galerías de Pintura. Also in the Galerías are several versions of *The Mystic Marriage of St. Catherine,* and his greatest work, an *Agony in the Garden,* comparable to that of the great Echave on the same subject. In a side chapel

27 *Documentos para la historia del arte en Andalucía,* p. 270.

140. Sebastián López de Arteaga. Marriage of the Virgin. Oil.
Pinacoteca Virreinal, Mexico City.

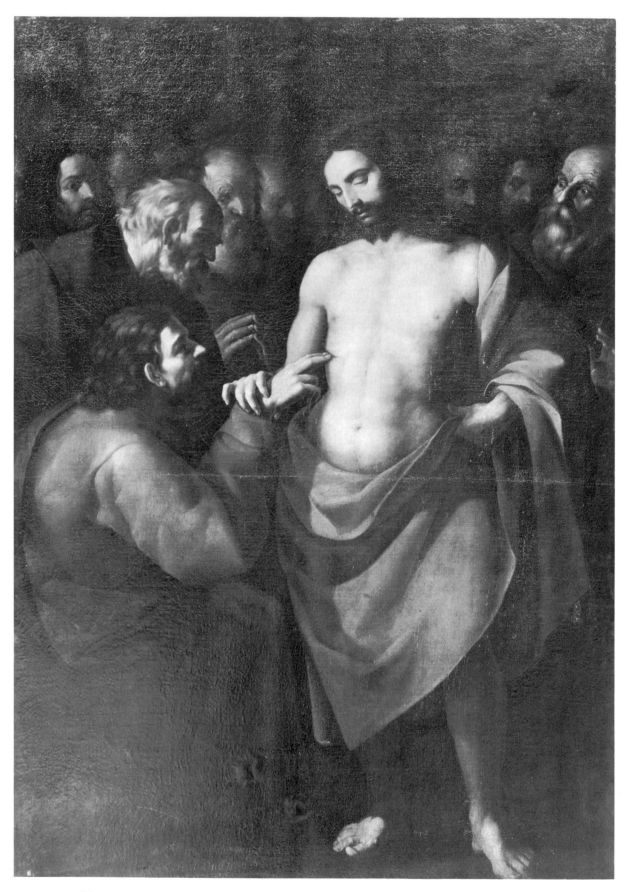

141. Sebastián López de Arteaga. Doubting Thomas. Oil. 2.26 x 1.56 m.
Pinacoteca Virreinal, Mexico City.

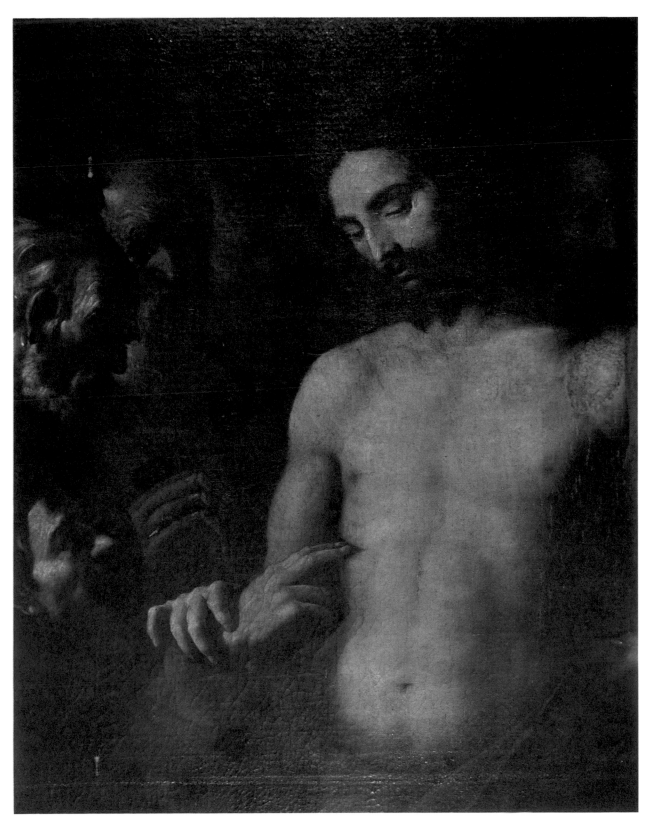

Sebastián López de Arteaga. Doubting Thomas (detail). Oil on canvas.
2.26 x 1.56 m. Pinacoteca Virreinal, Mexico City.

to have him released from the contract.[28] In 1638 he was a resident of Cádiz.

The fact that Arteaga stayed in Seville until 1638, and then moved to Cádiz, means that he was influenced by some of the great painters then working in Andalusia, above all the incomparable Francisco de Zurbarán. It is obvious that he also knew the paintings of José de Ribera, lo Spagnoletto, for one feels his influence clearly in Arteaga's work.

In any case, five years later he was in New Spain. In that year, 1643, he presented a petition to the Holy Office of the Inquisition in Mexico, in which, citing various members of his family who had worked for the Holy Office in Seville, he requested a position in the Tribunal. In view of the information submitted, the Tribunal, on May 3, directed that he be nominated for a notary's appointment while the requisite investigation of racial purity was being made. The position was authorized on the twenty-ninth of the month. What Arteaga actually wanted was a sinecure, and the appointment by the Holy Office was purely honorary; Couto is wrong when he says that the scarcity of Arteaga's paintings is because of his work as a notary.[29] He did not notarize a single document for the Inquisition; in fact his position there led to his producing more paintings, since in soliciting the position he had also offered the Tribunal his services as a painter. The Holy Office commissioned him to paint the portraits of the first Inquisitors of Mexico, and he painted sixteen of them; these portraits were preserved in the old building until the abolition of that regrettable Court.[30] Arteaga's appointment was simply honorary, as we have said, and in fact was provisional, since they were waiting for the genealogical data confirming purity of blood which was necessary for any definite appointment to the Inquisition. Consequently, in 1650, he was removed from the position because they had not succeeded in getting all the

information necessary about his family. Arteaga then protested proudly, "as a man of reputation, he said, with no stain on his character." He demanded that they complete the inquiry in Seville and the different places where his grandparents had been born. No records had been found for one of them; but when they presented the request for documents about this relative, on August 12, 1656, the painter was already dead. Arteaga married a relative of his, Doña Juana de Arteaga, the daughter of Juan Ambrosio Longón, a weaver of brocade, Milanese by birth and the son of Milanese parents. We do not know whether he had children.

Arteaga's oeuvre is smaller than that of any other painter of this period, but we must remember that his fifteen years in Mexico could hardly have produced as many paintings as other artists achieved in much longer lives. First of all we have the Portraits of the Inquisitors already mentioned. In the Barron Collection there was a St. Michael which later changed hands; it is important because it seems to be a predecessor of those archangels which were to be so popular in the time of Correa and Villalpando. In the Museo de la Catedral in Mexico City is a portrait of Archbishop Manzo y Zúñiga. In Couto's Diálogo he mentions an Adoration of the Kings in some convent, which may be the one now in the Municipal Art Gallery of Davenport, Iowa, in the United States.[31] A St. Francis, signed and dated 1650, which turned up in an antique shop, is now in the museum of the Basilica of Guadalupe. Sr. Díez Barrosa refers to a Madonna in a private collection, but this painting is not genuine. In the Basilica of Guadalupe they have a signed Crucifixion, dated 1643; its anatomy is hard, its style dry and rather disagreeable. A similar Crucifixion belongs to Don Luis Montes de Oca. The three most important paintings by Arteaga are undoubtedly those in the Galerías Nacionales de Pintura: the Marriage of the Virgin and the Doubting Thomas, both signed, and the Crucifixion. In the church of Santo Domingo in Mexico City there is an Investing of St. Ildephonsus, a beautiful picture formerly attributed to Luis Juárez but closer in feeling to Arteaga, which recalls the Adoration of the Davenport Municipal Art Gallery.

Comparison of the Marriage of the Virgin (140) and the Doubting Thomas (141; color, facing p. 148) has occasioned long and heated dispute. The learned professors of art, applying to the seventeenth century the concepts we use for contemporary painters, have discovered that the two pictures are not merely

[28] Celestino López Martínez, Notas para la historia del arte; arquitectos, escultores y pintores vecinos de Sevilla, p. 30.

[29] José Bernardo Couto, Diálogo sobre la historia de la pintura en México.

[30] Don José María Agreda y Sánchez told Don Luis González Obregón that he had seen these pictures in one of the rooms of the Inquisition building, which was then used as the Medical School of the National University, and is now the Academia Mexicana de Medicina.

[31] See Toussaint, "Pinturas mexicanas en Davenport," Anales del Instituto de Investigaciones Estéticas, 14 (1946), 25–32; Toussaint, "Mexican Colonial Paintings in Davenport," Gazette des Beaux-Arts, Ser. 6, 24 (1943), 167–174; Davenport Municipal Art Gallery, Catalogue of 334 Paintings.

different but antagonistic in style; therefore they cannot be by the same artist, and Arteaga will have to choose which one to be the author of. These gentlemen are a little forgetful of how things used to be in the world; among the paintings of El Greco, for example, there are plenty which today seem more contradictory than the two we are considering. They are forgetting that a painting by Zurbarán was attributed in the National Gallery in London to Velázquez, though there is nothing more distinct than the styles of these two great painters. They forget that factor which is of peculiar importance in all art: the man himself, who is subject to change, and does not always produce according to fixed rules like an automaton.

If we will be guided by historical reality, we can understand how both pictures can have been made by the same painter. To begin with, it should be said that distinguished critics of European painting find no more radical differences between these paintings than they are accustomed to in the *oeuvre* of other artists. Zurbarán works in different "manners" which are rather more marked. My feeling is that when Arteaga arrived in Mexico he found that the Colony delighted in the style which Echave had introduced and his pupils had faithfully followed: an agreeable style, Italianate in the brilliance of its coloring, softness of touch, and avoidance of the dramatic. The painter, who had to live, was not going to give up painting because the work required might not be exactly to his personal taste. This was not yet the time when an artist imposed his will on the public; he was a craftsman who was expected to attend to the commissions and the instructions, however frightful, of his clients. Thus Arteaga painted for the public taste a *Deposition,* the portrait of *Archbishop Manzo y Zúñiga, St. Michael,* perhaps the *Portraits of the Inquisitors,* and who knows how many other pictures now lost.

When, however, he had the support of the Inquisition, and could paint a picture without the imposition of any stipulation, his own personality and his own taste appear, and he produced a work of art which stands out from all the rest, like a banner in the history of Mexican painting: the *Doubting Thomas.* There are two inscriptions on this painting: one, the signature of the artist with the title of notary, and another which reads: *Hízose de los bienes del Capitán Francisco de Aguirre*—("Made from the estate of Captain Francisco de Aguirre"). Interpreted with strict historical accuracy, this inscription indicates that the Captain's estate had

been sold, and the proceeds used to pay for the painting. When it was simply a case of having a picture painted, the inscription would read *Hízose a devoción de fulano de tal* ("Made through the devotion of someone or other"), or *Hízose a costa de mengano* ("Made at the expense of so-and-so"). So it seems that this picture was painted, either to comply with a sentence of the Santo Oficio, which is quite likely in view of the subject, or by the terms of a will in which the whole estate was devoted to the production of a single picture, a pious act of noble dimensions. I tend to prefer the first possibility. That it was a painting important to the artist himself is indicated by the fact that he included a self-portrait, if my guess is correct. The face which appears at the left, looking out at us, behind the old man leaning forward, shows a young man with his hair dressed in the style of Philip IV; furthermore, the face agrees with the description given of him by his mother, in Seville in 1620, as having "a round face, with big eyes."

Unquestionably the picture was sensational: the artist had brought to it not only all his own genius, but all the vigor of the Spanish school of Zurbarán and Ribera, which came directly from Caravaggio. It had their strong contrast of light and shadow, obtained by a single source of light at one side, the sobriety of form, the suppression of detail, and, spiritually, the inner drama which means that painting is not a purely sensuous source of delight, that its purpose is to move us, to rouse ideas and passions in our spirit rather than simply to reproduce nature. With this picture the artistic movement we call the Baroque actually began in New Spain.

Such is my explanation of the mystery which has been created around Arteaga. When he could work freely, he did so, without allowing anything to impede the realization of his art. When he was constrained by necessity, he made whatever concessions his clients asked. There was no mystery about what they liked in the Colony, and the suave and objective art tó which the elder Echave had accustomed public taste was no problem for this painter. Thus one can understand the *oeuvre* of Arteaga; one can make a series ascending from the most charming and Italianate, like the *Marriage of the Virgin,* to the most sober and severe, the *St. Thomas.* The mistake, in my opinion, is to judge them separately, isolated not only from the rest of his *oeuvre,* but from the art of the period.

Arteaga thus brings a new factor to the painting of New Spain. To the Flemish and Italian influences which had reigned there, he adds this new quality: the vigorous chiaroscuro, the strong modelling, and the dark tonality which fills the picture with mystery and makes it suggestive, evocative, suffused with mystic spirit.

Arteaga undoubtedly ranks beside Echave the Elder, both in the vigor of his talent and in his questing spirit. His painting captivates us in an extraordinary way, possibly because it has that touch of mystery, of something not to be understood at the first glance.[32]

European Paintings in New Spain

We know from documents that a considerable number of European paintings reached Mexico in the second half of the sixteenth and the beginning of the following century. Although these are not Mexican paintings, they should be mentioned at least briefly, for they were important not only in forming public taste, but also as influences on the artists themselves.[33]

We know that in the Palace of the Viceroys there was a large *Portrait of Charles V* by Titian, the gift of the Emperor himself. He appeared in armor, on horseback, with a lance in his hand, as the chronicler Sariñana carefully describes the picture.[34] The description suggests a replica of the famous portrait in the Prado in Madrid. This painting may have been lost in the fire which destroyed the Palace in 1693.

Another portrait attributed to Titian used to be in the Franciscan church of Tzintzuntzan in Michoacán.[35] According to tradition this painting also was a gift from Charles V to the Franciscan church which had been the original cathedral of Michoacán. Actually, neither the documents we have, nor a study of the canvas itself confirms this story. It was not listed in the inventories of the church examined by Dr. Nicolás León until the first third of the seventeenth century. As for the painting itself, Titian was above all a colorist, the most notable colorist of the Venetian school, if not the most eminent who has ever painted anywhere; but this painting was characterized by its sombre tonality, which has suggested to some critics an attribution to El Greco. Furthermore, its subject, *The Entombment,* was paint-

142. Martín de Vos. St. John the Evangelist. Oil. Museo Nacional del Virreinato, Tepotzotlán, México.

ed by Titian in a totally different way, and the picture showed a weakness of composition which one could not attribute to the great Venetian. A comparison with our colonial painting shows clearly its relationship to the Echave group: there is the same musculature, the same conception of the body, the same ingenuousness in telling the story. This picture should be considered the work of some pupil of the Echave family, closer to the Younger than to the Elder.

Another artist whose pictures have been preserved in Mexico, and who had considerable influence, is Martín de Vos, as we remarked in connection with Echave

[32] See also Heinrich Berlin, "Sebastián de Arteaga, pintor de la Inquisición," *Anales del Instituto de Arte Americano e Investigaciones Estéticas,* 11 (1958), 53–56.

[33] Toussaint, *Pinturas europeas en México.*

[34] Isidro Sariñana, *Llanto del Occidente en el ocaso del mas claro Sol de las Españas,* fol. 14 r.

[35] This painting was destroyed in a fire on May 1, 1944.

Orio. His most important paintings are in the little Franciscan church of Cuautitlán, in the state of México. There are four pictures: a *St. Peter* and a *St. Paul*, figures of extraordinary grandeur, solemn of aspect, with noble drapery, a *St. Michael* and an *Immaculate Conception*. Only the *St. Michael*, dated 1581, is signed; it is a very important picture for the study of Mexican colonial painting, since this blond and dishevelled archangel set the type which all the angels in our painting were to follow, from Echave and Arteaga to Correa and Villalpando. In the museum of the Cathedral of Mexico is a magnificent *St. John the Evangelist*, writing, with a view of Jerusalem in the background (142); it is an excellent painting, as is the *Tobias and the Angel* in the Capilla de las Angustias in the Cathedral, which can certainly be attributed to him. I have also seen many engravings after drawings of this artist.[36]

In the Museo de Guadalajara are three pictures by Lucca Giordano, which show all his mastery and rich variety.

In the Augustinian monastery of Tlayacapan, in the state of Morelos, an old painting may be seen in a niche on the stairs: it represents *St. Augustine* giving his heart to the child Jesus, who is held by the Virgin. It seems to be a Flemish painting from the end of the fifteenth or the early sixteenth century, and is of great value.

In the Palacio de los Virreyes, to quote Sariñana again, there was a half-length portrait of *Philip II* by Alonso Sánchez Coello, a companion piece to the portrait of Charles V.[37]

We have also a fine group of paintings by Murillo. To begin with the Galerías de Pintura, there are a *St. John the Baptist*, a *St. John of God*, and various other paintings which have been attributed to his school. Recently Don Diego Angulo Íñiguez has reviewed these paintings and discarded the attribution to Murillo for some of them, without saying what he does think they are.[38] In Guadalajara are various paintings attributed to Murillo; a magnificent *Immaculate Conception* in the Cathedral is very characteristic of the master, both in style and in his typical interpretation of the subject. Quite another matter are the paintings bearing his name in the Museum there, which, according to the absurd label, were painted for the Franciscan monastery in Compostela and later brought to Guadalajara. A careful study of these paintings reveals iconographical de-tails which make such a history impossible: the *petates*, for instance—Mexican reed mats—shading St. Francis while he distributes bread, and the portraits, among them the Bishop of Nueva Galicia, the donor, which has been erroneously interpreted as a self-portrait of Murillo. It seems clear that these pictures were the work of a pupil of Murillo who passed through Guadalajara about the middle of the seventeenth century. In the museum of the Cathedral in Mexico City there is a *Virgin of Bethlehem* which does show the characteristic style of Murillo himself. There are also a number of his paintings in private collections. Among them is a *Virgin and Child* which is a replica of the one in St. James Palace in London, but quite superior to it, a very strong *Adoration of the Shepherds*, a *Child St. John the Baptist*, and a very interesting *St. Philip of Cantalicio*, besides many other pictures which are either old copies or later imitations such as have flooded the world markets.

Nor do we lack Zurbarán in our collections. One of his finest paintings is in the Galerías de Pintura, the *Christ at Emmaus*, signed and dated 1639. Other paintings by Zurbarán can be found elsewhere in the Republic. In Puebla, in the collection of Don José Luis Bello, is a *St. Peter Hearing the Cock Crow*, which may be a copy of a very similar one in the old Carmelite church in Atlixco. In Tlaxcala, in the Franciscan church, are two small paintings of full-length *Saints* whose style recalls the marvelous paintings of the museum in Cádiz.[39]

Such a quantity of European paintings—and we have mentioned only a small part of them, since we could collect a hundred or more masterpieces by studying the catalogues of private collections—shows that European art constantly shaped the colonial artists. They worked in touch with European fashions. At the same time they retained special qualities which occasionally transformed Mexican painting into something distinct from that of the Old World, as we have been able to observe in the course of this study.

[36] There is, for example, a Bible printed in Antwerp in 1595 which has a number of woodcuts after Martín de Vos, and I have some others in my collection. The influence of his drawing on Echave Orio is evident.

[37] Sariñana, *Llanto del Occidente*.

[38] Angulo Íñiguez, *La Academia de Bellas Artes de Méjico y sus pinturas españolas*.

[39] See Martín S. Soria, *The Paintings of Zurbarán*, pp. 174, 176–177, 187.

RENAISSANCE SCULPTURE

The Retables

E HAVE already considered a good deal of sculpture in speaking of Plateresque architecture, which was essentially sculpturesque. Now we turn to another category of Renaissance sculpture which can still be seen in Mexico. The most important manifestation of the Renaissance in colonial sculpture was the great altarpiece in the church. The apse was always filled with an immense Renaissance retable, classical in its general design, but in detail tending to be Plateresque. Of all these great retables, only three have survived intact. There is the retable of Huejotzingo, whose paintings Simón Pereyns made and signed in 1586, that of Xochimilco, whose author we do not know, but which we assume to be later, since its paintings are close to Echave Orío, and that of Cuautinchán, in the state of Puebla, which was the work of Juan de Arrúe, and which, as we have noted, was originally made for the church of Tehuacán in 1597 and two years later placed where it is now.

All three retables belong to the Renaissance. The purest of them is the one at Xochimilco, designed in a sober Renaissance style, its columns ornamented near the base by a band of figures in relief (143). The sculptured saints of this retable show great dignity and a superb amplitude of technique; they are the work of a sculptor of the first rank (144, 145). Along the bottom are busts of the Apostles, as was customary in all retables in this position.

The retable of Huejotzingo is more Plateresque, with its baluster columns (72, 132, 146, 147); the figures have neither the grandeur nor the simplicity of those at Xochimilco.[1]

The retable of Cuautinchán is still more sober; it has no sculpture except the framing, which consists of slender baluster columns (148). In the same church there is also a small side altar of Renaissance design, dedicated to San Diego of Alcalá. We assume that the paintings are the work of Pereyns, and it has been suggested that portraits of Philip II and his family may be found on its panels.

In the parish church of Tecali, in the state of Puebla, the retable from the former church of its Franciscan

---

[1] Heinrich Berlin, "The High Altar of Huejotzingo," *The Americas,* 15 (1958), 63–73.

143. Main altarpiece (detail). Polychrome and gilded wood; oil on canvas. Main altarpiece (detail). Church of the Franciscan monastery, Xochimilco, Distrito Federal.

144. Saint. Polychrome and gilded wood. Main altarpiece, church of the Franciscan monastery, Xochimilco, Distrito Federal.

145. Virgin Mary. Painted wood. Main altarpiece, church of the
Franciscan monastery, Xochimilco, Distrito Federal.

146. Main Altarpiece. Polychrome and gilded wood; oil
on canvas. Church of the Franciscan monastery,
Huejotzingo, Puebla.

147. Saint. Polychrome and gilded wood. Main
altarpiece, church of the Franciscan monastery,
Huejotzingo, Puebla.

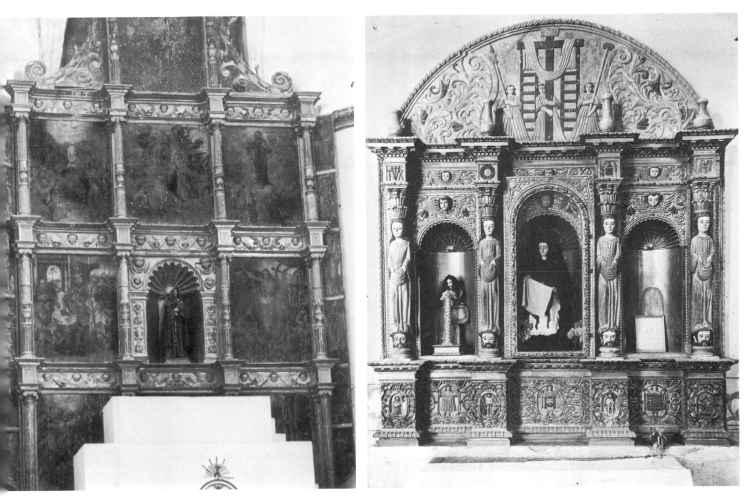

148. Main Altarpiece. Gilded wood; oil on canvas.
Church of the Franciscan monastery, Cuautinchán, Puebla.

149. Retable. Polychrome and gilded wood. Church of the
Franciscan monastery, Maní, Yucatán.

monastery is preserved. It is in the Renaissance style,
with pilasters in place of columns. Another small retable can be seen there, with a big painting of St. Francis.

In the church of the Franciscan monastery at Maní
in Yucatán there are some charming retables with caryatids and round arches at the top (149). They are
considered sixteenth-century work, but they may well
date from the early seventeenth; they are in full Renaissance style, and certainly the most interesting on the
Peninsula.

There are also in existence fragments of other retables from many monastic churches. Thus in the Franciscan church at Tlalmanalco is some large sculpture
which, along with the painted panels preserved there,
must have come from the original retable. At Tepeaca,

in the great Franciscan church, there are fragments of
the original retable: columns with reliefs around the
lower shaft and a kind of ring of cherubs at the top. A
fragment of the old Renaissance retable can also be
seen in the church of the Tercer Orden in Texcoco. In
the Franciscan church of Milpa Alta, in the Distrito
Federal, only the central relief of the retable has been
preserved, undoubtedly because of its great beauty; it
represents the *Assumption of the Virgin* and is very
large, polychrome, and gilded (150).

There is no doubt, therefore, that Mexico had a great
school of Renaissance sculpture, whatever some writers
have argued to the contrary. They based their opinion
on the ruling of the Third Council of the church that
"the images which are made in sculpture from now on

157

150. Assumption of the Virgin. Polychrome and gilded wood. Main altarpiece, Franciscan monastery, Milpa Alta, Distrito Federal.

continue their idolatrous practices. The clothing of images made it possible to conceal idols, and the church was trying to prevent this by having the sculpture made all of a piece.

The Guild

If the writers who so freely denied the existence of a colonial sculpture in Mexico before Tolsá had been acquainted with the ordinances of the guild of *escultores, entalladores,* and *ensambladores,* they would have had to change their opinion.

The ordinances of carpenters, carvers, joiners, and viol makers were enacted by the City of Mexico on August 30, 1568, and confirmed by the Real Audiencia on the following twenty-sixth of October. New ordinances for sculptors and carvers were enacted by the City of Mexico on April 17, 1589, and confirmed by the viceroy, the Marqués de Villa Manrique, on August 18 of the same year. These ordinances determine precisely what an *escultor* should know, and what an *entallador* should know. The sculptors were to be examined in making "a nude figure, and another clothed, giving satisfaction in its construction, in regard both to drawing and to style, and then to make it in the round, well proportioned and graceful, and if they know how to do this, they are to be given their certificate and presented to the Cabildo."

A wood carver "should know how to carve a capital, a column decorated with carving and foliage, a cherub, a bird, and know how to cut wood well, and to execute the background, and should know how to draw everything, and if they know this, they should be given their certificate in the form prescribed." The Indians were not bound by these ordinances and could freely pursue their crafts; but it was against the law for any Spaniard, even a master of the guild, to buy work from them to be resold in his shop.[3]

It should be pointed out that the sculptor and the wood carver worked *en blanco,* that is, in the raw

should be such that they do not need clothing; that is to say, the clothes should be made in the same material as the sculpture."[2] On the basis of this decree, critics have claimed that no sculpture was made before this time, arguing that if it is said that a certain thing should be done in the future, it means that it has not been done in the past. But it is wrong to interpret this injunction as prompted by purely aesthetic considerations; the Church was more concerned with ecclesiastical propriety, and especially that the Indians should not

[2] See *Concilium Mexicanum Provinciale III Celebratum Mexici Anno MDLXXXV.*

[3] I quote directly from a manuscript of Francisco del Barrio Lorenzot's in my collection, which I have cited above, "Compendio de las Ordenanzas de la Muy Noble, Insigne y Muy Leal e Imperial Ciudad de México." The publication edited by Genaro Estrada, *Ordenanzas de gremios de la Nueva España,* although useful if one has nothing else, is in fact quite deficient in comparison with various other manuscripts in existence. See also Francisco Santiago Cruz, *Las artes y los gremios en la Nueva España.*

wood, without finish. Both the gilding of columns and decorative detail and the finishing of figures—the *estofado* and *encarnación* by which drapery and flesh were painted and gilded—were done by the *dorador* (the gilder), whose craft was exactly defined. Many painters practised this craft in addition to the painting of pictures.

The Artists

There are very few documents concerning the sculptors of this period, but we do have some, and can hope that research will yield more data in the future.

To the craftsmen named in the first section of this book we can add the following. Three *entalladores* are mentioned in 1568: García de Salamanca, Juan Fernández, and Juan Rodríguez; they had worked together on the great retable of the Augustinian church at Malinalco for which Pereyns had made the paintings, and were witnesses at his trial.

In 1573 a Flemish artist of some prestige arrived in Mexico, Adrián Suster. He had been born in Antwerp in 1564, had gone to Seville, where he married, had learned his craft in Cádiz, and embarked from San Lúcar de Barrameda in the fleet of 1573. He worked for seven months in Veracruz, and then went to Puebla, and he worked in Michoacán and Tulancingo as well. In Mexico City he made the choir of the church of the monastery of Santo Domingo, but his most important work was the choir of the Old Cathedral, which he carved between 1584 and 1585 in collaboration with the sculptor Juan Montaño, of whom we shall speak shortly. In 1598 the Holy Office brought Suster to trial as a Lutheran, and all this information comes from the records of the Inquisition in the Archivo General de la Nación.[4]

In 1574 a retable was made for the Franciscan church at Tula, with paintings by Pereyns. The wood carver was Luis de Arciniega, and in view of this collaboration one is tempted to surmise that it was he who worked on the great retable at Huejotzingo also.[5]

We have already spoken of the remodelling of the Old Cathedral in Mexico City, between 1584 and 1585, to prepare for the convening of the Third Council. As we noted, the gilding of the nave and of the carving on the principal retable were done by Andrés de la Concha, a well-known painter. To appraise the cost of the retable experts were named: Pedro de Brizuela and Juan Montaño. Gestoso mentions a Brizuela in Seville in 1551;[6] the dates are not close enough to

refer to the same man, but the coincidence of the name, which is not common, suggests that they may be of the same family.

Juan Montaño, a sculptor of some fame in his day, appears in Seville in 1581, according to Gestoso.[7] He made the request that his servant, who was also an *entallador,* might accompany him to the New World, since he had contracted to teach him and get him into the guild. This document does not state his destination, but he appears in Mexico four years later. The most important work of Juan Montaño was the sculpture of the choir stalls in the Old Cathedral of Mexico, a considerable enterprise, which took three hundred and three days, and for which he received 924 pesos. In 1590 we find him *veedor* (overseer or inspector) for the guild of sculptors and carvers, together with Mateo Merodio.

Mateo Merodio's European background indicates an artist of prestige. The Conde de la Viñaza says of him:

Merodio Mateo—sculptor, resident of Seville. He carved in stone the decoration on the side doors of the church of of the Hospital de la Sangre in that city, in the year 1582. There should be statues in the niches of the upper story which are now vacant; if these existed, they would give us an idea of the quality of this artist.[8]

On March 6, 1595, two new overseers for the guild appear in the records of the Cabildo: Pedro Serrano and Martín de Oviedo. There is a Pedro Serrano, sculptor, documented in Toledo, but not before 1654, so that it could only be a relative, perhaps a son.[9] As for Martín de Oviedo, we know that he worked in Seville in 1592–1593, where he was associated with Alonso Vásquez, and that he made a retable for the church of Santiago in Alcalá de Guadaira.[10]

These data, fragmentary as they are, show that in this

[4] Archivo General de la Nación. Tomo *Inquisición*, No. 164.

[5] Cf. Berlin, "Huejotzingo"; Idem., "Artífices de la catedral de México," *Anales del Instituto de Investigaciones Estéticas*, 11 (1944), 22–23; Efraín Castro Morales, "Luis de Arciniega, maestro mayor de la Catedral de Puebla," *Anales del Instituto de Investigaciones Estéticas*, 27 (1958), 17–32.

[6] José Gestoso y Pérez, *Ensayo de un diccionario de los artífices que florecieron en Sevilla*, I, 176.

[7] *Ibid.*, I, 193.

[8] Cipriano Muñoz y Manzano Viñaza, *Adiciones al Diccionario histórico de los mas ilustres profesores de las Bellas Artes de D. Juan Céan Bermúdez*, III, 45.

[9] *Artífices de Toledo*, p. 185.

[10] Celestino López Martínez, *Notas para la historia del arte; arquitectos, escultores y pintores vecinos de Sevilla*, pp. 134–228.

151. Virgin and Child. Stone. Museo de Churubusco,
Distrito Federal.

There are among them very capable sculptors in the
round, and in this town of Santiago, among other able
craftsmen, there is an Indian, a native of the town, named
Miguel Mauricio, who is a very superior sculptor, and his
work is much more highly esteemed than that of some
Spanish sculptors; and besides being such an excellent
craftsman, he is not known to have any vice whatever . . .[12]

We also have some documentation from the provinces. Querétaro was always an important center for
sculpture. After 1606 we find the master sculptor
Francisco Martínez, who sculptured in that year a *San
Diego of Alcalá* for the church of the Franciscan mon-
astery there, and a *St. Francis* for the monastery of San
Antonio, of the Order of San Diego.[13] There was also
another distinguished sculptor active in Querétaro, Fray
Sebastián Gallegos. In 1630 he carved the image
known as *Jesús Nazareno de los Terceros,* a figure of
Christ carrying the Cross, for the church of the Third
Order of St. Francis, and a *Crucifix* for the chapel of
San Benito, which stood in the cemetery of the Fran-
ciscans; in 1632 the image called *Santa María del
Pueblito,* and also the *Christ of the Garden* for the
church of Guadalupe.[14]

We also know the name of the sculptor of the retable of the old parish church of Taxco, built between
1634 and 1637. He was Pedro de Torrejón, who
charged 1,000 pesos for his work, and the gilder was
Don Cristóbal de la Cruz, who got 1,050 pesos.[15]

Two sculptors appeared in Nueva Galicia around
1619: one was named Gandara, and he restored the
image of *Our Lady of San Juan de los Lagos;* the other
was Mateo de la Cerda, who was the father of Luis de
la Cerda, also a sculptor.[16]

Miscellaneous Sculpture

As for other sculpture of this period, there is a further group of figures which may have come from retables, or from other monuments which have been destroyed. One of the most important pieces is a *Virgin*

period there was already extensive activity in sculpture.
Since the character of the work does not change with
the century, we continue with our documentation into
the early seventeenth century. In 1610 Manuel de
Biera, sculptor, appears: he took Juan Lázaro, an Indian, as assistant for the time necessary to work off a
debt of forty pesos, which he had loaned him on the
tenth of August.[11] A year earlier, according to an action of the Cabildo taken on November 9, 1609, Manuel de Biera had sculptured the retable of St. Gregory
the Healer for the chapel of the Palacio del Ayuntamiento.

It seems that the Indians also were successful sculptors, for Torquemada relates:

[11] Document in the Archivo General de Notarías.
[12] Juan de Torquemada, *Monarquia Indiana,* III, 209.
[13] Carlos de Sigüenza y Góngora, *Glorias de Querétaro,* pp. 45,
61.
[14] *Ibid.,* pp. 50, 53, 91, 213.
[15] Toussaint, *Tasco,* p. 118.
[16] Alberto Santoscoy, *Historia de Nuestra Señora de San Juan
de los Lagos,* pp. 35, 40.

and Child in white stone, which was dug up in Mexico City about where the main portal of the church of San Francisco must have been (151); it is now in the Museo de Churubusco. In the same museum there is an *Adoration of the Magi,* a high relief on two slabs, of the greatest interest; its provenience is unknown (152).

The treasure of the Cathedral in Mexico City has three important images from this period. Two of them, a *Virgin* and a *St. John* seem to be the side figures of a Calvary, and perhaps came from the main retable of Santo Domingo in Mexico City, since they were found in Santa Catalina, the church of the Dominican nuns. In these figures one feels at once amplitude and severity; they have great dignity, and the technique of their *estofado* is very accomplished. Another figure of *St. John,* very similar to these, is preserved in the museum at Antigua, in Guatemala. The third sculpture in the Cathedral Treasure is a *St. Anne with the Virgin Mary,* whom she holds in her lap. The same subject appears in a magnificent group of *St. Anne, with the Virgin and Child* in the church at Cuautinchán; technically excellent, the feeling for volume is notable (153). Another *St. Anne with the Virgin* in the Museo de Santa Mónica in Puebla is of such superb quality that it is probably European work, no less than a Martínez Montañés. Of equal quality, and certainly by that sculptor, is the *Holy Child (Santo Niño Cautivo)* in the Cathedral of Mexico. Two sculptures in the sacristy of La Profesa in Mexico City, an *Ecce Homo* and a *Madonna of Sorrows,* have been identified as the work of Pedro de Mena.[17]

To come back to fragments remaining from sixteenth-century retables, we should mention again the great panel of *The Assumption* in the Franciscan church of Milpa Alta, in the Distrito Federal (150). Another, in Tochimilco, shows *St. Francis Receiving the Stigmata;* and there is a *Visitation,* considerably restored, on the high altar of the church of the Colegio de Niñas in Mexico City.

With thorough research, a comprehensive catalogue of the sculpture of this period preserved in the old churches of Mexico could be made. What we have given here is a fair sample of the high quality of this sculpture in the Renaissance style in New Spain.

[17] Diego Angulo Íñiguez, "Dos Menas en México," *Archivo español de arte y arqueología,* p. 13.

152. Adoration of the Magi (detail). Stone. Museo de Churubusco, Distrito Federal.

153. Virgin and Child with St. Anne. Painted and gilded wood. Franciscan monastery, Cuautinchán, Puebla.

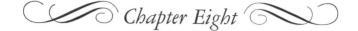

Chapter Eight

THE MINOR ARTS OF THE
RENAISSANCE PERIOD

Work in Gold and Silver

N OUR FIRST section we considered the beginnings of gold- and silverworking in the Colony. Now, in the second half of the sixteenth and the beginning of the following century, the craft developed remarkably along with the rich yield of the mines and the wealth of the colonists. A really marvelous body of work compares favorably with that of any European country.

Regulations of the Craft

In the beginning the metalworkers had been restricted by various prohibitions. In this period a series of regulations were imposed to control the craft, and above all to prevent evasion of the taxes required from silversmiths, especially the one called the *quinto*. The first ordinances concerning the refining of the metals which were being discovered in America had been enacted in a decree of December 10, 1512. On December 19, 1526, a new decree stipulated that silver could be worked so long as the *quinto real* (the King's fifth) was paid. Again, a decree of September 2, 1559, ordered that no piece of gold or silver which was not *quintado,* and so marked, could be used. A prohibition of November 9, 1526, was lightened by a succeeding

one of August 21, 1528, as we have remarked in the first section: while repeating that artisans must not have forges, furnaces, or crucibles in their shops, this gave them permission to work in the Casa de Fundición and so keep their shops operating. This establishes the modus operandi for metalworking for many years to come. Finally the goldbeaters received ordinances for their guild, issued by the Cabildo de México on July 12, 1598, on February 19, 1599, and again on January 3, 1665. Ordinances for the very noble art of the silversmiths were decreed by the Marqués de Cadereyta; and after being rewritten by the Conte de Fuenclara were proclaimed in 1746.[1]

The fact is that these regulations had been observed for a long time; the ordinances codify rules which had been in use since the sixteenth century, and for this reason they should be considered as the fundamental document in reference to this craft.

The main part of the ordinances is concerned with controlling fraud, especially evasions of the required

[1] See Francisco del Barrio Lorenzot, *Ordenanzas de gremios de la Nueva España*; Manuel Carrera Stampa, *Los gremios mexicanos*; Francisco Santiago Cruz, *Las artes y los gremios en la Nueva España.*

taxes, by the silversmiths and their assistants; another section deals with the organization of the guild, and a third part, very short, concerns technical matters of the craft.

This was the richest of the guilds, naturally, because of the value of their raw material. The ordinances begin by dividing the craft into four groups: goldsmiths, silversmiths, leafbeaters, and wiredrawers. They were given permission to form confraternities, and to celebrate each year the feast of their patron saint, St. Eligius, to whom a chapel was dedicated in the Cathedral of Mexico.[2] As one can see in the book by Señor Romero de Terreros,[3] the festivals organized by the Guild of Silversmiths in honor of their patron saint were quite sumptuous. Furthermore, in the famous Corpus Christi procession the silversmiths always had the first place and erected the most pretentious altars.

The ordinances fixed the value of the metals according to the Spanish standard, which went back to 1435: gold was to be of twenty-four carats, and silver of eleven *dineros* and four *granos*. We can reckon the value of the objects made of these precious metals by the following scale: gold was measured by the *castellano,* which was worth eight *reales* or *tomines;* silver by the *marco,* which was the equivalent of eight *onzas,* or a little over two hundred and thirty grams.

It was a requirement that every silversmith present the pieces he made to the Casa de Fundición, so that the *quinto* could be reckoned and paid. The *quinto* was marked by a punch with the royal crown, which might be framed in the Pillars of Hercules, or not. To test the quality of the material, the official in the Casa de Fundición scraped off a little piece which was called the *burilado.* This scraping was assayed by melting and comparing it with a piece of silver of the legal quality, which was called the *parangón,* the standard. Each piece was also to be marked with a punch indicating where it had been assayed and taxed; the mark for Mexico consisted of a capital *M* with a small *s* over it. The silversmith also had the obligation, expressly stated in the ordinances, of putting his personal mark on the piece. Consequently there are four marks which should appear on an authentic piece of colonial silver: the stamp of the *quinto,* the *burilado,* the stamp of the Casa de Fundición, and the maker's personal mark. Let me say at once that very few pieces are in existence which display all these marks.

With the object of controlling the guild more easily, it was stipulated in Mexico City, as in all cities where

silverworking flourished, that all the silversmiths should have their shops on the same street, which was called, naturally, "Calle de los Plateros." This regulation was put into effect on April 23, 1580, according to Fonseca y Urrutia;[4] but it appears in the Actas de Cabildo de México as approved on January 15 of that year.[5]

The place where the silversmiths worked in Mexico City was the first two blocks of San Francisco, which are now the first blocks of the Avenida Madero as one leaves the Plaza de la Constitución. It might be noted that *calles de los plateros* are still in existence in Lima and Cuzco in Peru.

To study the work in the precious metals systematically, it is convenient to divide it into two parts: religious and secular.

Religious Work in Gold and Silver

The pieces which were made for the churches were the most magnificent things imaginable. The splendor of the churches, with their Renaissance altarpieces all gilded and crowded with gilded and painted statues and the rich liturgical fabrics embroidered in gold and silver, demanded the same magnificence in the utensils of the cult. We have already considered the earliest gold objects made for the church; in the second half of the sixteenth century these cult objects became richer than ever.

First let us consider the custodias which were used for reserving or displaying the Sacrament. Just as the old Spanish cathedrals used great processional custodias —the work of that famous group of craftsmen headed by the Arfe family—at which we still marvel, the cathedrals of Mexico had their rich custodias. Thus we know that in the Cathedral of Puebla there was one called *la torrecilla*—the little tower—which measured almost three *varas* in height and was ornamented with thirty columns, forty-two bas-reliefs of Bible stories, and thirty-three figures of patriarchs, angels, and saints, all engraved.[6] The Cathedral of Mexico also treasured two processional custodias, which are minutely de-

[2] This chapel is now called the Capilla del Señor del Buen Despacho.

[3] Manuel Romero de Terreros, *Las artes industriales en la Nueva España.*

[4] Fonseca y Urrutia, *Historia de Real Hacienda,* I, 393.

[5] Mexico City, *Actas de Cabildo de la ciudad de México,* enero 15, 1580.

[6] *Diccionario universal de historia y geografía,* VI, 487.

scribed in the inventory of the church for the year 1588. The first weighed four hundred and eleven *marcos* of silver, and since at that time it was called *antigua,* it must have dated from at least the early part of the century. We do not know whether it had been brought from Spain or made in Mexico, but so renowned an object cannot be omitted from this history. It was hexagonal, three stories high. On the lowest level were groups of three columns, and between each group the figure of a Prophet, one third of a *vara* in height, with round finials, turned, and behind these a Virtue with the Signs of the Passion, including a little column. On the inside of this level the Last Supper could be seen, with the Twelve Apostles engraved; there were also reliefs on the pedestals. The second level consisted of six round pillars, turned, and engraved with babies holding the Instruments of the Passion as finials, and inside, a reliquary with the Twelve Apostles and the gold lunette to hold the Holy Sacrament. The third level also displayed six pillars; inside was a Descent from the Cross with five figures, and the Doctors of the Church around it, each one *jeme* high. At the top was a carved figure representing the Resurrected Christ with his banner, a third of a *vara* in height, and six pyramids to top it off. This custodia is clearly in full Renaissance style.

The other processional custodia is called in the inventory *custodia rica nueva*; this "rich, new custodia" was commissioned by the archbishop, Don Pedro Moya de Contreras. It weighed five hundred *marcos* of silver; it was square, and two stories high. At the top were eight nude figures with eight pyramids, and above all, St. Michael destroying the Devil. The second level was formed of twelve columns, hollow, with overlay and engraving, topped by four angels, each one *jeme* in height, carrying the Signs of the Passion, with two pyramids behind each angel; in the center, below the St. Michael, was the bell. The lower level, which was larger, had at each corner two columns ornamented with babies and fruit; in between the columns were pyramids a half-*vara* high, and in front of each column a Prophet on a pedestal; at the top of each column was an Evangelist, and there were also the four Fathers of the Church. Within the main story were shields with the figure of the Virgin and the coat of arms of Moya de Contreras in overlay. Inside, there was a silver casket with crystal windows half a *vara* wide and one *jeme*

high, with twelve hollow finials and four hollow pyramids, and in the center a gold cross between four pyramids of solid silver. One can see that these processional custodias were very rich, and in no way inferior to those of the Spanish cathedrals. This second custodia survived the centuries, until later in this book we shall note its appearance as the tabernacle in a Churrigueresque silver altar.

The same Archbishop Moya de Contreras left another custodia to the Cathedral. It was of gold, with a weight of nine hundred and four *castellanos,* five *tomines,* enamelled and set with amber and irregular pearls.

In the *Constituciones de la Provincia del Santo Evangelio* it is stipulated that custodias should not be made except *para con cáliz,* and that chalices should be three or four *marcos* in height, except those equipped with custodias, which would be larger.[7] There are some custodias of this type; the most important is the one in the town of Atzala, in the state of Guerrero. It is in two parts: a great chalice forty centimeters high, with an octagonal base, all very Gothic in feeling; and the custodia which sheathes it like a lantern, also forty centimeters high, and already Renaissance in style.[8] It is clear that the purpose of such custodias was to offer the bread and wine, symbols of the Body and Blood of Christ, to the adoration of the faithful.

The Cathedral of Mexico, in the days of Moya y Contreras, was thus already very rich in valuable ornaments for the cult. Beside the custodias, there are rich processional candleholders, candlesticks with caryatids, others with lions on their bases, others *"de media caña* with four claws and their long wicks, which have four echini superimposed, all engraved." Six rich verges. Two large dishes, one carved with a hunting frieze and a shield in the middle, the other ornamented with engraved archers and a shield in the center "of gold enamelled with blue and red, with six *romanitos* in black." There were four pyxes beside the antique one, some with precious stones, others engraved. Ten silver lamps are listed, of which two dated from the earlier period, all with their maniples and lighters, ornamented in various ways. In 1597 another lamp was recorded, which was called *la grande,* since it weighed seventy-two *marcos,* two and a half *onzas* of silver, *quintado*: "with its maniple and three chains of silver three feet long, and other smaller ones which hold the glass. The lower part terminates in a pineapple, with rings; at the top is a cross and pennant of silver."

[7] *Códice franciscano,* p. 151.
[8] Manuel Toussaint, *Tasco,* p. 117.

154. Platter. Silver. Museo Nacional del Virreinato, Tepotzotlán, México.

155. Thurible. Silver. Museo Nacional del Virreinato, Tepotzotlán, México.

In 1632 the Treasure of the Cathedral was magnificent; the Renaissance style was still the most richly represented (154, 155). There were four silver lavaboes. The finest, the work of Francisco de Eno, silversmith to the Cathedral, was decorated with masks and wildmen. There were two large bookstands in the choir, one of silver, the other of iron. In the chancel, two lecterns of the same materials, one of gilded iron, and one of silver, the work of Pedro Cebollos. Four rich large candlesticks which weighed more than five hundred *marcos* of silver had been a gift of Archbishop Bonilla. There were twenty-four chalices of different shapes and designs. The dean, Don Juan de Salcedo, gave a custodia loaded with precious stones, perhaps the first one to be ornamented in this way. The most valuable treasure of the church was the image of the *Virgin of the Assumption,* of gold and enamel, which measured a *vara* and a half in height, and was worth a fortune. It was made in 1610 by the silversmith Luis de Vargas, and in 1847 it was melted down by the Cabildo of the Cathedral, along with some large lamps we shall describe below, to pay for the high altar by Hidalga, a horror which fortunately has disappeared in its turn.[9]

The rest of the religious metalwork varied in style from the Gothic of the earlier period to the full Renaissance. The crosiers no longer displayed that bead ornament so reminiscent of the Gothic, but were decorated with spiral variations on plant forms, more or less fantastic. We have no examples of these crosiers; they can be documented only from paintings, where bishops and saints carry their staffs and other cult objects. The codices also furnish documentation of silverwork. In the Florentine Codex there are four examples,[10] one religious and the other three apparently secular, illustrated in the chapter on silverworking. The religious piece is a great thurible of gold, Gothic in general form. Because of the conventional drawing, one cannot be sure of the detail, but it seems to resemble a thurible in the Treasure of the Basilica of San Antonio in Padua which Burckhardt illustrates in his *Renaissance in Italy.* The three other objects are a wide-necked jar and two

Venetian goblets. In some other pictures also we find religious objects. The chalice of Echave Orio's *Gethsemane,* which may be dated at the beginning of the seventeenth century, is no longer Gothic, but Renaissance: it appears to have a turned base and foliate ornament on the cup. The crosiers which appear in the paintings of the Augustinian convent at Actopan are all of Renaissance design, with handsome interlacing curves, and the same thing is true of those in other paintings, as for example the *St. Augustine,* which we attribute here to Alonso López de Herrera. In this same painting the saint has a cross; it is formed of bars of gold set with emeralds cut in square bevel. In a painting of *The Immaculate Conception* by Baltasar de Echave Ibía—the one dated 1622—we see a mirror in full Renaissance style, with even a suggestion of the restrained Baroque.

Jewelry

There are abundant records of the jewelry of this period. I shall mention only a few important pieces to show that luxury had reached a height which perhaps surpassed even that of Spain, where there were often sumptuary laws (however flouted). The principal sources for this information are in the archives: the inventories taken by the Real Fisco de la Inquisición, and other documents in the Archivo de los Alcaldes Ordinarios y Corregidores de México. From the inventory of the property of Clara Henríquez in 1602 we take these excerpts:

One big necklace of irregular pearls, of thirty strings, with a mermaid of pearls and emeralds and rubies, and a knight on the mermaid also garnished with emeralds and rubies.

One Agnus Dei of gold, large, embroidered by the nuns, hanging on a rosary of heavy coral with golden ends.

Fifty clasps of gold, with four pearls at the sides and a bigger one in the middle.

One little gold spoon, called a *melindrito,* which has two figures of a courtier and a lady, and a heart, an eagle, and a *clavo* (nail).

One *melindre* (girdle?) with fifteen pieces of gold, emeralds and rubies, to be worn with a large skirt, where it joints the waist.

Some irregular pearls (*calabacitas de berrueco*) on earrings of gold, with Baroque pearls hanging from them.

Some little parrots of gold and emeralds for the ears, with their gold rings.

When the noble Alonso de Herrera married Doña

[9] All of this information comes from the inventories preserved in the Archivo de la Catedral de México. For further documentation see Toussaint's *La Catedral de México y el Sagrario Metropolitano.* See also Heinrich Berlin, "Artífices de la catedral de México," *Anales del Instituto de Investigaciones Estéticas,* 11 (1944), 25–27.

[10] Bernardino de Sahagún, *Historia general de las cosas de Nueva España.*

Agueda de Regil, he purchased the following jewels for his bride:

One ring of rock-crystal (*claveque*), and another sparkling one.
One Agnus Dei with a chain of *Bejuquillo*.[11]
One jewel consisting of a diadem (*risco*) of diamonds with eardrops to match.
One string of pearls for the neck.
Several pearl bracelets.

The document which best shows the high point which the jeweler's art had reached is the following, which I take from the Archivo de los Alcaldes in Mexico City. In 1646 Luis Ángel, resident of this city, entered an action against Don Pedro Díaz de la Barrera, *correo mayor* of this realm and *regidor,* stating as follows:

That it will be a matter of three years ago, more or less, that the said Don Pedro Díaz de la Barrera, recognizing that I am an eminent and ingenious craftsman in the art of working gold and making gold jewelry, asked me to make for him an exceptional piece, of unusual ingenuity and perfect workmanship, without sparing any effort, and that I should make with my skill whatever moulds should be necessary; and to make this he delivered to me one hundred and twenty-one emeralds, and at different times twelve *castellanos* of gold; and he promised to pay for my work and industry to my entire contentment and satisfaction. . . . I made the moulds, and worked and fabricated an exceptional jewel according to all the rules of the art and I put in it the said one hundred and twenty-one emeralds and it had fifty-four and a half *castellanos* of gold.

According to the goldsmith, his work was worth more than 450 pesos, "which is the least that you would give the most ordinary workman," and he demanded of the *correo mayor* 205 pesos, 6 *tomines,* which that official did not want to pay.

So we see to what magnificence the jewelry of this period had come. One can hardly imagine the beauty of such a piece, with such a quantity of emeralds—the most beautiful of stones, second only to the diamond in value. Surely Luis Ángel made other jewelry like this.

Household Silver

The success of the mines and the rich yield of minerals brought great wealth to many Spanish potentates of this period. Silver was the principal metal mined, and the mines of Mexico produced fabulous quantities of it to fill the coffers of the Spanish government. But a good part remained also in Mexico, both for coinage and for use in the houses of the nobility. There were people, like Alonso de Villaseca and Don Luis de Castilla, owners of the richest mines in Taxco, who in their houses had the most ordinary utensils made of silver, as if it were degrading to use pottery or porcelain at all.

The custom of silver table services lasted for a long time in Mexico; in the colonial period we always find, along with porcelain dishes from China, the silver dishes. In the nineteenth century the usage began to break down, since the very material of which it was made doomed the silverware. It could be converted directly into pesos when necessity arose, and these necessities were very frequent in the ups and downs of politics and of civil war. Even in the twentieth century many families still retained a good deal of colonial silver which at some moment of need was melted down and sold for simply the value of the metal. Objects of real artistic value have disappeared in this way.

A study of nonreligious silver would include all the pieces necessary for a table service, such as plates large and small, soup plates, cups, flat silver, saltcellars, platters, et cetera. They also made special pieces like compotes, incense burners, and chocolate cups.

It is natural, with such production, that silver should have been used for all sorts of things; but it was also subject to fluctuations in the economic condition of the country. Also, despite the enormous wealth of the period, old pieces were regularly melted down to make new, because of fashion. Thus there was a famous lavabo in the Cathedral of Mexico, formed of four eagles, which in time seemed old-fashioned, and was sent to be melted down without being replaced by anything equivalent or even comparable. Objects of silver carry their own death warrant, for the value of the metal they are made of excites men's greed, and they destroy them in order to get it.[12]

Furniture

The furniture of the Renaissance period was much more sumptuous than before, although Mexico did not lose its Oriental mood.

The only source we have for this information is doc-

[11] *Claveque* is, of course, rock crystal cut like a diamond; a *bejuquillo* is a very fine gold chain made in China.
[12] On silver and gold work in general, see Lawrence Anderson, *The Art of the Silversmith in Mexico*; Artemio de Valle Arizpe, *Notas de platería*; *Mexican Silverwork: Exhibition of Gold and Silver Organized by Rubin de la Borbolla.*

umentary; there are not enough examples in either public or private collections to allow serious study.

During the second half of the sixteenth and the beginning of the following century, furniture from Michoacán was much in fashion. Not only small objects like boxes, cups, saucers, or writing desks, but larger pieces appear; in the inventories we even find beds from Michoacán.

The chairs in the documents appear to be French chairs of the kind we use now, and sometimes those known as "Imperial." The older chairs which appear in the codices were almost all folding chairs, while the new chairs have the form we are accustomed to, in various styles and materials. In 1644 we find the following furniture listed: a small desk of walnut with turned legs; three ordinary black chairs of walnut; a bed of *granadillo* (West Indian ebony) with gilded bronze and a canopy of blue taffeta; a sewing box of walnut. The following items appear in 1642: a press of white walnut one *vara* and a half wide, with its lock and key; a flat-topped chest (*tumbado*) painted black and white; a writing case three quarters of a *vara* long, painted white and black; three little *tumbadillos,* two painted and the other covered with leather.

The following list is taken from the inventories made of his estate and goods by Don Alonso de Herrera at his marriage to Doña Agueda de Regil in 1645: a desk and writing case from Germany; a writing desk of ebony and ivory; three desks of mahogany from Havana; twelve black chairs with gilded nails; two mahogany benches; two large chests from China; a large chest of cedar from Havana, with gilded corners and hardware; a single bed of West Indian ebony with gilded bronze; a blue damask canopy; a large cupboard; a glass mirror with its ebony frame; a Turkish carpet; five pillows of blue and green velvet from China.

Among the furniture left by Luis Juárez, the likeable painter we have already discussed, appear: a little writing desk inlaid with ebony and tortoise shell and ornamented with ivory; eight pillows of worked velvet from China, four blue and four red; a single bed of *tapincerán* trimmed with gilded bronze; four stools of red leather with stitching in yellow silk; eight chairs of the same leather; a Mexican writing desk, one third of a *vara* high and three quarters of a *vara* wide, with silver handles; another Mexican desk, one *vara* long and more than a tercia (third of a *vara*) wide, covered with black leather; a small trunk covered with velvet; two

chests from Michoacán; a box covered with leather, with its top.

From various documents studied in the Archivo de Notarías we list the following furniture. In 1619: a writing desk painted in Michoacán, with its lock and key; large chairs called *imperiales*. In 1644: a Mexican desk and counting table, inlaid, made in Mexico with silver handles; four chairs with backs, and two stools. In 1650: a bed of West Indian ebony with bronze fittings, three coverlets, and a Chinese orange canopy; an Alcaraz rug, new; eight new chairs with backs, of Russian leather; a writing case of ebony and ivory with four drawers with lock and key; eight cocoanut shells ornamented with silver; a large beautiful gourd bowl from Michoacán. From 1686: a cupboard of white cedar, two and a quarter *varas* high, painted blue and white, and its doors with wire grilles, and its padlock.

At the beginning of the seventeenth century and for some years after, they made in Campeche desks and writing cases of fine woods, with geometrical designs of inlaid bone, indubitably of Mudejar tradition. These little works of art were exported; some are still to be seen in Venezuela.[13]

Moorish customs were still strong in New Spain in this period, as descriptions of the drawing rooms and interiors of the houses show. In 1624 the English traveller, Thomas Gage, describes in this way the cell of the prior of the convent of Santo Domingo in Veracruz:

His chamber was richly dressed and hung with many pictures, and with hangings, some made with cotton-wool, others with various colored feathers of Michoacan; his tables covered with carpets of silk; his cupboards adorned within with several dainties of sweetmeats and conserves.[14]

In the year 1688 drawing-room furniture of the most delightful kind appears:

Furniture for a drawing room which is composed of a new Moorish carpet six and a half *varas* long and five wide; fourteen cushions of scarlet plush *de dos ases* with their fine gold braid and tassels; a little desk of *tapincerán* three quarters of a *vara* in length; and a little Chinese lacquer trunk, of half a *vara,* with its lock and key.

---

[13] I owe this information to that cultivated Venezuelan connoisseur Don Carlos Moller, who has done so much to make known the art of his country.

[14] Thomas Gage, *Travels in the New World,* p. 34.

In the same inventory appears a cupboard of *tapince-rán*, with its wire grille, one and one-third *varas* in height, and three *tercias* wide, three shelves decorated with a variety of bric-a-brac in fine Chinese porcelain, blue and white, the last displaying curiosities in silver; and on the top a great glass jar and small jars of Chinese porcelain. Thus we find the furniture of this period evidencing considerable luxury, in harmony with the other arts.[15]

Embroideries and Weaving

We have seen that the art of embroidery was introduced to Mexico in the earliest days by the friars, who taught it to the Indians. In the period we are now considering this craft became really important, and produced work of the highest quality. Evidence of this can be found in the various ordinances which governed the guild of silkworkers, *del arte de la seda*.[16]

Since we can by no means review all the material here I shall confine myself to a few specific examples. In 1574 the Holy Office of the Inquisition commissioned an embroiderer by the name of Amaya to make its banner. The craftsman fulfilled his commission to the best of his ability, and presented his bill, which came to 1,560 pesos, plus 60 pesos for materials. The Inquisitors, secure in their power, did not agree to Amaya's bill, but had the work appraised by the embroiderers Fradique de León and Esteban Tufiño, who evaluated it at 1,176 pesos. The standard showed a St. Peter and a St. Michael with columns, their bases joined, and four shields: the King's, the Pope's, the Cardinal's, and St. Dominic's. It was embroidered on white satin, and the back was crimson damask with arabesque decoration. The Inquisitors, very well acquainted with Amaya's work, ordered that he should be paid the 1,176 pesos, and that this payment should include two chasubles of crimson and blue damask which he had also made. The embroiderer had no means of protest, given the character of his client. The same Amaya had formerly worked for the Marqués del Valle, Don Martín Cortés, between 1560 and 1565, when he embroidered with pearls the cloak the Marquesa used in the famous baptism of the twins, which made such a stir at the time. For the work alone he received 500 pesos. The tax on embroideries was figured

156. Marcos Maestre. Capa Pluvial (detail). Silk and metal embroidery. Museo Nacional del Virreinato, Tepotzotlán, México.

according to days of work, and was at the rate of a peso and a half per day.

A great deal of embroidery exists in Mexico; unfortunately there is as yet little documentation. When serious research is done in this field, it will undoubtedly yield important information. All we can do at this point is to offer such data as we have; though by no means complete, it may serve as a basis for future in-

---

[15] On furniture in general, see Abelardo Carrillo y Gariel, *Evolución del mueble en México*.
[16] See Barrio Lorenzot, *Ordenanzas*.

vestigation. First let us note the information which Romero de Terreros gives.[17] He says that Padre Pareja names two famous Mercedarian friars, Padre Fray Juan Galindo and Fray Andrés Nazari, who made the embroideries needed in their church. Among these things he mentions vestments of white cloth which cost 10,000 pesos; the cloth had been woven in Mexico, at 65 pesos a *vara*, which indicates its rich quality.

The most valuable existing collection of embroideries is without question in the Treasure of the Cathedral of Mexico, where one finds everything from the most brilliant Toledo embroidery to examples made by the Indians, with that ingenuousness in design which is so attractive. Among the European examples from this period we might mention a vestment made up of fragments of characteristic Toledo embroidery mounted on modern cloth to preserve it. The most notable example in this collection is a complete vestment signed by Marcos Maestre, the famous embroiderer of Seville at the beginning of the seventeenth century (156). The contract to make this vestment has been found in Seville. Its embroidery is like a series of paintings; the stitches are so fine that one needs a strong magnifying glass to distinguish them. I hope that the University of Seville will publish this contract, to provide important information on this interesting craft.

In conclusion we can give some names of silkworkers who are documented in this period. Besides those already cited, there are Antonio de Armenta, weaver of velvet, in 1608; Antón de Heredia, Alonso his son, and Hernando Martínez, all three weavers of velvet in 1609; Lázaro de Cuéllar, master of embroidery in 1622; Juan Bautista, Indian, embroiderer, who made some litters in 1619; Francisco de Cabrera, Spaniard, journeyman embroiderer, who in 1624 was working in the house of Francisco Vidales, embroiderer, in the Calle de San Francisco; Matías de Cerecedo, master of embroidery, 1626. Pedro Pérez, a journeyman weaver of velvet, had bought a loom in 1614, and was being bothered by the overseers of the guild because he had no certificate of examination; he requested six months to fulfill his examination requirements, which was granted. In the same situation was Antonio de Vega, a master in the weaving of lengths of cloth (*cortes de tela*), who asked permission to be examined in the weaving of velvet; this was granted in 1614. Diego Fernández in 1614 presented his credentials from Seville, as a master in the weaving of passementerie of silk; they were approved by the overseers. Cristóbal

Pérez, resident of Mexico City, a weaver of cloth of gold and silver and of *"cortes falsos,"* requested an appointment to be examined on October 12, 1615.

All this information indicates that the art of weaving rich fabrics, as well as embroidery, flourished in Mexico in this period. It is also undoubtedly true that they made fine lace. A notable example which belonged to the same Clara Henríquez should be mentioned: it was a netted bedspread showing all the scenes of the Passion. It was confiscated along with the rest of her goods by the Santo Oficio de la Inquisición in 1602.

The Ironworkers Guilds

Ironworking is properly divided into two crafts— blacksmiths and locksmiths—which had not been separated in the ordinances of 1524. Now each guild had its own ordinances. Those of the blacksmiths were enacted on April 6, 1568, and confirmed by the Real Audiencia de México. The locksmiths adopted a rule which had been instituted in Seville on July 9, 1502, and this was accepted by the city of Mexico.[18] The ordinances are precise as to the division of work: the locksmiths worked on everything having to do with locks, padlocks, keys, hinges, gudgeons (pivot hinges), hinge-posts, et cetera; the blacksmiths made everything else.

The ordinances of the blacksmiths required that a master should be examined in the making of a mallet, an axis, a plowshare, a hoe, a hatchet, and a claw hammer. Note that a man was examined as to what he knew how to do, and that he then confined his work to these categories. Other regulations protected the interest of the clients. No one should resell new ironwork, except a Biscayan plow; no one should sell as a new plow an *adobada* (wrought iron?) plowshare from Biscay. All masters must have their personal marks. Those who made things for the kitchen, such as grills, trivets, *azadores* or lamps, should make them well, whether soldered or wrought; and this was even more true of the work done for mines and for carts, where everything depended on the quality of the iron used.

The ordinances of the locksmiths divided the work into two kinds, *obra prima* and *obra baladí,* or as we say today, fine and ordinary work. The locksmith was

[17] Romero de Terreros, *Artes industriales.*

[18] It is curious that writers who have worked on this material— Romero de Terreros, *Artes industriales*; Enrique A. Cervantes, *Herreros y forjadores poblanos*; Antonio Cortés, *Hierros forjados* —do not make the distinction between blacksmiths and locksmiths.

to be examined in making a *cerrojo de mesa grande* (a large plate lock?), a padlock, and a *copada* lock—or some other kind he knew how to make—on which he must work alone. The other ordinances had to do with security, for since the locksmiths made the locks, the padlocks, and the keys, the safety of the residents was in their hands. Thus they were prohibited to make "bucket" padlocks, which could be opened with a bit of wool and a stick, except the sort called *de moro* (Moorish); and they were not to make keys from impressions in wax or plaster, but they could make the key for a lock which was brought them.

Examples of Ironwork

The best Renaissance pieces which have been preserved are obviously examples of *obra prima,* though we can hardly boast of such works of art in iron as were made in Renaissance Spain.

A few notable grilles of this period can be mentioned. In Mexico City there is a small one to be seen on the Calle de Roldán, with graceful curved bars. Grilles appear in that plan of the center of Mexico City at the end of the sixteenth century to which we have several times referred. They are Plateresque grilles: some are small and protruding, recalling those of the Casa de las Conchas in Salamanca; others are placed like great escutcheons over portals or decorating façades. I do not know why, but it seems fairly certain that no grille of this latter type has been preserved. The balconies of the Archiepiscopal Palace in Puebla were famous examples of ironwork; according to Carrión, one of them was still in place in 1898, with its balls and cornice. The iron for these balconies had been brought in the fleet of General Don Diego Flores de Valdés in 1567, and the work done a year later by the blacksmith Antonio de los Ríos.[19]

The grilles which Padre Ojea described in Mexico City in 1608 are already seventeenth-century work in a new style.[20] Still later is the screen of the Capilla del Santo Cristo in Tlacolula (157), which, like the pulpit there (191), is a wonderful example of early colonial wrought iron. Perhaps we should date in this same period, at the beginning of the seventeenth century, the wrought-iron railing which is still to be seen in the Capilla de las Ánimas, in the Cathedral of Mexico. As

[19] Romero de Terreros, *Artes industriales,* pp. 46–47.
[20] Hernando de Ojea, *Libro tercero de la Historia religioso de la provincia de México de la orden de Sto. Domingo.*

157. Grille and gate. Wrought iron.
Chapel of El Santo Cristo, Tlacolula, Oaxaca.

for the locksmith's art, the only examples from this period are the shield-shaped locks with Renaissance designs which can be seen in various private collections and in the Museo de Historia in Mexico City (158).

During the seventeenth century locks were generally in the form of a two-headed eagle, which was of course the device of the Austrian dynasty. The symmetry of this design gives the lock an heraldic quality. It may be noted that many of these iron locks were gilded *a fuego*; the name of a craftsman who did fire gilding, Andrés de Salinas, appears as early as 1615.

I can add here certain documentation which has come to my attention, though not very much. In the restorations to the Cathedral of Mexico in 1585 which we have so often cited, blacksmiths and locksmiths ap-

158. Chest. Inlaid wood with wrought iron. Museo Nacional de Historia, Mexico City.

pear; the following items come from the account books now in the Archivo General de la Nación:[21]

One peso, for two cross-shaped keys for two doors which the *obrero mayor* uses.

9 pesos, 4 *tomines,* to Melchor Vanegas, locksmith, for four *aldabonazos* for the pulpit, with their hinges and rosette nails and a handle and an *aldaba* (door knocker?).

2 pesos, for a lock for the choir-book stand.

4 pesos, 4 *tomines,* for the bolt for the Capilla del Crucifijo, with its lock, key, and eyes.

47 pesos, 7 *tomines,* to Gaspar de los Reyes, Spaniard, blacksmith, for six *arrobas* of iron, from which he made hooks (*gafas*) and nails for the joining of the braces of the framework of the church roof, at two and a half *tomines* a pound.

77 pesos, 1 *tomín,* 7 *granos* to Gaspar de los Reyes, blacksmith, for eight *arrobas,* 15 pounds of iron which he says he has put into the grille for the Puerta del Perdón, which was too small, and to make it as it is now the said iron was necessary, which at two and a half *reales* a pound came to 67 pesos, 1 *tomín,* 6 *granos,* and for his work in enlarging it and in repairing the mesh, that 10 pesos should be added, which together came to the said sum.

21 Archivo General de la Nación. Tomo *Historia,* No. 112.

To Andrés de Herrera, blacksmith, 124 pesos, for three hundred and thirty-two pounds of iron which he has used for nails for framing the roof of the church, and for the iron rods for the curtains of the retable and for the irons he made to set the pulpits of the Evangel and the Epistle, which at 3 *tomines* a pound came to the said sum.

To Juan Sánchez, locksmith, 36 pesos for twelve pair of hinges, with six nails for each pair, which were made for the doors of the choir. To the same, 10 pesos for a bolt, with its lock and eye for the said doors.

To Juan Cortés, locksmith, 2 pesos for twelve iron hinges. To the same, 14 pesos for eight angle-irons at 18 *reales* each. To the same, 24 pesos for three latches (*pestilleras*), two for the Puerta del Perdón, and one for the Puerta de los Canónigos; to the same, 4 pesos for two iron hinge-posts for the Puerta del Perdón, at 2 pesos each; to the same, 2 pesos, 4 *tomines* for another hinge-post for the Puerta de los Canónigos.

To Juan Sánchez, locksmith, 20 pesos for eight corner-irons for the doors, with six nails at 2 pesos, 4 *tomines* each.

To Diego López of Flanders, 2 pesos, 8 *tomines* for eighteen large nails.

To Francisco de Alarcón, 14 pesos, 3 *tomines* for one thousand five hundred and fifty wrought-iron nails.

To Andrés de Herrera, 16 pesos, 5 *tomines,* for an iron

screen for the Capilla del Santo Crucifijo, which weighed two *arrobas,* eleven pounds, which at 2 *tomines, 6 maravedíes* a pound, came to the said total. To the same Andrés de Herrera, 17 pesos, 7½ *tomines* for another screen that weighed sixty-six pounds of iron, which at 2 *tomines, 6 maravedíes* a pound came to the said sum.

To Juan Sánchez, locksmith, 54 pesos, 3 *tomines* for ninety-six hinges for the choir stalls and two large ones for the archbishop's chair.

16 pesos for a large knocker and lock for the new door of the Puerta del Perdón.

To Alonso Salas, locksmith, 50 pesos of common gold for his handiwork in casting a triangular iron foot, with its metal balls, for a bookstand for the choir of the church.

To Andrés de Herrera, blacksmith, 488 pesos, 4 *tomines,* for forty-nine *arrobas,* twelve pounds of large nails and the pin for the rafter crossing, which at 3 *tomines* a pound came to 416 pesos, 5 *tomines.*

To Juan Sánchez, locksmith, 64 pesos for the following things: for twelve pair of hinges with six nails apiece for the doors of the choir, at 3 pesos each: 36 pesos, for eight right-angles of iron for the said doors, with six nails apiece, that at 2½ pesos make 20 pesos; a bolt with its lock, eyes and key for the said doors, 18 pesos.

To Diego Muñoz, locksmith, 68 gold pesos for the locks and other hardware and ornaments for a screen and railing in the said church.

To Pedro López de Berlanga, 44 pesos, 4 *tomines* for lock hardware and a crosspiece (*crucero*) and other things for the Cathedral.

To these names we should also add the following ironworkers who appear in the seventeenth century: 1614, Roque Serrano, journeyman locksmith; Andrés Moreno, blacksmith and locksmith; Francisco Rodríguez, master blacksmith and locksmith. In 1616 we have Francisco González Grajeda and Luis Moreno, master blacksmiths and locksmiths; Lázaro Sánchez, journeyman locksmith. In 1632, Melchor Dávila, blacksmith and locksmith; 1639, Diego Priseño, master locksmith; 1642, Diego Domínguez, master blacksmith, resident of Tlalmanalco. In 1646, Nicolás de Trujillo, locksmith, and Sebastián de Nieva, blacksmith.

Iron was worked in the provinces of New Spain as well as in the capital; indeed, Puebla and Oaxaca were renowned for this industry. The town of Amozoc, near the city of Puebla, specialized in ironwork, as it has continued to do up to our own day; now it is especially noted for iron with silver inlay. Iron was also worked in Michoacán and in Querétaro, but rather later; this will be treated in the chapter on Baroque ironwork.[22]

Ceramics

The natives of New Spain were accomplished ceramists before the European conquest. The ceramic objects which have come down to us from the many pre-Hispanic cultures scattered over the country demonstrate consummate skill in the working of clay. The Indians did not know the use of glaze, however, so that this is a factor distinguishing post-Conquest ceramics. Recent excavations have shown that the Indians continued making their pottery as usual after the Conquest; this is reasonable, since it would be impossible to substitute the new methods at a single stroke. We see that not only general types, but specific details persisted from indigenous usage. We have found typical Indian *molcajetes,* the earthenware mortars used for grinding the ingredients for sauces, which have three feet in the shape of serpents, and are also glazed. Such proof of the persistence of an ancient form can hardly surprise us, since these very indigenous utensils are still in use in our kitchens, the *metate* (for grinding corn) as well as the *molcajete.* What is notable is the use of serpents for the feet of the pot, for it is well known that the serpent symbolised a pre-Hispanic deity, so that these *molcajetes* were made contrary to the teachings of the friars and even against government regulations.

It was not in this period, but toward the middle of the seventeenth century, that Mexican ceramics attained their highest development, with the type we call *talavera,* or majolica, in Puebla.

One problem about the ceramic industry in this period has now been definitely settled. The first scholar to work in Mexican ceramics was Edwin Atlee Barber; his book *The Maiolica of Mexico* is still useful, not only in showing how interesting the subject is, but also in giving considerable information.[23] Barber believed that the first potters arrived in Puebla in mid-sixteenth century, and that the guild which later was to be so splendid began to take shape at that time. He based this theory not, to be sure, on documents, but on tradition, and on a certain natural logic. One can hardly imagine that pottery in the Indian tradition suddenly stopped, and that then sometime later the European type appeared.

22 On ironwork in general, see Cortés, *Hierros forjados;* Cervantes, *Herreros poblanos;* Cervantes, *Hierros de Oaxaca;* Víctor Manuel Villegas, *Hierros coloniales en Toluca;* Víctor Manuel Villegas, *Hierros coloniales en Zacatecas.*

23 Edwin Atlee Barber, *The Maiolica of Mexico* and *The Emily Johnson De Forest Collection of Mexican Maiolica.*

159. Font. Ceramic. Church of the Franciscan monastery, Tepepan, Distrito Federal.

However, Barber's ideas were rudely attacked by a German scholar, Carlos C. Hoffman, in a lecture read in the Sociedad Científica "Antonio Alzate." Hoffman reached the conclusion that no Puebla tiles were made before 1630, that the master ceramists of Puebla arrived from Talavera de la Reina in Spain in the year 1662, and finally that Puebla was not the only center of so-called talavera pottery. Hoffman's argument denying

tile before 1630 was based on the building dates of the Puebla churches decorated with tiles; his single historical reference was from Gage, who visited Puebla in 1625 and does not mention glazed pottery. Hoffman's arguments are really weak. The dates of the construction of a church cannot prove anything about objects affixed to it—as if we were to take this date to apply to the pictures which decorate the interior. For that matter, many of the pictures in the Cathedral of Mexico came from the Old Cathedral and are consequently much older than the church. But if Hoffman had searched the archives, which he himself recommends as sources for the history of art, he would have realized that his assertion is entirely unsupported.

In fact, we know that there were potters in Puebla perhaps not at mid-century as Barber would have it, but at least as early as 1580, from documents published by Enrique A. Cervantes.[24] Thus we find Gaspar de Encinas, *maestro de locero* (master potter), documented in Puebla from 1580 to 1585; Juan García Carrillo, Gabriel Hernández, and Cristóbal de Olivares in 1593; Baltasar de los Reyes, apprentice in pottery, in 1599; and Antonio de Vega y Córdoba, master, from 1599 to 1637.

These names show beyond dispute that there were potters in Puebla at the end of the sixteenth century, but one can also give other proof. For example, the chapels of the second church of Santo Domingo in Mexico City, which was built at the end of the sixteenth century, were decorated with tiles, according to the account of Padre Ojea.[25] It could of course be argued that these tiles were imported, but there is other work which opens up the possibility that not only tile but pieces of glazed pottery of some importance were being made in Mexico. An example of this is the baptismal font which Federico Gómez de Orozco and I found in 1924 in the church of the Franciscan monastery of Tepepan, near Xochimilco (159). It is dated 1599; obviously it is pottery, with Renaissance designs and the Franciscan shield pressed into it, and recalls Sevillan ceramic ware in the same style.

For the rest, I think that Hoffman is right; certainly the great development of Puebla ceramics took place around the middle of the seventeenth century, and it is

[24] Cervantes, *Nómina de loceros poblanos durante el período virreinal.*
[25] Ojea, *Libro tercero,* p. 9.

a grave mistake to assume that this activity was confined to Puebla, as we shall show.

But before proceeding I am going to list the names of potters who worked in Puebla in the first half of the seventeenth century: 1612, Francisco de Vigas, apprentice; 1612–1623, Sebastián de Villardel, master; 1613, Salvador de Encian, master; 1613, Sebastián García apprentice; 1630, Juan González, apprentice; 1631, José de Cárdenas, apprentice in pottery; 1631, Juan Lozano Cerón, apprentice; 1631–1653, Andrés de Haro, master; 1632, Juan de Ortega, apprentice; 1632, Miguel de Vargas, apprentice; 1632–1642, Juan Rodríguez, master; 1633, Antonio López, apprentice; 1634, Diego de la Torre, master; 1634, Bartolomé de Sayabedra, apprentice; 1635, Juan Pérez de Espinosa, master; 1636, Nicolás de Castillo, apprentice; 1636, Juan Rodríguez de Miranda, apprentice; 1637, Francisco Varela, master; 1637, Juan de la Torre, master; 1637, Pedro de Terrazas, apprentice; 1637, Diego Rodríguez de Herrera, apprentice; 1637, Francisco Medel, apprentice; 1637, Nicolás de León, apprentice; 1637, Juan de Herrera, apprentice; 1637–1642, Juan de Valencia, master; 1638, Nicolás de Torre, master; 1642, Damián de Villardel, master; 1642, Juan de Celis, apprentice; 1642–1667, Juan de Sevilla Olmedo, master; 1644, Francisco López Bernal, master; 1644, another Antonio López, apprentice; 1645, José de los Santos, apprentice; 1645–1651, Diego Serrano y Peña, master; 1646, Alonso Sevillano, master; 1646, José de Sevilla, journeyman; 1646, Antonio Márquez de Santillana, master; 1646, Juan de la Feria, master; 1646, Juan Martín, apprentice; 1646, Nicolás Romero, apprentice.

Among the pieces which Cervantes records as of the early seventeenth century are some pots decorated in blue and black; the typical black decoration looks like lace or drawn work. Some tiles show a Mudejar influence in their strapwork designs, and this can also be seen in the pots which are decorated with geometrical patterns. Pieces like these have been found in excavating in Mexico City.

Puebla was not the only center for *talavera* ware; there were potteries more or less productive in a number of places in New Spain. The pottery of Dolores Hidalgo is a well-known example, although it is of course later in date, since it is supposed to have been established by the parish priest, Don Miguel Hidalgo.

We can point out, to begin with, that ordinances for a potters' guild in Mexico City were enacted on July 6,

160. Talavera vase, Mudejar type.
Metropolitan Museum of Art, New York.

1677, and confirmed by the Conde de Paredes on October 1, 1681, that is, a little more than twenty years after the ordinances of Puebla. That period belongs to a future chapter in this book.

To demonstrate the point at this time, however, I can list some potters who were active in the capital. These are names which I have come upon by chance, without doing any special research, in the archives—especially the Archivo de Notarías:

1626, Andrés de Haro, potter—his wife was named Leonor Hernández (as we have seen, this master appeared in Puebla after 1631; apparently he had worked in the capital of New Spain earlier); 1642, Gonzalo González, master potter; 1643, Diego de la Torre, journeyman, maker of earthenware, and Juan Rodríguez, master of the same craft.

1647, February 29, Diego de la Cruz Villanueva, master potter, resident in the district of Santiago, testified that he had sheltered an orphan, a little girl of two years and a half, more or less, and was now giving her to Diego Gutiérrez, master tailor, and to María de Zúñiga, his wife, to raise her and feed her, since he could not do so because of his poverty—which indicates that he did not earn enough by his art to live in comfort.

1648, Francisco Gómez Beltrán, master potter, resident in the district of San Lázaro. 1653, March 21, Juan Rodríguez de Borges, master potter, resident of Mexico City, makes for Francisco Gutiérrez Afanador, master of the apothecary's art, all the jars necessary for his shop, for 159 pesos, 6 *reales* of common gold.

Although few, these notices prove that a ceramic industry flourished also in the capital of the Viceroyalty. There is no doubt that special research would yield more material confirming this fact.

In this period Mexican ceramics are in direct imitation of the Spanish (160); there is none of the Chinese influence that was to modify their character later. It is easy to distinguish Spanish from Mexican pottery. Since the colonial potters applied their colors in heavy coats over the ground glaze, the colored parts were raised, a thing that would have appeared a serious defect to the Spanish craftsmen. Their tiles also show a certain convexity of surface, as if to show that they were used primarily for covering domes. This would have been considered an insupportable fault by the ceramists of Spain.

The high point in the importation of china and porcelain from China coincided with the high point in the production of pottery in the Colony. This Mexican pottery served the tables of the poor, while the mighty always enjoyed Oriental porcelain and services of silver.

PART THREE

Art in New Spain during the Formation of the Nation

The Baroque Style in Mexico, 1630–1730

Chapter Nine

BAROQUE ARCHITECTURE

THIS THIRD PERIOD in our survey brings us to the most interesting phenomenon in the history of Mexican art. The original conquistadors, after settling down as colonists, were dead. Their descendants enjoyed the immense fortunes they had left; these descendants had been born in Mexico and had married women born there, sometimes Indian women. So the group of Spaniards native to the New World began to be differentiated from the European Spaniards. As more Spaniards constantly arrived a desperate conflict developed between the *criollos,* who were the Spaniards born in Mexico, and the *gachupines,* the Spaniards who came from Spain to work in the country conquered by the ancestors of their rivals. The struggle between the two groups was bitter. Thomas Gage's account is undoubtedly exaggerated, since his book is all propaganda for England's seizing Mexico; but it has a basis of fact.[1] We should not forget that the first popular revolt occurred in 1624, and that those born in New Spain took the part of Archbishop Serna against the viceroy, the Marqués de Galves.

It is indeed to the social conditions in New Spain that we must look to understand the new style that informed the art of this time. This was an eminently aristocratic society, an aristocracy of wealth whose only lineage was descent from the conquistadors, and whose nobility was exhibited in the most splendid works of piety or charity. If in the earlier days churches and monasteries and even the cathedrals had been built in great part by funds from the Crown and compulsory subsidies of various sorts, in this period it was the potentates of the Colony themselves who were responsible for the high achievement in religious architecture. Enormous fortunes were devoted by the great landowners, the *mayorazgos,* and by simple gentlemen, to make themselves the patrons of churches and convents. One would say that there had been a kind of tacit agreement between these often licentious men and the church, which, at least in their opinion, would assure them of salvation in return for their immense contributions to the building of churches and monastic establishments.

In this period we see also the parishes beginning to be secularized. Administration of the parishes and missions was taken away from the friars, who had controlled them by special concession since the beginning of the Colony. The secular clergy began to take over

[1] Thomas Gage, *Travels in the New World.*

161. Façade, convent church of Las Monjas (Santa Catarina), Morelia, Michoacán.

all this administration, organizing the hierarchy of the Mexican Church. The friars complain, sometimes quite pitifully, of the way the parishes were seized by the archbishops and the bishops.[2]

As for art itself, we witness a complete change of taste. No longer was the Plateresque dominant in religious architecture; an entirely new style was being developed by combining elements from all the styles of the past. The same phenomenon had taken place in Spain, and this new style of both the Old and the New World is known as the Baroque.

Baroque—an Italian word, *barocco*—means impure, hybrid, bizarre, daring. It is evident that the internal sources of the Baroque derive from an abuse of the strict forms, and from that desire for change and renovation which sweeps from time to time over mankind, so disposed to variety, so subject in every activity to

that factor which, although essentially destructive, still includes a certain creative impulse—fashion.

Other more profound causes in Europe have been suggested as explanations of this style. For instance, the Baroque has been interpreted in Weisbach's interesting study as the expression of the Counter-Reformation in art. Actually the term is so broad, and its connotations so fluid, that it is difficult to agree on a definition. One thing is certain: that the Baroque style in Mexico evolves according to its own particular nature. Undoubtedly it derives from European Baroque, but its development is so special, so unique, that it would be foolish to try to explain it by reference to European theories. The relationship is rather one of similarity in mood, in these sumptuous church interiors in Mexico and in Portugal, for example. In the same way, South German Baroque shows resemblances to the Baroque of New Spain; we shall see how the engravings of Klauber may have influenced the Baroque architecture of Querétaro. At bottom the question is whether similar causes—the psychological state of a people, their religious feelings, their economic condition—produce these parallel effects in architecture. It is my belief that this is true.[3]

Religious Architecture

Before turning to the history of the Baroque style in New Spain, it will be useful to consider the history of three specific categories of buildings: the monasteries, the parish churches, and the great cathedrals.

Monastic architecture in this period is no longer so uniform as it was in mid-sixteenth century. As the new monasteries were built through private initiative and paid for by individuals, it was not possible to impose the strict rules which had obtained when the Crown carried the main costs of the work. As a result the monasteries built during the seventeenth century do not show a uniform program in their general planning, but only insofar as function determined the character of the various parts of the monastic establishment.

Thus we can follow the formulation of the nuns' church, which is more or less uniform and comes to be

[2] See for example the writings of Padre Francisco de Ayeta, complaining of the way the parishes which had been administered by the Franciscans were secularized, sometimes with blood and fire, as when the parishes of the bishopric of Puebla were taken over by Bishop Palafox.

[3] See Joseph A. Baird, "Mexican Architecture and the Baroque," in *International Congress of the History of Art, XX, New York, 1961,* 191–202.

a recognized architectural type. The convents themselves show little uniformity; they were often established in houses donated by their patrons, and had to adapt themselves to the disposition of the buildings, especially in densely populated areas, where it was difficult, if not impossible, to acquire more land. But the church, the essential part of the establishment, for which an ample site was always managed, developed a special plan to fit the requirements of the institution. The church had to be public—that is, open to the faithful for their attendance at all the ceremonies celebrated there—but the convent was cloistered, closing off the nuns in a world apart. Thus the church had to be built so that it could serve the nuns without infringing on their seclusion, and at the same time give free access to the populace. The solution is perfect (162). The church is a simple nave to make the most of the space; its principal axis is parallel to the street, which gives it good illumination and allows free access to the people, without disturbing the daughters of God living in the convent. The choir, at the end, is extended until it is sometimes nearly as large as the nave, and it is double, with an upper and lower story. The lower choir is divided from the nave by a screen which has terrible spikes toward the church, like dragon's claws to defend the nuns from the dangers of the world. One can see such a screen in the convent church of Santa Teresa la Nueva in Mexico City, one of the few which have survived. On either side of this screen two little grilled windows, the craticles, allowed the nuns to take communion without the priest's entering the cloister. The upper choir has a simpler and less formidable grille; it is shielded, like that below, by screens of cloth which allow those inside to look out while the public cannot observe what is going on in the choir. The church is vaulted, not with the Gothic vaults of the earlier period, but with a simple barrel vault with lunettes, or groin vaults. Often there is no transept, or only a short one; but there is always a dome and, at the end of the church, a tower. There are two portals, as if to symbolize the freedom of the people to attend the services, especially the ceremony of taking the veil, so marvelously rich with emotion and symbolism (161).

Another architectural category developed almost to monotony in this period is the parish church. The secular parish churches of Mexico have a Latin-cross plan with a marked transept from whose crossing a dome springs, which may or may not have a drum. The portal is at the end between two towers, and at the

162. Façade, convent church of La Concepción, Mexico City.

side is another doorway. In the spaces between the arms of the transept and the apse are located the sacristy, the parish offices (the *cuadrante*), the baptistry, and the chapels in which center the many confraternities, the groups of pious parishioners. This form of parish church persists all through the eighteenth century, and one is astonished if he finds any different kind of structure.

The Cathedrals

The great cathedrals, which had been begun in the preceding period, were brought in this period, if not to perfect completion (a thing achieved only after years of work), at least to a state in which they could be used for services, and consequently were dedicated.

The Cathedral of Mexico was dedicated formally in 1667 (163). Many different architects had had a part in building it; among the most important was Luis

163. Cathedral of Mexico and Sagrario Metropolitano, Mexico City.

164. Nave and choir, Cathedral of Mexico, Mexico City.

Gómez de Trasmonte, who worked between 1640 and 1661.[4] Rodrigo Díaz de Aguilera appears in 1668; another architect concerned with the construction was Melchor Pérez de Soto, who was tried by the Inquisition for astrology; and there were many others of less importance. The Cathedral was completed according to the plan established at the beginning of the seventeenth century. The only change proposed, it seems, had to do with the cupola. Gómez de Trasmonte suggested that the four columns on which it was to rest should be built heavier, but this proposal was not accepted. Also the system of construction was changed, and from the Capilla de San Isidro Labrador on, the roof was made in groin vaults of *tezontle* instead of the old ribbed

[4] See Heinrich Berlin, "Artífices de la catedral de México," *Anales del Instituto de Investigaciones Estéticas,* 11 (1944), 19–39.

vaults which they had been building since the sixteenth century (164). The portals were already Baroque, as we shall see in due course; the altars followed the same style, and the choir was furnished with magnificent Baroque stalls. The church had still only the base of one tower, but it was functioning in every way.

The Cathedral of Puebla was rapidly finished, in about nine years, by Bishop Palafox, who managed to dedicate it in 1649, just before returning to Spain (165). The guiding spirit was the architect, painter, and sculptor Mosén Pedro García Ferrer, from Valencia, advisor to the Bishop in matters of art. The Cathedral was finished with an important change in construction. According to the original plan, the nave and aisles were to be all the same height, and without a dome; that is, they intended to build a terrace-roofed church like that of Cuzco in Peru. We have already pointed

165. Cathedral of Puebla.

166. Nave and choir, Cathedral of Puebla.

out that the plans for this type of building came from a man who served as architect in both places, Francisco Becerra. Now, however, they raised the nave and the transept, and over the crossing placed a great dome on pendentives with a drum (166). The dome was designed by García Ferrer and built by the *maestro* Jerónimo de la Cruz, as were the vaults, while the walls, pillars, arches, and columns were under the direction of the architect Agustín Hernández.[5] Various other details of the church which date from this period, both sculpture and paintings, will be considered below in their proper contexts. This cathedral was left with a single tower; the other was not to be finished until the eighteenth century. Bishop Palafox had also planned a great cloister in front of the façade, where the Sagrario

and other offices would be located. Some of it was begun, but later torn down, and the church was left as we see it now.[6]

The Cathedral of Michoacán had been begun in Valladolid (Morelia) around 1660, but the work had met with great obstacles, and it went ahead only slowly (167, 168). The designer of this church was an *alarife* named Vicencio Barroso Escayola, who had worked on a number of buildings in Mexico City, such as the

[5] Antonio Tamariz de Carmona, *Relación y descripción del templo real de la ciudad de la Puebla de los Ángeles,* p. 18.
[6] See the plan published by Diego Angulo Íñiguez, "Las catedrales mejicanas del siglo XVI," *Boletín de la Real Academia de la Historia,* 113 (1943), 137 ff.; also the extensive file of documents concerning the razing of the structure, in the library of the Museo Nacional. See also Berlin, "Artífices," pp. 19–39.

167. Cathedral of Morelia, Michoacán.

168. Façade, Cathedral of Morelia, Michoacán.

169. Cathedral of San Cristóbal de las Casas, Chiapas.

Santo Oficio de la Inquisición and the Real Palacio de los Virreyes. After July, 1674, the Spanish architect Antonio de Echavira worked there; the building was finished only in 1774.[7]

The Cathedral of Mérida in Yucatán was finished, as we have seen, in the sixteenth century; from this century date only the mediocre campaniles which top the towers (112).

The Cathedral of Chiapas seems to date entirely from the seventeenth century (169). Its portals and its interior are Baroque in style, but it is in no way comparable to the other Mexican cathedrals. In fact it is closer to the churches of Antigua Guatemala, which date from this period.

The Cathedral of Nueva Galicia in Guadalajara had been finished, as we have said, in 1618 (115). Later it suffered a terrible earthquake which knocked down its towers, and these were rebuilt many years later in a ridiculous form.[8]

Civil Architecture

In civil architecture there are no developments which can be considered as new types, except perhaps in domestic architecture.

In the category of government buildings we have the Palacio de los Virreyes—the Viceregal Palace, now the Palacio Nacional. Except for the modern changes, the building really dates from the seventeenth century, since it was rebuilt after the insurrection of 1624 (170, 171). In structure, however, it was the same building as before: large patios were enclosed by arcades and corridors, with offices and apartments. This is essentially the design of all the public buildings.

The buildings devoted to education present more or less the same appearance. Perhaps one might say that their special function begins to show on the exterior, where the great walls have small high windows to indicate that the work of the mind should not be disturbed by the noise of the street. Such was the Colegio de Niñas, and such must have been the Colegio de San Pedro y San Pablo in Mexico City,[9] that of the Jesuit fathers in Puebla, and various other educational institutions. These buildings are still in use, their exteriors considerably altered, but their patios intact. That of Puebla, later the Colegio del Estado and now the University of Puebla, is said to have been built in 1690 by the Jesuit Juan Gómez (172). It retains its very handsome patios, with arcades on the lower floor and, on the second floor, walled-in arches, with windows—an

[7] See Berlin, "La catedral de Morelia y sus artistas," *Anales de la Sociedad de Geografía e Historia de Guatemala* (1953–1954), pp. 146–168; Ana María Liaño Pacheco, "La catedral de Morelia," *Arte en América y Filipinas*, 2 (1936), 95–113.

[8] See Manuel Romero de Terreros, "Las torres de la catedral de Guadalajara," *Anales del Instituto de Investigaciones Estéticas*, 34 (1965), 19–70.

[9] See Clementina Díaz y de Ovando, *El Colegio Máximo de San Pedro y San Pablo.*

170. National Palace, Mexico City.
Lithograph. From *México y sus alrededores*, 1860.

171. National Palace (after 1927), Mexico City.

172. Patio, Colegio de San Ignacio
(Universidad de Puebla), Puebla.

173. Casa Sola, Avenida Uruguay,
Mexico City.

arrangement favored by the Jesuits, which we find also in their colleges at Tepotzotlán and Pátzcuaro. The magnificent stairway leads to the assembly hall, formerly the Sala General, which is still richly furnished.

In this period dwellings begin to follow a special plan. Their form without doubt derives from earlier houses, but since they were almost all rebuilt in these times, our acquaintance with the colonial house dates in fact from this period. What happened was that the noble residences of the potentates who were descendants of the conquistadors or had been ennobled by the Crown began to be differentiated from the houses of the plebeian merchants, however wealthy.

At this time, probably, was also developed a special type of middle-class house: the *casa sola,* or "single house" (173). The *casa sola* is the house of the bourgeois who does not have much land but enjoys enough scope to make himself comfortable. These houses were almost always built by twos, so that in the documents they are spoken of as "a pair of houses." The patio, rectangular or square, is divided by a wall down the middle, so that one half belongs to one house and the other half to the other. An ample *zaguán,* the large entrance hall leading from the street doors to the patio, allows coaches to enter; there are shops opening on the street, and if the house is small, another *zaguán* on the same street gives access to the carriage house. The patio, or properly speaking, the half-patio, is narrow, with various apartments opening on it used for offices, storerooms and servants' quarters. Almost always one finds a second smaller patio for the stables and barns. Between the first and second patio is the stairway, which is usually of two flights, with a landing halfway up. Upstairs we have a "corridor" circling the first patio; occasionally this continues along the dividing wall over the two patios. On the side looking over the street is the *sala,* the drawing room where formal calls are received, with a small antechamber if there is space for it. On the long side of the patio are the bedrooms, and a sitting room called *la asistencia,* where friends are received and where the family passes most of the day. The dining room is at the back of the patio, opposite the *sala;* often it opens onto both of the patios. Over the second patio is the kitchen, the servants' room, and the *azotehuela,* the roof terrace. The baths and toilets are somewhere at the back.

This type of house, varying according to its area and the wealth of its owners, was common in Mexico City from this time on throughout the colonial era. It

174. Casa de Vecindad. Lithograph. From *Los Misterios de México,* 1852.

was still in use all through the nineteenth century, until it began to be supplanted in our day by houses built in the style of the United States, without patios, and without much local character.

A less important type than the *casa sola* is the *casa de vecindad,* a multiple dwelling (174). In the seventeenth century this usually consisted of a long central passage with the separate apartments, the *viviendas,* opening on both sides. Each of these consisted simply of two rooms and a kitchen, with perhaps a small patio. At the end of the central court would be a fountain, and a niche with an image lighted by a lamp. Occasionally the building was of two stories, and then the stairway was at the back, forming a kind of altar for the niche. There also were much larger *casas de vecindad,*

189

with from four to six apartments with more rooms, but the general arrangement remained the same, around a corridor or central patio, with stairways at the back or in front.

Very infrequently houses were built without patios; but they are in fact so rare that we mention the existence of a few in the center of Mexico City because they are unique examples.

The ultimate form of the multiple dwelling is what has been called a "cup-and-saucer apartment"—*accesoria de taza y plato*. It is an *accesoria,* that is, an apartment, which is part of another house, with one room opening on the street; over this room is built a mezzanine, often of wood, in which case it is called a *tapanco* (Indian cane hut). The *accesoria* has a doorway downstairs, the upstairs room, a window. The first floor is the shop; the second, the living quarters; and as the one rests on the other like a cup on a saucer, so it gets its name.

The houses of the other provinces of New Spain follow more or less the same form, varying only in their decoration. As we study the Baroque style in different parts of the country we shall note the differences in the dwellings.

The Baroque Style

Technically speaking, the term "Baroque" refers to a degeneration of Classical style. But since this degeneration seems in itself endowed with life, and its spirit carries the germ of its own development, there comes a moment when the architectural orders—the essential element of Classicism—are actually submerged beneath proliferating fantasy. Early Baroque appears to be simply a variation on the Classical mode; we can recognize in it all the components of the architectural orders. But already one feels an appetite for freedom that begins to modify the orders, that no longer respects the canons, that is willing to alter not only the proportion but the organization itself, as if a taste for mischief and rebellion were progressively growing within the ever-extended boundaries. Indeed it must be admitted that the monotony of the Classical orders invited attack, especially in young nations where a more vital art was wanted. And this rebellion could lead only to more complicated inventions which, falling short of traditional standards, yet had the capacity to revitalize art.

As we all know, Baroque is a term interpreted now with great latitude. The impulse we have noted, to escape the tyranny of the Classical orders, produced the

Baroque styles of Southern Europe, which have nothing to do with the Baroque of Latin America. Those fine gentlemen would laugh disdainfully at our Baroque, which in their opinion touches on madness. Their monuments represent a severe Baroque which handled the Classical canons with white gloves, even as it broke them.

American Baroque takes many forms. We do not want to compare it to an organism which keeps changing its nature, lest the philosophers, who insist that matters of the spirit cannot be compared to organic forms, should damn us. But there does seem to be a change, slow and systematic, which forces one to recognize a chronological development in the forms. Three varieties can be distinguished in this way—let us say three moods: sober Baroque, rich Baroque, and exuberant Baroque. Furthermore the style is prolonged throughout the colonial era, and sweeps through two stylistic periods; this prevents exact chronological boundaries, which would anyhow be excessively tiresome. It is important to realize that most of the civil architecture of the eighteenth century is still Baroque and not Churrigueresque.

Sober Baroque

The first Baroque architecture to appear in America was simply an imitation of Spanish Baroque.

In the early seventeenth century, as we have observed, a style related to the Herrerian style of Spain had made its appearance; but later a special style developed which we designate by the term "sober Baroque." It also was a Spanish style, whose antecedents are clear in Spanish architecture. It developed essentially as I have described: the Classical orders were retained, but with liberties; these changes consisted of altering the proportions of the columns, breaking the entablature, multiplying the projections, and, in effect, converting the supporting members into something purely decorative which functioned only among the ornamental devices of the building. There is also a multiplication of pediments, doorways, windows, niches, ornamental finials, and everything possible.

The development of the Baroque style in this period moved through three clearly defined phases, as we have said. Imported directly from Spain, it began by being "sober"; then, as the ornament preponderated, it became "rich"; and finally toward the end of the seventeenth century it reached such a stage of luxuriance in some places that it can only be termed "exuberant."

The first type of Baroque is represented by numerous examples in Mexico City. The church of San Lorenzo was finished about 1650 (175); that of Jesús María, whose architect was Pedro Briseño, was concluded around 1621, but later modified to its present form (369). The church of La Concepción (162) was finished in 1655 with its octagonal chapel opposite. (This charming chapel has been called the first church built in the capital by certain writers who do not understand that its style establishes its date in mid-seventeenth century.) The church of Balvanera, finished in 1671, has a Mudejar bell tower; that of La Encarnación, beautifully decorated with tiles, dates from 1648. In 1681 Santa Isabel, which unfortunately no longer exists, was built; and in 1661, San José de Gracia. From 1623 date both Santa Catalina de Siena and San Jerónimo; Santa Clara, which is austere enough to border on the Herrerian, is also of this period.

The friars also did some building at this time, notably the church of Santiago Tlatelolco, which was finished in 1610, and is consequently the prototype of the cruciform church in Mexico. Churches which also have Baroque portals are San Antonio Abad, of 1687—although the portal may be of later date—and its contemporary, the little church of Belén, which still exists although very much modified. Some of the orders achieved a certain uniformity of architectural type in this period, so that we find similarities in their buildings, for which a particular architect is in some cases responsible. Thus the Carmelites at this time employed that outstanding figure, Fray Andrés de San Miguel, originally from Segura in Spain, who built the magnificent monastery of San Ángel, the Desierto de los Leones, and the monastery of Salvatierra, where he died in 1644. He must have had a hand in many others, for there are always resemblances; that *espadaña,* the wall belfry of two or three stories so dear to the Carmelites, seems to have come from him. Various Carmelite establishments have been preserved in their original state: the house in Puebla, with the romantic cypresses in its churchyard; that of Morelia, which is dated 1621 on one of the portals; and what is now the parish church of Atlixco, with its red façade. The two Carmelite churches in Oaxaca, the Carmen Alto and the Carmen Bajo, have little interest; there is also one in Guadalajara. There are two hermitages, known as *de-*

[10] See Lauro E. Rosell, *Convento dieguino de Santa María de los Ángeles, Huitzilopochco-Churubusco.*

175. Façade, monastery church of San Lorenzo, Mexico City.

siertos: the Desierto de los Leones, which we have already mentioned, and the Desierto de Tenancingo, where the last work on the monastery dates from 1813, and tends toward Neoclassicism.

The Barefoot Franciscans of the Province of San Diego, who are called Dieguinos, were humble enough in their building. The best of their houses is at Churubusco, built by Don Diego del Castillo and Doña Elena de la Cruz, and finished around 1678 (176). With its little cloister, its church, and the adjoining chapel with its tiled dome, it is all, without being elaborate, quite charming. The Dirección de Monumentos Coloniales has taken it over as a museum, and is restoring the building.[10] The church of San Martín Texmelucan has

176. Façade, church and monastery of San Diego (Museo de Churubusco),
Churubusco, Distrito Federal.

a tiled façade and rich retables inside. Their monastery in Mexico City was finished by 1621 but shows evidence of later rebuilding; in Taxco also the monastery was entirely rebuilt after a fire in 1805. There is a very modest house in Acuitlapán; the one in Morelia has been converted into the Santuario de Guadalupe.

The Order of San Felipe Neri has left a handful of houses which range from La Concordia in Puebla, austere and sober, to that of Guadalajara, which is in a rich Baroque style. Their church in Oaxaca, which is of great beauty, dates from 1633; it is sumptuously decorated with retables of later date. The church in Mexico City must have been very beautiful, to judge by the façade, which is all that remains of it: sheltered by a great portal like a shell is a relief representing their patron saint. The house in San Miguel Allende was built at various times; its most interesting feature is the *camarín* of the Santa Casa de Loreto, of which we shall speak later.

The Baroque features of these churches can be quite specifically indicated. The structure has not changed; it is in the decorated areas that we recognize the style, especially in the entrance portals of the churches. These portals consist of a semicircular arch flanked by pilasters or columns, either single or double, with a niche or a window, or sometimes a relief, above.

This type of portal was so common in the seventeenth century as to be almost universal: all the churches have it, whether it is the parish church of Guanajuato or the old church of Tepotzotlán. Another type of Baroque portal typical of the sober style appears on the monasteries: a lintelled doorway with a coat of arms or a niche above. Such are the portals of the monastery of Jesús María in Mexico City, dated 1692, and of Santa Rosa in Puebla.

Residences in this style offer a variation: the portal opens between pilasters, with a window or balcony above, and higher up the coat of arms of the owner, if he has one (294). The jambs of doors and windows are prolonged upward to terminate either in a frieze or in a capital. Cornices are small, sometimes almost non-existent. If it was a noble house, there are battlements; sometimes there are small curving projections where the drain pipes open. In Mexico City the walls of the houses were covered with *tezontle,* which from this time on was cut in relatively small squared blocks, smoothed on the face, and known as *tezontle rostreado.* The jambs, lintels, cornices, and friezes are of cut stone, the pilasters are often rusticated, and the corner

177. House, Avenida 16 de Septiembre, Puebla.

of the building almost always has a niche, for the favorite saint of the householder, or the patron of the religious community.

The only rival to the secular Baroque of Mexico City is the Baroque which flourished in Puebla in the same period. Puebla, indeed, is a Baroque city which later takes on a unique Mudejar atmosphere not to be found in any other city in the world.

We can still glimpse the Puebla of Bishop Palafox in the few remains which the later inhabitants of the city have permitted to survive. The houses had portals

178. Portal, church of La Profesa (San José el Real), Mexico City.

acanthus pattern in relief, which seems to have been a favorite of Bishop Palafox's. The portal of the Colegio de San Pedro is ornamented in this way; it was finished in 1648, after drawings by Pedro García Ferrer, and cut by Lorenzo Abel in his shop, while Diego de Folco made the sculpture.[11]

Other Baroque buildings in Puebla show us what the city must have been like in the middle of the seventeenth century. It was a Baroque city *par excellence,* with an aristocratic air which Mexico City itself, although the capital of the Viceroyalty, could not equal. The portal of the church of La Santísima is an example of this; it was carved between 1670 and 1672 by Juan Jerónimo and his son Juan Antonio, who were mestizos.[12] The portal of the church of San Agustín was constructed around 1629 by Antonio Alonso, master stonecutter. The church of La Concepción was finished, in a somewhat popular Baroque style, in 1617, although the vaults and dome were not completed until 1732. The church of San Ildefonso dates from 1624; it is still quite Classical, but with rich interior decoration.

Examples of this moderate Baroque can be found in other regions of Mexico also. Thus we have in Oaxaca the church of San José, 1728; that of the Siete Príncipes, where a vaulted space makes an unusual portal, 1744–1782; La Defensa of 1792, and others.

In Querétaro the church of Santa Clara has two portals with pilasters topped by pinnacles, and a window on the second story. The same arrangement is found on Santa Rosa, except that a niche takes the place of the window. Within the bounds of this same sobriety, the church of La Compañía displays a richer ornamentation on its two portals, and above all, on the doorways of the fine patio of the College. Very austere are the portals of the church of Guadalupe, and those also of the church of the Capuchinas. The portals of the church of San Antonio also follow the same design.

In San Luis Potosí we find the church of San Francisco and the remains of the architectural complex around the monastery yard in this style, and also the Cathedral.

An isolated example which should not be overlooked is the parish church at Chalco, formerly the Franciscan

of cut stone, and corner balconies with a little column at the angle, of which only a few have been preserved intact. The walls began to be covered in a way to rival those of Mexico: where in Mexico they used a revetment of *tezontle,* in Puebla it was a combination of brick and glazed tile of extraordinary originality, which was undoubtedly devised in this period (177). The cornices are wider because the light is stronger, and little by little they are developed and elaborated in fantastic forms, in undulating curves, rich with ornament, always more Baroque. Civic buildings offer an architecture of greater solemnity: their portals are of grey stone, ornamented with reliefs and sculptures in white marble. The lintelled doorway is often framed in an

11 Enrique A. Cervantes, "Bosquejo del desarrollo de la ciudad de Puebla," *Universidad,* 4 (diciembre, 1937), 11–15; 5 (enero, 1938), 14–29.
12 *Ibid.*

179. Façade, convent church of Corpus Christi, Mexico City.

monastery. Its façade is built up with columns and entablatures, two stories crowned by a triangular extension ornamented with pinnacles to give a vigorous silhouette.

The Baroque churches of Morelia, in addition to the characteristics we have noted, offer a special device, a triangular piece above the façade. They sometimes have two portals, as on the magnificent church of Las Rosas, or that of Las Monjas (161), at other times just one, as on the church of the Capuchinas, or the Sanctuary of Guadalupe.

Rich Baroque

Paralleling the sober Baroque we have just reviewed, there also developed during the seventeenth and eighteenth centuries a type of Baroque church whose portals were decorated more lavishly, in rejection of the Spanish restraint.

It is not possible to draw up a complete catalogue of these monuments nor to establish a precise chronology. The style seems to develop through caprice and fantasy; it would be nonsense to try to impose order where every possibility except orderliness is explored.

This mood of refined lavishness appears in the churches of Mexico City by the middle of the seventeenth century. Thus we have the church of Santa Teresa la Antigua, 1678–1684, profusely decorated, and that of San Bernardo, finished in 1690 by the architect Juan de Zepeda, whose fine ornaments suggest Plateresque decoration brought up to date, as it were.[13] The magnificent church of San Agustín, finished in 1691 to replace an earlier one destroyed by fire (and now converted most unsuccessfully into the National Library) is an excellent example of this rich Baroque. When the church was made into a library, the architect Joaquín Heredia skillfully replaced the original elements of the facades. The main portal is organized with splendid twisted columns, and the central motif is a great relief representing St. Augustine as Protector (205). The Chapel of the Tercer Orden, in a simpler

13 Manuel Toussaint, *Paseos coloniales,* pp. 74–77.

195

180. Façade, church of San Cristóbal, Puebla.

which dates from 1724, was also his work (179). Its fine portal shows the influence of engravings, and indeed it seems like the frontispiece of an early eighteenth-century folio.[16] The church of the hospital of San Juan de Dios was finished in 1727; it is interesting for the large concave shell portico, with its excellent sculpture and undulating pilasters which seem to counterfeit, or at least to make the same effect as, spiral columns.

Puebla seems to have offered the ideal environment for this luxurious style. After the period of sober Baroque, in which Puebla was also pre-eminent, a guild of plasterworkers grew up there in mid-seventeenth century, and developed to perfection the art of relief in stucco. We have already mentioned the church of San Ildefonso, whose portal of 1624 is all but Herrerian in style, but whose interior begins to display the magnificent ornamentation in stucco relief which was to become typical later. Chronologically, Santo Domingo follows next; here the stucco work is more extensive, appearing on the choir vault, on a side portal, and on the spacious vaults of the nave. Later came San Cristóbal (180), which dates between 1676 and 1687 and was certainly the halfway stage to reach the greatest of all, the Capilla del Rosario of Santo Domingo. There one finds the full expression of Puebla Baroque, beginning in this period. From the very rich portal of grey stone with marble ornament, the reliefs of the Habsburg eagles at the base of the belfries (of which only one survives), to the interior with its Mudejar tile dado and its vaults completely covered with relief ornament, everything is an indication of what is to come later. A somewhat popular development of this style is found in the half-ruined buildings known as the Calvario de Tehuacán, in the state of Puebla.

We find this same type of ornament in the old Antequera, now called Oaxaca. We have already mentioned the church of San Felipe. We should note the church of La Compañía, with its curious mixture of influences, going back even to the Plateresque. The church of San

Baroque style, was covered over by an enlargement of the building, which for many years housed the Night Division; its portal is very interesting.[14] The church of San José el Real, known as "La Profesa" because it belonged to the Jesuit house of that name, was finished in 1720. It is one of the handsomest churches in the city, with its nave and wide aisles, its great crossing held up by clustered columns still Gothic in detail, its luminous cupola, and its two façades profusely covered with relief (178). It was designed by Pedro de Arrieta, the most famous architect of the period.[15] The church of the convent for Indian noblewomen, Corpus Christi,

[14] The façade of the Tercer Orden can be seen in one of Sylvester Baxter's illustrations for *Spanish-Colonial Architecture in Mexico*; the destruction had still not been completed in his day.

[15] Berlin, "Three Master Architects in New Spain," *Hispanic American Historical Review*, 27 (1947), 375–383.

[16] See Josefina Muriel de la Torre, "El convento de Corpus Christi," *Anales del Instituto de Investigaciones Estéticas*, 7 (1941), 10–57. See also Berlin, "El arquitecto Pedro de Arrieta," *Boletín del Archivo General de la Nación*, 16 (1945), 73–94; Berlin, "Three Master Architects," pp. 375–383.

181. Façade, church of La Soledad, Oaxaca.

182. Virgen de la Soledad. Façade, church of La Soledad, Oaxaca.

Agustín reproduces the façade of its older brother in Mexico City, relief and all; the sculpture is more realistic in scale, if less expressive. The masterpiece of this rich Baroque style is the church of La Soledad, a masterpiece unique in itself which belongs to no group or school (181). It dates from 1695, and was endowed by Don Pedro de Otálora, whose portrait appears on the portal—a memorial imperishable and deserved. The immense façade is spread out like a screen, like the façade of the University of Oñate in Spain, and is covered with sculpture of a high order (182). When we enter the church and see the decoration which covers the vault of the presbytery—as rich as anything in Oaxaca or Puebla—we realize that this church, like so many others, has suffered from a lapse of human taste.

The whole thing should have been decorated in this way.

In the state of Jalisco also are examples of this style, especially in its delightful capital, Guadalajara. The church of Santa Mónica, which dates from the beginning of the eighteenth century, follows the Spanish Baroque of the preceding period, yet its doorways and windows are richly decorated with twisted columns and the Hapsburg coat of arms (183). The figure of St. Christopher on the corner of the building seems like a medieval survival (184). The same motif appears on the church of Jesús María, although that is more consistent in its sober Baroque, as is that of Santa María de Gracia.

Outside Guadalajara developed a particularly rich

183. Portal, convent church of Santa Mónica,
Guadalajara, Jalisco.

184. St. Christopher. Convent church of
Santa Mónica, Guadalajara, Jalisco.

185. Façade, church of Santa Cruz de las Flores, Santa Cruz, Jalisco.

Baroque type of decorative sculpture, which should not be overlooked. The prototype seems to have been the ruined church of Santa Cruz de las Flores, which dates between 1692 and 1712, and whose remains are extremely interesting (185). Inside the church of Tlaquepaque is a first-class doorway, and the façade of the church of Santa Anita, of 1732, suggests that there must have been many examples of this rich stucco relief, which was perhaps inspired by the splendid pottery of the region.

Combined with popular art or, more precisely, with popular imitations of Baroque style, we find around Texcoco many churches which fall within the manner we are considering.[17] All the chapels around that old city have this decoration in stucco relief, more or less opulent, more or less popular, but always delightful. I mention here the more important of them, even though some actually date from the following period. First of all, the chapel of San Antonio, with its relief figures of children in rich foliate patterns, has a delightful popular flavor (186). The inscription which states that Padre Gante held his first school in this chapel is ridiculous. I do not know whether there may have been a primitive chapel on this site, where the worthy Franciscan might have carried on his admirable work, but I am perfectly sure that the present chapel dates from the late seventeenth or early eighteenth century. The church of La Concepción, the much altered chapel of the Molino de Flores, the very elaborate chapel of Tlaichiapan, dating from 1788, and many others are in this mood, including the famous "arcadas reales" of Papalotla, which we have already discussed.

The Mercedarian friars were very fond of this luxuriant Baroque decoration, as we can see from the examples they have left us. Only the cloister of the monastery remains in Mexico City, but this serves to describe the style (187). If the lower arcade, dating from mid-seventeenth century, is still sober, the upper cloister, built at the turn of the century, is the richest in the whole city—even richer than the cloister of San Francisco, which still survives hidden in a modern building on the Calle de Gante. It is designed with double arches in relation to the lower arcade, in the Mudejar manner, and the whole thing is covered with relief ornament—the profile of the arches carved in

[17] Raul Flores Guerrero, "El barroco popular de Texcoco," *Anales del Instituto de Investigaciones Estéticas,* 24 (1956), 35–51.

186. Façade, chapel of San Antonio, Texcoco, México.

diamond points—which makes a very rich effect. Their monastery in Puebla approaches it in luxury, though little remains of it. The church is modern, with its masonry façade and relief in white stone, but to the right stands the façade of the old monastery, very rich in stucco relief. It should be compared to the corresponding decoration on the monastery of Santo Domingo near by, from which it perhaps derives, since it is technically more perfect. The façade of the church of La

187. Cloister, monastery of La Merced, Mexico City.

Merced in Guadalajara shows a certain richness; but still more elaborate is the Mercedarian church in Atlixco, overflowing with relief and almost out of control in its Baroque exuberance (188). In the town of Quecholac, in the state of Puebla, the ruins of an admirable church may be seen; it is dated 1753 and is said to have been Mercedarian, though the insignia of the Order does not appear anywhere. The decoration is so superbly rich—though not without some indigenous flavor—that we may take it as a perfect example of the Baroque.

Durango's Cathedral, dating between 1695 and 1713, is quite solemn and serene. The decoration is in rich Baroque style, using twisted columns ornamented with reliefs. Over the façade is a beautiful weathervane, a cross of wrought iron, with its cock and all, like lace. The side doors, which are also richly decorated, are perhaps later, since incipient estípites appear. The decoration of the spacious interior is modern. The sacristy has very elegant cupboards and a good collection of paintings and works of art. The choir stalls much resemble those of San Agustín of Mexico City, which are now in the Escuela Preparatoria.

The Cathedral of Chihuahua, begun in 1726, shows

some characteristics of the rich Baroque style. There is a portal with columns and niches; there are two slender towers, and a dome with exterior ribs set on a drum. The side doors are still richer, with delightful popular detail, and the interior, a nave with two aisles, is also quite rich.[18]

Exuberant Baroque

By this term we designate a style which bursts all bounds in search of a lavishness of ornament which throws the others into the shade. This ornament still respects the architectonic structure; it is content to be decoration, but it covers over every space that is left free with reliefs in stucco, in plaster, or whatever will serve. Sometimes the relief is white or cream-colored with gold fillets, often it is frankly polychrome, in a prodigal luxury and extravagant fantasy which overwhelm us.

I do not know whether it is correct to say that Puebla, that Baroque and Mudejar city *par excellence,* is the cradle of this decorative art in New Spain. What is certainly true is that we find there the oldest examples of it, and that we know from documents that the workmen who made such decoration in other places, such as Oaxaca, came from there. The trajectory of this Baroque decoration in Puebla seems to begin in San Ildefonso, to continue in San Cristóbal (180), and to reach its climax in the Capilla del Rosario.

The Capilla del Rosario of the church of Santo Domingo in Puebla is indeed the masterpiece of this style (189). The year 1690 is given by the historians as the terminal date of this monument; it should be read as the date of a miracle in our colonial architecture.[19] This Rosary Chapel is the climax of a type of church which represents the Mexican mood of that time in an extraordinary way. They say it was not built by anyone of wealth and power, but from offerings of the pearl divers to the Virgin of the Rosary, their patron saint, and from contributions of the confraternities. With the profit from the jewels this little miracle was achieved. Here for the first time in the history of our country we

188. Façade (detail), monastery church of La Merced, Atlixco, Puebla.

can see the life of the nation embodied in unique form in a plastic creation. For the Catholic, for the historian, for the artist, the greatest marvels are assembled here. With a little imagination we can reconstruct the mood of those times, with all its intensity and religious fer-

[18] See Francisco de la Maza, "La catedral de Chihuahua," *Anales del Instituto de Investigaciones Estéticas,* 30 (1961), 21–38.

[19] *Octava maravilla del Nuevo Mundo en la gran capilla del Rosario.* See also José V. Medel M., *The Chapel of the Rosary;* Francisco de la Maza, "La decoración simbólica de la Capilla del Rosario de Puebla," *Anales del Instituto de Investigaciones Estéticas,* 23 (1955), 5–29; Toussaint, *Paseos coloniales,* pp. 137–139.

189. Rosary chapel, monastery church of Santo Domingo, Puebla.

vor. When we visit the chapel in the early afternoon, while the light floods through the windows of the cupola, our spirits soar free within its compass, and we are transported to those days at the end of the seventeenth century when multitudes gathered in the churches to participate in the splendid ceremonies. That dome richly decorated with saints, that interior embroidered in gold, that high altar where the Virgin seems to have mounted a throne such as she will have in Paradise,[20] the priests richly vested in precious silks and gold embroidery, the clouds of incense, the sacred singing from the little choir loft—We imagine the worshipper on his knees, his heart exhausted, his spirit open, infinitely aspiring; his eyes are fixed on the priests, but emotion overwhelms him; he lifts his face, looks at the tabernacle whose twisted columns seem to tremble, and finally in tears, raises his eyes to contemplate the marvellous cupola, where the saints are, all golden, like a simulacrum of heaven, amid the clouds of incense and the fervor which the whole ceremony gives off.

Even in an artificial picture like this, one can feel the identification of the religious life of the people with their art. Never has there been a more intimate union between the art and the life of a people than at this time. To find anything like it, we have to go back to the Gothic period, when the people built those prodigious cathedrals to nourish their religious spirit, or to the catacombs which the early Christians painted.

This exuberant Baroque moved out in various directions from Puebla, where it may have originated, and produced a series of interiors less magnificent perhaps, but in the same mood. First it went to Oaxaca, where the interior of the church of Santo Domingo was decorated, according to the documents, by craftsmen from Puebla. It is hard to appraise this work, because it has been so stupidly restored and repainted that one can just glimpse what it was originally. Nevertheless it is one of the most splendid interiors to be found in New Spain; it is like an Italian church, both in the amplitude of its form and in the magnificence of detail. There are parts of exceptional beauty: the vault under the choir loft, which is decorated with the tree of Jesse (190), and the figures in the round of famous Dominicans along the lower walls of the nave, the vault over

190. Tree of Jesse (detail). Painted and gilded stucco. Choir vault, monastery church of Santo Domingo, Oaxaca.

the choir—very high, with medallions of saints which diminish as they rise—and above all the vault (not a dome, as it has sometimes been called) over the crossing of the church, with its marvellous polychrome reliefs. The Capilla del Rosario adjoining the church is of later date; it is still Baroque, but was made in the first third of the eighteenth century, and has the quality of popular art.

Southeast of Oaxaca we find the Capilla del Santo Cristo de Tlacolula (191). It is a small version of the Capilla del Rosario in Puebla. Ironwork, which we have already mentioned, completes this magnificent work of art (157). Some of its details have a Classical look.[21]

There are two masterpieces of this style on the outskirts of Puebla: San Francisco Acatepec and Santa

[20] It was the work of Maestro Francisco Pinto.
[21] See Antonio Cortés and Genero García, *Iglesia de Santo Domingo en la ciudad de Oaxaca y Capilla del Santo Cristo en Tlacolula,* for excellent plates.

191. Chapel of El Santo Cristo, Dominican monastery, Tlacolula, Oaxaca.

María Tonantzintla. The exterior of the little church of Acatepec is a special kind of Baroque, completely covered with glazed tiles, *azulejos,* as they are called, some of which were certainly made expressly for this façade (192). The whole thing is extraordinary: it seems like a little china church which should be preserved under a glass bell. The interior was equally extraordinary (193, 194); in spite of its miniature proportions, it had a quality of grandeur.[22] Here the relief decoration of the Capilla del Rosario was interpreted in more popular form, as if it had been designed by European craftsmen but executed by workmen of the people. The exact date of this church is not known; hypothetically one can set it about 1730. The church of Santa María Tonantzintla, about one kilometer beyond San Francisco Acatepec, presents a simple façade in the Puebla style, faced with a combination of glazed and unglazed tile. Its interior, cruciform like that of Acatepec, is fantastic: the

whole thing is so covered over with relief ornament that it seems to be a miraculous grotto, or the sanctuary of some god (195). Studied in detail this church proves to be perhaps the most fascinating of them all. All the sculpture in relief, all the ornament which covers it and makes it a magnificent example of Puebla Baroque, is the work of Indians. Neither the Capilla del Rosario, nor the churches in Oaxaca, nor even San Francisco Acatepec has the Indian flavor of this church: the angels which abound in the decoration are little Indians, as if the Indians knew no other type of beauty to represent (196). Unfortunately this interior has lately been repainted and the original quality is gone, yet the magnificence of the ensemble and the ingenuous spirit of the detail are still eloquent.[23]

[22] The interior of this church was destroyed by arson on New Year's Eve, 1939; it has now been fully restored.
[23] See Pedro Mario Rojas Rodríguez, *Tonantzintla.*

192. Façade, church of San Francisco, Acatepec, Puebla.

193. Chancel. Painted and gilded stucco; painted and gilded wood; oil on canvas. Church of San Francisco, Acatepec, Puebla.

194. Charity (detail of decoration). Painted and gilded stucco. Nave, church of San Francisco, Acatepec, Puebla.

195. Chancel and dome. Painted and gilded stucco;
painted and gilded wood. Church of Santa María,
Tonantzintla, Puebla.

196. Decoration on pendentive (detail).
Painted and gilded stucco. Nave, church of
Santa María, Tonantzintla, Puebla.

197. Camarín of the Virgin. Sanctuary of Ocotlán, Tlaxcala.

199. Retable. Polychrome and gilded wood. Camarín of the Virgin of Loreto, church of San Felipe Neri, San Miguel Allende, Guanajuato.

Puebla Baroque decoration also moved into Tlaxcala, where we find so splendid an example as the *camarín* of the Virgin in the Sanctuary of Ocotlán (197). (The *camarín* is a special sacristy, a kind of dressing room, for a sacred image.) This interior differs from the customary Puebla formula in using the ornate twisted columns which we associate more with Mexico City.

Two other examples of exuberant Baroque interiors which resemble the work done in Puebla, though perhaps not derived from it, are the famous *camarines* of Tepotzotlán, dating from mid-eighteenth century (198), and that of San Miguel Allende, of the early eighteenth century (199). Each of these is covered by a vault on crossing arches, a characteristic Mudejar form.[24]

To conclude this report on Baroque buildings—cer-

tainly incomplete, but still abounding in magnificent examples—we must consider one more masterpiece: the Cathedral of Zacatecas. Its great façade, shaped like a shield, is related to the Baroque style of Jalisco, with twisted columns and a rose window in the center. Then the whole thing is covered with rich relief, in stone, a little flattened, like plaster decoration (200). Its date is 1752; it was the parish church before the bishopric of Zacatecas was established. One of the towers dates from the colonial period; the other was copied later so perfectly that both appear original.[25]

[24] See Angulo Íñiguez, "The Mudejar Style in Mexican Architecture," *Ars Islamica*, 2 (1935), 225–230.

[25] See Francisco de la Maza, "El arte en la ciudad de Nuestra Señora de los Zacatecas," *México en el arte*, 7 (1949), 5–16; José R. Benítez, *Las catedrales de Oaxaca, Morelia y Zacatecas*.

198. Camarín of the Virgin of Loreto, church of San Martín (Museo Nacional del Virreinato), Tepotzotlán, México.

200. Upper façade, Cathedral of Zacatecas.

Chapter Ten

BAROQUE SCULPTURE

Retables

MUCH THAT IS RELEVANT to the sculpture of this period will be found in the preceding chapter, for since the Baroque style is essentially sculptural, it is impossible to separate the architecture from its sculptured ornament.

We shall limit ourselves here, in consequence, to a study of the altarpieces of the period and the craftsmen who carved them. It is interesting to define the typical Baroque altarpiece and to compare it with the Renaissance type which preceded it and with what was to come later, the Churrigueresque. The Renaissance retables were constructed, as we have said, with columns, the classic Renaissance column with various ornaments on its shaft, or a special column we call *abalaustrada*, because it resembles a turned baluster (146). The Baroque retables also employ the complete architectural order, but the column, for all its Classical position, takes a special form: a heavy moulding is twisted around the shaft, its curve describing a helicoid, or spiral (201). This twisted column is called a salamonic column. The whole apparatus is covered with ornament, especially the columns, which are twined with vines and bunches of grapes (202). The keystones of

the arches, the brackets on which the columns rest, or the ornament in the intercolumnal space is made up of cherubs or birds devouring their own breasts. As for the Churrigueresque retable, it preserves only an echo of the classic orders; the perpendicular member is no longer a column but an estípite, that is, a square or rectangular pier of broken profile which is always larger at the middle than at the base (323). The entablatures are broken, indented or protruding, raised or lowered, according to the whim or the madness of the artist, and the whole effect is one of real vertigo.

There are countless examples of such Baroque retables as we have described (202). Some of the more important are the one in the Franciscan church at Tlalmanalco, a magnificent work of art; those decorating the church of San Agustín in Oaxaca; that of the Tercer Orden in Tlaxcala; one in the church at Ozumba (203), in the state of Mexico; and three which fill the Capilla de los Ángeles in the Cathedral in Mexico City, which date from early in the eighteenth century (204).

Reliefs and Figure Sculpture

Baroque architecture constantly employs sculpture, both reliefs and figures in the round, for the decoration

201. Main Altarpiece (detail). Polychrome and gilded wood. Church of the Augustinian monastery, Metztitlán, Hidalgo.

of buildings. All over the Republic are church façades ornamented with reliefs and statues. In Mexico City we might note first the two reliefs of the church of La Encarnación; the figures of the angels indicate that they are contemporary with the painting of Baltasar de Echave Orio. Over the door of the church of San Agustín, which is now the National Library, is a great relief representing St. Augustine sheltering a crowd of people under his cloak (205). We have already mentioned the reliefs of the façade of La Soledad in Oaxaca (181), and the relief over the portal of the church of San Agustín there, a smaller and less interesting copy of the one in Mexico City. In Puebla are many façade reliefs, like those we have mentioned on San Cristóbal (180). Over the doorway of the Colegio de San Pedro are reliefs and coats of arms made by Diego de Folco, according to a contract of August 8, 1648.[1] On the Cathedral of Puebla are reliefs and statues carved in a white stone known as *piedra de Villerías,* in strong contrast to the grey of the masonry. The four statues of the Portada del Perdón were made in 1662 by Juan de Sole González, master sculptor. While we are speaking of this church we might mention the sculpture inside which dates from this period. The four angels on the pendentives of the dome, excellent work in high relief, were made by Pedro García Ferrer, the famous artist who was at once architect, sculptor and painter. The tabernacle designed by García Ferrer was executed by Diego de Cárcamo, and the *Altar de los Reyes* was executed by Lucas Méndez in 1649, after a design by the famous Spanish sculptor, Martínez Montañés (379).

The churches of Mexico City also were decorated with sculpture. Among these are the figures of the principal portal of the Cathedral, a *St. Peter* signed by Miguel Jiménez in 1687, and a *St. Paul* by Nicolás Jiménez, of the same year. We do not know whether the magnificent marble reliefs which decorate the three portals of the façade were made by the same sculptors, but I can affirm that the work is excellent (206). On the church of San Bernardo, dedicated in 1696, two figures appear: one of *St. Bernard,* and the other of *The Virgin of Guadalupe,* both carved in that yellowish and almost translucent marble called *tecali,* after the town in the state of Puebla where it is quarried. The church of Las Capuchinas no longer exists, but we know from old photographs that there were reliefs over its two portals, one of them showing *The Crucifixion of St. Philip of Jesus.*

[1] Enrique A. Cervantes, "Bosquejo del desarrollo de la ciudad de Puebla," *Universidad,* 4 (diciembre, 1937), 11–15; 5 (enero, 1938), 14–29.

202. Main altarpiece. Polychrome and gilded wood. Monastery church of Santo Domingo, Puebla.

203. Main altarpiece. Polychrome and gilded wood. Church of the Franciscan monastery, Ozumba, México.

204. Archangel Gabriel. Polychrome and gilded wood. Capilla de los Angeles, Cathedral of Mexico.

205. St. Augustine as Protector. Façade, monastery church of San Agustín (Biblioteca Nacional), Mexico City.

206. Assumption of the Virgin. Façade, Cathedral of Mexico.

Sometimes there are isolated reliefs inside the churches: in San Bernardo a *Holy Family,* and in San Lorenzo an *Annunciation* (207). In Yanhuitlán, in the Mixteca Alta, there is such a relief in the sacristy of the Dominican church: it is a *Descent from the Cross* (208), a masterpiece, with figures somewhat over life size, painted, just as Padre Burgoa describes it in his chronicle.[2]

Possibly some of the sculpture in Querétaro should be dated in this period, such as the decoration of the façade and the cloister of San Agustín (258), or the relief on the façade of the church of San Francisco, among others. In Guadalajara we think at once of the great figure of *St. Christopher* in its niche at the corner of the church of Santa Mónica (184). But this sculp-

ture, so large in scale, with its ingenuous pose and simple drapery, seems earlier by a century than the date appropriate to a sculpture on a building of the early eighteenth century. The archaic quality of the figure, in contrast to the Baroque style of its pedestal, suggests that we have to do with a much older sculpture placed on the church when it was built.

Statues of donors were also made in stone or wood for churches and convents. Examples are that of Don Melchor de Covarrubias for the Jesuit College in Puebla, those of Cerón Zapata and of Bishop Santa Cruz for the church of Santa Mónica in the same city, that of Licenciado Buenaventura Medina Picazo for his chapel in the church of La Regina in Mexico City, that of Don Pedro Ruiz de Ahumada, the benefactor of Tepotzotlán (209), and others. These portraits are not of great worth, and often the priests, friars, or nuns to whose establishments they belong, wishing to brighten them up, have succeeded rather in destroying the venerable appearance of antiquity.[3]

For obvious reasons funereal sculpture did not achieve in Mexico the splendor it had in Spain.

Choir Stalls

The choir stalls made in this period offer decorative sculpture of the first importance. The most famous of these, which should be considered one of the most impressive pieces of sculpture in Mexico, is the choir of the church of San Agustín in Mexico City, which is preserved almost complete in the Salón de Actos of the Escuela Nacional Preparatoria of the National University (210). It is made up of many relief panels representing Bible stories (211), and should be dated between 1687, when the church suffered a severe fire, and 1690, when the rebuilding was completed, or within a few years after that. It was the work of Salvador de Ocampo.[4] Next in importance are the stalls which may still be seen in the choir of the Cathedral of Mexico (212, 224); these were the work of Juan de Rojas,

[2] Francisco de Burgoa, *Geográfica descripción,* I, 291–295.

[3] Manuel Toussaint, "La escultura funeraria en la Nueva España," *Anales del Instituto de Investigaciones Estéticas,* 11 (1944), 41–58.

[4] Rafael García Granados, *Sillería del coro de la antigua iglesia de San Agustín.* This monograph, published by the Instituto de Investigaciones Estéticas of the National University, reproduces all the known panels of this magnificent work of art. See also Heinrich Berlin's publication "Salvador de Ocampo: A Mexican Sculptor," *The Americas,* 4 (1948), 415–428, 510–518.

207. Annunciation. Gilded stone. Monastery church of San Lorenzo, Mexico City.

208. *(Right, above)* Descent from the Cross. Painted wood. Sacristy, church of the Dominican monastery, Yanhuitlán, Oaxaca.

209. Don Pedro Ruiz de Ahumada. Polychrome wood. Seminario de San Martín. (Museo Nacional del Virreinato), Tepotzotlán, México.

210. Choir stalls from the monastery church of San Agustín. Wood. Escuela Nacional Preparatoria, Mexico City.

211. God Creating the Sun and Moon. Choir stall from San Agustín. Wood. Escuela Nacional Preparatoria, Mexico City.

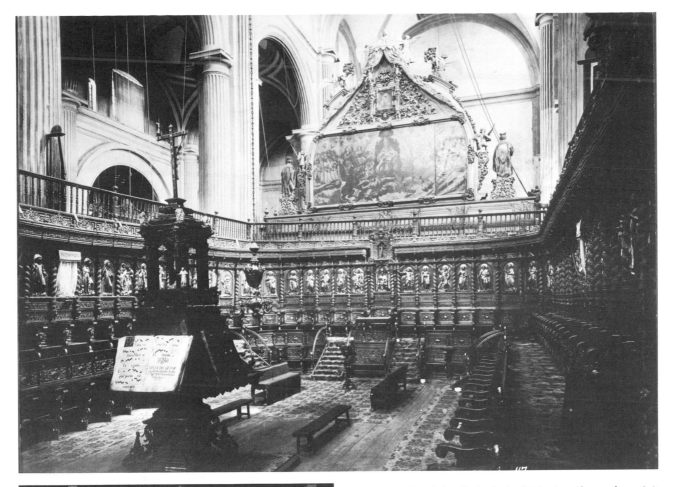

212. Choir of the Cathedral of Mexico (burned, 1967). Gilded wood.

213. Choir of the Cathedral of Mexico (detail; burned, 1967). Gilded wood.

214. Caryatid on a retable. Unpainted wood. Church of the Franciscan monastery, Quecholac, Puebla.

the making of these stalls, in which four master wood carvers took part: Juan de Rojas, who won it, Andrés de Roa, Tomás Juárez, and Joaquín Rendón. Since these sculptors must have been working in the second half of the seventeenth century, it is not unreasonable to suppose that some of them worked on the choir of San Agustín also.[6]

Parts of the Baroque choir of the Franciscan monastery at Xochimilco have been preserved. The choir of the Cathedral of Puebla, which is not properly a work of sculpture but of cabinetmaking, was directed by the master craftsman Pedro Muñoz between 1719 and 1722; it is of fine inlaid woods, in patterns deriving from the Mudejar tradition.

Fragments preserved from the choir stalls of the monastery of San Fernando are now in the Basilica of Guadalupe.

We should also mention the choir of the Cathedral of Durango, which is similar to that of San Agustín in its ornament.

Gilding and Estofado

This Baroque sculpture falls into various categories which are in fact the continuation of earlier types. On the one hand there was decorative sculpture in stone to ornament the buildings, on the other hand, the great retables to decorate the interior of the churches. There were also figures of saints and of Christ which might be part of the retable, or might stand alone on an altar or even in a private house. Since the great tradition of Baroque sculpture begins in this period, certain technical information should be given here.

Altarpieces were first carved of wood and left unfinished, *"en blanco"* (214); the kind of wood is specified in the contract. The gilder, or *dorador,* came next: after covering the carved wood with a thin coat of gesso to smooth out any roughness, he laid on a very fine bole, or *sisa,* which was red. Over this the gold was applied in genuine gold leaf, beaten out very thin by the goldbeater, the *batihoja.* When the gold leaf had adhered, it was burnished with a piece of agate. It is absurd to speak of retables *dorados a fuego;* the melting point of gold is so high that wood to which it was applied would certainly be burned: only metals can be fire-gilded.

For figure sculpture the technique is different. The

carved in 1696, and they are a good example of Baroque style.[5] They have twisted columns and high-relief panels with figures of saints, which were gilded later (213); some of the sculpture is of high quality. The Cabildo of the Cathedral held a competition for

[5] Cervantes, *Catedral metropolitana; sillería del coro.*
[6] See Berlin, "Salvador de Ocampo," *The Americas,* 1 (1948), pp. 420–428.

sculptor works in the same way *on blanco*, and then the statue also is covered with its coating of gesso, followed by the red bole, and the whole thing is gilded, except for the head and hands (215). Over the gold leaf which covers the robes designs are incised with a punch, in imitation of the embroidery and pattern of the fabric; then paint is applied over the gold, to imitate cloth like brocade. This technique is called *estofado,* a term which is correctly applied only when the gold leaf appears continuously under the color. Undoubtedly the term *estofado* has a French origin, related to the word *étoffe,* cloth. The face and hands are treated differently: instead of being gilded, they are covered with a paint imitating the color of flesh; this finish is called *encarnación.* The paint used for the flesh may be matte or glossy, according to whether it is left without polish, or burnished in a special way. This method of finishing wood sculpture goes back to the sixteenth century. It spread all over America; the most important centers of such work were New Spain, Quito, and Guatemala.

The Artists

I shall now give what further information I have on sculptors of this period. The following data come from the Archivo de los Alcaldes Ordinarios y Corregidores de México. Salvador de Ocampo, *maestro de escultor,* master sculptor, was active between 1699 and 1722.[7] The *maestro* Juan de Rojas, already mentioned, was still working in 1709.[8] Pedro Nolasco de Reina, master sculptor, made an appraisal in 1711, and Tomás Juárez, sculptor, whom we have also mentioned, made one in 1720. Antonio de Roa y Velasco, master sculptor, made an appraisal in 1704. Undoubtedly this Antonio de Roa would have been a relative, perhaps a son, of Andrés de Roa, who made the monument for the Cathedral of Mexico in the year 1698.[9] In 1645 we

215. St. Clare, from a retable. Polychrome and gilded wood. Chapel of the Virgen de Aránzazu, Guadalajara, Jalisco.

find Don Matías Juárez, master sculptor and painter, a mestizo; he is perhaps related to Tomás Juárez, who was active from 1695, when he competed for the choir of the Cathedral of Mexico, until 1721, when, as we have seen, he appraised some sculpture.[10]

The sculptors of Puebla are Pedro Maldonado, who made the retable of the church of Santo Domingo (202) between 1688 and 1690;[11] Laureano Ramírez, who had carved a retable of St. Francis Xavier for the church of the Colegio de San Pedro y San Pablo, and

[7] See also Berlin, "Salvador de Ocampo," pp. 415–428, 510–518; Berlin, "Dos estudios mexicanos: artistas y milagros; un tenebrario de Pedro Maldonado," *Anales del Instituto de Arte Americano e Investigaciones Estéticas,* 15 (1962), 109–124.

[8] Berlin, "Salvador de Ocampo," *ibid.,* pp. 510–518; Berlin, "Dos estudios mexicanos," *ibid.,* 119–124.

[9] See Berlin, "Artífices de la catedral de México," *Anales del Instituto de Investigaciones Estéticas,* 11 (1944), 19–39.

[10] On Tomás Xuárez, see Berlin, "Salvador de Ocampo," pp. 510–518; Berlin, "Artífices," pp. 38–39.

[11] The contract for this retable was published by Enrique A. Cervantes, "El colateral de Santo Domingo en la ciudad de Puebla," *Revista mexicana de estudios históricos,* 2 (1928), 10–17. See also Berlin, "Dos estudios mexicanos," pp. 119–124; Berlin, "Salvador de Ocampo," 419–420.

another artist who is spoken of by the name of Lucas, "the one from the quarter of Santa Ana."[12] The chroniclers refer to a sculptor of Puebla at this time who made the figure of St. Joseph in the church of San José, and that of the Virgin of the Rosary, but without giving his name. They say that he was brought before the Inquisition, and that he left his workshops with all his work to a pupil named Fernández de Sandrea or Sandreda, who continued the work his master had undertaken. Another sculptor of this period is Francisco López, who carved the statues for the retable of the parish church of Taxco (the church which preceded the present one). The retable for this church had been carved *en blanco* by a *maestro* Cayetano for the sum of 1,540 pesos, and later was gilded by the *maestro* Francisco Perea, for 2,400 pesos; it was inaugurated in 1728.

[12] Laureano Ramírez and Lucas are also named in the above contract.

Sculptors in Mexico City: Juan de Rojas, choir of the Cathedral of Mexico, 1695–1709; Andrés de Roa, monument, 1698; Tomás Juárez, 1695, choir, 1720; Joaquín Rendón, 1695, choir; Los Ximénez, Cathedral of Mexico; Laureano Ramírez, 1688–1690; Lucas, the one from the quarter of Santa Ana, 1688–1690; Matías Xuárez, mestizo, 1645.

Sculptors in Guadalajara: Gandara, 1619–1625; Matías de la Cerda, 1619–1625.

Sculptors in Puebla: Juan de Sole González, 1662; Lucas Méndez, 1649; Diego de Cárcamo; Pedro Maldonado, retable of Santo Domingo, 1688–1690; Francisco Pinto, Capilla del Rosario, 1690; Pedro García Ferrer; Laureano Ramírez, retable of St. Francis Xavier, in the church of the Colegio de San Pedro y San Pablo.

Sculptors in Querétaro: Maestro Francisco Martínez, 1606; Padre Fray Sebastián Gallegos, 1630.

Sculptors in Taxco: Pedro de Torrejón, 1634–1637.

Chapter Eleven

BAROQUE PAINTING

IN MEXICO CITY

The Beginning of the Pictorial Baroque

AROQUE ARCHITECTURE, so successful in expressing the spirit of the Colony, demands a special sort of painting consonant with the spirit of the ensemble. This subjugation of painting to the other forms of art means that in a certain sense it deteriorates: it must not be so strong in itself as to distract the attention of the spectator. In the total spectacle painting is just one of the actors playing its part in harmony with the others, and always subdued by them.

The moment was propitious for this. The mixture of foreign influences had produced an art which was not dominated by either the luminous serenity of the Renaissance or that struggle for dramatic effects which dims other esthetic interests. So the artists produced what their understanding allowed them to, and this production must be judged on its own merits. But as part of the monumental complex these paintings are always right. A moment was to come when the adaptation of painting to the Baroque interior was so perfect that it united with the other elements in a truly homogeneous artistic ensemble, and by so doing perhaps realized itself most fully. But this occurred at the end

of the period we are now studying, when the great Baroque interiors were achieved.

The Pupils of Sebastián de Arteaga

The term "pupil" is used here not in the strict sense, but to indicate the influence of the master on the younger painters.

José Juárez

The most important follower of Arteaga seems to have been José Juárez. He was the son of the painter Luis Juárez, whom we have already studied, and must have been born between 1615 and 1620, since in 1639 he was still a minor. Between 1639 and 1641 he married Doña Isabel de Contreras. They had a daughter, Antonia, who in 1659 married Antonio Rodríguez, painter, who was certainly a pupil of José Juárez. The sons of this marriage were the well-known painters Juan and Nicolás Rodríguez Juárez, who complete the dynasty begun at the end of the sixteenth century by Luis Juárez. We don't know when José Juárez died, but it seems likely from the dates of his paintings that it was in the decade after 1660.

216. José Juárez. The Sainted Children Justo and Pastor. Oil. 3.80 x 2.91 m.
Pinacoteca Virreinal, Mexico City.

The *oeuvre* of José Juárez is much smaller than that of his father, but he was a more powerful painter. He adopted the vigorous chiaroscuro of his master, Arteaga, though it was not his principal interest.

We find two manners in the paintings of this artist: one is soft in key with bright colors, the other is more somber, with dark backgrounds, and profoundly dramatic. For an example of the first manner we might first look at *The Holy Family* of 1655, which is in the Academia de Bellas Artes in Puebla, attributed to Rubens. The coloring is brilliant, reminiscent of the period of Echave, but there is more movement—in the little St. John who almost grabs at the Child Jesus, for instance. In this painting delightful Mexican details appear: a woven belt just like those used by the Indians of Mexico, and a basket of native fruit.

In this same manner is a *Virgin Investing St. Ildephonsus,* a powerful painting originally in the sacristy of Santo Domingo in Mexico City. The three paintings by Juárez in the Galerías de Pintura are also in this style. *The Adoration of the Magi,* dated 1655, shows an almost excessive influence of Arteaga in the hard profiles created by exaggerated chiaroscuro, but its composition is able and the color brilliant. The same thing is true of *The Apparition of the Virgin to St. Francis,* with its group of angels painted in a truly celestial way, and also of his masterpiece, the large painting representing *St. Justus and St. Pastor* (216). In the Franciscan church in Texcoco is a big painting of *The Last Supper* which has been attributed to José Juárez; if my attribution is correct, it belongs with this group.

The second manner of José Juárez is exemplified by three paintings: the large *St. Lawrence* which hangs in the library of the Escuela de Artes Plásticas (217), the lunette representing *The Crucifixion* in the church of La Profesa in Mexico City, and an *Adoration of the Shepherds* in the Academia of Puebla.

Three other paintings attributed to José Juárez are the great canvases decorating the stairwell of the Escuela de Artes Plásticas. They represent *Miracles of Blessed Salvator of Horta,* and came from the stairway leading to the Sala de Profundis in the monastery of San Francisco in Mexico City. If they are by José Juárez they show that he, like his contemporaries, knew how to absorb foreign influences, for they derive directly from Rubens. Another painting is in the Museo Nacional de México; it represents *The Death of St. Joseph* and is dated 1656.

217. José Juárez. Martyrdom of St. Lawrence. Oil. 5 x 3.29 m. Library of the Escuela de Artes Plásticas, Mexico City.

A further group of works by José Juárez is known only from literary references. Couto lists a *Child Jesus with St. John the Baptist* in the *portería* of the monastery of San Diego, signed and dated 1642;[1] in La Profesa, a *St. Alexis,* along with the *St. Justus and St.*

[1] José Bernardo Couto, *Diálogo sobre la historia de la pintura en México,* p. 42.

227

218. Pedro Ramírez. Christ Waited upon by Angels (detail). Oil. 5 x 3.50 m. Church of San Miguel, Mexico City.

Cross, St. Lawrence Giving Alms, Ananias Turning to St. Paul, St. Peter Curing the Paralytic, and *The Martyrdom of St. Sebastian.*[3] These attributions should not be taken too seriously, for we all know that critics may easily be mistaken, especially long ago when any sort of evidence was accepted.

In any case we do have enough authentic works by José Juárez to be able to give a specific description of his style. He is first of all a painter; the story doesn't matter to him. Where Echave would relate in detail just how the martyrdom of those poor little boys Justus and Pastor took place, for José Juárez it is simply a pictorial pretext: two figures of boys in a harmonious grey interior with angels marvellously drawn in silhouette flying around them and bringing the crowns of martyrdom. The anecdote, the narrative, and even the sentiment, remain peripheral. In front of this picture our experience is esthetic, it is a sensuous appreciation of painting itself.

Thus one can say that all the resources of the artist, his incomparable drawing, his understanding of perspective and composition, his color, his mastery of all the possibilities, all of this was used—in surprising anticipation of the future—to give us the feeling of what pure painting is.[4]

Pedro Ramírez

Pedro Ramírez was active in Mexico in mid-eighteenth century. Unfortunately we know nothing of his life; his biography is purely artistic.

Couto says that there was a *Nativity* in the Academia painted by Pedro Ramírez, but it is no longer there. He observed similarities between this and the paintings which were in the sacristy of the church of La Merced in Mexico City.[5] Couto also notes that Ceán Bermúdez mentions an artist called Pedro Ramírez who worked in Seville in 1660, and Lucio adds that Viardo mentions an artist by the same name in his work on the Spanish museums.

Gestoso, in his *Diccionario,* says that Pedro Ramírez, a painter of Seville, died on December 3, 1664.[6] On

Pastor we have already mentioned, which is dated 1653, and *An Angel Appearing to St. Francis,* dated 1658 (Couto erroneously reads this as 1698). Revilla mentions a *Life of St. Theresa,* the property of Señor Antonio Gutiérrez Víctory.[2] Ramírez Aparicio lists in the monastery of San Francisco a *Finding of the True*

[2] Manuel Revilla, *El arte en México en la época antigua y durante el gobierno virreinal,* p. 78.

[3] Manuel Ramírez Aparicio, *Los conventos suprimidos en Méjico,* p. 351.

[4] See also Justino Fernández, "Rubens y José Juárez," *Anales del Instituto de Investigaciones Estéticas,* 10 (1943), 51–57.

[5] Couto, *Diálogo,* p. 31.

[6] José Gestoso y Pérez, *Ensayo de un diccionario de los artífices que florecieron en Sevilla,* II, 83.

219. Pedro Ramírez. Liberation of St. Peter. Oil. 2.37 x 2.02 m. Museo Nacional
del Virreinato, Tepotzotlán, México.

220. Baltasar de Echave y Rioja (the Younger).
Martyrdom of St. Peter Arbues. Oil. 2.95 x 2.09 m.
Pinacoteca Virreinal, Mexico City.

the other hand, in the book describing the funerary honors paid to Philip IV in Mexico City which we have already spoken of, Sariñana says that the catafalque—that complicated Baroque invention—was made by a Pedro Ramírez.[7] If this is the artist who painted the Mexican pictures—which is not unlikely since painters did this type of work—he is not the painter of Seville, since that one had died two years before.

Other paintings attributed to Pedro Ramírez are the following: in the Capilla de la Soledad in the Cathedral of Mexico, the paintings of the principal retable, repre-

senting *The Agony in the Garden, Ecce Homo, The Dead Christ, The Flagellation,* and *The Road to Calvary;* in the fifteenth Exposición de Bellas Artes, of 1871, a *Virgin of the Rosary,* the property of the engraver Campa.

In the Museo Nacional de Historia there is a portrait of *Bishop Juan Bohórquez,* signed and dated 1653. In the church of San Miguel in Mexico City there is a *Christ Waited upon by Angels,* signed and dated 1656 (218), and in the Museo de Guadalajara, a *Christ Tied to the Column,* dated 1658. His masterpiece, the *St. Peter Weeping,* was discovered by the writer in the building called the Obispado, in Atzcapotzalco, and originally attributed to Zurbarán. The scholar Moreno Villa, who also at first believed the painting to be by Zurbarán, later discovered the signature of Pedro Ramírez.[8]

From the *Liberation of St. Peter* (219) and the great canvas of *St. Michael* in Mexico City a clear conception of this artist can be formed. He is the very type of a Baroque painter. The influences he reveals are multiple: on the one hand there is the vigorous chiaroscuro which he learned from Arteaga, on the other, the magnificence of foliage and angels which he brings from Rubens, and again, a delicacy in the drapery of the Angel with St. Peter which recalls the refinement of Zurbarán's canvases. Pedro Ramírez is unquestionably the most Baroque of Mexican artists.

Baltasar de Echave y Rioja

As we have said, the fourth painter of the Echave family was Baltasar de Echave y Rioja. He was born in Mexico, where he was baptized on October 20, 1632. He married Doña Ana del Castillo. In 1665 he appraised some paintings, and a year later painted for the Inquisition in Mexico City a *Martyrdom of St. Peter Arbues* (220), which is now in the Galerías de Pintura.[9] It was painted and then repainted: first they gave him an engraving to copy, and agreed to pay one hundred pesos; he finished the work, but it did not please the Inquisitors, who refused to pay the sum agreed, only eighty pesos. The artist then completely repainted it, without reference to the engraving; the

---

[7] Isidro Sariñana, *Llanto del Occidente.*

[8] See Heinrich Berlin, "Pintura colonial mexicana en Guatemala," *Anales de la Sociedad de Geografía e Historia,* 26 (1952), 118–128.

[9] Archivo General de la Nación. Tomo *Inquisición,* No. 454.

Inquisitors, seeing that the picture had been painted over and looked better, agreed to pay him eighteen pesos more. In any case, his painting is simply a copy of the one by Murillo.

In the Galerías de Pintura there is also an *Entombment,* dated 1668; in the Capilla de San Pedro in the Cathedral of Mexico, five canvases represent *The Life of St. Theresa*; and in the sacristy of the Cathedral of Puebla are two great canvases, *The Triumph of the Church* and *The Triumph of Religion,* copied from Rubens.

Echave died at fifty, on January 14, 1682. He was living at that time on the street which led from San Francisco to the Colegio de las Doncellas. He was buried in San Francisco, having made no will—probably because he had nothing to leave.

Such is the work of the fourth Echave, one of the smallest *oeuvres* of any colonial painter. His two large pictures in the Galerías permit an accurate evaluation of his art. He is almost excessively Baroque: he doesn't care about drawing, or about form, but is after the effect. Such is *The Entombment,* a deeply moving picture; Gillet speaks of it as a powerful painting, noting the effect as of smoky torches—like some canvases of Caravaggio—and the crowded figures, as in an *Entombment* of the School of Mazzoni and Baragelli in Modena.[10] Certainly Echave y Rioja deserves a monograph.

Secondary Painters of the Late Eighteenth Century

It is impossible to review in any detail the minor artists of this period; there are too many of them. I shall note the most important figures rapidly, if only to suggest the fecund environment of Baroque painting.

Antonio de Alvarado worked at the end of the seventeenth century. He collaborated with José Rodríguez de Carnero to make the triumphal arch for the Conde de Paredes in 1680, according to Don Carlos de Sigüenza y Góngora.[11] He was still living in 1702, old and poor; he must have died soon after.

Francisco de Angulo is a considerable painter; there are two pictures by him on the high altar of the Chapel of San Miguel Nonoalco in Mexico City; *The Angel Appearing to St. Joachim* and *The Annunciation to St. Anne.* They are signed and dated 1687, and are substantial works. He may have been the son of Nicolás de Angulo, who was active twenty years before.

Nicolás de Angulo is mentioned by Padre Florencia

as one of the most famous artists of Mexico in 1666.[12]

Fray Bartolomé de Arenas testified in the inquiry about the crucifix called El Señor de Santa Teresa in 1679.[13]

Fray Diego Becerra, a Franciscan, took his vows in Puebla on January 6, 1640, and worked on various projects in New Spain. In Puebla, his birthplace, there were paintings by him in the monasteries of San Agustín and San Francisco. Other important pictures, in the *portería* and outside chapels of the Franciscan monastery in Mexico City, were painted in 1648.[14] Apparently the only paintings by him which have been preserved are those representing *The Life of St. Augustine* in the Augustinian monastery in Morelia; they are signed, and also recorded by Fray Matías de Escobar, who dates them in 1682.[15]

Juan Becerra made an appraisal in 1688. There is a painting of *St. John of the Cross* by him in the sacristy of the Carmelite monastery in Villa Obregón, D.F. It is a picture somber in color and vigorous in execution.

Nicolás Becerra was active at the end of the seventeenth century. Couto refers to a picture of *St. Luquecius* which used to be in the Hospital de Terceros, dated 1693.

José del Castillo seems to be the artist who was married in Puebla on April 28, 1686, to Inés de Ávila.[16] His paintings are said to have decorated the monastery of San Francisco there. A *Virgin of Bethlehem* in Taxco signed by him seems to be a copy of an Italian picture, and a similar painting hangs in the Galerías de Pintura. Another painting in a private collection, *The Virgin with St. Catherine and St. John the Baptist,* is equally Italianate in style.

Tomás Conrado is listed by Padre Florencia among those who gave their opinions on the canvas of the Virgin of Guadalupe in 1666.[17] I do not know whether

---

[10] Louis Gillet, "L'art dans l'Amérique Latine," in André Michel's *Histoire de l'art,* VIII, 1068.

[11] Carlos de Sigüenza y Góngora, *Teatro de virtudes políticas,* p. 39.

[12] Francisco de Florencia, *La estrella de el norte de México,* fol. 60.

[13] Alfonso Alberto de Velasco, *Renovación por si mismo de la soberana imagen de Christo Señor Nuestro crucificado, que llamas de Ytzimiquilpan.*

[14] Agustín de Vetancurt, *Chrónica de la provincia del Santo Evangelio de México,* p. 37.

[15] Matías Escobar, *Americana Thebaida,* p. 418.

[16] Francisco Pérez Salazar, *Historia de la pintura en Puebla,* p. 170.

[17] Florencia, *La estrella de el norte.*

221. Antonio Rodríguez. St. Augustine. Oil. 1.69 x 1.21 m. Pinacoteca Virreinal, Mexico City.

or not he is the son of Gaspar Conrado, a painter active in Puebla some years earlier.

Nicolás de Fuen-Labrada is another artist mentioned in the Guadalupe inquiry.[18]

Juan de Herrera made the little pictures decorating the Capilla de las Reliquias in the Cathedral of Mexico, signed by him in 1698. They are acceptable and charming work, representing martyrs. All the writers confuse this artist with Alonso López de Herrera, so that they give him the epithet "El Divino," which is quite confusing, since these pictures are no more than unexceptionable. To apply the epithet to Alonso López de Herrera, as we have seen, clarifies the whole matter satisfactorily.

Sebastián López Dávalos also gave his opinion in the inquiry on the Guadalupe picture in 1666, according to Florencia.[19] We have eight paintings by him, representing scenes of *The Martyrdom of Saints Cosimo and Damian* in the chapel dedicated to these saints in the Cathedral of Mexico. They are quite adequate work, very typical of this period, and one of them seems to have a signature.

Antonio Rodríguez, as we have said, was a pupil of José Juárez, and married his daughter Antonia on September 8, 1659. We do not know when he died, but it is likely that he lived to the end of the seventeenth century, training his sons Juan and Nicolás Rodríguez Juárez. Antonio Rodríguez is a reputable painter; he continued to work in the severe style of his master, with the same dignified figures. A good many of his paintings are extant: three in the Galerías de Pintura, *St. Thomas Aquinas, St. Thomas of Villanova* (1665), and *St. Augustine* (221); a *St. Anthony* in the parish church of Coyoacán; a canvas of considerable scope and quality representing the *Souls in Purgatory,* in the sacristy of the church at Churubusco. In the church of La Profesa are several pictures with his signature, and more paintings by him are found from time to time. The style of Antonio Rodríguez represents the transition between the painting of the great colonial masters and the beginning of the eighteenth century, in which painting was to be subjected to such a variety of fashions and demands as to lose its integrity little by little, until it became thoroughly effete. The sons of Antonio Rodríguez, Juan and Nicolás, in their first period followed the style of their father—severe, clearly drawn, precisely composed; later, under the influence of Correa and Villalpando, they adopted the new style which we shall describe in due course.

José Rodríguez de Carnero was born in Mexico City, the son of Nicolás Rodríguez Carnero, who was also a painter. He married three times, and one of his sons, Domingo, took up the same profession. He died in Puebla on September 17, 1725.[20]

Collaborating with Antonio de Alvarado, José Rodríguez de Carnero made the arch which the Ayuntamiento erected in 1680 to welcome the Conde de Paredes as viceroy. It is described by Don Carlos de Sigüenza y Góngora in his *Teatro de virtudes políticas.*[21] In 1681 he appears with Antonio Rodríguez, whom we have discussed above, requesting a copy of the old ordinances of the painters' guild, which suggests that he was a person of some importance in his day.

His most interesting work is preserved in Puebla, where he spent the end of his life. There are four large pictures in the church of La Concordia, signed and dated 1693, representing *St. Margaret, St. Barbara, The Sorrows of the Virgin,* and *St. Joseph.* His most important paintings are the series of *The Life of the Virgin* which decorate the famous Capilla del Rosario. As with so many other artists of Mexico City and Puebla, two quite distinct manners appear: the paintings in the nave of the chapel have an almost excessively somber tonality, while *The Annunciation* and *The Institution of the Rosary* in the transepts are of a luminous light-blue tonality which unmistakably recalls the great *Assumption of the Virgin* of Pedro García Ferrer on the Altar de los Reyes of the Cathedral of Puebla. A lesser work by this artist is *The Triumph of the Jesuit Order* in the sacristy of the church of La Compañía in Puebla.

Juan Salguero appears among the painters who examined the Virgin of Guadalupe in 1666.[22] We know three of his paintings: the portrait of *Archbishop Don Juan Sáenz de Mañozca* in the Treasure of the Cathedral of Mexico, *Elijah and the Fiery Chariot* in the Museo Nacional, and *The Death of St. Theresa* in the monastery of Churubusco. These works show us an artist able, if not too inspired.

Bernabé Sánchez was active around 1684, when he appraised a painting. There are two signed canvases by

18 *Ibid.*
19 *Ibid.*
20 Pérez Salazar, in his *Historia* (pp. 71–73) treats Rodríguez de Carnero as a painter of Puebla. Considering his work in Mexico City, where he was born, this view is hardly justified.
21 Carlos de Sigüenza y Góngora, *Teatro.*
22 Florencia, *La estrella de el norte.*

222. Juan Sánchez Salmerón. Annunciation to Joachim. Oil. 1.88 x 1.26 m. Chapter room, Cathedral of Mexico.

Virgin of the Immaculate Conception. In Tulancingo, Hidalgo, there is a *Marriage of the Virgin* and a *Holy Family* in a chapel of the Cathedral, and in the museum of the Hospital de Jesús in Mexico City there is a large picture of *The Holy Family,* with St. Anne and St. Joachim, which resembles that of Tulancingo. In the Franciscan church of Tlalmanalco, in the state of México, are two paintings which may be attributed on style although they are not signed, a *Holy Family in Glory* and a *Virgin with St. Joachim and St. Anne.* Two pictures by him are listed in the catalogue of the Barron Collection: *St. Peter in Prison,* and *St. John the Evangelist.* Finally, in the upper cloister of the Franciscan monastery at Xochimilco, D.F., there is a little picture representing *The Last Judgment* which is of historical interest; although it appears to be a variant of a similar painting in the sacristy of the church of Loreto in Mexico City, it is in fact a copy of that painting, made by the French painter Cousin.[26]

Sánchez Salmerón is curiously eclectic. Some of his works show unmistakable artistic personality; but for the rest he submitted to the whims of his clients, and produced paintings of many kinds.

José de Villegas was active in 1675, when Bernardino Suárez, *bachiller,* apprenticed his son Juan Suárez Calderón to José de Villegas, master painter, to learn the art of painting.[27] We have a good painting signed by José de Villegas; it represents *The Crucifixion* and is in the arch of the vault on the Evangel side of the Capilla de las Reliquias in the Cathedral of Mexico. It is a strong work, showing genuine personality.

Antonio Alonso de Zárate, who in 1676 gave his opinion on the painting of Our Lady of Guadalupe, is referred to by Padre Florencia as among the outstanding artists of his time.[28]

Climax of Pictorial Baroque: The Formation of the Typical Style

The artists whom we have been considering were already moving in a completely Baroque environment, but their Baroque character consisted of putting together various pictorial devices whose sum was by no

him in the monastery of San Bernardino in Taxco which, although they are not exceptional, still show him to have been a respectable painter.[23]

Juan Sánchez Salmerón, a very uneven artist, appears with the other painters in 1666 to give his opinion on the Virgin of Guadalupe.[24] In 1679 he collaborated with Bartolomé de Arenas in the report on the Señor de Santa Teresa, as we have noted.[25] There are a lot of paintings by Sánchez Salmerón in existence; the most important are in the Treasure of the Cathedral of Mexico: *The Annunciation to St. Joachim* (222), *St. Joachim and St. Anne, The Birth of the Virgin,* and a

23 Manuel Toussaint, *Tasco.*
24 Florencia, *La estrella de el norte.*
25 Velasco, *Renovación.*
26 A reproduction of the French painting may be seen in André Michel's *Histoire de l'art,* IV, 762.
27 Archivo de Notarías.
28 Florencia, *La estrella de el norte.*

means a homogeneous style. From Arteaga's time on we have seen two modes in painting: the one, severe and austere, perhaps deriving from the *Doubting Thomas,* the other, luminous and brilliant in color, actually a continuation of the Renaissance style of the Echaves and López de Herrera. But toward the end of the seventeenth century a new style appears. If not actually produced by the Baroque concept of the sumptuous interior ensemble which was developing in New Spain, this style is certainly in close harmony with it. The principal exponents of this style were Juan Correa and Cristóbal de Villalpando, and they were followed, somewhat timidly, by the Rodríguez Juárez brothers, Juan and Nicolás. It is a luminous style that prefers a golden tonality; it has the flavor of autumn landscapes, now bluish, now rosy, but always sumptuous and rich. The figures are not the most important part of the picture; they are neglected, often intentionally subordinated to the effect of the whole—it is an eminently decorative style.

This is not to say that the artists we have named dedicated themselves exclusively to this sort of painting, since they also worked in the more serious style of their predecessors.

New Guild Ordinances

But before considering the personalities of these painters, we ought to discuss the new ordinances of the painters' guild, the *Ordinanzas del arte de la pintura,* which were set up in 1687, and which constitute an important document for the history of painting.

We have seen already how in mid-sixteenth century the painters tried to protect themselves by organizing a guild and soliciting the ordinances which were given them in 1557. These old regulations fell into disuse; it could be said that the Golden Age of Mexican painting, from Pereyns to José Juárez, happened without regard for the rules. When the painters in 1681 presented their petition requesting new ordinances, they said that the old ones "for a long time have not been used"—that is, that they had been forgotten. If in the sixteenth century the interference of the Church had threatened the painters' independence, it was now the great number of artists which made the more important of them band together to request new controls. The painters who presented the petition for the group were José Rodríguez de Carnero and Antonio Rodríguez. The artists themselves drew up the new ordinances, taking what seemed suitable from the old rules, and

throwing out what was antiquated. There was no longer any mention of fresco painting, for example.

The new ordinances consisted of sixteen articles, which can be divided into three groups. Technical standards are covered by articles IV, V, and IX; administrative matters, by articles I, II, III, VI, VII, VIII, X, XIII, XIV, and XV; while articles XI, XII, and XVI define the scope of the two crafts concerned, that is to say, painting and gilding.

The basis of the system, as in the sixteenth century and in all guilds, was an examination conducted by the alcaldes or *veedores,* the directors and supervisors, by which an artist obtained his *carta de examen,* his certificate, and the title of Master of the Painter's Art, *maestro del arte de pintor.*

Ordinance IV lists the things in which the painters must be examined. Artists were not divided into categories as in the sixteenth century; there was now a single craft, because only one medium was used—oil painting. The painter was required to know how to prepare canvas, and panels of wood and metal, to know drawing, foreshortening, coloring, drapery simple or complicated (*sueltos y combinados*), shading, medium tones and dark tones.

Furthermore the artist was required to make "a picture three *varas* high including various faces and nude bodies, a variety of beautiful faces, executing and explaining the proportions, position, or situation of each figure, and its coloring, lighting, and perspective, and demonstrating and executing architecture, flowers, landscape, animals, fruits, and vegetation."

The administration is exactly like that of all the guilds: the election of overseers, attendance at the fiesta, examination of paintings. An important stipulation is added: that no painter who has not received the title of *maestro* can make appraisals of paintings. This regulation was of financial importance to the artists, since they received substantial fees for their evaluations. We have learned many artists' names because they appraised paintings in the settling of estates. The ordinances submitted were approved, except for the one prohibiting the admission of Indians to the guild, and another which would have allowed sacred paintings to be sold at public auction.[29]

[29] See Francisco del Barrio Lorenzot, *Ordenanzas de gremios de la Nueva España*; Manuel Carrera Stampa, *Los gremios mexicanos*; Francisco Santiago Cruz, *Las artes y los gremios en la Nueva España.*

223. Juan Correa. Assumption of the Virgin. Oil. Sacristy, Cathedral of Mexico.

Juan Correa

We do not know any biographical facts about Juan Correa; we can only say that he was active from 1674 well into the eighteenth century, until at least 1739. There is an interesting possibility that Correa went to

Guatemala at the end of his life, since signed paintings by him dated in these last years have been found there. More probably, the pictures were exported, like those of Villalpando.[30]

In any case, we know that in 1674 he appraised a painting, and another in 1676, and that he continued in this activity through the early years of the eighteenth century. The catalogue of his paintings is very long,

[30] This information was given me by Salvador Toscano. See also Berlin, "Pintura colonial mexicana," pp. 118–128.

224. Juan Correa. The Apocalypse. Oil (burned, 1967). Choir, Cathedral of Mexico.

and I intend to note only the most important; as with all very productive artists his *oeuvre* is of uneven quality, and some of his paintings seem unworthy of his signature. The earliest I know is a *Child Jesus Appearing to St. Francis,* dated 1675, in the sacristy of the church of San Diego in Aguascalientes. It is a respectable canvas, although of somewhat ashen color. In the same place is another better picture, a *Scene from the Life of St. Francis,* dated 1681. From the same year dates a *Crucifixion* in a private collection in Budapest, and also the panels of *The Life of the Virgin* on the retable of the Capilla del Rosario in the parish church of Atzcapotzalco. The two great paintings decorating the sacristy of the Cathedral of Mexico are dated 1689 and 1691, and represent *The Assumption of the Virgin* (223) and *Christ Entering Jerusalem.* At the same time, Cristóbal de Villalpando did the other two [three] paintings there. Also in the Cathedral is the large painting of *The Apocalypse* (224), on the back of the Altar del Perdón facing the choir. The following works are signed but not dated: in the Galerías de Pintura, *St. Catherine, The Virgin of Sorrows,* and *St. Mary Magdalene;* in the church of Tepotzotlán, *The Expulsion, The Annunciation,* and *St. Nicholas.* A number of his paintings are in San Miguel Allende, in the sanctuary of Atotonilco, as well as in various city churches. Two paintings of his last period, *The Archangel Gabriel* and *The Archangel Michael,* dated 1739, are in the Philadelphia Museum of Art, in the United States.

A *St. Theresa* in the chapel of San Miguel Nonoalco is so close to the style of Antonio Rodríguez that one is tempted to assert that Correa was Rodríguez' pupil. Since, however, this sober and vigorous style was shared by all the painters of his period, we must wait for some documentary confirmation.

As we have said, Juan Correa is a very uneven painter. One feels the press of work urging his hand; although his knowledge is extraordinarily sound, his haste, the urgency to fill the enormous spaces of his canvases, results in his sometimes falling below his best level. As with all the painters of this group, one can

237

225. Cristóbal de Villalpando. The Immaculate Conception. Oil. Sacristy, Cathedral of Mexico.

ture and reliefs; it had to be responsive, above all, to its environment. Luminosity was the essential, so that the paintings would not be dark blemishes in those golden interiors. Correa succeeded admirably in this, as did his companions: they give us painting which is light and graceful, where the figures move in an atmosphere quivering and brilliant. It may indeed be true that we should search vainly in Spain for a parallel to this painting, just as we would not find there a Baroque decoration so sumptuous as our Baroque in the Capilla del Rosario in Puebla. Thus we have come to a definitive moment in Mexican art. We can disregard its weaknesses, for although our painter cannot be compared to the great artists of mid-century, he is important in achieving a new quality, in the creative impulse which he expresses, and which one cannot doubt embodies the eagerness of New Spain for an art of its own, breaking away from its Spanish lineage. Here New Spain attains its own personality, unique and unmistakable.

Cristóbal de Villalpando

Here we have a figure of the greatest interest for our colonial painting. In contrast to our ignorance of Correa's life we have considerable information about Cristóbal de Villalpando. We know that on the second of June, 1669, he married, in Mexico City, María de Mendoza, the daughter of Diego de Mendoza and Margarita Corcuera. Señor Pérez Salazar suggests that this Diego Mendoza was a painter of Puebla, active there around 1685, and that perhaps he was the father of an artist named Miguel de Mendoza, whom he supposes to be also from Puebla, although in fact he came from Oaxaca, as we shall see in due course. From the date of Villalpando's marriage it has been assumed without any real basis that he was born twenty years before; but if we presume that he would have been between twenty and twenty-five years old when he married, then it can be assumed that he was born somewhere between 1644 and 1649. He had two sons, Carlos, who was born in August, 1670, and was baptized on the thirtieth of that month, with Baltasar de Echave y Rioja as his godfather—which suggests that Echave was the teacher of Villalpando—and Cristóbal, who was born on February 5, 1690.

Cristóbal de Villalpando was a painter even more productive than Correa, and his *oeuvre* shows the same unevenness in quality. He painted two [three] immense pictures for the sacristy of the Cathedral of

distinguish in his work the two styles we have described: on the one hand, the more austere painting which goes back to Arteaga, on the other, a luminous style whose aim is harmony with the Baroque interiors. Such are the paintings in the sacristy of the Cathedral of Mexico and *The Apocalypse* in the choir there. If the architecture of these interiors sought to simulate Paradise, painting had the task of heightening this effect through a brilliance of color and a golden tonality which would hold its own with the real gold of sculp-

238

226. Cristóbal de Villalpando. An Allegory of the Church (detail). Oil. Sacristy, Cathedral of Mexico.

Mexico at the same time as Correa (225). Villalpando's represent *An Allegory of the Church* (226) and *The Triumph of the Eucharist* (227); we know from the payments that they were executed between October 1, 1684, and June 19, 1685.[31] He painted the dome of the Capilla de los Reyes in the Cathedral of Puebla, in oil; presumably this work was done before 1692, when Canon Castillo, the one who was interested in the work, died.[32] On October 14, 1702, he contracted to make paintings for the arch erected by the Cathedral of Mexico for the arrival of Viceroy Alburquerque, for 380 pesos; the poetry was provided by Licenciado Don Francisco Ayerra Santa María. They began putting up the arch on December 5, and the paintings represented

the story of Achilles. The arch erected by the Ayuntamiento had the myths of Jupiter and other gods, but unfortunately we do not know who painted that.[33] In 1709 Villalpando evaluated the paintings of Don José Bueno Basorí, and there is no doubt that he took part in many other professional activities. He died on Au-

[31] These receipts are in the Archivo de la Catedral de México. See also Francisco de la Maza, *El pintor Cristóbal de Villalpando*, p. 68. There has been confusion in the literature about the paintings in the sacristy of the Cathedral of Mexico, as to the subjects, and the number of them, which were painted by Correa and by Villalpando. As de la Maza comments, *aliquando bonus dormitat Homerus*: even Toussaint is in error here.

[32] Pérez Salazar, *Historia*, p. 118.

[33] Antonio de Robles, *Diario de sucesos notables; 1665–1703.*

227. Cristóbal de Villalpando. The Triumph of the Eucharist (detail). Oil. Sacristy, Cathedral of Mexico.

gust 21, 1714; already a widower, he was living on the Calle de la Concepción, and was buried in the church of San Agustín.

Besides the work already mentioned, I can list the following paintings by Villalpando: in the Cathedral of Puebla, a lunette dated 1683 representing *The Transfiguration and the Brazen Serpent*; in the Colegio del Estado of Puebla, two magnificent canvases: *St. Ignatius Loyola* and *St. Francis Xavier*; in the Cabrera Collection in Puebla, a *Presentation of the Virgin* and some representations of *The Marriage of the Virgin*;[34]

in the parish church of Cholula, a *St. Michael*. In the museum at Tepotzotlán are twenty-two canvases representing *The Life of St. Ignatius Loyola*; in the Museum of Guadalupe, near Zacatecas, a *Holy Family with St. Anne and St. Joachim*; in the Museum of Guadalajara, *Joseph Taken from the Well,* and a *Triumph of the Sacrament* which seems to be a copy after Rubens; in the Carmen in San Ángel, *St. Theresa Praying,* an *Agony in the Garden,* an *Ecce Homo,* a *Flagellation,*

34 Revilla, *El arte en México,* p. 83.

240

and *St. John of the Cross.* In the Museo Religioso of the Cathedral of Mexico are four magnificent pictures: an *Annunciation,* a *Marriage of the Virgin,* a *Flight into Egypt,* and an *Adoration of the Shepherds.* In the old Dominican church of Atzcapotzalco are paintings signed by Villalpando on a retable dedicated to St. Theresa. In the church of La Profesa in Mexico City, which is a veritable museum of painting, are some of the finest works of this painter: *The Death of Tobias, St. Theresa Receiving Her Habit from the Virgin, The Sermon on the Mount,* and others. According to Couto, the cloisters of San Francisco were decorated with pictures by Villalpando representing *Scenes of the Passion.*[35]

In the Museo Nacional de Guatemala are fifteen magnificent paintings of *The Life of St. Francis,* which originally decorated the cloisters of the Franciscan monastery in Antigua, and which for a long time were attributed to an imaginary "Francisco de Villalpando."[36] They are from his best period, and indicate how his fame had spread.

Villalpando shows the same unevenness in his work which we found in Correa, and which is undoubtedly explained by the haste in which he felt obliged to work. Because of the demand for painting to decorate the Baroque interiors the painter was deprived of tranquillity and the time to meditate on his work. Again we can observe in the series of paintings listed here that two styles appear clearly, as in Correa and some earlier painters; one is somber, dark in tone, with well-constructed figures; the other is light, luminous, with golden depths in which the figures move with incomparable grace. It is impossible to determine the originator of this second Baroque style, which was so admirably adapted to the architecture of the period. Rather than argue whether its author was Correa or Villalpando, we should recognize that the new style was called into being by necessity, a new mode perfectly consonant with those luminous interiors overflowing with gold and polychrome carving. In spite of the unevenness of Villalpando's *oeuvre,* he has left plenty of work which assures his position. His style is animated, his brush graceful, his imagination lively, his palette luminous. Among these paintings are some which are essential to the history of Mexican art, along with those of his inseparable friend, Correa.

The Rodríguez Juárez Brothers

If these two painters seem to have introduced the new pictorial style, two other painters are their able followers, another inseparable pair, until they are parted by death. I refer to Nicolás and Juan Rodríguez Juárez. As I have said, they were the sons of Antonio Rodríguez and Antonia Juárez, and therefore grandsons of the great artist José Juárez, and great-grandsons of Luis Juárez, the pupil of Echave Orio. Thus they complete an unbroken dynasty that stretches from the beginning of the seventeenth well into the eighteenth century.

Nicolás Rodríguez Juárez, the elder brother, was born in Mexico City, where he was baptized on the fifth of January, 1667. He studied with his father, Antonio Rodríguez, from the time he was a child, and his early works can be confused with his father's. When he was twenty-one he married Doña Josefa Ruiz Guerra, on September 8, 1688. They had only one daughter, María, who on the sixteenth of February, 1721, was married to Don Miguel de Contreras Villegas. The painter was already a widower at this time, and had taken holy orders: he was a priest.

We have few documents concerning his professional activities. In 1699 he made an appraisal of the pictures which belonged to Don Francisco Antonio Morantes Guerrero; in 1722, those of the estate of Don Domingo de Cuevas y Sandoval; in 1721 or 1722 he inspected the painting of Our Lady of Guadalupe, with his brother Juan and the painter Antonio de Torres; in 1734 he designed the triumphal car of the chandlers, confectioners, and dyers for the celebration of the capture of Orán.[37] Two years later, on June 10, 1734, he died in his house on the Calle del Amor de Dios; he lay in state in the church of San Agustín and was buried there.

Nicolás Rodríguez Juárez was a fairly productive artist, though less so than his brother Juan, and he worked, like other painters we have studied, in the two distinct styles. The first is sober and austere, with dark backgrounds and somber tonality; this work, as we have noted, bears an extraordinary resemblance to the art of his father, Antonio Rodríguez. The other style is light and luminous, and certainly in imitation of the later work of Correa and Villalpando. In the first manner we have *The Prophet Isaiah,* signed and dated

[35] Couto, *Diálogo.*
[36] Berlin, "Pintura colonial mexicana."
[37] It can be seen in the curious pamphlet published in honor of that event.

228. Nicolás Rodríguez Juárez. Marqués de Santa Cruz. Oil. 1.16 x 1.12 m.
Pinacoteca Virreinal, Mexico City.

1690, which makes a pair with *The Prophet Elias,* signed by his father, in the church of La Profesa in Mexico City. There used to be a *St. Gertrude* of the same date in the Galerías de Pintura. In the Alcázar Collection in the Museo Nacional de Historia is a *St. Theresa* with two angels, dated 1692; and in the Galerías de Pintura, the magnificent portrait of the *Marqués de Santa Cruz* (228) of 1675. In the second manner, we have a *Repentant Magdalene,* of 1718, in the Museo de Historia, and a *St. Christopher,* dated 1722, in the old Colegio de Guadalupe near Zacatecas.

Undated pictures are more numerous. There are many canvases by him in the Cathedral of Mexico: in the Capilla de la Antigua, *The Birth of the Virgin, The Presentation in the Temple,* and portraits of *Benedict VIII, Archbishop Vizarrón,* and *Philip V.* In the Museo de Historia there are three more portraits—*Viceroy Montañez,* the second *Viceroy Alburquerque,* and *Don Pedro Gutiérrez de Pisa;* in the monastery of Santo Domingo in Atzcapotzalco, two paintings, *St. Michael Archangel* and *The Annunciation to St. Anne;* in private collections, a *Virgin of the Rosary,* an *Image of the Virgin,* a *Holy Child,* and, listed in the catalogue of the Barron Collection, a *St. Giles Abbot.* In the old monastery of La Merced in Mexico City was a picture representing *The Baptizing of Maxiscatzin by Father Olmedo.*[38] A good deal of work by him is to be found outside the capital; besides the picture mentioned in Zacatecas, I have seen only a *St. Philip of Jesus* in the sacristy of San Diego in Aguascalientes, and two pictures in the Museo de Guadalajara, *St. Sebastian* and *St. Matthew.*

It is curious that the Spanish historians take him for a Spanish painter. Gestoso refers to him so in his *Diccionario,* mentioning a *Repentant Magdalene* which belonged to Don Luis de Mendoza, who lived at Mairena del Alcor.[39]

Nicolás Rodríguez Juárez seems to have been a serious artist, and his work is less uneven than that of other painters of his time. It recalls—and for this reason is pleasing to us—the dignified style of the end of the seventeenth century which his father Antonio Rodríguez had developed, and which is like a continuation of the style of the Golden Age taught him by his father-in-law, the great José Juárez. He seems less changeable than his brother Juan, although he was undoubtedly less gifted. He is one of the most attractive and sympathetic figures of this period.

Juan Rodríguez Juárez was born in Mexico City,

where he was baptized on July 14, 1675; he was therefore eight years younger than his brother Nicolás. He received his training from his father, and profited by it so well that already in 1694, that is to say, when he was nineteen years old, he signed a painting: the *Imagen de Nuestra Señora de San Juan.* He married Doña Juana Montes de Oca, when, we do not know; they had only one son, Francisco José, who was born in the capital on May 13, 1717. In 1701 he painted a portrait of *Philip V* for the ceremony of his inauguration, "full-length, dressed in Spanish style in a black suit with ruff and borders embroidered between bands of gold, wearing the sacred chain of the Order of the Golden Fleece."[40] As we have said, he inspected the image of the Virgin of Guadalupe, with his brother Nicolás and Antonio de Torres.[41] He made appraisals of paintings in 1726 and 1727. On January 14, 1728, he died in his house across from the Archbishop's palace, and was buried in the Cathedral.

The *oeuvre* of Juan Rodríguez Juárez is larger than that of his brother Nicolás, and shows a greater talent, though it too is of uneven quality. I do not believe a complete list of his work exists; I offer those I know.

Dated works are scarce; apart from those mentioned above, one should mention the portrait of *Don Juan Escalante y Colomeres,* of 1697, and perhaps that of *Don Manuel* of the same family; in 1714 the portrait of *Archbishop Lanciego y Equiluz* in the Cathedral of Mexico, magnificent in its color and realism; in 1720, *The Education of the Virgin* in the Museo de Guadalajara; of the same date, *The Assumption* and perhaps its companions, *The Transfiguration* and *Christ on the Sea of Galilee (Tempestad en la barca)* in the church of La Profesa in Mexico City; of 1724, a *St. Joseph* in the Capilla de La Antigua of the Cathedral of Mexico. Between 1718 and 1728, when he died, he made the paintings of the Altar de los Reyes in the Cathedral of Mexico: the immense *Assumption* and *Adoration of the Magi,* and the scenes from *The Life of the Virgin* which decorate the side altars and which were signed by him and dated 1726 (323, 324). The sketch for *The Adoration of the Magi* is in the Galerías

38 J. Laverrière, "El convento de la Merced," *El renacimiento.* 2, p. 34; J. Laverrière, "El convento de la Merced," in *México pintoresco.*

39 Gestoso, *Diccionario,* II, 387.

40 Miguel de la Cueva Luna y Arellano, *Sumptuoso festivo real aparato.*

41 Florencia, *La estrella de el norte.*

229. Juan Rodríguez Juárez. St. John of God. Oil.
1.75 x 1.10 m. Pinacoteca Virreinal, Mexico City.

de Pintura, with two other magnificent paintings:
St. John of God (229) and a *Self-Portrait*.

Undated works by Juan Rodríguez Juárez are the
portraits of two viceroys, the *Marqués de Casafuerte*
and the *Duque de Linares* (230), in the Museo Nacional de Historia. He made a large series of *The Life of
the Virgin* for the Seminary at Tepotzotlán. In Que-

rétaro three series of paintings could be seen: in San
Francisco, *The Life of St. Francis* and *The Life of St.
Anthony of Padua*; in La Congregación, *The Life of
St. Peter.*[42] In the Bush Collection there was a *St. John
of God* and a mediocre *St. Francis of Paola*; in the catalogue of the Barron Collection two paintings are listed,
St. Michael and an *Assumption*; finally, in a private
collection I have seen a *Virgin of Guadalupe,* with the
different apparitions, truly magnificent. On the exterior
wall of the choir of the Cathedral of Puebla are two
paintings which I consider the artist's best, *Scenes from
the Life of St. Ignatius Loyola.*

Juan Rodríguez Juárez can be considered the last
great painter of the colonial period. He had already felt
the influence of Murillo and assimilated it, but his work
still retains dignity. Some of his paintings can still be
called masterpieces, worthy of the century in which he
was born. Others are of inferior and uneven quality,
evidencing hurried work and consequent technical
weakness, yet one always finds in them a basic decorum
which we shall soon see disappear. He, too, works in
the two styles of Correa and Villalpando, though in a
form less marked than in their painting. So he was to
be the last in the group of great Baroque painters. The
painters contemporary with the Churrigueresque style
who followed him, despite their undeniable talent and
artistic ability, are obviously inferior. Perhaps the fact
is that painting itself became decadent in this period.

Secondary Painters of the Early Eighteenth Century

Around these eminent artists flourished a group of
painters whose names should be noted, since, although
their work was not of the highest quality, they were
active in the same period and contributed to its total
effect. Besides, as new pictures of this period are coming to light every day, I must mention these painters
to fill out the historical record. There are so many of
them, however, that I am forced to select only the most
important or the catalogue would be unmanageable.

Juan Aguilera painted a *Holy Family in the Shop of
St. Joseph* in the Capilla de San Pedro in the Cathedral
of Mexico, a quite respectable work. He also did a set
of *The Twelve Apostles* which used to be in the monastery of San Diego in Mexico City, and other work of
secondary importance.

Pedro Calderón was active in the first third of the
century. There are paintings by him in the church of

[42] José María Zelaa e Hidalgo, *Glorias de Querétaro.*

230. Juan Rodríguez Juárez. Duque de Linares, Viceroy of Mexico. Oil. 2.11 x 1.30 m.
Museo Nacional de Historia, Mexico City.

D.ª María Josepha de Aldaco y Fragoaga, Hija Legítima de D.ª Manuel de Aldaco y de D.ª Juana de Fagoaga y Aruzqueta: Nació dia 27 de Febrero de 1732.a., y fallecio el dia 10 de Henero de 1746.a. f. M...

231. Miguel de Herrera. María Josefa de Aldaco y Fragoaga. Oil. 1.79 x 1.28 m. Museo Nacional de Historia, Mexico City.

La Regina, among them a *St. Anthony of Padua,* signed in 1731. He seems to be the same Pedro López Calderón whom Couto mentions as the painter of a *Last Supper,* dated 1728, in the monastery of San Fernando in Mexico City.[43] In Guadalajara there was a *St. Anne* by him, and I have noted a *St. John Nepomucen,* signed and dated in Mexico City, 1723.

Padre Manuel was a Jesuit. We know of no historical documentation for him, nor even, with any exactitude, for the period of his activity. Several paintings are associated with this artist: one traditionally attributed to him is an *Immaculate Conception* in the Gale-

rías de Pintura, but it seems to be a copy of some European painting. Another, however, is authentic, a *Holy Family* in the Facultad de Medicina; it had been completely painted over, but the original painting shows indisputable artistic talent. In the parish church of Tacuba, in the sacristy, are some *Apostles* signed by this painter which evidence his considerable gifts. Fully Baroque in the movement of his draperies, he knows how to construct his figures solidly. His chromatic color, fresh and brilliant, is charming.

Fray Miguel de Herrera was an Augustinian monk, a very productive artist, variable in quality, but never reaching the level of the great masters. His earliest paintings dated from 1725, when he signed two pictures now in the Philadelphia Museum of Art. In 1729 he painted for the celebration of the canonization of St. John of the Cross a large canvas located in the *portería* of the monastery of El Carmen in Puebla. Other dated works continue until 1752. Among his best paintings should be noted the portrait of the child *María Josefa de Aldaco y Fragoaga,* dated 1746 and now in the Museo Nacional de Historia (231), a picture delightfully ingenuous although somewhat hard in its drawing, in which Fray Miguel is close to the popular portraitists, and a *St. Michael,* brilliant in color, which is in the museum of the Cathedral of Mexico.

Francisco de León is listed by Couto as a painter of this period; he mentions an excellent painting of *The Virgin of the Rosary in Glory* in the stairhall of the monastery of Santo Domingo, dated 1727.[44] I know a little panel by him in a private collection, a *Virgin of the Immaculate Conception* surrounded by angels; it reminds one somewhat of Murillo's, although it is less bland. The Barron Collection had a painting of *The Flight into Egypt* with his signature.

Francisco Martínez, a very productive painter somewhat older than Ibarra and Cabrera, was certainly one of the most famous of his day. Besides being a painter he was a gilder, and executed a work of tremendous importance, the gilding of the retable of the Altar de los Reyes in the Cathedral of Mexico, which we shall speak about in its place. He was a notary for the Holy Office of the Inquisition: the petition was presented on

[43] Couto, *Diálogo.*
[44] Couto, *Diálogo,* p. 64. See also Leopoldo I. Orendáin, "Francisco de León, pintor del siglo XVII," *Anales del Instituto de Investigaciones Estéticas,* 17 (1949), 17-21.

August 9, 1737, and the commission issued five days later; he took the oath on the twenty-third of the same month.[45] We have no other personal data about him. As early as 1718 he signed a large *Immaculate Conception* surrounded by angels in the sacristy of the Franciscan church in Tepeji del Rio. He appraised paintings in 1720 and during 1736–1737. For the Oath of Allegiance of Ferdinand VI he was commissioned, with Juan de Espinosa, to build the stages for the celebration; the eulogies addressed to him can be read in the book commemorating the festivities.[46] He was still living about the middle of the century; in 1753 he appears in the census with his apprentices: "Don Francisco Martínez, painter, widower; his brother-in-law is the Bachiller Don Pedro Cuellar, priest in this Archbishopric. His apprentices: Joseph Escobar, sixteen years old; Antonio Pardo, sixteen; Mariano de Estrada, Manuel Parra, fifteen years. The master and the apprentices say that they are Spaniards." Even in 1754 he appraised some painting, but the unsteadiness of his signature indicates an advanced age, and he died soon after, in 1758.[47]

The list of his paintings is long, but almost all of them are mediocre; if they were prized in his time, it merely indicates the decadence of taste. I am going to record only the principal ones I know: two on the outer wall of the choir of the Cathedral of Mexico, representing *The Martyrdom of St. Lawrence*, dated 1736; in the Galerías de Pintura, two *Evangelists* and an *Allegory of the Virgin with the Holy Trinity and Saints*; in the Colegio del Estado in Puebla, various canvases representing scenes from *The Life of St. Theresa*, some of them good enough, and a *St. Joseph* signed and dated 1738; in the parish church of Singuilucan, several paintings dealing with *The Passion of Christ*; in the sacristy of the church of Santo Domingo in Zacatecas, eight pictures on the same subject; various works in the church of La Profesa in Mexico City. In the Museo Nacional de Historia are several portraits, among them one of *The Duque de Linares*, dated 1723, which seems to be a copy of the one by Rodríguez Juárez, and two paintings, *Our Lord of Mercy* and a *St. Joseph*, which are interesting for the manner of painting the fabrics—it is evident that they were painted by an *estofador*. One of Martínez' most attractive paintings is *Our Lady of Mercy as Protectress*, which can be seen in the sacristy of the church of San Pablo in Mexico City; it is dated 1755, and considering the age of the artist, it is admirable. We shall have more to say about Martínez in the section on the gilding of retables.

José de la Mora was an unexceptional artist of the beginning of the century who appears to have been a pupil of Juan Correa.

José de la Mota was a quite active painter; a number of paintings by him are known.

Antonio de Torres was perhaps the most interesting painter of this group. He was very productive, and his paintings can be found all over; the greatest number are in San Luis Potosí, though there is no reason to believe that this city was his home. The dates of his paintings run from 1708 to 1728, but some without dates may well fall outside this twenty-year period. On his professional activities we have the following information: he inspected the painting of Our Lady of Guadalupe with the brothers Rodríguez Juárez in 1721–1722,[48] and between 1709 and 1727 he made numerous appraisals of painting.

The catalogue of his work is long, and I mention only the most important of which I have record. In the church of La Profesa is a series of *The Life of St. Philip Neri*, dated 1708–1709, and also an *Immaculate Conception* of 1714. A *Life of the Virgin*, dated 1728, came from the church of Romita to the museum of the Cathedral of Mexico, where there is also a *St. Francis*, sober and strong, and a *Coronation of the Virgin*, both dated 1728. In Aguascalientes is a painting of *Souls in Purgatory* in the *camarín* of San Diego, dated 1719; in the Colegio de Guadalupe near Zacatecas, a series of *The Life of the Virgin* in eight paintings. In the Museo Nacional de Historia are portraits of Franciscans in pairs, all evidently by the same hand, although only one of them is signed, with the date 1712; in the Cathedral of Mexico, other paintings of secondary value. His most important work is in San Luis Potosí, as we have said; it is a *Life of St. Francis*, a number of canvases now crowded into the sacristy of the church, which were removed from the cloister of the monastery. This painter deserves to have a detailed study devoted to his work, with a catalogue of the paintings

[45] Archivo General de la Nación. Tomo *Inquisición*, No. 862, fols. 37–39. This research was done by Francisco de la Maza.

[46] José Mariano Abarca, *El sol en León*.

[47] See Heinrich Berlin, "Dos estudios mexicanos: artistas y milagros," *Anales del Instituto de Arte Americano e Investigaciones Estéticas*, pp. 109–124.

[48] Florencia, *La estrella de el norte*.

and reproductions of the more important. Some of his paintings are worth more than the work of many artists who enjoyed more acclaim in his time.

The Decadence of Painting

In this summary review of the painters working in Mexico at the beginning of the eighteenth century, an enormous difference from the century before is obvious. We have considered painters who ought not properly to be mentioned in a history of art at all. The fact is that painting was entering a period of decadence from which it was not to rise during the rest of the colonial period. One reason seems to have been the commercialism which obliged the artists to paint in quantity, however low the quality; another and more important reason was the decadence of taste and of critical judgment among important people, the clergy, and hence the clients, who no longer wanted sound work from the artist's brush, but simply "pretty pictures" to decorate churches and houses. The underlying cause must be sought in the very concept of Baroque art. If one was interested in the effect of the ensemble, and not in its parts, it was not necessary, and in fact rather detrimental, that the painting should be of the highest quality. In the burst of frenzy that was a Churrigueresque retable—or even the exaggerated Baroque which preceded it—sculpture and painting, as distinct modes of expression, must disappear. Everything had to be submerged in the complex effect, to contribute to that spectacle which was unique and marvelous, not in its detail but as a whole, in the movement and the vertigo, in order to achieve the psychological effect for which they strove.

Chapter Twelve

PROVINCIAL PAINTING
IN NEW SPAIN

N THIS chapter I shall give what data I have on painting during the seventeenth and early eighteenth centuries in the provinces, outside the capital of New Spain. The abundance of documentation indicates a flowering of art all over the country. Our problem is to summarize this without devoting too much space to it, for it cannot be omitted from a history which claims to give a general view of the art of New Spain, and not merely of the capital of the Viceroyalty.

Painting in Puebla

All during the viceregal period the city most significant in all cultural activities was Puebla; not without reason was it considered the second city of the country. In studying the painting of Puebla, we can depend on the valuable research of Licenciado Don Francisco Pérez Salazar; if we had such publications in every region as Pérez Salazar has provided for Puebla, the history of painting in Mexico would be much easier to write.[1]

There were already painters in Puebla in the six-

teenth century; we have mentioned Nicolás de Tejeda, an inhabitant in 1557, and Juan Gersón, who painted the vault at Tecamachalco in 1562 and is mentioned in Puebla as Juan Garzón. In the seventeenth century the following artists appear.

Jerónimo Farfán was brought before the Inquisition in 1604 for using blasphemous language; he had made a painting of *The Apostles* in Tlaxcala for Luis Crespo. We have no other notices of him.

There seem to have been active in Puebla a whole family of artists called Lagarto whom the historians have lumped together under the one name of Luis Lagarto. Studying their works, with their various signatures, we can identify several painters of the family. First, there is Luis Lagarto, who signs his miniatures in capital letters, sometimes with a small lizard (*lagarto*) below. His work falls between the beginning of the century and 1624. He is said to have come from Spain, although no evidence has been found there except some paintings of later date, undoubtedly imported from New Spain. Concerning his activity in Mexico we know that in 1586 the Marqués de Villa Manrique appointed him examiner of candidates for teaching reading and writing; however this person is

---

[1] Francisco Pérez Salazar, *Historia de la pintura en Puebla.*

232. Luis Lagarto. Illumination from a choir book.
Watercolor on parchment. .34 x .33 m. Cathedral
of Puebla.

Frontera, in Spain; an excellent example of its kind, it
represents *The Mystic Marriage of St. Catherine,* and
is signed with an *L* and a little lizard.[3] Dated 1610 are
two miniatures in the collection of Don Mariano Bello;
in the Galerías de Pintura are two other miniatures, an
Annunciation, dated 1610, and a *Virgin of the Rosary,*
dated 1616. Don Luis MacGregor, the architect, has
an *Assumption,* signed, and dated 1612, of which the
white background has unfortunately darkened. There
were a *Holy Family* and an *Immaculate Conception,*
signed and dated 1624, in Seville, where Carderera
saw them.[4] In Durango, the capital city of the state, is
another beautiful miniature by Lagarto representing
The Birth of Christ. Pérez Salazar, the historian,
a little before his death had acquired a magnificent
St. Lawrence, with very rich ornament.

Luis Lagarto is an artist of great delicacy; his miniatures achieve the greatest perfection. They are painted
on fine vellum; gold is used profusely for the embroidered borders of the robes of the saints, and laid
down in fine rays for the haloes (233).

In the Museo Nacional de Historia is a miniature
signed by Andrés Lagarto in 1622; it represents *The
Virgin of the Immaculate Conception* and came from
the Alcázar Collection. Considering its similarity in
technique to Luis Lagarto's work, and the identical
surname, we suppose that Andrés was a relative; perhaps, considering the date of this single work we know
by him, his son.

Luis de la Vega Lagarto is the third member of this
family, who were certainly the most distinguished
illuminators in New Spain. He was active from 1632
to 1655, and the signature on his paintings is different
from those of the others: he signs his name in cursive
letters, often with a flourish. His miniatures are quite
delicate, although not so perfect as those of the first
Lagarto.

Pedro García Ferrer was the most important artist
in Puebla in the seventeenth century. Architect, sculp-

in some cases referred to as Juan Lagarto, which might
indicate that it was some older member of the family,
perhaps his father. In 1660 Luis Lagarto was a resident
of Puebla, and signed a contract with the Cabildo of
the Cathedral to paint, at his own cost, the illuminated
capitals for the choir books (232). He was to be paid
twenty pesos for each large letter and seven for each
smaller one. The texts were to be written by Alonso
de Villafañe. In view of these facts, the statement that
the one hundred and three choir books cost one hundred thousand pesos would appear to be an exaggeration.[2] A good many works by Luis Lagarto have been
preserved. From 1609 dates a miniature in Arcos de la

[2] Diego Antonio Bermúdez de Castro, "Teatro angelopolitano,"
in Nicolás León, *Bibliografía mexicana del siglo XVIII,* 121–
354.
[3] Published by Diego Angulo Íñiguez in the *Archivo español
de arte y arqueología,* 19 (1931).
[4] Cipriano Muñoz y Manzana Viñaza, *Adiciones al Diccionario
histórico de D. Juan Ceán Bermúdez.* 11-328-9. Conde de la
Viñaza assumed that this miniaturist had been employed by the
cathedral of Seville; however, it is plain from Gestoso's *Diccionario de los artífices* that no information on Lagarto is to be
found in the archives at Seville.

tor, and painter, he might be called the artistic personality of Don Juan de Palafox y Mendoza.

He was born in Alcoriza, Aragón, in 1583. He studied in Valencia, where he did a good deal of work, according to Jusepe Martínez.[5] Coming to Puebla with Bishop Palafox, he occupied himself at once in the building of the Cathedral, which had been entirely suspended. The idea of raising the nave, which was a change from the original plan, was perhaps his; he designed the dome, which was built by the *maestro* Jerónimo de la Cruz; he sculptured the four angels in relief on the pendentives, and painted the pictures for the Altar de los Reyes (379); he may have had a hand in the portraits of former bishops which Palafox had made for the chapter room of his church. He endured with Bishop Palafox all the difficulties created by the Jesuits, and returned with him to Spain. There he died, in Toledo in 1660, after having painted two pictures for the Cathedral, representing *St. Peter* and *St. Paul*.

García Ferrer is an artist of distinction, although his work in New Spain—which, as we have seen, is not plentiful—hardly permits a just appraisal of his ability. In his painting appear again the two styles which were general throughout the country: a somber style, of dark tones and contrasting brilliance, and a luminous style, of light tonality, which seemed to satisfy the needs of architectural decoration. Thus, in the first style we have the lower paintings of the Altar de los Reyes; and in the second, the great *Assumption of the Virgin* in the middle of the same altarpiece, painted in tones of rose and blue, its geometric composition of curves and fragments of circles reminiscent of Byzantine painting. There is no doubt that García Ferrer had a great influence on the painters who followed him in Puebla.

Diego de Borgraf was a Flemish painter who worked in Puebla, where he left paintings of a very interesting sort. He was born in Antwerp, the son of Luis de Borgraf and Juana Ruebens; this gave Pérez Salazar the idea that he was related to the great Rubens, which seems unlikely. He had settled in Puebla before 1649, when he took as apprentices Diego and Antonio de Espinosa and José Márquez. He was married three times: first, to María de Gasetas, with whom he had no children, so that the marriage was annulled, with the return of three hundred pesos of dowry; second, to

[5] Jusepe Martínez, *Discursos practicables del nobilísimo arte de pintura*, pp. 154–156.

233. Luis Lagarto. Nativity. Parchment. Pinacoteca Virreinal, Mexico City.

Francesca Rodríguez de Paredes, who brought him a dowry of a thousand and some pesos, and although there were children, they all died; and third, to Ana Jiménez, on the twenty-ninth of September, 1671, again without offspring. He died in March, 1686, and was buried in the church of San Agustín on the tenth day of that month.

There are a good many paintings by Borgraf in Puebla and Tlaxcala, important enough to justify a monograph which would reproduce all the pictures with the data on his life. He, too, followed two styles,

234. Diego de Borgraf. St. Francis. Oil. Pérez Salazar Collection, Mexico City.

the light and the dark. To the darker group belong: the large painting signed and dated 1652 which is now in the sacristy of the parish church of Cholula, representing *Christ Tied to the Column,* with four saints; a bust of *St. Francis* in the church of La Concordia in Puebla; and *The Death of St. Francis Xavier* in the church at Analco, perhaps his most powerful and moving work.

In the light manner are the painting of *The Apparition of St. Francis to St. Theresa,* signed and dated 1677, which is in the sacristy of the Franciscan church in Tlaxcala, and an *Immaculate Conception* which is in the Colegio del Estado of Puebla. I do not know whether the signature of Borgraf appears on a very similar picture in the anteroom of the chapter room of the Cathedral of Puebla; these paintings of the Virgin of the Immaculate Conception are in fact free copies after a painting by Francisco Rizi. Pérez Salazar attributes to Borgraf the two central paintings of the two retables which face the aisles of the parish church of San José in Puebla; they represent *The Virgin between St. Anne and St. Joachim,* and *The Flight into Egypt.*[6] In the sacristy of the church of the Santísima Trinidad in Puebla is a painting of *St. Leocadia,* interesting although somewhat hard in manner, and in the church of the Carmen of Puebla, a painting more curious than valuable, of *Christ Treading the Wine Press.* In the catalogue of the Barron Collection a *St. Catherine Martyr* is attributed to Borgraf, and Pérez Salazar owned a magnificent *St. Francis* (234). I have seen a *St. Joseph with the Child Jesus* on the market; it was signed, but the signature seemed dubious.

Borgraf, like all the Flemings, had a real feeling for painting. There are times when his brush plays graciously, as if at children's games. At other times, his art is meditative and abstracted, and succeeds in suggesting profound ideas and emotions. Such is the *St. Francis Xavier*: wrapped in a black robe, the saint is dying in a landscape, and the painting evokes the most terrible, and at the same time the noblest, feelings about sacrifice, tribulation, and suffering.

Gaspar Conrado was active in Puebla in mid-seventeenth century. He painted three altarpieces for the church of the convent of Santa Barbara, and there were paintings by him in the monastery of San Agustín in Puebla, before the fire of 1863.[7] In the storerooms of the Colegio del Estado in Puebla are eight canvases by him with scenes from *The Life of the Virgin.* He was a competent painter, but no more.

Antonio de Santander was the head of a family of painters, followed by his sons Antonio and José. He married Nicolasa de la Piedra, daughter of Rodrigo de la Piedra, who may have been his teacher. He did some

6 Pérez Salazar, *Historia,* p. 115.
7 Tirso Rafael Córdoba, *Mosaico mexicano.*

official work, such as the arch erected for the arrival of Bishop Santa Cruz, in 1675, on which he worked with the painter Juan Rubi de Marimón, and in 1680 the arch to welcome the Conde de Paredes. Two of his works are preserved in the Capilla de la Soledad in the Cathedral of Puebla, a *Crucifixion* and a *Descent from the Cross,* for which the contract was signed on August 31, 1679, and which are among the most important pictures to be found in the city. In the Chapel of San Antonio on the outskirts of the old city of Puebla are two paintings signed by him, a *Conception of the Virgin* and a *Saint,* which are notable for their fine linear drawing, their draperies almost excessively involuted, and their vigorously marked musculature. These same characteristics are found in a magnificent series of pictures, sadly deteriorated, which are preserved in the Academia de Bellas Artes in Puebla. They represent *Abraham and His Twelve Sons.* One hardly knows which to admire most in these paintings, the vigorous technique, the precise drawing, or the imagination which conceived such a group of exotic personages. Decked out in the most fantastic garments imaginable and posed in dramatic attitudes, they contrast with everything we are familiar with in the colonial painting of this period. If my attribution is correct, we must consider Antonio de Santander as one of the most important painters of the seventeenth century, not only the equal of Borgraf, but comparable to the Juárez family and the Arteagas. He also made the altarpiece for the church of La Concepción, which shows him to have been an eminent artist by any standard.

Rodrigo de la Piedra, a native of Cádiz, learned painting from Serafín Chacón. Later he appeared in Puebla, where he was the master of Antonio de Santander, if my suggestion is right. Unfortunately this is all we know about him.

We have no documentation about Juan Tinoco, except the many paintings from his hand which exist in Puebla. A set of *The Twelve Apostles, Jesus, and the Virgin* is in the Academia de Bellas Artes of Puebla; some of the Apostles are noble in conception and ably drawn (235). In the church of San Agustín is a *St. Rosalie,* signed and dated 1683, a quite adequate painting; in the vestibule of the chapter room of the Cathedral of Puebla, a *Biblical Battle*; and in the sacristy of La Concordia, *Our Lady as Protector,* attributed to him. The catalogue of the Barron Collection lists a signed painting by Tinoco, *The Mystic Marriage of*

235. Juan Tinoco. St. James. Oil. 1 x .50 m. Academia de Bellas Artes, Puebla.

St. Catharine. The name of Tinoco belongs among the best of the Puebla painters, immediately after Borgraf and Santander. His personality is very interesting; some historian might devote a little book to him.

Pascal Pérez was a mestizo; he was married on the first of November, 1683, in Puebla; by 1718 he was a master painter; he died in 1721 and was buried in the Cathedral. His work is very uneven. Among his pictures we may note: canvases representing *The Mysteries of the Rosary* listed by Pérez Salazar; and paintings of virgin martyrs, *St. Leocadia, St. Bibiana, St. Agueda, St. Barbara, St. Susanna, St. Quiteria,* and *St. Lucy,* all in the storerooms of the Colegio del Estado. In the portico of the parish church of San José are two large canvases of *The Crucifixion* and *The Descent from the Cross.* In the Capilla de San Felipe in the church of La Concordia in Puebla three quite acceptable canvases show scenes from the *Life of St. Cajetan*; this is perhaps the artist's best work, somber in tone like Borgraf's or Rodríguez Carnero's painting, and excellently handled. All the rest of his pictures seem mediocre, and some of them reach a rather low level, for example, a *Trinity* signed in 1708.

Cristóbal de Talavera was a painter of the end of the seventeenth century and the early eighteenth. He died on October 16, 1731. His sons were also painters, active in the following century, but quite mediocre. The father himself does not achieve a very high level of art, as we can see in a painting of *The Spiritual Lineage of St. Francis,* in the antesacristy of the church of San Francisco in Puebla, which is dated the year of his death, 1731.

Bernardino Polo was born in Huamantla, in the state of Tlaxcala, and headed a family of painters: his son, José Patricio (347),[8] and his nephew, José Aniceto. Some pictures by him exist in private collections; according to Pérez Salazar, they recall the color of Villalpando.

Juan de Villalobos married in Puebla in 1687, and died there on July 4, 1724. A good many of his paintings are preserved there, for example those decorating the sacristy of the Jesuit church, of which the best are *St. John the Evangelist, St. John the Baptist,* and, on the retable, *The Communion of St. Louis Gonzaga, The Holy Family,* and *The Virgin with St. Anne and*

St. Joachim. In the sacristy of San Francisco is a double portrait of *Bishop Santa Cruz and Bishop Gorozpe*; in the Sagrario, a *Baptism of Christ* and a *Washing of the Feet.* His best-known paintings are those decorating the *camarín* of the Sanctuary of Ocotlán (197); one of these is signed and dated 1723, and they represent scenes from *The Life of the Virgin.* To these we should add the painting of *St. Barbara with Madre María de Guadalupe* which is in the Museo Nacional de Historia in Mexico City; the portrait of the nun is magnificent, rendering the face with great sensual veracity. In San Martín Texmelucan are some pictures in the church of the Dieguinos; in the Museo del Carmen in San Ángel (Villa Obregón, Distrito Federal), a *Birth of the Virgin*; and other pictures in the Museo de Santa Mónica in Puebla. Such is the *oeuvre* we know for this artist, who for his time was indeed quite admirable.

Painting in Michoacán

We have already given some information about painting in Michoacán in the early days of the Colony, and have considered the painting of *The Entombment of Christ* which has been attributed to Titian. We should add the cult image now known as the *Perpetuo Socorro,* which was brought to Pátzcuaro by Don Vasco de Quiroga, and was so esteemed by him that it was hung in the place where he was buried.

As for early wall painting in churches and convents, we might note the painted vault of the old sacristy in the church of San Agustín in Morelia; it is of the type we have seen everywhere, though it has been spoiled by making the faces "pretty." Concerning indigenous painting, we know that the Indians of Tiripitío and Pátzcuaro were great painters; however, even by the seventeenth century we no longer find local artists, but paintings sent out from the metropolis to decorate the churches of Michoacán. Of this kind are two very interesting paintings in the Cathedral of Morelos, representing *The Circumcision* and *Jesus Disputing with the Doctors,* which recall the painting on the retable in the church of Xochimilco near Mexico City. Luis Juárez is represented by paintings in the Carmelite monastery, as we have noted, and also by a *Vesting of St. Ildefonsus* in the Cathedral. We have also noted the paintings by Becerra and Antonio Rodríguez in the church of San Agustín.

When we look for local painters of the region only three names appear: the Augustinian friars Pedro and

---

[8] See the ex-voto of Joseph Patricio Polo, dated 1741, in Huamantla, in the collection of Mr. and Mrs. Donald Weismann, Austin, Texas.

Simón Salguero, and the Franciscan Alberto Enríquez. Fray Matías Escobar speaks of the first two.[9] Of Fray Simón Salguero he says that he painted three portraits in the monastery of Charo, and later, in describing the Franciscan monastery in Morelia, that "the main stairway likewise has many and very numerous portraits, and the Death of Our Father St. Augustine, which is above the cornice, is from the hand of the *presentado* Fray Simón Salguero." (A *presentado* is a student who has finished his reading in theology and is candidate for the degree of *maestro*.)

More interesting are the documents concerning the Franciscan, Alberto Enríquez, who is generally called Fray Francisco Manuel de Cuadros. He was a Peruvian and made his living in Pátzcuaro as a *curandero*, a healer. On October 1, 1663, the *fiscal* entered a complaint of heresy against him. Testimony was taken, and he went to prison on December 14. He was then taken to Mexico City and there, after a trial full of incidents, his body was burned on March 21, 1678, in front of the church of San Diego. He had been executed by garroting because he gave signs of repentance.[10] I offer as pure conjecture the idea that the painting in oil on the wall of a very small cell opening in the wall of the church of San Francisco in Pátzcuaro may be the work of this painter, when he was confined there before being sent to Mexico City. The apparent date of the painting and the abnormal character of the artist make this hypothesis seem not impossible. This painting of *St. Francis* is of some quality; the saint is appearing to a dead Pope, attended by a friar.

Painting in Oaxaca

The large region which we know today as the state of Oaxaca had its colonial painting like the other parts of New Spain. As early as the sixteenth century we find codices and mural painting. Indeed, the monasteries of Yanhuitlán, Etla, and Cuilapan have magnificent examples of fresco painting on their walls. We also know that several great painters worked in Oaxaca: Andrés de la Concha at Yanhuitlán, Pereyns at Coixtlahuaca, and Arrúe in the city of Oaxaca, Etla, Tlacochahuaya, Huitzo, and Huajolotitlán.

There are some European paintings of considerable quality in the city of Oaxaca (the old Antequera), for example, a panel of *St. Sebastian* in the sacristy of the Cathedral, and a *St. Michael* of moderate interest, also on a panel, in the chapel of Guadalupe. In the church of La Soledad are six paintings of some value which Don Pedro Otálora brought from Europe. Two of them, *St. Mary Magdalene* and *St. Margaret,* are certainly Flemish, and the others, *St. Jerome, St. Theresa, St. Catherine,* and *St. Benedict Abbot,* are said to be Italian, although the *St. Jerome* would appear rather to be Spanish.

Among the artists of the early seventeenth century we should mention Marcial de Santaella, who seems to be a local painter; a *St. Christopher,* signed by him in 1726, and *Archangels in Glory* by him are in the Cathedral.

Painting in Yucatán

There is little information on the development of painting in Yucatán, though from the beginning of the Colony it is as lively as in other parts of Mexico. Thus we read that

among the friars whom the saintly Bishop Landa brought to this Province was Padre Fray Julián de Quartas: he was a native of Almagro and took the habit in the Province of Castille . . . he loved the Indians deeply, and taught them painting, gilding, and carving . . . and this was how it came about that there are very many of them who are painters, gilders, and sculptors . . . They were so well trained by Spanish masters that today there are in this land artists unsurpassed in skill by the best in the world.[11]

Bishop Landa arrived in 1549; so if, as the chronicler states, Padre Quartas was nineteen years old when he arrived, and died at the age of fifty-seven, he must have been born about 1530, and died in 1587.

Padre Lizana also mentions other painters, and this does suggest that there were a great number of artists there. When Padre Fray Pedro Cardete died in 1619, his portrait was painted on the bier, though it did not look like him because the body had swollen after death; the chronicler explains that the painter wanted to paint him before he died, but the friar would not permit it.[12]

He also tells us that in the chapel of the monastery of Izamal there were painted *The Miracles of the Virgin,*[13] though he does not indicate whether these were murals or paintings on an altarpiece.

[9] Matías Escobar, *Americana Thebaida,* pp. 218, 418.
[10] See José Toribio Medina, *Historia del tribunal del Santo Oficio de la Inquisición en México* for documentation on this trial.
[11] Bernardo de Lizana, *Historia y conquista espiritual de Yucatán,* fol. 97 v.
[12] *Ibid.,* fol. 110.
[13] *Ibid.,* fol. 31 v.

In spite of the eulogies paid to the Yucatecan artists by Padre Lizana, the fact is that in the year 1621 painting was in decline, or at least had fallen into religious impropriety, since the Inquisition intervened, ordering that a watch be kept over the paintings which the Indians owned.[14]

I know only two Yucatecan paintings from this period which, without being important work, are worth mentioning: a *St. Augustine* and a *St. Ambrose* which are in a private collection and which from photographs appear to be distinguished work. Studying the pictures themselves, one sees that they are of only moderate quality; but they are interesting because they are quite different from colonial painting in any other part of Mexico. Painted in large strokes on a dark ground, they are not without a certain force.

Painting in Tlaxcala

The ancient nation of Tlaxcala was always a land of painters. Both in the murals decorating the monasteries and in the painting of post-Hispanic codices, the Tlaxcaltecans ranked among the first, as we have seen. Some of this work in Tlaxcala is quite different from similar work elsewhere in New Spain—for example, the murals decorating the old open chapel of Tizatlán, which was built, according to tradition, on the site of the Palace of Xicoténcatl.[15]

The privileges granted to the Indians of Tlaxcala by the Crown in return for their assistance in the Conquest worked to make Tlaxcala little more than a dead city, and naturally there were fewer European artists here than elsewhere. Documents concerning painting are scarce in this city. In regard to European painting, we have already mentioned two small pictures in the church of San Francisco which can be attributed to Zurbarán. The painters who were active in Tlaxcala were usually from Puebla; there is the *St. Theresa* by Borgraf, already mentioned, and the pictures by Juan de Villalobos in the *camarín* of the Sanctuary of Ocotlán (197). The only reference which seems to be clearly Tlaxcaltecan refers to a dynasty of painters, the Caro family. The oldest, Antonio Caro, appears in 1676 as master painter in Tlaxcala. In 1751 Manuel Caro was born there, and in 1763, his brother Mariano. Another member of the family who signed his paintings in Tlaxcala was José Caro de Ayala, but these last three are artists of the eighteenth century. This does clear up one problem: Pérez Salazar supposed that the Caro family came from Puebla, but in fact they were from Tlaxcala.

Miguel Lucas de Bedolla signed paintings in the Sanctuary of Ocotlán which can be dated in this period. They have very little importance.

Painting in Nueva Galicia

Unhappily we do not have enough data to write the history of art in this important region. One could not claim that painting flourished there as abundantly and as continuously as in some other places—Puebla, for instance—but there are indications that it did achieve some importance in Nueva Galicia.

Primitive painting in fresco was used to decorate the conventual establishments just as elsewhere; we know, for instance, that the portraits of the founding friars could be seen in the *portería* of the Franciscan monastery in Guadalajara.[16]

Padre Tello repeatedly gives information about paintings, but never so precisely as we should like. Thus, from a letter of the viceroy, Don Luis de Velasco, written in Mexico City on April 13, 1594, to the President of the Audiencia de Nueva Galicia, we learn that Capitán Juan Ochoa had requested the paint to make seven retables. From this we deduce that there were artists capable of painting them, and that only pigments were needed. Again, he tells us of an image of *St. Michael* painted on leather which shone with radiance on Michaelmas of 1536 or 1540, because of a victory of the Spaniards over the Indians; this was the reason why the residents of Guadalajara committed their city to the holy archangel as patron.[17]

This chronicler also gives some information about painting in the northern cities which belonged to the Audiencia de Nueva Galicia. He says that in the Llanos de las Vacas certain nomadic Indians tanned the hides of the cows they killed to make clothing, and in some places these hides were very finely painted.[18] In the region of Tiguex and Marsata, he reports, the portraits of some friars who had been martyred by the Indians were found, so realistic that it was plain that they had been killed by sticks and stones. These martyrs were

[14] Archivo General de la Nación. Tomo *Inquisición*, No. 486.

[15] Manuel Toussaint, "Un templo cristiano sobre el palacio de Xicoténcatl en Tizatlán," in *Paseos coloniales*, pp. 44–46.

[16] José Ignacio Paulino Dávila Garibi, *Breves apuntes acerca de los chimalhuacanos*.

[17] Antonio Tello, *Libro segundo de la Crónica miscelanea de la santa provincia de Xalisco*, p. 237.

[18] *Ibid.*, p. 430.

Fray Agustín Ramírez and Fray Francisco López, and the converts who were accompanying them were killed with them.[19]

For the seventeenth century the records continue to be scarce. Juan Ibáñez, *maestro de pintor,* was buried in Guadalajara on April 16, 1626; Francisco Flores, also a painter, testified in the inquiry concerning the miraculous image Nuestra Señora de San Juan de los Lagos in 1668.[20] Concerning Ibáñez, we know that he decorated the Cathedral of Guadalajara, between 1618 and 1625, with frescoes of subjects from Holy Scripture.[21]

Don Tadeo Ortiz mentions Lavandera, who, he says, worked as a painter in the city of Jalisco; but this reference has little value, since Ortiz' book is hardly serious.[22]

An artist who seems to date from this period is José Aguilar, whose painting of *The Holy Trinity with Saints* is preserved in the Museo de Guadalajara.

The most important artist of Nueva Galicia, in the early eighteenth century, was Diego de Cuentas, although his work is very uneven. It is not certain, in fact, that he was from Jalisco, since there are pictures by him in Guadalajara, Morelia, Zacatecas, and Mexico City; but I place him in Guadalajara because his paintings are more numerous there. There are five in the Museo de Guadalajara: an *Immaculate Conception,* signed in 1739; *St. John of the Cross; The Virgin of the Apocalypse;* seven *Archangels;* and a *Trinity,* of 1737; also, the portrait of *Fray Felipe Galán,* bishop of Nueva Galicia from 1696 to 1702, and founder of the Seminary. In the Museo Michoacana in Morelia is a mediocre portrait of *Don Vasco de Quiroga,* and in the Museo de Pintura of the Colegio de Zacatecas, the portrait of *Fray José Guerra,* signed and dated 1730, which is a quite acceptable painting. Somewhat better are the four *Evangelists* in the church of La Profesa in Mexico City, certainly his most interesting work. They show mastery and vigor of touch, as it were a recollection of seventeenth-century painting.[23]

It only remains to recall that there are magnificent European paintings in Guadalajara, as we have already mentioned. One should also bear in mind that many of the paintings which make up the collections in Guadalajara are by the great colonial painters, from Luis Juárez on.

Painting in Querétaro

In this period documentation on painting in Querétaro is as scarce as it is abundant for sculpture; later we have more material.

Concerning seventeenth-century artists there is only a reference to the *Guadalupana,* which, according to Sigüenza y Góngora's *Glorias de Querétaro,* was painted by Baltasar de Echave y Rioja for the church of Guadalupe, along with six angels by him.[24]

In studying a private collection from Querétaro, I found two artists who can be placed in the seventeenth century. The first signed his paintings Peralta; these were a *Head of John the Baptist,* signed in 1679, *St. Peter, St. Ignatius,* and *St. Francis Xavier,* and an oval picture of *Several Saints,* signed and dated 1659. He is an artist of some worth, sober in technique, using vigorous chiaroscuro like Arteaga's. In the eighteenth century we shall find several artists in Querétaro by the name of Peralta; probably we have to do with a family of painters, of whom this is the first.

In the same collection was a *St. Anne Teaching the Virgin to Write,* signed by Camacho. It is quite acceptable, and in style recalls the four little *Evangelists* of Echave Ibía.

José García, painter, gilder, and *estofador,* appears to have been active in the first half of the eighteenth century. In the corridor of the Congregación de Guadalupe there are several *Apostles,* signed by him in 1723; in the church of San Antonio, *Christ Carrying the Cross,* of the same year; also a nun's coat of arms without date. His most important work, however, is a piece of sculpture which we consider elsewhere in this volume.

Such is the information, little enough, to be sure, which we have about painting in Querétaro during this period. In the eighteenth century we shall find a number of painters there.

19 *Ibid.,* p. 494.

20 Alberto Santoscoy, *Historia de Nuestra Señora de San Juan de los Lagos,* p. 35.

21 F. P. Laris, *Guadalajara desconocida,* I, 2.

22 Tadeo Ortiz de Ayala, *México considerado como nación independiente y libre,* pp. 228–229.

23 See Leopoldo I. Orendáin, "El pintor Diego A. de Cuentas," *Anales del Instituto de Investigaciones Estéticas,* 19 (1951), 75–85.

24 Carlos de Sigüenza y Góngora, *Glorias de Querétaro.*

Chapter Thirteen

THE MINOR ARTS DURING
THE EARLY BAROQUE PERIOD

Work in Gold and Silver

THE ART of working precious metals reaches its climax, as one might expect, in the Baroque period. Following our system of arrangement, we shall first discuss valuable examples of the jeweller's art—both religious and secular gold work—and then silverware. The documentation is very extensive; we shall have to limit ourselves to the most important examples for our discussion.

Religious Artifacts

First of all we must consider the great custodia of Santo Domingo de la Calzada in Spain, which was the gift of a Mexican, Don Gaspar Osio, a wealthy resident of San Miguel el Grande, in 1655. It is one meter, twenty centimeters in height; "the Baroque decoration is light, the architectonic line dominates; beautiful, severe, and untinctured by the Rococo."[1] It is of silver, gold-plated, with enamelled decoration, red geometric designs on a white ground. There is a monstrance in the Treasure of the Cathedral of Mexico which, though small, has exactly the same Baroque form.

Among the most outstanding religious artifacts should be listed also the gold crown of the Virgen de los Desamparados in Toledo, which was made in Mex-

ico in the seventeenth century. It is in the form of a basket of flowers, delicate in design and loaded with emeralds, and was the work of the Guatemaltecan silversmith Andrés Martínez, in 1641.[2]

In the study we have frequently referred to, Señor Romero de Terreros describes other splendid religious ornaments, such as those which gave luster to the canonization of St. John of God in the city of Mexico in October of 1700. "The images of the saints which were carried in procession were loaded with jewelry, the image of St. Augustine and of St. John himself outstanding among them." Robles says that St. Augustine was "carried by an eagle, and held in his hand a church made of crystal and gold, with a clock in it which told time; and the eagle carried an inkwell of diamonds, emeralds, and pearls in its beak." St. John of God wore a robe which had been given by Doña Andrea de Guzmán, Duquesa de Atlixco, wife of the viceroy. It was "embroidered and fringed most intricately in gold

---

[1] Manuel Romero de Terreros, *Las artes industriales en la Nueva España*, p. 33. He quotes this description from the work of Anselmo Gascón de Gotor, *El Corpus Christi y las custodias procesionales de España*.
[2] *Ibid.*, p. 33.

258

and silver thread, with patterns of flowers and pomegranates, the cuffs all of emeralds, garnished with gold, and the pomegranate seeds were rubies, also set in gold; the diadem was of diamonds and pearls." In 1728 the Virgen del Rosario of the Dominican monastery in Puebla had a robe embroidered with pearls valued at 230,000 pesos, and a gown with diamonds, rubies, and emeralds worth 52,500, which were enormous sums at that time. Her two crowns, according to the *Gaceta*, were worth 32,000 pesos, and "the headdress which is made of diamonds, 8,000."[3]

The Treasure of the Cathedral of Mexico was enriched in this period by a good many very valuable vessels (236). Most important in the inventories is the *custodia* given by the Dean, Don Juan de Salcedo. It was remarkable for the wealth of precious stones decorating it: amethysts, jacinths, sapphires, pearls, emeralds, rubies, topazes, pearls, garnets. On the base appeared the coat of arms of the Valle de Salcedo.

In the inventory of 1649 appear the objects from the legacy of Archbishop Feliciano de la Vega. Among them are: a chalice with its paten of gold, its base of enamelled silver; a crucifix of gilded silver with blue enamel; an image of Our Lady with the Child Jesus, all in silver, seated on a pedestal of the same metal. In 1654 a cross of gilded silver is listed, the gift of Archbishop Guerrero and restored by Mañozca; it seems to be the base of a tabernacle in the form of a Greek cross.

The inventory of 1704 lists four exquisite silver altar fronts for the high altar. The first was decorated with the Virgin of the Assumption, with cherubim. The second, the gift of Dean Malpartida, was of engraved silver and displayed the Last Supper in the center and the coat of arms of St. Peter. In 1706 the inventory lists a pyx of gold which consisted of a chalice, pall (*hijuela*), and cover; it was enamelled on the outside, with four overlays of gold with figures of babies, and was the gift of Canon Don Nicolás Orrego. In 1713 we find the magnificent silver lavabo which decorated the sacristy. It had appeared in 1704, and is described in this way: ". . . a silver font which is in the sacristy of this holy church, which the Señor Deán Don Diego Malpartida y Zenteno gave in the year 1689 so that the *señores sacerdotes,* the priests, could wash their hands, with a scroll which says that it is commended to God." A note in the inventory provides that if the lavabo was about to be destroyed or made into something else, it

3 *Ibid.*, pp. 38–39.

236. Monstrance. Silver. Museo Nacional del Virreinato, Tepotzotlán, México.

should go to the oratory of San Felipe Neri. From its description we learn that it consisted of a support of silver on a base of painted stone; a large basin rested on this support, and above this basin another support held a smaller basin. The Cabildo added a finial of silver in the form of an eagle, with the shield of St. Peter in gilded silver on its breast.

237. Brooch. Silver and jewels. Private collection.

238. Brooch, reverse. Silver. Private collection.

From the inventory of 1713 we learn of another smaller font of gilded silver with statues of mermaids and three nude figures enclosed by lattice and vines. This is apparently an object in Renaissance style which had been acquired later.

Jewelry

If the treasures of the church were such jewels as these, personal jewelry was no less lavish (237, 238). Unhappily we have no examples securely dated from this period, but we do have descriptions in the inventories which allow us to appraise its quality. The information comes from testamentary evaluations, from the appraisals made by master silversmiths when the inventory of each estate was made. We shall quote only selected items, to avoid tiresome repetition.

In 1683 we find some earrings: *chambergos* (hatshaped?) of gold and pearls, others crescent-shaped, others of almond-shaped crystal, and several bracelets of small pearls (*pulseras de rostrillo*).[4]

In 1704, pendant earrings of emeralds, with pearshaped drops (*asardinados*), valued at 250 pesos.

In 1711, in the estate of Don Joseph Estrada, bracelets of seed pearls, others of smaller pearls, a ring in the form of a feather, some *negras* of gold and pearls,

[4] The term *rostrillo* refers, of course, to small, irregular pearls. The very curious manner in which they were graded is worth noting, since the terms were in common usage: the *rostrillo* was an irregular pearl which weighed 600 to the ounce; the *rostrillo grueso* weighed 500 pearls to the ounce; *rostrillo menudo,* 700 pearls to the ounce; *medio rostrillo,* 1,200 pearls to the ounce; *medio rostrillo grueso,* 850 pearls to the ounce; *medio rostrillo mejor,* 1,000 pearls to the ounce.

some earrings like woven straw (*petatillos*) with two knots at the top, some *bamboyas* ("show-offs") of gold and pearl, some mermaids with their chains of gold and pearls, a jewel of the Immaculate Conception, of jacinths and pearls, four pendants of *berruecos*,[5] a spoon and *mancerina* (a chocolate-cup holder) of tortoise shell with a silver base.

In the same year, 1711, we find in another inventory: two drop earrings *de chiquihuite* (basket-shaped?); some earrings with parrots (*cochos*) set with irregular pearls, weighing ten *granos*; other small earrings of gold with their little drops (*chorritos*); a memorial ring of four bands and a rosette of gold with a diamond.

In 1722, in the estate of Don Domingo de Cuevas y Sandoval, a master candlemaker who seems to have earned more as a pawnbroker than by his craft, we find the following items: a set of emeralds, consisting of some large pear-shaped eardrops, a cabochon on each, and four little cabochons, a pendant (*joya de pecho*) with one hundred and six emeralds, a plume with sixty-one emeralds, another smaller one with six small cabochons and forty emeralds; a choker of three strands, with nine emeralds on each one. These jewels belonged to Capitán Miguel Hipólito de Cuevas, who had pawned them for 388 pesos.

A small gold reliquary with the Virgin of Loreto and St. Cajetan, enamelled, which belonged to Doña María Montalvo, wife of Don Bartolomé Calderón, and had been pawned for 20 *reales*.

Some earrings in the form of little baskets of gold and small pearls; they belonged to Nicolás Antonio, an Indian sculptor, who had borrowed 20 pesos, 4 *reales* on them.

In 1720 we find the following entry, a really magnificent object, in the estate of Doña Teresa Ramírez de la Torre: a set composed of a bowknot, with another smaller one pendant, made in the antique style, garnished with diamonds set in silver and emeralds in gold, enamelled white on the back, and decorated with purple; some eardrops in three pieces with the same stones and the same form, and a gold watch of painted porcelain, in bad condition, ornamented with the said stones. All these jewels, with 384 diamonds, some rose-cut and some flat-cut, and 93 emeralds, were appraised at the sum of 1,120 pesos.

The jewels which Romero de Terreros describes in the book we so often refer to should also be mentioned. From the estate of Capitán Don Ginés Gómez de

Valdés, he mentions the following, listed in the inventory of his possessions in 1723: ". . . two pearl chokers, one of three strands made up of 126 beads, *garbanzos, garbanzón y pimienta*; the other of two strands with 164 pearls, *culantro y calabacitas*. Since the pearls are apparently graded by vegetable terms—chick-peas, large peas, pepper, coriander, and little squashes—Romero de Terreros observes that we seem to be dealing rather with horticulture than with gems![6]

Household Silver

Silversmiths were as busy as the jewellers. The artisans had increased considerably in number. We know this from various documents, for instance the *matrícula* or register of silversmiths, makers of gold thread and beaters of gold leaf in Mexico City in 1685, as recorded by Francisco Pérez de León, Contador de Monedas de la Real Audiencia.[7] Forty-three silversmiths are listed with their shops; there are fourteen wiredrawers and fifteen goldbeaters, which is indeed a good number for Mexico City at that time. Many names of workers in the precious metals can be found by going through the archives of the Secretaría de Hacienda, which are now preserved in the Archivo General de la Nación, especially in the documents referring to the *media anata*. From these documents one can see what an extraordinary level the art of the silversmith had reached in New Spain.

It is interesting to have the names of objects made in silver which were used in the Baroque period, and we can give two such lists. One consists of the prizes offered in the poetry contests sponsored by the University; they are reported by Don Carlos de Sigüenza y Góngora in his *Triumpho Parthénico*:[8]

A clasp-knife (*flamenca*) of silver with relief engravings
A silver box for tobacco
A salver of silver, gilt
A silver tray
A large cocoanut shell set in silver
A little salver and narrow-necked vessel of silver
An elegant rose in silver filigree
A Mendoza saltcellar of silver
A big silver plate

---

[5] The *berrueco*, as we all know, is a pearl of irregular shape—a Baroque pearl.

[6] Romero de Terreros, *Artes industriales*, p. 34.

[7] Published by José Torre Revello in his interesting study, *El gremio de plateros en las Indias Occidentales*.

[8] Carlos de Sigüenza y Góngora, *Triumpho parthénico*.

239. Chair from the Old Cabildo of Mexico City. Wood with embroidered leather. Cathedral of Mexico.

240. Chair. Wood with embroidered velvet. Franz Mayer Collection, Mexico City.

A, little holy-water font
A half-dozen china cups decorated with silver
A silver mug
A silver drinking cup (*vernegal*)
Two handsome candlesticks of silver
A powder box
A delicate bowl (*tembladera*) of silver, *quintada*
A silver writing-case
A scalloped plate (*vandeja*) of silver
A handsome bowl of silver (*avellanada*)
A gilded silver apple for perfumed water

The other list comes from the Inquisition. Maestro Nicolás Ruiz, silversmith of Puebla de los Ángeles, presented his bill to the Inquisition in Mexico City in 1675 for making the following pieces: "Four candlesticks, a dozen plates, two salvers, two dishes (*fuentes*), and a candlestick, eight spoons, and two knife-handles."

Furniture

Baroque furniture continued to be enormously influenced by Moorish customs, and it was not until well into the eighteenth century that this attitude was to change, with a search for new forms. Characteristic of Baroque furniture are legs in the form of twisted columns, and certain ornamental details very similar to what we find on the large carved retables. Such permanent church fixtures as choir stalls have already been discussed under sculpture; many writers consider them simply as furniture, but I feel that they are an integral part of the building, like the retables and pulpits.

Certainly the great cupboards (*cajoneras*) which ornament the sacristies of the churches should be considered among ecclesiastical furniture. We note therefore those of the Cathedral of Mexico, those of the Cathedral of Puebla, and, among the most sumptuous, those which were in the church of San Francisco Acatepec, now destroyed. These cupboards belong to a period of transition from Renaissance to Baroque style. The vertical supports are the typical uprights of a Baroque retable, while the fronts of the drawers are covered with Renaissance relief, although their excessive ornament could also be considered Baroque in feeling.

The chair—the most interesting piece of furniture in the colonial period, as we have said—takes on a characteristic form in this period. It is no longer the French chair which appeared in earlier inventories, nor the Italian chair which they used at the time of the Conquest, but the type of armchair which we know as a *sillón*. Certainly some chairs of this type were made even in the sixteenth century; an example can be seen in the sacristy of the church in Mixquic, in the Federal District, covered in red velvet with Renaissance embroidery. In all the paintings of the seventeenth century we see these armchairs of dignified design. Extant examples are those now in the Cathedral of Mexico, which belonged to the Old Cabildo (239); the back and the seat are of leather decorated with very fine embroidery in maguey fiber. Little by little these Baroque chairs grew more and more complicated, not only in ornament, but in the form itself, until their lines were indeed capricious, and the carving of the legs was in such high relief that it must have been frightfully uncomfortable (240).

Cupboards (*armarios*) continued to be used, as in the preceding period. The beds are the same beds of West Indian ebony (*granadillo*), with legs in the form of twisted columns which continue upward to hold the canopy. Some beds were painted; red was the favorite color, and they were ornamented with gilded carving.

Ironwork

Magnificent examples of wrought iron were created in the Baroque period; naturally, as time passed, the work became more expert, and the craftsmen could achieve results which would have been impossible earlier. Practically all the grilles and railings we have now are Baroque. Outstanding among them are those of the Cathedral of Puebla. In 1691 the dean, Victoria Salazar, commissioned the transept railings, and six years later, the grille of the choir, to be painted and gilded, with a frieze of cherubim and egg-and-dart halfway up, crowned with volutes and balls. This was the work of the master blacksmith Mateo de la Cruz; it cost 4,600 pesos and weighed 269 *arrobas*.[9] The grilles of

241. Grille and gate. Wrought iron and sheet iron. Church of El Santo Angel, Analco, Puebla.

the chapels were the work of the *maestro* Juan de Leyva Pavón, and each one weighed 500 *quintales*. They are all alike, with variations in the decorative detail at the top and the symbols of the advocacy of each chapel.[10] All these grilles were gilded. There are also Baroque grilles in the church of El Santo Ángel de Analco in Puebla (241). The most important of these, which seems to date from 1751, was the gift of Roque Jacinto de Illescas; the other is dated 1723. These grilles combine wrought iron with various figures cut out of sheet iron.

[9] Romero de Terreros, *Artes industriales,* referring to Diego Bermúdez de Castro's *Teatro angelopolitano.*
[10] Romero de Terreros, *Artes industriales,* p. 99.

263

242. Lock and hinges. Wrought iron.
Museo Nacional de Historia, Mexico City.

The *oeuvre* of the master locksmiths in the seventeenth century continues to be the same direct and artistic work as in the preceding period. The keyholes of chests and boxes have a typical form at this time: they are usually shields drawn in reverse curves. Often, as we have noted, the two-headed eagle of the Habsburgs appears as a decorative motif. The iron is not merely wrought but often engraved as well; that is, the basic forging of the metal is supplemented by cold-chiselling, to give a more elaborate result (242). From this time on we begin to have very rich work.

There are a great number of magnificent examples from this period in private and public collections. The most important public collection is that of the Museo

de Historia, and of the private collections, the Museo Bello in Puebla.

There is very little documentation on blacksmiths of this period. The following description of a valuable example comes from the evaluation in 1702 of the estate of Francisco de Izarrazábal:

. . . iron stirrups, with openwork below, their plates of gold enamelled in white, green, and red, and the border around them of gilded silver; their worth or value: one cannot estimate what it may be, since in order to measure it, they would have to be taken apart and broken up, which would spoil them and destroy them, and so, as an estimate, in their present state, they are here valued at 150 pesos, more or less.[11]

Ceramics

During the seventeenth century the art of ceramics took on extraordinary importance. The Puebla ware called *talavera* was developed to a high level; it was the only product that could compete with Chinese porcelain. It took on an architectural role, furthermore. Now in Mexico an effect was achieved which can be found in only a few places in the world, as the whole façades of buildings were covered with glazed tile, of the sort called *azulejos*.

The ordinances governing the craft were decreed in this period. The ordinances for potters in the city of Puebla were published on August 22, 1666; those for the city of Mexico were issued on July 6, 1677, and confirmed by the viceroy, the Conde de Paredes, on October 1, 1681.

The ordinances of the potters are like those of all the other guilds in regard to administration. It should be noted that these ordinances deal with the whole ceramic industry, and not only with what we know today as *talavera poblana*. The fifth article of the ordinances of Puebla distinguishes three categories of pottery: fine pottery (*loza fina*), plain pottery (*loza común*), and yellow ware (*loza amarilla*). "Yellow ware" means cooking utensils—jugs, pots, casseroles—and those who make this type of pottery are forbidden to make either "fine" or "plain" pottery. This prohibition is followed by the further caution that each master potter can work only in the category in which he has been examined, and in no other. The eighth article dictates technical standards for the craft: that the clay

[11] Archivo de los Alcaldes Ordinarios y Corregidores de México.

be well strained and clean; that the glaze for *loza fina* must be made with one *arroba* of lead and six pounds of tin; that if it is painted it must be outlined with black; and that each piece must be *delgado por parejo*, equally thin, that is to say, uniform in thickness. For plain white pottery the glaze must be made with one *arroba* of lead and two pounds of tin, and the same for medium-quality painted ware. Finally, each master should have his mark and should put it on each piece he makes.[12]

The ordinances of the potters of Mexico City are similar. They direct that the master potters should convene in the church of the parish of Santa Veracruz, the meeting place of their Confraternity of Santa Justina y Rufina, to elect their overseers. To be examined for the craft one must be a Spaniard or a mestizo, not a Negro or a mulatto; Negroes and mulattoes cannot be master craftsmen, only journeymen. The article dealing with technical standards sets the following requirements: in the glaze for plain pottery there must be two pounds of tin for each *arroba* of lead, rather more than less. The clay must be of good quality and strained, and

. . . each straining must have ten basketloads (*guacales o chiquigüites*) of white clay and twelve of dark, so that the clay will be strong and will take colors well. The same should be done in the case of fine pottery, keeping to the good colors which are requisite, rejecting the color green so that the said pottery should not be painted with it, since it is not permanent and exposes the pottery to the danger of crackling. And in the case of plain pottery there should be painted in the center a small blue *berenjena* (eggplant), so that it will be known for plain pottery; and in imitations the pottery must be carefully painted blue in the middle, and no other grade should be painted blue. . . . And for medium quality the glaze is to be prepared with one *arroba* of lead and four pounds of tin, painting this pottery only with interlacing or dots, and in types of colors which are superior and of great variety. And fine pottery, for each *arroba* of lead should have six pounds of tin, and should be painted in blue and black; and each master should place on what he makes a mark which should be exhibited at the time of his examination by the court and should be affixed to his certificate. And pottery which is not made according to this specification will be held spurious, and anyone who complains will be supported, and a fine will be imposed of twenty pesos, to be paid in quarters.[13]

[12] Enrique A. Cervantes, *Loza blanca y azulejo de Puebla*.
[13] Francisco del Barrio Lorenzot, *Ordenanzas de gremios de la Nueva España*.

243. Talavera flowerpot, Chinese type.
Metropolitan Museum of Art, New York.

The Mexican ordinances also distinguish three types of pottery, but not the same as those of Puebla: white ware, yellow ware, and red ware.

Examples from the second half of the seventeenth century show a pronounced Chinese influence (243); they are decorated in two tones of blue, a light blue in dots, and another dark blue, in thick coats which form the designs. It is not only the technique which imitates Chinese porcelain; the decorative motifs are similarly inspired, to the point where Chinese people appear in the bottoms of the bowls. Some of this pottery is truly splendid. Throughout the century they continued to use the same formula, characterized by a light blue combined with a strong blue. Sometimes the blue glaze of the pattern is so thick it has actual relief, so that the bowl seems not merely glazed but carved.

As we have said, the ceramics of Puebla had a decisive influence on the architecture of that city. In fact these buildings have a unique appearance: their façades are covered with tile, glazed and unglazed, of various kinds and in various combinations. Though one cannot prove it, this form of decoration certainly recalls the famous Mudejar pavements known as *olambrilla,* except that in those the brick is usually large and the glazed tile a tiny piece completing the decoration, while on the houses of Puebla the *azulejo,* the glazed tile, is about half the size of the brick, which allows a great variety of patterns. Some of the notable buildings of this period should be mentioned. The most important of them, without any doubt, is the church of San Francisco Acatepec, near Cholula (192). This façade, in a lavish Baroque style, where Churrigueresque forms begin to emerge in the timid estípites, is completely executed in glazed tile. These tiles were designed expressly for this façade; there are special pieces indispensable to the architectural motifs, such as the small ceramic units which build up the twisted columns, or the pieces which form the mouldings. So splendid is this façade that it seems like a porcelain church which ought to be protected by a dome of glass.

Among other churches of Puebla, one must mention the famous Capilla del Rosario, whose decorative sculpture we have already discussed. A good deal of glazed tile is used there, both outside and inside. The outside of the dome is decorated with tile, which covers the columns between the windows above the *lucernas* and also those of the lantern. Between the broken pediments over the windows are ceramic sculptures of distinctly popular flavor. The tiles of the interior are magnificent, especially those in Mudejar patterns which form the dado, finished by a frieze of cherubim in relief alternating with the fleur-de-lys insignia of the Dominican Order (189). These tiles are very fine, and they have occasioned the most absurd opinions; such as that they were brought from Persia expressly for this chapel—which reveals a total ignorance of Persian art. These tiles are indeed lovely, but they do not have the technical perfection of Persian tiles, nor even of the ceramics of Talavera de la Reina or Seville in Spain. The Capilla del Rosario, as we have said, was dedicated in 1690.

The tiles from certain rooms of the monastery of La Soledad in Puebla (now in the collections of Don Mariano Bello and of the Museo del Estado in Puebla) seem earlier, since they still show Renaissance designs.

The drawing is delicate and the colors are simple: light blue, yellow, and green, with dark outlines.

We should also note the tiles which cover the dome of the Cathedral of Puebla, which date from 1649, as we have said, and which give it an unusual appearance.

The *azulejos* of Puebla in the seventeenth century have certain specific characteristics which are easily identifiable. The costumes represented have naturally served as a means of dating, since it is unlikely that people would be represented in clothing long out of fashion, and even less likely in clothing which was not yet in use. Barber has accurately identified certain tiles of the middle of the seventeenth century; among them we should note the very characteristic ones with the mark *F,* and others with the mark of a bee.[14] Although these marks have not been identified, one can establish the period from the costume of the people represented, and so by similarities of style attribute other ceramics which do not offer such details of costume.

In Mexico City tile was not so generally used as in Puebla. *Tezontle* was the typical decoration for buildings there, and indeed that decorative resource may have inspired in rival cities the adoption of tile revetment. But this is not to say that tile was not used in a good number of houses in the capital. The outstanding, if somewhat exotic, example is the incomparable Casa de los Azulejos, or House of Tiles (289). Actually domes were usually decorated with tile all over the country, and we see churches of this period in Mexico City in which tile is richly used. Among seventeenth-century buildings there is the bell tower of the church of La Encarnación, handsomely decorated with *azulejos,* and that of the church of Balvanera, which, with its very beautiful yellow and blue tile, is as fine as any of the towers of Puebla.

There are really magnificent examples of pottery from this period in private collections; one hardly knows whether to admire the audacity of their size, or their decoration and the excellence of the designs that cover them. It must be admitted, all the same, that in spite of our enthusiasm they are far from being perfect pieces, nor are they comparable to European ceramics of the time. They have a quality which, if for some it is an attraction, unquestionably constitutes a defect for others: the quality of popular art. Technically they had not achieved the perfection of European work; they were dominated by the Baroque, which was an emi-

---

[14] Edwin Atlee Barber, *The Maiolica of Mexico.*

244. Grille and gallery of the choir. Cathedral of Mexico.

nently "popular" style. Indeed, we must repeat, very few pieces are worthy to be compared, not only to the ceramics of Renaissance Italy, but even to the famous Hispano-Moorish ceramics of the Middle Ages, which produced the marvels of Valencian pottery with its metallic reflections.

Bronze

The use of bronze was not known in Mexico before the Conquest. The Indians used copper and tin, but they had not discovered the secret of combining them. At the time of the Conquest military necessity forced the Spanish to undertake to make bronze, since cannon were cast in that metal in those days. To obtain it, Hernán Cortés, who knew that there were tin mines in the Taxco region, sent prospectors to look for the coveted metal and to report on the mineral resources of the region. Cortés succeeded in casting his bronze cannon and later, when the Conquest had been achieved and spirits were somewhat pacified, bronze served a purpose more peaceful and welcome: to make the many

bells which were needed for the new churches being built.

A few bells of the sixteenth century have been preserved; they have a characteristic long shape which little by little changed until the bells had less length and greater diameter. Among these early bells are those of the monastery of Acolman, on which the place glyph of the town appears in relief.

As an appendix to this section I am publishing the complete catalogue of the bells of the Cathedral of Mexico, with their dates and makers when these are known, from a document of 1796 in the Cathedral archives, and also a list of the more important bells of the Cathedral of Puebla.

In the seventeenth century small bells which had a special distinction were also cast: they were consecrated to the task of helping the faithful to a good death. These bells are extraordinarily fine because they were finished on a lathe, and they are composed of a series of concentric mouldings which give them a great elegance.

Bronze was also used to make grilles and railings

for sumptuous buildings. We do not know whether some may have been made in the seventeenth century; those we have now all date from the eighteenth. We must mention, however, the great screen of the choir in the Cathedral of Mexico (244). Although this was not executed in New Spain, it should be considered a part of our colonial heritage, since it was designed by the painter Nicolás Rodríguez Juárez, whom we have already discussed. The drawings were taken to China and the work was done in the city of Macao by the Chinese craftsman Quiauló. It is curious but natural that the Chinese metalworkers could not understand the drawings of the Mexican painter, which had to be explained to them by a Franciscan friar. What with one thing and another, the screen did not come out exactly right in its dimensions, and it was necessary to have it cut down in Mexico, which was done by Jerónimo de Balbás, who also installed it. It was inaugurated on March 10, 1730.[15]

This is without any doubt the most sumptuous choir screen in the New World. It is made not simply of bronze, but of two Oriental alloys of precious metals, called *tumbago* and *calain*. Tombac is a fine bronze, of a rich, ruddy color, which contains a considerable proportion of gold. *Calain* is a similar alloy, but much lighter in tone, so that it is like a high light against the darkness of the tombac. The balusters of the screen are perfect, and the doorway is a semicircular arch in the center; a variety of ornaments finish the top, and the screen itself is topped by a Calvary, as usual.

The railings of the *crujía,* the passageway from the choir to the high altar, were made in Mexico, contrary to the opinion often published. It is of bronze, and is a piece of Baroque art of the first order, with its balusters and railings and the angels bearing candelabra. The author of this magnificent work was Don José de Lemus, master worker in brass and copper, whose shop was in the Calle de Tacuba; he finished it in 1745, assisted by another master of the same craft, Don Manuel del Castillo.

We should also note a bust of Philip V placed over a portal in the Casa de Moneda (now the Museo de

Antropología) where it still is,[16] and the magnificent St. Michael on the tower of the church of the Hospital de Jesús, which may also date from the seventeenth century.

In 1625 the name of Baltasar Ferra, brassworker, appears in the documents; in 1622, Hernán Sánchez *el mozo* (the Younger) is working as a journeyman bell caster. Many other bell casters are named in the following lists.

BELLS OF THE CATHEDRAL OF MEXICO ACCORDING TO A DOCUMENT OF 1796

SIXTEENTH CENTURY

Simón and Juan Buenaventura. *Doña María.*	1578
Presumably the above. *San Joseph.*	
Unknown. *Santa Bárbara.*	1589

SEVENTEENTH CENTURY

Hernán Sánchez. *Santa María de los Ángeles.*	1616
Unknown. *María Santísima de Guadalupe* (treble).	1654
Unknown. *Señor San José.*	1658
Unknown. *San Miguel Arcángel.*	1658
Parra. *San Miguel* (small, *esquila*).	1684
Unknown. *San Agustín.*	1684

EIGHTEENTH CENTURY

Manuel López. *San Gregorio.*	1707
Unknown. *Santa Bárbara* (treble).	1731
Juan Soriano. *San Rafael.*	1745
Unknown. *Nuestra Señora del Carmen* (treble).	1746
Juan Soriano. *San Juan Bautista y Evangelista* (*esquila,* small).	1751
José Contreras, Atzcapotzalco. *San Pedro y San Pablo.*	1752
Unknown. *San José* (treble).	1757
Unknown. *San Paulino Obispo* (small, *esquila*).	1758
Bartolomé and Antonio Carrillo, Tacubaya. *San Joaquín y Santa Ana* (small).	1766
Bartolomé Espinosa. *La Purísima* (small, *esquilón*).	1767
Bartolomé Espinosa. *Santiago Apóstol.*	1784
Bartolomé Espinosa. *Santo Ángel Custodio* (*esquila,* small).	1784
Bartolomé Espinosa. *Nuestra Señora de la Piedad* (treble).	1787
D. Salvador de la Vega, Tacubaya. *Santa María de Guadalupe.*	1791
D. Salvador de la Vega. *Los Santos Ángeles.*	1791

[15] See Manuel Toussaint, *La Catedral de México y el Sagrario Metropolitano,* on the history of this work. See also Alberto María Carreno, "Los órganos, el Altar del Perdón y las tribunas de la Catedral metropolitana de México," *Memorias de la Academia Mexicana de la Historia,* 16 (1957), 326–338.

[16] See Heinrich Berlin, "Three Master Architects in New Spain," *Hispanic American Historical Review,* 27 (1947), 375–383.

D. Salvador de la Vega. *Jesús* (*esquilón*). 1791
Unknown. *Santo Domingo de Guzmán* (treble).

PRINCIPAL BELLS OF THE CATHEDRAL
OF PUEBLA

SEVENTEENTH CENTURY

Francisco Márquez. *Doña María.* 1637
Diego Márquez Bello. *San José.* 1638
Antonio Campos Herrera. Several bells. 1673

EIGHTEENTH CENTURY

Antonio de Herrera and Mateo Peregrina.
   Jesús Nazareno. 1731

Embroidery

The arts of weaving and embroidering silk continued during the Baroque period, as is evident from the names of craftsmen I shall give here and the descriptions of the most notable pieces. An epoch of luxury, of magnificence in everything that would exalt divinity in the churches and human grandeur in its sphere, produced artifacts of incomparable quality.

Among the innumerable treasures which stir one to covetousness in the inventories of the Cathedral of Mexico, the following are the most important from this period. In the inventory of 1649, among the bequests of the Archbishop Don Feliciano de la Vega, a cope of gold and silver cloth, embroidered in gold, and a white pectoral ornamented with twenty emerald studs, and a rose formed of seventeen small diamonds; it also had four silver clasps. Another cope was of red cloth, with flowers of gold and silver, gold fringe and four clasps likewise. One sees indeed that, in harmony with the spirit of the times, luxury and sumptuousness were more esteemed than legitimate art.

In the inventory of 1654 appears a magnificent set of vestments for which the viceroy, the Duque de Alburquerque, gave the cloth. It consisted of a cope, a chasuble, dalmatics, maniples, and stoles, all in the best brocade, of three levels, white and buff, with panels embroidered in *obra de corte de canutillo*—that is, with spirals of gold thread.

Embroidery, as Romero de Terreros observes, is also used to decorate furniture. Thus he notes in his book that in 1666 the chairs of the *oidores* in the palace were decorated with the coats of arms of Castile and Leon embroidered on their backs, and also that the dais of the Audience Chamber of the Holy Office was embroidered by Roque Zenón in 1712.[17]

The most important piece from this period preserved in the Museo de Arte Religioso of the Cathedral of Mexico is, without any doubt, the enormous pluvial cope which Don Diego de Malpartida y Zenteno had made for the image of St. Peter. This embroidery on crimson damask in two tones of gold, representing enormous flowers of incomparable harmony, seems to express the very spirit of that humble, manual art of embroidery. Yet it can hold its own in the great Baroque symphony of the late seventeenth century, among the architecture and the decorative sculpture and painting. It was made by a Mexican embroiderer, Antonio Rangel, and the date 1699 appears on it.

Baroque Silk Weavers and Embroiderers: 1635, Pascual de la Cruz, mestizo, weaver of bedding, both wide and narrow; 1642, Luis de Arenas, master weaver of velvet; 1646, Gabriel de Mesa, master of the art of silk; 1646, Gregorio de Villasana, master of the art of silk; 1649, Nicolás de Barrientos, master embroiderer; 1683, Joseph de Avecilla, master of the art of cloth of gold and of wool; 1683, Juan Hernández, apprentice of the preceding; 1699, Antonio Rangel; 1712, Roque Zenón.

Glass

The art of making glass has flourished since the most remote times, but the Indians who inhabited what was to become New Spain did not know it. When the Spaniards established themselves in the new country, the glass industry was one of the last to develop, and it was only in mid-sixteenth century that glass blowers appeared.

Even when master glass blowers had come to New Spain they did not manage to provide flat glass for windows and doors. These openings were closed by painted cloths which had been covered with melted wax, and which were called generically *encerados*. The windows of the original Cathedral of Mexico were of this kind.[18] Later, window glass was made, but not in the large flat sheets to which we are accustomed; instead, small pieces of glass, more or less regular in shape, were joined by lead to form the window. In fact this is a continuation of Gothic glassworking, or more accurately a degeneration, since the Mexican windows are much simpler and are without color. We have a record of the original glass of the present Cathedral of Mexico

---

[17] Romero de Terreros, *Artes industriales,* pp. 188–189.
[18] Toussaint, "La primitiva catedral de México," in *Paseos coloniales,* pp. 1–5.

in the book in which Sariñana describes the funerary ceremonies of Philip IV.[19] These windows were filled with small panes in a geometric pattern, simple, but at the same time harmonious and agreeable.[20]

The only colonial glass which has been preserved in Mexico City is what little still exists, in bad condition, in the church of La Profesa, dating from the first third of the eighteenth century. It too is laid in geometrical pattern, but on the basis of circles, with that glass we call *fondo de vaso* (bottom-of-a-glass). These damaged windows allow the passage of a warm light which softly illuminates the interior of the magnificent church.

To take the place of glass in the windows there were often used thin sheets of that yellowish marble called *tecali* after the town near which it is found. At Puebla, in various buildings such as the Academia de Bellas Artes—on the dome which covers the stairway—and in other places, like the Cathedral of Morelia, one can still see these panels of translucent stone through which a warm milky light falls to illuminate the interior softly. The use of sheets of marble for windows was not confined to Mexico; they were also used in South America, even in the Argentine, where they were called *berenguelas*.

By mid-sixteenth century glassmaking flourished in Puebla de los Ángeles. One master, Rodrigo de Espinosa, can be found established in Puebla as early as 1542. His furnace was on the Calle del Venado, and he was so active that the Cabildo in 1543 had to prohibit his cutting wood within a zone of two leagues from the city.[21] He continued to work, and in 1547 could state that Puebla was the only place in New Spain where glass was made, so that it was exported as far as Guatemala and Peru. Three classes of glass were produced: white crystal, green glass, and blue glass. This furnace ceased to exist between 1712 and 1723.

In 1728 Antonio Pardo, master glass maker, had his furnace in the street called Calle del Horno del Vidrio, which is to say that his glass furnace had given its name to the street. It continued to function for almost a century, while different members of the family succeeded him: Alonso Pardo in 1744, José Mariano Pardo from 1773 to 1800. Another member of the Pardo family had a furnace in the Calle de Arista. At the beginning of the nineteenth century glass furnaces are mentioned in the Calle de Iglesias, and also, in 1806 in the Calle de Rementería.[22]

We can add some other notices referring to glass in New Spain. In 1617 an ordinance of the viceroy, the Marqués de Guadalcázar, executed on January 30, says literally: "It is prohibited to pick the herb *barilla*, of which glass is made; only glassmakers and smelters of gold and silver being permitted to do so."[23]

The plant referred to in this ordinance is called *barilla* also by Basalenque, who says that when the Lake of Cuitzeo dried up and no longer sheltered the little fish called *charay*, which was the means of support for the towns on the lake, it produced in compensation great quantities of the herb called *barilla*, which is used in making glass.[24]

Other notes about the glass industry are the following: in 1642 we find Diego Becerra, master of *bedriera del candil*, though we do not know whether this designation implies that he was already making lamps of glass. In 1721 we have Miguel Maldonado, master of glass and gilding, and in the following year, Don Antonio de Quiñones, an expert in mirrors and crystal.

Such are the historical data, very sparse, to be sure, which I can immediately furnish, and which indicate the need of assembling a special monograph on the art of making glass in Mexico.[25]

What sort of glass objects should be classified as art? If the glassmaker simply knew how to make glasses and bottles, window glass and flasks for chemists, he would have little place in a history of art. To answer this question, let us list some of the antique pieces which are much sought after by collectors today, and which have reached fabulous prices where before they were unappreciated. For example, there are those great vases, often a half meter in height, with designs engraved or cut on the surface; or the bottles from wine shops, which also may have engraved decorations, or

---

[19] Isidro Sariñana, *Llanto del Occidente.*

[20] It is to be hoped that when a serious restoration of our cathedral is undertaken these simple windows which are so easy to make may be restored.

[21] Francisco R. de los Ríos Arce, *Puebla de los Ángeles y la orden dominicana*, I, 98.

[22] All of these notes on glassmakers in Puebla come from the book of Hugo Leicht, *Las calles de Puebla*, pp. 188, 459.

[23] "Ordenanzas," *Boletín del Archivo General de la Nación*, Ser. 1, No. 11 (1940), 2–327.

[24] Diego Basalenque, *Historia de la provincia de San Nicolás de Tolentino de Michoacán del orden de n. p. S. Agustín*, p. 292.

[25] See Alice Wilson Frothingham, *Hispanic Glass; with Examples in the Collection of the Hispanic Society of America*, pp. 121–126.

small seed-shaped indentations, or which may be ground or gilded. There are the large glass bells used to cover small images, the large and small screens which were used to shelter candles and lamps from drafts, and those great globes in bright colors, coated with quicksilver, which used to shine as decoration on drawing-room tables and then degenerated, as they became common, to ornamenting the vulgar pulque shops. And finally, there are the great crystal flasks filled with colored water which apothecaries used in their shops; the colored light which fell through them always lent some gaiety to the gloom of the drugstore, that home of poultices, pills, and purges.

PART FOUR

Pride and Wealth

The Climax of the Baroque in Mexico, 1730–1781

Chapter Fourteen

THE GREAT RELIGIOUS

ARCHITECTURE

The Churrigueresque Style

THE TERM "Churrigueresque" is used to designate a very specific mode of the Baroque. It has been suggested that we substitute the term "Ultra-Baroque" for Churrigueresque; but the fact is that we are not dealing with a single style which developed until it surpassed itself, but with two distinct styles. The term is derived, of course, from the name of a Spanish architect, Don José de Churriguera, because—although this has now been shown to be inaccurate—he was believed to have created this new style. But the very word *churrigueresco,* so complicated and emotional, seems to evoke this mad and fantastic expression of eighteenth-century art, and it is for this reason that I have retained it.

The Churrigueresque is a purely ornamental style. The plans of buildings are the same as in the preceding century; the elevations are covered with ornament, outside and inside, and both painting and sculpture are subordinated to the total decorative design. Generally it was the cruciform church bequeathed by the seventeenth century which was repeated to the point of monotony in the rebuilding or remodelling of parish and conventual churches. The occasional exceptions are not

enough to give any real variety to the group, as far as structure is concerned.

The Churrigueresque style reflects the social condition of a brilliant and prosperous colony. Magnanimous viceroys like Bucareli or Revillagigedo and zealous archbishops like Lorenzana guided a peaceful government through an era of well-being, disturbed only by famines or epidemics. The mines were producing fabulous fortunes, like those of Borda, the Counts of Regla and Valenciana. Agriculture had established itself in the pattern it was to retain almost into modern times, with large estates, the latifundia and the hacienda. This wealth, in the hands of the new nobility which the king was establishing, produced a new sort of civil architecture: the noble residence, of which, as we shall see, admirable examples still remain.

The piety of the colonists continued the same; at times superstitious, they were ostentatious and openhanded, lovers of ceremony and also of the carnivals where, in the name of some revered image, unrestrained bacchanals occurred. The church was rich as never before; custodias and sacred vessels incorporated fortunes in jewels; emeralds and diamonds were count-

275

245. Main altarpiece. Polychrome and gilded wood. Church of Santa Prisca, Taxco, Guerrero.

ed by the thousands. Gentlemen crammed the churches with riches, or built them complete and new: *"Dios a darle a Borda y Borda a darle a Dios."* And God did give Borda treasures, and Borda returned the treasures to God.

But we cannot help seeing also in the complexity of those retables, in their infinity of ornament which leaves not a single space free, a reminiscence of the old indigenous art—not in any resurrection of pagan motifs, but in their esthetic spirit. This *horror vacui,* this excessive supercharging of detail, executed as if for a golden reliquary, involved a resurgence of the Indian genius, to be admired and praised as the deepest and most sincere expression of the Mexican spirit in art. No other art has expressed more truly than this our national character, already formed during the colonial epoch.

Differences between Churrigueresque and Baroque

Two fundamental differences separate these two styles. First, while the Baroque still respects the structure of the building and the architectural orders, with their members clearly visible (202), the Churrigueresque little by little moves away from the logic of Classical art, in favor of altering the proportions, varying the profiles, and attacking that basic principle of all structure which requires a lightening as one ascends and clear respect for the laws of gravity (245). The Churrigueresque not only is not a structural style, but at its climax boasts of not being so. Secondly, for the habitual supporting member of the Baroque style—the column, whether cylindrical or twisted, always covered with ornament—the Churrigueresque substitutes the estípite (250, 251). This is a supporting member, square or rectangular in section, and formed of multiple elements: pyramids and truncated prisms, parallelepipeds, superposed foliage, medallions, garlands, bouquets, festoons. The ornament is all vegetable, applied to geometric forms. The estípite may be free-standing or attached to the retable, when it is called an engaged estípite. Its evolution follows an historical development of ascending complication, as in all Baroque: it is timid at the beginning, then daring, and finally mad.

The artist who introduced the estípite into New Spain seems to have been Jerónimo de Balbás, who worked on the Altar de los Reyes of the Cathedral of Mexico from 1718 on (323), and later made the *ciprés* (the high altar) and other things there. The new form was adopted by the Colony quickly, and we see engaged

estípites on the portal of the old Archbishop's Palace, dated 1743, and very simple ones at the doorways of the church of the Colegio de Niñas of 1744, both in the capital.

Another characteristic of the Churrigueresque style is the transmutation of materials of construction—thus breaking the most elemental law of architecture. Stone is worked as if it were wood, or vice versa; sometimes one reads that the stone is to be cut to imitate draperies, curtains, ropes, and tassels. Furniture influences architecture, and there are portals, like that of the house of the Conde de Santiago de Calimaya in Mexico City, which rest on four claw feet, as if it were architecture in the Chippendale style (294). Sometimes the yellowish tone of the stone, with the patina of centuries, looks like old ivory, as on the façade of the church of the Santísima Trinidad in Mexico City (251) or the tower of the church at Tepotzotlán (273). Like pieces delicately carved in balsam wood, Asiatic perhaps, are those finials of the incomparable church of Santa Prisca in Taxco, as if they had come to Acapulco on the China galleon.

The Architects and Their Ordinances

In the year 1736 a group of the most important architects of Mexico City waited upon the Cabildo and submitted a set of ordinances drawn up by them to control their profession. It was signed by Pedro de Arrieta, Miguel José Rivera, José Eduardo de Herrera, Miguel Custodio Durán, Manuel M. Juárez, and Francisco Valdés. The document was dated December 7, 1735, and submitted on February 20, 1736; on the eighth of June following, the Procurador announced that the ordinances had been approved.[1]

These ordinances consisted of a group of provisions intended to protect the personal interests of the architects in such a way as to prohibit anyone else from building anything. But let us take it step by step. They began by saying that, although ordinances did exist and the guild functioned according to them—apparently those of 1599, since Barrio Lorenzot gives us no others—they had been much abused. For this reason the overseers and master architects of the guild had drawn up new ordinances which they were herewith submitting for approval to the authorities.

[1] Archivos del Antigua Ayuntamiento de México. *Expediente,* No. 2983, legajo 14. My thanks are due to my pupil Manuel Carrera Stampa for the copy of these ordinances.

The chapters concerning administration give the following directives: that the guild should have its altar in the church of the Espíritu Santo, and its patron should be Nuestra Señora de los Gozos; that in the procession of the Holy Entombment each year the guild should carry the group of the Holy Angel Gudiel with the insignia of the Crown and the Lashes. All members were to contribute for fiestas, but they were not to join other guilds, since the subsidiaries of their own guild— the foremen (*sobrestantes*), stonecutters, and masons— would be enough. They should meet once a year in their church and, after hearing mass, choose an alcalde or director, and two overseers or inspectors (*veedores*) to govern the guild and give examinations to the journeymen (*oficiales*) who wished to become master architects. Another duty required of them was to make an inspection in the city each month to ascertain that all building was being directed by proper architects according to good building practice. When any extraordinary situation threatened the public safety they were to offer a remedy without charging any fee, unless some private individual would profit by it.

In practice, the ordinances were framed to protect the members of the guild. No one could be a master of architecture but a Spaniard of recognized standing and good character, with all qualifications supported by testimonials. That is to say, Indians and mestizos were excluded from the profession; at this time to be "Spanish" did not necessarily imply having been born in Spain, but simply being the legitimate descendant of Spanish parents, even though born in the Indies. In fact, the greater part of the architects were of this class; they were *criollos*—what today we would call Mexicans.

Anyone who wished to be a master architect must have worked as a journeyman for six years under a master architect who had passed a written examination in one of three crafts: building in masonry (*mampostear*), building with cut stone (*asentar cantería*), or draughting. In addition he must know how to read, write, and figure, to apply the principles of "geometry," and to *"montear, reducir, cuadrear y cubicar"*— that is, to draft plans and elevations to scale, and to compute areas and volumes. The examination had two parts: a practical demonstration on some public work for whatever time the *alcalde* and the overseers required, and a technical or theoretical examination, to take place in the house of the alcalde or of the candidate's sponsor, if he had one. A stranger must submit his certificate (*carta de examen*), which would be accepted if it came from some important city of the kingdom; if not, he would be required to submit to an examination.

The rest of the ordinances protected the prerogatives of the guild. No major-domo of a monastery should build on his own, later getting an architect's signature for a small fee. No private individual should build by himself or with only a foreman. No stonecutter, mason, or carpenter should supervise building, claiming that it was just "repairs"; they were restricted to such repairs as stopping leaks or whitewashing, and this only with permission from the alcalde and supervisors.

Finally there is a small group of provisions concerned with standards of materials. They indicate the proper proportion of lime, the measurements of wood, such as planks, beams, and those for framing openings. They direct that the sand should be from San Joaquín or Tacubaya, "since its good quality and lack of impurity is known, and the others are adulterated with clay and *tequesquite* (harmful salts)." On the subject of stone they say:

Cut stone should be of the following sizes: the runner (*atravesado*), three quarters of a *vara* long, half a *vara* wide, and one third of a *vara* thick; the binder (*piedra de lazo*), half a *vara* long, one third of a *vara* wide, and one quarter of a *vara* thick. Stone two to the cartload (*de dos en carreta*), or three, or four, or one, should conform to a width and length which seems proper, according to the discretion of the masters, and that those specially cut should be correct for their purpose, the said stone being of good quality, and not *tepetate* (caliche or soft limestone), which is unsound. That soft stone (*guijarro*) should not be substituted for *chiluca* stone. That a *braza* of hard stone or *tezontle* should be four *varas* long, two wide, and one high, according to custom. Brick should be of good quality and manufacture, and should measure one third of a *vara* long, one sixth of a *vara* wide and three fingers thick.

Further articles oblige the architect to visit the work at least every third day, and to find out the rights-of-way in new areas, and that the alcaldes and supervisors should have a map of the city, with the prices of land in each part.

Such are the ordinances. Their completeness, if we disregard a certain disorder, indicates the stage to which architecture had progressed in New Spain. They are of great interest, because the monuments which have been preserved up to the present date from this period on.

246. Convent church of Santa Brígida (destroyed, 1933), Mexico City.

Baroque Churches of the Eighteenth Century

Throughout the eighteenth century, the Baroque style continues, in varying degrees of complexity, side by side with the Churrigueresque in both religious and civil buildings. Let us begin with those of Mexico City.

San Hipólito (1739), with its great Baroque portal, is still in the style of the seventeenth century, with Mudejar reminiscences in the reliefs. The monument at the corner of the churchyard wall is already Neoclassical, as we shall see: apparently the work of José Damián Ortiz de Castro (360).

Santa Brígida, built between 1740 and 1745, was the unique example in this city of an oval plan, distinguished in this way from all the common cruciform churches, and also by its fine portal of white marble and other details (246). It was stupidly destroyed to widen a street, so that now where an example of exquisite art once stood there are mediocre buildings dedicated to commercialism.[2]

Of the College of San Miguel de Belén, founded by the Mercedarians outside the city, only the church, finished in 1735, remains. Its lovely portal strikes a romantic note beyond the little garden, and inside there are still interesting retables in the most delightful Churrigueresque style.[3]

The church of Santa Inés, of the old convent of the same name, was finished in 1770. Its coarse portals already show Neoclassicism struggling with the Baroque; the carved panels of its two doors are the best things to be seen there now.

The great and spacious church of La Soledad de Santa Cruz was built between 1731 and 1792. The late date is indeed apparent in its already Neoclassical details, and we shall discuss it later.

At the middle of the century, in 1755, the church of San Fernando was finished for the friars of the Propaganda Fide. The great façade of *tezontle* with its

[2] Justino Fernández, "Santa Brígida de México," in *Congreso Internacional de Historia de América, II, 1937,* 438–454.

[3] See Heinrich Berlin, "Three Master Architects in New Spain," *Hispanic American Historical Review,* 27 (1947), 375–383.

247. Chapel of El Pocito, Villa Madero, Distrito Federal.

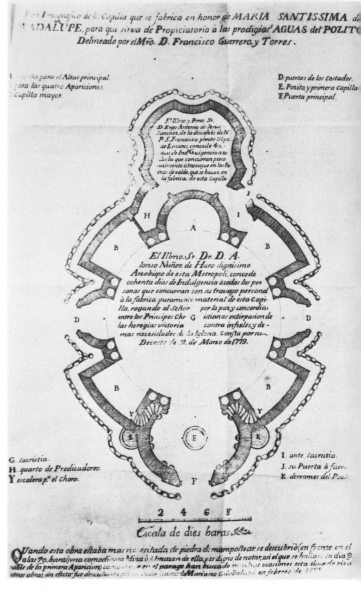

248. Plan, chapel of El Pocito, Villa Madero, Distrito Federal.

carved stone portal may still be seen, but the fine Churrigueresque retables which used to be inside were destroyed in the nineteenth century.[4]

A fine example, a chapel which because of its position became a parish church, is the church called the "Salto del Agua" because it stands across from the

[4] See Berlin, "El arquitecto Joseph Eduardo de Herrera," *Anales del Instituto de Arte Americano e Investigaciones Estéticas*, 17 (1964), 90–98; Berlin, "Three Master Architects," *ibid.*, 375–383.

fountain which dispensed the water of the Chapultepec aqueduct. Begun in 1750, it was finished in 1761, and it is a building of great elegance and proportion. It can still be admired; at present rebuilding has been completed on the south side, where it had been left isolated in the replanning of the whole area. This reconstruction has been carried out so skillfully that it will be difficult in the future to distinguish the original from the new construction.

The monastic church of Santo Domingo, finished in

249. Sagrario Metropolitano, Mexico City.

1736—the third church to be built on this site—is probably the most typical example of Mexican Baroque with Churrigueresque elements. It conforms to the taste of its time, but it is of excellent quality. Cruciform in plan, with an ample transept and rows of chapels along the nave, an airy dome, a rectangular apse—which unfortunately no longer has its original retable as the ends of the transepts do—it can be taken as the most perfect and the most Mexican church of its period. Outside we see a spacious building of *tezontle,* with a great portal of cut stone, a slender tower roofed with glazed tile, and an elegant cupola. It has lost two of its exterior chapels, the Rosario,[5] and the Tercer Orden, which was the work of Lorenzo Rodríguez. Now only the chapel of the Señor de la Expiración remains, at the end of the stupidest street yet cut through by man—it neither leads anywhere nor comes from anywhere; its purpose was simply to cut in two the splendid Dominican monastery.

An incomparable jewel of eighteenth-century Baroque is the Capilla del Pocito—the Chapel of the Well—in the Villa de Guadalupe in the Distrito Federal (247, 248). It was built between 1777 and 1791, as an act of charity by masons, painters, and stonecutters, and even by the architect himself, the celebrated Don Francisco de Guerrero y Torres. He seems to have been inspired by the plan of a Roman temple, but the solution of the elevation is entirely his own. The chapel consists of a large oval space, with a circular room in front and another, a mixtilinear octagon, behind, all three crowned by splendid domes. The lower structure is of *tezontle,* with portals and windows of stone, and the domes, with the parapet uniting them to the lower part, are covered with blue-and-white tiles, which gives the building an incomparable color scheme. As if this were not enough, the elegance and sensitivity of the sculpture on the main doorway is so moving that we are shaken by its beauty every time we look at it.[6]

Churrigueresque Churches of Mexico City

The most important are the Sagrario, the Santísima Trinidad, the Santa Veracruz, San Francisco (the side door), and the Enseñanza.

The Sagrario Metropolitano is a magnificent demonstration of the style (163, 249). On a Greek-cross plan the two naves cross at the center to support a cupola; in the corners are the chapels and the offices of the church, which serves as the parish church of the Cathedral. A richly carved doorway leads to the Cathedral.

The exterior consists of three walls, elegant in silhouette, built of dark red *tezontle,* the volcanic stone so popular in this period. On the south and west fronts two great façades symmetrically frame the portals, designed with pairs of estípites and niches between them on either side (250). At the outer edges are smaller doorways, vigorously ornamented to maintain an equilibrium, and between them and the great portals are windows of fine design with rusticated frames and discreet finials. Thus the decoration is concentrated in certain areas, rhythmically, on a pyramidal design.

These great façades are made up in the same way as the altarpieces of gilded wood. This monument was the work of the architect Lorenzo Rodríguez, and it was built between 1749 and 1768. The foundations were inadequate, perhaps because the architect counted too much on the platform on which the Cathedral stands, and the church was deteriorating so that it would have collapsed if it had not been restored in time. Thanks to the interest of President Cárdenas, various architects worked from 1935 to 1939 at stabilizing the foundations.[7]

The church of the Santísima Trinidad originally belonged to a hospital and hospice for priests. It has the usual cruciform plan with a cupola at the crossing and two façades, the principal one very similar in design to that of the Sagrario (251), the lateral one unusual in the depth of its relief. Inside the church the original retables have not been preserved. It was built between 1755 and 1783. It too is thought to have been the work of Lorenzo Rodríguez, but if it was, he did not see it finished, since he died on the third of July, 1774.[8] The tower, which is most original in having its roof shaped like a papal tiara, is unfinished in some parts.

The church of San Francisco dates from the seven-

[5] Berlin, *Herrera.*

[6] Manuel Toussaint, "La Capilla del Pocito en Guadalupe," in *Paseos coloniales,* pp. 63–65. See also Berlin, "Three Master Architects," 380–383; Glenn N. Patton, *Francisco Antonio Guerrero y Torres and the Baroque Architecture of Mexico City in the Eighteenth Century.*

[7] See Toussaint, *La Catedral de México y el Sagrario Metropolitano;* M. Álvarez Cortina and Alberto Le Duc, "Sagrario de México," *Archivo español de arte y arqueología,* 11 (1935), 97–101; Manuel Romero de Terreros, "La carta de esamen de Lorenzo Rodríguez," *Anales del Instituto de Investigaciones Estéticas,* 15 (1947), 105–108; Margaret Collier, "New Documents on Lorenzo Rodríguez and His Style," in *International Congress of the History of Art, XX, 1961; New York.*

[8] See Berlin, "Artífices de la catedral de México," *Anales del Instituto de Investigaciones Estéticas,* 11 (1944), 36.

250. South portal, Sagrario Metropolitano, Mexico City.

251. Church of the Santísima Trinidad, Mexico City.

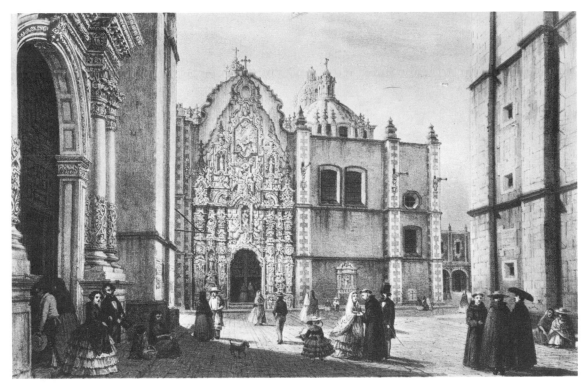

252. Balvanera Chapel, monastery of San Francisco, Mexico City.
Lithograph. From *México y sus alrededores,* 1856.

253. Nave, convent church of La Enseñanza, Mexico City.

254. Nave, convent church of Santa Clara, Querétaro.

and 1764. On the other hand, the west front, which seems to date from 1776, as does one of the towers, is cold in feeling, as if these estípites were drawn with T-square and compass. The other tower was built much later.

The church of La Enseñanza, the only part remaining of the old convent school built by the venerable Madre Azlor under the advocacy of Nuestra Señora del Pilar, is a fine example of the style we are considering. It was built around 1754, and no one who visits it will forget it. The façade is Baroque, of ample proportions, perhaps a little excessive for the small space in front of it. The design of the interior is especially resourceful; it is like a theatre where the aim was to provide all the galleries possible for the pupils of the school (253). The retables are excellent, especially the principal one with its interesting and unusual vertical emphasis. The architect of this church seems to have been Guerrero y Torres.

Churriguersque Churches in Other Regions

Querétaro

The art of Querétaro is a splendid exhibition of the eighteenth century. Although some of the buildings date from the seventeenth century, its artistic peak was reached after 1700. Cloisters, portals of churches and houses, stairways, all were rendered in a rosy stone, smooth and hard, which permitted the greatest delicacy. The exteriors are in general Baroque, but the interiors exuberate in fantasies which we cannot but feel as Churrigueresque, not only in period, but in character.

The Churrigueresque of Querétaro is distinguished from other Churrigueresque by a marked French quality: Rococo motifs, symmetrical or asymmetrical, as in the styles of Louis XIV and Louis XV, appear frequently. Furthermore, the gilding is of great virtuosity; some passages are not only golden, but reflect metallic greens, reds, and blues, in contrast to the Churrigueresque of the capital, which never allows itself such liberties. Still more, the estípite, which as we have seen is the characteristic Churrigueresque motif, is interpreted quite licentiously, so that within the mood of the times and of the style we get the most fascinating of altarpieces and cloisters. Taking the estípite as a pilaster, they flatten it and extend it until it is no more than low relief, but so wide that within its outlines they can fit niches, statues, angels, or whatever they like. The

teenth century; but the Balvanera chapel, later known as the chapel of La Escala Santa, offers a rich Churrigueresque portal (252). Its statues disappeared around 1864. Inside, another portal of fine Baroque design leads to the church.

The Church of the Santa Veracruz is one of the oldest in Mexico City; a confraternity of conquistadors was once attached to it. The present building dates from 1730. Its south façade is a delightful example of ingenuous Churrigueresque; it displays the dates 1759

255. Grille, convent church of Santa Clara, Querétaro.

Churrigueresque of Mexico City delights in angles, because it works in terms of light and shade like any good Baroque design; in Querétaro they prefer the curved, the rounded, the soft, the tender. It feels oriental, at least in its mood and ensemble, if not historically.

There are two churches in Querétaro which rank among the most important examples of the Churrigueresque: Santa Clara and Santa Rosa. Santa Clara, a convent church finished in 1633, whose exterior shows certain archaistic details, such as the statues on the façade, in the eighteenth century was decorated inside in the most fantastic manner conceivable. Imagination has burst its bounds and runs wild. Retables, pulpits, the marvellous gallery with its grille which seems a netting of fine cords, everything is overwhelming (254). The screens of the upper and lower choirs are works of art of the first quality (255). Unhappily we are ignorant of the designer of this prodigious decoration; from its

date, and by comparison with his work, it may well be the creation of Mariano de las Casas. He did draw the plans for the church of Santa Rosa, which was dedicated in 1752, although he did not build it. The construction was so unsound that buttresses had to be added; these are the work of Gudiño, and quite original in form. The decoration of the interior, as fine as that of Santa Clara, and no doubt by the same artist, is perhaps later than the building of the church (256, 257). In both of these churches the Churrigueresque of Querétaro can be studied infinitely: in both, one's emotion overflows, overwhelmed by so much beauty.

There are no Churrigueresque church façades in Querétaro. They prefer the more sober Baroque exterior, leaving fantasy to proliferate within. Only the façade of the Capilla del Rosario of the monastery of Santo Domingo, finished in 1760, ventures to give us something like flattened pilasters, with a niche, termi-

287

256. Choir, convent church of Santa Rosa de Viterbo, Querétaro.

257. Retable of the Virgin. Polychrome and gilded wood; oil on canvas. Convent church of Santa Rosa de Viterbo, Querétaro.

nating in caryatids. This theme, developed with genius, can be seen again in the cloister of the monastery of San Agustín, finished in 1745, which is attributed to Mariano de las Casas. The church has a Baroque façade, with prismatic columns bound by stiff diagonal bands; but the cloister shows a high quality of imagination and invention (258). On the second story the arches appear to be supported by caryatids in high relief; they are youths with their arms extended and their hands in various positions. People say that they are demonstrating an alphabet for deaf-mutes; it is possible that they represent the positions taken by the priest's hands in saying Mass.

The architects and sculptors of Querétaro recorded in this period are Mariano de las Casas, Mariano Paz, Gudiño, Ortiz, Zápari, and García.

Puebla de los Angeles

This city, famous for its Baroque architecture in the seventeenth century, and for its Mudejar then and later, also fell under the spell of the Churrigueresque. San Francisco, a church of noble lineage, with its great nave covered by Gothic vaults and its side door which still shows the coat of arms of Tlaxcala, acquired a new façade where typical Puebla decoration—panels of glazed tile set into unglazed tile, certainly very handsome—was combined with elegantly carved estípites of stone (259). It dates from between 1743 and 1767, and its designer was José Buitrago.

The churches of Puebla were famous for the richness and elegance of their interiors; but only a few examples are left to recall this. It is sad to have to say it,

288

258. Cloister, monastery of San Agustín (Palacio Municipal), Querétaro.

259. Façade, monastery church of San Francisco, Puebla.

but most of them have lost all interest and value. Nowhere can we see more plainly the phenomenon of commendable piety and religious feeling joined to the worst ignorance and bad taste concerning art. Confraternities, societies, and clubs, led by priests quite innocent of the harm they were doing, have renovated these interiors, destroying incomparable treasures in altarpieces and paintings to follow the fashion of a Neoclassicism of dubious artistic quality, sadly impoverished in materials and invention.

The most noteworthy Churrigueresque interior is that of the beautiful parish church of San José, which is like a little cathedral. It has preserved its retables intact, and they are of the highest quality, even though the church dates from the seventeenth century and was decorated in 1771. Another example is the convent church of Santa Catarina. Its nave lies parallel to the street, with two portals and a little bell tower, all in the typical Puebla style of tile and brick. The interior is as fine as the exterior, all embroidered with gold and polychrome sculpture; its retables are still Baroque, although one of them has estípites. In other places, for

260. Façade, church of La Valenciana, Guanajuato.

261. Dome and chancel, church of La Valenciana, Guanajuato.

262. Retable of St. Joseph. Polychrome and gilded wood. Monastery church of San Agustín, Salamanca, Guanajuato.

instance in the magnificent seventeenth-century Baroque church of Santo Domingo, there are Churrigueresque retables to be seen. Santo Domingo has two, which go unnoticed, or rather, are eclipsed by the marvellous Capilla del Rosario. They are, however, good examples of the Puebla Churrigueresque, and afford an opportunity for pointing out its characteristics. They are deeply cut, technically of high quality, and greatly influenced by French design; this is a vigorous Rococo in high relief, like the best of Louis XV decoration.

Guanajuato

This region is very rich in examples of Churriguer-

esque art. In the city of Guanajuato there is first of all the delightful façade of the church of San Diego (1775). The monumental ensemble of the church of La Compañía (1765) provides one of the richest Churrigueresque exteriors. Because it is built on a hillside, the façade is elevated above the street, with great cypresses in front of it growing over the roofs of the buildings below: there is a complete harmony between the slender shape of the trees and the delicate form, daring but deliberate, of the estípites. The sculpture is also of high quality. The city of Guanajuato is surrounded by a ring of churches, each more beautiful than the other, built in the towns around the various mines. First of them all is that of La Valenciana, which was built between 1765 and 1788, mainly by Don Antonio Escandón, Conde de Valencia.[9] The Valenciana is one of the prime examples of Churrigueresque art, with its great sculptured façade and its magnificent retables (260, 261). The little church of the mines of Cata has a superb façade with estípites, decorated with small medallions on which are sculptured tiny figures of saints in all sorts of positions. The design of the upper part of the doorway recalls the work of Lorenzo Rodríguez. No less rich, though quite different in character, is the portal of the ruined church of San Juan de Rayas, a veritable filigree in stone; this has been moved into Guanajuato, much to the credit of that noble city. Finally, there was the old church of Marfil, long in ruins; its portals have been salvaged and moved to the University of Guanajuato.

The city of Salamanca has two jewels in this style: the façade of the parish church, profusely ornamented with estípites, niches, medallions, and reliefs, and the interior of the church of San Agustín, whose retables embody the most daring of fantasies (262). There we feel that we are moving in an atmosphere of richness and luxury, among forms extravagantly capricious, and yet of the greatest elegance.

In the other direction lie the cities of San Miguel de Allende and Dolores Hidalgo. In the first we find the façade, still timid but none the less beautiful, of Santa Clara, sheltered in a niche formed by a great shell (263). The façade of San Francisco, 1780, merits an honorable place in this account,[10] as does its twin, the façade of the parish church of Dolores, which was

[9] See the interesting monograph by Antonio Cortés, *Valenciana.* See also Armando Nicolau, *Valenciana.*
[10] See Francisco de la Maza, *San Miguel de Allende.*

built between 1750 and 1778 and has two magnificent Churrigueresque retables, one gold and the other ungilded.

Moving northward we come to San Luis Potosí, which has one of the rarest and most valuable examples of this art: the chapel of Aránzazu. Cruciform in plan, with a cupola, the whole interior is decorated with stucco work organized in a design of engaged estípites. A window carries the same style to the exterior; its engaged estípites and reliefs representing children are worked with incomparable delicacy. The church of the old Carmelite convent here has two portals in this style, interesting for their originality, not to say their daring: twisted columns on the first story, estípites on the second and third, niches between the verticals, and all sheltered by a drapery of stone. The stories are divided by cornices and friezes which are prudently horizontal. Inside, greater daring appears: a great portal and two retables of masonry in a Churrigueresque *sui generis,* in which the mouldings are creased so fine that it might be called a "pleated Churrigueresque" (264). It is somewhat reminiscent of the main retable of La Enseñanza in Mexico City; here the ambiguity of the line gives an evanescent effect. Still further north we find the Cathedral of Saltillo, the last example of Churrigueresque, or rather of a Baroque which has listened to the siren song of the Churrigueresque and tried to resist it. In spite of the profuse reliefs on its columns and estípites, it is more solid and firm than the hallucinatory examples to the south.

Other States

Michoacán. Westward there is little to be seen in this style: Michoacán, so hospitable to the Baroque, offers only scattered examples. In Morelia, capital of the state, there is nothing to speak of besides a delicate retable in the church of Las Rosas. Since the two central estípites are missing, the middle has a strange feeling of flatness. Of exteriors, there is the portal of the church of La Merced, a curious example of monstrous estípites, and the decoration over a doorway of the old prison for men, whose superposing of scrolls, mouldings, fragments of pediments, and other ornament is characteristic of the Churrigueresque.

Hidalgo. In the state of Hidalgo two distinguished examples can be pointed out. One is the façade of the

11 Toussaint, "La parroquia de Atitalaquia," in *Paseos coloniales,* pp. 58–60.

263. Church of La Salud, San Miguel de Allende, Guanajuato.

parish church of Atitalaquia, elegantly carved in a rosy stone which seems to anticipate that of Querétaro.[11] The other, the parish church of Apan, is seldom mentioned, but its main retable should be placed among the finest examples of Mexican Churrigueresque. Al-

264. Retable. Polychrome and gilded wood. Monastery church of El Carmen, San Luis Potosí.

though it is less daring, the chapel of El Carmen in Ixmiquilpan is also admirable, especially for the harmony between its façade and the retables inside.[12]

Jalisco. Guadalajara, capital of the state of Jalisco, abounds in Baroque churches. The chapel of Aránzazu, which was part of the monastery of San Francisco, has a good Churrigueresque portal and retables in the same style, some restrained and some daring, but all of excellent quality. The parish church of Lagos de Moreno in the same state is an elegant example of discreet Churrigueresque, with its portico of flattened pilasters recessed in a shallow trapezoid, and a side door of simpler, but still Churrigueresque, design. Inside, the doorway to the sacristy is framed in the twisted columns of the Baroque; the vigorous relief above it seems earlier in style and may have come from some older building.

The parish church of Tlalpujahua should be noted as a very interesting example. Its façade is a special kind of Baroque, with very rich carving. They say it was built to compete with the church of Santa Prisca in Taxco, but there is no proof of this, nor is such competition likely. And without reference to the Taxco church, this one has its own individual merit.

Oaxaca. In Oaxaca, the noble city *par excellence,* we find a Churrigueresque relic in the ruined church of San Francisco. The façade is still intact, with carving of great refinement and statues of excellent quality. Earthquakes have left the interior in ruins, but I remember having seen it in 1926 still crammed with magnificent Churrigueresque retables.

Yucatán. One can even find examples of the Churrigueresque in Yucatán among the few retables which have survived. We have already mentioned the retables at Maní, which are certainly the finest in the state, but are in the Renaissance style. The later retables, as far as I have been able to observe, present special characteristics: a timidity in design—they cling to horizontal cornices—and the use of bright colors, red or blue, and a white background. One cannot be sure that this color is original, for here more than almost anywhere colonial art has suffered the desecration of ignorance in the guise of renovation. The retable at Sacalcen, which has blue pilasters with gold fillets on a red background, is one of the most important. There is one at Sotuta, with estípites and painted panels; one at Telchac, with seven

[12] See the *Catálogo de construcciones religiosas del Estado de Hidalgo.*

265. Church of Santa Prisca and San Sebastián, Taxco, Guerrero.

old paintings and some figures; one in the Franciscan monastery of Valladolid, with engaged estípites and horizontal cornices, painted red; and a similar one at Ixcabá. At Dzemel there are three retables in the parish church; two are of little importance, while the largest, three stories high with sculptures between the columns, is unpainted, displaying the natural color of the cedar

266. Nave and choir, church of Santa Prisca, Taxco, Guerrero.

in which it is carved. A retable at Hocabá is similar in form, but polychrome; the one at Mame has been crudely repainted. At Maní, beside those of Renaissance design, there are also several later retables, for example, the main altarpiece, its three stories divided by Corinthian columns with figures in the niches be-

tween—it has been painted white, red, and gold quite recently. The altarpiece of the church of La Candelaria in Mérida probably dates from the preceding period, since it has twisted columns.[13]

Three Superior Examples

We have left to the end of this essay on the Churrigueresque style in Mexico three prime examples which would in themselves be enough to bring honor to any country: the parish church of Taxco, the church of Ocotlán in Tlaxcala, and that of the seminary of San Martín in Tepotzotlán.

The parish church of Santa Prisca y San Sebastián in Taxco (incorrectly called a cathedral in tourist literature) was paid for and built under the direction of the important Spanish mine owner Don José de la Borda (265). Although he was not a professional, his judgment in matters of art was sure and sound. After he obtained the permission of the viceroy and the archbishop to build his church, his enthusiasm never faltered until he had seen it completed. There were two architects: one called Durán (either the Diego Durán who appears in the census of 1754, or Miguel Custodio Durán, whom we have noted above), and Juan Caballero. The designer of the retables was Isidro Vicente de Balbás, perhaps a son of that Jerónimo Balbás who introduced the Churrigueresque style to Mexico. It was begun in 1751 and finished seven years later. A homogeneous work of art, and of a beauty which cannot be described, the church of Taxco dominates the delightful town, where nature and man have cooperated to create a privileged place, a little earthly paradise where life is easy, the climate kind, and the setting beautiful. But to return to the church: its exterior is Baroque, with a tinge of the Churrigueresque, and with large-scale sculpture which suggests wood carving. The interior, with its magnificent altarpieces, is an astonishing Churrigueresque work of art (245, 266, 267, 268). For all that, madness is held within bounds, no doubt under the influence of Borda. The retables repeat identically across the nave; reason inexorably controls the effect, and fantasy develops just so far as the restraints of reason permit.[14]

In the sanctuary of Nuestra Señora de Ocotlán, the interior is an example of great Churrigueresque art cre-

[13] All of this information comes from the interesting *Catálogo de construcciones religiosas del Estado de Yucatán.*
[14] See Toussaint, *Tasco.*

267. Retable. Polychrome and gilded wood; oil on canvas. Capilla de Jesús Nazareno,
Church of Santa Prisca, Taxco, Guerrero.

268. Sacristy, church of Santa Prisca, Taxco, Guerrero.

269. Façade, sanctuary of Nuestra Señora de Ocotlán, Tlaxcala.

ated by an Indian, Francisco Miguel, or so it is said. The façade is like a piece of popular art (269). The parish church of Tlaxcala seems to be its model; but at Ocotlán imagination, joined with the most ingenuous piety, has created something unique. Technically, the building is imperfect: these estípites and figures have not been cut from stone, but built up by hand, with stones and plaster, in what we call *mampostería.* Hence it is necessary to whitewash them every year after the rainy season; and this is what makes the whole thing look like frosting (270). Nothing could be more attractive, more affecting, than this great façade flanked

by its two towers, which look as if they had been nailed onto the blue sky above us as we approach the hill on which the sanctuary stands. The interior is rich in retables from the transept to the apse, and it undoubtedly had more formerly (197). In our time we have seen how misguided piety (or disguised cupidity—one cannot judge) has damaged the interior, to the detriment of art and the true service of God. We do not have exact dates; the façade and towers seem to have been the last to be made.

The church of the seminary of the Jesuits in Tepotzotlán, dedicated to San Martín, is one of the most

298

270. Façade (detail), sanctuary of Nuestra Señora de Ocotlán, Tlaxcala.

271. Capilla de San José, church of the Seminary of San Martín (Museo Nacional del Virreinato), Tepotzotlán, México.

extraordinary examples of Churrigueresque art. Even if everything else should disappear, this one building would suffice to bring honor and glory to the style. The church is not of homogeneous construction: an old, spacious Baroque church, dating from 1670 to 1678, was brought up to date in the eighteenth century. Perhaps its size encouraged the making of the great altarpieces and the majestic façade (273). Even if we disregard the chapel known as the Relicario de San José (St. Joseph's Reliquary), dated 1737 (271), and the Casa de Loreto (The House of Loreto), with its *camarín* (198) which we have already studied, the group of retables covering the apse and transepts of the church

is incomparable. There are eleven retables: three in the apse, dating from 1755, six in the two arms of the transept, from 1756, and two more in the nave—that of Our Lady of Light, and that of St. Joseph, dating from 1758 (272). When we come face to face with them, standing at the crossing of the transept under the wide dome which seems to concentrate our emotion, a strange feeling invades us. It is as if we were in another world, better than this one we know, where the human spirit, transmuted into the divine, could speak to us with the genius of its creative power and

272. Nave, church of the Seminary of San Martín (Museo Nacional del Virreinato),
Tepotzotlán, México.

273. Façade, church of the Seminary of San Martín,
(Museo Nacional del Virreinato), Tepotzotlán, México.

imagination. The carving seems to have life: it climbs up the walls, scales the windows, and penetrates them. We think of grottoes below the sea, covered with mother-of-pearl and coral, of palaces built by fairies and magicians. For a time Christianity is forgotten, as it changes into something pantheistic and universal— or rather, let us say that anyone of artistic sensibility, be he pagan, Protestant, or atheist, will be able to enjoy this marvellous spectacle. The intimate, the unique emotion which pervades this work of art and springs from it is a feeling of great catholicity: it is indeed the humility of man that speaks here—man who can create such magnificent prayers as are here given tangible form, who can exalt with the most effusive hymns, though without words, the glory of God.

The façade and the tower at Tepotzotlán are later; they were built between 1760 and 1762, and certainly by a different artist (272). Technically, the relief sculpture in golden stone is excellent, and the whole thing is imposing. In design, however, it is less audacious, less fanciful, than other Churrigueresque exteriors, whether because the artist was made to restrain himself, or, what is more likely, because his own temperament and judgment restrained him. However that may be, the building is incomparable.[15]

[15] See Alexander von Wuthenau, *Tepotzotlán*; Toussaint, *Paseos coloniales*, pp. 47–57; Pablo C. de Gante, *Tepotzotlán: su historia y sus tesoros artísticos*; Berlin, "Three Master Architects," pp. 375–383; "Tepotzotlán," *Artes de México*, pp. 62–63 (1965), 7–38.

Chapter Fifteen

CIVIL ARCHITECTURE

OF THE EIGHTEENTH CENTURY

HE ARCHITECTURE of the buildings in which the inhabitants of New Spain passed their daily lives in this period is of great importance. It fixed the types of Mexican architecture from that distant time almost up to our own day, in spite of the influence of France or the parvenu imitation of architecture in the United States. This Baroque architecture, clearly Spanish, but marvellously suited to the Mexican environment in all its variety, along with the splendid Baroque-Churrigueresque of the great churches, is the most profound manifestation of the Mexican spirit in art during the colonial period. To facilitate study, we are grouping the civil buildings here by their functions, leaving to the last the most interesting group, the dwellings.

Public Buildings

Government Buildings

First come the government buildings. The old Palacio de los Virreyes in this period took on the final appearance we know (except for the additions of the nineteenth century) with the so-called "Puerta Mariana" and its cramped patios. It remained, for all that, a dignified building, with a majesty appropriate to its function, the seat of the executive power (170). The later changes, particularly the addition of the third story, have taken away something of its special heritage and excellence, giving the façade an inexplicably frivolous air (171). The upper patios are faithful copies, as if one could do nothing but reproduce the lower floors.

The ancient palace of the Cabildo of Mexico City, the Diputación, the Ayuntamiento, or whatever it may call itself, also has suffered reconstruction, with the third story and its little arcade. It was built between 1720 and 1724, and its classic design can still be admired in lithographs of mid-nineteenth century (274).

The Palacio de la Audiencia de Nueva Galicia still exists in Guadalajara, a spacious building, with its great Baroque portal, a little extravagant and swaggering, like the natives of that delightful city (275). It was built between 1751 and 1775, and the architects seem to have been Don Nicolás Enríquez del Castillo and Don José Conique. The stairwell has been decorated by Orozco.[1]

---

[1] Diego Angulo Íñiguez, *Planos de monumentos arquitectónicos de América y Filipinas*, I, 330.

274. Palace of the Ayuntamiento (Cabildo), Mexico City.

Less sumptuous, but also impressive, is the building of the Cabildo in Aguascalientes, now the Palacio de Gobierno; it governs, from one corner of the plaza, what the church—which occupies the opposite side—permits it to.

Among less important government buildings there are magnificent examples in Mexico City. Such is the Real Aduana de México, the Royal Customs House, finished in 1731, which one can still contemplate, if contemplation can disregard its vulgar and squalid situation (276). A spacious building built of *tezontle,* with portals and balconies of stone, it has two patios from which a single monumental stairway leads to the upper floor. If only this building, given over now to the most sordid activities of the city, might recover its dignity and, adequately restored, be put to some nobler purpose—archives, library, or school!

The building called "La Acordada," which was the prison connected with the law court of the same name, was built on the corner of what are now the Avenidas Juárez and Balderas. It appears that it was begun on July 17, 1757, under the direction of Lorenzo Rodríguez.[2] Completely in ruins, it was rebuilt between 1777

and 1781, at the expense of the Tribunal del Consulado.[3] One can see a view of the building, with a brief description, in the *Libro de mis recuerdos.*[4] It was of *tezontle,* with windows and doors framed in cut stone and, in the center, a great portal of the height of the whole building, with the appropriate coats of arms.

The building known as "El Apartado," which gave its name to the street, still exists, but it has no architectural quality and looks more like a prison. Here metals were assayed for minting, for the payment of the *quinto* and so on, and it now houses the Mint. The beautiful building originally used for the Mint, the Casa de Moneda, is now the Museo Nacional de Arqueología. It is an outstanding monument of Baroque art, with its walls of *tezontle,* its noble fenestration, and its rich portal. This building was the work of Bernardino de Orduña, and bears the date 1734, when it was finished.[5] Dependencies of the Real Hacienda,

[2] Manuel Orozco y Berra, *Memoria para el plano de la ciudad de México.*
[3] Angulo Íñiguez, *Planos,* I, 326.
[4] Antonio García Cubas, *El libro de mis recuerdos.*
[5] See four articles by Heinrich Berlin: "El arquitecto Pedro de

called "Cajas Reales," were also built in mining centers. There is such a building in Pachuca, by José Joaquín de Torres (1774), and one in Zimapán, by Guerrero y Torres (1776).[6]

On the north side of Mexico City, in the old section of Peralvillo, the old Garita, or excise building, has been preserved. Now used as a school, it is a pleasant structure of *tezontle* with stone ornament and an ample portal.

Little needs to be said about the various barracks. One can just identify the one known as the "Cuartel de los Gallos" in Mexico City. It has a large portal and, at the corners of the façade, some sculptured dogs perhaps much older than the building itself, which dates from 1782.[7]

Religious Buildings

If we turn to religious buildings other than the churches and convents, we find a little group of interesting work. First of all, the diocesan residences. The Palace of the Archbishop in Mexico City took its present form in this period, with the work done by Archbishop Vizarrón between 1730 and 1747; Núñez de Haro later enlarged it by adding another house. It is a building of great sobriety, with a skyline of inverted arches and merlons, and plenty of balconies. The portal, which we have discussed as an early example of the Churrigueresque, and a patio of simple flat arches complete the ensemble.

Larger, more elegant, and exemplifying the typical local style, the Archbishop's Palace in Puebla deserves more attention than it has received, especially since its skillful restoration and remodelling by the Secretaría de Hacienda. It was begun in the seventeenth century, but its present form is the work of Bishop Santa Cruz and his successors.

A splendid building, perfectly homogeneous and constructed all of cut stone, with exotic finials of Asiatic flavor at the ends of the façade, is the old Semi-

Arrieta," *Boletín del Archivo General de la Nación*, 16 (1945), 73–94; "Three Master Architects in New Spain," *Hispanic American Historical Review*, 27 (1947), 375–383; "El arquitecto Joseph Eduardo de Herrera," *Anales del Instituto de Arte Americano e Investigaciones Estéticas*, 17 (1964), 90–98; "El ingeniero Luis Díez Navarro en México," *Anales de la Sociedad de Geografía e Historia de Guatemala*, 22 (1947), 89–95.

6 Angulo Íñiguez, *Planos*, I, 375, 379.

7 *Ibid.*, I, 381. This building has been converted into a motion picture theater; what is extraordinary is that it retains some traces of its past.

275. Palace of the Audiencia de Nueva Galicia (Palacio de Gobierno), Guadalajara, Jalisco.

nario de Valladolid, now used for the Palacio de Gobierno in Morelia (277).

There was also a great episcopal residence in Oaxaca; but we can no longer guess what its façade was like before the present one was built in an absurd style derived from the ruins of Mitla.

276. Royal Customs House, Mexico City.

277. Seminary (Palacio de Gobierno), Morelia, Michoacán.

278. Patio, Holy Office of the Inquisition, Mexico City.

A building in the religious category which should be considered here is that of the famous Inquisition of Mexico City. From the beginning it occupied the same location on the Plaza de Santo Domingo, facing the monastery with whose friars the officials of the Holy Office were fraternally associated. After many successive campaigns of construction, beginning in 1571 when the dread Tribunal was established in Mexico, their building finally received its definitive form between 1732 and 1736. It was then as we see it today, except for the third story and various changes made in the attempt to adapt it to the impossible—a School of Medicine. The architect was Pedro de Arrieta. Before establishing the Medical School there in the nineteenth century, they had thought of using it for the Academia de San Carlos, and the plans exist for this conversion, drawn by Joaquín Heredia. It is built of *tezontle* and cut stone, with its large portal cutting across the corner —the terrible *puerta chata* of which they spoke in colo-

nial times. The most interesting parts now preserved are the stairway and the great patio with pendant arches—unsupported by columns—at the corners (278). The construction is obvious, in spite of the illusion of levitation which only this period would credit. Two arches cross, and their voussoirs are continued downward at the intersection to give the impression that they are suspended without supports.[8]

Academic Buildings

The design of the typical school building is one of the most important developments; for it is at last in this period that a distinct academic type appears. Except for the University, which, as we have seen, took its definitive form after much experimentation about 1584, all the early schools had to adapt themselves to

[8] See Francisco de la Maza, *El Palacio de la Inquisición*; Berlin, "Pedro de Arrieta," pp. 73–94; Berlin, "Three Master Architects," pp. 375–380; Berlin, "Herrera," pp. 92–95.

279. Façade, College of San Ildefonso (National Preparatory School), Mexico City.

280. Patio, College of San Ildefonso, Mexico City.

the buildings in which they were established, remodelling them to fit their most urgent needs. The type we are describing here is actually the type built by those outstanding educators, the Jesuit fathers, and their associates. The most important of their schools was the College of San Ildefonso, a fine building now poorly adapted for a school of quite different character, the Preparatoria (279). It was completed in 1749 and its architect was Padre Cristóbal de Escobar y Llamas of the Society of Jesus.[9] It is composed of three great patios with arcades, or *"corredores"* (280), a large chapel—today the library—and a great salon, now the General de los Actos, or assembly room, which is called the "Generalito." The façade has a quality of great majesty, hinting at the Churrigueresque, with its wide areas of *tezontle* and its carved stone portals, not so much rich as solemn (281), and its windows very high above the street to avoid as far as possible all "worldly noise."

Another imposing building, whose date is not clear, is the large Jesuit college in Morelia, which is still properly used as a school. The date, *"año 1582,"* carved on the seventeenth-century tower of the church may be intended to commemorate the arrival of the Jesuits in Michoacán.

The college in Pátzcuaro presents a delightful appearance at once rustic and well-bred, in the ensemble of its roofs, for instance, or its large patios.

Seminaries did not follow a standard plan, but some of these also had considerable architectural quality. The one in Mexico City, established beside the Cathedral in the seventeenth century, was moved to the monastery of San Camilo and completely rebuilt; now only the houses belonging to it on each side remain. That of Morelia, as we have noted, is the present Palacio de Gobierno, a fine building. That of Guadalajara has been ably restored as the Museo del Estado, so that one can still enjoy its fine stone façade and spacious patio.

As beautiful as the College of San Ildefonso, if not more beautiful, the College of San Ignacio in Mexico City—known as "Las Vizcaínas"—illustrates perfectly the type of the colonial school (282). It was constructed between 1734 and 1767, and although one could believe that the architect was the same as San Ildefonso's, since the buildings seem like twins in their

281. Portal, College of San Ildefonso, Mexico City.

broad façades of *tezontle,* their carved stone portals and their patios, two other names appear. The plans seem to have been drawn by Don Pedro Bueno Basorí, who had died before they began to build, and the land grant was received on November 27, 1733, by the master architect Miguel José de Quiera, who perhaps built it. Here the skyline of pyramidal pinnacles and the great

[9] J. M. Marroquí, *La ciudad de México.* He refers to a MS of *México católico* by Ignacio Carrillo y Pérez. See also José Rojas Garcidueñas, *El antiguo colegio de San Ildefonso.*

282. Façade, College of San Ignacio (Las Vizcaínas), Mexico City.

framed windows give the building an unmistakable quality of majesty. The portal of the chapel, dated 1786, was the work of Lorenzo Rodríguez (283). Four main patios, conveniently connected by passages and arcades, constitute the core of the structure (284), and nothing could be more impressive than the monumental stairway. The chapel has retained its Churrigueresque retables, and a modest museum has been assembled from the works of art which were scattered through the building—furniture, paintings, goldwork.[10]

The Real y Pontificia Universidad, whose early history we have followed, was rebuilt during the reign of Charles III:

One's attention was particularly attracted by a handsome portal three stories high, rich with ornament in the Churrigueresque style, and decorated with statues of Civil Law, Medicine, Philosophy, Theology, and Canon Law, with busts of the three Charleses and the royal coat of arms. . . . [But] all this very beautiful, elegant, striking and costly portal was demolished, smoothed off to allow the decorations for the inaugural oath of Señor Don Carlos IV, leaving the whole façade simply painted in perspective, with ornament of the Tuscan Order.[11]

The complete demolishing of the University was accomplished in 1910. The lower staircase, with its profuse carving, was taken to the old monastery at Churubusco; one Churrigueresque doorway was placed in the

[10] Enrique de Olavarría y Ferrari, *El Real Colegio de San Ignacio de Loyola.* See also Gonzalo Obregón, "La capilla del Colegio de las Vizcaínas," *Anales del Instituto de Investigaciones Estéticas,* 8 (1942), 19–25; Antonio Toussaint, "Colegio de las Vizcaínas," *Artes de México,* 42 (1962).

[11] See Joaquín García Icazbalceta's introduction to the first dialogue of Francisco Cervantes de Salazar, *México en 1554; tres diálogos latinos,* p. 13. The quotation is from Carrillo y Pérez, *México católico,* Lib. 7, Cap. 1, Para. 8. See also Romero de Terreros, *Medallas relativas a la antigua Universidad de México;* Berlin, "Three Master Architects," pp. 375–383.

old College of San Pedro y San Pablo, and another installed in a library on the outskirts of the city.

The Colegio del Cristo in Mexico City is still relatively well preserved. Founded in 1612, the present building dates from the middle of the eighteenth century; the most interesting features are a charming Baroque portal and the patio.

Hospices

Of the hospices, which were at once penal and educational institutions, we have data on one, a large building across from the Paseo de la Alameda, in the middle of the street of La Acordada. It dated from 1774, but had small architectural interest, and it was demolished a long time ago.

The hospice of Santo Tomás de Villanueva, on the present Avenida Hidalgo in Mexico City, bears the date 1780 on a delightful Baroque portal which recalls Spanish Churrigueresque. Its walls are of *tezontle*; its patio has been rebuilt.

Hospitals

The hospitals of New Spain were all rebuilt during the eighteenth century. They do not follow a uniform plan, but had to be adapted to old sites and even to earlier buildings. A brief list of them follows.

Let us look first at the hospitals of Mexico City. The Hospital Real de Indias was perhaps the most important in size and social significance, if not in architecture. The plan was a large patio surrounded by arcades, with shops and offices downstairs, and big wards for the sick upstairs. Architecturally, only the portal with its panelled pilasters, flat arch, and balcony, and the patio with the same arches, pilasters, and buttresses, are of interest. The building was constructed over many periods, but finished in 1754. The portal seems to date from 1726 and to be the work of Jerónimo de Balbás. Lorenzo Rodríguez had a part in the building later. The vicissitudes of the little church with its elegant Baroque doorway, in which the most famous architects of the times were involved, can be found in detail in the *Estudio* of Señor Angulo Íñiguez. Now the whole

283. Chapel portal, College of San Ignacio (Las Vizcaínas), Mexico City.

thing has disappeared in the enlarging of the Avenida San Juan de Letrán.[12]

The hospital of the Terceros de San Francisco was built where the Post Office now stands. It was an old mansion, with doorways and balconies in the typical manner. It would be absurd today to think of establishing a hospital in such a situation, one of the noisiest places in the city; but in 1756, when it was inaugurated, it was on the extreme edge of the colonial capital.

[12] Angulo Íñiguez, *Planos*. I, 246–260. On the hospital, see Justino Fernández, "El Hospital Real de los Indios de la ciudad de México," *Anales del Instituto de Investigaciones Estéticas*, 3 (1938), 25–47. The portal, which they managed to save, now stands in a house, 3 Plaza de los Licenciados, in the old town of San Ángel (Villa Obregón, D.F.).

284. Patio, College of San Ignacio (Las Vizcaínas), Mexico City.

By this time the hospital of San Hipólito had lost the austere character given it by its admirable founder, Bernardino Álvarez; probably it was already concerned with the male insane. A heavy construction of *tezontle,* it can be seen adjoining the church of the same name, and, through the doorways of shops which have invaded it, can be glimpsed a patio with a neglected garden—all that remains of the hospital building.

If men go mad, so do women, and perhaps more often. José de Sáyago, a charitable carpenter who made several retables in the seventeenth century, with the help of his wife dedicated himself to gathering in the insane women who were wandering in the streets. With the aid of Archbishop Aguiar y Seijas he persisted in his project, and in 1700 the Congregación del Divino Salvador established the hospital by this name in the old Calle de la Canoa. It was rebuilt in the eighteenth century, and after various vicissitudes became the Secretaría de la Asistencia Pública. Only one original doorway remains.

The order of Hospitalers of San Juan de Dios, the *"juaninos,"* established hospitals in several cities of New Spain. That some of them are still in use proves their efficiency. The one in Mexico City, repaired after a fire on March 10, 1766, retains even older parts, like the Mudejar covering of its outer walls.

The Hospital de San Juan de Dios in Atlixco still functions in its original building, its halls lined with fine Puebla tile, which was the most hygienic material available at that time (285). At Tehuacán there is another still in use, but less well preserved.

In Puebla a magnificent example of a hospital building can be found, though so changed and put to such different use that it has only archeological interest: the Hospital de San Pedro, which was later given the magnificent title "Real y General." It is very old; Veytia says that it had already been established in 1545.[13] The building itself, a large construction with walls of unglazed tile, a fine coat of arms of the Cathedral of Puebla—a vase with lilies—and an immense patio, has

[13] Mariano Veytia, *Historia de la fundación de la ciudad de la Puebla de los Ángeles en la Nueva España.*

312

285. Patio, Hospital de San Juan de Dios, Atlixco, Puebla.

Markets

There was no typical form of building for the markets. The custom of the Indian markets, or *tianguis,* persisted: the merchants simply set up *puestos,* temporary stalls, displaying their wares in some plaza. They still do this, and there is nothing pleasanter or more lively than these market days, *días de plaza,* in the villages of Mexico. But there were also markets somewhat better organized. One recalls, for instance, the Alcaicería (Silk Exchange), which was established early in the seventeenth century in part of the establishment of the Marquesado del Valle in Mexico City—a project which in fact was the first to break into the Conquistador's property. The idea was to establish something like the Alcaicería in Granada, where the Moors held their silk market. Although the project seems not to have been successful, the principal passage which was cut through kept its name until our own day.

Other markets established in buildings were called by the name *parián.* The Parián in Mexico City, a rectangular structure opposite the Palacio del Ayuntamiento, brought a good income to that body from the rental of its stalls or *cajones* (351). It was begun in 1695 and finished in 1757. The government pulled it down in 1843, but rather for political reasons than to

been remodelled inside and outside for a variety of unsuitable uses. The church, which has no special interest, is still in use.

The Hospital de Belén in Guadalajara is one of the most venerable in the country, and has been able to retain its old building. It was built by the worthy Bishop Alcalde, who did not live to see its completion in 1797. As Angulo observes, it is one of the last examples of the hospitals on a cruciform plan which go back to the time of Ferdinand and Isabella (286). Here a second crossing of corridors, with arms leading to the four corners, has been added, so that there are eight wards enclosed within the rectangle. The chapel, which is small and unimportant, occupies the center of the façade and the hall behind it.[14]

[14] Angulo Íñiguez, *Planos,* I, 267. Cf. Alberto Santoscoy, *Historia del Hospital Real de San Miguel; época colonial.*

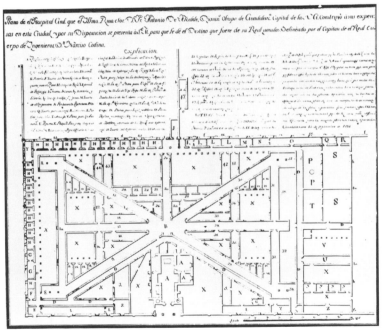

286. Plan of the Hospital Real de San Miguel (Hospital de Belén), Guadalajara, Jalisco.

287. Biblioteca Palafoxiana (Biblioteca del Estado), Puebla.

improve the city. Actually it was a ridiculous thing to have on the main plaza.[15]

The Parián of Puebla still exists, in its own quarter, but has no interest. Around it is a series of rooms whose doorways are sheltered by basket-handle vaults, which make a sort of portico, or arcade without supports; it is the most Mexican thing you can find.

The Palafoxian Library

Another building of this period in Puebla merits a paragraph for itself because it is unique: the Biblioteca Palafoxiana (287). There is no other library building in Mexico which was expressly built in colonial times for a library. It belonged to the college of San Juan, but was connected also with the bishop's palace. It was completed in 1773 and its name properly commemorates the venerable Palafox. It is a long room, with groin vaults, a rich entrance doorway, and two stories

[15] Mexico City, Ayuntamiento, *Colección de documentos oficiales relativos a la construcción y demolición del Parián.*

of fine bookshelves, with grilles to guard its treasures. It has a floor of ornamental tile, and great balconies over the garden, where one can go out and read with all the pleasure that comes from a good book and a congenial place.

Private Buildings

Noble Residences in Mexico City

The Baroque house which reached its typical form in Mexico City during the seventeenth century, in imitation of the Andalusian house, persisted to the end of the colonial period and even into the nineteenth century. It was the normal dwelling before the arrival of North American influences which—working with other circumstances like the costliness and scarcity of property in the center of the city, changing customs, and new means of transportation—have produced the present domestic architecture of the capital, so different from that Spanish tradition which still continues, not without a struggle, in the provinces. The great portal with a more or less sumptuous balcony above it is typical of Andalusia, as are the gate, the patio, and the *zaguán,* or hallway from portal to patio. The railings of wrought iron, the grilles, the supports for exterior curtains, all come from there. However, in Mexico in the eighteenth century there developed from these details a special type of house, the noble residence.

It corresponds to a new rank in the social hierarchy. Some colonists, Creoles—which means Spaniards born in America—who had grown rich from their mines or their haciendas and other property, were given titles of nobility by the King of Spain, and thus a new class was created—the titled nobility. But it is not enough to have a title and enjoy it: one must make it visible by means of a luxurious residence which constitutes the seat of the title, where the estate was established at its foundation. Now the simple house, whether detached or not, great or small, neither implies nor demonstrates anything but provision for daily life. There seems to be a difference between "residing" and "living": to "reside" is to live in ease, without the necessity of work which simply "to live" demands. Furthermore, a residence is fixed; the social position of the landed gentry imposes obligations and rights unknown to the man who merely owns, or lives in, a house. Receptions, balls, and banquets require special arrangements, and the privilege of holding certain religious ceremonies in one's house implies the need of a chapel or oratory furnished with the greatest propriety.

All these observations are apposite in a consideration of the arrangement and the parts which made up a noble residence. Straightforward and—as we would say today—functional, viceregal architecture expresses, as few styles do, its purpose and the means of achieving it. The architect's program speaks clearly in each project: a church cannot be anything but a church, a college is a college, a theatre, a theatre, a residence nothing but a residence. Neoclassicism never understood this, and so the façade of the Parthenon served for a church, like the Madeleine, or for the Bourse in Paris, for a theatre in Berlin, for various museums in London, and for all the houses of any distinction in Washington!

It must also be admitted that we owe a group of splendid works of art to what many would feel a most undesirable circumstance: the creation of an aristocracy, which in some cases might boast an ancient lineage, but which was nonetheless autocratic. I wonder whether the creation of this social class may not have functioned in the concepts which moved the Creoles to fight for the independence of Mexico, but I do not know. If it did,

we must be grateful also for that, as well as for its having left to independent Mexico this series of monuments in which the spirit of Spain remains, not as the power of an empire, but as the generosity of a vanished parent.

Let us then describe the characteristics which distinguish the noble residence. The exterior, first of all, shows us that we are looking at the dwelling of an important person. They worked not only for symmetry, usually so disdained by the Baroque, but for solemnity. Sometimes the façade itself is a monument. The building could be made important by indicating the number of stories, by making the portal stand out, by placing the coat of arms of the nobleman in a very visible place, by crenellating the top of the building—and adding cannon if the owner had been a captain-general—by adding those little towers which originated on the conquistadors' houses but serve now only for decoration and display. When we enter the palace we are astonished by the size of the patio with its fountain, by the richness of the principal stairway, the spaciousness of the galleries. If we visit the living quarters, we find that it is in fact the ordinary house, built on the scale and with the luxury that the owner's fortune can support. There are huge salons, one with a dais where the faithful vassal, in expectation of a visit some day from his sovereign, has prepared a seat of honor under a canopy—meanwhile hanging a portrait of His Majesty. The chapel, with its rich portal, is found at the head of the stairs, the other rooms occupy the side galleries—the bedrooms, the service rooms, and so on. The dining room is very spacious and is situated off the gallery parallel to the street, beyond the patio. There is almost always a second patio, with its service stair for the servants. A special characteristic of these residences is the mezzanine with low ceilings to accommodate offices, or sometimes apartments with independent access to the street. For the nobleman was not too proud to have his house earn what it could for him; shops opened on the ground floor, a custom dating back to the houses of Cortés himself.

Beyond the practical arrangements—which of course are not identical in the examples that have survived—comes the skill of the architects who made the plans, of the sculptors who cut the stone ornament, and of the masons who built the walls. Their art is perhaps more ennobling than the writ of nobility itself. Time, whose hand alone can create a patina, or evoke tradition like a seamless garment to veil and lend mystery to the archi-

288. The Plaza de Guardiola: House of the Marqués de Santa Fe de Guardiola, house of the Conde del Valle de Orizaba, and monastery of San Francisco, Mexico City. Lithograph. From *El Album Mexicano,* 1855–1856.

tecture, finishes the work. Thus these buildings have come down to us and fill us with pride; they are genuine creations of Hispano-Mexican art.

There are about forty houses in Mexico City which can be considered in this category as noble residences. Considering their great number, and remembering the number of other buildings—conventual buildings, buildings concerned with government, with charity, and with education—which we have looked at, remembering that they all fit into an area which hardly exceeded the original area of the city, and that most of them were of monumental character, one feels that the term "The City of Palaces" (attributed to Baron von Humboldt, although it is not to be found in his works) was justified in the early nineteenth century.

Now I shall give a brief survey of these residences, at least naming all that have come to my attention. Even

this simple list, more complete than any yet published, was difficult enough to prepare. But it should be useful for future work, such as a serious monograph, well illustrated with plans, cross sections, elevations, and photographs of these valuable buildings. Many of them are in danger of destruction, from greed whipped up by the exaggerated rise in real estate values.[16]

House of the Conde de Miravalle (Isabel la Católica 30). This may be the oldest of all the mansions, perhaps dating from the seventeenth century. Walls of *tezontle,* doors and windows of rusticated stone, and low mezzanines. The ground floor, much rebuilt, and the cornice indicate that various houses were thrown

[16] Romero de Terreros, *Residencias coloniales de la ciudad de México*; Idem, "La casa colonial," *Anales del Museo Nacional de Arqueología, Historia y Etnología,* 5 (1913), 161–181; Federico Mariscal, *La patria y la arquitectura nacional.*

316

House of the Conde del Valle de Orizaba (Casa de los Azulejos), Mexico City.

into one. It was remodelled in the nineteenth century, and was used for a hotel—the Hotel del Bazar—for many years.

House of the Marqués de Santa Fe de Guardiola. This house gave its name to the little plaza in front of it, at the west end of the present Avenida Madero (288). It too seems to have been quite ancient. Of only two stories, with large balconies upstairs, and doors with iron grilles downstairs; above the larger balcony, which was over the portal, a pediment for the coat of arms. Crenellated roof line. It was demolished in the nineteenth century to make way for an imposing building in European style, and this, in turn, for the construction of the Edificio Guardiola, a branch of the Bank of Mexico.[17]

House of the Marqués de Ciria, Mariscal de Castilla (corner of Avenida Hidalgo and Aquiles Serdán). Recently demolished in the prolongation of Avenida San Juan de Letrán. The exterior had lost all character in a commercial clutter. There was still a charming patio with columns and arches, apparently dating from the seventeenth century.

House of the Conde del Valle de Orizaba; also called "Casa de los Azulejos," "The House of Tiles" (Madero 4). One of the richest examples, a house worthy of any city, anywhere (288). The title of the Conde del Valle de Orizaba was bestowed by Philip III on Don Rodrigo de Vivero in 1657, in recompense for his services. One of his descendants built this house. Legend has it that the young man was a prodigal spendthrift, and that his father reproached him with the Spanish proverb: "You will never build a house of tile!"—that is, accomplish anything worthwhile, and that when he reformed in time, he rebuilt the house, covering it with *azulejos*. The truth seems to have been rather different. The fifth Condesa del Valle de Orizaba married and lived in Puebla until her husband died in 1708, when she returned to her home in Mexico City. In her will, drawn in 1737, she says that she had rebuilt the mansion of the estate, since it was in bad condition, and much enlarged it. I do not believe that this "rebuilding" was limited to facing the façade with tile; this would not have corrected the deterioration, and besides the word *reconstruir* is used in such a way that it can mean only that the House of Tiles was for practical purposes built at this time. Whether because the Countess brought back a taste for the houses

[17] Federico Gómez de Orozco, *La Plaza de Guardiola.*

289. House of the Conde del Valle de Orizaba (Casa de los Azulejos), Mexico City.

of Puebla, or for whatever reason, this mansion is unique; neither in Mexico City nor in Puebla, nor anywhere else, is there a house completely covered outside with glazed tile (289; color, facing p. 316). If it were not for the perfection of the whole building, such a revetment would prove ridiculous—suitable for a kitchen, a bathroom, or a water-closet. But the artist knew what he was doing: a dado of cut stone, fillets, pilasters, mouldings, window frames and doorframes in the same stone; strong cornices marking the horizontals, so that the tiles—with their several exquisite shades of blue and the high lights of the glaze—are framed in panels by

290. House of the Marqués de Jaral de Berrio, Mexico City.

the soft grey tone of the stone. If the ensemble is beautiful, the profile against the sky is magnificent: a niche over the great portal, another at the corner, and a silhouette of festooning mouldings ornamenting a horizontal, with pinnacles and Chinese urns also in ceramic.

The interior is no less fine, in spite of what it has suffered in being put to another use: the great patio with its slender columns and its beautiful fountain; the monumental stairway with its superb tile dado, perhaps older than the tile of the façade (where one of the best murals of our great Clemente Orozco can be admired); the galleries whose railings were made, it is said, in Asia; the doorway to the chapel, the great rooms, the roofs—it is all of a richness and a taste which one can-

not but admire, especially as it is so rare to find these two qualities together.[18]

House of the Marqués de Jaral de Berrio, or *House of the Marqués de Moncada,* or *Hotel Iturbide* (Avenida Madero 17). This palace is the most important in the group (290). Its luxuriousness and magnificence are explained, according to tradition, by the fact that its owner, the Conde de San Mateo de Valparaiso, to prevent his fortune's falling into the hands of his daughter's suitor, the Marqués de Moncada, ordered his architect to build a house whose cost would be equal to the girl's dowry. Thus are waste and ostenta-

[18] Romero de Terreros, *La Casa de los Azulejos*; Gómez de Orozco, *La Plaza de Guardiola.*

tion redeemed by art! The wide façade is symmetrical; there is a very high first floor, with a mezzanine, a second floor, and a third story formed of two towers joined by a loggia or gallery. The decoration of finely carved stone on the portal with its two Atlantes, on the pilasters and the window frames, is all excellent (291). The patio is of amazing proportions, and different from the old colonial patios (292); one seems to be in Italy, in one of those Milanese or Florentine *palazzi*. The chapel doorway is all filigree. There are many similarities between the decorative detail of this building and the decoration of those built by Guerrero y Torres, such as the broken mouldings of the doorframes and of the bases of columns and pilasters. It is fairly safe to assume that he was the architect, as he was of the earlier house of the Conde de San Mateo, which he signed (see below). This palace has no signature, a rare omission with so important a building, but it is possible that the inscription may have disappeared in one of its many remodellings.[19] The building was used by Iturbide as his palace. Much later it was remodelled as a hotel, bearing the name of our great patriot, by which it is still known.

House of the Marqués de Prado Alegre (Avenida Madero 39). A large residence, much modified in later remodellings. Today one sees only the great façade, of two stories and a mezzanine, with its very rich doorway carved in relief, and its large balcony and finial to carry the coat of arms. Balconies with rusticated frames and crenellated roof line.

Houses of Don José de la Borda (Madero, Bolívar, 16 de Septiembre, and Motolinía). The great Spanish gentleman who has bequeathed us both his fortune, in the church at Taxco, and his spirit in his charities, had the idea of building a house which would occupy a whole block in the city, like Cortés' own house long before. It was to be bounded by the four streets named above, and a long continuous balcony was to permit him to walk all around his property. This purpose never was realized, but various houses on the present Avenida Madero and the Calle de Bolívar are bound together by such a balcony. This was not properly speaking a noble residence, nor did the buildings present a homogeneous appearance, but there is no doubt that they were important.

Houses of the Marqués de Uluapa. There was no house bearing this title on the Calle 5 de Febrero, as is

19 See Berlin, "Three Master Architects," pp. 375–383.

291. Portal, house of the Marqués de Jaral de Berrio, Mexico City.

commonly believed. Two houses belonged to the family: one at the corner of Las Damas and Ortega (now Bolívar and Uruguay) where it was long erroneously believed that Bolívar himself had lodged, and the other in the Calle de San Francisco (now Madero) which has not been identified. The first is without artistic interest.

House of the Marqués de la Colina. Between 1803 and 1806 this was located in the Calle de San Francisco, now the Avenida Madero. We have no information about this house.

292. Patio, house of the Marqués de Jaral de Berrio, Mexico City.

293. House of the Conde de Santiago de Calimaya, Mexico City.

House of the Marqués de San Román. In 1820 this house appears in the first block of the Calle de San Francisco, we know nothing more about it.

House of the Marqués de Rivas Cacho. This stood on the Callejón de Betlemitas, now called Filomena Mata, and was destroyed a good while ago.

Houses of the Mayorazgo del Valle de Oaxaca (Today the Nacional Monte de Piedad, Calle del Monte de Piedad 7, between the Avenida 5 de Mayo and Calle de la Palma). This is what remains of the residence of Cortés, whose early history we have already given. As long ago as the seventeenth century the great estate had been cut up; but the house seems to have remained unchanged from the last remodelling of the eighteenth century, in 1758, until a story was added in our time. The institution of the Monte Pio acquired the house in 1836 for the national pawnshop. It is an immense building of *tezontle* with doors and windows framed in stone. The part to the right of the portal was originally lower than the rest, and its pinnacle and merlons much richer, but today it has all been made uniform. The interior, completely reconstructed, has only bits of old detail.

House of the Conde de Santiago de Calimaya (Pino Suárez 30). Perhaps the house that is best preserved, still inhabited by descendants of the family (293). It is dated 1779 and was perhaps the work of Francisco de Guerrero y Torres. There is a noble air about the exterior, partly due to the absence of a mezzanine, and to the great portal with claw feet copied from furniture and its coat of arms above between two Atlantean figures (294). The silhouette of the roof is very ornate, with drain spouts in the form of cannon. The interior is intact: the spacious patio, with a fine arcade in whose spandrels there are coats of arms of the families related to the house of Santiago, and a delightful shell-shaped fountain with its mermaid (295). The portal of the chapel is likewise excellent.

House of the Marqueses de San Mateo de Valparaíso (Now the Banco Nacional, corner of Venustiano Carranza and Isabel la Católica). This is one of the most famous noble residences of the Colony (296). Built between 1769 and 1772 by Francisco Antonio Guerrero y Torres, it has a superb façade with a tower at the corner, a rich portal, and a large patio which has been converted as gracefully as possible into a bank.

[20] Toussaint, *Paseos coloniales*, pp. 65–70; Berlin, "Three Master Architects," pp. 375–383.

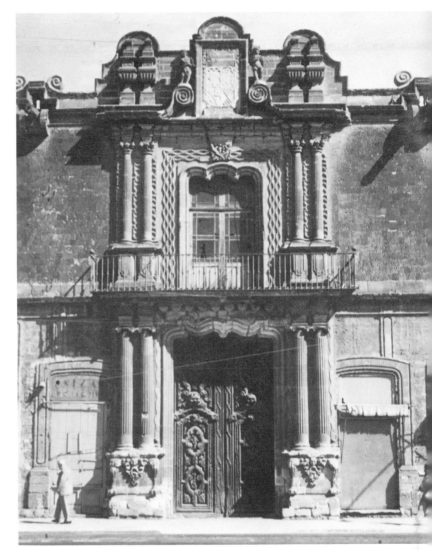

294. Portal, house of the Conde de Santiago de Calimaya, Mexico City.

One of its most astonishing features is the stairway, a unique example of the double spiral, which would serve for the gentlefolk and the servants at the same time.[20]

House of the Conde de Heras Soto (Corner of Chile and Donceles). There is perhaps no house to equal this in the elegance of its stone decoration. The portal is at once sumptuous and in excellent taste, with the rich bronze railing of the balcony above, and the exuberant surrounding frame of sculpture (297). The sculpture which decorates the corner window has the same qual-

295. Patio, house of the Conde de Santiago de Calimaya, Mexico City.

296. House of the Marqueses de San Mateo de Valparaíso (Banco Nacional), Mexico City.

297. Portal, house of the Conde de Heras Soto, Mexico City.

298. Corner decoration, house of the Conde de Heras Soto, Mexico City.

ity: a child standing on a lion holds a basket of fruit on his head; on either side, like a tapestry, extends a panel in relief, rather French in feeling (298). Of the interior there remains only the patio with its arcade of small columns.

House of the Marqués de Herrera. There is no longer a trace of this residence, which used to stand at Venustiano Carranza 42, where the Banco de Commercio now is. It appears that Bolívar lived in it when he passed through Mexico City. In the nineteenth century

and the early twentieth the President of the Republic, General Don Porfirio Díaz, lived there.

House of the Marqués de Salvatierra. In 1820 this house was located on the Calle de los Bajos de San Agustín, now the Calle 5 de Febrero, between Uruguay and El Salvador.

House in the Calle de la Palma (Palma 35). In this street, in the one stretch that dates from the colonial period, can be seen a large house with a façade of *tezontle* and openings framed in stone. The top floor is

299. House of the Conde de la Cortina, Mexico City.

new. We do not know whom it belonged to. The street is said to have been named from a palm tree in relief on the front of this house.

House of the Marqués de Santa Cruz de Inguanzo. By deduction from the old address, I have identified this as the two-story house now numbered 62-A on the Calle Venustiano Carranza. The upper story is higher than the ground story, which makes an effect of disproportion, as does the heavy parapet of inverted arches

and crenellations. Its walls of *tezontle* with stone framing give it, nonetheless, a pleasant air of antiquity.

House of the Conde de San Bartolomé de Xala (Venustiano Carranza 73). This was the work of Lorenzo Rodríguez, finished in 1764, according to the inscription on an arch of the patio. The exterior looks like a three-story building because the mezzanine has become more important. One cannot appraise Rodríguez' work, because of the changes it has suffered.[21]

House of the Marqués de San Miguel de Aguayo. This house was located in the old Calle de Zuleta, and one can still see what is left of it. A simple two-story house without mezzanine, with its wide portal, a balcony over it, and above that the coat of arms.

House of the Conde de Medina y Torres. According to the *Calendario* of Zúñiga y Ontiveros for the year 1802, this house was on the Calle de San Pedro y San Paulo. It would be difficult to identify it today.

House of the Marqués de Castañiza. On the old Calle de San Ildefonso, named for the college, can be seen an ancient large house in very bad condition, which may have been the mansion of this nobleman. One of the holders of the title was Bishop of Durango.

House of the Conde de la Torre de Cosío (Uruguay 90). The façade of this mansion, much altered, still exists. We can still admire the great stairway, but the interior has been entirely modernized. On the outside wall of a room at the top, which retains the form of a tower, may be seen the coat of arms and its crenellated parapet, now surmounted by a rude iron railing. There are downspouts in the form of cannon; but as a whole the building has lost its character.

House of the Conde de la Cortina (Uruguay 92). Next door to the one above is to be found this residence, which must have been magnificent in its time (299). We can still identify its big façade, its great portal with the balcony above, its windows and doors framed in rusticated stone, and the tower at the corner. The needs of the city, which required opening the Avenida 20 de Noviembre, cut off a large part of the building and took away its old impressiveness.

House of the Conde de Regla (Salvador 59). From what we can see in an old painting, the house of this magnanimous man did not show the slightest ostentation outside. Two stories high, built of *tezontle,* with pilasters and doorframes of stone, the only unusual

21 Romero de Terreros, *Una casa del siglo XVIII en México, la del conde de San Bartolomé de Xala.*

324

300. Houses of the Mayorazgo de Guerrero (Academia Nacional de Música), Mexico City.

thing is the arrangement of the portal: only the coat of arms is over the entrance, and the balcony is divided between two doors, at either side. There are descriptions of its luxurious interior, but the house has been vilely cut up to make it into what they call, with barefaced cynicism, a *casa de productos,* a factory.

House of the Marqués de Selva Nevada (Venustiano Carranza 49). A great residence, its walls covered with *tezontle,* its doors and windows framed in stone. Completely remodelled to convert it into a hotel, with shops on the street.

House of the Marqués de San Juan de Rayas. This nobleman, owner of one of the most famous mines of Guanajuato—where he built a marvel of a church as we have seen—had his residence in Mexico City on the Calle de los Medinas. I have not been able to identify it.

Houses of the Mayorazgo de Guerrero (Corner of Zapata and Correo Mayor). Twin houses can still be seen here; they belonged to this estate whose title goes back to the sixteenth century (300). Both have towers

on the corner, and they seem to carry on a dialogue about the grandeur of the past and the misery of the present. The first of them, opposite the Museo Nacional, seems to have been the residence of the noble family; the other, which contains several apartments, is like a faithful servant. From the style of its façade of *tezontle* and cut stone, above all from the great portal, we identify the first as the work of Guerrero y Torres. The date on an arch of the patio—1713—seems to be earlier than the façade.[22]

The second building, no less beautiful, is less symmetrical on the outside, but perhaps for this reason more delightful. It consists of two *casas solas* of the usual kind, with their appendages. These two houses, with the old building of the Museum, the churches of Santa Inés and La Santísima to the east, the venerable Palacio Nacional and the no less ancient Archbishop's Palace, with the majestic Cathedral to the west, all together constitute one of the most beautiful parts of the

[22] See Berlin, "Three Master Architects," pp. 375–383.

325

301. Country house of the Conde del Valle de Orizaba (Casa de los Mascarones), Mexico City.

city today, and one of the most evocative of Viceregal days.

House of Chavarría (Donceles 147). A spacious residence built of *tezontle* with stone framing, only two stories high, the lower floor roughly rebuilt. In the niche at the corner it has, not a saint as was usual in these shrines, but a hand holding a custodia. It is known that the owner of the house, Juan de Chavarría, at the time of the terrible fire in the church of San Agustín in 1676, saved the custodia with the Holy Sacrament at the peril of his life. The King granted him the right to honor his house with the symbol we see. Chavarría had his tomb made, with his portrait praying, in the church of San Lorenzo.[23]

House of Don Antonio Bassoco. From 1802 to 1806 the house of this grandee appears on the Calle de Don Juan Manuel. Probably it was one of those showing a graceful tower at one corner. To this gentleman we owe no less than the church of Loreto, a unique masterpiece, as we shall see.

House of the Marqués de Apartado. This building is now occupied by the Secretaría de la Economia Nacional. Since it is in the Neoclassic style, it will be considered in a later chapter. We have also discovered that there were other houses belonging to this estate, on the Puente de Leguízamo.

House, Avenida Uruguay 117. At this address there is a noble residence whose owner we have not been able to identify. It is not very impressive, but its proportions and the arrangement of the façade indicate that it belongs to the type we are listing.

House, Calle 5 de Febrero, 18. Wrongly ascribed to the Marquesa de Uluapa. Properly speaking it is not a noble residence, but a house whose owner, a gentleman of excellent taste, ornamented it with the finest tiles to be found in the capital (343). Recently it has been possible to prove that these *azulejos,* which had been admired as some of the finest to come from the potters of Puebla, were actually made in Mexico City. In any case, they are splendid and unique in that they depict people busy with daily life, instead of saints.[24]

Casa de los Mascarones. This building was the country house of the Conde del Valle de Orizaba; its construction dates from 1766 to 1771, but it was left un-

[23] Toussaint, "La escultura funeraria en la Nueva España," *Anales del Instituto de Investigaciones Estéticas,* 11 (1944), 41–58.

[24] Francisco J. Rhode, "Azulejos de México," unpublished MS; Alberto Le Duc, Roberto Álvarez Espinosa, and Jorge Enciso, *Una casa habitación del siglo XVIII en la ciudad de México*; Romero de Terreros, "Una casa habitación del siglo XVIII en la ciudad de México," *Anales del Instituto de Investigaciones Estéticas,* 4 (1939), 64–66.

completed. The façade is composed with very fine estí-pites holding up caryatids, which stand between the no less beautiful windows, very richly carved (301). The caryatids have given the house its name—the House of the Masks.

Houses in Other Cities of New Spain

After the seventeenth century, with prosperity throughout the Colony, a variety of types of houses developed in the various regions of the Viceroyalty. Conditions of climate and location determined their form, just as they had in the motherland. In a general way one can say that on the plateau we have flat-roofed houses around a patio, in the ports there are types adapted to that climate, and in the mining towns, which are in the mountains, a different type.

Puebla. The second city of New Spain, which was no mean rival to the capital, developed its own unique type of house or residence. We have suggested that a desire to compete with the *tezontle* façades of the houses of Mexico City may have encouraged the development in Puebla of the façade of brick and tile so marvellously harmonious with the Mudejar mood of the city. However that may be, it is undeniable that this type of house is unique, not only in Mexico, but in the whole world. So we must lament that these houses, irreplaceable examples, their interiors as fine as their imaginative façades, are being systematically demolished to make room for *"casas coloniales modernas."* One hardly knows which is more shocking, the crass ignorance of proprietors and architects, or the boundless greed of both in complicity with the local authorities. If some control is not imposed, Puebla will be in ten years' time a vulgar city which the tourists visit to see whatever churches are left and to buy candy which may well be inferior to that of Mexico City and other places.

So there is an urgent need to preserve, if only in our modest descriptions, these treasures threatened by the disease of commerce. There are examples of archaic houses whose balconies are held up by two great carved stones like brackets. Others, later in date, have façades covered with unglazed tile (177). After these comes the typical, unique form: combinations in the most original ways of glazed and unglazed tile covering the whole façade (302, 303). The interior always has a patio with more or less ample galleries, with those flattened arches typical of the city. There are railings also constructed of the same masonry, with rectangular pris-

302. Detail of two houses, Puebla.

matic supports joined by curves. Arcades are frequent, even in houses of a later date, with every sort of arch imaginable. Thus a house developed which was derived, just as elsewhere on the plateau, from the Andalusian house, but which was without precedent in its decoration.

As for the types of houses to be found in Puebla,

303. Casa de los Muñecos, Puebla.

304. Casa del Alfeñique (Museo de la Ciudad), Puebla.

there was everything from the humblest—but no less picturesque—to the noble residence, although examples in this highest category were not so numerous as in Mexico City. *Casas de vecindad,* where, beyond a semicircular or mixtilinear arch, a Sevillan patio opens, with its paving of irregular stones, its fig tree at one side, and whitewashed doorways in every corner. *Casas de viviendas,* two apartments at the front, two at the back, and others around the patio. *Casas solas,* like those of Mexico City, but more spacious, with a larger patio and bigger rooms, all paved with glazed brick. The noble residence is of the same type as in Mexico City, but raised to the maximum size and dignity.

In Puebla, furthermore, there are houses which, more than any others, exemplify the Churrigueresque, with engaged estípites worked in masonry, in stucco, or in stone flanking doors and windows. One could name a handful of admirable dwellings in this style, usually in a popular vein. One that cannot be omitted is the so-called Casa del Alfeñique—"The House of Marzipan," "The Candy House"—because its delicate and complicated reliefs recall the decoration of that Moorish sweet made of ground almonds and sugar (304). Its architect, at the end of the eighteenth century, was Don Antonio de Santa María Incháurregui, the most famous of the period. This house has now been converted into the museum of the city.[25]

Querétaro. The houses of Querétaro have special characteristics. Their balconies are supported by brackets in the form of dogs, sometimes very well carved, as on the Casa de los Perros, the House of the Dogs. The arches of patios and galleries offer the greatest possible variety of curves, countercurves, volutes, and so on. They have a Mudejar quality, but even more of the Baroque (305). An outstanding example of this type of house is the one owned by Don Rosendo Rivera. Quite different, with a quality of popular art, but full of flavor and interest is the Casa del Faldón. The prize, elegantly carved in rosy stone, is the house which is said to have belonged to the Marqués de la Villa del Villar del Águila; a true noble palace, worthy of any capital, it looks magnificent here (306). It is too bad that a little window has been cut through where the coat of arms used to be displayed, sheltered under a proud canopy.

Oaxaca. The house in Oaxaca deserves an extended

25 Toussaint, "La casa de alfeñique en Puebla," in *Paseos coloniales,* pp. 60–63.

305. Patio of a house, Querétaro.

study; there is such a variety of types in this city of noble lineage that a monograph is wanted. These are some of the distinctive types: a one-story building with a patio and apartments on the four sides; a house of which a part is higher; a two-story house. The different rooms are arranged in the usual way. The characteristic quality of the Oaxaca house in general is solidity (307). Notably—or rather, unfortunately—earthquake country, its houses like its churches and palaces had to stand firm on the ground to resist the quakes as much as possible. At the corners are buttresses, and the whole city presents a solemn appearance of robustness and solidity which contrasts with the friendly and slangy character of its citizens.

Morelia. In contrast to Oaxaca we have the no less

306. House of the Marqués de la Villa del Villar del Águila, Querétaro.

noble city of Valladolid, as it was originally called. Here, although there is some danger of earthquake, they seem not to fear it so much because the gentle hill on which the city stands is of solid rock. However that may be, the houses of Morelia are delicate; their patios have slender columns and daring arches. Their arrangement does not differ from the normal type we have described.

San Luis Potosí. The three cities above, Oaxaca, Morelia, and San Luis, are most like the cities of Castile. In all three of them the use of stone predominates in the buildings, in contrast to the Andalusian stucco which brightens Guadalajara, Cuernavaca, or Pátzcuaro, for example. The houses of San Luis are all of noble proportions and antique appearance. A special detail, which I have not seen elsewhere, is the character of the supports for the balcony in the few examples remaining. Instead of the brackets of Querétaro, or the

cantilevered slab of Puebla, here it is a real console, with sculptured reliefs.

Guanajuato. Here the houses fit themselves to the broken terrain, doing the best they can. This is the typical house of the mining town, entirely different from the houses of the central plateau. One can indeed find houses with patios, as elsewhere in New Spain, but the majority are made up of a puzzle of rooms, passageways, stairways, and intersections. This is what gives the city its special and unique charm.

Taxco. One can say the same of this town, which we have already discussed. The houses there have great variety. Few have patios, for here it is not necessary: galleries are more desirable, their arched or lintelled arcades turned to the most beautiful view. There is one real seignorial residence, the house of Borda, the creator of Taxco. From the front it is a proper house of two stories facing the main plaza; behind, it seems to be riding over a ravine, and its levels are multiple and astonishing. The Casa de Humboldt, so called because Humboldt once spent the night there, is a handsome example which illustrates the rule. Its one-story façade, with a rich portal and elegant windows, hides a delightful variety of levels within, which give the house its special quality. One can find similar arrangements in other mining towns which have been converted into cities by the success of the mines. The architecture has faithfully adapted itself to the exigencies of the terrain. I am thinking of Zacatecas, that city of noble lineage, of Pachuca, where they have chosen not to follow the tradition, of Tlalpujahua, where it has been preserved more agreeably.

San Miguel de Allende. A city notable for its old mansions, perhaps more than for its churches. The conservatism of the inhabitants can be seen in the zealous care of their houses. There are a handful of these which would not be out of place in any city. The house of Allende, where he was born, is an example from this period, an elegant mansion with a rich portal and hospitable plan. We shall refer to other houses of San Miguel later.

Veracruz. The houses in seaports always have the same character, imposed by the climate and by that relentless tyrant, the sea. In small ports which are not yet cities the houses take various forms, provisional, and usually without style. In the great ports, like Veracruz, they have created a real civil architecture, where the solution of the basic problems has not prevented architectural excellence and charm. The building mate-

307. Noble House, Oaxaca.

rial there is principally what is called *piedra múcara,* a crustaceous limestone which has much the same recommendations as the *tezontle* of Mexico City. The houses in the center of the city are high, of two or three stories, with narrow, shadowed patios which serve to combat the heat. Country houses are spacious and well ventilated, and have large balconies with awnings and curtains, where one can even hang a hammock.

Metal is not used much, because the salt air corrodes it, but woods resistant to decay, like *zapote.* Outside the city the houses are small, built of wood painted in bright colors, and have porches. The dwellings known locally as *patios* are frightful: there is a large courtyard around which open the most miserable of apartments, often only a single room.

Gardens

Very few examples of colonial gardens have come down to us, and these in such abandon that they can hardly be said to have survived.[26] Mexico, a land of the richest vegetation, is wonderfully suited to the making of gardens and orchards, and indeed there have been many of them, and still are. But when we think of gardens which are works of art, like the gardens of Italy, Spain, or France, where architecture and sculpture and beautiful fountains are combined in a harmonious ensemble, there have been very few of these. First of all there was the famous garden of Borda in Cuernavaca, built not by Don José, as most people think, but by Don Manuel, his son, around 1783, and apparently designed by José Manuel Arrieta. Making the most of the hillside, numerous terraces, ramps, and stairways were laid out. There were plenty of fountains, and the lake is impressive.

Next in importance is the garden known as El Pensil Mexicano in Tacuba, in the Distrito Federal. It seems to date from the eighteenth century, with fine gateways and stone benches. Apparently it belonged to Don

26 Romero de Terreros, *Los jardines de la Nueva España.*

331

Manuel Marco de Ibarra, whose coat of arms appears on the shield over one of the gateways.

In Tlalpan there was preserved until recently a charming garden, square in plan, with paths and circles, decorated with stucco reliefs. It was destroyed in cutting through the highway to Acapulco, leaving the house, which also has artistic importance, mutilated.

I used to know another little garden with a high terrace, on the hacienda of Cuadra, near Taxco. Whether it still exists I cannot say.[27]

The monastery orchards were often laid out like gardens; we should not forget those of the Carmelites in San Ángel and in Puebla. When they established hermitages, they were veritable parks, like the famous Desierto de los Leones, the work of Fray Andrés de San Miguel, the famous architect of his order whose secular name had been Andrés de Segura.[28] There, as at the Desierto of Tenancingo, the wonderful forest and the delightful countryside are more interesting than the architecture.

To ornament patios and gardens they built fountains, some of them real masterpieces, like that at Acámbaro. Or they decorated them with jars and dishes of pottery from China or Puebla, like the "Risco" ("The Cliff"), still preserved, though much deteriorated, in the house named after it in San Ángel, D.F.

[27] Toussaint, *Tasco,* p. 105.
[28] Toussaint, "Fray Andrés de San Miguel, arquitecto de la Nueva España," *Anales del Instituto de Investigaciones Estéticas,* 13 (1945), 5–14.

Chapter Sixteen

PAINTING IN MEXICO CITY DURING
THE EIGHTEENTH CENTURY

E HAVE briefly outlined the causes of the decline in painting in the eighteenth century, which were not peculiar to New Spain but functioned all over the world. This decadence is the more to be lamented in Mexico, as we realize that appreciable talents were stifled in its soft and rosy vulgarity, talents which in another environment would have come to something—at least as much as their predecessors. It is an unavoidable law of art that the environment submerges the artist unless he is a genius of such rank that he succeeds in dominating the environment.

Two Famous Painters

Don José de Ibarra

The first famous painter of the century was Don José de Ibarra, who was born in Guadalajara, Nueva Galicia, in 1688 and died in Mexico City in 1756. He and his wife, Doña Juana Navarijo, had two sons with the same name as their father. He was a pupil of Juan Correa, as he himself tells us, but he was apparently influenced by the most important painters of the early eighteenth century, by Villalpando, Correa's friend, and the Rodríguez Juárez brothers.

One of the characteristics of the painters of this period is fecundity. Since they are not original, but reproduce any painting or print that falls into their hands, and since technique counts for little except in the general effect of the picture, the studios or workshops turned out work by the hundreds. Furthermore the artist was, as we should say today, primarily a director of a workshop; he was not the sole author of the pictures that came from it, even though they bore his signature.

Ibarra still preserves a certain propriety in this disorderly and frenetic environment; we can see qualities which relate his work to the previous period, and which make one regret that he might not have worked earlier. He is technically proficient—proficiency is perhaps the best quality we can cite in these men—his drawing is easy, his figures still have character, he knows how to construct a composition. But his faults bear witness pitilessly that he does not try to represent reality, neither its form nor its strength. He works with conventions, or rather formulae, which deprive his work of personality. He likes effects of contrast in

308. José de Ibarra. Self-Portrait. Oil. .63 x .55 m.
Pinacoteca Virreinal, Mexico City.

color, but his repertory becomes more and more reduced as he uses only a small number of colors. His
ideal is the theatrical, the grandiloquent, the exaggerated. All of these painters try to strike the note of the
Churrigueresque, but they lack the talent to achieve
the daring and fantasy of the style.

Of the large production of Ibarra, which is far from
having been catalogued, we might indicate the most
important. There are a number in the Galerías de San
Carlos: the canvases of *The Women of the Gospel,* the
series of scenes of *The Life of the Virgin* (although
some of them do not seem to be originals), and his
Self-Portrait (308), which has been mistaken for that
of Cabrera.[1] To these may be added the paintings decorating the reliquary of San José at Tepotzotlán, the
paintings on the outside of the choir of the Cathedral
of Puebla—whose weakness is so evident in contrast to
those by Juan Rodríguez Juárez in the same location—
twelve large panels of *Passages of Holy Scripture,*
which were in the Bach Collection, and several paintings in the Cathedral of Mexico.[2]

Don Miguel Cabrera

After Don José de Ibarra comes Don Miguel Cabrera, who shares the same characteristics. He was either more able or more fortunate, for his fame has obscured not only his predecessor but all the painters of
the century. It stuns one to realize what a pitch of ignorance and blindness not only the illiterate public but
even the people of culture had come to at this time.
We have already touched upon some historical reasons
for this phenomenon. Cabrera's fame persisted un-
blemished throughout the nineteenth century, when it
was a real source of pride to own a picture by him.
Finally criticism, looking at the classical painting of
Europe, and back at the colonial painting of earlier
days, turned against the idol, denying him not only all
prestige but all quality. Cabrera changed from the most
excellent painter of all time to the most despicable that
could be imagined. Both evaluations are unjust; they
show how criticism, deriving from what is most human
in man, is impulsive and passionate.

In short, Cabrera is not the superior painter that his
contemporaries dreamed—they seem to have judged art
like sleight-of-hand; neither is he deserving of scorn as
insignificant. He was a man of his time, like all of us,
but if one knows how to look with a selective eye, reading between the strokes, Cabrera shows himself as,
first, an audacious salesman, and, secondly, a painter—
not of genius—but still not unworthy of the great colo-

[1] Abelardo Carrillo y Gariel, *Técnica de la pintura de Nueva España.*
[2] See Heinrich Berlin, "Dos estudios mexicanos; artistas y milagros," *Anales del Instituto de Arte Americano e Investigacio- nes Estéticas,* 15 (1962), 109–119.

309. Miguel Cabrera. Assumption of the Virgin.
Oil on canvas. Sacristy, church of Santa Prisca,
Taxco, Guerrero.

310. Miguel Cabrera. Doña María de la
Luz Padilla y Cervantes. Oil on canvas.
Brooklyn Museum, Brooklyn, New York.

nial tradition. Ibarra is always more controlled, but by the same token we do not find in his work those sincere bursts of spirit.

Cabrera was born in Oaxaca in 1695; he learned to paint there and moved to Mexico City in 1719. We do not know what master he worked with—Correa, Villalpando, and the Rodríguez Juárez brothers were still living. He tells us nothing. He was a friend of Ibarra's, whom he doubtless respected, but this gives us no rea-

son to suppose that he was a pupil of Correa. One can state with assurance that Ibarra had a great influence on Cabrera's art; they seem like brothers. It takes a good eye and experience to distinguish the paintings of one from those of the other. Within their limited field of color Ibarra is colder, more sober, and more timid. Cabrera is more daring and imaginative.

He married in 1740 Doña María Solano y Herrera, and they had a big family. He was *pintor de cámara* to

311. Miguel Cabrera. Sor Juana Inés de la Cruz. Oil. 2.07 x 1.48 m. Museo Nacional de Historia, Mexico City.

Archbishop Rubio y Salinas, which contributed considerably to his fame. In 1756 he published a pamphlet on Our Lady of Guadalupe entitled *Maravilla americana,*[3] which is interesting for the information it gives about the painters of the period. He was permanent president of a private academy of painting founded by the artists of Mexico City in 1753, which we must not confuse with the Academia de San Carlos (of which we shall speak later), as some writers have done. He died in 1768 and was buried in the church of Santa Inés in Mexico City, at the foot of an altar maintained by the painters.[4]

The *oeuvre* of Cabrera, as we have said, consists of an overwhelming number of pictures painted to decorate churches and convents (309), or to satisfy the people who wanted to own a work by him, since this was the categorical imperative of art in the eighteenth century. There is also a much smaller number of canvases in which the artist succeeds in bequeathing his true spirit to us. For the French historian, Louis Gillet, Cabrera is still a decorous portrait painter (310), whose portraits carry on intact the great tradition of Spanish portraiture inherited by the Colony.[5] And indeed one can cite the magnificent *Sor Juana Inés de la Cruz;* inspired by the early portrait of a mediocre painter, it is superior in breadth, in skill, and in feeling (311). Cabrera undoubtedly felt all the attraction of this exceptional woman, and gives her to us, if not as our affection and imagination would picture her, at least in a most acceptable form. Some of his saints, like the *St. Anselm,* wrapped in his ample white robe, reveal his gifts. The portrait of a nun, *Sor María Josefa Agustina Dolores,* in silvery grey tones and a technique anticipatory of modern work, is charming (312). His paintings in the church at Taxco must be counted among the best of his work.

The catalogue of his known work is immense; there is almost no colonial church which doesn't have one or two or more of his paintings, whether in the capital or in the provinces. There are many in private collections, and they went even to Spain.[6]

312. Miguel Cabrera. Sor María Josepha Augustina Dolores. Oil. 1.68 x 1.05 m. Museo Nacional del Virreinato, Tepotzotlán, México.

[3] Miguel Cabrera, *Maravilla americana.*

[4] Luis González Obregón, *México viejo,* Ser. 2, 147. See also Javier Castro Mantecón and Manuel Zárate Aquino, *Miguel Cabrera, pintor oaxaqueño del siglo XVIII.*

[5] Louis Gillet, "L'art dans l'Amérique Latine," in André Michel, *Histoire de l'art,* VIII, 1070.

[6] See Berlin, "Pintura colonial mexicana en Guatemala," *Anales de la Sociedad de Geografía e Historia de Guatemala,* 26 (1952), 118–128.

When we think of formulating a judgment of this artist, we cannot but remember that while for some he was a stupendous artist, for others he was no more than mediocre. If we make a real effort to identify ourselves with the art itself, taking into account the times in which he worked, we see him as truly a victim of the period—producing like a machine hundreds of paint-

313. Juan Patricio Morlete Ruiz. St. Louis Gonzaga.
Oil on canvas. .51 x .63 m. Pinacoteca Virreinal,
Mexico City.

ings by formula, without substance, empty. Fleeing
from this bondage, escaping occasionally from his own
commercialism, which reduced art to an unseemly
thing, he blossoms in a small number of paintings
which, if they do not fully redeem him, at least reveal
a creative potential, and indicate that in another environment he might have been a great artist.

Painters Contemporary with Cabrera

A small group of artists seem to center around Cabrera. When he published the pamphlet on the painting of the Virgin of Guadalupe, some took part in the
examination of the picture, and all gave their opinions.
They are Don Manuel de Ossorio, Don Juan Patricio
Morlete Ruiz, Don Francisco Antonio Vallejo, Don
José de Alcíbar, and Don José Ventura Arnáez. All of
them suffered an enormous influence from Cabrera,
and from the bad taste of the period, such as to smoth-
er the real talent of some of them.

Don Manuel de Ossorio was born in 1793 and was
active for a good part of the century. His style is said
to have been very similar to Cabrera's, a fact which explains the scarcity of pictures by him—for although
Couto says they were numerous in his time,[7] today we
do not know a single one. The explanation must be
that his works were given apocryphal Cabrera signatures in the period when there was such enthusiasm for
owning Cabrera's work.

We know that Don Juan Patricio Morlete Ruiz was
born in 1715; he married Doña María Careaga very
young, and had many children. The face of this artist,
which is extremely appealing, agrees with his work,
which is characterized by a taste unusual in his time.
Although he cannot free himself from the period, he
chooses silvery grey tones from which emerge the soft
faces, especially that of *St. Louis Gonzaga,* his favorite
subject (313). His *oeuvre* is not very large; we might
mention the portraits of three viceroys—*Amarillas,
Cajigal,* and *Croix*—all in the Museo de Historia at
Chapultepec.[8]

Don Francisco Antonio Vallejo was the most productive of the group. The catalogue of his works is
large, but they are without strength or marked personality: he is a second Cabrera. We suggest as the most
worthwhile three groups of large mural canvases: those
which decorate the church of La Enseñanza in Mexico
City; those which cover the walls of the sacristy in the
chapel of the Colegio de San Ildefonso (now used as a
library), and the great series of *The Life of St. Elias,*
perhaps his most enterprising work, in the monastery
of El Carmen in San Luis Potosí. In these pictures we

[7] José Bernardo Couto, *Diálogo sobre la historia de la pintura
en México.*
[8] See José Rojas Garcidueñas, "Un oleo mexicano en Santiago
de Compostela," *Anales del Instituto de Investigaciones Estéticas,*
34 (1965), 71–74.

can see that, although he was dominated by the bad taste of the period, with its false and monotonous color, this artist was gifted as a composer of monumental paintings.

Don José de Alcíbar was the dean of the group; I have seen paintings by him dated 1801. Since his earliest paintings date from 1751, Alcíbar must have been producing pictures for half a century, both on canvas and on metal, which he was partial to. The catalogue of his work, although certainly incomplete, is very large. The great picture of the *Adoration of the Kings,* in the sacristy of the church of San Marcos in Aguascalientes, has been considered the masterpiece of Alcíbar. It does show great skill, but it is not original; I have seen a small painting attributed to Orrente, from which Alcíbar took the greater part of his painting, while other figures were copied from the painting of the same subject by Rubens, now in the Museum at Lyons. So our colonial artists worked! For this reason I consider his best work to be the portrait of *Sor María Ignacia de la Sangre de Cristo* in the Museo de Historia (314). It is the portrait of a nun as she makes her profession: she is dressed in a very rich cloak and her crown and bunch of flowers are no less rich. But he has really seen the face; the spirit of this young girl, timid and curious at the same time, captured so perfectly by the painter, reveals a true artist.

Don José Ventura Arnáez worked as an assistant to Cabrera after 1750, but seven years later he seems to have had his own workshop. In 1771 he collaborated with another painter, Don Pedro Quintana, in making the triumphal arch to welcome Viceroy Bucareli to Mexico City. His work, like that of Ossorio, was abundant in the time of Couto; but today we have nothing.

To these artists of Cabrera's group we should add two more who deserve to be mentioned here: José de Páez and Antonio Pérez de Aguilar.

José de Páez inundated the second half of the eighteenth century with his paintings. Among this infinity of pictures, some have interest, as with all these artists; but it is difficult to name one that is entirely respectable. We might mention the portraits of the *Judges of La Acordada* in the Museo de Historia.[9]

Antonio Pérez de Aguilar was a rather ingenious artist of the period, discovered by accident. There was a delightful *bodegón, The Cupboard Filled with Things,*

9 See Berlin, "Pintura colonial," pp. 118–128.

314. José de Alcíbar. Sor María Ignacia de la Sangre de Cristo (detail). Oil. 1.80 x .98 m. Museo Nacional de Historia, Mexico City.

in the Galerías de Pintura, attributed to Morlete Ruiz (315). When this painting was taken down in 1934 to be photographed and measured for the catalogue of the colonial paintings which I was making, I found on the back of the canvas this inscription: *Antonio Pérez de*

315. Antonio Pérez de Aguilar. The Cupboard. Oil.
1.26 x .98 m. Pinacoteca Virreinal, Mexico City.

Aguilar faciebat. Año de 1769 en México. The writing
is contemporary, so that there was no doubt that we
had a new colonial painter, and from the quality of this
painting, an excellent one for his time. Now we know
that he was active as early as 1749, when he signed a
portrait of the *Venerable Palafox,* which hangs in the
antesacristy of the parish church of Real del Monte, in
the state of Hidalgo.[10]

Secondary Painters

In another book, devoted to colonial painting, I have
catalogued the multitude of artists who worked in this
period. Here I want simply to point out the most distinguished of them, those who to some extent stand out
against the autocracy of the official painters and the
monotony of the group.

Ignacio María Barreda was a very productive portrait painter, whose most impressive work was a large
painting for the Seminary in Mexico City, which represents *Archbishop Nuñez de Haro Awarding Prizes to
the Students.* The portraits from his hand all show
identical mannerisms (354; color, facing p. 388).

Manuel Carcanio was born in 1689, and seems to
have lived for almost a century, since he appears in the
Real Academia de San Carlos, which was founded in
1783. He must have done a lot of work in so long a
life, but we know only a few pictures by him, which do
not indicate a great painter. From Couto we know that
he painted a *Life of the Virgin* for the *antecoro* of the
choir of the Dominican monastery in Mexico City.
That is all of our information about this painter.[11]

The great work of José Joaquín Esquivel seems to
have been a *Life of St. Peter Nolasco* for the monastery
of La Merced in Mexico City, which no longer exists.
It was dated 1797. Couto praises some of his paintings.
We have in the Museo de Historia a series of portraits
of the *Deputies of the Congregación del Señor de
Burgos*; they are respectable work in the conventional
style of that type of painting. There are twelve of
them, painted between 1781 and 1785.

Andrés Islas was a mediocre painter, whose works
are very numerous without doing him any credit. He
specialized in portraits, which undoubtedly paid best.
So we have two portraits by him of the *Venerable
Palafox* in the Cathedral of Mexico, one of *Don José
Escandón* in Querétaro, portraits of *Charles III, Bucareli,* and the *Conde de Regla* in the Monte de Piedad,
and one of *Clement XIV*—perhaps the least weak—in
the Museo de Historia, dated 1769.

Andrés López and his brother Cristóbal worked together, and they both enjoyed a deserved prestige. The
most famous work of the brothers, who were active at
least from 1777 to 1812, is the series of large mural
paintings covering the walls of the church of El Señor
del Encino in Aguascalientes. They are dated in Mexico
City from 1798 to 1800. We do not know if they are
original work or copies—a matter which was of no
concern to the painters—but they show considerable
talent, and many a church in Mexico would be fortunate to have similar decorations. There are a large
number of works by the brothers López, but none that
can rival these.

10 *Catálogo de construcciones religiosos del estado de Hidalgo,*
I, 527.
11 Couto, *Diálogo.*

Carlos Clemente López was active in mid-eighteenth century, and his pictures often turn up on the market. One might surmise that he was the father of the brothers Andrés and Cristóbal López; but we have no documentation. I know quite a few paintings of his; in some he seems to be freeing himself from Cabrera's influence, which is something in itself.

The work of José Padilla can be found easily in the old Jesuit seminary at Tepotzotlán. There we can see his principal victim, *St. Stanislaus of Kostka.* One would not have expected the saint to suffer two martyrdoms, first in life and then in art! This time the torture was inflicted by Padilla. But in spite of its ridiculous inadequacies, the series is in fact interesting: one must simply consider it in the category of popular or folk art, even though it is by a known painter. What wins us in this sort of painting is not an academic proficiency, but its ingenuousness.

Don Pedro Quintana was well thought of in his time, but we do not know a single work by him. He seems to have been a son-in-law of Cabrera, and must have made the most of the relationship.

Pedro Sandoval is known to us as the painter of the *Sybils* of the old University of Mexico which are now in the Paraninfo, the Assembly Room of the new University, badly hung above the seats which line the wall.

Mariano Vásquez was active in 1787; he is said to have been a pupil of Cabrera's, and he painted some excellent portraits. We do not know whether he may have been the father of José María Vásquez, who worked in the period of the Academy, and whom we shall consider in due time.

Chapter Seventeen

PAINTING IN THE PROVINCES

OF NEW SPAIN

IN THE EIGHTEENTH CENTURY

PAINTING FLOURISHED all over Mexico, just as it did in the capital of the Viceroyalty, especially in the cities with a good number of Spanish and Creole residents. Its character is the same everywhere, its decadence perhaps accentuated by the distance from metropolitan standards. The most important centers are Puebla, Querétaro, Michoacán, Guadalajara, Tlaxcala, and Oaxaca. We shall discuss each of them briefly, as our material permits.

Puebla

Of the numerous painters working in Puebla at this time, only a few merit a place in this review. The research of Pérez Salazar makes our task easier; anyone who wants more information should consult his work.[1] We can add a few things from our own files.

There are six painters named Berrueco in Puebla:

Diego, Miguel, Pablo José, José Mariano, Nicolás, and Luis. They were not all of one family. The most famous was Luis Berrueco, who belongs to the first half of the century and was perhaps a pupil of Juan Correa (316). He has a large *oeuvre*; we might mention a *St. Michael of the Miracle* in the Cathedral of Puebla.

Salvador del Huerto was a mediocre artist of the turn of the century, one of the group which established the Academia de Bellas Artes in Puebla.

Manuel López Guerrero was like Salvador del Huerto, but rather better. Two canvases by him in the sacristy of the church of La Concordia are worth looking at.

José Joaquín Magón is the Puebla painter who most deserves notice, although Zendejas enjoys that reputation. Magón, one might say, is the Ibarra of Puebla, while Zendejas might be called the Cabrera. His *oeuvre* is large, and far from fully catalogued (317). I should list, as his best paintings, *Our Lady of Mercy as Protectress,* in the church of La Merced at Atlixco, and the

[1] Francisco Pérez Salazar, *Historia de la pintura en Puebla.*

342

316. Luis Berrueco. St. Catherine. Oil.
Private collection, Mexico City.

317. Joseph Joaquín Magón. Doña María Manuela
de Ovancado. Oil. Private collection, Mexico City.

St. Pulcheria in the University of Puebla. Among smaller ones, a *Virgin of Light* in the church of San Agustín in Puebla; the portrait of the donor, whose head measures barely ten centimeters, is delightful.

Miguel Jerónimo Zendejas has been the subject of much controversy: while some place him high above the clouds, others completely denigrate his art. He is said to have been born in 1724, either in Puebla or in Acatzingo, where he decorated the Sanctuary. If this is true—the baptismal record has not been found—he lived to be ninety-two, since his death occurred on

May 20, 1815. His production was enormous; one can hardly find a church in Puebla which does not have one or more of his works (318). He is an uneven artist if there ever was one, and this is what causes the controversy. In general he was careless, but one cannot deny him a great manual dexterity and an inventive imagination. Some of his paintings are like distant precursors of Impressionism. His best work is perhaps in the four large canvases dated between 1775 and 1778 which decorate the walls of the sanctuary of the Virgen de los Dolores in Acatzingo, representing *Christ Carrying the*

318. Miguel Jerónimo Zendejas. Death of St. Joseph.
Oil. Church of San José, Puebla.

Cross, The Apostles Comforting the Virgin, The Descent from the Cross and Pietà, and *The Crucifixion.*
Very curious is his *Decoration for the Interior of an Apothecary's Shop,* now in the Museo de Historia.

Lorenzo Zendejas, the son of Miguel Jerónimo, was less sprightly and less pleasing. His work is frankly mediocre, for all it shows occasionally a certain influence of French painting.

A group of painters by the name of Talavera, certainly of the same family, were active in Puebla from the end of the seventeenth century to the early nineteenth. The most important was Pablo José Talavera.

In the church of La Soledad there are two large canvases of his, one on each side below the choir, which are decent enough.

Benito Velásquez is the author of a large *St. Christopher,* very pleasing, in the Cathedral of Puebla.

An artist of Puebla whom no one has yet studied was Marimón, who was active in the early eighteenth century. His most interesting work is a large picture in the sacristy of the Sagrario in the church of San José in Puebla, *Christ Carrying the Cross Followed by Three Priests*: each of the priests has his cross, and at the left there are many more who have thrown away their crosses. There are paintings by him in San Francisco in Tlaxcala, where he signed all the canvases on one retable, and in the church of La Santísima and the Museo de Santa Mónica in Puebla. I am not sure whether the portrait of *José Rubí* belonging to Pérez Salazar is by Marimón.

Querétaro

Although many artists were active in Querétaro during the eighteenth century, painting was not so important as sculpture, for reasons we have already indicated. Nor does there appear a single name with the prestige of an Ibarra or Cabrera, or of a Magón or Zendejas in Puebla. I list here the names of those who in my opinion deserve some notice.

I have seen a *Virgin of Refuge Surrounded by Saints,* by José Manuel Aguilar y Cabello, which came from Querétaro. Pleasing, it is influenced by popular painting.

Francisco Báez was born in Mexico City in 1726, but moved to Querétaro, where he was registered in the census of 1791 as a painter.

Miguel Ballejo y Mandirano signed a *Crucifixion* which is on the stairway of the Jesuit college in Querétaro—it is of no great value.

José García, painter, gilder, and painter of sculpture, was active in the first half of the century. In the Congregación de Guadalupe in Querétaro there are some paintings by him of *Apostles,* signed in 1723. I wonder whether he may also have been a sculptor in wood; it is difficult to believe, since the guild ordinances prohibited it. However, there is a fine relief of *An Angel Taking his Heart from the Dead St. Augustine,* signed by Joseph García in 1745, which we shall consider in discussing sculpture.

Victoriano Granados was an Indian painter; his son, a mestizo named Ignacio, was also a painter. The census of 1791 lists them, but I have found none of their work.

Certain paintings of this period are signed simply Noriega. I know a *St. John of the Cross* by him, and an admirable canvas in the sacristy of the Sagrario in Querétaro.

José Peralta was obviously a descendant of the Peralta listed in the seventeenth century. He was born in Querétaro in 1769 and is listed as a painter in the census of 1791, which has given us so much information about art in Querétaro.

Michoacán

This was a region of great painters, and offers some of the finest work of the eighteenth century. Two centers are important: Valladolid (now Morelia) and Pátzcuaro. The work of two painters stands out from the quantity of eighteenth-century canvases in the churches of Morelia. They are not masterpieces, nor even by famous artists, but if you know how to look at them you will find them charming.

The first is a group of three canvases in the sacristy of the church of San Agustín, where I saw them originally. (When the room was done over later and the fine vault of the sixteenth century uncovered, they were put in a dark storeroom, from which they were returned finally to their original place.) They represent *The Judging of Christ, The Tormenting of Christ,* and *The Crucifixion.* They date from 1732 and were signed by Manuel Xavier Tapia, who seems to have been an Indian. His representation of the *Judging* is the most curious and interesting imaginable, with a strong influence of popular art. The costumes of the judges, the luxurious appearance of the room, and the statements on scrolls issuing from the mouths of the characters—it is all unique.

The other painting, which is unhappily anonymous, is in the sacristy of the church known as Las Monjas: it represents the moving of the community from the convent of Las Rosas to their new house, in 1738. All of colonial Valladolid is portrayed assisting at this great event: richly gowned ladies—all wearing aprons and rebozos—on the balconies; horsemen, friars from all the communities with their patron saints on litters, dancing Indians, the people, everything. It is one of those paintings which—without being a masterpiece, and far from it—has such an attraction that we can spend hours looking at it, discovering new details, interesting and ingenuous, every time we return to it.

In the same church of Las Monjas may be seen a series of canvases of *The Passion of Christ,* signed by Marcos Fernández; but it is inferior work.

There are a lot of paintings in Pátzcuaro, though fewer than in Morelia. In the basilica of La Salud are numerous portraits, among them one of *Don Vasco de Quiroga* dated 1755, and all signed by Manuel de la Cerda. They are not of great merit. Manuel's brother Juan de la Cerda was also a painter. There used to be interesting pictures also in the old monastery of San Agustín; when the monastery buildings, and the church as well, were put to other uses these were moved to the church of San Juan de Dios.

Guadalajara

The old capital of Nueva Galicia is quite rich in paintings, both colonial and European; a visit to the Museo del Estado will give satisfaction to the most demanding historian of art. If one is in search of local artists, however, we can offer only two, and these without assurance; they are Antonio and Nicolás Enríquez.

I assume that Antonio Enríquez was a native of Guadalajara, because his work is found only there: a *Way of the Cross* in four paintings, of which one is signed in 1749, and a *St. Dominic Preaching to the Nobility* of 1747, both from the convent of Santa Teresa and now in the Museo del Estado.

It is more difficult to be sure of the birthplace of Nicolás Enríquez. Although there is work by him in Guadalajara, the eight panels of *Scenes of the Passion* in the Museo were signed by him in Mexico City in 1768. There is signed work by him in many places, and his reputation was high enough in his day. He is not inferior to other secondary painters we have mentioned in this period.

Tlaxcala

A good many artists from Tlaxcala are known in this century; we shall mention the most important. In the Sanctuary of Ocotlán there are various pictures by Miguel Lucas Bedolla: a *Virgin Mary, St. Christopher,* and a *Visit of the Holy Family to St. Anne and St. Joaquim.* They indicate a painter of not very lofty aims.

A dynasty of painters in Tlaxcala are the Caro family. The first, Antonio Caro, was active in the last third of the seventeenth century. Afterwards José Caro de Ayala appeared—he painted *Our Lady of Europe* in the church of San Francisco in Tlaxcala—and Manuel and Mariano Caro. From the information in the census, we assume that the last two were sons of José and grandsons of Antonio. Manuel was born in Tlaxcala in 1751, and his wife was called Gertrudis Martín. Mariano was born in 1763, and he married his sister-in-law, whose name we don't know. Manuel was the most famous of the Caros, but he was assumed to be a native of Puebla. Obviously he moved to Puebla because he could not find a suitable environment for his art in the provincial atmosphere of Tlaxcala, and there lived the rest of his life, dying on September 2, 1820. His *oeuvre* is quite large; we have pictures from as early as 1781 and up to 1814, but there is probably much more. The dates show that he belonged to two epochs: the expiring Baroque and the Neoclassic, which was emerging. An example of the older style is to be found in the five large canvases which tell the legend of *The Apparition of the Virgin of Ocotlán* in the Sanctuary at Tlaxcala (197); these date from 1781, and may be said to show that he had not yet gone to Puebla. Caro, who was able and talented, adapted himself to the new style admirably. I believe, and certainly he himself also believed, that he should be judged as a Neoclassic rather than as a Baroque painter.

A worthy painter of the period was Juan Manuel Illanes, who made a faithful copy of the Lienzo de Tlaxcala, as we have said (36). Work of his may be seen in Tlaxcala and Tehuacán.

A certain painter, Gregorio Lara Priego, is mentioned among the masters of Zendejas. I have found a painter by this name in Tlaxcala; he has a painting in the sanctuary of Ocotlán, and six in Puebla in the Capilla de los Terceros of Santo Domingo, dated 1756. Since Zendejas' wife is called "Pliego," it is just about certain that he married the daughter of his master.

Oaxaca

My notes include the following work by artists whom I presume to be from Oaxaca, although there must be many more. A *St. Bartholomew* signed by José Palacios in 1787, now in the sacristy of the Cathedral. Isidro de Castro signed with only his family name two large canvases to be seen in the church of La Soledad; they show the influence of Cabrera.

In Oaxaca and the villages of the Mixteca there are many paintings by Don Miguel de Mendoza, and on one of his paintings the signature reads: *"natural de estas Mixtecas,"* "native of the Mixtec region." Hence he was not from Puebla, as it had been believed, and this explains why there are so few works by him in Puebla. I know only the series of *The Way of the Cross* in the church of La Luz, dated 1737, which is respectable enough. In the incomplete notes of Señor Bonequi of Oaxaca it is stated that there are paintings by Mendoza in Etla, in Teposcolula, in Oaxaca, and in almost all the towns of the Mixteca.

Bonequi mentions also a *Life of St. Dominic* in the cloister of the Dominican monastery by Padre Chávez, "an ecclesiastic who according to his portrait had only one eye, and who was a native of Oaxaca." There is no such series of paintings in existence now.

I have some records of other paintings from Oaxaca. In the parish church of Ixcatlán a *Holy Trinity with Donor,* of medium size, signed by Antonio de Lara and dated 1765. In Teposcolula a painting of popular flavor with many figures, dated 1748, by Martínez de Roxas. In the church of Tejupan a retable dedicated to the Virgin of Guadalupe; the Virgin had originally been a statue, but a painting was substituted. It dates from 1779, and the artist who made the whole thing, according to an inscription, was Juan José Suárez.[2]

Such is the brief outline of provincial painting in New Spain in the eighteenth century. If this is added to the corresponding chapter from the preceding century, it will be seen that we have given more information than all that has been known previously. It is not enough, however. We need a monograph on each region, and this work should be done by local scholars.

2 This note was given me by Don Alfonso Caso.

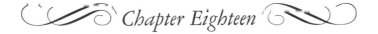

Chapter Eighteen

SCULPTURE IN THE

EIGHTEENTH CENTURY

Artistic Values

HE ART of this period found its strongest expression in sculpture. The great Baroque and Churrigueresque churches we have described at such length are indeed essentially works of sculpture rather than of architecture. The façade is like a retable which has emerged from the nave to stand in front of the church, metamorphosed into stone to resist the elements. The towers clothe themselves in sculpture, the cupola flaunts it, and often the whole building looks like the fabrication of a confectioner, all frosting and colored paper. Painting declines; it is a secondary ornament filling the open spaces left when the sculptor has exhausted himself.

Every apogee carries the germ of its decadence. The splendid Baroque sculpture that fills our whole eighteenth century is perhaps unrivalled in the whole world as a decorative element in these ensembles which are contrived to lead the viewer into ecstasy (254, 266, 272). Yet in the sense of personal creations the individual statues are often inferior. This is understandable, but still a pity. After the Renaissance sculpture, so grave and noble (145), after the dramatic Baroque of the seventeenth century, a worthy heir to Spanish tradition (204), what the eighteenth century offers is

a striking technical perfection in the finishing of faces and draperies—the *encarnación* and *estofado* (319)—but an almost total lack of the creative spirit which imbues a unique work of art, powerful and original (320). All the sculpture of this period is bombastic; the drapery is too full of folds, the attitudes are too exaggerated, melodramatic to a degree which can easily pass over into comedy, if not farce (321).

Furthermore, the sculptors fell into the habit of certain facile devices which had up to now been used with discretion, which they believed to increase the realism of their work, and which the pious but ignorant public loved. I refer to those eyes made of crystal, the real teeth, and human hair and eyelashes, and to the images made to be dressed in real clothing (322). The church councils had long prohibited this clothing of images, so destructive of art, but the vulgar and somewhat heterodox enthusiasm of both the clergy and the faithful only increased, until they achieved the ultimate abuses in this vein.

On the other hand there is popular art which commands real esteem, unpretentiously when it is genuine. In this category are a series of images of the highest artistic value: the *Santiago* with his machete and pistols

319. St. Joachim with the Virgin Mary, from the retable of St. Joachim.
Polychrome and gilded wood. Church of San Cosmé, Mexico City.

Angel from a retable. Polychrome and gilded wood. Museo Nacional
del Virreinato, Tepotzotlán, México.

321. St. Francis (detail). Polychrome and gilded wood.
Museo Nacional del Virreinato, Tepotzotlán, México.

320. Virgin of the Immaculate Conception (La Purísima).
Polychrome and gilded wood. 1.50 m. Museo de la Basílica
de Guadalupe, Villa Madero, Distrito Federal.

322. Virgin of Loreto. Painted wood. Church of San Martín (Museo Nacional del Virreinato), Tepotzotlán, México.

(345), or *St. Isidore the Worker* with his yoke of oxen, the flayed and bleeding Christ, and all the others that any cultured visitor—for only he will appreciate this art—can find in the thousands and thousands of churches scattered over the generous soil of Mexico.

We turn now to specific works of sculpture, to report what we have succeeded in finding out about their makers. Like everything else in this book, this has the character of a preliminary essay. Some valuable and apposite contributions have been made by Moreno Villa in his study of Mexican sculpture.[1]

We have been accustomed to think of three cities as the centers of sculpture in this century: Mexico City, Puebla, and Querétaro. The fact is that we have documentation for these three cities; it could hardly be denied that there were many sculptors in other places as well. It will be for the scholars of the future to complete our comments.

We ought to include also the sculpture of the southeast of New Spain—Chiapas, Campeche, and Yucatán—which shows an appreciable influence from the work of the Guatemalan sculptors.

Sculpture in Mexico City
Jerónimo de Balbás

Churrigueresque sculpture seems to begin in Mexico City with the arrival of the great Spanish artist Jerónimo de Balbás. In 1709, on the sixth of December, he had completed the high altar of the Sagrario in the Cathedral of Seville, which cost 1,227,390 *reales de vellón*.[2] It seems to have been very like the retable which he then made for the Capilla Real in the Cathedral of Mexico. This retable, known as the Altar de los Reyes (323, 324), was made between 1718 and 1737, although the gilding was done only in 1743, by the painter Francisco Martínez.[3] Balbás was an eminent man, who soon became the favorite sculptor of the Cathedral chapter—he was sometimes referred to as *arquitecto,* but this was frequently the case with *entalladores,* the carvers of wooden altarpieces, as early as the seventeenth century. He made the high altar of the Cathedral, a precipitous edifice with marble columns on the first story, destroyed in the middle of the nineteenth century (325). He was also sent to Acapulco, as we have seen, to receive that masterpiece, the screen for the Cathedral choir, which he later installed (244). There is no doubt that he must have done a lot of work for the churches in Mexico City, which were changing the style of their decoration in these years. However he seems eventually to have returned to Spain, since in 1761 we find Jerónimo de Balbás in Seville, presenting the design for a monstrance for the Cathedral, which was executed.[4] Unless we have come

[1] José Moreno Villa, *La escultura colonial mexicana.*
[2] Juan Agustín Ceán Bermúdez, *Diccionario histórico de los más ilustres profesores de las bellas artes en España,* I, 92.
[3] See Justino Fernández, *El Retablo de los Reyes; estética del arte de la Nueva España.*
[4] Gascón de Gotor, *El Corpus Christi y las custodias procesionales de España,* p. 138.

323. Altar de los Reyes. Polychrome and gilded wood; oil on canvas. Cathedral of Mexico.

324. Altar de los Reyes (detail). Polychrome and gilded wood; oil on canvas. Cathedral of Mexico.

upon another man of the same name—a son of his perhaps?—we must accept his return to Spain, in view of the dates.

Isidro Vicente de Balbás

In the second half of the century another Balbás appears in New Spain, Isidro Vicente. From the work that we know by him—the splendid retables of the church of Santa Prisca in Taxco (245, 266), and a

project for completing the façade of the Cathedral of Mexico—we can feel almost sure that he was the son of Jerónimo. Earlier, he had repaired the high altar of the Cathedral, the work of the first Balbás, because its weight had caused it to deteriorate. Obviously this second Balbás also must have done a great deal of work in his time.[5]

[5] See Heinrich Berlin, "Artífices de la catedral de México," *Anales del Instituto de Investigaciones Estéticas,* 11 (1944), 37.

Other Sculpture

A notable combination of sculpture with architecture can be seen in the galleries which surround the choir of the Cathedral (164, 244). We know that they were the work of the architect José Eduardo de Herrera[6] and of Domingo Arrieta, who may have been the sculptor. They belong actually to the exuberant full Baroque style, with large figures of youths supporting the corners, and everything covered with ornamental foliage. They date from 1734.

To the group of Mexico City belong the unknown sculptors of Tepotzotlán (271, 272), those of Taxco, whom we know, and a small number of artists who carved the enormous quantity of retables and statues which at present we have to call anonymous. The Ureña brothers, Don Felipe, José, Carlos, and Hipólito, we meet as the authors of the altarpiece of the Galicians, dedicated to Santiago in the Capilla del Tercer Orden in San Francisco in Mexico City.[7] It was gilded, like the Altar de los Reyes in the Cathedral, by Francisco Martínez, and consecrated in 1741. The retables and the table of the sacristy of San Francisco in Toluca, dedicated in 1729, were also their work. These altarpieces are undeniably Churrigueresque, though moderately so for the date, as can be seen in the plates published in that curious book on the Church, *Mano religiosa del M. R. P. Fr. Joseph Cillero.*[8] From these examples one can assume that this big family of wood carvers had a large output in their day. The same should be said of the Sáyago—or Sállagos—family, which goes back to the seventeenth century and the generous founder of the hospital for insane women, as we have seen. In the eighteenth century we find Don Juan de Sállagos, who was active in 1753 in the same craft as his ancestor. He too must have made lots of sculpture and retables.

There are other secondary names which we prefer to group in a list at the end of the chapter; otherwise it would seem like a catalogue, for we are ignorant of the work they did.

The characteristic quality of the Mexico City group is to be found in the technical perfection of the carving

325. The Coronation of Iturbide (detail showing the high altar of the Cathedral of Mexico). Oil on silk. c. 1822. Museo Nacional de Historia, Mexico City.

[6] See Heinrich Berlin, "El arquitecto Joseph Eduardo de Herrera," *Anales del Instituto de Arte Americano e Investigaciones Estéticas,* 17 (1964), 90–98.

[7] These original documents are in my possession.

[8] Antonio Díaz del Castillo, *Mano religioso del M. R. P. Fr. Joseph Cillero.*

and *estofado*—the result of the severe regulations of the guild to which they were subject—and in their loyalty to Spanish style in their choice of forms and decorative motifs. The Rococo of Versailles enjoyed much less popularity in the capital than in Puebla or Querétaro, where the reliefs sometimes seem really French.

Sculpture in Puebla

The sculpture of Puebla during the eighteenth century has been very little studied. If only we knew everything about the image makers and the carvers, as we know each and every one of the painters! All the sculpture in Puebla is attached to a single name whose prestige smothers all judgment and discrimination: Cora. The same thing that happens with Tresguerras in the Bajío occurs with Cora in Puebla: any work of any value is attributed to Tresguerras, even if it is in the Baroque style he detested. In Puebla the situation is even worse, because the ennobling name Cora covers three separate persons, and any sculpture not only good but even "pretty" has to be by Cora, without saying which of the three.

We will try to find our way through this labyrinth, though it is certainly a difficult task. At the outset it must be made clear that all of this is subject to correction when archives and records have been studied, a task which Francisco Pérez Salazar—that lamented friend and irreplaceable scholar—has done for painting. Our information comes entirely from the printed material available to everyone. It must be explained also that all of these sculptors belong to two different periods, the Baroque, which we are studying now, and the Neoclassic, which follows it.

José Villegas Cora (the Elder)

The first sculptor of this name is called José Villegas Cora. According to his biographers, he was born in Puebla in 1713; he died there on the fourteenth of July, 1785, and was buried in Analco. Thus his art coincides with the period of full Churrigueresque style, between 1733 and 1785. His biography is legendary; no one offers the least documentation. They say that he studied with the Jesuits, that he learned Italian, Latin, and even philosophy. That he then dedicated himself to architecture and sculpture, and passed the examination for master sculptor. That in a competition at Rome he won third place—first place went to the Pope's sculptor, and second to the sculptor of the King of Spain—and that this was published in a Madrid periodical called *Mercurio.* That the Bishop of Puebla, Don Antonio Joaquín Pérez, returning from the court in Madrid, brought a charming figure of the Holy Child, which he showed to Cora, with the admonition: "Learn to make sculpture!" And that the artist's reply

to this was to split the head of the Child and take out from inside a piece of parchment on which was written *José Villegas de Cora.*[9] Revilla says—and Moreno Villa accepts without question—that Cora principally made images which were meant to be dressed in real clothes. Some of these he may well have made, but it was not until later that such images became the rule. The evident anachronisms in this supposed biography are enough to indicate that, apart from the dates of birth and death, we know nothing about his life.

In short, we should accept the following attributions of sculpture to Cora the Elder with all possible reservations. In the church of San Cristóbal, an *Immaculate Conception* and a *St. Anne* and *St. Joachim,* signed; in San Pablo, a *St. Joseph*; in San Francisco, a *St. Francis* and a *Virgin of Sorrows*; in the Mercedarian and Carmelite churches, the appropriate figures of *The Virgin*; in the former, two other statues, *The Saviour* and a *Patriarch,* and in the latter, figures of *St. Ignatius* and *St. Francis Xavier* as well. In San Matías, an image of St. Matthew, and in San Antonio (formerly Santa Bárbara) a *St. Peter of Alcantara,* a *Virgin of the Immaculate Conception,* and a *St. John Nepomucen.* A statue of *St. Rock* is also listed.

Criticism is no less elusive. They say that Cora the Elder was an idealist, who represented what he dreamed rather than what he saw, in contrast to his nephew Zacarías, who studied reality and imitated it as far as possible. This opinion is to be interpreted, in my opinion, to suit the dates when the two artists lived: it means that the first was a Baroque artist, and the second, Neoclassic.

José Zacarías Cora

In fact, the second Cora, José Zacarías Cora, the nephew of the first, was born in Puebla on the ninth of June, 1752, and died there on the same day in 1816. From the time he was a child he worked, as apprentice and then as journeyman and assistant, with his uncle, from whom he learned his perfect technique. Many images in Puebla are attributed to him; the most important, undoubtedly, is the large *St. Christopher* in the church of San Cristóbal. It might be described as a

---

[9] This is Revilla's account, a masterpiece of anachronism. Cora died in 1785; at that time Bishop Pérez was twenty-two years old. He was not elected to the bishopric until 1814, and took possession only in 1816. See Manuel G. Revilla, *El arte en México en la época antigua y durante el gobierno virreinal.*

Baroque sculpture improved by Neoclassic knowledge. The athlete stands erect, exhibiting a powerful musculature perfectly represented; but his drapery is blown back in a way that comes from the Baroque sculpture that was admired in Puebla. José Zacarías Cora's great triumph was to be called to Mexico City to make statues for the towers of the Cathedral—all the figures for one of the towers, plus two for the other. The director of the work, Tolsá, had no better assistant. But this belongs to the next chapter in the history of sculpture.

José Villegas Cora (the Younger)

The third Cora, according to the writers, was a pupil who also had the name José Villegas, and who adopted Cora as his second surname in gratitude for the teaching of the master. There is a *St. Theresa* by him in the church of Santa Teresa in Puebla. We know nothing else about him.

Sculpture in Querétaro[10]

The two most gifted Baroque sculptors of Querétaro seem to have been Don Ignacio Mariano de las Casas and Francisco Martínez Gudiño. Tresguerras' remarks about them are expressive enough, if one discounts his passionate and willful personality.

Ignacio Mariano de las Casas

Speaking of Las Casas this author says that "in the assembling or architecture of altarpieces he had the worst taste possible"—this we should interpret as meaning that he carved excellent Churrigueresque retables, which Tresguerras abominated. If Las Casas built the monastery of San Agustín, with its church and fine cloister, it is not hard to imagine that he may have been responsible for the retables of Santa Rosa, where we know he was engaged. There must be many other things by him, not only in Querétaro but in other towns of the region. The choir of the church of Santa Clara, which displays the talent and invention of a fantastic Baroque sculptor, is also attributed to him.[11]

---

[10] See Joseph A. Baird, "Eighteenth Century Retables of the Bajío, Mexico: The Querétaro Style," *Art Bulletin,* 35 (1953), 197–216.

[11] See Francisco de la Maza, *Arquitectura de los coros de monjas en México.*

[12] See Francisco Eduardo Tresguerras, *Ocios literarios.* The famous architect Pietro Borromino might be called the Churriguera of Italy. Ignace Klauber was a German engraver of the eighteenth century, some of whose prints Tresguerras seems to have known.

Francisco Martínez Gudiño

Concerning Gudiño, Tresguerras is even more expressive. According to him, Gudiño was from Guadalajara, and was a building supervisor with some experience in sculpture. In constructing buildings his work was acceptable, we are told, solid and even imposing; but in "the architecture of altarpieces, he followed the confusion of Klauber, and went even beyond the dreams of Borromino."[12] This description can apply only to the retables of Santa Clara, and so we shall assume Gudiño to be the creator of those marvels unless documents are found to prove otherwise. Another paragraph of Tresguerras' referring to both Casas and Gudiño reveals at once his genuine sincerity and their worth: "I do not wish to give the impression that they were not skillful, but that in compliance with the bad taste reigning at that time, they laid bets as to who could be the most extravagant, without any respect for the writings of Vitruvius, Serlio, and other architects." This seems in some way to confirm my supposition, since there is not in Querétaro, nor in the whole world, a competition more brilliant, more sublime, than that between the interiors of Santa Rosa and Santa Clara.

Roxas

Tresguerras also mentions a third sculptor: "Roxas, from Mexico City, has left us as his only claim to fame some disorderly retables, all alike; he did use figures on them, but for the most part ready-made (as the Italians say) and chronically lazy nymphs . . . In Celaya, Salvatierra, and this city [Querétaro] I have seen and considered works by Roxas which support this opinion."

Tresguerras speaks of these craftsmen as dead and gone; but he also mentions some artists of his own time, and with more rancor, naturally. Although they appear as architects—*"arquitetes,"* as he calls them in his bantering vein—some were primarily sculptors. Tresguerras even called himself a *tallista,* a wood carver. He was very likely obliged in the early days to work at commissions which were not to his taste, but which helped to support him. He takes care not to tell us what retables, what portals, or what buildings he had had to make to earn a living. His own style, springing from himself as a complete autodidact, is admirable, and will be studied in the final section of this book; but it should be noted here that, by his own admission, he began as a Baroque sculptor.

Sculptors of the Turn of the Century

Querétaro was always a city of artists and of sculptors above all. In the eighteenth century an important group appeared, who were to continue into the following century, with names among them famous even in the capital.

To begin with we have Bartolico, very famous in his day:

He has left us an imperishable memory of his skill in the sacred image called *Jesus of Nazareth of the Three Falls,* which is venerated in the church of the Franciscan fathers in the said city [Querétaro]. The countenance is divine, the body well proportioned, the impulse and attitude of falling and struggling up with the cross is so naturally rendered, owing to the ingenious and effective mechanism, that every year the residents of Querétaro are delighted to see this scene represented just exactly as the ungrateful people saw it actually happen to the Supreme Author of Life.[13]

Zelaa attributes to him a *St. Peter* (around 1760) in the sacristy of the same church, a *St. John Nepomucen* in the nave of the church of Guadalupe, and a *Crucifixion* which was placed on an altar of the church of the Hermanos del Cordón de San Francisco in 1807.[14] By 1778, when Padre Granados published his book, Bartolico had died.

Tresguerras speaks of a group of four architects who were active in Querétaro and Celaya, and who, as we have seen to be common, also made retables. They are Zápari, García, Ortiz, and Paz. "Paz," Tresguerras remarks, "... has filled Querétaro with ridiculous monuments." "But now all are well known: Zápari, far too renowned; Ortiz, removed in disrepute from the work on Las Teresas in Querétaro; García's life finished; and Paz derided for his manner and his materials alike."[15]

Zápari sounds like an Italian name; all I know about him is that he made the altarpieces facing the aisles in the Cathedral of Morelia.[16] Early in the nineteenth century he was in Mérida.

By Joseph García, whom we have noted as a painter,

I know only one little panel skillfully executed in high relief. It represents *St. Augustine,* dead, with two angels taking away his heart. As a matter of fact, there are three identical reliefs of this subject: one which belonged to Don Joaquín García Icazbalceta, another from the Alcázar Collection, now in the Museo de Historia, and this one which has the signature and the date 1745. But in view of the date, this is perhaps not the García to whom Tresguerras is referring.

Of Ortiz I know nothing, unless the reference is to Ortiz de Castro, the famous architect of the façade of the Cathedral of Mexico, whom we shall study in the Neoclassic period. Paz is presumably the Mariano Paz who was working years later in the capital, a student of the Academy of San Carlos, and famous in spite of Tresguerras.

The *Padrón* of Querétaro

In 1791 the *Padrón General de Nueva España,* a census list for the purpose of taxation, was drawn up by order of the second Viceroy Revillagigedo. A few volumes of this have come down to us, preserved in the Archivo General de la Nación. Among these is the *Padrón* of Querétaro, from which we have obtained the names of many sculptors and carvers. These are transcribed at the end of this chapter, but I want to excerpt one item because of the importance it holds for the history of sculpture in Querétaro. It reads:

Francisco Escóvar, mestizo, native of Querétaro, 56 years old, sculptor, exempt. A journeyman, Mariano Perusquía, Spaniard, 20 years old, 5 feet and one inch; good disposition, first class. Another, Mariano Montenegro, Spaniard of 18 years, 5 feet and one inch. Good disposition, first class.

So we know the first master of two sculptors of Querétaro who were later to be famous: Perusquía and Montenegro. Also their birth dates, the first in 1771, the second in 1773. This information will be pursued in the discussion of Neoclassic sculpture.

Sculpture in Southeastern Mexico

There were three important centers of sculpture in the Southeast: Chiapas, Campeche, and Yucatán. All three seem to have been affected by Guatemalan influence. The characteristic works always have a theatrical appearance, as if they were permanent processional figures for Holy Week in Seville. The ornamentation imi-

13 Joseph Granados y Gálvez, *Tardes americanas.* pp. 421–422.
14 José María Zelaa e Hidalgo, *Glorias de Querétaro.*
15 See Romero de Terreros, "El arquitecto Tresguerras," *Anales del Museo Nacional,* Ep. 4, Vol. 5 (1927), pp. 55–63.
16 José Guadalupe Romero, *Noticias para formar la historia y la estadística del obispado de Michoacán.*

Side altar, convent church of La Enseñanza, Mexico City.

tating rich fabric, the great silver haloes, the grandiloquent attitudes, sometimes conceal authentic quality

Chiapas

In Chiapas a good deal of sculpture worth consideration is preserved. Some of the figures are influenced by the Guatemalan style, others represent rather a popular art of real profundity. Such is that Juan Diego dressed like a Chamula Indian, which may be admired in the church of Guadalupe in San Cristóbal de las Casas.[17]

Campeche

There is less information about Campeche. We know a figure of Christ, called the *Cristo de San Román,* in the hermitage of that saint. It is not different in character from the usual figure of this type.

Yucatán

Very little is known about Yucatecan sculpture. We have already spoken of the retables preserved in the churches. We know much less about individual sculptures; most of them were wantonly destroyed. The famous *Cristo de las Ampollas* of the Cathedral of Mérida, which was destroyed during the revolution, seems to have dated from the seventeenth century. I know a *Christ Carrying the Cross* in the Candelaria, an excellent figure with a terribly heavy cross of timbers covered by silver decorations and pitilessly weighed down by massive silver cornerpieces. Our Lord is clothed, to his greater suffering, in a thick tunic with heavy embroidery, and above the crown of thorns shines, almost ironically, a great halo of silver which was probably added later. It seems, as I say, a processional figure from Seville, like the *Cachorro* or the *Señor del Gran Poder.*[18]

Sculptors of the Eighteenth Century in Mexico City:

1704: Antonio de Roa y Velasco, master sculptor

1709: Juan de Rojas, joiner, appraises the estate of Don José Bueno Basorí

1711: Pedro Nolasco de Reyna

1713: Antonio Sáyago, master carpenter
Salvador de Ocampo, master sculptor

1720: Tomás Xuárez

1765: Don Joseph Joachím Benites, master of carving and gilding

Sculptors of Querétaro in 1791 Tax List:

Francisco Fernández, 35 years

Manuel Cortés

Ignacio Núñez, mestizo, 30 years

José Trinidad García, 25 years

Pedro Yamas; 40 years, born in 1751

Mariano Escóvar, 35 years; his son, Bartolomé Escóvar, 15 years

Atanasio Luna, *cacique,* 41 years

Cosme Luna, 25 years

Vicente Luna, 16 years

José Luna, *cacique,* wood carver, 28 years

José Prado, mestizo, 26 years

Toribio Aguillón, 20 years

Juan Izguerra, 25 years

Antonio Guevara, mestizo, 64 years

Vicente Ximénez, *cacique,* 50 years; born in 1741

José Rodas, mestizo, wood carver, 25 years

José Arreguín, mestizo, wood carver, 40 years

[17] For more information about sculpture in Chiapas, see an article by Salvador Toscano, "Chiapas: su arte y su historia coloniales," *Anales del Instituto de Investigaciones Estéticas,* 8 (1942), 27–43.

[18] See the *Catálogo de construcciones religiosas del Estado de Yucatán.*

THE MINOR ARTS OF THE CHURRIGUERESQUE PERIOD

N THE eighteenth century every form of art lay under the spell of the extravagant Baroque. In the churches, so fantastically decorated, all the objects of daily use—furniture, cult objects and ornaments—had to be equally dazzling. The same thing happened in the residences of the nobility, and even in less pretentious houses. One of the characteristics, and perhaps the most admirable, of colonial art—and indeed of all art in the past—was that there was no division between the artistic and the utilitarian. Any object whatever, however humble its purpose, was made as if it were a work of art—which in fact it became.

Two categories must be distinguished in the things we shall now examine. One is the category of real works of art, artifacts which become museum pieces when they are unfortunately removed from the situation they were made for. The other category is made up of objects which served the men of their time in daily use. Histories of art are, for the most part, concerned only with the first category, with "masterpieces." I believe that—without depreciating the masterpiece, of course—one should pay attention also to the other category of things, to the furniture, the silver, the jewelry, and all the other objects used in daily life, because this seems to me the most vital part of the art of an epoch, as it is the most human. Without any intention of providing a guide for dealers or collectors, but rather as an integral part of this study, I feel it suitable to note the character of such artistic manifestations.

All the same this undertaking is obviously difficult, and indeed rash. Not that I am afraid of corrections from the specialists; I should indeed welcome that help. The fact is that they are willing only to attack one's mistakes, preferring to keep their knowledge exclusive, whether for business reasons or for self-gratification. But we are now at the point where a beginning must be made in writing the total history of our art: if our only fault is recklessness, so much the better.

From the beginning of this study I have avoided describing the category we are considering as "industrial arts"—a term one uses today to show how modern he is. I prefer the classical term "minor arts," because I am not ready to resolve the questions opened up by the new term. What, indeed, can be the relationship between the two concepts, "art" and "industry"? To me they seem antithetical. The weakness of the term appears immediately in not knowing whether to speak of

326. Cupboard. Wood.
Museo de Churubusco, Distrito Federal.

327. Wardrobes, table, and chairs. Wood with leather.
Museo Regional, Querétaro.

"industrial arts," or "artistic industries." So I prefer the old term, which I base on the idea I have just expressed, that every object, however humble its purpose, may be a work of art.

Furniture[1]

Domestic Furniture

Furniture in this period was influenced mainly by the country which has created the most enduring styles —England. The secret of this perhaps lies in the fact that since the furniture was comfortable—the basic requirement—it was inevitably excellent in design. But let us go step by step. The traditional types of Spanish furniture of the seventeenth century of course persisted: the ecclesiastical armchairs, wide and commodious

[1] See Abelardo Carrillo y Gariel, *Evolución del mueble en México.*

(239), the cupboards with coffered panels (326), the chests and boxes, the beds with their turned posts and canopies, the tables with diagonal legs and supports of wrought iron (327).

An interesting fact is that architecture did not influence furniture as it had in earlier periods; at least it is very unusual to find a piece of furniture decorated with estípites. On the other hand, as we have pointed out, furniture had an appreciable influence on architecture.

As we say, it was England which established the styles: Queen Anne and Chippendale. Mexican antique dealers call all furniture with claw feet below and complications above, Chippendale. Actually most of the furniture with curving shoulders and a plain middle, with more or less ornament of a relatively superficial type, is of the Queen Anne style. Chippendale is heavier, more daring, more Baroque. The Mexican quality of these pieces is to be found in a less elegant

328. Chair. Painted wood with reed seat.

329. Chair. Wood with damask seat.
Museo Nacional de Historia, Mexico City.

workmanship; they are somewhat popular versions of the European models. The principal items of furniture in the eighteenth century are as follows.

Chairs. Examples range from the modest chair of the simple people (328), with its rattan seat—brought from Andalusia, where it is still made—to the most sumptuous. The set of furniture for a salon is called an *ajuar,* and consists of a sofa or two, various *sillones* or other armchairs, some rocking chairs, and a dozen simple plain chairs, *sillas. Taburetes,* benches without backs, were also very fashionable. There are chairs of

a special type in which the back does not rise above the arms, which bend around one very comfortably (331). We illustrate a perfect example of the Chippendale chair—so perfect that one cannot be sure whether it is colonial or European (329)—and I have seen a model Queen Anne armchair which is known to have been made in Mexico.

In eighteenth-century portraits we find chairs in the fashionable French styles of Louis XIV, XV, and XVI. One cannot of course prove that examples like this actually existed in Mexico; but we can see that the paint-

330. Wardrobe. Inlaid wood.
Martínez del Río Collection, Mexico City.

331. Chest of drawers, mirrors. Private collection.

ers knew them well, and if they represented them so faithfully, it was probably because they were looking at them.

Tables. The tables of the eighteenth century followed the same styles as the chairs. The legs contort themselves and rear up as if they wished to upset everything. The most impressive tables were in the churches, and we shall speak of them below.

Beds. I suppose that the old beds of West Indian red ebony (*granadillo*), with their finely turned posts, continued to be used; but now the style demanded that

they be painted in lively colors, in the technique known as *maque* (lacquer) and decorated with gilded carving and with real oil paintings. They are painted green, red, yellow, tawny.

Cupboards. On the one hand the cupboards (or wardrobes) of the seventeenth century continue, with their panelled walls and doors and their little drawers. But large decorated cupboards were also made, inlaid with mosaics of fine wood, of bone, or of mother-of-pearl, in intarsia, or as we now say, marquetry (330).

Desks. There is no proof whether those splendid

361

332. Sacristy table. Church of La Valenciana,
Guanajuato.

two supports drawn out from the cupboard itself to
make a writing shelf. The back is full of cubbyholes,
drawers, secrets. Undoubtedly it too is European in origin, but it has nothing to do with the classic *bargueño*.
The *escribanía* appears to have been a smaller piece, a
writing case to be placed on a table; its opened door is
covered with green baize, suitable for writing. Inside
were kept the paper, ink, pouncer, waters, quills, and
penknife for cutting them—everything in fact that was
properly known as "writing materials." The writing
case may be more or less decorated; there are some
which are real jewels.

Commodes. It may have been in this period that the
commode, or chest of drawers, was born. Its name explains it. Ladies and gentlemen had been keeping their
personal effects in chests where, as we all know, everything is jumbled and mixed together. This piece of
furniture, of the same general shape as the large chest,
but higher, with shelves or drawers, allows things to be
kept in better order and got at more easily, or commo-
diously. Hence its name. Naturally there are chests of
drawers in many styles, from the simplest—a true chest
with drawers—to fine examples in Chippendale or
Louis XV, made of rich woods, like the one we illustrate (331).

Mirrors. The rooms of residences, whether simple or
noble, were decorated in this period with mirrors on
their walls. The mirrors have rich frames of carved and
often gilded wood; sometimes the frames are decorated
with small mirrors inset (331). The best mirrors were
Venetian. A device called a "cornucopia" was attached
to the wall, carrying one or more holders for candles.
They had been used since the seventeenth century,
when a typical form was the two-headed eagle of the
Habsburgs. They do not necessarily have mirrors, but
since it is obvious that this doubles the power of the
light, they usually do.

Ecclesiastical Furniture

The richest furniture in this period is undoubtedly
found in the churches. This will be briefly described;
but it should be noted that I do not consider as furniture the choir stalls, pulpits, ambones, or anything else
which has an established place in the church. The reason is obvious: these things are not furniture (which is
movable), but permanent fixtures. Like retables, they
fall in the category of decorative sculpture. The most
important pieces of ecclesiastical furniture are the tables and cabinets of the sacristy, the chairs of the pres-

desks called *bargueños* were made in Mexico, but I
incline to the negative. Nor do I know any inventory
which mentions one by the name that indicates their
provenience, the town of Bargas in the province of
Toledo.

Anyway, there are no examples of the *bargueño* to
be found in Mexico, except those imported in modern
times from Spain. *Escritorios* and *escribanías* are frequently mentioned, but they seem different. The *escritorio* of the eighteenth century is a desk, a big cupboard
with a door in the middle which opens down to rest on

bytery, the credence—the small table beside the altar—and the confessionals.

The sacristy tables are sometimes rectangular, sometimes polygonal or round. They are always of great size to accommodate the objects which have to be laid out on them (268, 332). I can mention three of very high quality: the one in the sacristy of the sanctuary of Ocotlán in Tlaxcala, that of Santa Rosa in Querétaro—interesting for its shape and for its disguised drawers and little cupboards—and one conserved in the Museo de Historia at Chapultepec, a magnificent example of unknown provenience.

The great *cajoneras* which are used to keep the robes and ornaments required by the ritual are simply large chests of drawers. They may fill a whole wall of the sacristy, sometimes three walls in a cathedral (268). They are decorated in various ways, but there are some with very rich relief carved in fine wood, ungilded.

The three armchairs of the presbytery are usually true works of art of very high quality. Many of the chairs now in private collections came from churches. Among the finest examples are the presbytery chairs of the church of Santa Prisca in Taxco (309), which form a set with the pulpit, the ambones, the Tenebrae candelabrum, and the cupboards of the sacristy—all undoubtedly the work of a single artist. They are rich, like the magnificent interior, and their perfection is illustrated by the fact that the upper part of the chair backs can be folded down, so that the back of the priest's vestments can hang freely. Another three chairs almost as rich as those of Taxco are to be found in the parish church of Totimehuacán, Puebla. They perhaps came, like the retables, from the old monumental Franciscan church there, which is now in ruins.

The *credenza,* as it is called in Italian, is a small table on which are placed the cruets and the towel, the *tercerilla* needed for the Mass. Usually it has no artistic quality; sometimes, as at Taxco, it is part of the set.

Confessionals also were sometimes treated as works of art. I recall, as a supreme example, that known as the Penitenciario of the Cathedral of Mexico (333) and also those of the Cathedral of Puebla, and an extraordinary one which I photographed in the parish church (the old church of the Dominican monastery) of Teposcolula, in the Mixteca Alta of Oaxaca. This jewel is carved in a style saturated with French feeling.

Among ecclesiastical furniture we should consider also lecterns and *facistoles.* Some of the lecterns which are placed on the altar for celebrating Mass are real

333. Confessional (Confesionario del Penitenciario), Cathedral of Mexico.

works of art, of richly carved and gilded wood, others are made of metal, some even of gold and silver. Other lecterns stand on the floor and can be moved from place to place; we might cite one in the Cathedral of Mexico, a rich example of Baroque art.

Facistoles are the large lecterns which stand in the middle of the choir; they are not fixed to the floor but stand on a large base (334). They consist of two parts: the heavy base, and the upper part which turns, on which are placed the great choir books which they have in all the cathedrals. Some of these lecterns are sumptuous. The most important one is in the Cathedral of Mexico; it came from the Philippines (335). It is made of fine woods, ebony and *tíndalo,* decorated with twelve beautiful ivory statuettes, and crowned by the

334. Choir lectern. Wood. Monastery church of San Francisco, Querétaro.

335. Choir lectern. Wood and ivory. Cathedral of Mexico.

Virgin of the Assumption, the patron saint of the church. This splendid object was the gift of the Archbishop of Manila, Don Manuel Rojo, who had formerly held an important position in the chapter of our Cathedral and wished to honor his old church with this gift. The work took so long that the Archbishop did not live to see it completed, but he directed in his will that it should be finished and sent to Mexico, where it arrived, after many adventures, in 1770.[2]

[2] See Manuel Toussaint, *La Catedral de México y el Sagrario Metropolitano.*

Work in Gold and Silver

Various observations can be made about work in the fine metals in this period. In goldwork, both religious and secular, artistic quality yields to the value of the precious stones which cover it, while silverwork reaches its climax of technical perfection.

There is also a change in the organization of the work. Instead of only *maestros de platero,* another title, *patrones de platero,* also appears frequently at this time. We have not succeeded in distinguishing the difference between these two titles with complete historical accurary. Apparently the industry had become so important that men who were not masters of the craft were permitted to operate silver shops and invest their money in them. Obviously the *maestros* could be, and in fact were, also *patrones*—that is, owners of their shops; but the appearance of this title which refers not so much to the craft as to the direction, ownership, or administration of the shop suggests this conclusion. There is confirmation in the fact that the only time the word *patrón* appears in the ordinances of the guild (Ordinance 36, of those of Fuenclara in 1746)[3] it is in the statement that neither *patrones* nor *maestros* can take on apprentices of mixed blood, but only certified Spaniards—a purely administrative rule. The hypothesis seems to be confirmed also in the *Padrón de la Ciudad de México,* the census made in 1753, in which are listed the names of ten *dueños,* or proprietors, of silver shops, as well as many others who appear as *maestros* or simply silversmiths. Furthermore, the widows of silversmiths could continue to operate the shops of their defunct husbands, as can be seen in the list of silversmiths preserved in the Archivo de Hacienda, the most complete one we have, which was drawn up for collecting the tax of the *media annata.*

The style of gold- and silverwork has the same characteristics we have noted in the other arts in this period. Contorted forms, curved lines, above all abundant French influence in the Rococo of the Louis. Architectural elements are not frequent. The estípite is rare in these artifacts, which seek effects more capricious, more fantastic, more suitable to the rich materials of which they are formed. It does appear, however, in some work of architectonic character, as we shall see in speaking of the sanctuary of Ocotlán in Tlaxcala.

Ecclesiastical Artifacts

The richest repositories, as always, are the cathedrals. First, that of Mexico City, then Puebla and the Basilica of Guadalupe, but also the other cathedrals, Valladolid, Oaxaca, Guadalajara. The sanctuaries—Ocotlán in Tlaxcala, that of the Señor de Chalma, and of San Juan de los Lagos—are a blaze of gold. Churches and chapels dedicated to the Virgin Mary in her various advocacies are not far behind: the wealth of the Virgen del Rosario in Puebla, of the Virgen de la Soledad in Oaxaca, of the Virgen de los Remedios outside Mexico City, and above all, of the Virgin of Guadalupe, is well known.

Since it is impossible to describe all of these treasures, which can be found in the special studies,[4] only the most important pieces will be considered here.

The Cathedral of Mexico. The Cathedral of Mexico, which already owned extremely valuable artifacts, was still further enriched in this period by acquiring the treasure which Don José de la Borda had had made for the church of Santa Prisca in Taxco. He had retained the ownership, and in one of his financial crises he decided to sell them to the Cathedral of Mexico. It was the one place worthy of such objects besides the church which he had built in Taxco, and which is itself no less rich a jewel. Borda offered the Cathedral the treasure; but he needed the money in cash to satisfy his creditors, and the Cathedral did not have it. So he turned over the treasure to his most ferocious creditor, Doña Josefa Arósqueta, viuda de Fagoaga, who in turn sold them to the Cathedral by a contract of March 31, 1772, for the sum of 102,466 pesos and 2 *tomines.* The payments were made in quite leisurely installments.

Borda's custodia, which has become a myth, was adorned with 4,107 diamonds on one side, and 1,750 emeralds on the other. This was only the monstrance itself—what we call "the sun"—so a base no less rich was ordered by the church in 1777 from the silversmith José Antonio del Castillo. This base was also of gold, and showed 1,065 diamonds, 896 emeralds, 544 rubies, 8 sapphires, and 106 amethysts. The subsequent history of the custodia is dramatic; we quote from another writer, although we have no proof of his statements. "It was stolen on the night of January 17, 1861. Later the government sold it for 180,000 pesos to Señora Doña Cándida Añorga de Barrón, who took it with her to Europe, and part of this magnificent piece still exists in Notre Dame." Every effort to see this custodia has proved vain; my purely historical interest in studying a masterpiece of eighteenth-century Mexican gold work was rebuffed by that suspicion so typical of cathedral chapters.[5] The ciborium of Borda's treasure was octagonal, weighing six hundred *castellanos* and displaying 1,701 rose diamonds, while the chalice had 1,920 similar stones.

The pieces of silver purchased from Borda consti-

3 "Ordenanzas de Platería de Fuenclara," in *Legislacion del trabajo en los siglos XVI, XVII, XVIII,* pp. 135–150.
4 See Manuel Romero de Terreros, *Las artes industriales en la Nueva España*; Lawrence Anderson, *The Art of the Silversmith in Mexico*; Artemio de Valle-Arizpe, *Notas de platería.*
5 See Rafael García Granados, "La custodia de Borda," *Anales del Instituto de Investigaciones Estéticas,* 1 (1937), 28–32.

336. Altar text *(palabrero)*. Silver. Museo Nacional del Virreinato, Tepotzotlán, México.

tuted an extraordinary collection: a cover for the tabernacle door, two pyxes, two large candlesticks, three altar texts *(palabreros)* (336), two lecterns, three altar fronts, three bases for crosses or processional candlesticks, four torch holders and two chandeliers.

Another custodia appears in the inventories of this period; it was of silver gilt, with the monstrance of gold and two silver bases, one larger than the other. The larger had fifty-seven gold overlays without jewels. The smaller, oval in shape, was decorated with twenty-four gold overlays, in which were four emeralds, five jacinths, and four fine "white Bohemian stones." In the rays of the monstrance appeared sixteen cherubs of gold.

The Cathedral was also enriched at this time from the treasure of the expelled Jesuits, which was brought from the Junta de Temporalidades. There was a chalice of gold decorated with 199 diamonds, 246 emeralds, 40 rubies, and 20 amethysts on the cup, and 9 flat diamonds and 9 emeralds on the cover. This came from the church of San Pedro y San Pablo. Listed also among items purchased from the treasure of Tepotzotlán are a gold chalice with diamonds and emeralds, fourteen small candlesticks, and four torch holders of silver.

But the most sumptuous and renowned piece was a shrine of silver, *repoussé* and engraved, which belonged to the high altar of gilded wood made by Jerónimo de Balbás (325). Churrigueresque forms were interpreted sensitively by the goldsmith, in pilasters, fillets, pediments, tympana, cartouches, and other elegant detail. It was the gift of Archbishop Vizarrón y Eguiarreta, and cost 29,628 pesos. In the time of Rubio y Salinas, and by his orders, this shrine was ruined. They added to the upper part four little Doctors of the Church whose pedestals balance on branches like waterspouts, and below, four gigantic Evangelists on enormous brackets which completely destroy the scale. This absurdity cost 16,000 pesos. Inside the shrine could be seen a tabernacle made out of part of the great Renaissance custodia of Moya de Contreras, which we have described above; Vizarrón had it gilded.

The Cathedral of Puebla. The Cathedral of Puebla was also very rich. They still had the custodia called *la torrecilla* (the little tower) which we have described above, and considerable other treasure. From this period we find a *custodia* of gold for the feast of Corpus Christi; it measured more than a *vara* in height and was adorned with diamonds and emeralds. It was first used in 1727. The immense lamp which hung from the cupola, the work of the *patrón* Diego Larios, was first used in 1751; it was of *plata mestiza,* with gilded overlays, and cost 67,000 pesos. Also forty-eight large candlesticks, a *vara* and a half in height, and four candlesticks of two and three-quarter *varas,* four urns of the same height, and four more a third of a *vara* high. Finally there are listed twenty-five chandeliers *(candiles),* among them six lamps.[6]

Descriptions of the most notable pieces of silver and the treasures of the Basilica of Guadalupe can be found in Romero de Terreros' book.[7] These are the most important: the shrine, reconstructed in 1703 by Fray Antonio de Jura, with a silver frame for the painting; two gold chandeliers which weighed 1,213 *castellanos,* and a silver lamp of 650 *marcos.* The choir screen, a real work of art, dates from this time; its rail and finials are of silver, and, like the choir screen of Guadalupe in Spain, it is crowned by the image. It was made in 1752 by the silversmith Eugenio Batán.

The famous Sanctuary of Ocotlán in Tlaxcala—famous for the fervor which it raises in the faithful, as

[6] This information was taken from the description of the Cathedral by Señor José Manzo, *La catedral de Puebla, 1844.*
[7] Romero de Terreros, *Artes industriales.*

well as for the treasures of art which they apparently do not appreciate, since they destroy them so zealously —still retains beautiful examples of silverwork in its altar furniture. There is a splendid altar front, with its ornaments and tabernacle. The principal silver and the beautiful gold custodia are described in a little known work edited by Francisco Pérez Salazar.[8] The custodia has an exaggeratedly Baroque base, with little bells, and an angel supports the monstrance, which is more restrained but has at the end of each ray a circle of engraved stars surrounding a jewel. The silver tabernacle has engaged estípites and a profusion of reliefs. The altar front also is covered with reliefs, but less accomplished and indeed frankly popular in style. Of finer quality are two covers for the tabernacle door, one of open work and the other with a fine relief in the middle. The less sophisticated work seems to have been done by Antonio Fernández, who did it without pay as an act of devotion, and the finer work, by the silversmith José de Isunza of Puebla, about 1789. Other pieces are listed, but we do not know their present whereabouts.

Another type of valuable object which should not be overlooked is the pedestal used for a famous image. That of the Virgin of Guadalupe, apparently seventeenth-century work, is a marvel: it is of three stories like a piece of architecture, with pilasters and a multitude of figures, all carved in silver. That of Our Lady of Ocotlán in Tlaxcala, which is not described in the above document, is very beautiful. In a lavish eighteenth-century Baroque style, it is hexagonal, with large protruding motifs at the corners and magnificent reliefs on the convex sides. The little Virgin, freed of her voluminous robes, sits with affecting simplicity on the magnificent throne. There are many other such pedestals for the images venerated in the famous sanctuaries of Mexico.

Jewelry

We can acquaint ourselves with the jewelry worn by the ladies and gentlemen of New Spain in the portraits of the period. In 1757 a lady displays a necklace of three strands of pearls with a pendant in front; her jewelled earrings consist of an ear-piece and a drop; her bracelets are of metal. In 1777 bracelets are of many strands of pearls; the necklace of large pearls

with a *calabacita* (a pumpkin-shaped pearl?) in the center, the earrings pear-shaped, jewelled rings on the little fingers and two large watches hanging from the belt. Such was jewelry throughout the eighteenth century, with variations on the theme. Gentlemen used the precious metals and jewels for buttons, snuffboxes, sword hilts, shoe buckles and the heads of their canes. The honorary decorations and insignia are masterpieces, bright with jewels and enamel.

Household Silver

Domestic silver is the same as in earlier periods: bowls, platters, saltcellars, washbasins, water jugs, candlesticks, scissors, candle sockets, large and small salvers, trays, bowls, holy-water stoups. Inkwells should be noted; they are composed generally of three parts— the container for ink, the wafer holder, and the pounce box, all on a plate or tray.

Silversmiths

The roster of silversmiths in this period is very long. In the list of 1753 we find twelve silver shops in the Calles de San Francisco and elsewhere. By the end of the century the number is still greater. And not only in the capital, but in all the important cities the noble art of silverworking flourished: in Puebla, Querétaro, Oaxaca, Valladolid, Guanajuato, and others. The use of silver was so common that even in middle-class houses there were dishes and flat silver, bowls and washbasins of so precious a material.

Bronze, Brass, and Copper

Expert work in bronze and brass (or latten, as it was called in the colonial era) continued during the period we are now considering. We have already observed that the bell casters turned out excellent work during the whole eighteenth century. Bronzeworkers were called both *latoneros* (braziers) and *cobreros* (coppersmiths); they knew how to make the alloys—bronze, of copper and tin; brass, of copper and zinc.

Bronze was used for the balusters of balconies and other railings—often of great perfection, since after casting they were turned and polished; for the hinges of church doors, some of them quite beautiful; for ornamental nails on the same doors, also turned on the lathe; and for candlesticks. For architectural ornament it was often fire-gilded with gold of specified purity, so that such details are very rich. It was used also for inscriptions, of which the finest is the well-known eulogy

[8] Carlos Céspedes Aznar, *La plata labrada del Santuario de Nuestra Señora de Ocotlán,* ed. Francisco Pérez Salazar.

of Viceroy Bucareli in the Basilica of Guadalupe, the work of Francisco Ortúzar.

Also of bronze were countless small objects of daily use which have come down to us and are often a delight: inkwells, in their three parts, from the simple octagonal prism to the convex cylinder, later balustraded, and finally in the shape of little urns; mortars with figures in relief on the outside; table bells still in the Renaissance tradition; corners for the great choir books; thousands of crucifixes, hollow-cast, and scarcely finished, which belong to the category of popular art.

Brass lent itself to a series of important domestic uses. There was the handsome candlestick (*palmatoria*) with a device for expelling the candle-end and a hook for the snuffers, which were also of brass. I do not know whether the oil lamp called a *velón* was used as widely in New Spain as in Spain—those I have seen came from Europe. The *velón* is a masterpiece, with its turned or octagonal base raising rather high the lamp proper, with its four wicks, and a movable screen attached to the base, all topped by a handle for carrying it to the required place.

Finally we have copper, the humblest, though most necessary of these metals. It was relegated to the kitchen, and a great variety of objects were made out of it. Yet all are beautiful in line and harmonious in proportion, and one at least can be called an object of art, or at least an object sought after by collectors and antiquaries: the chocolate pot, in its typical and traditional form.

Finally, we can give the names of craftsmen which have been preserved in the 1753 census of Mexico City:

Cristóbal de Ortega, master brazier
Juan Guzmán, brazier
Antonio Rodríguez, brazier
Luis Herrera, master brassworker
Manuel Herrera, brazier
Mariano Hurtado, brazier
Juan de Saldaña, also brazier

Certain other notices about this guild are to be found in the Archivo Histórico de la Secretaría de Hacienda. These follow below.

Brassworkers: Don Salvador Vega and Don Ignacio Torres, overseers for 1796–1797. Manuel Mendoza and José Machorro, overseers for 1798. Don Salvador de la Vega and Juan Palomino, overseers in 1781. Examination of José Valdés Pérez and Ignacio Torres,

1781. Examination of Juan Cirilo de la Vega, 1769. Juan Cirilo de la Vega, overseer in 1771.

Record from 1754 to 1788: Pedro Jijón, overseer in 1763, Calle de Chiconautla. Examination of Joseph Parra, March, 1739. Examination of Francisco Sánchez, 1759. Francisco Sánchez, overseer in 1761. Examination of Mariano Hurtado de Mendoza. Examination of Luis Mendoza, 1759, Callejón de Dolores. Cayetano García Cornejo, Santa María. Don Manuel Mendoza and Don José Valdés Pérez, overseer for the kettlemakers. Examination of Luis Moneda, 1784. Don Manuel Guerrero and Don Bartolomé Espinosa, overseers, 1785. Examination of Don Vicente Torres, 1786. Don Vicente Torres and Don Ignacio Díaz, overseers, 1788.

Wrought Iron and Steel

Churrigueresque art makes use of wrought iron just as it does of wood or stone. Obviously one cannot expect from the blacksmith anything so rich in fantasy as the retables, but still within the character of the material great effects are achieved, as one can see in the screens of Santa Prisca in Taxco or those of the galleries of Santa Clara and Santa Rosa in Querétaro.

Architectural Ironwork

Grilles. The role of wrought iron in the architecture of this period is very important. There is, first of all, the grille. As we have seen in previous chapters, iron grilles were used profusely from the sixteenth century on, both in churches and convents and in private residences. From the simple grille of bars, square in section, sunk or protruding from the embrasure of a window, to the large ones, richly patterned, of Oaxaca; the variety is infinite, especially in those which we might call "full-length grilles" in the doorways of the ground floor. We can mention here only outstanding examples. The grilles of the three churches of San Francisco, Santa Clara, and Santa Rosa in Querétaro seem to be the richest, even though they imitate early Spanish ironwork, as Romero de Terreros observes. In fact, the grille of the gallery of Santa Rosa, formed by spirals which fill the squares constructed by vertical and horizontal bars is indeed a Gothic survival (256). That of Santa Clara is Renaissance in flavor; its simplicity and uniformity contrast with the unrestrained luxury of the carving which surrounds it (255).

More delicate, although less striking, are the grilles

covering the mixtilinear windows of the parish church of Santa Prisca in Taxco. Virtual filigree in iron, they are in harmony with the spirit of the monument, true Churrigueresque grilles.

Puebla is a city rich in wrought iron.[9] Among its remarkable grilles we should note that on the south side of the Cathedral, rough in workmanship but grandiose, which seems to be the only colonial ironwork on the exterior.[10] Others are those of the portal of the church of La Compañía, which are strong and proud, those of the parish church of San José, and one of the grilles at Analco (241), the most sumptuous of them, which was made by Roque Jacinto de Illescas and which apparently dates from around 1758. Other blacksmiths of this family were Andrés, active around 1714, and Juan, active around 1767, all residents of Analco.

In Mexico City the magnificent grilles of the Sagrario should be mentioned; well organized in design, they have vertical bars and also balusters, an important development. We find the same technique in those of the house next to the Valenciana mine near Guanajuato, which are very fine. So is the well pulley there, which we mention here out of place because it is one of the very few examples to be found in Mexico.

Oaxaca also is rich in iron grilles of the greatest variety of design; there is hardly an old house without them.[11]

Balconies and railings. The subject of balconies and railings is very important, for they are very numerous in all the viceregal cities. In the seaboard cities they had to be made of wood because the salt sea air quickly destroys iron; but the interior towns offer a truly prodigal display, so that we can enjoy balconies in Oaxaca (307), in Puebla (177), in Querétaro, or in the capital of New Spain itself. Sometimes the railings are simple, of twisted bars, sometimes these open out to form trefoils, motifs in the shape of a C, lozenges, or any combinations of these elements. The balcony is held up by brackets which we call *pies de gallo* in Mexico—cock's feet—while above, another support in the form of an arch fastens the railing to the wall. In some places, like Oaxaca, these members are decorated with flowers, so that the very iron seems to have come to life.

We shall cite only a few outstanding examples. The tower of the church at Tepotzotlán is circled at the roof line by a balcony with a fine railing, notable as an example of wrought iron, although architecturally an unsuitable addition (273). The Capilla del Pocito also has fine railings upon its bell towers.

In Puebla there are the balconies of the Casa de Alfeñique and many others (302, 304).

In Querétaro the balconies of the house of Fernández de Jáuregui in the Plaza del Marqués de la Villa del Villar del Águila are real works of art. Those of the house of López de Cala are signed by Juan Ignacio Vielma.

In San Miguel de Allende the delightful house where the leader Allende was born has balconies whose railings bear the inscription: *D. Domingo—Mayo 4 de 85 años—Narciso, de Allende.*

Weathervanes. After railings, the cross of the weathervane is perhaps the most decorative element of wrought iron in architecture. Almost all the colonial churches had a great iron cross over the lantern of the cupola, with a cut-out cock which served as weathervane, moving around the shaft of the cross to show the direction of the wind. This was the custom as far back as the sixteenth century and such crosses persisted throughout the colonial period. For example, there was one on the Cathedral of Mexico, above the dome which preceded the present one. On the seventeenth of September, 1752,

. . . there was placed on the crown of the dome of this Holy Cathedral Church a very beautiful cross of iron, of more than three *varas,* with its weathervane, with the prayer of *Sanctus Deus* engraved on both sides, and in the middle an oval, of a quarter *'vara,* in which there is on one side a very beautiful *cera de Agnus* in its glass case, and on the other side a plate on which is carved Señora Santa Prisca, the patron saint against lightning. The shaft of the said cross is two *varas* and its total weight fourteen *arrobas;* it is set in a handsome pedestal of masonry.[12]

The painstaking Marmolejo reports that on the sixth of January, 1764, in the city of Guanajuato "with great pomp and solemnity, and with the most extraordinary ceremonies, there was put in place the iron cross which formerly crowned the old dome of the Compañía, and which had fallen down."[13]

[9] Enrique A. Cervantes, *Herreros y forjadores poblanos.*

[10] Francisco Díez Barroso in his *El arte en Nueva España* mistakenly assumed the other grilles of the atrio to be colonial. Actually the date 1893 can be read on them.

[11] Cervantes, *Hierros de Oaxaca.*

[12] José Manuel de Castro Santa-Anna, *Diario de sucesos notables, 1752–1754.*

[13] Lucio Marmolejo, *Efemérides guanajuatenses.* See enero 6, 1764.

337. Door pull and studs. Wrought iron.
Church of San José, Puebla.

Other crosses are to be found on the sanctuary of Ocotlán in Tlaxcala (269), on the Cathedral of Zacatecas, and on San Martín Texmelucan, as well as two on the charming church of San Francisco Acatepec, near Cholula, which have no vanes but are very elegant.

Iron in Daily Use

From the enormous group of objects made of iron for daily use we mention only such as have some artistic quality in form or decoration. Such are finely wrought candlesticks, steelyards or scales, an iron for baking wafers made in 1703 which imprints a clear design with fine lettering. There are covers for the jars in which chocolate was kept, snuffers, trivets, and a thousand other things. I do not know whether those fantastic decorative kitchen racks which one sees in Spain were ever used in Mexico.

Among the things necessary for riding horses there are a good many made of iron. We have already studied stirrups, which they continued to make in this period, as well as bits, spurs, and buckles. The style of decorating such objects with fine incrustations of silver, practiced in the neighborhood of Amozoc, near Puebla, perhaps dates from this period. Despite the popular character of this work, the objects give such an impression of luxury, or richness and splendor, that all the charros are glad to use them.

The blacksmiths themselves used tools which were skillfully decorated. Thus in the collection of the Museo de Historia there is a hoof-parer covered with reliefs, and some very extraordinary veterinary lancets.

Little art is to be found in agricultural tools. Still, we should mention one which is an indigenous survival translated into iron, the *coa*. It is a kind of hoe, in the form of a leaf folded back, about twelve centimeters wide, fastened to a handle measuring a meter or more in length. It is used for everything, and before the Conquest was made of wood. Tools for the other crafts, such as forging, carpentry, masonry, mining, et cetera, make as little pretense of art. An anvil is beautiful inasmuch as its form, adapted to the necessities of the smith and his work, has to be balanced and economical; but it was not intentionally created as art.

It is perhaps in the production of the locksmiths that we find the finest work. It is not strictly speaking the lock, but the keyhole, which is ornate, and by extension this is called the *chapa*, or lock. The richest examples are those on chests; usually this keyhole has the shape of a shield or disk. The shield often displays the two-headed eagle of the House of Habsburg; one should not assume for this reason alone that the lock dates from the seventeenth century, however. Frequently this device—certainly very decorative—continued in use well into the following century.

The most valuable collection of locks is preserved in the Museo Bello in Puebla, originally collected in Mexico City by Don Salvador Miranda. That of the Museo de Historia comes next, and there are also magnificent examples in private collections. The early keyhole plate of the sixteenth century has a plain surface, and the curves of the outline constitute the decoration. Later they were cut out in more complicated shapes, in the seventeenth century in the typical form of the shield with volutes and palmettes. The greater luxury of the eighteenth century produced a plate pierced, carved, and sometimes engraved with designs. The decorative motifs are foliate, or simply interlaced fillets among which appear animals or babies. The keys, the latches, the corner-pieces all make a very rich ensemble. Some locks are real marvels of craftsmanship, in their complicated invention and richness of conception.

The locksmith's work includes many other activities, most of which have some artistic character. They are the ones who make padlocks, knockers, latches, bolts, hinges, nails, and studs for decoration. Ornamental nailheads were used to decorate and strengthen wooden doors, and those used on the churches were often splendid (337). The complete hardware of such a door included pivots and hinge-posts, knockers, and nails; sometimes there were also handles (*tiraderas*). On church doors this hardware might also be of bronze, but most were iron.

Finally we should speak of the door knockers for houses, whose most interesting motifs are animal forms —dogs, lions, lizards, serpents. Especially interesting are those still to be seen in the venerable city of San Cristóbal de las Casas in Chiapas. Other forms are a grotesque mask of a man, a lion, or a dragon quite Asiatic in style. Although many of these are made of bronze, there are also some of iron.

Objects of Steel

Steel, as well as iron, was skillfully worked, above all for weapons. The swordmakers' guild was organized very early, and although the best blades came from Europe—especially from Toledo—and the armorers were satisfied to work the hilts, it cannot be doubted that swords were also made in Mexico, along with all the other offensive weapons: daggers, halberds, lances, muskets, blunderbusses, shotguns, et cetera.

They also made defensive armor. If the conquistadors soon exchanged their armor for the *escaupiles,* the cotton-padded armor which was an adequate protection from Indian arrows, it is still indubitable that steel cuirasses, breastplates, coats of mail, helmets of various types (*cascos, yelmos*), shields, and bucklers were soon being made.

Among the lesser objects of steel for daily life— spoons, scissors, needles, razors, and penknives—there

is one which might be mentioned because it almost always has some artistic character: the *eslabón,* the steel for striking fire with a flint. These exist in such a variety of forms, from the simplest to the most complicated—from a plain rectangular plate to a lion, a dog, or a monkey biting its tail—that a special monograph would be needed to do them justice. The Museo de Historia has the best collection of these small works of art.

Textiles and Embroidery

According to the historians, silk weaving had practically ceased in New Spain by the end of the seventeenth century. They explain this by the indolence of the Indians in cultivating mulberry trees and in making silk, combined with the excellence of the Chinese and European silks which came to Mexico. Thus silk culture continued in only a few places, and naturally silk weaving diminished. The weaving of wool and cotton continued, but it is not until the end of the eighteenth century that this can be considered as an art. Romero de Terreros, whose observations we quote here, mentions a rebozo of the Condesa de Xala dating from 1786, which he illustrates; it is charming.[14] As a matter of fact, this type, like the men's sarapes, falls into a new category, that of "popular art."

As for the needlework crafts, far from declining, they increased to satisfy the needs of the cult in the sumptuous Churrigueresque churches. We have an impressive heritage of magnificent vestments, made of rich fabrics and admirably embroidered.

In the incomparable collection preserved in the Treasure of the Cathedral of Mexico we can follow the development of the art of embroidery, from the gremial of Bishop Zumárraga, with its timid Renaissance design (62), to the luxurious Neoclassic vestments of Bishop Núñez de Haro y Peralta.

From the period we are now considering we offer two cardinal examples of eighteenth-century work, one executed by Europeans, the other by Indians. The first is embroidered in gold and silver on red silk, with floral motifs symmetrically arranged in the Neoclassic manner (338). There is still a certain Baroque feeling in the breadth allowed to the borders, as if the brilliance of the metal counted for more than the elegance of the design.

14 Romero de Terreros, *Artes industriales.*

338. Dalmatic. Embroidered in silk, silver, and gold. Museo Nacional del Virreinato, Tepotzotlán, México.

The other example can be called Churrigueresque (339). Here there is no lineal concept of design, as in the first: these dancing angels in ascent are in concept like the ideal estípite, where movement rather than form is sought. Against the gold background are flowers of vivid color—they are the Mexican poppies we love so much—and little musical angels busy playing their parts. The enchanting thing is that these flowers, so rich and plentiful, and these actors in the ecclesiastical fiesta are alike Indian (340). Their simple faces remind us of the dolls of pottery or papier-maché which are sold at carnivals, or of the angels in that Indian paradise we have already visited, the church of Santa María Tonantzintla. This vestment comes from a church in Puebla, and the Dominican insignia ornamenting it indicates that it was made in a Dominican community.

We have abundant documentation on the embroiderers of this period. In 1712 Roque Zenón embroidered hangings for the hall of the Audiencia of the Holy Office.[15] The guild of embroiderers, who had taken as their patron the Virgen de las Angustias in the church of the Hospital del Amor de Dios, moved to the chapel of the Hospital de San Andrés, where the image was taken at the time the other hospital was closed.[16]

As for personal notices of embroiderers, the following notes come from the Archivo Histórico de Hacienda.

Embroiderers of the Eighteenth Century:

1754. Juan Cadena, Guild member and overseer, Calle de Chiquis
Tadeo Sánchez, Calle de Chavarría
Master Juan Castellanos, Halbardier, Calle de San Francisco
1756. Manuel Nieto, Overseer, Bajos de San Agustín
Javier Ontiveros, Calle de las Golosas
Phelipe Escalona, Calle de las Golosas
Master Suárez, Puente de Solano

[15] Manuel Ramírez Aparicio, *Los conventos suprimidos en Méjico,* p. 90.
[16] J. M. Marroquí, *La ciudad de México,* I, 324.

Master Leandro, Calzada de la Piedad
Master Vicente, Calle de Cadena
Pedro Aguilar, Calle de Montealegre

1764. Don Vicente Vallarta, master embroiderer, with a public shop on the Calle de Cadena. His father had taught the craft to the master Don Jerónimo de Miranda, deceased, and now they were assessing him the *media annata* for the three years that he had been overseer. Miranda had taken Vicente as a child and maintained him and taught him the craft: the boy called him father. As he did not wish to pay, he testified with the following witnesses:

1. Don Juan Castellanos, forty-nine years old, halbardier in the Viceroy's guard, master embroiderer, with his shop on the Calle de la Profesa. It was about thirty-five years ago that he entered as a jour-

339. *(Opposite)* Chasuble. Embroidered in silk, silver, and gold. Museo Nacional del Virreinato, Tepotzotlán, México.

340. *(Below)* Fluting angels (detail of Chasuble No. 339). Embroidered in silk, silver, and gold. Museo Nacional del Virreinato, Tepotzotlán, México.

neyman into the household of Don Sebastián Vayarta (the father of Vicente), who died in the fourth or fifth year; and he was taken in by Jerónimo de Miranda, who died in 1764. The craft had so declined that he had hardly enough to eat.

2. Don Miguel de Zavala, more than fifty years old, master embroiderer with shop in the Calle del Hospicio, in a house belonging to the monastery of San Nicolás, of the Augustinians of Michoacán. He made more or less the same statement.

3. Juan Esteban del Castillo, *indio ladino,* as he proved himself to be. A *cacique,* married to Joachina Díaz, a Spanish woman, master embroiderer living on the Callejón de la Condesa, in a *casa de vecindad.* In 1764 he was an examiner and overseer.

1770. Juan Esteban del Castillo and Juan Castellanos, overseers

1772. Francisco Xavier Ontiveros and Francisco Nieto, overseers

1775. Examination of Mathias de Quiñones

1781. Don Ignacio Murguía and Don Francisco Ontiveros, overseers
Examination of Don Mariano José de Orona

1783. Don Juan del Castillo, alcalde
Don Agustín Nieto, overseer

1784. Mariano Orona and José Torino, overseers

1785. José Castellanos and Ignacio Murguía, overseers
Examination of Francisco Velásquez de la Cadena

1786. Agustín Nieto and Francisco Cadena, overseers

1787. Examination of Don Ramón Ortuño and of Manuel Bonifacio González

1788. Don Ignacio Murguía and Don Juan de Dios Castellanos, overseers
Examination of Don Manuel Bernal and Don Franciso Camacho

1789. Examination of Jaime Pons and José Zamora

1796. Don Manuel Bernal and Don Josef Suárez, overseers

1798. Don Rafael Morales and Don Gaspar Ortuño, overseers

Ceramics

It was in the second half of the eighteenth century that colonial ceramics began to decline in quality, to end in a sad decadence. As an unlikely compensation, it was in this period that the finest architecture using tile ornament was achieved.

The continuity of forms and motifs is notable; one needs a good eye, very experienced in distinguishing one from the other, to recognize the period of a piece. They continued to imitate Chinese ceramics, not only in the forms but also in the decorative motifs (243). Other influences are discernible also, that of silver for instance: platters and plates of glazed china have scalloped edges imitating the pieces made by silversmiths.

The use of two tones of blue in the glaze continued: a light color which seems to serve as background, and another, darker, applied in heavy glaze which stands out under the smooth surface of the cover glaze.

By the end of the eighteenth century the technique was coarse and the quality had declined miserably, while the designs followed the models of the Academy, as we shall see in due time.

The best collections of colonial ceramics are those in Puebla, that of the Museo Bello and that of Señor José Luis Bello, but there are some valuable ones also in Mexico City, such as the collection in the Museo de Historia, that of the widow of Señor Pérez de Salazar, that of Señor Franz Mayer, and others. The most interesting pieces are the large *lebrillos,* or tubs, the great jars, urns, bowls, flowerpots, dishes, chocolate cups, and the *albarellos,* called in Mexico *camillas,* which are simply the jars of the colonial apothecary.

Ceramic Architecture

The *azulejo,* the glazed tile, became very important as a decorative element in architecture. The best came from Puebla, though tiles no less beautiful were also made in Mexico City. The Puebla tile is made of a clay which after firing has a yellowish color and dense appearance; it is more than a centimeter thick. The tiles made in Mexico City are of an inferior clay, red in color; their glaze is thinner, and they are only half as thick as the Puebla tiles.[17] There is no doubt that glazed tile was manufactured also in other cities of New Spain, but the two most important centers were Puebla and the capital.

We can only mention cursorily the most important examples of architecture decorated with *azulejos* in both cities.

In Puebla the masterpiece is the kitchen of Santa Rosa, where the whole interior is covered with smooth white tile and decorated with blue tile—walls, handkerchief vaults, doorways, windows, and stoves (341).

[17] See an unpublished MS by Francisco J. Rhode, "Azulejos de México."

374

341. Kitchen, convent of Santa Rosa, Puebla.

It is an anticipation of modern hygienic equipment, but artistic. We do not know exactly when this work of art was made; some historians date it at the end of the seventeenth century, as a reward from the illustrious Bishop Santa Cruz to the nuns who had discovered that extraordinary dish, turkey with *mole* sauce, but others place it a century later. Actually it seems rather older, although one must take into account that it has been restored at various times. It has been designated a Museum of Ceramics, although it is at present quite inadequately organized for such a purpose.

A superlative example of the architect's joining hands with the ceramist—or rather, of the potter's faithfully following the architect's conception—is the façade superimposed on the venerable church of San Francisco in Puebla (259). The façade dates from 1743 to 1767, and it is logical to assume that the tile panels were placed last. They are of such fine quality, in both design and technique, they harmonize so admirably with the unglazed red tile of the walls and the grey stone of the portal, that it would be difficult to find a Churrigueresque work with greater unity. This

is not a matter of popular art, but of the deep esthetic sensitivity which the ceramists of Puebla had attained.

The churches of Puebla are prodigal with tiles, as if they were in competition with the houses. They go so far as to commit real esthetic crimes, as for instance in the romantic and evocative churchyard of the Carmen. Heavy excrescences of tile piled onto the seventeenth-century Baroque portals of stone have destroyed the silhouette and the noble proportions.

The finest patio in Puebla, if not in all of Mexico, is that of the Casa de Ejercicios belonging to the church of La Concordia (342). Everything is admirable: the sober architecture with its great buttresses, the design, and the proportions. It is decorated with tile, but not in the popular style of Puebla; we seem rather to be in Italy, in a noble palace of splendid quality. How sad it is to speak of this building which would have been preserved as a monument in any civilized country! It is now a tenement, crudely cut up and dirty. Its stupid tenants, unaware of the artistic value of the building they live in, do their best to destroy it, to get even for the miserable rent they pay.

375

342. Patio of the Casa de Ejercicios,
church of La Concordia, Puebla.

The church of Guadalupe is one of the most attractive in its tile decoration. On the fine Baroque façade —perhaps a good bit earlier in date—the tile panels relating the episodes of the legend strike a note of color and of brilliance in a neighborhood cluttered with stupid imitations of colonial art.

Near the Guadalupe is San Marcos, which offers the same combination: the large façade covered with unglazed tile in which are set ornamental panels of *azulejos* dating from the end of the eighteenth century.

The last church exterior to be decorated with glazed tile seems to have been the sanctuary of Nuestra Señora de la Luz, a beautiful church which we have already discussed. Its red walls and its large ceramic pictures make an unforgettable effect.

Much might be said about the domes of Puebla. Especially in Cholula, that city of countless churches, the semicircular dome, *media naranja,* was popular. This dome rests directly on the crossing without a drum; covered with yellow and blue tiles it is indeed like the half rind of a great orange, inlaid with blue to make it more brilliant.

But we should consider the finest cupolas of this period in Puebla. First, that of the church of La Compañía. I doubt if this should really be called a dome; its base is square, and on it rest the panels which form the roof. In any case, the outside is entirely covered with tile, which apparently dates from the middle of the eighteenth century. The cupola of the church of the Soledad, formerly a part of that important convent, seems to be of the same period. Its lines are graceful and its decoration, in black and white tile, is unique. Historians are not in agreement as to the date of the tower and the cupola of the church of Santa Catalina. The architectural forms would seem to date from the seventeenth century, but the tile revetment may have been added a century later, as at the Carmen. However that may be, the dome and bell tower are among the most beautiful to be found in old Puebla. We have already referred to the archiepiscopal palace, an excellent piece of work which has been well preserved by proper restoration. Its magnificent tile decoration seems to date from this period (1758–1763); it was appraised by the master architect J. M. de Santa María.[18]

If the patio of the Oratorio de La Concordia is magnificent, there are others which we should not overlook, although they are less important. One is in the old convent of Santa Mónica, now converted into a museum: fresh and cool, its walls of rosy unglazed tile and *azulejos* make the perfect foil to the green plants, and vice versa.

The patio of Santa Rosa, outside the famous kitchen, is less sumptuous, but still of high quality, and there are many others which the traveller or the critic cannot easily visit because they are closed away.

One cannot possibly pretend to make a study of colonial ceramics in the eighteenth century without devoting some sentences, however brief, to the houses of

18 Cervantes, *Loza blanca y azulejo de Puebla.*

376

Puebla in this period, whose decoration is unparalleled in the world.

The development of the façades of these houses follows a curve from the simplest to the most complex. First we have balconies resting on large stone brackets, smooth masonry walls, and no cornice, to be followed by a façade covered with unglazed tile and a moderate cornice (177); the door and window openings are marked by white frames which extend to the top of the façade, as in Mexico City. The third and last stage of this development presents the walls covered with a combination of glazed and unglazed tile in the most complicated and delightful patterns (302). Balconies were very salient, resting on large cantilevered stones without corbels or any support, and with flat or vaulted canopies over them as prominent as the balcony itself. They served as corridors, with several doors opening onto them. Sometimes a single enormous balcony went across the whole façade (303). To crown the façade a very daring cornice thrust itself out, undulating or simple in profile, but always very fancy. To get to the great examples, there is the Casa del Alfeñique (304), which we have discussed, or the one called the Casa de los Gigantes, because of the grotesque figures filling the huge ceramic panels of its façade.

The decoration of these walls is of such variety that one could fill a fine album with all the designs in which the fantasy of the potters and the dexterity of the masons of Puebla—famous beyond all others in New Spain—lavished itself.

This is all the more desirable since—as I have repeatedly observed in this book, but must say once more —these houses are fated to disappear through the ignorance and greed of their owners and the unconcern of the authorities. At least we might preserve in this way the memory of what Puebla once was, which her sons have not known how to respect.

In Mexico City also there is great architecture decorated in tile. The foremost and unique example is of course the house we call by that name, the *Casa de los Azulejos*; as we have said, it dates from this period (289). Its most valuable tiles may be the panels which give the noble coats of arms of the Viveros family and their relatives. These date from after 1751, according to the genealogists.

But the finest examples of ceramic art are in the house erroneously presumed to belong to the Marquesa de Uluapa, on the street formerly called Calle de la Monterilla, and now the Cinco de Febrero. Around the

343. Gardener. Glazed tile panel. Roof garden of a house, Cinco de Febrero 18, Mexico City.

flat roof of this house are large panels with genre figures: the major-domo, the laundress, the ice-cream vendor, and so on, all a little under life size, perfect in character and color (343). The background is decorated with Mudejar patterns. These tiles, which for a long time were thought to be from Puebla, were made in Mexico City; the clay shows it, as does the technique of the painting.[19]

[19] Cf. Rhode, Azulejos; also Alberto Le Duc and Roberto Álvarez Espinosa and Jorge Enciso, *Una casa habitación del siglo XVIII en la ciudad de México.*

Almost all the noble residences have decorations in tile; they are indispensable in the kitchen (350), they are often used for a dado in corridors and on stairways, and often they decorate the lifts of the stairs.

Fountains are commonly covered with tile, and some reach monumental proportions, like that of the convent of La Regina, which can still be admired in the patio of the Hospital Béistegui. Nothing is more romantic than one of these convent patios where the little octagonal fountain of tile is shaded by the branches of blossoming orange trees. Such is the cloister at San Angel, which seems a pictorial illusion rather than a work of architecture.

Many churches in Mexico City were decorated with tile, their dadoes and interior chapels as well as their towers, domes, and other details. To note a few: the church of La Santísima, whose dome has great panels with pontifical coats of arms, and that of Santa Inés, with bands on the dome which remind us of rebozos.

The most important of them all is the Capilla del Pocito in the Villa de Guadalupe (247), which we have already discussed. The concept of the architect, Guerrero y Torres, is complete: the cupolas covered with tile contrast marvellously with the velvety red of the *tezontle,* the grey of the stone, and the ivory tone to which the reliefs have weathered.

I offer now some data about the potters of Mexico City, in the hope that some scholar may complete them. These come from the Archivo Histórico de Hacienda.

Potters of Mexico City:

José Sánchez and José Guarneros, overseers, 1796
Mariano Hernández and José Paz, overseers, 1797
Manuel Echeverría and José Rodríguez, overseers, 1798
Tosian Nava, *Ex. y V. 54,* opposite the Calvario
Simón Naranjo, *Ex. y V. 65*
Manuel Caro, *63 y Ex.*
José Romero, *54 y Ex,* Sta. María
José Bergara, *56 y Ex.*
Juan de Dios Sánchez, *56 y Ex.*
Athanasio Mendoza, *62 y Ex.*
Lucas, *Calle 61 y Ex.*
Manuel Barba, *60 y Ex.* S. Lázaro
Martín Hernández, *64 y Ex.*
　Joseph Rivas, *Ex.*
1696. Overseers, Antonio Bravo and Sebastián Delgado

1697. Antonio Martínez and Francisco Moreno
1698. Nicolás Ramírez and Gregorio de Urrola
　Examination of Joseph de Talabera and of Damián Molina
1699. *Ex.* Antonio de Lara
　Gregorio de Urrola and Joseph de Talabera
1700. Sebastián de Nava and Sebastián Delgado
1701. Sebastián de Nava and Sebastián Delgado
　Ex. Juan González
1702. Francisco Moreno and Juo González
1703. Anto Martz. and Grego Vrriolo
　Ex. Tomás Anto de Medina
1704. Tomás de Medina and Sebastián Delgado
1705. Francisco Moreno and Diego de Almanza
　Ex. Nicolás Sánchez
1706. *Ex.* Gabriel de Alcázar
1707. Gregorio de Urrola and Gabriel de Alcántara
1707. Miguel de Tapia; Miguel Vecerra
1713. Overseers, Miguel Román and Marcos Caballero
1714. Overseers, Diego Velásquez and Diego de Almanza
1715. Overseers, Damián de la Pena and Juan de la Pena
1754–1765. Antonio Bergara. *Ex.* In the Ornillo.
　Antonio Enríquez, Cjon. S. Juan
　Joseph Vicente Herra, *Ex.*
　Joseph Cariaga, *Ex. y V.* 65
1765. Overseers, Simón Naranjo and José Cariaga
1766. Examination, José Mariano Ojeda
1767. Overseers, Joseph Rivas and Antonio Enríquez
1768. Examination, Joseph Rodríguez, Joseph Francisco Senteno
1770. *Id.* Antonio Valbas
1771. Examination of Mariano Oyanguren y Espínola, maker of whiteware
1775. José Mariano Hernández
1781. Josef Rodríguez and Don Atanasio José Mendoza
1784. Overseer, Mariano Hernández
1785. Examination of Juan Antonio Alfaro
1789. Examined: Ignacio Illescas, José Joaquín Sandoval, José Rodríguez, Andrés Salgador, José Paz and José Antonio Romero

Other Crafts
Ivory

There is no documentation on ivory carving in Mexico. Neither in the ordinances, nor in any of the lists of craftsmen we have, does there appear a carver of ivory; there is only a cabinetmaker (*ensamblador*) who works with ebony and ivory, Marcos de Espinosa, active between 1649 and 1660. Yet it is a fact that ivory carvings are abundant in New Spain, and there is no church or house without its ivory crucifix, large or small, more or less beautiful. The Holy Child, the Virgin, and all sorts of saints are also found in ivory. Here we have a problem which has not been resolved: Did all these pieces come from Asia? There is no doubt that the majority of the important ivory sculptures in our museums—in the Treasure of the Cathedral of Mexico, the Museo Nacional—are of Asiatic provenience. We have proof, for example, that the statuettes of the Cathedral's choir lectern came from Manila. There are also two sorts of internal evidence which go to prove this: in the first place, the perfection of technique, which is proficient in the highest degree, and, secondly, the absence of Christian feeling in these images. They are impassive, without emotion, like the material of which they are made.

It is not possible to speak conclusively, because of the lack of historical data. This very lack, however, indicates that there was in fact no guild of ivory carvers, and that this valuable material was worked by wood carvers only occasionally and on a small scale in repairing figures, or by joiners and cabinetmakers who used it for intarsia and marquetry.

One can assume that the supply of ivory pieces was perhaps greater in New Spain than in Europe, since more than once they were sent to the Old World. In 1669 the Congregation of the Oratorio de Padres Felipensis in Puebla sent to Rome certain papers concerning important affairs, and "they sent together with these papers a great ivory Crucifix, with its cross of ebony and silver finials, which is the one venerated on the high altar of the Oratory in Rome."[20] This means that the Christ was of such high quality that only the principal church of the Order of San Felipe Neri was worthy of it.

Among the famous pieces of ivory in Mexico are the twelve charming figures we have mentioned, made in Manila for the lectern around 1765 (335). They have a smooth and milky quality, as if the ivory had turned to jasper. In the Capilla de las Reliquias, set into the

[20] *Memorias históricas de la Congregación de El Oratorio de la ciudad de México*, ed. Juan Mariano.

344. Holy Family. Ivory.
Museo de Arte Religioso, Mexico City.

retable, there is a high relief, small in its proportions but very fine. However, it is in the Museo de Arte Religioso that the best pieces are kept. There is a collection of crucifixes of various periods and varying artistic value, and a *St. Michael* on a Baroque pedestal of the seventeenth century. The prize is the *Sacred Family*, remarkable for both the size of the figures and their technical elegance (344). A gracious tenderness emanates from the Virgin and St. Joseph—their figures gently curved, following the form of the tusks from which they are made—toward the Child, who receives their diffident homage with open arms.

In the Museo de Historia there are some excellent pieces which came from the collection of Don Ramón Alcázar: a *St. Michael* of considerable vivacity, a *St. Joseph with the Child Jesus,* a *Virgin Mary,* and other objects.

In Puebla, in the collection of Don Mariano Bello there is a very beautiful *Crucifix,* a real work of art, whose realism suggests a Spanish carving of the seventeenth century. In the Museo de Santa Mónica there is another beautiful ivory *Christ,* which has been confused with one which, according to legend, belonged to Diego de Alvarado, a Jew who used to whip it. That crucifix, after having remained for many years in the church of the convent of Santa Mónica, was moved to the Cathedral of Puebla, where it was kept on the altar of St. John Nepomucen. There is undoubtedly other valuable ivory sculpture in the Cathedral.

Shell

There is very little historical documentation about the art of tortoise shell, although objects decorated with shell are abundant. The antiquary Meneses owned a chest of tortoise shell with decorations of brass and silver, and engravings of animals. The inscription on it gives us the name of a craftsman, and shows that tortoise shell was worked in New Spain. It says: *Guadalaxara, Año de 1716. Francisco Xavier Pan y Agua me fecit.*

We remember having seen on one of the side altars of the church of Santa Rosa in Querétaro a magnificent tortoise-shell reliquary of this period, in the form of a shield, perforated, and with rich ornament.

A remarkable piece, which has been allowed to disappear through carelessness and lack of appreciation, was the great candlestick for the Easter candle in the Cathedral of Mexico. More than three meters tall, its form was Baroque, and the whole structure was covered with plates of tortoise shell and silver reliefs. Only the upper part has been preserved, in the Treasure of the church.

Tortoise shell was used extensively to decorate pulpits, lecterns, the Good Friday candelabra, commodes, and chests of drawers in churches and cathedrals. The large Spanish combs intricately carved of shell must have been fashionable in colonial times, although they certainly did not reach the enormous size of the combs

which the ladies of Buenos Aires carried in their hair. Small objects, snuff boxes, cigarette cases, were made of tortoise shell, as were ordinary combs.

Intarsia or Marquetry

This craft consists in decorating furniture, chests, pulpits, or choir stalls with an inlay of fine woods, bone or ivory, and shell (158, 330). There are fine designs, either geometric, in the Mudejar manner, or with foliate motifs.

The masterpiece of this kind of work is indubitably the choir stalls of the Cathedral of Puebla, made by a group of workmen under the direction of the master craftsman Pedro Muñoz between 1719 and 1722. It is the richest and most delicate example we have of Mudejar decoration in ecclesiastical furniture.

Although they have already a quality of popular art, we should not omit the objects made of fine woods by the Indians of Peribán and Paracho in Michoacán, or the exquisite small chests with bone inlay which are made in the town of Santa María del Río, near the city of San Luis Potosí.

In conclusion we offer the names we have found—sadly few—of artists in this craft:

1649–1660. Marcos de Espinosa, master joiner in ebony and ivory
1660. Joseph Díaz de Rivera, apprentice to the above
1720. Gabriel Gómez, master cabinetmaker
Diego de Arellano, cabinetmaker
1727. Juan de Alvarado, master cabinetmaker

Leatherwork

There is fuller documentation about leather workers, especially those who made harness, which in olden times had the quality of a work of art. Thus we have the ordinances of the guild of harnessmakers published on May 2, 1549, other ordinances of March 24, 1572, and a third set of 1609. To provide an idea of the work of these craftsmen, we transcribe from the ordinances of 1609 the paragraph listing the objects which a workman must make in his examination for master craftsman:

A packsaddle girth with tassels of black or white leather. A French crupper with rings. A saddlegirth with flowers of black or white leather. A sword belt lined with dressed sheepskin, and the same backstitched with Mixtec silk. A shot bag, of cordovan or sheepskin. A box of cordovan and another of sheepskin, stitched with Mixtec silk. A scabbard for a knife or machete, made as requested.

An infinity of other objects were also executed in leather, many of which offered an opportunity for artistic work. Such were trunks, richly embroidered with maguey fiber or tooled with designs in relief; the seats and backs of chairs, large and small, sometimes embossed, sometimes embroidered; boots, so called, which were actually only leggings and were almost always covered with fine tooling in relief; and a great variety of utensils and articles of clothing.

Chapter Twenty

POPULAR ART IN MEXICO

Preliminary Considerations

THE CONCEPT "popular art" has come into being in our time. Popular art in fact paralleled the development of the other arts right through the colonial period, but only in recent times has it been recognized and appreciated as a separate category which has its own values. What used to be looked on as a curiosity, or at best a piece of admirable manual dexterity, is now taken to be a work of art. This comes about from a new feeling for the significance of the human spirit in all its forms of expression—an interest which is realized in the discipline of anthropology.

In this way the field of art studies has been enriched with a new area unimagined by traditional historians. Not that any studies of popular art have yet appeared which could claim to be definitive, or even thorough. People appreciate it, they extoll it, they break into raptures of admiration before the more distinguished objects—but up to now they have not written a single study which meets the needs of the simple observer or collector, much less of the critic. What studies have been published are no doubt estimable,[1] but they have not fulfilled the expectations aroused by the objects. They limit themselves to cataloguing whatever popular art they happen to know, without even doing that ex-

haustively. And since they mix together literature, verse and prose, music, and everything they come upon, it is clear that without knowing it, or at least without admitting it, they are working rather in the field of folklore. Undoubtedly popular art is a branch of this lore; but its field is limited to the plastic arts, and it is stupid not to realize this.

It is not possible in a general work like this to attempt a profound study of this material which in itself deserves at least a volume, if not several, nor should it be expected. All I can do is to sum up my ideas on the subject, and make such observations as seem pertinent.

When we speak of popular art, we make, in using this adjective, a clear distinction: there is a "popular"

---

[1] On popular art in general, see Gerardo Murillo (Dr. Atl), *Las artes populares en México*; Roberto Montenegro, "Folk Art," in *Twenty Centuries of Mexican Art*. Since this chapter was written the literature on popular art, which the author was one of the first to discuss seriously, has increased considerably. See further Daniel F. Rubín de la Borbolla's two articles, "Arte popular y artesanías de México," *Artes de México,* 43–44 (1962), 1-275; and "Las artes populares indígenas de América, supervivencia y fomento," *América indígena,* 19 (enero 1959), 5–42; Abelardo Carrillo y Gariel, *Imaginería popular novo-española*; Frances Toor, *A Treasury of Mexican Folkways*; Gerd Doerner, *Mexikanische Volkskunst*; José Guadalupe Zuno, *Las artes populares en Jalisco*; Leopoldo I. Orendáin, *Pintura popular.*

art which seems to confront and oppose another kind of art—the art which is not of "the people," not popular. These two types represent the two faces of a single phenomenon.

If it is a difficult thing (and one which has not yet been achieved) to understand the essence of the phenomenon we call "art," it is even more difficult to clarify the subsidiary phenomena, of which this so-called "popular" art is one.

In the first place, careful observation will show that we lump together under this term a number of quite diverse types. Some are authentic products of popular art, while others are popular imitations of the art which is not "popular."

Perhaps the following may help to put our ideas in order. The primary examples of legitimate popular art are things made without consideration of art as such: household utensils, toys, sarapes, rebozos, pots, gourds, et cetera. Their purpose is practical, and their decoration, which is traditional, is continually repeated over long periods of time, like the names which are given to the children of a certain family.

But manual skill and the impulse to art are both innate in man. Thus a man does his best, in working on the little objects for daily use, to make them agreeable. Are they then works of art? If we consult the man himself on this point, he will laugh at us, or swear at us, according to his character. And yet for us these pots, this crude glassware, these knife handles have the qualities of an enchanting art. We buy the pieces for a few cents and put them in our cabinet, where they arouse the admiration and envy of all our friends.

The explanation is plain. The man has made the things in the best way he can. He did not create works of art, because he lacked a consciousness of art; it was an unconscious talent which functioned in his work. But we others, conscious observers with some experience of art, recognize the merit of his productions and acquire them and enjoy them.

In the phenomenon called art three factors are present: the creator, the work of art, and the person who contemplates it. When the communion of these three is realized, the phenomenon is complete: two spirits, and an object which has joined them. In the case of popular art, the creator is unaware, but the contemplator appreciates and gives value to the object. Artistic phenomena exist in the subjective sphere: the contemplator, in appreciating the value of the object which its maker cannot appreciate, is the real creator of the qual-

345. Santiago Matamoros (St. James the Moor-Killer). Painted wood. Church of Santiago Tlachichilco, Santiago de Anaya, Hidalgo.

ity of art in it, and to this extent, of the "work of art."

The foregoing considerations are applicable only to legitimate popular art; the popular imitation of Fine Art has to be evaluated in quite a different way. This whole interest in popular art is, as we have said, a creation of our time. When the world shook off the bonds of academicism, it was discovered that esthetic quality had manifested itself in many modes. Those which were outside the academic canons had up to now been dismissed as curiosities: Negro art, Indian art (formerly considered only as anthropological material), the art of children, of the insane, and so on. From the study of primitive art—which can hold its own with any other on the basis of esthetic quality—came the idea of studying all the nonorthodox varieties of art, and they have markedly influenced our own contemporary art.

I will not pretend to make a definitive study of Mexican popular art. I must content myself with sketching the principal types, and noting a related phenomenon, the popular imitation of art which is not popular.

Furthermore, one has to emphasize a distinction between the indigenous art which survived in colonial times and the popular imitation of European art. These considerations are subtle, and they still need critical examination. Obviously, from a point of view which tends to generalize, all the work which one historian has called *tequitqui*[2] can be grouped with popular art.

But looking at the phenomenon in specific examples, I am convinced that it should not be so considered. The fact is that the art of Indian sculptors who continued to work in their Indian manner under Spanish domination has characteristics so distinct, so individual, that we are forced to view it as a separate category of art which existed within the sphere of normal viceregal art. Examples will illustrate this distinction: the lion of the museum at Tuxtla Gutiérrez in Chiapas (56) or the animals from Tepeaca (55) are not popular sculpture, but Indian sculpture carved after the Conquest in the same technique used before the Conquest. In contrast, a Santiago on horseback (345) with his pistols, his machete, and his charro pants, *is* popular art, and so is a St. Isidore the Laborer, with his plow, his yoke of oxen and his straw sombrero.

With these notions sorted out, I can arrange the enormous bulk of our material in three large groups:

I. Survivals of indigenous art
II. True manifestations of popular art
III. Popular imitations of works of art which are not popular

Indigenous Survivals

The objects which belong in this first category, apart from what we have considered already, are often not works of art, but simply artifacts in the anthropological sense. They include Indian utensils, pots, furniture, and also buildings—which naturally continued to be made after the Conquest, since the conquistadors did not annihilate the natives. Without pretending to be a spe-

cialist in this material, I believe this to be an approximate list of them:

Buildings

Jacalli, the Indian huts or cabins, called *jacal* or *choza.* This includes all the regional types of small Indian dwellings.

Temaxcalli, or *temascal.* The Indian bathhouse, like our Turkish bath, but with its special type of building.

Granaries. I am ignorant of the Indian name for these granaries, but in the state of Morelos they are built in a special form: they look like enormous clay eggs.

Sculpture

All the sculpture designated *tequitqui,* which we have considered in the first section of this book.

Furniture

The *equipal,* a distortion of the word *icpalli,* which means simply "chair" in Nahuatl. These are made in Jalisco, of wood and leather, and are very comfortable. The modern examples with paintings or fringes or other decoration are ridiculous.

Petate, or *pétatl,* a mat. Used daily in every Indian family, past and present. They are made in all sizes and of various thicknesses, from the large and heavy ones which serve as mattresses, to the small ones so finely woven that they seem like cloth. The craft is extended to make dolls, fire fans, bags or baskets, and many other objects of woven reeds (*tule*). A *petate* is not a work of art in itself; but in the same technique very fine *petates* woven in different colors do attain the character of real art, as the collection which used to be in the house of Don Mariano Bello demonstrates. Incomparable elegance in technique, imaginative design, a variety of colors, they were rich in all of this. They were comparable to old European tapestries. These *petates* came especially from Coatlatlauhcan, near Huajuapan, in the state of Oaxaca.

In this same mat-weaving technique objects in enormous variety are made, from fans to little purses, which can be found at present in any popular market. They are lively in color, and they are properly classified as popular art, since the original function of the craft has been lost sight of.[3]

---

[2] José Moreno Villa, *La escultura colonial mexicana,* p. 16.
[3] See also George M. Foster, *Culture and Conquest,* pp. 93–95.

Utensils

Metate. Perhaps the most important indigenous survival is the ancient *métlatl* for grinding maize, the sacred grain (350). Usually they are not works of art, unless in respect to their more or less elegant form; but sometimes they are covered with reliefs, and inscriptions, and become admirable pieces of decorative sculpture. Already made by mestizo craftsmen in colonial times (as they still are in our day), they are indeed objects of popular art.

Metlapil. This is the pestle to use with the metate, what grinds the *nixcómel,* the corn prepared to make tortillas. It has the shape of a spindle, and is of necessity smooth.

Molcajete. A tripod mortar of rough stone or pottery, used to grind chilis and tomatoes for sauce.

Tejolote, or *texolotl.* The stone, in the form of a cylinder with rounded ends, which is used as a pestle with the *molcajete;* it is shaped rapidly by hand grinding.

Comal, or *comalli.* The pottery griddle, almost flat, on which tortillas are cooked.

Xiquepextle (no Spanish equivalent). A straw basket, double-woven, round at the top and square at the bottom, which is used to keep tortillas hot, with a cloth which is placed on the bottom and folded over the top.

Masks

Masks seem to have been used in many cultures, by the Egyptians, who placed them on their mummies, by the Greeks and the Japanese in their theatres. The Indians of America used ritual masks in certain totemistic dances, and for their dead. During the colonial period they began to make masks in the European style, but some of the indigenous types persisted (346). Nowadays there is an extensive manufacture, still imitating the ancient types, or inventing new ones frankly popular in style.

Naturally, as I have said, I cannot pretend to have covered this material; it is waiting, intact, for the study of the anthropologists. A serious publication is urgently needed, with the best possible illustrations.

True Popular Art

The study of true popular art is broader and more varied. It is as if the styles of all the periods were applied to objects which were not expected to be artistic,

346. Mask of a Christian, from the Dance "Moros y Cristianos." Painted wood. Brooklyn Museum, Brooklyn, New York.

and which the makers firmly believed they were making without artistic intent.

I shall attempt here to continue the plan of organization which I have followed throughout this volume, but I am not sure that it will work; for art is so inconstant a thing, so lively, at times so slippery, that no one, without the grossest pedantry, can set up absolute categories.

Architecture

When the *chozas* of the Indians are eliminated, what remains that really deserves to be called popular architecture? Many buildings, indeed, so many that we cannot possibly enumerate them. The churches of Yucatán and Campeche, which have their special form, with a great *espadaña,* a wall belfry of many bells, on the façade. The houses of certain parts of Oaxaca—Tehuantepec and Juchitán, for example—marvellously adapted to the climate and without architectural pretensions, are magnificent examples of popular architecture. Certain churches in the Huasteca, whose façades are built of logs and sticks arranged in patterns, a purely practical device. The *casa de vecindad* of Mexico City, Puebla, Oaxaca, or any other Mexican city, is very typical. There may be chance resemblances to buildings in Europe, or in cultured Mexican architecture, but certainly there was neither the intention nor the opportunity of copying them. Here you have to do with the inspiration of mestizo contractors and builders who have left the imprint of their spirit on their creations. In the name of specious standards of hygiene, our so-called civilization, with its eagerness to exploit the poor (since the rich have already been exploited to the limit) is destroying these dwellings in which entire generations have lived out their lives for centuries.[4]

Sculpture

Popular sculpture may be found in two kinds of work: images of saints which differ from the traditional types accepted by the church, and decorative sculpture. I have commented already on the images of Santiago (345)[5] and San Isidro Labrador. It is relevant that these personages are engaged in activities of the common people: war and agriculture. So the artist in making his image neglects the classic formula, and looks to the daily life of the people around him. And he is especially concerned that these saints may be easily identified by their attributes.

Objects decorated with sculpture are very numerous. Among them we might point out:

The saltcellars of pulque shops—great stone objects, quite heavy, so that the devotees cannot easily carry them off, and decorated in a delightful way.

Knives and razors with horn handles, often shaped like an animal.

Slingshots. I have seen magnificent ones in Otomi villages, of hard wood with humorous carvings of animals: a monkey drinking pulque from the wineskin, a dog, a lizard.

Very fine examples of carving are the cocoanuts covered with reliefs which are made in the prisons. A whole romantic story—the abduction of the girl, the duel with pistols, the final tears—will be represented. Others are historical: the War of the Intervention and the Empire appear with their characters faithfully portrayed.

From cocoanuts we pass to walnuts, and to apricot and cherry pits, a diminutive sculpture which is not less impressive for being tiny: the monkey biting his tails, a half-centimeter high, attains a surprising assurance of form and minuteness of detail. The large hunting horns made of bulls' horns and covered with reliefs should not be overlooked.

Painting

There seems to be only one type here: the so-called *retablos,* which are in fact ex-votos in which pious people give thanks for some divine favor received, illustrating at once the evil and its cure through the intervention of a sacred image. Charming, evocative, and ingenuous in the way they state the theme, and in its plastic solution, these little pictures painted in oil on wood, tin, or cardboard are plentiful in the sanctuaries of the famous images. The oldest that have been found date from the seventeenth century (347), but they are still being made even today. They are not works of art, but of ritual, and they are not like any other painting, ancient or modern. And yet their artistic value is immense, in their authentic—that is, childlike—interpretation of forms, of perspective, of the affections and emotions which suffuse their characters with life.[6]

Minor Arts

It is naturally in this area of art that the most abundant and the richest examples of popular invention are to be found.

Ceramics, first of all. This is a great chapter in popular art (350). There is no important region of the

---

[4] See Gabriel García Maroto and Enrique Yáñez, *Arquitectura popular de México*; Sergio Zaldívar G., *Arquitectura barroco popular.*

[5] See Rafael Heliodoro Valle, *Santiago en América.*

[6] See Roberto Montenegro, *Retablos de México: Mexican Votive Paintings.*

Dia de el Glorioso San Lorenzo, entrando Joseph Patricio Polo dela Calle en un cavallo alborotado, no pudie
u Jetarlo en el patio, se entró enla Sala donde resbalando los quatro pies, cayó sobre el Ginete, è invocando es
dulce nombre de Jesus, ysu Esposa à nuestra Sᵃ de el Rosario, quedo libre y el bruto tan quieto como si fuera
de t... en Hu...

347. Anonymous. Ex-voto of Joseph Patricio Polo. Oil on canvas. Collection of Mr. and Mrs. Donald Weismann, Austin, Texas.

country where pottery is not made. To study it, and distinguish the indigenous survivals from the popular work, is not easy.[7] Faced with a task of this size, I shall merely indicate some important types. In the first place, two large divisions are distinguishable: common pottery and whiteware. In the state of Jalisco there is a brilliant ceramic industry, whose centers are Tlaquepaque, Tonalá,[8] El Rosario, and Santa Cruz. One must distinguish between the genuine popular pottery, a

glossy grey crockery with charming painting, and the crude imitation of majolica, in the worst taste, which they are now manufacturing.

Next in importance is Oaxaca, with the centers at Coyotepec, Santa María Atzompa, and Tehuantepec. The pottery of Coyotepec is fired black, and also painted with graphite; there is a great range of objects, from

[7] See Foster, *Culture and Conquest,* pp. 87–93.
[8] See Isabel Marín de Paalen, *Alfarería: Tonalá.*

387

great pots to the little bells of metallic tone which so astonished the poet Ramón López Velarde. He has immortalized them in a line of his *Suave Patria*: "your earthenware rings like silver . . . "[9] Other pottery is glazed black or a very dark green. But the ceramics of Oaxaca are of such variety that it is impossible to sum them up in a few lines. A visit to the great Saturday market in the city of Oaxaca makes one feel that there should be a chair of ethnography, or better still, of popular art.

The state of México has a rich ceramic industry. Pottery is made in Cuautitlán, Metepec, Valle de Bravo, Texcoco, Temascalcingo, Toluca, Tecaxic, Almoloya, San Marcos, and Coscomatepec. Everyone knows the magnificent pitchers and casseroles from Texcoco, of reddish pottery, with an excellent glaze and a great variety of shapes. That of Metepec is a brilliant black with light decoration, or has a fine dark green glaze.

Puebla is a state which produces a great quantity of ceramics. The so-called *talavera* of the city of Puebla, which we have already discussed in treating the minor arts, is not popular art, and for this reason some writers are excessively abusive toward it, especially Dr. Atl. There is an important ceramic industry besides this in the city, thanks to the quality of the clay available there. This popular pottery, famous all over the country for its strength and impermeability, is made in a particular section of the city where the potters live, called La Luz. Here they make utensils of red clay, and also whiteware. Other centers of production in the state are Amozoc, where the technique of making diminutive animals is far superior to that of Jalisco, Izúcar de Matamoros, Santa Marta, and Tepeji.

In Guerrero there are two important centers: Tlapa and Tolimán. The jugs from Tlapa, unglazed and painted with serpents in sepia, remind us of the vases of archaic Greece.

Michoacán offers the fine burnished red pots of Tzintzuntzan, whose smooth and glossy quality recalls pre-Conquest Tarascan ceramics. Another center of production is Ocumicho.

In Guanajuato we find three foci of potters: Dolores Hidalgo, where they were established and encouraged by the Father of Our Country, Father Hidalgo; San Miguel de Allende, with an important output of whiteware, and San Felipe Torres Mochas.

The pottery of Aguascalientes includes finely shaped vessels with a stylized decoration which one would think an anticipation of modern art.

In various other states pottery of various kinds is made. It is impossible to specify their characteristics in a work like this. We shall be satisfied with mentioning some names, in the hope that a specialist will work on them: Morelos (San Antón near Cuernavaca), San Luis Potosí, Chiapas, Chihuahua, and Tlaxcala.

Textiles.[10] Let us begin with the famous sarapes known all over the world as a specialty of Mexico. With sarapes, as in all popular art, it is necessary to distinguish the genuine artifacts—those which follow the traditional, unsophisticated patterns, free from all foreign influence—from those which copy exotic motifs, whether it be the national coat of arms, or pre-Conquest fretwork, or worst of all, idols. Such imitation strips the essential from popular art, under the poor excuse of civilizing it, or the powerful stimulus of exploitation and profit. The most famous sarapes are those of Saltillo, characterized by graduated or contrasting stripes of bright colors. This technique is new, for no ancient prototypes are known; it appears that they are woven for the most part in San Luis Potosí.

Other important centers of sarape weaving are Aguascalientes and San Juan de los Lagos in Jalisco. Santa Ana Chiautempan, Tlaxcala, is a place important for wool weaving, both sarapes of fine design and suitings which imitate English cloth to perfection. Oaxaca offers splendid examples, heavy and warm; those of Teotitlán del Valle are famous, although they include perhaps the most exaggerated examples of unsuitable influence, with archeological designs which belie their genuine primitive tradition. Sarapes are made in Texcoco, México, and in the state of Jalisco, both in the capital, Guadalajara, and in the towns of Xocotepec and Etzatlán.

The rebozo, or shawl, although oriental in origin, has come to be the garment symbolical of the Indian woman of Mexico. She uses it in a thousand ways: as a headdress, wrapped in a crown for protection from the sun, as a proper rebozo or scarf, covering the face to leave only a part visible, as a shawl against the cold, as finery to enhance and ornament her personal charms. The weaving of the rebozo is a highly skilled technique, in spite of the primitive looms which are used. Some are made of silk, so fine that they can be drawn through a ring; some are made of cotton thread, *de*

[9] See Paul van de Velde and Henriette Romeike, *The Black Pottery of Coyotepec, Oaxaca, Mexico.*
[10] See Foster, *Culture and Conquest,* pp. 98–99.

388

Ignacio María Barreda. Doña Juana María Romero. Oil on canvas.
1.42 x 1.16 m. Museo Nacional de Historia, Mexico City.

bolita, as they are called. The colors are referred to in a delightful terminology which may well evade a dry historian of art: some are *palomas* (doves), others *coyotes*: the doves are grey-blue, the coyotes, tawny in color. The most important places where rebozos are woven on primitive looms are Santa María del Río in the state of San Luis Potosí, Guadalajara in Jalisco, and Tenancingo, Texcoco, and Temascalcingo in the state of México.

Silverwork. Almost all the work which is done in silver, and what little goldwork is made in Mexico, is either a popular art or a popular imitation of European work. And this may be said to go back to the colonial period; there are in fact very few Mexican pieces which have achieved the perfection of European work. Among the objects which are true popular art one might mention the *milagros,* ex-votos which are offerings of the pious, and which almost always represent an objective memorial of the grace received: eyes, an arm, a leg, or breasts cured of some infirmity, or a bull, a cow, or a donkey recovered. The principal centers of production are: Oaxaca, whose silversmiths recall the work of their Mixtec and Zapotec ancestors; Pátzcuaro, which offers artifacts with a genuine popular flavor; Mexico City, Puebla, and Taxco, where in recent times great numbers of silver shops have been established. The promoter of this activity, the architect William Spratling, began with popular work and imitations of European silver; at present he is one of the few silversmiths with a feeling for modern style. The rest of the shops continue to work as they always have.

Lacquer. The technique of lacquer is assumed to be an importation from the Orient, especially China. However, the matter is not so simple, for pre-Hispanic lacquers are known, and in those which are being made today native materials are used. However it is, two categories must be distinguished: one, authentic lacquers, and the other, imitations of lacquer work. The first group has flourished since the earliest colonial times in two centers: Uruapan in Michoacán, and Olinalá in Guerrero. The technique of genuine lacquer work consists in first covering the whole object—gourd, wooden tray, or calabash—with a heavy coat of paint mixed with special substances which are the secret of the work. This is later burnished. Next, the pattern of the decoration is marked with a sharp punch, and the paint is removed down to the original material to form the design. Then the same sort of paint, in other desired colors, is applied in the hollowed-out

parts, to complete the decoration. This technique is like the champlevé process of enamel. When the decoration is complete, the object is burnished all over, and then no difference can be seen between the background and the areas which have been filled in.

The best quality of lacquer is characterized by flat colors, which one finds in all the old pieces. At present the work has degenerated, with an attempt to variegate the colors in imitation of cheap chromos. The favorite color scheme of typical lacquer from Uruapan is a black background with a decoration of flowers in vivid colors.[11] In Olinalá they work on a fine orange ground with designs in green and in wine-red, in excellent taste.

I have found imitation lacquer in Quiroga (formerly called Cocupao de Michoacán), in Chiapa de Corzo in the state of Chiapas, and in other smaller places. This technique consists of painting the whole piece to give a brilliant surface like lacquer, and then painting the decoration over this. Its showy appearance cannot compare at all to the fine quality and the glossy smoothness of the genuine work.

Furniture. Popular furniture is a matter of only some few types. The reed chair, of *tule,* in four sizes for all ages. The table of white wood, with its drawer and its turned legs. The *trastero,* a very simple cupboard without doors, and the chests—*cajas* or *cofres*—the popular descendants of the old *arcones.* When the chest is painted and decorated with the view of a cathedral and many birds and bunches of flowers, it is an object of elegance in imitation of the lacquer we have been speaking of (348). Such furniture is made in Toluca and Tenancingo in the state of México, in the Villa de Guadalupe, and in some places in Michoacán.

Toys. Toys are objects which almost always express the artistic spirit of the people. Of course we refer to the toys of the poor, which are sold at fairs and markets. They are made of clay, of cardboard, of wood, of tin. They do not make the slightest pretension of being art, but they must be "pretty"—attractive in form and color. And in these toys the artist and the cultivated person find an inextinguishable source of art. The stylization, the resemblance to primitive art, the unconscious harmony of color, the occasional caricature—everything works to make these toys at times perfect

[11] Francisco de P. León, *Los esmaltes de Uruapan;* José Guadalupe Zuno, *Las llamadas lacas michoacanas de Uruapan no proceden de las orientales.*

389

348. Painted chest. Wood.

works of art in the popular vein. It is a great pity that mechanization and imitation are steadily destroying this expression of the creative and artistic genius of the Mexican people. If we add to this the vulgar cheap toys manufactured in Japan and Germany, we have all the more reason to appreciate the popular toys of Mexico, which, if they gave us hours of joy as children, now enchant us as examples of a recondite art.

Popular Imitation of Fine Arts

Here is a chapter which might be as long as this whole book. Every manifestation of sophisticated art, in all its varieties, has an echo, a reflection, a double, as we say today, embodied or expressed in popular idiom. The qualifying characteristic is very subtle; at times it may be reduced to matters of technique, while at other times it will be summed up as a taste for the picturesque, which is alien to official art in all periods that lack the Baroque spirit.

I limit myself here to observations about the three large divisions of art: architecture, painting, and sculpture.

Architecture

Throughout the colonial period we find popular types of architecture parallel to the other, proper, architecture. The reason is obvious: opposite the architect or *alarife* from Spain works the unsophisticated builder or *maestro de obras* who imitates his buildings. They understand the methods of construction empirically, or by practical experience, and it is in the decoration that their invention and their memory work to reproduce what they have seen in other buildings. As the essential element is lacking—the feeling for classical design, for architectural proportion, for measure and the laws of composition—the work which results is a delightful, but popular, piece of art.

It is impossible to attempt even a list of monuments of this kind. Anyway, the most important of them have already been pointed out in this book. Here I shall

349. Anonymous. Painted screen: Country Pleasures. Oil. Museo Nacional de Historia, Mexico City.

content myself with discussing three important examples which will illustrate my conception of this type of architecture.

The first typical example of imitation in the popular mood is to be found in the façades of the ancient Augustinian church at Yuririapúndaro (96). The structure itself does not fall into this classification, but only the façades, where they were trying to imitate the façade of the church of Acolman (89). At Acolman, whose sculpture displays the perfection of technique and the rich sobriety of Spanish Plateresque, in a Renaissance design of great purity, we cannot but see a cultured European hand. In the façades of Yuriria we recognize a copy, but carried out with less authority, and with additions which destroy the basic character of the Plateresque. They are more picturesque, less severe, inferior in design and composition.

The second example is afforded by the church of the Tercer Orden in Cuernavaca, Morelos. It is a Baroque structure, cruciform, with two portals, one in front, and one at the side which is sheltered by a great portico in the form of a shell. The lack of proportion in pilasters and columns, the execution—crude if picturesque —of reliefs and statues, all recalls the popular art we have been considering.

The third example is no more nor less than the façade of the famous sanctuary of Ocotlán in Tlaxcala (269), an outstanding example of Churrigueresque architecture, as we have said. For all its ingenuous charm, it cannot be compared, either in conception or in execution, to the work of the great Churrigueresque designers who created the Sagrario in Mexico City, or the churches of Tepotzotlán and Taxco. It too falls into the classification of popular architecture.

350. Anonymous. A Mexican Kitchen. Oil on canvas. Museo Nacional de Historia, Mexico City.

Painting

The popular painting of the eighteenth century which imitates the work of the great artists is very important. It may be subdivided as follows: first, mural painting; second, pictures and screens with genre scenes, either historical or of popular life; third, sacred images; and fourth, portraits.

Mural painting. The murals of the sixteenth century painted in fresco by Indians in the churches and convents belong to this category (31). In the seventeenth century they disappeared under heavy coats of plaster and the walls of the cloisters were decorated with large oil paintings on canvas. Sometimes the popular quality persists, as in the series of the *Life of St. Stanislaus of Kostka* by Padilla at Tepotzotlán. The most interesting

survival of this popular mural art was the decoration of the outside walls of pulque shops. This has unhappily disappeared without being recorded, thanks to time and mistaken notions of sanitation.[12]

Genre scenes. In the colonial period screens were very common. Often one side showed episodes from the conquest of New Spain and the other side a view of Mexico City. The one preserved in the Museo de Historia is of this kind (349); it came from Madrid, where it was acquired by the Mexican government.[13] There are also a good many pictures which show typical Mexican scenes of popular life (350).[14] Such is the painting which shows a *puesto,* or stall, in a Mexico City market, in the Museo de Historia. One can recognize even the quality of the peanuts, not to mention a whole display of food and vegetables. But the prize of this type of painting, and one of the most important pictures of the eighteenth century, is the one which shows *The Plaza Mayor* of the capital in the second half of the century, formerly owned by Señor Alcázar (351). The evocative power of the artist is boundless. The picture is crowded with the whole life of the Colony; from the viceroy, who is going to the Cathedral in his sumptuous carriage accompanied by the *oidores* of the Real Audiencia, to the lowest of the rabble, who is stealing what he can for food, the whole colonial society is here faithfully represented.[15]

There are a number of paintings of this type: a *Procession in the Villa de Guadalupe,* which belongs to the Condesa de Corzana in Madrid; a screen showing a bull fight opposite the castle of Chapultepec, belonging to Señor Villar Villamil, and others which we cannot begin to list.

Sacred images. This group is so numerous that an attempt even to catalogue them is impossible. There is no

12 See Emily Edwards, *Painted Walls of Mexico,* pp. 145–164.
13 Cf. Salvador Moreno, "Un biombo mexicano del siglo XVIII," *Anales del Instituto de Investigaciones Estéticas,* 28 (1959), 29–32.
14 See "Pintura popular y costumbrista del siglo XIX," *Artes de México,* 61 (1965); Walter Pach, "Unknown Aspects of Mexican Painting," *Gazette des Beaux-Arts,* Ser. 6, Vol. 24 (1943), pp. 208–220; "Bodegones mexicanos," *Artes de México,* 41 (1962); Manuel Romero de Terreros, "Bodegones y floreros en la pintura mexicana," *Anales del Instituto de Investigaciones Estéticas,* 14 (1946), 55–60; Leopoldo I. Orendáin, *Pintura popular.*
15 See Romero de Terreros, *La Plaza Mayor de México en el siglo XVIII.*

351. Anonymous. The Plaza Mayor of Mexico City. Oil on canvas. 2.12 x 2.66 m. Museo Nacional de Historia, Mexico City.

village church without at least one saint painted in a popular style. One hardly knows which is more extraordinary, the complacency of the priests, or their lack of artistic judgment. Probably both attitudes play a part in filling the churches with popular paintings, along with their zeal to encourage the faith by any means. The colonial paintings they replace may have been more or less valuable, but they were certainly more orthodox examples of religious art.

The popular touch is betrayed first in the clothing. Saints, male and female—even the Virgin Mary—appear bedecked in native dress (352). And then the details of the picture refer to local customs with obvious anachronisms. I have seen a charming picture in

353. Blas Bisente. Archangel Raphael with Donor.
Oil on canvas. Private collection.

352. Anonymous. St. Marina. Oil on canvas.
Museo de Guadalupe, Zacatecas.

which the Virgin Mary is grinding corn for their tortillas in a modest metate, while the Child fans the charcoal stove with his *aventador* to help his Mother, and St. Joseph is working in an unmistakably Mexican carpenter shop. At other times the popular quality appears in a determination to realize what defies realization, as in the countless representations of the *Ecce Homo* or of the *Flagellation of Christ,* where one is shown the sanguinary ribs and all but the viscera of the thorax, as if it would be possible for a man to live in such a condition.

Many images of this sort have ornaments that are not painted, like real jewelry, pearls, diadems and haloes of metal. I have even seen a Virgin with genuine emeralds for earrings and another on her breast; beside the value of the gems, the painting made a poor showing.

Real treasures can be found among these images: such is the *Archangel Raphael* I illustrate (353), photographed near Pátzcuaro by Weston. The slender figure, richly garbed, with the tiny, pretty donor at his feet, makes a picture at once ingenuously charming and pictorially powerful.

Portraits. Many of the eighteenth-century portraits are popular imitations of high style. The painters Barreda (354; color, facing p. 388) and Islas specialized in this kind of portrait, and flooded the drawing rooms of New Spain with ostentatious figures leaning on fantastic furniture which pretended to be authentic Louis XIV or Louis XV, or at the least Chippendale. As iconographical documents they are valuable indeed; as art they rank far below the portraits of Cabrera, who was able to maintain the distinction and nobility of the colonial portrait.

These popular portraits were to reach their height in the first half of the nineteenth century, in the hands of provincial painters; Montiel in Veracruz, Estrada in Jalisco, and Bustos in Guanajuato are the foremost. They continued the colonial tradition, especially Estrada, but they fall outside the boundaries of our concern historically.

Sculpture

The same characteristics are to be found in the plentiful religious sculpture which has decorated our churches since the earliest days of the Colony (355). Artistic in intention, inspired by Classical or Baroque models, their makers were not equipped to work "with

354. Ignacio María Barreda.
María Manuela Esquivel y Serruto. Oil.
Museo Nacional de Historia, Mexico City.

all the rules of art," and their shortcomings of conception and of technique are replaced—or better, compensated—by their gifts of candor and childlike directness. Everything—from the magnificent statues decorating the parish church at Teposcolula in the Mixteca Alta of Oaxaca to the multitude of figures of Christ (356, 357), of the Virgin of Sorrows, of St. Francis, and of the whole celestial court which inhabit the churches of Mexico—belongs in this category.

355. Our Lord of Patience (Cristo del Cacao).
Corn pith, painted. 1.40 m. Cathedral of Mexico.

356. Crucifix. Church of the Franciscan monastery,
Tlaxcala.

In some regions there were formed, if not schools, at least groups with special characteristics. An example of this is the sculpture which flourished in New Mexico, once a colony of New Spain and now a state of the United States. This religious sculpture was something unique. And it is an extraordinary phenomenon that the folk artists, imitating conventional sculptures of saints, and then imitating the imitations, managed sometimes to create sculpture which vividly recalls the work of the primitive sculptors of Europe. Nothing could be more moving than these figures of Christ, with their big heads and treelike bodies, their arms perpendicular at their sides, the great eyes, the hair and beard falling in heavy locks, gazing down, amazed, on the primitive faith of the pious and the ingenuousness

of the imagemakers. Art and religion go hand in hand in the first steps of a culture. But these saints present themselves so pure, so innocent, and achieve their purpose with such artistic assurance, that they leave us overwhelmed with astonishment and emotion.[16]

Decorative sculpture shows the same characteristics, as we have noted, and it runs alike over the exteriors of buildings—façades, portals, towers, windows—and the interiors, where it is a matter of retables, or of covering the whole structure with relief in stucco or plaster. The masterpiece in this genre is certainly the stone retable from the Cathedral of Santa Fe in New Mexico, which is now in the church of Cristo Rey (358). It is

[16] See Mitchell A. Wilder and Edgar Breitenbach, *Santos.*

357. Crucifix. Corn pith, painted. Church of the Dominican monastery, Tlacachahuaya, Oaxaca.

358. Retable from La Castrense chapel. Painted stone. Church of Cristo Rey, Santa Fe, New Mexico.

a delicious popular imitation of the timid Churrigueresque type. Engaged estípites in the form of caryatids organize the design, with sculptures between them, and it apparently dates from 1761. It is all softly painted, and some of the figures seem to be the work of sculptors who cannot be dismissed as popular. However that may be, nothing could be more affecting, more touch-

[17] See Alexander von Wuthenau, "The Spanish Military Chapels in Santa Fe and the Reredos of Our Lady of Light," *New Mexico Historical Review* (July, 1935); Pál Kelemen, "The Significance of the Stone Retable of Cristo Rey," *Palacio,* 61 (1954), 243–272.

ing, than this genuine work of art where Spanish forms and Indian execution come together in a single expression of the Christian spirit.[17]

Within the category of popular art great stores of material await the scholar; but the eye must be indeed discerning to distinguish their characteristics, and the judgment very delicate, to neither underrate nor exaggerate their qualities. A firm and accomplished hand is needed to steer through the complicated and often stormy seas of our popular art.

PART FIVE

Art and the Independence of Mexico

Neoclassic Art, 1781–1821

Chapter Twenty-one

THE ROYAL ACADEMY OF SAN CARLOS OF NEW SPAIN

 THE ACADEMIES which were founded in Europe after the seventeenth century were a product of Rationalism. After the *Discours sur la Méthode* of Descartes men learned again that they could think. But this discovery, in its very breadth, held many dangers. It was clearly a great gain in freedom, but the political and religious situation of the people made such free expression of the spirit a terribly risky thing for established society. So apparently this thesis was developed: man is free to think, so long as he thinks properly. Reason, unless it wants to plunge into imprudence, must follow the road of the true faith, of propriety and the established order. Thinking men must band together and study the models afforded by history in philosophy and literature, in science, and in art. Only in this way can that divine gift, creative thought, produce splendid fruit. Such ideas, encouraged by those in the best position to give encouragement—the monarchs—resulted in the founding of academies, which were named after the academies of ancient Greece without the slightest resemblance to their character. As it turned out, however, history soon proved this device inadequate for controlling the explosion of energy released by reason. France,

the center of Rationalism, cradle of the academies, was first to suffer the fatal and redeeming outcome: revolution. Men could not only think freely, but act in the same way. From metaphysical liberty they moved naturally to real liberty—political liberty.

The repercussions of these phenomena reached New Spain not in their elemental simplicity, but in much more complex forms. The only connection between the founding of the Academia de San Carlos and the idea of independence is chronological, and it would be absurd to claim that the Academy played any part in the revolt. Rationalist concepts appear mainly in a horror of the Baroque, and in that desire to return to Classical art which shows up in all the "cultured" writers and artists. At the same time, the French philosophers and Encyclopædists were read avidly by those working for political emancipation. So without the relationship's being causal, Neoclassic art, like all legitimate art, is still related to a certain condition of society—just as all the artistic manifestations we have surveyed in this fatiguing history have been. This condition of our society and this kind of art represent the end of our tour through the art of the Viceroyalty. The Neoclassic attitude continues to be the only significant one throughout the first half of the nineteenth century, appearing first in Romantic, and then in Neo-Renaissance style.

The Founding of the Royal Academy of San Carlos[1]

A man of great energy and a master of the graphic arts, Don Jerónimo Antonio Gil, was the guiding spirit of our Academy in its inception (color, facing p. 444). Without him the project might not have been realized, at least not so rapidly and effectively as it was. His special characteristic was action; Gil was busy at work even before royal authorization had been received. He was appointed chief engraver of the Royal Mint of Mexico when Don Alejo Madero retired; he came to Mexico with his two sons and two of his most promising pupils from the Academy of San Fernando, Tomás Suría and José Estebe. He had been instructed to establish a school of engraving in the Mint, and for this he brought a selected library, prints, drawings, and tools, besides a collection of replicas (in sulphur) of the Greek and Roman coins belonging to the Academy of San Fernando. This collection was first consigned to him by a royal decree of September 21, 1778.

As soon as he arrived in Mexico he began his teaching with the three scholarship students in the Mint, and later accepted any student who wanted to attend.

His success in those classes suggested to Gil the establishment of an academy of the three Fine Arts, like that of San Fernando of Madrid and San Carlos of Valencia. He presented the plan to the Superintendent of the Mint, Don Fernando José Mangino, who, when he had been convinced, presented the project to the viceroy, Don Martín de Mayorga on August 29, 1781. The Viceroy received the idea enthusiastically and appointed a committee of which he was the chairman, and which was made up of Mangino, Gil, the *corregidor* of the city of Mexico, the *regidor decano del Cabildo,* the *prior del Consulado,* the *administrador del Tribunal de Minería,* the Marqués de Ciria, the Marqués de San Miguel de Aguayo, the senior consul, who was Don Antonio Bassoco, and the *director del Tribunal de Minería,* Don Joaquín Velásquez de León. Don Ignacio Bartolache was secretary.

On November 4 of the same year, 1781, the name-day of Charles III, under whose patronage the new Academy was established, classes began—long before they could be sure of royal approval. The classes of the Academy were first held in the Mint, like the school of engraving.

For its support the new Academy depended on subsidies from official institutions. The Consulado contributed 3,000 pesos annually; the Tribunal de Minería, 5,000; the City of Mexico, 1,000; the city of Veracruz, 200; Querétaro, 100; Guanajuato, 200; the town of San Miguel el Grande, 50; and the cities of Córdoba and Orizaba, 15 each. Beyond this annual subsidy they relied on a number of single gifts by individuals.

After taking this action, official sanction was necessary. On August 1, 1782, the Viceroy made a report to His Majesty, soliciting his approval as well as a subsidy of 12,500 pesos annually, which, with that already procured, was considered sufficient for the development of the new institution. Charles III directed Viceroy Don Matías de Gálvez to inform him in detail, and, in view of his warm support, approved the establishment of the Academy by a royal decree of December 25, 1783. A year later, on November 18, 1784, he issued the Royal Decree of Foundation, together with the statutes by which it was to be run. It was endowed with 9,000 pesos annually, with an additional 4,000 from the Ramo de Temporalidades de Regulares Extinguidos, or in default of that, from the Vacantes Mayores y Menores of the Viceroyalty.

The official inauguration of the Academy took place on November 4, 1785, the name-day of His Majesty, under the Conde de Gálvez, who as viceroy sent a detailed report of the function. Classes were begun with all solemnity, the Viceroy distributed prizes to thirty students, while five others, to show their ability, each demonstrated his special skill in painting, sculpture, architecture, engraving, and die casting.[2]

The Academy counted among its members some of the most illustrious of the viceregal aristocracy. The governing board was composed in this way: the viceroy was vice-patron; the president of the board was Don Fernando José Mangino; the director general, Don Jerónimo Antonio Gil. Members of the Council were:

---

[1] The bibliography of the Academy of San Carlos is already extensive. We cite four works of importance: Jesús Galindo y Villa, "Reseña histórica de la Academia Nacional de Bellas Artes, antigua de San Carlos," *Anales de la Academia Nacional de Bellas Artes en México,* 1 (1913), 9–32; Diego Angulo Íñiguez, *La Academia de Bellas Artes de Méjico y sus pinturas españolas;* Abelardo Carrillo y Gariel, *Datos sobre la Academia de San Carlos;* Justino Fernández, *Catálogo de la Real Academia de San Carlos de Nueva España* (in preparation). See also Jean Charlot, *Mexican Art and the Academy of San Carlos, 1785–1915;* Arturo Arnáiz y Freg, "Noticias sobre la Academia de Bellas Artes de San Carlos," *Anales del Instituto de Investigaciones Estéticas,* 2 (1938), 21–43.

[2] Angulo Íñiguez, *La Academia de Bellas Artes,* p. 15.

TA DE LA PLAZA DE MEXICO, NUEVAMENTE ADORNADA, PARA LA

LOS IV. *que se colocó en ella el 9 de Diciembre de 1796, cumple años de*

Miguel la Grua, Marques de Branciforte, Virrey de Nueva España, quien

tud y consuelo general de todo este Reyno, e hizo grabar esta Estampa, que

ESTATUA EQUESTRE DE NUESTRO AUGUSTO MONARCA REYNANTE:

la Reyna Nuestra Señora MARIA LUISA DE BORBON, su amada Esposa,

solicito y logro de la Real Clemencia erigir este Monumento para desahogo de su

dedica á Sus Magestades, en nuevo testimonio de su fidelidad, amor y respeto

359. Rafael Jimeno y Planes and José Joaquín Fabregat. The Plaza Mayor of Mexico City 1797. Engraving.

Don Ramón de Pasada; Colonel Don Francisco Antonio Crespo; Don José Ángel de Cuevas Aguirre y Avendaño; Don Antonio Barroso y Torrubia; Don Antonio Bassoco; Don José Gorráez y Malo, Mariscal de Castillo and Marqués de Ciria; and Don Pedro Ignacio de Valdivieso y Azlor, Marqués de San Miguel de Aguayo. It was not noble blood that the new Academy lacked!

Various Locations of the Academy

The Academy was first located in the Mint itself, the Casa de Moneda, where the idea had originated. This is the building at present occupied by the Museo de Arqueología. For four years the Academy continued there. As the space was inadequate, Gil requested and obtained the building of the ancient Hospital del Amor de Dios, founded by Fray Juan de Zumárraga, which had been abandoned when the hospital was absorbed into the Hospital de San Andrés. The engraver moved into this building in 1791, and continued alone there for a year until some of the colonial artists came to assist him. Later they acquired a piece of land called "Nipaltongo" across from the Hospital de San Andrés, with the idea of erecting a suitable and adequate building there, for which plans were drawn by Director of Architecture Don J. Antonio González Velásquez.[3]

[3] *Ibid.,* p. 366.

403

But this site was sold to the Real Tribunal de Minería —whom nobody could refuse—to build their School of Mines, as we shall see. Some time later, after Independence, they considered installing the Academy in the building of the Inquisition, and their architect, Don Joaquín Heredia, drew up the necessary plans.[4] This project also fell through, and when the Academy was reorganized in 1842, it was still renting the same old building. Through the efforts of its new directors this building was purchased, and it was later enlarged by adding the three adjoining houses. And there, with various remodellings which have brought it to its present form, the worthy Academy has remained, only changing its name from time to time.

The First Professors

As we have said, Don José Antonio Gil, who dominated all the activities of the Academy, at first had to resort to employing some of the old colonial craftsmen. These were José de Alcíbar, Francisco Clapera, Santiago Sandoval, Gutiérrez, López, Sáenz, Vásquez, Serna, and García. But this did not solve the problem. These men were not adequate for their new role because of their old-fashioned attitude, nor, by the same token, could the Academy appreciate their efforts and the work they accomplished. The Academy urgently needed academic teachers, who would have to come from Spain. And that was what happened.

In answer to the Academy's request, by a royal decree dated April 12, 1786, nine professors, or special directors, as they were called, arrived in Mexico. Don

[4] These plans can be seen in the library of the Academia, now known as the Escuela Nacional de Artes Plasticas.

Ginés Andrés de Aguirre was director of painting, and Don Cosme de Acuña, assistant director. Don José Arias was named director of sculpture, and Don Antonio González Velásquez, director of architecture. Don Jerónimo Antonio Gil continued in charge of die casting, retaining also his position as director general. For engraving, Don Fernando Selma was appointed, but as he did not accept the position, a royal order of November 21, 1787, appointed Don José Joaquín Fabregat.

The divisions of painting and sculpture had bad luck. The men appointed were in fact mediocrities. Poor health, and conflicts with the sometimes exaggeratedly energetic Gil—who had in any case preferred other candidates—made a mess of things. Acuña did not want to stay in Mexico, Arias lost his mind and then his life, while Aguirre, for better or worse, kept on working until he died, we don't know when. But this bad luck was to work for the best: the arrival as directors of sculpture and painting, respectively, of Don Manuel Tolsá and Don Rafael Jimeno y Planes. The Academy had been saved.

In the following chapters we shall study these personalities, and what we know of their lives and their art. The Academy reached its highest point while Mexico was still a colony. We have a valuable work of art which is a kind of cooperative expression of the staff, the engraving showing *The Plaza Mayor of Mexico* in 1796 (359). There we have the great plan: the architectonic concept is the work of González Velásquez; the statue of Charles IV, installed several years later, was to be the masterpiece of Tolsá; the drawing was made by Jimeno; and the engraving was done by Fabregat. Gil, no doubt, made trouble.

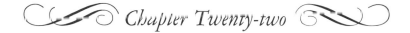

Chapter Twenty-two

NEOCLASSIC ARCHITECTURE
IN NEW SPAIN

The New Ideas

THE CONTRAST between Churrigueresque architecture and the Academic or Neoclassic style is so violent that it seems like the art of two different worlds. The Baroque, in all its forms, had satisfied the needs of the country. It had left that astonishing series of religious monuments and palaces, houses and colleges in which today we take pride as the legacy of the artistic geniuses of Spain and Indian Mexico. Now, however, that art began to suffer the consequences of criticism founded on the Academic principles.

The Neoclassic period of the Colony covers only forty years, eleven of them taken up with the War of Independence, which impoverished the country. Because of the briefness of the period and its poverty, Neoclassic monuments are much less numerous than Baroque. Today the historical sequence seems natural and logical. Released from the iconoclastic fury of the Academic attitude, we can appreciate both phenomena as powerful expressions in art of their different social epochs. But if the Colony had been able to continue at the economic level it enjoyed under the second Viceroy Revillagigedo, many of the buildings which now enchant us as the very embodiment of the Mexican spirit, would have been replaced by Neoclassic monuments.

Certain statements have been preserved which express the academicians' opinions of Baroque architecture, and at the same time show the methods they devised for controlling the Baroque architects. The most important device was to admit to the Academy, as *académicos de mérito,* all the architects approved by the Ayuntamiento, "with the absolute condition that before beginning any work, whether church, convent, or other considerable building, they must present the plans directly to our Junta Superior de Gobierno, and submit, without objection or excuse whatsoever, to the corrections made in them, and with the warning that, in case of disobedience, they will be severely disciplined."[1]

Thus, sweetening the pill and the discipline beforehand, they hoped to prevent a city "deformed," as they felt so many of the old buildings to be. The following opinion was written in 1795:

[1] Abelardo Carrillo y Gariel, *Datos sobre la Academia de San Carlos,* p. 35.

The architects' unwillingness to subject themselves to the rules of their art is the cause of the deformity which one sees in the public buildings of this city. Some houses rise to a height which the notorious instability of the terrain makes unwise, at the imminent risk of collapse. In all of them there is a disregard of that selectivity and taste in façade decoration which determines the elegance and exterior beauty of a building. In many of them one perceives with horror a confused and disagreeable mixing of the Three Orders; doors and windows are placed arbitrarily, without balance or symmetry; the stairways are as perilous as they are unsightly; and the interior plan offers none of that ease and convenience which was the precise object of its invention.

Finally, one can hardly find a single building in which the different members which should compose it can be distinguished clearly, and in none of them does one note the least sense of proportion, of that relationship of the whole with the parts, and of the part to the whole, which constitutes the elegance of a good design. The root of these defects is that the architects are accustomed to begin building before putting their ideas together on paper, because they are generally ignorant of rendering and mechanical drawing. Precisely from this lack of composition there results the general monstrosity of the constructions which disfigure the streets of this fair capital and are a matter of ridicule in the eyes of every intelligent man, for all they have cost their owners large sums of money.[2]

The gruff, bad-tempered Costansó, who emerges as a figure of the first importance in this period, quarrelled with everyone, even poor González Velásquez. He attacked Castera, who was *maestro mayor* of the city—director of public works—with unremitting jealousy. Castera, a very energetic man, had made himself the favorite architect of Viceroy Revillagigedo, working on such improvements to the city as pavements, drains, and fountains, even overriding the authority of the Ayuntamiento. Describing a house which Castera was building, Costansó writes in this way in 1788:

The termination of the portes-cocheres makes a very good impression, and propriety ought to be maintained in designing the doors and windows of the wings, avoiding the multiplicity of superposed projections. Employed economically, these are eloquent, but in exaggerated number they botch up the whole effect, and for this reason those over the windows should be suppressed. It will be desirable as

well to suppress the niche at the top. Images of the saints are very little venerated in the streets and their proper place is in the church. A coat of arms or some allusive trophies are more appropriate, and make a finer finial.[3]

Obviously what is criticized here is not Castera's ability, but Baroque architecture.

Costansó's second angry charge is that Castera did not know how to draw, and had engaged a student of the Academy, José Reyes, who had abandoned his career for the good pay. Costansó himself was an admirable draughtsman. I have seen his fine drawings for a convent of Santa Teresa in San Miguel el Grande, which have the further interest that the church much resembles that of the Loreto in Mexico City, which is, in fact, attributed to Castera. Costansó asserted that all the architects should attend the Academy to learn to draw. Even a *maestro mayor* of the city of Mexico, favorite of the viceroy, whose accounts were paid on his signature alone, and under whose orders the most noted architects of his time worked, should go and learn draughting like a schoolboy! Actually, in hiring a draughtsman Castera was ahead of his day, and had moved up almost into our own time. Anyhow, did the architects of the great monuments of the eighteenth century know draughting? Lorenzo Rodríguez, Guerrero y Torres, the designer of Tepotzotlán, were they able draughtsmen? No, they were not. Their spirit conceived the creation, and the "drawing" was revealed in the stone itself. If one considers seriously and without prejudice, this is indeed the specific criticism that can be brought against Neoclassic architecture—besides its having destroyed incomparable Baroque buildings—too much drawing and too little spirit. The Academic rules, making everything dependent on "composition" and subjecting this to fixed canons, were able to produce adequate and correct works, but not works of genius. They had clipped the wings of the imagination on a drawing board.[4]

The period, like all periods of crisis, was saved by its few great personalities: genius has its way, however oppressively it is chained. In architecture these outstanding figures are: in Mexico City—José Damián Ortiz de Castro, Manuel Tolsá, and Miguel Costansó; in the whole region of the Bajío—Francisco Eduardo Tresguerras; and in Puebla—the less gifted José Manzo.

There is also a group of craftsmen of secondary importance, who are still significant for the Neoclassic

[2] *Ibid.*, pp. 33–34.
[3] *Ibid.*, p. 36.
[4] See Diego Angulo Íñiguez, *La arquitectura neoclásica en Méjico.*

movement. From all of these, the architects of high quality and the others, we have formed our catalogue of the monuments of the period. They are not, as we have already remarked, so abundant, or so distinguished as the Baroque monuments. And even in this smaller group, we are troubled by the same old problems of sound attribution, of identifying the designers of well-known buildings.

Neoclassic Architects

First we shall consider the documented work of the architects of the period; then we can take up the buildings whose designers are not known.

Don Miguel Costansó, *ingeniero*

He was born in Barcelona in 1741, and after working in Catalonia and the coast of Granada, first as a draughtsman and later as an engineer, he reached New Spain with the expedition of Lieutenant General Don Juan de Villalba, in 1764. He continued his military as well as scientific career; in 1808, when he offered his services to the viceroy on the occasion of Iturrigaray's dismissal, he had the rank of brigadier general.[5]

His most important work seems to have been in cartography; we have the following data on this subject. When he first came to Mexico, he worked under the orders of Don Antonio Ricardos on the map of the Gulf of Mexico. In 1767 he moved inland. In 1768 he drew a map of the bay of La Paz and Puerto Cortés with Don José de Urrutia,[6] and in the same year one of the bay of San Bernabé.[7] The following year he was a member of the expedition of Portolá (1769–1770) up the Pacific coast to survey and found the ports of San Francisco, San Diego, and Monterey in California, and brought back an interesting diary.[8] A result of this journey was the *Carta del Mar del Sur* (*Map of the Pacific Ocean*), dated in Mexico October 31, 1770. A *Carta de Gran Parte de la Nueva España* is mentioned in 1777, and another of the same subject two years later. The last appearance of his name in reference to map making is in 1800, when he approved the map of Veracruz drawn by his pupil and collaborator, Manuel Mascaró. The history of geography in Mexico is much in debt to this man.

His ability made it almost certain that the need for able architects would bring him to civil architecture. His first work seems to have been an enlargement of the Casa de Moneda (the Mint) in Mexico City, which he planned in 1772 and carried out between that year

and 1780. I suppose that the façade on Correo Mayor is his work, and represents this enlargement. It is decorated with those "allusive trophies" of which he speaks in criticizing Castera.[9] In 1779 he designed the gunpowder factory of Santa Fe, which he built in two years and a half. The rebuilding of a similar factory at Chapultepec, destroyed by a fire in 1784, was also his work.[10]

The cigar factory of Mexico City is said to have been designed by the director of architecture of the Academy, Don José Antonio González Velásquez, and built by Costansó, who finished it in 1807. It still exists, now known as "La Ciudadela," "the Citadel." In fact its plan is more that of a fortress than a factory, and its strategic situation at the gate of the city, dominating one of the principal approaches, has resulted in its being taken over for military purposes and even becoming the focus of riots and revolutions throughout our history. Its architectural quality may be seen in the elegant design of its portals.

The most important work of Costansó in the field of architecture was the main cloister of the convent of La Encarnación, finished at the end of the eighteenth century. It is an enormous enclosure, its lower floor rusticated and the upper one sober in design. After the thousand changes it has undergone, it forms today the *patio de honor* of the Secretaría de Educación Pública, where one can admire some of the best murals of Diego Rivera.

An unrealized project of Costansó's was the Botanical Garden of which Angulo gives a detailed account in his interesting *Estudio*. The plan was drawn in 1788, and discussions continued in the following years, but nothing was accomplished, not even a decision as to the site. There are interesting references to the house of

[5] *Gazeta*, octubre 1, 1808.

[6] Pedro Torres Lanzas, *Relación descriptiva de los mapas, planos et c. de México y Florida existentes en el Archivo General de Indias*, I, No. 245.

[7] *Ibid.*, I, No. 246.

[8] Miguel Costansó, *Diario histórico de los viages de mar, y tierra hechos al norte de la California*.

[9] See also these articles by Heinrich Berlin: "Three Master Architects in New Spain," *Hispanic American Historical Review*, 27 (1947), 375–383; "El arquitecto Pedro de Arrieta," *Boletín del Archivo General de la Nación*, 16 (1945), 73–94; "El arquitecto Joseph Eduardo de Herrera," *Anales del Instituto de Arte Americano e Investigaciones Estéticas*, 17 (1964), 90–98; "El ingeniero Luis Díez de Navarro en México," *Anales de la Sociedad de Geografía e Historia de Guatemala*, 22 (1947), 89–95.

[10] Angulo Iñiguez, *Planos de monumentos arquitectónicos de América y Filipinas*, I, 358–361.

360. José Damián Ortiz de Castro. Commemorative monument.
Stone. Church of San Hipólito, Mexico City.

Castera, an architect, which we shall use in discussing his work.

Thus one can sketch in Costansó's *oeuvre,* subject to corrections and additions. Considering his personality and his importance, it calls for a special monograph.

Don Manuel Mascaró, *ingeniero*

This fellow countryman of Costansó's seems to have been intimately connected with him, first as his pupil and finally as associate. Mascaró figures as a cartographer, and we can assign to him various additions to the map of New Spain drawn by Costansó in 1777. In 1791 he laid out part of the road from Mexico City to Toluca, and in 1800 he drew the plan for the expansion of Veracruz, which we have mentioned as approved by Costansó. He must have been engaged in architecture to some extent, since there is a record of his working on the Castle of Chapultepec from 1785 to 1787.[11]

Don José Damián Ortiz de Castro, *arquitecto*

A shooting star in our artistic history, without doubt the most eminent Mexican architect of his time. He was born in Jalapa (or in Coatepec nearby) on September 28, 1750, and died in Tacubaya on May 6, 1793, at just forty-three years of age. He was buried in the parish church there; whether his remains were later removed to the Cathedral, "to the tomb of cut stone which the Illustrious and Venerable Cabildo in token of their esteem dedicated to him in the Capilla de los Santos Ángeles below the new tower," is not known.[12]

Little architecture by Castro is known. We know that he had a part, like practically all the architects of his time, in the rebuilding of the city undertaken by Revillagigedo. In 1790 he supervised the paving of the Plaza Mayor; in 1793 he contracted to build the fountains at its corners; he made a drawing of the conduits, sidewalks, and drains which the viceroy sent to Spain. For his admission to the Academy he presented in 1787 a project for the rebuilding of the old church of Tulancingo.[13]

As for other activities, we can cite his opinion, with Castera, on the Cuartel de los Gallos.[14] In 1785 he mapped the piece of land called "Nipaltongo," which the Academy had bought for its building, and which was later sold to the Tribunal de Minería for the School of Mines which Tolsá built. In 1787 he appeared in a lawsuit concerning the customs house at Campeche.[15] It was he, according to Costansó, who introduced the proper use of plaster in architecture. But in none of these activities do we see the artist; for that we must look to the graceful commemorative monument at the corner of the wall around the atrium of the church of San Hipólito in Mexico City (360).[16]

His most important work, however, an achievement which would immortalize any architect, was the completing of the towers and façade of the Cathedral of Mexico (163). The appearance of the church was deplorable. Only the first story of the east tower had been built, there were three portals in the façade which dated from the seventeenth century but had never been finished, and there was only the base of the west tower, in quite bad condition. The Cabildo of the Cathedral announced a competition to complete the façade. We know of only three entries: that of Don José Damián Ortiz de Castro, which was chosen, that of Don José Joaquín de Torres, and that of Isidro Vicente de Balbás, which seems to have arrived late, since it is in the archives of the Academy while the others are in the Cathedral. Since the members of the Academy played some role in the contest, it was very likely they who awarded the prize to Ortiz' project, the only one in a Neoclassic style. The other two are wildly Baroque, especially that of Balbás, which in its general design somewhat recalls the famous façade of the Obradoiro of the Cathedral of Santiago de Compostela, the Bible of Spanish Churrigueresque. A disorganized design, poorly proportioned in many respects, it was most fortunate that it was not adopted.

When Ortiz' project had been chosen, the next step was the estimate, made in 1787 by "Don Joseph Ortiz, director of this project, *maestro mayor de la Santa Iglesia de la Nobilisima Ciudad y académico de mérito de la Real Academia de San Carlos,* and by Don Ignacio Castera, *maestro mayor y veedor de esta N.C. y Real Desague,* and Don Joseph Delgadillo, architect, who has a major responsibility in the Cathedral works."[17]

---

[11] *Ibid.,* I, 315.

[12] A document in the Archivo de la Catedral de México. "Cuentas de la fachada y torres."

[13] Carrillo y Gariel, *Datos sobre la Academia,* p. 31.

[14] Angulo Íñiguez, *Planos,* I, 383.

[15] *Ibid.,* I, 349.

[16] I have seen the document which affirms that this monument is by Ortiz. Unhappily I have lost the reference to identify it.

[17] The data we give here come from the summary of this estimate and the description of work done by Juan José de Gamboa, signed in Mexico City on October 29, 1796. This is kept in the Cathedral archives. The quotations also are from this document.

361. Cupola of the Cathedral of Mexico.

The estimate includes: one tower base of *chiluca* stone and cut stone; two second stories of the same stones, and two tops for the towers. To remove the top of the façade, taking down the stone to rework it, and to replace it; also seven statues. The cost of the whole thing was set at 133,748 pesos, 5 *reales, 4 granos.* Since not all of the work was done—the statues, for instance, and the bolts for the bells—there was a saving of more than 11,000 pesos.

In the estimate were included simple iron crosses for the tops of the towers. The motif was retained, but not the material, partly for fear of lightning at that height, partly in favor of the more impressive and harmonious aspect of stone crosses on globes of stone, an admirable project of distinguished architecture, especially the rings four *pulgadas* thick on which rests the unbelievable weight of the globes, which are two *varas* in diameter, and the crosses, which measure two and a half *varas,* by one-half *vara,* and one-third *vara* in each arm. These have neither bore nor bolts of iron, but from the center of the globes a spike, fifteen or sixteen *varas* long goes down to the crossing of diagonal cedar beams in the interior of the towers, where the top of the tower begins.

We have called it a distinguished architectural project, but one should add, an alarming project, which aroused the secret activity of a committee, whose misgivings, however, were in the end allayed. The commissioners, whose individual duty it was to avoid risks, were satisfied when they proceeded to put these crosses and globes in place that they would not be a danger in winds or earthquakes, which has proved true. This achievement is due to the ingenuity and architectural inspiration of the director of the work, Don José Damián Ortiz, who deserves the greatest praise for his faithful concern and integrity, and for his outstanding and distinguished knowledge in his noble profession. The Real Academia de San Carlos recognized this and bestowed on him the title of *académico de mérito* even before he was given the commission for this work.

Sedano, in the interesting book in which he collects *Noticias de México,* reports the dates when the towers were finished: the west tower on April 18, 1791, and the other on May 13 of the same year. He adds that

Inside each globe, in a case of wood lined with lead, was placed *Lignum Crucis* (Wood of the True Cross), relics, commemorative coins of Charles IV, with devout prayers and testimony authorized by the secretary to the Cabildo of the Holy Church as a record for the future.[18]

Disregarding all the stylistic implications of this enormous construction—begun laboriously in the sixteenth century, finished in respect to its interior and its portals in the seventeenth century, and ornamented with the profusion and frenzy of the eighteenth century—Ortiz de Castro found the only possible solution. As a man of his own time, without archeological feeling, he made an original design which took care of topping the towers and finishing the façade discreetly with statues. Just as styles are superimposed in the old Euro-

[18] Francisco Sedano, *Noticias de México.*

410

362. Façade, College of Mines, Mexico City.

pean cathedrals until some of them seem like hand-books of architecture, ours combines all the styles of architecture which flourished during the colonial period. The secret of Ortiz' success lies in the harmony and proportion of his design. The towers may appear a little heavy, but from the area of their bases and the width of the church there is no reason to believe that the towers of Agüero's original plan (which we do not have) would have been lighter. To achieve a certain effect of lightness, Ortiz opened up the second story. The unusual bell-shaped tops, which seem to be of heavy stone, are in fact of thin *tezontle* covered by a veneer of cut stone bound with hoops of iron. Only by this means have they been able to withstand the earthquakes of a century and a half.[19]

Don Manuel Tolsá

After Ortiz, the Valencian Manuel Tolsá took over the completion of the Cathedral (381). He was not an architect, but, as we have seen, a sculptor who came to Mexico as director of sculpture for the Academy. As a sculptor, he will be considered in the relevant chapter; only his architectural work is under consideration here. Certainly the factors we have often described functioned to turn Tolsá to architecture: the lack of trained men and the abundance of work to be done. An educated man of excellent taste, he was quite capable, in a

country where anyone could be an architect, of being one himself. He was admitted to the architectural division of the Academy, and has left a handful of constructions in New Spain.

First among these works we must put the completion of the Cathedral, which was suspended at the death of Ortiz de Castro. After that unhappy event his brother, Francisco Ortiz, continued directing the work, but apparently he did not have José's ability, for he soon disappeared. To Tolsá we owe the cupola, the top of the façade with its clock and statues, and the ornamenting of the towers—whose upper stories seemed too bare—with large stone figures.

The cupola was a heavy seventeenth-century dome, with a large drum and appropriate lantern. To Tolsá it seemed low and out of scale with the towers. So, perhaps making use of the old construction, he covered it

[19] We can neither affirm nor deny that Ortiz was familiar with the towers of the cathedral of Pamplona, finished in 1783, and the way they are topped. The dates of the competition to finish the façade of the Cathedral of Mexico are just about contemporary with the work at Pamplona. The top of the Pamplona towers seems normal, also, except for being bell-shaped, while that of the towers in Mexico City is extraordinarily emphasized. There are repercussions from these towers in several cities of New Spain, and even as far away as Quito in Ecuador, where their influence can be seen in the tower of the church of San Agustín. On Ortiz de Castro's work for the Cathedral, see also Berlin, *Artífices*, pp. 37–38.

411

363. Side door, main façade, College of Mines, Mexico City.

of the design appeared too small for the façade, which is to say that Ortiz had not succeeded so well as with the towers. Tolsá began by raising the middle of the façade, to echo the rising of the nave above the aisles inside; this was topped by a curved member which supported a cube holding the clock and the group of the Theological Virtues. Instead of the four Evangelists on the façade, sixteen large statues were put at the corners of the towers, which had seemed too bare and cold. Tolsá himself executed the center group, Zacharías Coro and the Sandovals did the figures for the towers. We shall give further details in the chapter on sculpture.

So Tolsá, with an eye for correlating detail, undeniably good taste, and that sense of proportion, of scale, without which good architecture cannot exist, succeeded in unifying and ennobling the exterior of the church. The competition of the different styles gives it vitality, and it is in itself a symbol of all the architecture of the Viceroyalty, completed just as the War of Independence began. It is as though the mother country, in granting political autonomy, bequeathed to us in our great cathedral her whole spirit embodied in architecture.

Tolsá's second great architectural work (probably the first that was entirely his own) is the great palace of the Colegio de Minería—the College of Mines—a building in which we can still take pride in this much abused city (362).

The history of the building can be outlined briefly.[20] The Real Tribunal de la Minería, established in 1777, wanted to build a School of Mines, since their situation on the Calle del Hospicio de San Nicolás was in every way inadequate. On October 22, 1792, they determined to buy from the Academy the land called "Nipaltongo," and this was effected for the sum of 30,000 pesos on May 14, 1793. They seem to have considered having Costansó build it, but on May 17, 1797, Don Manuel Tolsá presented his plans, which were approved on the twenty-seventh of July following. He was named director of the work, with an annual salary of 1,000 pesos. The building was begun soon after, and in 1811, after the Ministros del Tribunal had inspected it, they gave orders that some of the rooms should be equipped for lectures, so that they could stop paying rent, and

with stone and enlarged the ring of the lantern, giving it an elegant curve (361). The lantern itself he replaced with one perhaps too high for the dome, but in scale with the height of the towers and the mass of the church.

Then he resolved the problem of the façade (153). Ortiz had planned a slightly curved rise in the center, which would be crowned by statues of the Theological Virtues, with statues of the Evangelists on the horizontal sections over the doors. As a matter of fact this part

[20] See Santiago Ramírez, *Datos para la historia del Colegio de Minería*; Manuel F. Álvarez, *El Palacio de Minería*; Justino Fernández, *El Palacio de Minería*.

364. Stairway and patios, College of Mines, Mexico City.

that dependencies should be constructed for leasing. On April 13, 1813, the work was completed, at a cost of 1,596,435 pesos. Apparently they had money to burn.

Eleven years later, in 1824, the building was threatened with destruction because of the excessive weight of the dome over the stairs. The architects Paz and Heredia presented an estimate of 400,000 pesos to save it. This was too great an expense for the now independent Mexican government, and nothing was done. In 1830, however, the French architect Antoine Villard offered to restore it for only 97,435 pesos, and was given the commission. So this monument of art was saved for the time being. It continues to be endangered by the uneven settling, which has also altered its proportions.

The Palacio de Minería is a monument in the style of Louis XVI; everything about it is symmetrical and ordered, portals and balconies alike (363). Its patio and stairway are the most beautiful, the most sumptu-

ous in Mexico (364). This was the setting for the most elegant balls of the nineteenth century, and "elegant" is indeed in my opinion the adjective to describe it. This building would be at home in any French city. Nonetheless, visiting it from time to time, and listening to the comments of foreigners who accompany me, I cannot help feeling how pedantic, cold, and devoid of feeling it really is, in comparison not only with our great Baroque buildings, but with many a modest village church. After all, the Baroque and its popular interpretations came from Spain, from that dramatic and brutal Spain that gave us being, while these preciosities of periwig and brocade coat, pretending to flatter our poor vanity, only humiliate us. In any case, the Palacio de Minería is a great monument.

There are some residences in Mexico City which are Tolsá's work, or attributed to him. One is the palace of the Marqués del Apartado, today the Secretaría de la Economía Nacional, an imposing building with a large patio. The house of Pérez Gálvez o Pinillos on the old

413

365. House of Pérez Gálvez, Mexico City.

Puente de Alvarado is a fine residence whose façade with its bowed-in half ellipse is most original, and whose gardens were indeed magnificent (365). When it was given by Maximilian as a wedding present to Marshal Bazaine, he must have found it most congenial. The house of Tolsá himself is on the same street, and he undoubtedly built others which we do not know about. He also made the plans for the bull ring, working with another architect, Mazo.[21]

Concerning other architectural activities of Tolsá's we have the following data. In 1797 he drew the plans for the convent of Santa Teresa in Querétaro.[22] It is said that this building was built later, between 1803 and 1807, by Tresguerras, though this is not documented, and we cannot be sure whether he used Tolsá's plans if indeed he did build it. In 1802 Tolsá drew the plan for the house of the Propaganda Fide in Orizaba; in December of that year building was begun under

the direction of José María Manzano.[23] In 1809 he planned a large college for missionaries in Mexico City, but it was never built. In the capital also he built a Casa de Ejercicios for the Congregation of San Felipe Neri, near the church of La Profesa. According to a document which we saw at the Dirección de Monumentos Coloniales, the splendid Hospicio—the Orphanage—in Guadalajara was built after his plans (366). Its central dome, raised on columns, is most original; in recent years it has been decorated with fine frescoes by José Clemente Orozco.

For the Cathedral of Puebla Tolsá designed the magnificent high altar, which is still there to be admired. He

21 Nicolás Rangel, *Historia del toreo en México; época colonial, 1529–1821,* p. 242.
22 Angulo Íñiguez, *Planos,* I, 226.
23 *Ibid.,* I, 243.

414

366. Hospicio Cabañas, Guadalajara, Jalisco.

first made a drawing, and then a model; the altar was begun on September 1, 1797, while Biempica was bishop, and finished and dedicated on December 8, 1818 under Pérez Martínez. The artists who cooperated in this masterpiece were: Tolsá, who designed and directed the work and made a wood figure of *La Purísima* to be cast in bronze; Don Simón Salmón, a Mexican, who gilded it; Patiño Ixtolinque, Zacarías Cora, and Legaspi, who worked on the other sculpture; Pedro Pablo Lezama, the marblework and masonry; Don José Ramírez, the stuccowork; Don Manuel Caamaño, the bronzes and silver; Don Joaquín Inocencio, the carving; and Don Mariano Vargas, who constructed the mechanism for opening the doors of the tabernacle. The work was completed under the supervision of Don José Manzo y Jaramillo.[24] Manuel Francisco Álvarez, the engineer, says that Tolsá was inspired by one of the altars of the Gesù in Rome.[25] This altar has been criticized as exaggerated in size; Tolsá himself suffers most

24 "La catedral de Puebla," in *Noticias curiosas.*
25 On Tolsá, see especially the monograph of Alfredo Escontría, *Breve estudio de la obra y personalidad del escultor y arquitecto Don Manuel Tolsá.*

from this, since the only work of his hand, the statue of the *Purísima,* is practically invisible. Tolsá was not an original artist, but he was endowed with good taste and a sense of form which in spite of all saved him. The richness of this tabernacle, the amplitude of conception, the excellence of the sculpture and the fine detail of the ornament are valuable in themselves. Other altars by Tolsá will be discussed in considering his sculpture.

Don José Antonio González Velásquez

He came to the Academy as director of architecture in 1783, as we have said. He filled the post until his death in 1810. He was no genius, and he left little work. The massive church of San Pablo el Nuevo, finished in 1803, is the only one extant. His chapel for the crucifix called El Señor de Santa Teresa, whose cornerstone was laid on December 17, 1798, and which was inaugurated on May 13, 1813, when its designer was already dead, was almost totally destroyed in the earthquake of April 7, 1845. He drew up three projects for the school which the Academy hoped to build on its land called "Nipaltongo," but none of them was used. The cigar factory later known as La Ciudadela was also projected by González, but we owe its execution to Costansó, who, as we have seen, completed it in 1807. He drew plans for a college of the Propaganda Fide for Orizaba between 1795 and 1797, but it was not built; later Tolsá designed and built this college, as we have seen. His most vigorous and tasteful work was certainly the redesigning of the Plaza Mayor of Mexico City, as a setting for the equestrian statue of Charles IV in 1796 (359). A great esplanade, slightly elliptical, was formed by a high balustrade, with four high crested gates at the axes. In the center on a graceful pedestal stood the monument, and outside the balustrade in the corners, the fountains built by Don José del Mazo. Laid out in this way, the Plaza Mayor, with the imposing Cathedral beyond, the Palace of the Viceroys at one side, and that of the Cabildo on the other, was one of the most beautiful squares in the world. It was razed in 1822 for a bullfight to celebrate the coronation of Iturbide. The statue was stuck away in the patio of the University, and the Plaza reverted to an empty field, as it had been before Revillagigedo's time, and as it is now. The balustrade was later used for benches in the Alameda. Another achievement of Velásquez' was the destruction of the Churrigueresque portal of the University, substituting one "of the composite Ionic order." This was done for the literary assembly celebrated on December 28, 1790.[26]

For the funeral ceremonies of Charles III in 1789, he built the customary catafalque, and an engraving of it was made by Tomás Suría under Gil's direction. Likewise the monument for the proclaiming of Charles IV as King was built by González and engraved by Suría in 1790. Finally, he presented, with Don Ignacio Castera, an estimate for the repairs necessary in the college of San Ignacio, called Las Vizcaínas, after the earthquake of March 7, 1800. He must have been involved also in other building of which we are at present ignorant.

Don Ignacio Castera

He was one of the most discussed personalities of his time. Whether they admired him or envied him, everyone talked about him. His name is intimately linked with the second Viceroy Revillagigedo, whose right-hand man he seems to have been in the work of transforming the colonial capital. In the official report on the Viceroy's term of office we find Castera's name

at every step.[27] He was criticized for everything, even for cutting through the street named Revillagigedo: they charged that he wanted to give his own property access to the Alameda. That is obvious; but the street was useful, and has been retained, name and all. As for the allegation that Castera was not an architect but simply a colonial craftsman, this too is doubtful. Traces of his house have survived, and a description of it by Costansó himself shows it to have been indeed a mansion. As Angulo says:

In these drawings Castera gives us a handsome house in Neoclassical style, none other than the house he built for himself. Indeed it has quite the air of a small palace. Classical taste rules in every detail: in its sober façade with the typical urns against the sky, and its garland on a chaste panel, in the first patio with its entablature on Doric columns and more garlands, fasces, and rectangular panels on the inner walls.[28]

The ground area of the house, according to Don José del Mazo y Avilés, who appraised it in 1789, was 18,166 square *varas,* no less. It filled the whole area between the Calle de Revillagigedo and the Paseo de Bucareli. Though not completed, the house had everything one could wish for, from a billiard room to a pool faced with stone and tiles. This architect knew how to enjoy life. In this house, at the outbreak of the War of Independence, Castera buried his treasure, pots full of shining gold doubloons. It was found some years ago by the workmen who were demolishing part of the building to extend the Avenida de la Independencia.

Castera was involved in all sorts of projects. We see him designing fountains,[29] drawing up reports about the old church at Tláhuac, about the pavements of Mexico City, the barracks known as Los Gallos, the cockfighting ring, and an infinity of matters which were his responsibility, important as he was at the time. As an example of elegant decoration, we might note the façade which Castera designed for the ceremony to celebrate Charles IV's taking the oath of office on December 27, 1789. We have a delightful engraving of this façade, which was superimposed on the Ayunta-

[26] *Obras de eloqüencia y poesía,* xviii–xix.

[27] This has been published by the Archivo General de la Nación.

[28] Angulo Íñiguez, *Planos,* I, 360.

[29] Manuel Carrera Stampa, "Fuentes o pilas 'económicas' del México colonial," *Anales del Instituto de Investigaciones Estéticas,* 8 (1942), 61–75.

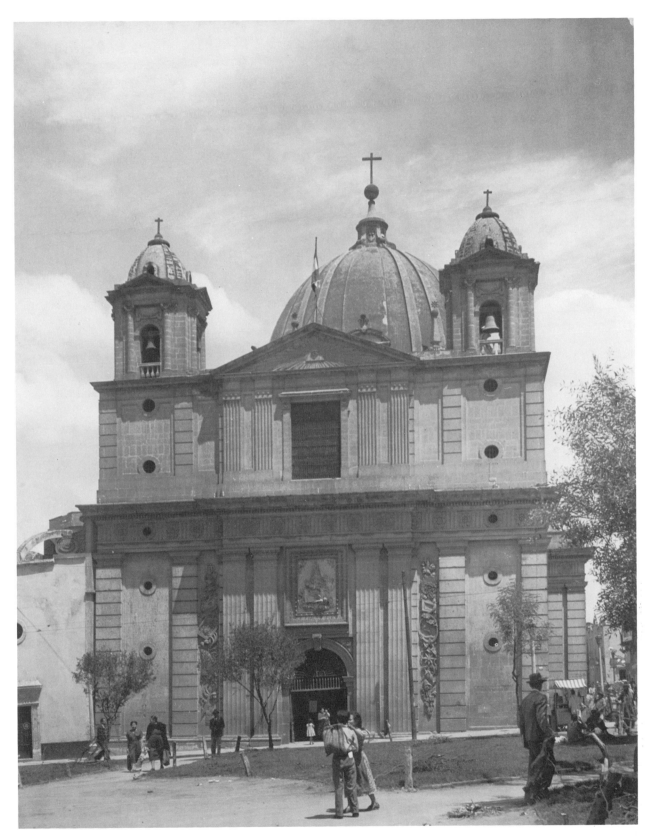

367. Façade, church of Loreto, Mexico City.

368. Interior, church of Loreto, Mexico City.

miento. Its legend reads: "Don Ignacio Castera designed it; J. de Reies drew it—Don Joaquín Fabregat, director of the Real Academia de San Carlos of Mexico engraved it." (Fabregat was in fact not director general of the Academy, but simply director of engraving.) The façade is in two stories, the lower formed by an arch adorned with garlands, and the upper a rhythmic line of coupled columns between which stand statues of the kings of Spain, from Ferdinand V through Charles IV. Above this there are trophies over each pair of columns, and in the center a higher part with a triangular pediment, which has a genealogical tree of the Spanish royal family below, and above, two portraits and a medallion with a bust of the King, and in the triangle more trophies with the royal arms. The whole thing is crowned by Apollo's chariot drawn by four horses and stirring up a cloud of dust. The cor-

[30] See Francisco de la Maza, "El urbanismo neoclásico de Ignacio de Castera," *Anales del Instituto de Investigaciones Estéticas,* 22 (1954), 93–101.

rectness of proportion and the elegance of the detail are clear. Castera deserves a monograph, for the vigor of his personality almost more than for his art; it should deal with the artistic life in the time of Viceroy Revillagigedo.[30]

One of the finest churches in Mexico City, the Loreto, has been attributed to Castera (367). Tradition and reputation have given it to Tolsá, but a document signed by the son of the nobleman who paid for its building, the Conde de Bassoco, has clarified matters. In the beginning they went to Tolsá, and he presented the plan of a rotunda, which they did not accept. Then they approved the plan of the architects Ignacio Castera and José Agustín Paz, and according to this the church was built. The cornerstone was laid in 1809, and the church was consecrated on August 29, 1816. At his death, before the completion of the building, the patron had already spent 217,194 pesos, and his widow continued to subsidize it, to the sum of 300,000 pesos.

The architects did not know how to estimate the

character of the ground, and they built the east side of heavy cut stone, while the west was of *tezontle*. Inevitably, the church sank toward the heavier side; but astonishingly enough, the bonding was so perfect that there is not the slightest sign of collapse. So it stands, leaning like the Tower of Pisa, and will continue to stand for many years—at least we hope so.

The church of Loreto is so different from our Baroque buildings, so daring in its scope, that we cannot but recognize it as something exceptional. It is unique in its period, because, for all its basic conformity to the Academic principles, it clearly expresses a strong personality. We can find antecedents among the domes of classical architecture, from the Pantheon through the great French examples—but how ample, how noble, how artistic is the space one feels below this immense dome! The gods of harmony and proportion consort in this place (368). The effect of the exterior is also commanding: the very sober portal, the modest bell towers dwarfed by the great dome, which can be seen from anywhere in the city. At the outside corners of the transepts there are blind façades, monuments of proportion and taste. The painted decoration which covers the interior of this noble temple is in the highest degree unworthy of the architecture.

Don José Gutiérrez

He came from Spain on a scholarship to the Academy, where he studied with Costansó and González Velásquez. In 1792 he was allotted by the governing board a stipend of four hundred pesos a year in place of his scholarship, and in a meeting of May 3, 1794, he was declared *académico de mérito,* having submitted a project for a royal palace and two chapels. He collaborated with Costansó on the Ciudadela in 1795. By 1794 he was substituting in the department of architecture for González, who was ill, and he continued to serve without pay until 1799, when he was given an annual salary of seven hundred pesos. He gave up the position in 1804 when, at Tolsá's suggestion, he went to Guadalajara to build the Casa de Misericordia and the Sagrario of the Cathedral.[31] We have records of other work by him: in 1795 he drew plans, as we have noted, for the college of the Propaganda Fide in Orizaba; in 1818 he submitted plans for a convent of Santa Teresa which was to be built in Valladolid, though I do not know whether it ever was. His talent can be appreciated in the fine cupola of the Sagrario in Guadalajara: elegant in proportions and refined in or-

nament, it is not unworthy of comparison to the work of his masters.

Don José del Mazo y Avilés

He passed his examinations as *maestro de arquitectura* in 1784, and continued to follow the profession in Mexico after the War of Independence. In 1791 he took part, with other important architects of his time, in the construction of a conduit along the Calle de los Mesones, from the Calle de San Juan to the Puente Blanquillo. I presume this was a matter of piping the drain which ran through this district. For the Plaza Mayor of Mexico City he made the corner fountains, as we have seen. In 1803 he presented a plan for a college for Indian girls which was to be built in the Santuario de los Ángeles. He appears as late as 1826, making a new Fuente de la Aguilita for the Plaza de Santo Domingo, to replace the one Castera had made in 1793.[32]

Don Joaquín Heredia

He appears as *académico de mérito* in architecture at least as early as 1803, and many years before as an additional *maestro mayor* acting with Mazo and Castera, the official *maestros mayores* of Mexico City. Later he took over Castera's position, and the supernumerary was J. M. Echeandía; then in 1820 Echeandía and Paz held the official positions. In 1831 he described himself as "the chief citizen Joaquín Heredia, the most venerable architect of this federal city, *académico de mérito* and director of architecture in the Academia Nacional de Bellas Artes, etc." Of the many things he must have built, I know only the plan to remodel the old Inquisition building for the use of the Academy, which I have mentioned. A son of his by the same name was the architect who remodelled the church of San Agustín for the National Library, a project successful enough esthetically, though fundamentally absurd. Architects of the same name, undoubtedly his descendants, appear throughout the nineteenth century.

Don José Agustín Paz

His name appears with Castera's in reference to the church of Loreto (367). He too was a member of the Academy, and he was *maestro mayor* of the city with J. M. Echeandía after 1820. He collaborated with Or-

---

31 All this information comes from Carrillo y Gariel, *Datos sobre la Academia,* pp. 64–65.
32 Carrera Stampa, *Fuentes,* p. 61.

369. Portal, convent church of Jesús María,
Mexico City.

tiz de Castro in the decoration of the Cathedral, and
certainly executed many other works which will be
identified in time. He seems to have been the Paz
whom Tresguerras censured for his Churrigueresque
work; if so, he was a convert to Neoclassicism, like so
many others.

Monuments by Unidentified Architects

Before turning to Neoclassic architecture in the provinces, it would be well to note some Neoclassic buildings of Mexico City whose designers have not been

identified. There are several churches dating from the
beginning of the nineteenth century, such as the parish
church of San José, which is crowded between older
buildings so that its cupola and Classical portals can
hardly be appreciated. The church of San Diego is
much older, but its portal and tower were refinished in
a Neoclassic style of some elegance. One can say the
same of the fine tower of the old convent church of the
nuns of Jesús María, and its large portals, with their
Classical columns and curvilinear pediments, urns and
garlands (369). The central portal of the Soledad,
with its pediment and the Eye of the Trinity carved in
a triangle, is typical of the period. The next to the last
Carmelite church was also Neoclassical (the last one
got no farther than the foundations). The chapel of
the cemetery of the Campo Florido, somewhat dry in
style in spite of its name, belongs in the group.

Some houses by anonymous architects are evidently
of this period—built in stone, with symmetrical masses
and voids, soberly decorated with garlands, candelabra,
and curved pediments over doors and windows.

An anonymous work of real quality, the fountain
known as the *Salto del Agua,* which was finished in
1779, rightly belongs to this period (370). It is thoroughly French in style, with its rusticated tank and
mythological symbols, mermaids and dolphins, as well
as twisted columns. It is a miracle that it has been preserved where it stood, at the end of the aqueduct of
Chapultepec. Its condition was deplorable, however,
and the original stones have been moved to the museum at Churubusco, replaced *in situ* by a replica so
that we can at least enjoy its appearance. Another fountain on this same aqueduct, dating from 1755 to 1760,
was moved to Chapultepec, where the reconstruction
can be seen. At the end of the other aqueduct which
brought water to the city there was also a fine fountain,
called *La Tlaxpana,* which has disappeared. Other
fountains worthy of mention are the fountain of San
Miguel in Puebla, dated 1777 (371), and one of
graceful Baroque design which still stands in a garden
at Acámbaro.

Neoclassic Architecture in the Provinces

Francisco Eduardo de Tresguerras

The figure of this man is one of the most fascinating
in Mexican art, as much for his engaging and lively
spirit as for his work (372). This is notwithstanding
the fact that his name has become a legend, so that

Francisco Eduardo Tresguerras. Portrait of his Wife, María Guadalupe Ramírez.
Oil on canvas. Museo Nacional de Historia, Mexico City.

370. Fountain, Salto del Agua, Mexico City. Lithograph. From *México y sus alrededores,*
1836–1864.

371. Fountain of San Miguel, Puebla.

372. Francisco Eduardo Tresguerras. Self-Portrait.
Oil on canvas. Salomon Hale Collection, Mexico City.

distinguished sons of the era, was self-taught and never attended an art school except for one year at the Academia de San Carlos when he was already mature, and had broken away from a mistaken religious vocation. On his return to Celaya he married María Guadalupe Ramírez, of whom he made a charming portrait in oil in 1787 (color, facing p. 420). He was a painter, a sculptor, a wood carver, and an engraver, as well as a musician and a poet. Finally he devoted himself to architecture, and was most productive in this field. Studying from the prints and treatises of the period, he calls himself the disciple of Ponz, Polomino (*sic*), and Mengs; his concept of architecture was firmly based on the classics—Vitruvius, Vignola, and Serlio. It is almost certain that he began by designing some Churrigueresque retables, but of little quality, since otherwise he would have mentioned them. It is absurd to attribute to him the altarpieces of Santa Clara and Santa Rosa in Querétaro, as Baxter does; in any case these retables were carved about the time of Tresguerras' birth, or very little later.

In 1794 he requested the approval of the Academy "to exercise the profession of architecture freely." He says he had "complied with all the requirements, as is shown by the Plan and Elevation as assigned, and executed by me in the Sala de Arquitectura, of my own invention without copying or fraud (as confirmed by the affidavit of the Señor Director Dr. Antonio Velásquez attached to this plan)."[34] In spite of this, I do not believe, for two reasons, that he was granted the title of *académico de mérito*: he does not appear on the appropriate lists, and furthermore he would never have stopped broadcasting the fact if he had been. He confines himself to saying only that "the Academy recognizes me as its disciple and has licensed me for work of any kind."[35] If Tresguerras had been an *académico de mérito,* the whole Bajío would have rung with his

every cupola that resembles that of the Carmen in Celaya, every tower that looks Neoclassical, every doorway and window with a curved pediment, and indeed every nice building tends to be attributed to him—and in fact is. Tresguerras remains interesting. The very mania for believing him the unique architect of the Bajío region, which makes it difficult to determine his real work among these buildings ascribed to him without rhyme or reason, only makes him more interesting.[33]

He was born in Celaya on October 13, 1759 (not 1745, as often stated), and was the son of Pedro Tresguerras, a native of Santillana del Mar in Spain, and a mother of Mexican birth. Eduardo, like all the

33 On Tresguerras: Manuel de Terreros, "El arquitecto Tresguerras," *Anales del Museo Nacional,* Ép. 4, Vol. 5 (1927), pp. 55–63; José Rodríguez Familiar, *Francisco Eduardo de Tresguerras*; M. Payno, "Don Francisco Eduardo Tresguerras," *El museo mexicano,* II, 16. See also the *Ocios literarios* of Francisco Eduardo Tresguerras; and three articles by Francisco de la Maza: "Dibujos y proyectos de Tresguerras," *Anales del Instituto de Investigaciones Estéticas,* 18 (1950), 27–33; "En el segundo centenario de Tresguerras," *Anales del Instituto de Investigaciones Estéticas,* 29 (1966), 9–14; and "Otra vez Tresguerras," *Anales del Instituto de Investigaciones Estéticas,* 32 (1963), 53–58.
34 Carrillo y Gariel, *Datos sobre la Academia,* p. 31.
35 Payno, *Tresguerras.*

triumph. Indeed he deserved to be one; his work is by no means inferior to that of his metropolitan contemporaries, within the narrow range imposed by Neoclassicism. Tresguerras died of cholera on August 13, 1833.

It is very difficult to catalogue his work. A serious monograph is urgently needed, with research in the archives to check mere tradition. Here we can only indicate what is known, what is reported, and what is assumed. If Tresguerras should be listening, he would be pleased.

In Celaya, his native city, parts of the church of San Francisco are attributed to him: the portico, which may well be his work, the altars, the dome, which is nothing but a replica of the Carmen's, and a tower in three stories, which recalls the old Baroque towers of the seventeenth century. Within this same archaic monastery is found the little chapel which Tresguerras designed as his own tomb. A great artist, he could build his own mansion for immortality, and everything about it speaks of him when we visit it—invokes him, so that, leaving, we feel that Tresguerras is not dead, that his spirit inhabits this place. It consists of a small vaulted space with an altar at the back. The façade has a touching grace, with its Neoclassic pilasters and pediment, medallions, garlands, and finials. The delicacy of its ornament is enchanting.[36]

Celaya boasts also the great bridge which Tresguerras built across the Río de la Laja. It rests on elegant basket-handle arches with projecting voussoirs, and prow-shaped piers with vigorous cutwaters. It is dated 1809, and still serves the incessant coming and going of travellers.

A small but elegant obelisk in the main Plaza of Celaya follows Tresguerras' drawings, if we are to believe tradition. It was erected after the Independence of Mexico.

It was here in Celaya, furthermore, that Tresguerras made his great statement, in rebuilding the church of the Carmen (373). I suspect that the old Baroque church was of the greatest interest, very likely more valuable than the one we have; but we are concerned here with Neoclassic architecture, and as such this building cannot but rouse the liveliest admiration.

The old church suffered a fire in 1802, from a carelessly placed candle or whatever, and was completely

373. Church of El Carmen, Celaya, Guanajuato.

ruined. The Carmelites, who always had plenty of means, began reconstruction of the church at once. Tresguerras got the commission, in spite of his rivals, and this admirable building is the result. The cornerstone was laid on November 4 of the same year, 1802, and the dedication took place on October 13, 1807; the building cost 225,000 pesos.

The church is cruciform in plan, just like those of the mid-eighteenth century; it may be that Tresguerras was able to use part of the old church, perhaps the walls as well as the foundations. The new things are to be found in the projecting portico, with its three Classical façades formed of columns, pediments, and all

36 See Maza, "La tumba de Tresguerras," *Anales del Instituto de Investigaciones Estéticas,* 19 (1951), 105–118.

374. Portal, church of El Carmen, Celaya, Guanajuato.

375. Side portal, church of El Carmen,
Celaya, Guanajuato.

the proper details, and the tower, of two stories and a pinnacle, which rests upon it (374). Over the crossing the cupola rises, tall and elegant, on a Classical drum supported by paired columns, with corresponding projections on the entablature, and pedestals for statues or urns which were never put in place. The dome, elegantly curved, is covered with yellow and green tiles whose diminishing bands correspond to the projections of the drum. The lantern is of fine proportions, with a balustrade. The whole thing has an air of harmony and grateful tranquillity. The interior, which is also Tresguerras' work, displays the same quality, both in the ornamentation of the structure, its pilasters and vaults, and in the altarpieces and images. The effect is one of

unusual unity, verging on monotony—the very antithesis of the Baroque.

The side door, quite French in its grace, is one of the jewels of the period, fine in proportions, elegant and inventive in design (375).

The Capilla de los Cofrades is also very agreeable; here we find the most spirited example of Tresguerras' painting, of which we shall speak later.

A theatre on the Calle de Nuevafrente is also said to have been designed by Tresguerras, but there is no documentation for this.

In Querétaro, the church of Santa Teresa is attributed to him, but again without proof. I am not convinced by this heavy portico of a Greek temple, with

Ionic bases and capitals used badly on a structure drier than the driest Doric temple in existence. Tresguerras writes of "Ortiz [de Castro?] thrown out from his work for the Teresas in Querétaro," and we do know that Tolsá drew up a plan for the building. But whoever may have been responsible for this pseudo Parthenon, we can be sure that it is not in Tresguerras' style. The cornerstone was laid in 1803, and it was finished by 1807, which is to say, at exactly the time that Tresguerras was rebuilding the Carmen in Celaya.

We know that he designed the small but attractive fountain of Neptune in Querétaro; it is characteristic of his style, and dates from 1797. The statue is not his work. He also erected the dais and triumphal arch in that city for the proclamation of Charles IV as King.

One of Tresguerras' masterpieces is to be found in Guanajuato, the palace of the Conde de Casa Rul, owner of the famous Valenciana mine (376). There is no documentation. We know that it was finished in 1803 when Humboldt visited the city; he bursts into dithyrambic eulogy, and says that it cost 40,000 pesos. The building has an indisputable elegance and sobriety. The lower floor is lightly rusticated, with frieze and cornice which carry a balcony across the whole façade. On the second floor, Ionic pilasters in pairs separate doors with triangular pediments, and in the middle a central balcony projects with paired columns of the same order and a curved pediment; above, there is a refined entablature and a triangular pediment with the owner's coat of arms. It is all cut in that handsome yellowish stone which is the pride of the Bajío. One might feel that the lower floor is not robust enough for the upper structure, or that the principal doorway seems meager, but even so the solution of the second floor would do honor to any architect. The patio and the galleries, though less vigorous, are extremely elegant.

In San Luis Potosí he is said to have built the theatre later called after Ruiz de Alarcón, and the Column of Independence inaugurated on September 16, 1827. The famous Caja de Agua, a delightful piece of Neoclassic art, was not Tresguerras' work, as people keep insisting (377). It may be said that it was either by a pupil of his or inspired by his style, but according to Muro, the historian of the city, it was designed by an engineer, Juan N. Sanabria, and finished in 1832.[37]

In San Miguel el Grande, now called San Miguel de

376. House of the Conde de Casa Rul, Guanajuato.

Allende, they attribute to him the tower of the church of San Francisco, the crypt of the parish church, and the house of the Conde de la Canal. A handsome Neoclassic house, like others in this admirable city, it does not show any definite characteristics of Tresguerras, so that the attribution is more than doubtful.

In Salvatierra "the parish church was not built until the great period of Tresguerras, whose plan and design were painstakingly followed."[38]

In Salamanca the high altar of the parish church, now destroyed, was attributed to him.

In Irapuato the building of the convent of La Enseñanza was supervised by an overseer named Riaño, under the direction of Tresguerras. It was finished in 1810.

Finally, the terrace of the hacienda El Cabejón in

---

[37] Manuel Muro, *Historia de San Luis Potosí.*
[38] Pedro González, *Geografía local del Estado de Guanajuato.*

377. Caja de Agua, San Luis Potosí.

Jalisco is supposed to have been designed by Tresguerras. It consists of an open space surrounded by balustrades of stone, with an unusual fountain in the center.

From all that has been said, one can form an idea of the importance of Tresguerras in Mexican architecture, of his refined personality and his polished taste. At the same time one is assailed by a doubt as to whether we may be praising in his name the work of a group of men, since his own *oeuvre* is really uncertain. Let us hope that this essay of appreciation may serve to inspire more specific research which in the end will substantiate the contribution of this artist, so beloved and actually so unknown.

Neoclassic Architecture in Puebla

Don José Manzo

This artist was born in Puebla on April 29, 1789 (378). His parents were Don Francisco Manzo y Vargas and Doña Bárbara Jaramillo. He was a pupil of Salvador del Huerto, a painter of Puebla, and of the silversmith Antonio Villafaña.

As we have seen, he finished Tolsá's high altar for the Cathedral, and then by order of Bishop Pérez undertook the decoration and arrangement of the whole church. The appearance of the interior of the Cathedral of Puebla is Manzo's work (166). It was he who replaced the old Baroque retables with the Neoclassic altarpieces we see today; even the Retablo de los Reyes, designed by Martínez Montañés, was completely reconstructed (379). There is a practically contemporary engraving of it in its original state, and, comparing it with the present altarpiece, we can see that Manzo kept the original contours, the paintings, and the marble columns, and made everything else new. The old retable would have been of carved and gilded wood, which makes no mean effect with onyx columns, as we can see in the tabernacle of the Rosary Chapel in Puebla and in the old altar of the Cathedral of Mexico; Manzo built an altarpiece of white plaster with gilded fillets and ornaments. The antique wooden statues of polychrome and gold were supplanted by Neoclassic ones whose robes give off metallic reflections, in the style of Zacarías Cora. All the altars were made in the same new style; the whole interior of the church is decorated in a consistent scheme of gold and white, even the vaults. The stone of the columns is revealed, but bases and capitals are gilded, and the floor is covered with fine stone from Santo Tomás. Manzo left the building fresh and new, as if it had just been finished. It makes an impression of cleanliness and harmony which we do not find in the Cathedral of Mexico, but at the considerable sacrifice of nobility and the patina of antiquity. If we did not know the history of this great church, we might think, judging solely from the interior, that it dated from no earlier than the first half of the last century. The reform was complete.

All the churches of Puebla suffered the same loss as the Cathedral; we have seen how scarce Churrigueresque retables are in this city.

In 1824 Manzo travelled abroad, as attaché to the Mexican Legation in Rome, and took advantage of his journey to visit the United States, London, the Nether-

378. José Manzo. Self-Portrait. Pastel.
José Luis Bello Collection, Puebla.

379. Altar de los Reyes. Painted and gilded
wood; oil on canvas. Cathedral of Puebla.

lands, and Paris. In Paris he fell ill from the change of climate, but would not go back to Mexico without learning as much as possible about lithography and other things. He did not, as his biographers claim, introduce lithography into Mexico; this matter is clearly documented.[39] Manzo died in Puebla on July 24, 1860; at that time he was living in the Calle de Infantes.[40]

[39] Manuel Toussaint, *La litografía en México en el siglo XIX.* See also Justino Fernández and Edmundo O'Gorman, *Documentos para la historia de la litografía en México.*
[40] This information was given me by Señor Medel of Puebla.

Manzo is a figure of the first importance for Neoclassic art in Puebla. If we cannot agree with his opinion that appreciation of a new style requires the destruction of our inheritance from the past, the same charge can be brought against Tresguerras and Tolsá. One would like to have a fuller account of his life, his times, and his work.

Other Provincial Architecture

There are other Neoclassic monuments scattered about the provinces. One of the most notable examples

427

380. Alhóndiga de Granaditas, Guanajuato.

of civic architecture is in Guanajuato: the Alhóndiga de Granaditas, the grain market and granary (380). Famous in the War of Independence, it was later used as a prison and is now in very bad condition, almost in ruins. Like all the outstanding buildings of this region, it has been attributed to Tresguerras, but the diligent Marmolejo gives us the following facts. The plans and budget for the building were presented to the Ayuntamiento on March 12, 1796; they were the work of an architect of Guanajuato, Don José Alejandro Durán y Villaseñor. Professors from the Academia de San Carlos later revised these plans. The cost was estimated at 164,775 pesos. In August, 1796, the Ayuntamiento applied to the viceroy for permission to spend this sum, which was granted on July 7, 1797. On the first day of August the Cabildo directed that steps should be taken toward building, and at the end of the same year they paid 25,843 pesos, 5 *reales*, 2 *granos* for twenty houses, to free the land which the building was to occupy. Work began on January 5, 1798, and

was finished November 7, 1809. A year later the building was to receive its baptism of fire and blood.[41]

The Alhóndiga—the "Corn Palace," as it has been called—is a great block of masonry with few windows and a well-designed Classical portal. The interior offers a fine patio with columns, surrounded by galleries into which open the offices and granaries.

In Oaxaca the Palacio de Gobierno is a fine Neoclassic building, but later than our period. Perhaps the façade of the church known as the Iglesia del Marquesado, so restrained and delicate, with its portraits in sculpture and its refined ornament, does fall within our limits.

Morelia, that noble Baroque city, has no monuments of this period. Nonetheless, there can be seen, hidden away in a second patio off the Escuela de Derecho, the Law School, some little arches so pure in design and construction as to be models of Neoclassic design.

41 Lucio Marmolejo, *Efemérides guanajuatenses.*

428

Here we should mention, perhaps, the tombs and funerary monuments from the end of the eighteenth and the beginning of the nineteenth century. Just as all through the colonial period, they followed the dominant style, and so we have some magnificent Neoclassic examples. I will note two of them. One, a masterpiece, was the "catafalque erected in the Holy Church of Guadalaxara for the obsequies of D.ª M.ª Isabel Francisca de Braganza, Queen of Spain." The fine engraving is signed: *Inv. y dib. por Dionisio Sancho Escult. de Cam. de S.M.,* that is, "Designed and drawn by Dionisio Sancho, Chamber Sculptor to His Majesty." It was erected in 1819.[42]

The other was put up in Puebla in honor of the soldiers killed in Buenos Aires in 1808. It seems to have been the work of José Luis Rodríguez de Alconedo.

And so we bring this chapter to an end, the shortest of all, and the nearest to us. The fact is that this period has not been studied so well as the earlier ones: the Baroque has absorbed us too much. At least we have laid the first stone of a future construction: the history of Neoclassic architecture in Mexico.

Architects and Engineers, 1781–1821:

Don José Antonio González Velásquez (d. 1810). Architect, Academy
Don José Eligio Delgadillo and his father. Study 381
Don José Damián Ortiz de Castro. Arch. Acad.

Don José Joaquín García de Torres. Arch. Acad.
Don Francisco Antonio Guerrero y Torres. Arch.
Don José del Mazo y Áviles. Arch. Acad.
Don José Buitrón y Velasco. Arch.
Don Juan Manuel Chango
Don Juan Man. Master architect
Don José Gutiérrez. Arch. Acad.
Don Manuel Mascaró. Engineer
Mariano Sánchez. Master stonemason
Don Antonio de Urrutia. Master architect
Francisco Eduardo Tresguerras. Arch.
Don Joaquín Heredia. Acad. Arch.
Don Esteban González. Acad. Arch.
Don Luis Martín. Acad. Arch.
Don Manuel Tolsá. Acad. Arch.
Don Luis Tola y Salcedo. Acad. Arch.
Don Ignacio Castera. Acad. Arch.
Don José Velasco y Buitrón. Acad. Arch.
Don José Ávila y Rojano. Acad. Arch.
Don José Agustín Paz. Acad. Arch.
Don José Echeandía. Acad. Arch.
Don José Mariano Mendoza. Acad. *Super.* Arch.
Don Manuel Pavedilla. Acad. *Super.* Arch.
Don Miguel Costansó. Engineer
Don Francisco Ortiz de Castro

[42] Maza, *Las piras funerarias en la historia y en el arte de México.*

Chapter Twenty-three

NEOCLASSIC SCULPTURE

Neoclassic Ideology

THIS CHAPTER is so intimately related, on the one hand to Neoclassic architecture and on the other to sculpture before the founding of the Academy, that I set it apart only to be consistent with my plan. The same names parade through the two periods, and the work of the sculptors is confused with that of the architects. Retables, which formerly were works of sculpture, are now examples of architecture, because of a fundamental change of attitude.

To demonstrate this change in attitude, let us quote one opinion about the sculpture of the retables, as a companion piece to the Neoclassic architect's opinion of Baroque buildings given in the preceding chapter. This statement of ideology appears in the celebrated periodical edited by Don José Joaquín Fernández de Lizardi, *Pensador Mexicano*—the *Thinker of Mexico.* Considering the prestige of the author and the wide diffusion of his papers and books, it is not rash to assume that in his time—the early years of the nineteenth century—the opinions of Fernández de Lizardi were those of the cultivated public of New Spain.

It is a dialogue between an Italian and a Frenchman; the Frenchman is speaking of our capital to the Italian, who has just arrived from Europe. Of the Cathedral he says:

"It is the largest church, not only of Mexico City, but of the realm. The architecture is not refined: it is much too complicated and heavy. At the crossing there is a high altar, old-fashioned work by which modern taste must be repelled; it is more like a great growth than an altar (*tiene un pino que parece pinal*). Inside it there is a tabernacle of silver, crude in workmanship, which encloses one of gold —its value is solely in the material. Beyond this pyramid, this so-called high altar, at the end of the church there is a retable known as the *Altar de los Reyes,* which is nothing but a cluttered up woodpile, gilded in the antique style, and altogether indecent. The side chapels, with the exception of three which are redecorated in the modern style and quite nice, are more like prison cells than chapels, since they are very dark, cramped, and totally without propriety . . ."

"What would you say then of the other churches, if this is your opinion of the most important one?"

"There are all kinds. Some are very sad, dark, and ancient; others, elegant, light, and tastefully decorated. Among the latter, the convent church of the nuns of Jesús María in my opinion deserves first place, not for size and grandeur, but for its orderly and tasteful arrangement. Its altars are very comely and simple; above a black base rises a beautiful course of alabaster, so that the whole church has this color, and light is permitted to penetrate freely, catching the gold fillets of the mouldings which stand out strikingly on the white—and so we have a church decent, orderly, and cheerful,"[1]

Three fundamental concepts emerge from these paragraphs: clarity, modernity, and order. Churches should be bright and full of light, not like those of the past, which are dismal, shadowy, black. Any idea that the Catholic ritual prefers dim and shadowy interiors is disclaimed. Although it is not specifically expressed—and in that period might indeed have put the author in real danger—one word rings quite clearly through this censure—obscurantism. The second idea is concerned not so much with antiquity (which in itself could not be considered a fault, since the fashionable architecture imitated the much more antique Roman and Greek styles), but with *colonial* antiquity; that is to say, they were against the system, against the colonial idea. The new style, imported from France and Italy, just as the imaginary people discussing it came from those countries, implies a relationship between artistic emancipation from the old forms and political independence. Order, the third element they insist on, is expressed by a very Mexican term *curiosidad*: it means what is tidy, refined, and nicely made (completely unrelated to the other "curiosity," which is inquisitiveness). So we see how rationalism and the efforts for independence do reveal themselves in the apparently innocent phenomena of art.

Don Manuel Tolsá

Don Manuel Tolsá is clearly not only the most notable sculptor but the dominant figure of the period (381). He was born in the town of Enguerra in Valencia on December 24, 1757; his parents were Don Pedro Juan Tolsá and Doña Josefa Sarrión y Gómez. He seems to have studied in Valencia and to have received the degree of *académico de mérito* from the Academia de San Carlos there, which later was incorporated with the Academia de San Fernando in Ma-

381. Rafael Jimeno y Planes. Portrait of Manuel Tolsá. Oil. 1.03 x .82 m.
Pinacoteca Virreinal, Mexico City.

drid. When the first director of sculpture in Mexico, Don José Arias, died after losing his mind, Tolsá was appointed to his place by a decree of September 6, 1790. His salary was 1,800 pesos a year, with the provision that an additional 200 pesos should go as pensions for the sisters of Arias, Doña Francisca and Doña Paula.[2]

He left Valencia for Cádiz the same year, on December 24, 1790. The Spanish government entrusted to

1 *El pensador mexicano,* diciembre 23, 1813.

2 Alfredo Escontría, *Breve estudio de la obra y personalidad del escultor y arquitecto Don Manuel Tolsá.* A brief but well-documented monograph. See also Francisco de la Maza, "Algunas obras desconocidas de Manuel Tolsá," *Anales del Instituto de Investigaciones Estéticas,* 14 (1946), 33–54; Manuel Romero de Terreros, "Méritos y servicios de D. Manuel Tolsá," *Anales del Instituto de Investigaciones Estéticas,* 12 (1945), 33–42.

382. Manuel Tolsá (?). Virgin of the Immaculate
Conception. Polychrome and gilded wood.
Church of La Profesa, Mexico City.

him the care and transporting of the seventy-six chests full of books and other things and the famous plaster casts of Classical sculpture from the Academia de San Carlos and the Vatican. The tradition that these were a gift from Charles III is false: they were bought and paid for. Tolsá and his precious baggage left Cádiz on the frigate *Santa Paula* of the royal fleet on February 20, 1791, for Havana, where he had to wait for another ship to take him to Veracruz. He reached Mexico on the following twenty-second of July, with the casts. His assistant, Baltasar Pombo, travelled as his servant, but was in reality a maker of plaster casts. It was he who repaired the casts, and he held the position of director of plaster casting until it was abolished.[3]

Tolsá brought with him a niece who later became a nun in the convent of Santa Clara in Mexico City, and he married Doña Luisa Sanz Téllez Girón Espinosa de los Monteros. Escontría suggests that the marriage took place in Veracruz, where he landed, since she was a native of the port and no record of the marriage has been found in the parish archives of Mexico City. They had nine children, and the sculptor died in the capital, where he was buried on December 25, 1816. His wife survived him for ten years.[4]

As we have said, Tolsá came as director of sculpture. Later he obtained the title of *académico de mérito* in architecture, submitting his plans for the School of Mines, a retable, and a cell for the Marquesa de Selva Nevada in the convent of La Regina.[5] When González Velásquez died in 1810 Tolsá succeeded him as director of architecture, but he was never director general, as some writers state. At the death of Gil, Don Rafael Jimeno y Planes, who had been director of painting, moved into the position, which he filled until his death in 1825.

No complete catalogue of Tolsá's sculpture has been made, and in fact only seven pieces by him are known. Even with the variety of his artistic activities, this is an insignificant amount of sculpture, and it is reasonable to suppose that we do not know all of his work.

We have spoken of the high altar of the Cathedral of Puebla, which included a figure of *La Purísima, The*

[3] Abelardo Carrillo y Gariel, *Datos sobre la Academia de San Carlos*, p. 76.

[4] Salvador Toscano, "Testamento de Manuel Tolsá," *Anales del Instituto de Investigaciones Estéticas*, I (1937), 50–54.

[5] Carrillo y Gariel, *Datos sobre la Academia*, p. 37.

383. Manuel Tolsá. Charles IV. Bronze.
Mexico City.

384. Manuel Tolsá. Charles IV (detail of horse).
Bronze. Mexico City.

Virgin of the Immaculate Conception, by him. As it was of wood, we assume that his original carving was retained, gilded and painted in the Baroque manner. The *Purísima* which is now in the church of La Profesa in Mexico City may be the same one: it shows just Tolsá's characteristics, Classical in anatomy, and Baroque in its drapery (382).

A *Virgin of Sorrows* in the Profesa is also mentioned, and for this church he built the altarpiece, which is still in place. It is well proportioned, with a tabernacle formed of columns and a bell-shaped top. The mediocre sculptures are not by him; they are said to have been made by Patiño Ixtolinque. The altarpiece of the church of Santo Domingo in Mexico City is also his work; a magnificent Churrigueresque retable must have been sacrificed for it, to judge by those which have miraculously survived in the transepts. Tolsá's is of handsome proportions, with Classical columns, a curved pediment below and a triangular one above; as a work of its time it is acceptable, but it is totally out of harmony with a Baroque church. Actually the period is revolutionary in the most serious sense of the word: they felt it necessary not only to build, but to destroy the vestiges of the past. It is on this score that we must censure the Neoclassic artists most seriously, for not valuing the historical development of art, which is profoundly significant in a way they did not realize. Everyone has a right to create his own art; no one has the right to destroy the art of the past, which represents ideals that are no less valid for being different.

Tolsá's first great work in sculpture is the magnificent group of the Theological Virtues, *Faith, Hope,* and *Charity,* which crown the principal façade of the Cathedral of Mexico.

As early as 1793 the stone for them had been obtained from the town of San Bartolo Naucalpan, but as the workmen of Sandoval, the sculptor whose business it was to see to the dressing of the stone, spoiled the one intended for the *Faith,* Tolsá would not use it. Only in 1809 does he write that at last he has the pieces of stone which were intrusted to Don Mateo León, and which cost 968 pesos and three quarters of a *real.* In December, 1812, he gives his receipt for 4,500 pesos for the three statues, and 3,500 for the cross, chalice, anchor, and flame of gilded bronze.[6]

These three figures are full of movement and of life. Not that Tolsá is original; at least the *Charity* is copied from one only a few meters away in the Sagrario, the work of some obscure Baroque stonecutter. But the amplitude of the forms, the masterly draping of the robes, the timidity of the child clinging to the woman, all reveal an artist of the first rank.

Tolsá's masterpiece as a sculptor is the colossal equestrian statue of Charles IV (383, 384). A result of the adulation of one of the most worthless viceroys New Spain ever had, it demonstrates how the most miserable factors can lead to valuable results when genius takes over. The adulation produced a portrait of two animals; but the work of art is of the highest order.

Its history can be outlined briefly. On November 30, 1795, the Marqués de Branciforte requested Godoy's permission to erect an equestrian statue of the King, after the accompanying model, and at a cost of ten to twenty thousand pesos according to the estimate likewise included, the money to be contributed by his well-to-do subjects. The Prince of Peace replied from Jerez on May 5, 1796, that His Majesty granted the necessary permission, on condition that the busts of royal persons should be omitted from the base.[7]

The Viceroy communicated the royal approval of his project to an assembly of the Audiencia, the Archbishopric, the Ayuntamiento, University, Tribunales, and ecclesiastical and secular bodies on the fifteenth of June following. They then proceeded to the planning of the Plaza and the pedestal for the monument, according to a project by González Velásquez (359). The first stone of the Plaza was laid on July 18 of the same year. On the ninth of December following it was inaugurated, with a temporary statue of wood, carved and gilded in the Academy, since Tolsá had not finished his. It was cast on August 2, 1803, in furnaces built in the old College of San Gregorio, under the direction of Don Salvador de la Vega, a skilled bell caster. On the ninth of the following December it was inaugurated by Viceroy Iturrigaray in solemn ceremonies, including "Songs of the Mexican Muses."

For all our pride in it, the statue of Charles IV is not original. Tolsá's inspiration was Girardon's equestrian portrait of Louis XIV; his statue can almost be called a copy of it. There is now in the Museo de His-

---

[6] Archivo de la Catedral de México. On Tolsá's work for the Cathedral see also Toussaint, *La Catedral de México y el Sagrario Metropolitano.*

[7] Federico Gómez de Orozco, "Documentos acerca de la estatua de Carlos IV," *Anales del Instituto de Investigaciones Estéticas,* 5 (1940), 77–83. See also Luis González Obregón, "La estatua de Carlos IV," in *México pintoresco.*

toria a small bronze which came from the García Cubas family, which is said to have been Tolsá's work, and to have been his model. I have also seen a bronze statue, about half life size, in the collection of Don José Luis Bello in Puebla; I do not know whether the signature "Girardon" on it is authentic; but I can affirm that the sculpture is identical with our Charles IV.[8]

Be that as it may, no one can deny the beauty and perfection of this great bronze. Within the Neoclassic canon, an effect of true realism is achieved in the rendering of horse and rider. If Goya had not portrayed Charles IV so cruelly, this monument might have succeeded in immortalizing that mediocre ruler. But the personality is of small account; it is the work of art that matters, the majesty of the forms, the grandeur of the monument and its superb pedestal, the high technical perfection—the stamp of genius. Tolsá indeed rises above his model here.

Other Neoclassic Sculptors of Mexico City

The Sandovals

Don Santiago Cristóbal Sandoval, whom Sedano calls an Indian cacique from the section of Santiago, and his son, Ignacio, figure in this period.[9] They are not sculptors of importance, but rather assistants to others. The elder Sandoval must have been a successful Baroque sculptor in the second half of the eighteenth century. When the Academy was founded, he was the first professor of sculpture until Arias arrived, for lack of a more suitable incumbent. Later father and son appear together in various work. We know that Don Ignacio had a fellowship in the Academy. The father again appears as acting director of sculpture before Tolsá's arrival, and is the teacher of Patiño Ixtolinque.[10] Later we find the Sandovals working on the statues for the old tower of the Cathedral; they are supposed to have made only six of them, since two were carved by José Zacarías Cora, as we shall see. On July 5, 1793, they were paid 1,200 pesos for six statues of soft stone: St. Ambrose, St. Jerome, St. Philip of Jesus, St. Hippolytus, St. Cassian, and St. Isidore. This was at the rate of 200 pesos each, while Señor Tolsá received 2,500 pesos per figure. As some of the figures were injured in installing them, Ignacio Sandoval was paid 18 pesos on August 10 of the same year, for fifteen pieces of fingers which he "put on" St. Isidore, one new hand "because the fingers were entirely broken," repairs to

another hand and the pen of St. Jerome, as well as various repairs to the robes of the other saints. Such is our information about these men, besides the fact that Sandoval made the statue of Charles IV which stood on the Plaza, opposite the Calle de la Moneda, before they had thought of erecting Tolsá's.[11] Their humbleness is affecting, and we should like to know and to praise all that they achieved, as artists and as Indians.

Don Dionisio Sancho

He was the second director of sculpture in the Academy. After González Velásquez died in 1810 and Tolsá was made director of architecture, Sancho was appointed to the position by a royal order of August 20 of that year. He set out at once, but did not take over the position until February 17, 1811. After the War of Independence began, the Academy had a hard time. Sancho went to Guadalajara, though we don't know exactly when, to direct the Casa de Moneda. There they made use of his abilities to design the catafalque of Queen María Isabel Francisca de Braganza in 1820, as we noted in discussing architecture. When speaking of himself, Sancho always used the title *escultor de cámara de Su Majestad*—"chamber sculptor to His Majesty."

Pedro Patiño Ixtolinque

He was born on May 30, 1774, in San Pedro Ecatzingo, the son of a Spaniard and a mestiza. He was therefore classified, according to the castes descriptive of the intermarriage of people of different races, as a *castizo*, which in this context doesn't signify "noble" by any means. In adopting his mother's Indian name, which doesn't even appear on the baptismal record,[12] this man showed a fine spirit of independence and rebellion. In fact his mother's lineage was more important than his father's; tradition describes him as a *cacique*. In the beginning he was a pupil of Don Santiago Sandoval, and in 1788 he received one of the two fellowships established for Indians, along with another Indian, Don Juan de la Cruz. He studied with Arias during the short period of his teaching at the Academy,

[8] The French critic Louis Gillet has noted this antecedent in "L'art dans l'Amérique Latine," in André Michel, *Histoire de l'art*, VIII, 1061–1062.

[9] Francisco Sedano, *Noticias de México*, p. 230.

[10] Carrillo y Gariel, *Datos sobre la Academia*, pp. 54, 78.

[11] Sedano, *Noticias*, p. 230.

[12] Carrillo y Gariel, *Datos sobre la Academia*, p. 78.

and after 1791 with Tolsá, whose favorite pupil he was. He very nearly went to Europe, since his name appears among the six scholarship holders whom they planned to send to Rome in 1793. He was awarded the rank of *académico de mérito* on January 18, 1817, for his relief representing *King Wamba,* and an extemporary problem. Revilla states that after being admitted to the Academy he took part in the War of Independence, but gives no proof of it. It seems to be true that he made a death mask of Morelos in San Cristóbal Ecatepec. Patiño married a lady named Carrizosa, though we don't know when, and had at least one child, named Pedro like himself. In 1825 he figures as a member of the Ayuntamiento of Mexico City. He was the third director general of the Academy, named on January 28, 1826, to take the place of Jimeno, who died a year earlier.[13] He died in Mexico City in 1835.[14]

We know few works by Patiño, considering how much he must have done in his long life. I can name only these: the main altarpiece of the Sagrario in Mexico City, which is so much like all the others of the period and lacking in personality; the statues for the retables of Santo Domingo and La Profesa in Mexico City; the *Angels* and the *St. Peter* of the high altar of the Cathedral of Puebla; a *Virgin of Sorrows* which is still in La Profesa; three statues of the *Virgin of the Immaculate Conception* for the churches of Santa Teresa and San Diego in Mexico City and that of San Antonio in Querétaro. The crucifix which was used for the swearing in of members of the Constitutional Convention of 1857 was acquired from his son by Ponciano Arriaga—if we are to believe Revilla, who gives these last attributions. Besides the relief of Wamba, the most academic of his works and now almost ruined by neglect, there are two allegorical figures by him, stuck away below the staircase in the Escuela de Artes Plásticas, which were carved for a mausoleum in honor of Morelos that was never completed. One feels a certain dignity in his figures, and a mobility in the drapery, which show him for a pupil of Tolsá.

Three Other Sculptors

Among the many craftsmen active in this period, there are other obscure workmen who deserve to be saved from oblivion. Such were three sculptors who collaborated with Ortiz de Castro on the façade of the Cathedral of Mexico: José Santos Castillo, Mariano Paz, and Nicolás Xirón. To them we owe all the decorative sculpture: festoons, candelabra, urns, garlands.

They were all three paid for this work in 1790, before the death of the great architect Ortiz de Castro.

Sculptors of Puebla

José Zacarías Cora

Since he was born in the middle of the eighteenth century and lived only sixteen years into the nineteenth, we have presented the facts of Cora's biography in discussing eighteenth-century sculpture. We described him as a Baroque artist who came to Neoclassicism through the study of anatomy.

Putting aside for the time being numerous sculptures attributed to him in Puebla, we shall at this point consider his part in completing the Cathedral of Mexico. He was brought from Puebla expressly to do this work, as he himself states in his bill presented on January 26, 1793. He collected 3,662 pesos, 4 *reales,* for the following sculpture:

For the new tower—for 8 statues of stone, 3 *varas* high with their bases, each of one piece (except for the first two, which are of two pieces each), of the following saints: *St. Gregory the Pope, St. Augustine, St. Leander, St. Fulgentius, St. Cassian, St. Francis Xavier, St. Primitivus,* and *St. Barbara,* at 300 pesos each one—in consideration of my having come from my home, the city of Puebla de los Ángeles, for this sole purpose, and having had to be at the quarry with my assistants since the month of February of the year 1791, wishing to complete them so that they could be brought to the churchyard needing only the final polishing—2400 pesos. For the said *St. Primitivus,* which when it was already finished at the quarry and needed only to be polished, a stone fell on it and broke it to pieces, leaving it useless—275 pesos.

St. Primitivus did not want to go up on the tower, and got broken again in transport, so that it was necessary "to work a stone, with the base and the legs halfway up the thigh, and a head," for all of which he charged 137 pesos, 4 *reales.* "For two groups of three seraphim each between the columns at the base of the west side of the tower at 115 pesos for each group." For the old tower: "Two statues of the same size and stone, of *St. Emygdius* and *St. Rose of St. Mary*" at the same price,

---

[13] Jesús Galindo y Villa calls him the fourth director general, because he mistakenly believes Tolsá to have been the second. "Reseña histórico de la Academia Nacional de Bellas Artes, antigua de San Carlos," *Anales de la Academia Nacional de Bellas Artes de México,* 1 (1913), 9–32. The fact is that Tolsá was originally director of sculpture, and later director of architecture.

[14] Manuel G. Revilla, *Biografías de artistas,* pp. 3–21.

and 20 pesos for various repairs.[15] It should be noted that all the writers assert that Tolsá did drawings for these statues and also for the six made by Sandoval; the documents themselves say nothing of this, however.

By comparison with work definitely by Cora, such as the sculpture in the church of San Cristóbal in Puebla —one of which, the *St. Joachim,* is signed *Año de 1786. Cora*—we can attribute other sculpture to him. There is a *Crucifix,* the property of Don Carlos Alonso Miyar, which shows the same technique of modelling as the St. Christopher, especially in the hair (the moustache is identical), although the veins are not so exaggerated. A vigorous *St. Sebastian* in a private collection shows a treatment of the hair, eyes, and mouth similar to these two. A very realistic *St. Philip Neri* in the church of La Concordia, a *St. Augustine* in the church of San Agustín, and a *St. Rock* (I don't know whether it is the one mentioned as being in the church of San Roque) can be added to the group—these last three figures are dressed in real clothing.

Other Sculptors

We should also mention José Villegas here, although there is nothing to add to the notice given above. He certainly would have continued to produce plenty of saints, and since he had been an apprentice of Cora the Elder, they would be similar in style.

A Legaspi is named in the documents for the sculpture of the high altar of the Cathedral of Puebla, without specifying his contribution.[16] He is probably the same man who appears in the *Guía de Forasteros de Puebla* (*Guide to Foreigners in Puebla*) in 1852. Of the sculptors listed there—Don José María Legaspi, Don José María Olivares, Don José María del Castillo, Don José Dolores, and Don Santiago—some were undoubtedly active in this period. There is evidence for assuming that Legaspi was not the only one who worked through several periods: Manzo, for example, was still living, and appears with Arrieta, Ordóñez, and Morales among the painters.

[15] Documents in the Archivo de la Catedral de México: "Cuenta de torres y fachada." Perhaps my notes are in error, since they indicate that both Cora and the Sandovals were paid for the statue of *San Casiano.*

[16] "La catedral de Puebla" in *Noticias curiosas.*

[17] I should like to express my sincere thanks to Señor Licenciado Don Manuel Septien for having given me a copy of this essay by Canon Don Vicente Acosta.

[18] José María Zelaa e Hidalgo, *Glorias de Querétaro.*

Neoclassic Sculptors of Querétaro

In the census taken in Querétaro in 1791 numerous sculptors are listed, as we have said. Three of them stand out as the most important in the Neoclassic movement: Mariano Perusquía, Mariano Arce, and Mariano Montenegro—the three Marianos. We can study them now with some satisfaction, giving new data, thanks to the unpublished research of Canon Don Vicente Acosta on the sculpture of Querétaro.[17]

Mariano Perusquía

He was born in Querétaro in 1771, as we have seen. Twenty years later he was working with the mestizo sculptor Francisco Escobar, and then he went to Mexico City, where according to tradition he was a pupil of Manuel Tolsá's. When he returned to Querétaro, he set up a workshop with Mariano Arce, his friend and collaborator. This is all the information we have about him, none of it documented except what the census gives, and the fact that in 1795 he won the sculpture prize of the Academy. The list of work attributed to him is immense. First of all we have those in Querétaro which Zelaa cites.[18] Dating from 1803 are a *Purísima*—a *Virgin of the Immaculate Conception*— for the monastery of San Antonio and a *Crucifix* for the Barefoot Carmelites; these two seem to have been made while he was still in Mexico City. From 1804 dates a similar *Crucifix,* copied after that of Santa Teresa in Mexico City, for the Cofradía del Santo Cristo de los Trabajos. In 1808 he made a figure of the *Blessed Sebastian of Aparicio,* for the church of the Hermanos del Cordón; in 1809, *Mary* and *St. John* on either side of the *Crucifix* by Bartolico in the same church; a *Guardian Angel* for the Capilla de la Santa Escala in the parish church of Santiago, and a *Purísima* for San Francisco. Canon Acosta adds the following works: in the church of Santa Teresa—*Jesus of Nazareth, St. Theresa, St. John of the Cross, The Sacred Heart*; in the church of San Agustín—*The Virgin of Succour.*

According to the Canon, again, Perusquía left the following work in Guadalajara. In the Cathedral—*St. Martin, St. Paul, St. James, St. Nicholas of Tolentino, St. Francis of Assisi, St. Francis Xavier, St. John Nepomucen, St. Clement, St. Theresa,* and *The Assumption.* Also *Archangels,* such as those in the church of San Francisco. In the Sagrario—*St. Rose* and *St. Peter and St. Paul.* In the church of San Antonio—*St.*

437

385. Mariano Arce. Pietà. Polychrome wood. Church of San Francisco, Querétaro.

Anthony with the Holy Child. In San Diego, the figure of its patron saint, which originally belonged to the Cathedral. In San Francisco, the heads of *The Virgin* and *St. Joseph*; in the Carmen and the Merced—the two appropriate figures of *The Virgin.* He lists a *Virgin of the Rosary* in the church of Zapotlán el Grande, and in the sanctuary of Nuestra Señora de San Juan de los Lagos, figures of *St. Joachim, St. Anne, St. Sebastian, St. Catherine Martyr,* and possibly the figures of the *Virgin of the Assumption, St. Joseph,* and *St. John.* Let us hope that this copious list of attributions may in time serve some local writer as a basis for the monograph this sculptor deserves.

Perusquía had great technical skill, but he idealizes his figures almost to a formula. His Virgin and his Child are always beings of unreal beauty, and his saints, like *St. Louis the King,* seem spirits from beyond this world. It is no small thing, to be sure, to embody pure spirit; but in our day an intensity of realism is more prized.

Mariano Arce

This second Mariano had a more original and serious talent. Unhappily we have not one biographical notice of him; he does not appear in the 1791 census, and tradition reports only that he was a pupil of Tolsá, and that he set up a shop in his native city with his friend Perusquía. So his history is limited to his works, or rather to those attributed to him.

The most famous of them are certainly the *Pietà* in San Francisco and the *St. James* of the old Cathedral of Querétaro. Inspired by a long tradition, including Michelangelo, this dramatic *Pietà,* with its fine triangular composition, does indeed stand out among all the sculpture we have seen in this exhausting history (385). A fecund imagination and the skill to embody it, undeniable technical proficiency and intense emotion are all found in this work. It may be true that it is theatrical and bombastic; but, for my part, I frankly prefer this to the monotonous series of saccharine Virgins and placid Christs.

Arce's second important work is the *St. James* of the old Cathedral of Querétaro; it was given by the artist to the Ayuntamiento of the city in 1815. The saint, dressed as a pilgrim, stands in wonder at the moment when the Virgin appears to him in Zaragoza; all the technical and spiritual gifts of the sculptor are evident here.[19]

On the basis of these two masterworks, the relationship of all the sculpture attributed to him has to be worked out. There is a *Virgin of Sorrows* for the church of San Felipe in Querétaro, *St. Christopher* for the church of the Montecillo in San Luis Potosí, and the statue of *Liberty* for the Plaza de la Constitución in Querétaro, made in 1820. According to Canon Acosta there are also in Querétaro two *Crucifixes* by Arce, one in the Cathedral and the other for the sacristy of the church of La Congregación; also in the Cathedral are the three *Theological Virtues, St. Philip Neri,* and *The Holy Martyrs John and Paul.* A fine statue of *St. Sebastian Valfré* was destroyed in the Carranza revolution. The Canon lists the following sculpture by Arce in the Cathedral of Guadalajara: *St. Joachim, St. Dom-*

19 Revilla, *El arte en México.*

438

inic, St. Thomas Aquinas, St. Joseph, and *St. Anne.* The *St. Peter* and *St. Paul* in the choir also appear to be his work.

Mariano Montenegro

Of Montenegro we can say only that he was born in Querétaro in 1773, that, along with Perusquía, he worked with Francisco Escobar, a mestizo, and that afterwards he achieved great fame, as did Perusquía and Arce. Unfortunately we can add nothing more.

Querétaro was always a city rich in artists, most of all in the Baroque and Neoclassic periods. The list appended to the chapter on Baroque sculpture—taken from the census of 1791, with a few names from other sources—applies as well to this period. Let us hope that local historians, searching the archives which still remain in the city, will be able to write a more comprehensive history of sculpture there. In quality and importance it deserves no less.[20]

---

[20] I have placed the *nómina* of sculptors of Querétaro at the end of the chapter on Baroque sculpture, since, as we have pointed out, these craftsmen belong to both the Baroque and the Neoclassic periods.

Chapter Twenty-four

ACADEMIC PAINTING

IN NEW SPAIN

Pictorial Concepts

THE PICTORIAL ART of this period is not very different from the art in other media which we have been considering. The same criteria obtain: forms as precise as possible, controlled emotion, and an approach, however superficial, to Classical art. But one cannot deny a certain intensity and power to the movement, and two quite antithetical influences can be observed. On the one hand, there is Tiepolo, who shows how to decorate great spaces with airy figures moving freely in the ambient which vaults and cupolas provide. On the other hand, the example of Goya, a genius in all his creations, seems to demand inexorable realism as the unique quality possible in painting. We shall find both influences in Mexico—but without losing our sense of proportion, for we do not pretend to offer any masterpieces in this period.

The painting of this era was not, nor could it have been, comparable to that of earlier times. It may be superior in quality and technique to that of the Baroque painters immediately preceding, but it has neither their freshness nor their candor. Compared to the painting of the great centuries it is cold and conventional. But in spite of such criticisms we should not disdain this painting, for it is, after all, the expression of an epoch. Following the tradition of a history of art as impartial as may be, I wish to appraise whatever is good—though it would be autocratic to pretend to absolute judgment. Moreover, Neoclassic painting shows a sincerity of purpose comparable to that of the architecture. The sculptors were still more or less Baroque artists wearing a Classical disguise. In painting this is not so common, perhaps because it was less possible. In any case, a Neoclassic painter reveals himself as such in every brush stroke.[1]

The Professors of Painting at the Academy

José de Alcíbar and Francisco Clapera

Since there were at first no European painters to teach in the Academy, they made use of two colonial painters who were still active: José de Alcíbar and Francisco Clapera. We have already studied Alcíbar as a Baroque painter from the group around Cabrera; it remains only to add that he was acting director in the Academy until 1806, four years before the end of his

---

[1] See Justino Fernández, "Dibujos neoclásicos," *El hijo pródigo*, 2 (1943), 163-165.

long life (we have paintings by him dated as early as 1751). Clapera also began as a Baroque painter, and one can see traces of Cabrera's style in his work, although later he oriented himself to Neoclassicism. He painted an altarpiece of *Our Lady of Mercy* for the Sagrario of Mexico City. He held the same rank as Alcíbar until his death on March 10, 1810.

Don Andrés Ginés de Aguirre and
Don Cosme de Acuña

These two artists arrived in 1786 with that first boatload of European artists who proved so unlucky. The following year the Governing Board, mentioning Aguirre's irresponsibility, directed that Acuña should take over his pupils. But Acuña didn't want to stay in Mexico. He wanted to return to Spain, and gave the excuse of family troubles. The real reason was the enmity of Gil, who had intended to have other artists for his Academy; the charges he makes against Acuña are terrible, going so far as to hold him guilty of Arias' death. Acuña's petitions were refused, first in 1787 and then in 1789, but he persisted and returned to Spain, exactly when we do not know. In 1798 the King named him *pintor de cámara,* and on the thirteenth of September of the same year approved his nomination by the Academy of San Fernando as assistant director of painting; after the death of Don Francisco Bayeu, the director was no less than Don Francisco de Goya y Lucientes.[2] Busy as he was in the Academy, Acuña seems to have left little work in Mexico. Some drawings are mentioned, and a *St. Nicholas* in the Gutiérrez Victory Collection, besides his paintings—representing the baptisms of Christ, of St. Augustine, of Constantine, and of St. Philip of Jesus—which used to decorate the vault of the baptistry in the Sagrario of Mexico City.[3] Don Andrés Ginés de Aguirre continued in his position as director of painting under Jimeno's direction until he died. We do not know the date of his death, but Couto's note is explicit: "At the death of Aguirre in the beginning of this century,

the Government wished to have our compatriot Don Atanasio Echeverría for the second director of that section."[4] As for his painting, we can cite only a portrait, adequate enough, of *Don Ignacio Avila Bustamante,* which is dated 1788 and signed with the surname alone.

Don Rafael Jimeno y Planes

This distinguished and worthy professor was named to take Acuña's position. He had been born in Valencia in 1759, studied at the Academia de San Carlos there, and had won the third prize in 1773. The following year he had a scholarship to the Academia de San Fernando in Madrid, where he continued his studies with Mengs, and possibly with Bayeu. In 1777 he returned to Valencia and in 1783 was given a fellowship to study in Rome, where he stayed for three years. Back in Valencia he was named acting director of the Academy, and there he received the appointment as director of painting in the Academia de San Carlos of New Spain, which he accepted. The appointment is dated July 3, 1793, and Jimeno reached Mexico in May of the following year. He was married in Mexico, although it is not known when or to whom. At the death of Gil in 1798 he was named director general of the Academy; he was the second director, not the third, as is claimed by those who believe that Tolsá was the second. He died in the middle of 1825, at which time— if we are to believe Revilla—several months' salary was owing him. The Academy was weathering its first storms.

I shall speak first of the work of Jimeno in his native land, before going on to what he did in Mexico. In the Museo Provincial in Valencia there are two pictures by him: a figure copied from Raphael's *School of Athens,*[5] surely done while he was a student, and a *St. Sebastian.* In the edition of *Don Quixote* which the Academia de la Lengua published in 1780 can be found various plates drawn by him; and he made copies of the *Virgen de las Angustias,* a sculpture by Juan Adán, for the Escuelas Pias de San Fernando in Madrid. He also painted portraits in the Spanish capital from 1775 on, such as that of *Mengs,* his teacher, and one of the *Marquesa de los Llanos.*[6]

Now to outline his work in New Spain. A minor example, of which we have already spoken, is the drawing for the large engraving representing the Plaza Mayor of Mexico City (359). The only easel paintings mentioned in the literature are the following: an *Im-*

---

[2] Abelardo Carrillo y Gariel, *Datos sobre la Academia de San Carlos,* pp. 45–46.

[3] Manuel G. Revilla, *El arte en México en la época antigua y durante el gobierno virreinal,* p. 97.

[4] José Bernardo Couto, *Diálogo sobre la historia de la pintura en México,* p. 92.

[5] Cipriano Muñoz y Manzana Viñaza, *Adiciones al Diccionario histórico de D. Juan Ceán Bermúdez,* II, 225–226.

[6] For these references I am indebted to the kindness of Don J. M. González de Mendoza.

386. Rafael Jimeno y Planes. Miracle of the Well. Oil. Chapel of the College of Mines, Mexico City.

387. Rafael Jimeno y Planes. Assumption of the Virgin (detail). Oil. Cupola of the Cathedral of Mexico.

maculate Conception of great size, which Clavé considered his best painting[7] and which was owned by Señor Escandón; a *St. Joseph with the Child Jesus* in the Galería Buch; and, listed in the catalogue of the Fifteenth Exhibition of the Academy, a small portrait of *Tolsá,* belonging to Señor Garay, and a sketch, *Jesus Disputing with the Doctors,* owned by Señor Lucio.

In the Galerías de Pintura in Mexico City are his two magnificent portraits, one of *Don Jerónimo Antonio Gil* (color, facing p. 444)—a strong characterization showing him with the professional tools of the engraver—and one of *Don Manuel Tolsá* (381), a very fine Goyesque interpretation. There are several sketches: one, the *Miracle of the Well,* is for the large mural in the chapel of the School of Mines, where it can still be seen along with his *Assumption.* Other sketches are for a *Crucifixion,* and for *Our Lady of Carmel.* There is also a painting of *The Woman Taken in Adultery* in the Gallery.

In the Academia de Bellas Artes in Puebla there are a number of works by Jimeno which cannot be disregarded. There is a series of portraits in which the cold tonality does not detract from the precision of form and the trenchant interpretation of character. I believe there is another painting by Jimeno in the Davenport Municipal Art Gallery, in Davenport, Iowa, in the United States: a *Virgin and Child,* which combines a Tiepolesque airiness with the artist's Classical feeling.[8]

We must, however, look to Jimeno's mural paintings for his most ambitious work and the source of his fame. Painted in tempera (not fresco, as some say), they consist of: the decoration of the chapel of the Señor de Santa Teresa, the cupola of the Cathedral of Mexico, and the large rectangles of the chapel ceiling in the Colegio de Minería.

We have already spoken of the chapel rebuilt by González Velásquez between 1798 and 1813 for the crucifix called the *Señor de Santa Teresa.* Jimeno painted the legend of its restoration in the dome, and in the apse, the disturbances which occurred in the village of El Cardonal when they tried to bring the image to the capital.[9] Couto says that he acquired the sketch for the apse painting and put it in the Gallery of the Academy; at some time it disappeared from there, but has recently turned up on the antique market in Mexico. All of Jimeno's painting in this chapel was lost on April 7, 1845, when a frightful earthquake brought the building to the ground.

For the Colegio de Minería Jimeno did two large

tempera paintings, which still decorate the chapel ceiling. As we have said, one represents *The Miracle of the Well* (386), and the other is an *Assumption of the Virgin.* In these paintings we see Jimeno as neither a talented painter nor one who understood the problem of decorating such a situation. They are wrong in scale, and they are painted in perspective so that they would look right on a wall, and only there—instead of which one finds them on the ceiling, where they cannot be seen at all.

The work which brought Jimeno his greatest fame was the painting, in tempera, of the inside of the cupola of the Cathedral of Mexico (387). The most splendid building, the center of the Mexican Church, required the greatest painter of the time. It was finished on August 15, 1810. It represents the *Assumption of the Virgin,* to whom the church is dedicated, with a great multitude of figures filling up the space. Many European influences show in this work. It was Tiepolo who conceived this program—that one should superimpose on the actual architecture another, pictorial, architecture. Thus in a handsome cupola, derived from the Renaissance but interpreted by the Baroque, the imagination constructs an elegant balustrade, which opens up unbounded space where one can put anything one wishes. The general idea of the groups of figures comes from Tiepolo; some of them, like the Faith, Hope, and Charity, even show a more specific influence, if compared to the Italian artist's painting in the Scuola dei Carmini in Venice. The dependence is obvious, but when we examine Jimeno's figures in detail we find unmistakable traces of Goya's style also. There is, of course, nothing unusual in this; as we have seen, one was expected to copy everything.[10] It is said that the cupola was begun by Sáenz and finished by Jimeno; actually Sáenz seems to have been Jimeno's pupil and assistant there. That Jimeno was the author of the

[7] Couto, *Diálogo,* p. 94.

[8] See Toussaint, "Pinturas mexicanas en Davenport," *Anales del Instituto de Investigaciones Estéticas,* 14 (1946), 25–32; Justino Fernández, "Tiepolo, Mengs and Don Rafael Ximeno y Planes," *Gazette des Beaux-Arts,* Ser. 6, 23 (June, 1943), 345–362.

[9] Jimeno's source of inspiration was certainly the book by Dr. Alfonso Alberto de Velasco, *Renovación por si mismo de la soberana imagen de Christo Señor Nuestro crucificado, que llamas de Ytzimiquilpan.* Republished in 1698 as *Historia de la renovación del Santo Cristo del Cardonal,* it has been reprinted many times, with variations in title.

[10] Rafael Lucio, *Reseña histórica de la pintura mexicana en los siglos XVII y XVIII.*

388. José María Vásquez. Doña María Luisa Gonzaga
Foncerrada y Labarrieta. Oil. 1.03 x .79 m.
Pinacoteca Virreinal, Mexico City.

pletely destroys the architecture of the building. But it creates another architecture of its own, a celestial architecture, and within this his world floats. It is a pity that the tempera medium lacks the quality of purity and permanence of fresco painting. The work has deteriorated terribly with time, and restorations, however good they are, never succeed exactly in giving us what the artist left, to say nothing of his spirit.[11]

Students of the Academy

The first students to receive scholarships in painting were José María Guerrero, José María Vásquez, Augusto Cerezo, and Manuel García.[12] Of Guerrero—if he is the José Guerrero for whom I have documents—we know only that he copied the image of the Virgin of Guadalupe for Bartolache,[13] and that in 1808 he signed a really magnificent miniature, a portrait of his son, *José Manuel.* José María Vásquez has more personality. We have signed works by him from 1790 on; he was a follower of Jimeno and held the rank of *académico de mérito* and the position of acting director of painting—at least there is a picture of his so signed, dated 1801. When Jimeno died, he became director general of the Academy, to be succeeded in 1826 by Patiño Ixtolinque. Two works of his can be seen in the Galerías de Pintura, a delightful portrait of *Doña María Luisa Gonzaga Foncerrada y Labarrieta,* full of sincerity and feeling, signed in 1806 (388), and a *Crucifixion* of 1817. Manuel García appears in 1787, when with others, he inspected the Guadalupe picture for Bartolache's study. I can add nothing more. Of Cerezo, the single notice we have is his scholarship.

From the beginning it was planned that six students should be sent to Spain, to the Academia de San Carlos. In 1790 the Academy was asked to propose a suitable arrangement, if they could not themselves carry the expense of this. It is clear that some students did go to Spain on scholarships, where they worked with Don Cosme de Acuña after his return there. Thus there is record that in 1802 the stipend of the Indian *cacique* José Mariano del Águila should be extended, and that since Don Pablo de la Vega had died after making

whole design is shown by his drawings for the work. These belonged to Dr. Lucio, and are now treasured as the unique thing they are by Don Aniceto Castellanos. There are about ninety of them, a whole working set. In these one can appreciate the elegance of line and the artistic ability of Jimeno; it would be a pleasure to have a monograph on this artist.

The decoration of the cupola, as we have said, com-

[11] For these and other murals, see Raul Flores Guerrero, "Los muralistas del siglo XIX," *Artes de México,* 4 (1954), 31–56.

[12] Carrillo y Gariel, *Datos sobre la Academia,* p. 54.

[13] Francisco Javier Conde y Oquendo, *Disertación histórica sobre la aparición de la portentosa imagen de María Sma. de Guadalupe de México,* I, 270.

444

Rafael Jimeno y Planes. Portrait of Jerónimo Antonio Gil. Oil on canvas.
1.18 x .82 m. Pinacoteca Virreinal, Mexico City.

great progress in painting under Acuña, his stipend should be given to his brother, Don Francisco de la Vega, who was studying architecture.[14]

Other Painters in Mexico City

José Antonio Castro

He was a pupil of Jimeno, the most gifted of his pupils according to Revilla, who remarks that he had seen a little painting by Castro representing an allegory of the alliance of Spain and England against Napoleon at the beginning of the nineteenth century. Revilla also says that Castro moved to Guadalajara with Acuña, the sculptor from Querétaro, a little after Independence to take charge of the Academy of Drawing there.[15]

Juan de Sáenz

Also a pupil of Jimeno's, he worked with him on the painting of the cupola of the Cathedral of Mexico. The group of *St. Michael and the Rebel Angels* is attributed to him. Fernández Villa asserts, without any proof, that he died because of having misplaced one of Jimeno's drawings for this project. I have records of certain works by Sáenz, though certainly there must be many more. In the Colegio de Guadalupe near Zacatecas (now the Museo de Pinturas) there is a signed *Virgin of Light,* and in the same city a *Virgin of Bethlehem* owned by the Urízar family. The church of the Soledad in Mexico City has two large canvases dealing with *The Finding of the True Cross by St. Helena.* In the church of Tepalcingo in Morelos there are mural paintings imitating retables; this suggests that Sáenz, before entering the Academy, had a career as a Baroque painter.

Atanasio Echeverría

A draughtsman and naturalist, he was a member of the Noutka Expedition, which was directed by Sessé and included the naturalist Don José Mociño. This was in 1771.[16] Don Juan Cerda collaborated in the drawings, and in 1793 the viceregal government decreed that certain prints and drawings should be copied in the Academy to be sent to the court of Spain. Couto gives this note about Echeverría, although he makes a mistake in his name, calling him "Anastasio":

When Aguirre died, at the beginning of this century, the government wished to appoint as second director of the branch (of painting) our compatriot Don Anastasio Echeverría, the celebrated artist of the botanical expedition of Sessé and Mociño, whose magnificent *Flora Mexicana* is presumably in Madrid. Humboldt, who saw it, said that his drawings of plants and animals can compare to the best that Europe has produced in that genre. I have heard the same from Don Pedro de la Llave and others who know his work. However, there were circumstances which worked against his receiving the appointment to the Academy.[17]

Felipe Fabris

Curiously enough it is because of his bad reputation and misbehavior that we can give biographical data for this foreign-born painter, while we have nothing on the Mexicans. To be tried before the Inquisition was in those days the equivalent of full newspaper publicity. Fabris painted a portrait of the second Viceroy Revillagigedo, who seems to have been his patron; it is thought to be the portrait hanging in the Archivo General. He was born in Udine, in the Venetian Federation, in 1750. He stayed there until he was eighteen, when he set out to see the world—his world, Europe. He was in Rome for two or three years, where he studied with Geronimo Ricci. Then, for the adventure, he came to New Spain in 1784, and was an assiduous student at the night classes of the Academy. He struck up a friendship with the old Clapera, and even more intimately with the sons of Gil and with Tomás Suría, all three engravers. The Holy Office brought charges against him: heresy, erotic painting, and Freemasonry —especially the last, the fashionable crime of the time. There is no proof that he was a pornographic painter, but it does appear that he painted some things of this sort. Locked up in the prison of the Inquisition, he tried to escape; he had a bad fall and made his situation worse. It appears that Revillagigedo interceded for him, and that he was sent to Spain in 1791. He had stayed in Mexico about seven years, most of the time in jail.[18]

---

[14] Carrillo y Gariel, *Datos sobre la Academia,* p. 49.

[15] Revilla, *El arte en México,* p. 99.

[16] Archivo General de la Nación, Tomo 67, "Viajes y descubrimientos," No. 15. See also *Antología del Centenario,* ed. Luis Gonzaga Urbina, II, 884.

[17] Couto, *Diálogo,* p. 92.

[18] "Fragmento del proceso de Felipe Fabris," *Publicaciones del Archivo General de la Nación,* 21 (1932), 25–130. A partial account has been published by Francisco Pérez Salazar in his *Historia de la pintura en Puebla,* pp. 126–128.

José Perovani

There is another Italian, less boisterous, in this period. He seems to have come to Mexico at the turn of the century, since he appears among the followers of Patiño Ixtolinque. He is said to have been an *académico de mérito.* He painted portraits of two viceroys, *Calleja* and the *Conde del Venadito,* which are in the Museo de Historia. His painting is in no way extraordinary; it employs the same modest style used by the colonial painters in their commissions.

Francisco Ibar

Another figure of this period is Francisco Ibar, who besides being a painter wrote on politics—the times were right for this. In regard to his artistic *oeuvre* I can only state that he had some part in the catafalques erected in Mexico City, for Queen María Isabel Francisca de Braganza in 1810 and for the Queen Mother María Luisa de Bourbon in 1821. As a political writer he is best known for his *Muerte política de la República Mexicana* of 1829 and 1830, which was followed by the *Regeneración política de la República Mexicana,* a rare work more curious than useful.

José María de Uriarte

In 1817 the president of the Audiencia de Guadalajara, Don José de la Cruz, brought him to Guadalajara from Mexico City. He did various work there, and in 1819 and 1820 supervised the making of the catafalque for the obsequies of Queen María Isabel Francisca de Braganza.

Painting in Puebla

A group of artists of no great scope worked in Puebla at this time; they were active through the period of the War of Independence almost to the middle of the century. It is too bad that we have so little record of these good people.

Agustín Arrieta

This artist was an ingenuous and painstaking painter of the still-lifes—*bodegones* ("taverns") or *mesas revueltas* ("banquet-tables") as they call them—in which the Puebla collections are so rich.

Lorenzo Zendejas

The son of Jerónimo, shows neither the invention nor the productivity of his father. There are some pictures by him in Puebla churches; his *Self-Portrait* is unimportant. He died on the second of May, 1830.

José Julián Ordóñez

He was active in founding the Academy of Puebla. He painted the *Four Evangelists* for the Cathedral there, and some other things.

Salvador del Huerto

He was active at the end of the eighteenth century and the beginning of the nineteenth; there are pictures by him, though of no particular importance, dating from 1796 and 1798. In 1812 he signed, with other artists, an agreement to teach drawing without pay in an annex of the primary school; this was the beginning of the Academia de Bellas Artes of Puebla.

Miguel Carranza

A painter of the last days of the Colony, he married María Gertrudis García on June 9, 1818. He did work for the Cathedral of Puebla in the period after Independence.

Manuel López Guerrero

This artist is more interesting. He obviously goes back to the colonial period, since he married Doña María Gertrudis Romero on December 21, 1789, but he also took part in the founding of the Academy in Puebla. We know some pictures by him, of average quality.

José Luis Rodríguez de Alconedo

The figure of this man, the last great painter of the Colony, is notable in every way, and brings the story of colonial painting in Mexico to a distinguished conclusion. As if it were not enough to bequeath us his spirit in art, he gives also his life, as a patriot and revolutionary. He attained that greatest glory that man can attain: to die for his country. But before this he had achieved fame as an artist; like all great men, he was active in many fields. Primarily he was a silversmith, and as such we shall study him in the following chapter. He was a skilled craftsman, using the technique of fire gilding, and executed some very important work. Painting seems to have been a secondary interest which served for relaxation and pleasure, or to fill up the time when he was not working at something else. He would never have guessed that two of his pastel portraits would bring him immortality.

He was born in Puebla, where he was baptized on June 23, 1761, the son of Don José Rodríguez Alconedo and Doña Ignacia Sandoval y Rojas. There in 1780 he married Doña María Gertrudis de Acuña. He then went to Mexico City, and after an examination on October 22, 1791, was licensed as a silversmith. In 1794 he was granted the rank of *académico de mérito* in engraving. After he was established in the capital, his belief in the independence of Mexico involved him in more than one conflict. A man of great frankness, whose sincerity shines out—as one can see in his self-portrait—he was unable to hold his tongue, and so was enmeshed in the unhappy net which was to carry him to prison and finally to execution. Because of rash talk when Viceroy Iturrigaray was imprisoned, Alconedo was brought into court and his house was broken into. In the end he was sent to Spain under arrest with his brother Don José Ignacio, a pharmacist and botanist who was considered his accomplice. After many adventures he reached Cádiz on February 15, 1810. He was imprisoned and tried, and then the following year, on February 17, re-embarked for Mexico, to arrive at home on April 27, 1811. Although he had been acquitted in Spain, he was again thrown into prison, and was freed only after an energetic defense presented by his wife, on May 27. But a quiet life was impossible, especially as the War of Independence of which he had dreamed was being pressed by the great Morelos. Alconedo went south to join him. We do not know how long he was with the soldiers, but he was in Zacatlán when the town was unexpectedly taken by the royalist leader Luis del Águila. He seized Alconedo, who was taken to Apan and shot by order of Calleja, on March 1, 1815. So ended the hero's life.

His silverwork belongs to the following chapter, but we can look at his painting here. Six portraits are attributed to him, although only two are signed, the *Self-Portrait* and the portrait of *Señora Doña Teresa Hernández Moro* (389). The other four portraits are of *Francisco Pizarro,* the painter *José Manzo, Ferdinand VII,* and a *Lady with her Son.* The portrait of Señora Hernández Moro was signed in Cádiz in 1810, which may indicate that it was in Spain that Alconedo turned to portrait painting to earn some money. We need not wonder that this lady refused her portrait: her appearance and her spirit have been exposed so cruelly

389. José Luis Rodríguez de Alconedo. Doña Teresa Hernández Moro. Pastel. Academia de Bellas Artes, Puebla.

that one ought to thank her for letting us see it at all. When we look at this astonishing work of art, one name comes to our lips: Goya! Although it is impossible to show that the Mexican painter was a pupil of Goya's, it is his very spirit, realistic and pitiless, taking pleasure in a perfect representation of human imperfection, which breathes in this pastel. She sits as if at some all-too-human gathering, her fat soul shining out of her face, and indeed from every pore. Alconedo may have painted his own portrait on shipboard during the tedious days of his return voyage in February of 1811

447

390. José Luis Rodríguez de Alconedo. Self-Portrait. Pastel. Academia de Bellas Artes, Puebla.

the vulgarity of the face, he twines a garland of flowers on a classical bust. The assurance of the drawing, and the character which animates the painting make it a real masterpiece. The portrait of the lady with her child is less interesting; greater concessions are made to "beauty" and to making a good appearance. These three paintings are in the Academia de Bellas Artes of Puebla.

In the Museo del Alfeñique in the same city there is another portrait in pastel—a technique which seems to have been used in Puebla at that time only by Alconedo—representing *Ferdinand VII*. If it is by our painter, it should be grouped with the pastel of the lady and child; it is in fact quite mediocre.

In a private house I have seen twelve pictures in pastel of *The Apostles*. One of them has the signature of Alconedo and is dated 1813 in Mexico. Although they do not seem to be original work, but copies from engravings, possibly by Tiepolo, the hand of Alconedo is discernible in them.

The other two pictures attributed to him are probably not his work. Both portraits were in the collection of Don Rodolfo Bello in Puebla which is now the property of his son. The small *Portrait of Manzo* shows a skillful resemblance but little character; it is no more than a likeness. I am inclined to believe it is a self-portrait by Manzo. The so-called *Portrait of Pizarro* is simply a repainted picture of mid-nineteenth century, the work of some recalcitrant academician.[19]

(390). If he is cruel to the others, he is no less candid with himself. His hair disordered, his shirt open á la Byron, we are shown this swarthy man with his large, sensual mouth and his good-natured eyes. To balance

[19] On Alconedo, see Pérez Salazar, *Historia,* pp. 88–95, 198–200; three articles by Francisco de la Maza: "José Rodríguez de Alconedo," *Anales del Instituto de Investigaciones Estéticas,* 6 (1940), 39–56; "Nuevos datos sobre el artista José Luis Rodríguez Alconedo," *Anales del Instituto de Investigaciones Estéticas,* 11 (1944), 93–94; and "Las estampas de Alconedo," *Anales del Instituto de Investigaciones Estéticas,* 23 (1955), 69–74; and José Luis Bello and Gustavo Ariza, *Pinturas poblanas, siglos XVIII–XIX.*

Chapter Twenty-five

MINOR AND GRAPHIC ARTS

The Tolsá Style

THE METALWORK which dazzled us in the earlier parts of this history—so sumptuous in the Baroque period—now turns into something very conventional, very architectonic, and very monotonous. Its uniformity is such that we assume the style to have been fathered by a single man—Tolsá. In this period, to say "the Neoclassic style" is to say "the style of Tolsá," although we must admit that here, as in all his work, there is little originality. Referring to these artifacts, Romero de Terreros remarks with his usual circumspection: "It is our opinion that Don Manuel, if he did not copy them, at least was inspired by the models which were made popular at this time by a new edition of the *Varia conmesuración* of Juan de Arfe y Villafañe, published in 1806 in Madrid by Asencio y Torres, in two quarto volumes. The original illustrations were replaced by plentiful new plates drawn by Francisco Cremona, and in the second volume can be found those which certainly provided Don Manuel Tolsá with the models for his bronzes."[1] It is a fact, furthermore, that it was he who introduced the technique of bronze-gilt, thus adding,

so to speak, falsity to dullness, since an object made honestly of bronze, such as we see in the Baroque period, is preferable to a conventional piece of bronze hidden under a thin coating of gold. The Neoclassic period delights in mystification: they invented stucco as a substitute for marble and onyx, wood was painted like alabaster, bronze had to be gilded. In colonial times they gilded wood, but with no pretense whatever that the retable or pulpit was made of metal, much less of gold. They sometimes gilded iron, as on the grilles of the Cathedral of Puebla, but this was simply for decoration; just as they would paint with any other color, they painted in gold, even chairs or beds.

But we must distinguish the characteristics of this style we are censuring so freely, and point out its virtues. Instead of passing judgment, let us begin in this way. The positive qualities of the style of Tolsá are to be found in its logical articulation, its precision of drawing, and its technical perfection. After such vituperation, this is no faint praise: Señor Tolsá would, we imagine, be satisfied.

The bases of candelabra and monstrances are bell-shaped, more or less elevated, their flutings perfectly spaced and graduated (391). The perimeters are wreathed with strings of pearls or egg-and-dart, all very

---

[1] Manuel Romero de Terreros, *Artes industriales en Nueva España,* p. 72. See Juan de Arfe y Villafañe, *Varia conmesuración.*

391. Monstrance. Silver. Museo Nacional del Virreinato, Tepotzotlán, México.

classical. The shafts follow the Renaissance pattern for candelabra, but a goblet form is preferred, with hanging garlands harmoniously arranged on the outside, and with a fluted top, inversely curved, to hold the socket, or in the case of a custodia, the monstrance.

One should also remark that, as all this silver was cast in sections and put together with brass pins and bolts, there are examples which show the style of two or three periods in their parts.[2]

Frames are rectangular, avoiding Baroque fantasy. They have floral ornaments, or Classical moulding the same all around, and then at the top a *copete,* a central motif between the garlands which extend across the top to fall discreetly on both sides.

Inkwells and cruets for the Mass alike take on the shape of goblets and urns, and vary from a classicizing Baroque to a Louis XVI style, with even a few Empire

pieces. There are also pieces which are examples of popular art imitating the style of preceding periods.

Neoclassic Work in Gold and Silver

The quantity of artifacts in the precious metals in museums and private collections is so great that we must limit ourselves here to the most important.

In the inventory of the Cathedral of Mexico drawn up in the year 1819 we find a number of new and very rich pieces. Some of these are antique, some come from Europe, but many are the work of the great Mexican silversmiths of the period. Among the gifts of Señor Rubio y Salinas appears a gold chalice with its paten, which weighed 242 *castellanos,* and was decorated with 308 emeralds. Also a ciborium of gilded silver in the form of a shell.

The *maestraescuelas,* Señor Navarijo, presented a chalice, with a gold cup and octagonal base with reliefs in the Gothic style. From the estate of the prebendary, Don José Calderón, the church bought a chalice of gold made in France, adorned with ninety-six brilliants, twenty-eight emeralds, fifteen amethysts, thirty-six rubies and fifty-three pearls.

From the estate of Señor Núñez de Haro came a whole set of gold: a chalice with its paten and two spoons, a bell, cruets, and plate. When Señor Fonte took this chalice to Spain, his attorney, Don Atílano Sánchez, on August 6, 1842, turned over to the church in the name of the executors, "a chalice with paten, a spoon, cruets and plate, all of gold beautifully made, *quintado,* and weighing nine *marcos,* which cost, including the work, 2,000 pesos, according to the reckoning of the *patrón de platería,* Don José María Martínez." This note appears in the inventory of Osores.

The most important silversmith of the period, Don José María Rodallega, was born in Guadalajara in 1741. He passed his examinations in 1772, and must have died around 1812. He made fifty-nine articles for the Cathedral between 1780 and 1807, at a cost of more than 67,000 pesos.[3]

---

[2] For example, see Fig. 125 in Lawrence L. Anderson's unorganized and unwieldy volume, *The Art of the Silversmith in Mexico.* This shows a Neoclassic base, with a Baroque shaft, while the top, which has been turned on the lathe, may well be older. And this whole candlestick is called a genuine example of the style of Tolsá!

[3] This is Anderson's estimate (*Art of the Silversmith,* pp. 244–245). According to the material I give below, the number of his works for the Cathedral was far greater: for instance, there are sixty large candlesticks (*blandones*) alone.

We can mention only the more important of his works. Two crosses: one of plain silver with a base of the same, with gilded fillets and mouldings, on it a Christ about one *vara* long, of gilded bronze or calamine, the crown and nails of gilded silver, made in 1807; the other of gold with its Christ, and the pedestal loaded with precious stones, at a cost of 10,546 pesos and 3 *reales*. In 1805 sixty large candlesticks of *mestiza* silver. Six vases of *mestiza* silver with their garlands and twenty-four of white silver to hold flowers. Four urns of *mestiza* silver for the presbytery, with their pedestals, also of silver, which weigh 1,042 *marcos*, for which Rodallega was paid 16,672 pesos. In 1807 these were converted into incense burners, by putting bronze braziers in them. Two bronze lecterns given by the dean, Don Leandro Tarralba, with very fine frames of brass, fire-gilded; for these Rodallega charged 4,922 pesos, 5 *reales*.

Bruno, the treasurer of the Cathedral and its Mæcenas in this period, had Rodallega make eighteen lecterns, two of *mestiza* silver with tiaras embroidered on crimson velvet, eight of white silver with tiaras embroidered on velvet, and the other eight of white silver with the pontifical coat of arms gilded in the center. When one of these lecterns was stolen in 1825, it was replaced by melting up the silver from very old and much finer things. Rodallega was involved also in the work on the candlestick for the pascal candle which we have mentioned, although his part was confined to the silver overlay; for this he charged 15,400 pesos. Neither the patrons nor the silversmiths dreamed that their efforts would end in the melting pot.

When the church was low in funds, they paid for these objects partly in money and partly in old silver, a deplorable custom, since to make new things they destroyed the old pieces which were undoubtedly of greater artistic value. But as we have seen, this was the attitude of the period.

Such examples of liturgical art show how the churches and cathedrals were enriched in this era. In Puebla likewise, in Morelia or Guadalajara, there is a similar wealth of magnificent objects, which display the taste of the time and are rich with the precious stones that the faithful delighted in offering to the glory of God.

Gilded Bronze

We have already discussed this manifestation of Neoclassic taste. Although false in principle, it permits

392. José Luis Rodríguez de Alconedo. Charles IV. Silver. Museo Nacional de Historia, Mexico City.

a sumptuous ornamentation of buildings and altars, and its technical perfection combines with the fact that gold does not tarnish, to produce a practically permanent decoration.

We do not know whether Don Manuel Tolsá had his own shop for fire gilding or commissioned his work from other craftsmen. What we do know is that he paid 3,500 pesos for the gilding of the anchor, the cross, the chalice, and the flame, the attributes of his Virtues, on the Cathedral; the work is said to have

451

393. Juan Ortiz. Virgin of the Rosary. Woodcut. Archivo General de la Nación, Mexico City.

been done by Don Jerónimo Antonio Gil. His *Purísima* for the high altar of the Cathedral of Puebla was cast in bronze and gilded by Don Simón Salmón, and everyone was full of praise for the perfection of the work. The bust of Hernán Cortés for his tomb in the church of the Hospital de Jesús, and the coat of arms as well, were also of gilded bronze. One supposes that the bust was of considerable quality, but the tomb was destroyed in 1822 and the two pieces of bronze were sent to Italy.

All the famous silversmiths of the period worked in gilded bronze. Thus Antonio Caamaño is the author of the bronzes that decorate the often-mentioned high al-

tar of the Cathedral of Puebla, and of the very fine and restrained gilded bronze ornaments in the chapel of the College of Mines.

Rodríguez Alconedo, whose varied activities we have mentioned, achieved the rank of *académico de mérito* in the section of die cutting by making a silver relief portrait of Charles IV—a splendid work now in the Museo de Historia (392). But he also devoted himself to the meticulous task of gilding bronze, as we can see from the receipt for payment, on February 22, 1794, of 6,282 pesos, 3 *reales* for work on the façade of the Cathedral of Mexico. He had fire gilded, with twenty-four–carat gold, the trophies, crown, Order of the Golden Fleece, and Order of Charles III placed over the central door, and the crown and keys of the tiaras over the side doors.[4] Knowing this, we can understand the disappearance of these ornaments, "because of the carats of the gold."

Many more objects of gilded bronze were made in those days, but this is enough to demonstrate the taste, and to show the satisfaction which both the public and the craftsmen found in the technique.

Neoclassic Furniture

Like all forms of art, furniture follows the decrees of fashion. Of course I suppose that they did continue to use their Baroque furniture for a long time; nevertheless, in New Spain as in Spain itself and everywhere, they began to make a series of popular adaptations of Classical furniture. In the most fashionable mansions of the nobility one finds chairs, armchairs, tables in the style of Louis XVI; at least we see them in the portraits of the period, but never in such great number or of such quality as Baroque furniture. We can indeed say that, with some exceptions, Neoclassic furniture had no great development in New Spain because of the insecurity of the times.

Wood Engraving and Metal Engraving

Our history of the plastic arts in the colonial era would not be complete without some pages on the art of engraving, a medium highly refined and well suited to delicate expression.

The first appearance of engraving in New Spain is intimately connected with printing. It was necessary to decorate the books which were issuing from the new printing presses, and it was also necessary to make sa-

---

[4] See Francisco Pérez Salazar, *Historia de la pintura en Puebla.*

cred prints to be distributed at low cost among the recent converts. The first presses established in Mexico brought with them a certain number of blocks cut in Europe, but these were by no means sufficient. Hence the first wood engravers were improvised, so to speak. The most notable was Juan Ortiz, or whatever his name was—for he was French and a real adventurer, to judge by his trial (for a quite trivial crime) before the Inquisition in Mexico. His engraving of the *Virgin of the Rosary* (393), which made him so much trouble, shows us a medieval image, ably designed, with what may be portraits of contemporary people.[5]

The art of the pictorial woodcut, which in Europe was enriched by names like Dürer and Holbein, developed more modestly in New Spain, but it is interesting for the same reasons. We should perhaps make some technical comments of a simple didactic sort, if this is not presumptuous. The woodcut is made on a block of wood, cut with the grain; the artist is called a *cortador de tablas.* His task, certainly difficult enough, consists in leaving in relief an image or figure drawn by him or someone else. The block can then be used as part of the typographical composition, since its height and quality are identical with those of the printing type.

At the end of the sixteenth century another type of engraving appears in Mexico: they speak of sheets of brass called "plates" (*láminas*) and special paper to print from them. This was the copper engraving which had already produced fine work in Europe.

If a woodcut can be called *positive,* since every raised surface makes its mark on the paper, we should describe copper engraving in the opposite way, as *negative.* In this case it is the cuts made on the blank plate of copper which print on the paper. These indentations can be developed in two ways. The first, the more noble and difficult, is what we call "dry point." This is made by delicately scratching the copper with the burin. In prints made in this way the spirit seems to work directly. But human ingenuity, always looking for an easier way, discovered a chemical process for engraving the plate: it is covered with a varnish resistant to acid, and the drawing cuts through this to leave the copper exposed. When the plate is bathed in acid the

394. Alejo Infante. Our Lady of Refuge. Engraving.

parts penetrated by the drawing tool are eaten away. This operation can be repeated time after time, perfecting the drawing, and also printing successive copies which are called "states." This technique is known as "etching"; Rembrandt used it for some of his most remarkable creations.

During the seventeenth and eighteenth centuries wood engravings continued to be used for small decorations in books, while metal engraving, and especially etching, were introduced and developed. Most of this engraving had a popular character which fell far short of perfection (however appealing it may be to collectors!) (394). The list of engravers at the end of the chapter shows the importance of this activity in the colonial era.[6]

[5] On this point, see Edmundo O'Gorman, "An Early Mexican Xylograph Incunabula," *Mexican Art and Life* 7 (1939), 16–19; Manuel Toussaint, *El grabado en madera en México del siglo XVI a nuestros días.*

[6] Romero de Terreros, *Grabados y grabadores en la Nueva España.*

It was of course the founding of the Academy which introduced correct drawing and improved techniques. For the chair of metal engraving they had expected Don Fernando Selma, an excellent engraver, but as he did not accept the position, Don José Joaquín Fabregat was appointed instead. He reached Mexico in 1788 and died in 1807. The most important engravings of this artist are the print of the *Plaza Mayor de México* of which we have spoken (359), and the monumental *Plan of Mexico City* which Don Diego García Conde had drawn and Fabregat engraved in 1807. As Gil had wanted Selma, who was his son-in-law, to have the appointment, he was frightfully hard on the substitute:

Don Joaquín Fabregat, being no more than a middling professor of his Art, is very selfish and jealous and it is frankly he who has influenced everyone, holding meetings with them, to the end that the Academy should prohibit its students from working for the public for pay, so that no one else should be excessively recompensed as he is; because he has been provided, at the cost of the Academy, with all the tools necessary for printing and teaching his pupils, of whom the first were Marchena and Águila, and he was crafty enough to collect 300 pesos for the teaching of the said printing . . .[7]

The first three students in metal engraving were indeed Julián Marchena, José Mariano del Águila, and Ignacio Guerrero. Guerrero had his scholarship taken away for lack of application; it was given to Atanasio Echeverría, who in turn left it to go on the Botanical Expedition of Sessé, as we have seen. Finally it came to Luis Marenco, who requested that it be changed to painting, for which he had more talent.[8] Mariano del Águila received a scholarship to Spain, where we find him studying with Acuña when his grant was extended in 1802.[9]

At Fabregat's death he was succeeded as director of metal engraving by Pedro Vicente Rodríguez, who had been assistant director, and whose position was taken by Francisco Jordán. The last Academic engraver was Manuel Aráoz. One should note that Jerónimo Antonio Gil practised the art of copper engraving, as did his pupil Tomás Suría, although both were primarily die-casters, and we shall consider them in that category.[10]

Medallists

The art of making coins and medals has had an important place in man's artistic history. From the primitive coins of the Greeks and Romans, so precious to collectors, through the beautiful medals of the Renaissance, which rank with their sculpture and painting, we find exquisite works of art. The diemaker is actually a sculptor of miniature bas-reliefs, who must know how to make a concave carving on the steel dies which by pressure will strike the coins or medals from gold, silver, or bronze.

The first coins of New Spain, those called *macuquinas,* or crosses, are rudimentary and not really coins at all, but simply metal disks with the official seal. People cut them up when they could not be exchanged for pieces of lesser value. Next came the *columnaria,* named after the Columns of Hercules, which appeared on them. The dies with which the first money was made came from Spain; a blow by a hammer stamped them into the soft metal. We know that in 1619 Diego Martínez was coiner in the Real Casa de Moneda, the Royal Mint; in 1636 Juan Ambrosio held the position; and in that year Antonio Maldonado had died. In 1646 Vicente Hernández had the same title.

It appears that there was no diecutter at the Mint until the eighteenth century. The first name mentioned in this office is Francisco Prieto in 1767.[11] Next appears Don Alejo Madero, to whose pensioning we owe the appointment of Don Jerónimo Antonio Gil on January 26, 1778. Gil arrived on December 24, and, as we have seen, played a great role in the founding of the Academia de San Carlos. However, he was first and foremost a die cutter, and for that reason we have waited until now to take up his biography. He was born in Zamora, in Spain, on November 2, 1731. He studied at the Academia de San Fernando in Madrid, and received a scholarship to complete his artistic education under Don Tomás Prieto. In 1756 he was awarded a first prize for the second class in painting. But his natural interest was in medals, and his production in this field was such that he can be considered one of the outstanding craftsmen of the period. It was his medal for the Montepío de los Cosecheros de Málaga which, according to Ceán Bermúdez,[12] brought him the posi-

---

[7] Abelardo Carrillo y Gariel, *Datos sobre la Academia de San Carlos.*

[8] *Ibid.,* p. 54.   [9] *Ibid.,* p. 59.

[10] Justino Fernández, *El grabado en lámina en la Academia de San Carlos durante el siglo XIX.*

[11] Sebastián C. Navallón, *El grabado en México.* For the history of money, see the article by Manuel Orozco y Berra in the *Diccionario universal de historia y geografía.* See also Romero de Terreros, *La moneda mexicana; bosquejo histórico-numismático.*

[12] Juan Agustín Ceán Bermúdez, *Diccionario histórico de los mas ilustres profesores de las bellas artes en España,* II, 187.

tion of *grabador mayor*—that is, chief engraver—to the Royal Mint in Mexico. We have already seen that one of his tasks was the establishment of a school of engraving, and how, through his efforts and with the approval of Mangino, the Academia de San Carlos de Nueva España grew out of this school. Gil brought with him his two sons, Bernardo and Gabriel, though his wife, Doña Magdalena Ramos, refused to leave the Spanish court, and was later put in a convent. As in all great enterprises, Gil had to suffer the consequences of his zeal, especially when the first professors arrived from Europe. In the first place, instead of the artists he had wanted, other and less talented men were sent; and secondly, they seem to have made their "Voyage to the Indies" as a pleasure trip, without worrying about the good salaries they enjoyed. Hence the director of the Academy of San Carlos—granted that nothing turned out right—became exacting, lost his head, and finished by quarrelling with everyone who did not satisfy him. We have referred to some of these incidents. Gil died on April 18, 1798, and was buried in the church of the Tercer Orden de San Francisco. Jimeno has left us his portrait in the gallery of the venerable Academy (color, facing p. 446). We see an energetic countenance, the vigorous personality clearly expressed; he holds a die in his hand.

One must separate this personal life, with all its turmoil of large or petty problems, from the artist's *oeuvre*, and the indelible influence of his spirit on his pupils. Besides the medals he made in Spain, which quickly won him the rank of *académico de mérito* in the Academia de San Fernando in Madrid, there are a number which he struck in New Spain. Ceán lists the following: the medals and coins for the proclamation of Charles IV as King, six for the Consulado and another for the Tribunal de Minería, also two for Guadalajara and others for Querétaro, Oaxaca, and Veracruz. He also made two medals commemorative of the statue of Charles IV. The medals commemorating the founding of the Academy in Mexico were naturally also his work (395).

Like practically all die casters he also engraved on copper, although this work, which must have seemed so easy, is not of the same quality. Some writers mix up the two media as if we were speaking of only one.

Gil began engraving in Europe, where he illustrated the *Reinas Católicas* of Padre Flores; he also engraved the *Proporciones del cuerpo humano* and the portrait of Charles III for the works of the V. Palafox, and

395. Jerónimo Antonio Gil. Medal Commemorating the Founding of the Academia de San Carlos. Silver. Museo Nacional de Historia, Mexico City.

very likely others. These engravings are inferior to his work in Mexico. The portraits of the *Conde de Gálvez* and of *Don Miguel,* his son, and above all that of the *Marqués de Sonora,* of 1787, are perfect in technique and in their classical interpretation. Some—and I among them—may prefer the popular engravings of the eighteenth century, but the fact is indisputable: these are as perfect as the best of European engraving.

Gil's favorite pupil was Tomás Suría. A restless spirit, who seems never to have found his proper vocation, we see him as an artist with the Malaspina Expedition, as a die cutter, and as an engraver.[13] He was born in 1761 and came to Mexico as Gil's pupil; on December 21, 1778, he was given a stipend in the Casa de Moneda. He was a member of Malaspina's fruitless expedition in search of a northwest passage: they sailed from Acapulco in 1791, but returned in November of the same year. The drawings he made on this trip have only a scientific, or rather an anthropological value. He went back to his engraving, which he should never have left, and filled Gil's place as director of engraving (diemaking) at his death in 1798. In 1806 he was promoted to *contador ordinario de pagos* (third class). He seems to have died in Mexico City sometime after 1834.

Suría, like his teacher Gil, worked both as die cutter and as engraver, probably because there were more commissions for engraving than for medals. In both media Suría shows himself a conscientious and adequate craftsman. Concerning his medals, Don José Toribio Medina remarks: ". . . they are of much more note [than his engravings]; he made a good many medals which in size, drawing, and composition are not surpassed by the Peninsular artists of the epoch."[14]

The two sons of Gil, Gabriel and Bernardo, were also among his first pupils, as were Juan Ignacio Bacerot, José Esteve, Manuel López, and José Cervantes. Unfortunately the art of engraving was dying out—be it wood, metal, or die cutting. In vain did professors like Periam and Bagally arrive; all they could produce were Academic works, technically perfect, but colder and less significant the more skillful they became. Technology was to put an end to all these things, and even to the lithography which reached such artistic heights in mid-nineteenth century. But art never dies, although it has its decadent or discouraged periods. So, just as Mexican painting has risen from the Academic

corpse, so to speak, to produce one of the most vital movements in contemporary art, wood engraving, etching, and lithography have begun a brilliant new life in our time.

List of Metal Engravers:

Samuel Stradanus (1606–1622); C. Rosillo (1679); Antonio Isarti (1682); Miguel Guerrero (1694); Francisco de Torres (1688); Villegas (1686); Alberto de Castro (1696); Andrade; Antonio de Castro (1691–1732); Bernadino Alemán (1701); Mota (1712); Francisco Silverio (1721–1761); Amado (1727); Santillán (1728); Pedro Rodríguez (1732); Joaquín Sotomayor (1728–1738); Baltasar Troncoso (1743–1760); Balbás (1746–1747); Ponce (1747); Francisco Amador (1734–1748); Antonio Onofre Moreno (1734–1774); José Benito Ortuño (1751–1765); Villegas (1757); Salcedo (1753–1758); Francisco Rodríguez (1753–1759); José Morales (1753–1763); Francisco Márquez (1753); Fray Francisco Jiménez (1755–1756); Sotomayor (1756); S. T. M. (1756); Andrade (1757–1777); Sandoval (1762); M. Villavicencio (1762–1795?); J. de Naxera (1767); José Mariano Navarro (1769–1774); Francisco Casanova (1769–1791); Agustín Moreno (1774); Espejo (1775); I. García de las Prietas (1775–1802); Benavides (1788); Parra (1780); Pavía (1780–1793); Mera (1782); J. Joaquín Fabregat (d. 1807); Julián Marchena; José Mariano del Águila; Ignacio Guerrero; Tomás Suría (1785–1813); Atanasio Echeverría; Francisco Eduardo Tresguerras; Manuel López López; Pedro Vicente Rodríguez; Francisco Jordán; Manuel Aráoz.

List of Die Cutters:

Francisco Prieto (1767); Alexo Madero; Jerónimo Antonio Gil; Tomás Suría; José Esteve; J. Ignacio Gordillo; José Ignacio Bacerot; Manuel López; José Cervantes; Bruno Gómez; José Molina y Garrido; Bernardo Gil; Gabriel Gil; Echeverría; Cerda.

13 Justino Fernández, *Tomás Suría y su viage con Malaspina.*
14 José Toribio Medina, *La imprenta en México, 1539–1821,* Introduction.

CONCLUSION

After a long and ardent journey through our Mexican art, we find ourselves at the end of the road. From the heights which we have so laboriously attained, let us cast a glance back at the landscape through which we have passed. How varied, how intense, how full of life is the panorama of Mexican art in the colonial period! The most diverse moods, the most contrasting personalities, have worked to bequeath us this great legacy of Hispanic art.

Such interesting phenomena as the living prolongation of the Middle Ages in America, the flowering of a Renaissance worthy of Spain herself, or the submerged survival of the Indian spirit which imparts to all the creations that its mind conceives and its hands execute an ineluctable stamp of melancholy, of rich complication, of nostalgia. And in contrast to such things, the brilliant production of art in the European mode, which gives way little by little to other ideas and new achievements of the Mexican mind and spirit. It is not without emotion that one attends the birth of a new culture and a new nation. If early evidence of Mexico as a nation distinct from the rest of the world is not so plain in our political history, it reveals itself clearly in the plastic arts of the colonial period. The different ethnic elements begin to fuse; and a new group of men appear—men who realize that along with their Spanish origin they have received a heritage of intellectual independence and an endowment of the soundest and most noble principles. Before our eyes there emerges the artistic expression of a new nation which has found its own language in forms universally comprehensible. The Baroque style comes to perfection in Mexico—if we can so describe a thing which becomes more perfect the less pure it is. We are overwhelmed by the great religious architecture of eighteenth-century Mexico, which makes New Spain the equal, if not the superior, of any Baroque country in the world.

At the end of the colonial period, just before our day, the Neoclassic movement, inspired by the Academy and its professors from Europe, presumes to extinguish the protean, chaotic life of the Baroque. It succeeds merely in producing monuments which are clearly importations and which contrast miserably with the relics of the great preceding period. Yet it was then, within these very Neoclassic concepts, that Mexico achieved her independence. Fortunately she had already recorded her real history in art. I trust that I have faithfully interpreted that history in the review which I here offer to the students of American art, with my most heartfelt enthusiasm.

México, November 27, 1945

SOURCES OF ILLUSTRATIONS

Berko
182

Hugo Brehme
122, 288, 370

The Brooklyn Museum
310, 346

Gabriel Ibarra
114, 115

Instituto de Investigaciones Estéticas
12, 13, 17, 33, 34, 42, 45, 65, 79, 94, 109, 110, 114, 115, 121, 123, 127, 130, 131, 133, 134, 135, 136, 139, 148, 169, 177, 183, 187, 188, 197, 201, 216, 217, 218, 220, 221, 226, 227, 228, 229, 230, 232, 233, 234, 235, 237, 238, 245, 249, 264, 287, 308, 310, 313, 318, 331, 376, 382, 383, 385, 392, 394, 395. *Color Plates* 1, 2, 3, 9.

Instituto Nacional de Antropología e Historia, Archivo de Monumentos Coloniales y de la República
2, 3, 5, 6, 9, 10, 11, 14, 15, 18, 19, 20, 22, 23, 24, 26, 27, 29, 30, 31, 32, 35, 40, 41, 46, 49, 51, 52, 54, 56, 60, 61, 66, 67, 69, 70, 71, 72, 73, 75, 76, 78, 80, 87, 90, 91, 92, 95, 98, 99, 100, 101, 102, 106, 108, 111, 112, 113, 117, 118, 119, 120, 125, 126, 128, 129, 132, 143, 144, 145, 146, 147, 149, 150, 155, 157, 159, 161, 162, 163, 164, 166, 167, 168, 170, 171, 172, 173, 174, 175, 176, 178, 179, 180, 184, 185, 186, 189, 191, 192, 193, 194, 199, 202, 203, 206, 207, 208, 210, 212, 219, 223, 225, 231, 236, 239, 240, 241, 242, 244, 246, 248, 251, 252, 253, 254, 255, 256, 259, 260, 262, 263, 266, 268, 269, 271, 274, 275, 276, 277, 278, 279, 280, 281, 282, 283, 284, 289, 290, 291, 292, 293, 294, 295, 296, 297, 298, 299, 300, 301, 302, 303, 304, 305, 306, 307, 311, 312, 319, 322, 325, 327, 328, 329, 330, 332, 333, 334, 335, 337, 342, 343, 345, 348, 350, 352, 354, 357, 362, 366, 368, 369, 373, 374, 375, 377, 379, 384, 390

Guillermo Kahlo
47, 164, 198, 205, 250, 272, 323, 360

Elisabeth Kelemen
211

Laboratories Julio
183

The Library of Congress
28, 36, 37, 351

Luis Limón
137, 138, 140, 141, 142, 228, 315

John McAndrew
39, 43, 77, 81, 82, 83, 84, 85, 86, 107, 153, 190

Luis Márquez
58, 59, 121, 142, 154, 204, 213, 215, 222, 224, 265, 314, 320, 321, 336, 344, 355, 363, 364, 371, 372, 384, 386, 388, 389, 391

The Metropolitan Museum of Art
160, 243

Loren Mozley
89, 200, 261, 273, 365

Museo de Arte Religioso
57, 62, 156, 338, 339, 340, 391

Museo Nacional de Antropología
63

Museo Nacional de Historia
58, 311, 312, 395

Museum of New Mexico
358

Mario Octavio Peralta
Color 5

Raul Pulido
Color 7, 8

Walter Reuter
Color 4

F. J. Rhode
45

Ricardo Salazar
229

Martin Soria
7, 316, 317

Suárez
387

Salvador Toscano
53

The University of Texas
4, 16, 165, 181, 247, 286, 341, 365, 367

Elizabeth Wilder Weismann
21, 25, 38, 44, 48, 50, 55, 68, 88, 93, 103, 104, 105, 116, 151, 152, 209, 214, 258, 270, 285, 347

Marianne Yampolsky
Color 6

BIBLIOGRAPHY

Abarca, José Mariano. *El sol en León; solemnes aplausos conque el rey nuestro Señor D. Fernando VI . . . fué celebrado el dia II de febrero del año de 1747*. México: María de Ribera, 1748.

Acosta, Jorge R., José Gorbea Trueba, and Pablo Martínez del Río. *Tula, guía oficial*. México: Instituto Nacional de Antropología e Historia, 1957.

Advertimientos generales que los Virreyes dejaron a sus sucesores para el gobierno de Nueva España, 1590–1604. Ed. France V. Scholes and Eleanor B. Adams. México: Porrua, 1956.

Aguilar, Gilberto F. *Hospitales de antaño*. México: Hospital Juárez, 1944.

Alamán, Lucas. *Disertaciones sobre la historia de la República Megicana*. Mégico: J. M. Lara, 1844.

Album mexicano; colección de paisajes, monumentos, costumbres y ciudades principales. México: Antigua Litografía Debray Sucs., n.d.

Aldaña, Cristóbal de. *Crónica de la Merced de México*. Ed. Jorge Gurria Lacroix. México: Biblioteca Nacional, 1953.

Alemán, Mateo. *The Sucesos of Mateo Alemán*. Ed. Alice H. Bushee. Paris: Macon Pretat Frères, 1911.

Almela y Vives, Francisco, and A. Igual Ubeda. *El arquitecto y escultor valenciano Manuel Tolsá, 1757–1816*. Valencia: Diputación Provincial, 1950.

Álvarez, Federico. *El Palacio Nacional*. México: Editorial Espartaco, 1959.

Álvarez, Manuel F. *Apuntes biográficos de arquitectos mexicanos*. México: Vargas Rea, 1955.

————. *El Palacio de Minería*. México: Ministerio de Instrucción Pública y Bellas Artes, 1910.

————. *Las pinturas de la Academia Nacional de Bellas Artes*. México: 1917.

Álvarez Cortina, M. and Alberto Le Duc. "Sagrario de México," *Archivo español de arte y archaeología,* 11 (1935), 97–101.

Anderson, Lawrence Leslie. *The Art of the Silversmith in Mexico*. New York: Oxford University Press, 1941.

Angulo Íñiguez, Diego. *La Academia de Bellas Artes de Méjico y sus pinturas españoles*. Sevilla: La Gavidia, 1935.

————. *Arquitectura mudéjar sevillana de los siglos XIII, XIV, XV*. Sevilla: Gráficas Marinas, 1932.

————. *La arquitectura neoclásica en Méjico*. Madrid: Real Academia de Bellas Artes de San Fernando, 1958.

————. *Bautista Antonelli*. Madrid: 1942.

————. "La capilla de indios de Teposcolula y la catedral de Siena," *Archivo español de arte,* 25 (1952), 170–172.

————. "Las catedrales mejicanas del siglo XVI," *Boletín de la Real Academia de la Historia,* 113 (1943), 137 ff.

————. *La cerámica de Puebla (Méjico)*. Madrid: 1946.

————. "Eighteenth-Century Church Fronts in Mexico City," *Journal of the Society of Architectural Historians,* 5 (1945–1946), 27–32.

————. "Mudejar Style in Mexican Architecture," *Ars Islamica,* 2 (1935), 225–230.

————. "Pereyns y Martín de Vos," *Anales del Instituto de Arte Americano e Investigaciones Estéticas,* 2 (1949), 25–27.

————. *Planos de monumentos arquitectónicos de América y Filipinas*. Sevilla: Universidad de Sevilla, 1933–1940.

Angulo Íñiguez, Diego, Enrique Marco Dorta, and Mario Buschiazzo. *Historia del arte hispanoamericano*. Barcelona and Buenos Aires: Salvat, 1945–1956.

Antología del Centenario. Ed. Luis Gonzaga Urbina. México: M. León Sánchez, 1910.

Arellano Garza, Humberto. "Arts and Crafts in Mexico," *Texas Quarterly,* 2 (Spring 1959), 156–167.

Arfe y Villafañe, Juan de. *Varia conmesuración para la escultura y arquitectura* (1585). Madrid: Imprenta Real, 1806.

Armando, Nicolau. *Valenciana*. México: Dirección de Monumentos Coloniales, Instituto Nacional de Antropología e Historia, 1961.

Arnaiz y Freg, Arturo. "Noticias sobre la Academia de Bellas Artes de San Carlos," *Anales del Instituto de Investigaciones Estéticas,* 2 (1938), 21–43.

Arroyo, Antonio. *El monumental convento de Santo Domingo de Oaxaca*. Oaxaca: 1955.

Arroyo, Esteban. *La reconstrucción del altar mayor del templo de Santo Domingo de Oaxaca*. Oaxaca: 1959.

Atl, Dr. See Murillo, Gerardo.

Baird, Joseph A. *The Churches of Mexico, 1530–1810.* Berkeley: University of California Press, 1962.

———. "The Eighteenth Century Retable in the South of Spain, Portugal, and Mexico." Unpublished doctoral thesis, Harvard University, 1951.

———. "Eighteenth Century Retables of the Bajío, Mexico: the Querétaro Style," *Art Bulletin,* 35 (1953), 197–216.

———. "Mexican Architecture and the Baroque," *International Congress of the History of Art, XX, New York, 1961.* Princeton, New Jersey: Princeton University Press, 1963, 191–202.

Balbuena, Bernardo de. See Valbuena.

Barber, Edwin Atlee. *The Emily Johnston De Forest Collection of Mexican Maiolica.* New York: Metropolitan Museum of Art, 1914.

———. *The Maiolica of Mexico.* Philadelphia: Pennsylvania Museum, 1905.

Barrio Lorenzot, Francisco del. *Ordenanzas de gremios de la Nueva España.* Ed. Genaro García. México: Secretaría de Industria, Comercio y Trabajo, 1920–1921.

Basalenque, Diego. *Historia de la provincia de San Nicolás de Tolentino de Michoacán del orden de n. p. S. Agustín* (1673). México: Voz de México, 1886.

Baxter, Sylvester. *La arquitectura hispano colonial en México.* Trans. with notes by Manuel Toussaint. México: Departamento de Bellas Artes, 1934.

———. *Spanish-Colonial Architecture in Mexico.* Boston: J. B. Millet, 1901.

Beaumont, Pablo de la Purísima Concepción. *Crónica de la Provincia de los Santos Apóstoles S. Pedro y S. Pablo de Michoacán, de la regular observancia de N.P.S. Francisco.* México: Archivo General de la Nación, 1932.

Bello, José Luis, and Gustavo Ariza. *Pinturas poblanas: Siglos XVII–XIX.* México: Atlante, 1943.

Benevente, Toribio de. See Motolinía.

Benítez, Fernando. *La vida criolla en el siglo XVI.* México: Colegio de México, 1953.

Benítez, José R. *Algunas noticias inéditas o poco conocidas referentes a pintores y alarifes de la Nueva España.* Guadalajara: 1948.

———. *Alonso García Bravo, planeador de la ciudad de México y su primer director de obras públicas.* México: Cía. de Fomento y Urbanización, 1933.

———. *Las catedrales de Oaxaca, Morelia y Zacatecas.* México: Talleres Gráficos de la Nación, 1934.

———. *La fuente monumental de Chiapa de Corzo.* Guadalajara: 1941.

———. *Morelia.* México: Talleres Gráficos de la Nación, 1935.

Berlin, Heinrich. "El arquitecto Joseph Eduardo de He-rrera," *Anales del Instituto de Arte Americano e Investigaciones Estéticas,* 17 (1964), 90–98.

———. "El arquitecto Pedro de Arrieta," *Boletín del Archivo General de la Nación,* 16 (1945), 73–94.

———. "Artífices de la catedral de México," *Anales del Instituto de Investigaciones Estéticas,* 11 (1944), 19–39.

———. "La catedral de Morelia y sus artistas," *Anales de la Sociedad de Geografía e Historia de Guatemala,* 27 (1953–1954), 146–168.

———. "El convento de Tecbatán," *Anales del Instituto de Investigaciones Estéticas,* 9 (1942), 5–13.

———. "Dos estudios mexicanos: Artistas y milagros; un tenebrario de Pedro Maldonado," *Anales del Instituto de Arte Americano e Investigaciones Estéticas,* 15 (1962), 109–124.

———. *Fragmentos desconocidos del Códice de Yanhuitlán y otras investigaciones mixtecas.* México: Antigua Librería Robredo de J. Porrua, 1947.

———. "The High Altar of Huejotzingo," *The Americas,* 15 (1958), 63–73.

———. "El ingeniero Luis Diez Navarro en México," *Anales de la Sociedad de Geografía e Historia de Guatemala,* 22 (1947), 89–95.

———. "Pintura colonial mexicana en Guatemala," *Anales de la Sociedad de Geografía e Historia de Guatemala,* 26 (1952), 118–128.

———. "Salvador de Ocampo, a Mexican Sculptor: Documents," *The Americas,* 1 (1948), 415–428, 510–518.

———. "Sebastián de Arteaga, pintor de la Inquisición," *Anales del Instituto de Arte Americano e Investigaciones Estéticas,* 11 (1958), 53–56.

———. "Three Master Architects in New Spain," *Hispanic American Historical Review,* 27 (1947), 375–383.

Bermúdez de Castro, Diego Antonio. "Teatro angelopolitano, o histórica de la ciudad de la Puebla," in Nicolás León, *Bibliografía mexicana del siglo XVIII.* México: 1908.

"Bodegones mexicanos," *Artes de México,* 41 (1962), 3–16.

Bonavit, Julián. "Esculturas tarascas de caña de maíz y orquídeas," *Anales del Museo Michoacana,* Ep. 2, No. 3 (1944), 65–78.

Borah, Woodrow W. *Silk Raising in Colonial Mexico.* Berkeley: University of California, 1951.

Burgoa, Francisco de. *Geográfica descripción* (1674). México: Archivo General de la Nación, 1934.

———. *Palestra historial de virtudes y exemplares apostólicos* (1670). México: Archivo General de la Nación, 1934.

Buschiazzo, Mario. *Estudios de arquitectura colonial hispanoamericana.* Buenos Aires: Kraft, 1944.

————. *Historia de la arquitectura colonial en Ibero-américa*. Buenos Aires: Emecé, 1961.

Cabrera, Miguel. *Maravilla americana*. México: Real mas Antigua Colegio de San Ildefonso, 1756.

Calderón Quijano, José Antonio. *Historia de las fortificaciones en Nueva España*. Sevilla: Escuela de Estudios Hispano-Americanos, 1953.

Calí, François. *L'art des conquistadors*. Paris: B. Arthaud, 1960.

————. *The Art of the Conquistadors*. London: Thames and Hudson, 1961.

Carreño, Alberto María. "Los órganos, el Altar del Perdón y las tribunas de la catedral metropolitana de México," *Memorias de la Academia Mexicana de la Historia*, 16 (1957), 326–338.

Carrera Stampa, Manuel. "Fuentes o pilas 'económicas' del México colonial," *Anales del Instituto de Investigaciones Estéticas*, 8 (1942), 61–75.

————. *Los gremios mexicanos; la organización gremial en Nueva España, 1521–1861*. México: Ibero-americano, 1954.

————. *Guía artística de la ciudad de México y sus delegaciones*. México: Secretaría de Educación Pública, 1955.

Carrillo y Ancona, Cresencio. *El obispado de Yucatán; historia de su fundación y de sus obispos*. Mérida: R. B. Caballero, 1895.

Carrillo y Gariel, Abelardo. *Autógrafos de pintores coloniales*. México: Instituto de Investigaciones Estéticas, Universidad Nacional Autónoma de México, 1953.

————. *El Cristo de Mexicaltzingo; técnica de las esculturas en caña*. México: Dirección de Monumentos Coloniales, Instituto Nacional de Antropología e Historia, 1949.

————. *Datos sobre la Academia de San Carlos*. México: 1939.

————. *Evolución del mueble en México*. Dirección de Monumentos Coloniales, Instituto Nacional de Antropología e Historia, 1957.

————. *Las galerías de pintura de la Academia de San Carlos*. México: Instituto de Investigaciones Estéticas, Universidad Nacional Autónoma de México, 1950.

————. *Imaginería popular novo-española*. México: Ediciones Mexicanas, 1950.

————. *Ixmiquilpan*. México: Dirección de Monumentos Coloniales, 1961.

————. *Técnica de la pintura de Nueva España*. México: Instituto de Investigaciones Estéticas, Universidad Nacional Autónoma de México, 1946.

Cartas de Indias. Madrid: Ministerio de Fomento, 1877.

Casas, Bartolomé de las. *(Apologética) Historia de las Indias*. Ed. Marqués de la Fuensanta del Valle and José Sancho Rayón. Madrid: M. Ginesta, 1875–1876.

Castro Mantecón, Javier, and Manuel Zárate Aquino. *Miguel Cabrera, pintor oaxaqueño del siglo XVIII*. México: Dirección de Monumentos Coloniales, 1958.

Castro Morales, Efraín, "La catedral de Puebla y Juan Gómez de Trasmonte," *Anales del Instituto de Investigaciones Estéticas*, 32 (1963), 21–36.

————. "Francisco Becerra en el valle de Puebla, México," *Anales del Instituto de Arte Americano e Investigaciones Estéticas*, 13 (1960), 11–26.

————. "Un grabado neoclásico," *Anales del Instituto de Investigaciones Estéticas*, 33 (1964), 107–109.

————. "Luis de Arciniega, maestro mayor de la Catedral de Puebla," *Anales del Instituto de Investigaciones Estéticas*, 27 (1958), 17–32.

————. "Las yeserias de la iglesia vieja de 'La Compañía' de Puebla," *Anales del Instituto de Investigaciones Estéticas*, 28 (1959), 85–90.

Castro Santa-Anna, José Manuel de. *Diario de sucesos notables, 1752–1754*. Méjico: 1854.

Catálogo de construcciones religiosas del Estado de Hidalgo. México: Dirección General de Bienes Nacionales, 1940.

Catálogo de construcciones religiosas del Estado de Yucatán. México: Dirección General de Bienes Nacionales, 1945.

La catedral y el sagrario de México. México: Dirección General de las Bellas Artes, 1917.

Ceán Bermúdez, Juan Agustín. *Diccionario histórico de los mas ilustres profesores de las bellas artes en España*. Madrid: Vda. de Ibarra, 1800.

Cedulario. See Puga, Vasco de.

Cervantes, Enrique A. "Bosquejo del desarrollo de la ciudad de Puebla," *Universidad*, 4 (diciembre, 1937), 11–15; 5 (enero, 1938), 14–29.

————. *Catedral metropolitana: sillería del coro*. México: Secretaría de Hacienda, 1936.

————. "El colateral de Santo Domingo en la ciudad de Puebla," *Revista mexicana de estudios históricos*, 2 (1928), 10–17.

————. *Herreros y forjadores poblanos*. México: M. Casas, 1933.

————. *Hierros de Oaxaca*. Oaxaca: Gobierno del Estado, 1932.

————. *Loza blanca y azulejo de Puebla*. México: 1939.

————. *Nómina de loceros poblanos durante el período virreinal*. México: 1933.

Cervantes de Salazar, Francisco. *Life in the Imperial and Loyal City of Mexico in New Spain and the Royal and Pontifical University of Mexico, as described in the Dialogues for the Study of the Latin Language*. Trans. Minnie L. B. Shepard, Intr. Carlos E. Castañeda. Austin: University of Texas Press, 1953.

————. *Mexico en 1554; Tres diálogos latinos de la*

Nueva España. Trans. J. García Icazbalceta. México: Andrade y Morales, 1815.

———. *Túmulo imperial de la gran ciudad de México* (1560). Ed. Justino Fernández, Edmundo O'Gorman, Federico Gómez de Orozco. México: Alcancía, 1939.

Cetto, Max. *Modern Architecture in Mexico.* New York: Praeger, 1961.

Céspedes Aznar, Carlos. *La plata labrada del Santuario de Nuestra Señora de Ocotlán.* Ed. Francisco Pérez Salazar.

Charlot, Jean. *Mexican Art and the Academy of San Carlos, 1785–1915.* Austin: University of Texas Press, 1962.

Chauvet, Fidel de Jesús. "The Church of San Francisco in Mexico City," *The Americas,* 7 (1950–1951), 13–30.

———. *Los franciscanos y sus construcciones en Tlaxcala.* México: Talleres Junípero Serra, 1950.

———. *Tlatelolco; interesante recopilación histórica.* México: Parroquia de Santiago Tlatelolco, 1945.

Chueca Goitia, Fernando, and Leopoldo Torres Balbás. *Planos de ciudades ibero-americanas y filipinas existentes en el Archivo de Indias.* Madrid: Instituto de Estudios de Administración Local, 1951.

Cisneros, Luis de. *Historia de el principio, y origen progressos venidas a México, y milagros de la Santa Ymagen de nuestra Señora de los Remedios, extramuros de México.* México: Iuan Blanco de Alcaçar, 1621.

"La ciudad de México," *Artes de México,* 49–50 (1964) I, 53–54.

"Ciudad Sahagún y sus alrededores," *Artes de México,* 56–57 (1964).

Codex Chimalpopócatl. *Anales de Cuautitlán.* Trans. Faustino Galicia Chimalpopoca, Gumesindo Mendoza, Felipe Sánchez Solís. México: Museo Nacional, 1885.

Codex Durán. See Durán, Diego.

Codex, Florentine. See Sahagún, Bernardino de.

Codex Jucutácato. *Lienzo de Jucutácato.* México: Vargas Rea, 1951.

Codex Kingsborough. *Códice Kingsborough; memorial de los indios de Tepetláoztoc al monarca español.* Ed. Francisco del Paso y Troncoso. Madrid: Hauser y Menet, 1912.

Codex Mendoza. *The Mexican Manuscript Known as the Collection of Mendoza.* Trans. James C. Clark. London: Waterlow and Sons, 1938.

Codex Michoacán. *Crónicas de Michoacán.* Ed. Federico Gómez de Orozco. México: Universidad Nacional Autónoma, 1940.

Codex Osuna. *Pintura del gobernador, alcalde y regidores de México; códice en geroglíficos mexicanos y en lenguas castellana y azteca (1564).* Madrid: M. G. Hernández, 1878.

Codex Sahagún. See Sahagún, Bernardino de.

Codex Sierra. *Códice Sierra; fragmento de una nómina de gastos del pueblo de Santa Catarina Texupan.* Ed. N. León. México: Poulat, 1906.

Codex Tepetláoztoc. See Codex Kingsborough.

Codex Tlaltelolco. *Anales de Tlaltelolco.* Ed. Heinrich Berlin and Robert H. Barlow. México: Antigua Librería Robredo de J. Porrua, 1948.

Codex Tlaxcala. *Lienzo de Tlaxcala; homenaje a Cristóbal Colón: antigüedades mexicanas.* México: Secretaría de Fomento, 1892.

———. "Lienzo de Tlaxcalla; la conquista de México," *Artes de México,* 51–52 (1964), 1–80.

Codex Yanhuitlán. *Códice de Yanhuitlán.* Ed. Wigberto Jiménez Moreno and Salvador Mateos Higuera. México: Instituto Nacional de Antropología, n.d.

Códice franciscano. Intr. Joaquín García Icazbalceta. México: Salvador Chávez Hayhoe, 1889.

Cogolludo. See López de Cogolludo, Diego.

Colín, Mario. *Crónicos de una ciudad.* Toluca: 1955.

Collier, Margaret. "New documents on Lorenzo Rodríguez and his style," in *International Congress of the History of Art, XX, New York, 1961.* Princeton: University Press, 1963, 203–218.

Concilios provinciales primero y segunda de México. See Lorenzana, Francisco Antonio.

Concilium Mexicanum Provinciale III Celebratum Mexici Anno MDLXXXV. México: 1770.

Conde y Oquendo, Francisco Javier. *Disertación histórica sobre la aparición de la portentosa imagen de María Sma. de Guadalupe de México.* México: La Voz de la Religión, 1852.

Constituciones sinodales. México: Juan Pablos, 1556.

Córdoba, Tirso Rafael. *Mosaico mexicano.* Veracruz-Puebla: Librerías La Ilustración, n.d.

Cornejo Franco, José. *Guadalajara.* México: Monografías Mexicanas, 1946.

———. *Guadalaxara colonial.* Guadalajara: Imprenta Font, 1938.

Corona Núñez, José. *Rincones michoacanos; leyendas y breves datos históricos de algunos pueblos de Michoacán.* México: Cámara de Diputados, 1938.

Cortés, Antonio. *Hierros forjados.* México: Museo Nacional de Arqueología, Historia y Etnografía, 1935.

———. *Valenciana; Guanajuato, México.* México: Secretaría de Educación Pública, 1933.

Cortés, Antonio, and Genaro García. *Iglesia de Santo Domingo en la ciudad de Oaxaca y Capilla del Santo Cristo en Tlacolula, Estado de Oaxaca.* México: Museo Nacional de Arqueología, Historia y Etnografía, 1924.

Cortés, Antonio, and Genaro García and Federico Mariscal. *La arquitectura en México: iglesias.* México: Museo Nacional, 1914–1932.

Cortés, Hernán (Hernando). *Five Letters: 1519–1526.*

Trans. J. Bayard Morris. London: George Routledge and Sons, 1928.

Costansó, Miguel. *Diario histórico de los viages de mar, y tierra hechos al norte de la California.* Berkeley: University of California Press, 1911.

Couto, José Bernardo. *Diálogo sobre la historia de la pintura en México* (1860–1861). Ed. Manuel Toussaint. México: Fondo de Cultura Económica, 1947.

Crónicas de Michoacán. See Codex Michoacán.

Cruz, Salvador. "Algunos artistas y artesanos del México de Cervantes de Salazar (1550–1560)," *Anales del Instituto de Investigaciones Estéticas,* 28 (1959), 91–98.

————. "Algunos pintores y escultores de la ciudad de México en el siglo XVIII," *Anales del Instituto de Investigaciones Estéticas,* 33 (1964), 103–106.

Cuevas, Mariano. *Cartas y otros documentos de Hernán Cortés.* Sevilla: F. Díaz, 1915.

Danes, Gibson. "Baltasar de Echave Ibía: Some Critical Notes on the Stylistic Character of his Art," *Anales del Instituto de Investigaciones Estéticas,* 9 (1942), 15–26.

Davenport Municipal Art Gallery. *Catalogue of 334 Paintings.* Davenport, Iowa: 1925.

Dávila Padilla, Agustín. *Historia de la fundación y discurso de la provincia de Santiago de México de la orden de Predicadores . . .* (1596). México: Academia Literaria, 1955.

Un desconocido cedulario del siglo XVI perteneciente a la Catedral Metropolitana de México. Intr. José Castillo y Piña; notes, Alberto María Carrillo. México: Victoria, 1944.

Díaz del Castillo, Antonio. *Mano religiosa del M. R. P. Fr. Joseph Cillero.* México: Imprenta Real de el Superior Govierno, 1730.

Díaz del Castillo, Bernal. *Historia verdadera de la conquista de la Nueva España.* Ed. Ramón Iglesia. México: 1943.

————. *The True History of the Conquest of New Spain.* Ed. Genaro García, trans. A. P. Maudslay. London: Hakluyt Society, 1908–1916. Vols. 23–25, 30, 40.

Díaz y de Ovando, Clementina. *El Colegio Máximo de San Pedro y San Pablo.* México: Universidad Nacional Autónoma de México, 1951.

Diccionario universal de historia y geografía. México: Tipografía de Rafael, 1853–1855.

Díez Barroso, Francisco. *El arte en Nueva España.* México: 1921.

Dirección de Monumentos Coloniales. *Edificios coloniales artísticos y históricos de la República Mexicana que han sido declarados monumentos.* México: Instituto Nacional de Antropología e Historia, 1939.

————. *Three Centuries of Mexican Colonial Architecture.* New York: D. Appleton-Century, 1933.

Documentos inéditos del siglo XVI para la historia de México. Ed. Mariano Cuevas. México: Museo Nacional de Arqueología, Historia y Etnología, 1914.

Documentos inéditos o muy raros para la historia de México. Ed. Genaro García and Carlos Pereyra. México: Vda. de C. Bouret, 1905–1911.

Documentos inéditos relativos a Hernán Cortés y su familia. México: Archivo General de la Nación, 1935.

Documentos para la historia del arte en Andalucía. Sevilla: 1930.

Doerner, Gerd. *Mexikanische Volkskunst.* Wien: Wilhelm Andermann Metropol Bücher, 1962.

Durán, Diego. *Historia de las Indias de Nueva-España y islas de tierra firme* (1579–1581). Ed. José F. Ramírez. México: Andrade y Escalante, 1867–1880.

Echave Orio, Baltasar de. *Discursos de la antigüedad de la lengua cantabra bascongada.* México: Henrico Martínez, 1607.

Edwards, Emily and Manuel Álvarez Bravo. *Painted Walls of Mexico: From Prehistoric Times until Today.* Austin: University of Texas Press, 1966.

Enciclopedia universal ilustrada europeo-americana. Barcelona: Espasa-Calpe, 1907–1930.

Epistolario de Nueva España, 1505–1818. Ed. Francisco del Paso y Troncoso. México: Antigua Librería Robredo, 1939–1942.

Escobar, Matías. *Americana Thebaida.* (1729) México: Victoria, 1924.

Escontría, Alfredo. *Breve estudio de la obra y personalidad del escultor y arquitecto Don Manuel Tolsá.* México: Ingeniería y Arquitetura, 1929.

Estrada, Genaro. *El arte mexicano en España.* México: Porrua Hnos., 1937.

Fernández, Justino. *Arte mexicano; de sus orígenes a nuestros días.* México: Porrua, 1958.

————. *Arte moderno y contemporáneo de México.* México: Instituto de Investigaciones Estéticas, Universidad Nacional Autónoma de México, 1952.

————. "El códice del Tecpan de Tlaltelolco," *Investigación histórica,* 3.

————. "Composiciones barrocas de pinturas coloniales," *Anales del Instituto de Investigaciones Estéticas,* 28 (1959), 5–24.

————. "Dibujos neoclásicos," *El hijo pródigo,* 2 (1943), 163–165.

————. "Una escultura tequitqui en Monterrey," *Anales del Instituto de Investigaciones Estéticas,* 12 (1945), 15–17.

————. *El grabado en lámina en la Academia de San Carlos durante el siglo XIX.* La Habana: Universidad de la Habana, 1938.

————. "El Hospital Real de los Indios de la ciudad de

México," *Anales del Instituto de Investigaciones Estéticas,* 3 (1938), 25–47.

———. "Las ilustraciones en el libro mexicano durante cuatro siglos, 1539–1939," *Maso Finiguerra,* 4 (1939), 125–154.

———. *Morelia; su situación, historia, características, monumentos y nomenclaturas.* México: Secretaría de Hacienda y Crédito Público, 1936.

———. *El Palacio de Minería.* México: Instituto de Investigaciones Estéticas, Universidad Nacional Autónoma de México, 1951.

———. *Pátzcuaro; su situación, historia, características, monumentos y nomenclaturas.* México: Talleres Estampillas y Valores, 1936.

———. "Una pintura desconocida de la Plaza Mayor de México," *Anales del Instituto de Investigaciones Estéticas,* 17 (1949), 27–39.

———. *El Retablo de los Reyes; estética del arte de la Nueva España.* México: Universidad Nacional Autónoma de México, 1959.

———. "Rubens y José Juárez," *Anales del Instituto de Investigaciones Estéticas,* 10 (1943), 51–57.

———. "Santa Brígida de México," in *Congreso Internacional de Historia de América, II, 1937.* Buenos Aires: Academia Nacional de la Historia, 1938.

———. "Tiepolo, Mengs and Don Rafael Ximeno y Planes," *Gazette des Beaux-Arts,* Ser. 6, 23 (June, 1943), 345–362.

———. *Tomás Suría y su viaje con Malaspina, 1791.* México: Porrúa Hnos., 1939.

Fernández, Justino, and Edmundo O'Gorman. *Documentos para la historia de la litografía en México.* México: Instituto de Investigaciones Estéticas, Universidad Nacional Autónoma de México, 1955.

———. *Santo Tomás More y "La Utopia de Tomás Moro en la Nueva España."* México: Alcancía, 1937.

Fernández, Justino, Federico Gómez de Orozco, and Manuel Toussaint. *Planos de la ciudad de México, siglos XVI y XVII.* México: Universidad, 1938.

Fernández de Lizardi, José Joaquín. *El Pensador Mexicano.* 23 diciembre, 1813.

Fernández de Velasco, Manuel. *El artesano en la Nueva España en el siglo XVI* (Thesis). México: Universidad Nacional Autónoma de México, 1963.

Ferrer de Mendiola, Gabriel. *Nuestra ciudad, Mérida de Yucatán, 1542–1938.* Mérida: Basso, 1938.

Florencia, Francisco de. *La estrella de el norte de México.* México: María de Benavides, Vda. de J. de Ribera, 1688.

Flores Guerrero, Raul. "El barroco popular de Texcoco," *Anales del Instituto de Investigaciones Estéticas,* 24 (1956), 35–31.

———. *Las capillas posas de México.* México: Ediciones Mexicanas, 1951.

———. "El convento de Charo y sus murales," *Anales del Instituto de Investigaciones Estéticas,* 22 (1954), 123–132.

———. "Los muralistas del siglo XIX," *Artes de México,* 3 (1954), 31–56.

Foster, George M. *Culture and Conquest; America's Spanish Heritage.* Chicago: Quadrangle, 1960.

Franco y Ortega, Alonso. *Segunda parte de la historia de la provincia de Santiago de México, orden de Predicadores en la Nueva España; año de 1645.* México: Museo Nacional, 1900.

Frias, Valentín F. *La conquista de Querétaro.* Querétaro: Escuela de Artes de Señor San José, 1906.

Frothingham, Alice Wilson. *Hispanic Glass; With Examples in the Collection of the Hispanic Society of America.* New York: Hispanic Society of America, 1941.

Gacetas de México, 1703–1731. México: F. Escalente, 1854.

Gage, Thomas. *Travels in the New World.* Norman: University of Oklahoma Press, 1958.

Galindo y Villa, Jesús. *Historia sumaria de la ciudad de México.* México: Cultura, 1925.

———. "Reseña histórica de la Academia Nacional de Bellas Artes, antigua de San Carlos," *Anales de la Academia Nacional de Bellas Artes de México,* 1 (1913), 9–32.

Gante, Pablo C. de. *La arquitectura de México en el siglo XVI.* México: Porrua, 1954.

———. *Tepotzotlán; su historia y sus tesoros artísticos.* México: Porrua, 1958.

García Cubas, Antonio. *El libro de mis recuerdos* (1885). México: A. García Cubas, Hermanos Sucs., 1904.

García Granados, Rafael. "Calpan," *Universidad de México,* 1 (1931), 370–376.

———. "Capillas de indios en Nueva España, 1530–1605," *Archivo español de arte y arqueología,* 11 (1935), 3–29.

———. "La custodia de Borda," *Anales del Instituto de Investigaciones Estéticas,* 1 (1937), 28–32.

———. "Reminiscencias idolátricas en monumentos coloniales," *Anales del Instituto de Investigaciones Estéticas,* 5 (1940), 54–56.

———. *Sillería del coro de la antigua iglesia de San Agustín.* México: Imprenta Universitaria, 1941.

———. *Xochimilco.* México: Talleres Gráficos de la Nación, 1934.

García Granados, Rafael, and Luis MacGregor. *La ciudad de Oaxaca.* México: Talleres Gráficos de la Nación, 1933.

———. *Huejotzingo; la ciudad y el convento franciscano.* México: Secretaría de Educación, 1934.

466

García Icazbalceta, Joaquín. *Don fray Juan de Zumárraga.* México: Andrade y Morales, 1881.

García Maroto, Gabriel, and Enrique Yáñez. *Arquitectura popular de México.* México: Instituto Nacional de Bellas Artes, 1954.

García Preciat, José. "La catedral de Mérida," *Archivo español de arte y arqueología,* 11 (1935), 73–93.

———. "La catedral de Campeche," *Anales del Instituto de Investigaciones Estéticas,* 6 (1940), 9–38.

Gestoso y Pérez, José. *Ensayo de un diccionario de los artífices que florecieron en Sevilla desde el siglo XIII al XVIII inclusive.* Sevilla: Andalucía Moderna, 1899–1900.

Gibson, Charles. *Tlaxcala in the Sixteenth Century.* New Haven, Connecticut: Yale University Press, 1952.

Gillet, Louis. "L'art dans l'Amérique Latine," in André Michel's *Histoire de l'art,* VIII, No. 3. Paris: Colin, 1929.

Gómez de Orozco, Federico. *El convento franciscano de Cuernavaca.* México: Centro de Estudios Franciscanos, 1943.

———. "La decoración en los manuscritos hispano-mexicanos primitivos," *Anales del Instituto de Investigaciones Estéticas,* 3 (1938), 48–52.

———. "Documentos acerca de la estátua de Carlos IV," *Anales del Instituto de Investigaciones Estéticas,* 5 (1940), 77–83.

———. "¿El ex-voto de Hernán Cortés?" *Anales del Instituto de Investigaciones Estéticas,* 8 (1942), 51–54.

———. "Monasterios de la Orden de San Agustín en Nueva España, siglo XVI," *Revista mexicana de estudios históricos,* 1 (1927), 40–54.

———. "Las pinturas de Alonso de Villasana en el Santuario de los Remedios," *Anales del Instituto de Investigaciones Estéticas,* 14 (1946), 65–80.

———. *La Plaza de Guardiola.* México: Banco de México, 1942.

González de la Puente, Juan. *Primera parte de la chorónica augustiniana de Mechoacán.* (1624) Ed. Francisco Plancarte y Navarrete. Cuernavaca: Miranda, 1907.

González Galván, Manuel. "Modalidades del barroco mexicano," *Anales del Instituto de Investigaciones Estéticas,* 30 (1961), 39–68.

González Obregón, Luis. "La estatua de Carlos IV," in *México pintoresco.* Ed. Adelberto A. Estera. México: La Europea, 1905.

———. *México viejo.* Paris and México: Vda. de C. Bouret, 1900.

Gorbea Trueba, José. *Culhuacán.* México: Instituto Nacional de Antropología e Historia, 1959.

———. *Tepeapulco.* México: Instituto Nacional de Antropología e Historia, 1957.

———. *Yanhuitlán.* México: Instituto Nacional de Antropología e Historia, 1962.

———. *Yuriria.* México: Instituto Nacional de Antropología e Historia, 1960.

Granados y Gálvez, Joseph Joaquín. *Tardes americanas.* México: Zúñiga y Ontiveros, 1778.

Grancsay, Stephen V. "A Gift of Mexican Conquistador Stirrups," *Bulletin of the Metropolitan Museum of Art,* 33 (1938), 73–76.

Grijalva, Juan de. *Crónica de la orden de n.p. S. Agustín en las provincias de la Nueva España* (1624). México: Victoria, 1924.

Guerrero Moctezuma, Francisco. *Las plazas en las ciudades de la Nueva España en relación con las ordenanzas de nuevas poblaciones de Felipe II.* México: 1934.

Harth-Terré, Emilio. *Francisco Becerra, maestro de arquitectura; sus últimos años en el Perú.* Madrid: Instituto "Gonzalo Fernández de Oviedo," 1952.

———. "Juan García Salguero, un criollo de México, escultor en Lima," *Anales del Instituto de Investigaciones Estéticas,* 30 (1961), 69–90.

Hijuelos F., Fausto A. *Mérida; monografía.* México: Secretaría de Educación Pública, 1942.

Icaza, Francisco A. de. *Conquistadores y pobladores de Nueva España; diccionario autobiográfico.* Madrid: El Adelantado de Segovia, 1923.

Iglesias de México. Ed. Dr. Atl, Manuel Toussaint, José R. Benítez. México: Secretaría de Hacienda, 1924–1927.

Información de méritos y servicios de Alonso García Bravo alarife que trazó la ciudad de México. Ed. J. I. Mantecón and Manuel Toussaint. México: Imprenta Universitaria, 1956.

Instrucciones que los virreyes de Nueva España dejaron a sus sucesores. México: Imprenta Imperial, 1867.

Journal of the Society of Architectural Historians, 5 (1945–1946). Special issue on Latin-American architecture.

Kelemen, Pál. *Baroque and Rococo in Latin America.* New York: Macmillan, 1951.

———. "Religious Sculpture of Colonial Mexico," *Art in America,* 32 (1944), 109–117.

———. "The significance of the stone retable of Cristo Rey," *Palacio,* 61, No. 8 (August 1954), 243–272.

Kubler, George. "Architects and Builders in Mexico; 1521–1550," *Journal of the Warburg and Courtauld Institutes,* VII, 1–2 (1944), 7–19.

———. *Mexican Architecture of the Sixteenth Century.* New Haven: Yale University Press, 1948.

———. "Mexican Urbanism in the Sixteenth Century," *Art Bulletin,* 34 (1942), 160–171.

———. "On the Colonial Extinction of the Motifs of

Pre-Conquest Art," in Samuel K. Lathrop. *Essays in Pre-Columbian Art and Archaeology.* Cambridge: Harvard University Press, 1961, 13–34.

————. "Ucareo and the Escorial," *Anales del Instituto de Investigaciones Estéticas,* 8 (1942), 5–12.

Kubler, George, and Charles Gibson. *The Tovar Calendar.* Memoirs of the Connecticut Academy of Arts and Sciences, 11 (1951).

Kubler, George, and Martin S. Soria. *Art and Architecture in Spain and Portugal and their American Dominions, 1500–1800.* The Pelican History of Art, 17. Baltimore: Penguin, 1959.

Laverrière, J. "El convento de la Merced," in *México pintoresco.* Ed. Adelberto A. Estera. México: La Europea, 1905.

Le Duc, Alberto, Roberto Álvarez Espinosa, and Jorge Enciso. *Una casa habitación del siglo XVIII en la ciudad de México.* México: Cultura, 1938.

Legislación del trabajo en los siglos XVI, XVII, XVIII. México: Departamento Autónomo del Trabajo, 1938.

Leicht, Hugo. *Las calles de Puebla; estudio histórico.* Puebla: Mijares, 1934.

León, Francisco de P. *Los esmaltes de Uruapan.* México: DAPP, 1939.

León, Nicolás. *Bibliografía mexicana del siglo XVIII.* México: 1908.

————. "La relación de Michoacán," *Revista mexicana de estudios históricos,* 1 (1927), 191–213.

————. *El Ylmo. Señor Don Vasco de Quiroga, primer obispo de Michoacán.* México: Sucs. de F. Díaz de León, 1904.

Liaño Pacheco, Ana María. "La catedral de Morelia," *Arte en América y Filipinas,* 2 (1936), 95–113.

Lienzo de Tlaxcala. See Codex Tlaxcala.

Lizana, Bernardo de. *Historia y conquista espiritual de Yucatán* (1633). México: Museo Nacional, 1892.

Llaguno y Amírola, Eugenio. *Noticias de los arquitectos y arquitectura de España desde su restauración.* Ed. Juan Agustín Ceán Bermúdez. Madrid: Imprenta Real, 1829.

López de Cogolludo, Diego. *Historia de Yucatán (siglo XVII).* Mérida: M. Aldana Rivas, 1867–1868.

López González, Valentín. *El palacio de Cortés en Cuernavaca.* Cuernavaca: Universidad de Morelos, 1958.

López Martínez, Celestino. *Notas para la historia del arte; arquitectos, escultores y pintores vecinos de Sevilla.* Sevilla: Rodríguez, Giménez, 1928–1930.

Lorenzana, Francisco Antonio. *Concilios provinciales primero y segundo celebrados en la muy noble y muy leal ciudad de México . . . 1555 y 1565.* México: Imprenta de El Superior Gobierno, 1769.

Louchheim, Aline B. "The Church Façades of Lorenzo Rodríguez." Unpublished M.A. thesis. New York University, 1941.

Lozoya, Marqués de (Juan Contreras y López de Ayala). *Historia del arte hispánico.* Barcelona: Salvat, 1931————.

Lucio, Rafael. *Reseña histórica de la pintura mexicana en los siglos XVII y XVIII.* México: Secretaría de Fomento, n.d.

McAndrew, John. "Fortress Monasteries?" *Anales del Instituto de Investigaciones Estéticas,* 23 (1955), 31–38.

————. *The Open-Air Churches of Sixteenth-Century Mexico.* Cambridge: Harvard University Press, 1965.

McAndrew, John, and Manuel Toussaint. "Tecali, Zacatlán and the *Renacimiento Purista* in Mexico," *Art Bulletin,* 34 (1942), 311–325.

MacGregor, Luis. *Actopan.* México: Secretaría de Educación Pública, 1955.

————. "Cien ejemplares de plateresco mexicano," *Archivo español de arte y arqueología,* XI, 35 (enero–abril, 1935), 31–45.

————. *Estudios sobre arte colonial mexicano.* México: Publicaciones Mundiales, 1946.

————. *Huejotzingo.* México: Instituto Nacional de Antropología e Historia, 1957.

————. *El plateresco en México.* México: Porrúa, 1954.

————. *Tepoztlán.* México: Instituto Nacional de Antropología e Historia, 1958.

Maler, J. "Un primoroso ropaje de plumas," *Anales del Museo Nacional.* época 1, 33 (1886), 1–3.

Manrique, José Alberto. "Artificio del arte; estudio de algunos relieves barrocos mexicanos," *Anales del Instituto de Investigaciones Estéticas,* 31 (1962), 19–36.

Manzo, José. *La catedral de Puebla, 1844.* Puebla: El Escritorio, 1911.

Marco Dorta, Enrique. "Arquitectura colonial; Francisco Becerra," *Archivo español de arte,* 16 (1943).

————. "Un biombo mejicano del siglo dieciocho," *Archivo español de arte,* 62 (1944), 70–75.

————. *Fuentes para la historia del arte hispanoamericano.* Sevilla: Escuela de Estudios Hispano-Americanos, 1951.

Marín de Paalen, Isabel. *Alfarería: Tonalá.* Guadalajara: Planeación y Promoción, 1960.

Mariscal, Federico E. *La arquitectura en México; iglesias.* México: Museo Nacional, 1932.

————. *La patria y la arquitectura nacional.* México: Stephan y Torres, 1915.

Marmolejo, Lucio. *Efemérides guanajuatenses.* Guanajuato: Colegio de Artes y Oficios, 1883.

Marroquí, José María. *La ciudad de México.* México: J. Aguilar Vera, 1900–1913.

Marroquín, Alejandro. *La ciudad mercado, Tlaxiaco.* México: Universidad, 1957.

Martínez, Jusepe. *Discursos practicables del nobilísimo arte de la pintura.* Ed. Julián Gallego. Barcelona: 1950.

Martínez de Cossío, Leopoldo. "Documentos para la historia de la catedral de México," *Anales del Instituto de Investigaciones Estéticas*, 33 (1964), 93–101.

Mayer, August Liebmann. *Historia de la pintura española.* Madrid: Espasa-Calpe, 1928.

Maza, Francisco de la. "Algunas obras desconocidas de Manuel Tolsá," *Anales del Instituto de Investigaciones Estéticas*, 14 (1946), 33–54.

———. *Arquitectura de los coros de monjas en México.* México: Universidad Nacional Autónoma de México, 1956.

———. "Arte colonial de México," *Cuadernos americanos*, 8 (1949), 232–236.

———. "Arte colonial en Chiapas," *Ateneo de Tuxtla Gutiérrez*, 6 (1956), 59–122.

———. "El arte en la ciudad de Nuestra Señora de los Zacatecas," *México en el arte*, 7 (1949), 5–16.

———. *La capilla de San José Chiapa.* México: Instituto Nacional de Antropología e Historia, 1960.

———. "La catedral de Chihuahua," *Anales del Instituto de Investigaciones Estéticas*, 30 (1961), 21–38.

———. *La ciudad de Cholula y sus iglesias.* México: Instituto de Investigaciones Estéticas, 1959.

———. "La decoración simbólica de la Capilla del Rosario de Puebla," *Anales del Instituto de Investigaciones Estéticas*, 23 (1955), 5–29.

———. "Dibujos y proyectos de Tresguerras," *Anales del Instituto de Investigaciones Estéticas*, 18 (1950), 27–33.

———. "En el segundo centenario de Tresguerras," *Anales del Instituto de Investigaciones Estéticas*, 29 (1960), 9–14.

———. "Las estampas de Alconedo," *Anales del Instituto de Investigaciones Estéticas*, 23 (1955), 69–74.

———. "Fray Diego Valadés, escultor y grabador franciscano del siglo XVI," *Anales del Instituto de Investigaciones Estéticas*, 13 (1945), 15–44.

———. "José Rodríguez de Alconedo," *Anales del Instituto de Investigaciones Estéticas*, 6 (1940), 39–56.

———. "La mitra mexicana de plumas de El Escorial," in *Homenaje a Rafael García Granados.* México: Instituto Nacional de Antropología e Historia, 1960.

———. "Noticias sobre arquitectura colonial," *Anales del Instituto de Investigaciones Estéticas*, 21 (1953), 19–25.

———. "Nuevos datos sobre el artista José Luis Rodríguez Alconedo," *Anales del Instituto de Investigaciones Estéticas*, 11 (1944), 93–94.

———. "Otra vez Tresguerras," *Anales del Instituto de Investigaciones Estéticas*, 32 (1963), 53–58.

———. *El Palacio de la Inquisición.* México: Instituto de Investigaciones Estéticas, 1951.

———. "Un pintor colonial desconocido," *Anales del Instituto de Investigaciones Estéticas*, 18 (1950), 89–90.

———. *El pintor Cristóbal de Villalpando.* México: Instituto Nacional de Antropología e Historia, 1964.

———. "Las pinturas de la Casa del Deán," *Artes de México*, 2 (1954), 17–24.

———. *Las piras funerarias en la historia y en el arte de México.* México: Instituto de Investigaciones Estéticas, 1946.

———. *Los retablos dorados de Nueva España.* México: Ediciones Mexicanas, 1950.

———. *San Miguel Allende; su historia, sus monumentos.* México: Instituto de Investigaciones Estéticas, 1939.

———. "La tumba de Tresguerras," *Anales del Instituto de Investigaciones Estéticas*, 19 (1951), 105–118.

———. "El urbanismo neoclásico de Ignacio de Castera," *Anales del Instituto de Investigaciones Estéticas*, 22 (1954), 93–101.

Medel M., José V. *The Chapel of the Rosary, Puebla.* Puebla: 1940.

Medina, José Toribio. *Historia del tribunal del Santo Oficio de la Inquisición en México.* Santiago de Chile: Imprenta Elziviriana, 1905.

———. *La imprenta en México; 1539–1821.* Santiago de Chile: 1907–1912.

Mendieta, Gerónimo de. *Historia Eclesiastica Indiana.* Ed. Joaquín García Icazbalceta. México: Antigua Librería, 1870.

Mexican Silverwork: Exhibition of Gold and Silver Organized by Rubín de la Borbolla. México: Museo Nacional de Artes e Industrias Populares, 1952.

Mexico, Archivo General de la Nación. "Fragmento del proceso de Felipe Fabris," *Publicaciones,* 21 (1932), 25–30.

Mexico, Archivo General de la Nación. *Los judíos en la Nueva España.* México: Talleres Gráficos de la Nación, 1932.

Mexico City, Ayuntamiento. *Colección de documentos oficiales relativos a la construcción y demolición del Parián.* México: I. Cumplido, 1843.

Mexico City, Cabildo. *Actas de Cabildo de la ciudad de México.* México: 1889–1919.

México a través de los siglos. Ed. Vicente Riva Palacio. Barcelona: Espasa, 1888–1889.

México pintoresco. Ed. Adelberto A. Esteva. México: La Europea, 1905.

México y sus alrededores. México: Decaén, 1855–1864.

Michel, André. *Histoire de l'art,* VIII, No. 3. Paris: Colin, 1929.

Moedano Koer, Hugo. "Tizatlán, asiento del señor Xochipilli," *Cuadernos americanos,* Año 2, Vol. II, No. 5 (1943), 133–142.

Molina, Alonso de. *Confesionario breve, en lengua Mexi-*

cana y Castellana. México: Antonio de Espinosa, 1569.

Montejano y Aguiñaga, Rafael. *Guía de la ciudad de San Luis Potosí.* San Luis Potosí, 1960.

Montenegro, Roberto. *Retablos de México; Mexican Votive Paintings.* Trans. Irene Nicholson. México: Ediciones Mexicanas, n.d.

Mora, Joaquín A. "El palacio de Nuestra Señora de Guadalupe," *Universidad* (Monterrey), 8–9 (1950), 203–234.

Moreno, Salvador. "Un biombo mexicano del siglo XVIII," *Anales del Instituto de Investigaciones Estéticas,* 28 (1959), 29–32.

Moreno Villa, José. *La escultura colonial mexicana.* México: Colegio de México, 1942.

———. *Lo mexicano en las artes plásticas.* México: Colegio de México, 1948.

Motolinía (Toribio de Benevente). *Motolinía's History of the Indians of New Spain.* Trans. Francis Borgia Steck. Washington: Academy of American Franciscan History, 1951.

———. *Memoriales.* Ed. Luis García Pimentel. México-Paris-Madrid: 1903.

Moyssén, Xavier. "Las cruces de Toluca," *Anales del Instituto de Investigaciones Estéticas,* 27 (1958), 33–46.

———. "La primera academia de pintura en México," *Anales del Instituto de Investigaciones Estéticas,* 34 (1965), 15–30.

———. "Tecamachalco y el pintor indígena Juan Gersón," *Anales del Instituto de Investigaciones Estéticas,* 33 (1964), 23–40.

Muriel, Josefina. *Conventos de monjas en la Nueva España.* México: Santiago, 1946.

Murillo, Gerardo (Dr. Atl, pseud.). *Los altares (Iglesias de México,* 5). México: Secretaría de Hacienda, 1925.

———. *Las artes populares en México.* México: Secretaría de Industria y Comercio, 1922.

Muro, Manuel. *Historia de San Luis Potosí.* San Luis Potosí: M. Esquivel, 1910.

Museo de Arte Religioso. *Guía oficial.* México: Instituto Nacional de Antropología e Historia.

El museo mexicano, ó miscelanea pintoresca de amenidades curiosas é instructivas. Tomo tercero. México: Ignacio Cumplido, 1844.

Museo Nacional de Artes Plásticas. *Catálogo de pintura; sección colonial.* Ed. Manuel Toussaint. México: 1934.

Navallón, Sebastián C. *El grabado en México.* México: Museo Nacional, 1933.

Neumayer, Alfred. "The Indian Contribution to Architectural Decoration in Spanish Colonial America," *Art Bulletin,* 30 (1948), 104–121.

Noticias curiosas. Puebla: 1867.

Nuttall, Zelia. *Ancient Mexican feather work at the Columbian Historical Exposition at Madrid.* Washington: Government Printing Office, 1895.

———. *Datos históricos relativos a la llamada "Casa de Cortés," o Casa Municipal en Coyoacán.* México: Secretaría de Gobernación, 1922.

———. "The Gardens of Ancient Mexico," in *Smithsonian Institution Annual Report, 1923.* Washington: 1925.

———. "Ordinances Concerning the Laying Out of New Towns," *Hispanic American Historical Review,* 5 (1922), 249–254.

"Oaxaca," *Artes de México,* 70–71 (1965).

Obras de eloqüencia y poesía premiadas por la Real Universidad de México en el certamen literario que celebró el día 28 de diciembre de 1790. México: Felipe de Zúñiga y Ontiveros, 1791.

Obregón, Gonzalo. "La capilla del Colegio de las Vizcaínas," *Anales del Instituto de Investigaciones Estéticas,* 8 (1942), 19–25.

———. "La iglesia del Colegio de Niñas," *Anales del Instituto de Investigaciones Estéticas,* 20 (1952), 21–39.

———. "Un sepulcro plateresco en México," *Anales del Instituto de Investigaciones Estéticas,* 33 (1964), 45–50.

Ochoa V., Ángel S. *El convento de S. Francisco de Guadalajara, 1554–1954.* Guadalajara: Font, 1959.

Octava maravilla del Nuevo Mundo en la gran Capilla del Rosario. Puebla: Plantiniana de Diego Fernández de León, 1690.

O'Gorman, Edmundo. "An Early Mexican Xylograph Incunabula," *Mexican Art and Craft,* 7 (1939), 16–19.

———. "Una estampa del siglo XVI," *Anales del Instituto de Investigaciones Estéticas,* 4 (1939), 30–36.

Ojea, Hernando de. *Libro tercero de la Historia Religiosa de la provincia de México de la orden de Sto. Domingo.* México: Museo Nacional, 1897.

Olavarría y Ferrari, Enrique de. *El Real Colegio de San Ignacio de Loyola, vulgarmente Colegio de las Vizcaínas, en la actualidad, Colegio de la Paz.* México: F. Díaz de León, 1889.

Olvera, Jorge. "La catedral metropolitana de México, I," *Artes de México,* 32 (1960), 3–76.

———. "Copanaguastla, joya del plateresco en Chiapas," *Ateneo de Tuxtla Gutiérrez,* 1 (1951).

"Ordenanzas," *Boletín del Archivo General de la Nación,* Ser. 1, 11 (1940), 2–327.

Orendáin, Leopoldo I. "Francisco de León, pintor del siglo XVII," *Anales del Instituto de Investigaciones Estéticas,* 17 (1949), 17–21.

———. "Iconografía popular jalisciense," *Anales del*

Instituto de Investigaciones Estéticas, 34 (1965), 79–84.

———. "Libros corales en la catedral de Guadalajara," *Anales del Instituto de Investigaciones Estéticas,* 29 (1960), 37–46.

———. "El pintor Diego A. de Cuentas," *Anales del Instituto de Investigaciones Estéticas,* 19 (1951), 75–85.

———. *Pintura popular.* Guadalajara: 1950.

Orozco y Berra, Manuel. "La Alhóndiga de Granaditas, Guanajuato," in *México pintoresco.* Ed. Adelberto A. Esteva. México: La Europea, 1905.

———. *Memoria para el plano de la ciudad de México.* México: Ministerio de Fomento, 1867.

———. "Puerta lateral de San Francisco," in *México pintoresco.* Ed Adelberto A. Esteva. México: La Europea, 1905.

Ortiz de Ayala, Tadeo. *México considerado como nación independiente y libre.* Burdeos: C. Lavalle Sobrino, 1832.

Pach, Walter. "Unknown Aspects of Mexican Painting," *Gazette des Beaux-Arts,* Ser. 6, 24 (1943), 208–220.

Palacio y Basave, Luis del Refugio de. *La catedral de Guadalajara.* Guadalajara: 1948.

———. *Joyas franciscanas en Puebla y Tlaxcala.* México: Centro de Estudios Históricos Franciscanos, 1944.

———. *Visita de curioso al convento de Huexotzinco, Cholula.* Guadalajara: Parangón, 1937.

Palacios, Enrique Juan. *Iglesias mexicanas.* México: Müller Hnos., 1920.

Palm, Erwin Walter. "Las capillas abiertas americanas y sus antecedentes en el Occidente cristiano," *Anales del Instituto de Arte Americano e Investigaciones Estéticas,* 6 (1953), 45–64.

———. "Estilo y época en el arte colonial," *Anales del Instituto de Arte Americana e Investigaciones Estéticas,* 2 (1949), 7–24.

Papeles de Nueva España, Ser. 2. Ed. Francisco del Paso y Troncoso. Madrid: Sucs. de Rivadeneyra, 1905–1941.

Pareja, Francisco de. *Crónica de la Provincia de la Visitación de ntra. Sra. de la Merced de la Nueva España* (1688). México: J. R. Barbedillo, 1882–1883.

Paris, Musée National d'Art Moderne. *Art mexicain, du précolombien à nos jours; Paris . . . mai-juillet 1952, I.* Paris: Les Presses Artistiques, 1952.

Paso y Troncoso, Francisco del. See *Papeles de Nueva España.*

Patton, Glenn Neil. "Francisco Antonio Guerrero y Torres and the Baroque Architecture of Mexico City in the Eighteenth Century." Unpublished thesis, University of Michigan. Ann Arbor: University Microfilms, 1958.

Peñafiel, Antonio. *Cerámica mexicana y loza de Talavera de Puebla; época colonial y moderna.* México: Secretaría de Fomento, 1910.

———. *Ciudades coloniales y capitales de la República Mexicana; Las cinco ciudades coloniales de Puebla: Cholula, Huexotzingo, Tepeaca, Atlixco y Tehuacán.* México: Secretaría de Fomento, 1914.

———. *Ciudades coloniales y capitales de la República Mexicana; Estado de Tlaxcala.* México: Secretaría de Fomento, 1909.

———. *Ciudades coloniales y capitales de la República Mexicana; Historia colonial de Querétaro.* México: Secretaría de Fomento, 1911.

Pérez Embid, Fiorentino. *El mudejarismo en la arquitectura portuguesa de la época manuelina.* Sevilla: Editorial Católica Española, 1944.

Pérez Salazar, Francisco. *Historia de la pintura en Puebla.* 3 ed. Notes, Elisa Vargas Lugo. México: Instituto de Investigaciones Estéticas, 1963.

Pol, Ferrán de. *Cuernavaca.* México: Edición de Artes, 1948.

Ponce, Alonso. *Relación breve y verdadera de algunas cosas de las muchas que sucedieron al padre fray Alonso Ponce en las provincias de la Nueva España.* Madrid: Vda. de Calero, 1873.

Puga, Vasco de. *Provisiões, cédulas, instrucciones de Su Magestad (Cedulario de Puga).* México: El Sistema Postal, 1878.

Quevedo, F. G. de. *Así es Oaxaca.* México: Font, 1948.

Quintana, José Miguel. *Las artes gráficas en Puebla.* México: Antigua Librería Robredo, 1960.

Quiroz y Gutiérrez, Nicanor. *Historia de la aparición de Nuestra Señora de Ocotlán y de su culto en cuatro siglos (1541–1941).* Puebla: 1940.

Ramírez, Santiago. *Datos para la historia del Colegio de Minería.* México: Imprenta del Gobierno Federal, 1890.

Ramírez Álvarez, J. Guadalupe. *Querétaro; visión de mi ciudad.* 2 ed. Querétaro: Ediciones Provincia, 1956.

Ramírez Aparicio, Manuel. *Los conventos suprimidos en Méjico.* Méjico: J. M. Aguilar, 1861–1862.

Rangel, Nicolás. *Historia del toreo en México, época colonial; 1529–1821.* México: M. L. Sánchez, 1924.

Rea, Alonso de la. *Crónica de la orden de N. Seráfico P. S. Francisco, Provincia de San Pedro y San Pablo de Mechoacán en la Nueva España* (1639). México: Voz de México, 1882.

"Real disposición para destenar las deformidades arquitectónicas de los edificios (1777)," *Anales del Instituto de Investigaciones Estéticas,* 31 (1962), 144–146.

Revilla, Manuel G. *El arte en México en la época antigua y durante el gobierno virreinal.* México: Secretaría de Fomento, 1893.

Reyes Valerio, Constantino. *Tepalcingo.* México: Instituto Nacional de Antropología e Historia, 1960.

————. *Trilogía barroca.* México: Instituto Nacional de Antropología e Historia, 1960.

Rhode, Francisco José. "Angahuan," *Anales del Instituto de Investigaciones Estéticas,* 14 (1946), 5–18.

————. "Azulejos de Mexico." Unpublished MS.

Ricard, Robert. *La "conquête spirituelle" du Mexique.* Paris: Institut d'Ethnologie, 1933.

————. "La plaza mayor en España y en América española," *Estudios geográficos,* 11 (1950), 321–327.

Ríos, Enrique. "Una obra ignorada de Simón Pereyns," *Anales del Instituto de Investigaciones Estéticas,* 9 (1942), 61–65.

Ríos Arce, Francisco R. de los. *Puebla de los Ángeles y la orden dominicana.* Puebla: Escritorio, 1910.

Riva Palacio, Vicente. *México a través de los siglos.* Barcelona: Espasa, 1886–1889.

Rivera Cambas, Manuel. *México pintoresco, artístico y monumental* (1880). México: Editora Nacional, 1957.

Rivero Carvallo, José. *Totimehuacán, convento y templo franciscanos.* Puebla: López, 1961.

Robertson, Donald. *Mexican Manuscript Painting of the Early Colonial Period: The Metropolitan Schools.* New Haven: Yale University Press, 1959.

Robles, Antonio de. *Diario de sucesos notables; 1665–1703.* Méjico: J. R. Navarro, 1853.

Rodríguez Familiar, José. *Francisco Eduardo de Tresguerras.* México: 1933.

Rodríguez Lozano, Manuel, and Manuel Toussaint. *Imaginaría colonial.* México: Universidad nacional, 1941.

Rojas Garcidueñas, José. *El antiguo colegio de San Ildefonso.* México: Universidad Nacional Autónoma de México, 1951.

————. "Un oleo mexicano en Santiago de Compostela," *Anales del Instituto de Investigaciones Estéticas,* 34 (1965), 71–74.

————. "San Miguel del Milagro," *Anales del Instituto de Investigaciones Estéticas,* 4 (1939), 55–63.

Rojas Rodríguez, Pedro. "Copandaro," *Anales del Instituto de Investigaciones Estéticas,* 22 (1954), 115–122.

————. "Un relieve herético," *Anales del Instituto de Investigaciones Estéticas,* 26 (1957), 77–78.

————. *Tonantzintla.* México: Universidad Nacional Autónoma de México, 1956.

Romero, José Guadalupe. *Noticias para formar la historia de la estadística del obispado de Michoacán.* México: García Torres, 1862.

Romero de Terreros y Vinent, Manuel, Marqués de San Francisco. *Los acueductos de México en la historia y en el arte.* México: Instituto de Investigaciones Estéticas, 1949.

————. "Una antigua casa de campo," *Anales del Instituto de Investigaciones Estéticas,* 21 (1953), 27–29.

————. "El antiguo convento franciscano de Topoyanco," *Memorias de la Academia Mexicana de Historia,* 12 (1953), 299–305.

————. "El antiguo monasterio agustiniano de San Miguel Acatlán," *Anales del Instituto de Investigaciones Estéticas,* 34 (1965), 63–64.

————. *Antiguas haciendas de México.* México: Editorial Patria, 1956.

————. "El arquitecto Tresguerras," *Anales del Museo Nacional,* época 4, 5 (1927), 55–63.

————. *Arte colonial; apuntes reunidos.* México: J. Ballesca, 1916.

————. *Arte colonial; segunda serie de apuntes reunidos.* México: Pedro Robredo, 1918.

————. *Arte colonial; tercera serie de apuntes reunidos.* México: Librería Cultura, 1921.

————. *El arte en México durante el virreinato; resumen histórico.* México: Porrúa, 1951.

————. *Las artes industriales en la Nueva España.* México: P. Robredo, 1923.

————. *Atlatlaúhcan; el antiguo monasterio agustiniano.* México: Dirección de Monumentos Coloniales, Instituto Nacional de Antropología e Historia, 1956.

————. *Ayotzingo.* México: Dirección de Monumentos Coloniales, Instituto Nacional de Antropología e Historia, 1959.

————. "Azulería sepulcral," *Anales del Instituto de Investigaciones Estéticas,* 23 (1955), 49–51.

————. *La biblioteca de Luis Lagarto.* México: 1950.

————. "Bodegones y floreros en la pintura mexicana," *Anales del Instituto de Investigaciones Estéticas,* 14 (1946), 55–60.

————. *Breves apuntes sobre la escultura colonial de los siglos XVII y XVIII.* México: Secretaría de Educación Pública, 1930.

————. "La carta de examen de Lorenzo Rodríguez," *Anales del Instituto de Investigaciones Estéticas,* 15 (1947), 105–108.

————. "La casa colonial," *Anales del Museo Nacional de Arqueología, Historia y Etnología,* 5 (1913), 161–181.

————. *La Casa de los Azulejos.* México: Bland Bros., 1919.

————. *La casa de los virreyes en Huehuetoca.* México: Secretaría de Gobierno, 1921.

————. *La casa de Parada.* Madrid: Rivadeneyra, 1917.

————. *Una casa del siglo XVIII en México; la del conde de San Bartolomé de Xala.* México: Universidad Nacional Autónoma de México, 1957.

————. "Una casa habitación del siglo XVIII en la ciudad de México," *Anales del Instituto de Investigaciones Estéticas,* 4 (1939), 64–66.

———. *Catálogos de las exposiciones de la antigua Academia de San Carlos de México, 1850–1898.* México.

———. "El convento de San Francisco de Ozumba y las pinturas de su portería," *Anales del Instituto de Investigaciones Estéticas,* 24 (1956), 9–21.

———. "El convento dominicano de Chimalhuacán-Chalco," *Anales del Instituto de Investigaciones Estéticas,* 30 (1961), 91–96.

———. *La escultura colonial en México.* México. 1923.

———. *Grabados y grabadores en la Nueva España.* México: Ediciones Arte Mexicano, 1948.

———. *Historia sintética del arte colonial de México (1521–1821).* México: Porrúa Hnos., 1922.

———. "Huexotla," *Anales del Instituto de Investigaciones Estéticas,* 26 (1957), 51–54.

———. "La iglesia de San Francisco de México," *Anales del Instituto de Investigaciones Estéticas,* 20 (1952), 41–43.

———. *La iglesia y convento de San Agustín.* México: Instituto de Investigaciones Estéticas, 1951.

———. *Los jardines de la Nueva España.* 2 ed. México: Antigua Librería Robredo de J. Porrúa, 1945.

———. "José Guerrero, grabador mexicano," *Anales del Instituto de Investigaciones Estéticas,* 34 (1965), 75–78.

———. *Medallas relativas a la antigua Universidad de México.* México: Universidad Nacional Autónoma de México, 1945.

———. "Méritos y servicios de D. Manuel Tolsá," *Anales del Instituto de Investigaciones Estéticas,* 12 (1945), 33–42.

———. *La moneda mexicana; bosquejo histórico-numismático.* México: Banco de México, 1952.

———. "El pintor Alonso López de Herrera," *Anales del Instituto de Investigaciones Estéticas,* 34 (1965), 5–14.

———. *La plaza mayor de México en el siglo XVIII.* México: Universidad Nacional Autónoma de México, 1946.

———. "Los principales pintores de la Nueva España," in *Congreso Internacional de Historia de América, II, Buenos Aires, 1937.* Buenos Aires: Academia de la Historia, 1938.

———. *Residencias coloniales de la ciudad de México.* México: Secretaría de Hacienda, 1918.

———. "Las torres de la catedral de Guadalajara," *Anales del Instituto de Investigaciones Estéticas,* 34 (1965), 69–70.

Romero Flores, Jesús. *Apuntes para una bibliografía geográfica e histórica de Michoacán.* México: Secretaría de Relaciones Exteriores, 1932.

———. *Iconografía colonial; retratos de personajes notables en la historia colonial de México.* México: Museo Nacional, 1940.

Rosell, Lauro E. *Convento dieguino de Santa María de los Ángeles; Huitzilopochco-Churubusco, Museo Histórico.* México: Dirección de Monumentos Coloniales, Instituto Nacional de Antropología e Historia, 1947.

———. *Iglesias y conventos coloniales de la ciudad de México.* México: Patria, 1946.

Rubín de la Borbolla, Daniel F. "Las artes populares indígenas de América, supervivencia y fomento," *América indígena,* 19 (enero, 1959), 5–42.

Rubín de la Borbolla, Daniel F., ed. "Arte popular y artesanías de México," *Artes de México,* 43–44 (1962), 1–275.

Rubio Mañé, Jorge Ignacio, and Manuel Toussaint. *La casa de Montejo en Mérida de Yucatán.* México: Imprenta Universitaria, 1941.

Sahagún, Bernardino de. *Historia general de las cosas de Nueva España* (Florentine Codex). Madrid: Hauser y Menet, 1905–1907.

Salazar, L. "Arquería de Zempoala," *Anales del Ministerio de Fomento,* 2 (1877), 141.

Salazar Monroy, Melitón. *Convento de San Francisco y Capilla de Tercer Orden en la ciudad de Tlaxcala.* Tlaxcala: Oficina de Turismo del Estado, 1938.

———. *Convento franciscano de Huejotzingo.* Puebla: López, 1940.

Santiago Cruz, Francisco. *Las artes y los gremios en la Nueva España.* México: Jus, 1960.

Santoscoy, Alberto. *Historia del Hospital Real de San Miguel; época colonial.* Guadalajara: Diario de Jalisco, n.d.

Sariñana, Isidro. *Llanto del Occidente en el ocaso del mas claro sol de las Españas.* México: B. Calderón, 1666.

Saville, Marshall H. *The Goldsmith's Art in Ancient Mexico.* New York: Museum of the American Indian, 1920.

Schurz, William Lytle. *The Manila Galleon.* New York: Dutton, 1939.

Schuster, Alfred B. *The Art of Two Worlds; Studies in Pre-Columbian and European Cultures.* New York: Praeger, 1959.

Sedano, Francisco. *Noticias de México.* México: J. R. Barbedillo, 1880.

Sescosse, Federico. "La portada de San Mateo y la Lonja de los Ganaderos Zacatecanos," *Anales del Instituto de Investigaciones Estéticas,* 34 (1965), 65–68.

Sigüenza y Góngora, Carlos de. *Glorias de Querétaro en la nueva congregación eclesiástica de María Santíssima de Guadalupe.* México: Vda. de Bernardo Calderón, 1680.

———. *Teatro de virtudes políticas* (1680). México: 1856.

———. *Triunfo parténico* (1683). México: Ediciones Xochitl, 1945.

Sitwell, Sacheverell. *Spanish Baroque Art, with Buildings in Portugal, Mexico, and Other Colonies.* London: Duckworth, 1931.

Smith, Robert C., and Elizabeth Wilder (Weismann). *A Guide to the Art of Latin America.* Washington: Library of Congress, 1948.

Smith, Robert C. "Colonial Towns of Spanish and Portuguese America," *Journal of the Society of Architectural Historians,* 14 (1955).

Sociedad Española de Amigos del Arte. *Aportación al estudio de la cultura española en las Indias; catálogo general ilustrado.* Prólogo, José Gabriel Navarro. Madrid: Espasa-Calpe, 1930.

Sodi de Pallares, María Elena. *Historia del traje religioso en México.* México: Stylo, 1950.

Solá, Miguel. *Historia del arte hispanoamericano; arquitectura, escultura, pintura y artes menores en la América Española durante los siglos XVI, XVII, XVIII.* Barcelona-Buenos Aires: Labor, 1935.

Soria, Martin S. "Colonial Painting in Latin America," *Art in America,* Vol. 47, No. 3 (1959), 32–39.

———. "Notes on Early Murals in Mexico," in *Studies in the Renaissance,* VI, 236–242. New York: Renaissance Society, 1959.

Stanislawski, Dan. "Early Town Planning in the New World," *Geographical Review,* 37 (1947), 95–105.

———. "The Origin and Spread of the Grid-Pattern Town," *Geographical Review,* 36 (1946), 105–120.

Steck, Francis Borgia. *El primer colegio de América, Santa Cruz de Tlaltelolco, con un estudio del Códice de Tlaltelolco por R. H. Barlow.* México: Centro de Estudios Franciscanos, 1944.

Studies in Latin American Art. Ed. Elizabeth Wilder (Weismann). Washington: American Council of Learned Societies, 1949.

Tablada, José Juan. *Historia del arte en México.* México: Cía. Nacional Editoria, 1927.

Tamariz de Carmona, Antonio. *Relación y descripción del templo real de la ciudad de la Puebla de los Ángeles.* Puebla: 1649.

Tello, Antonio. *Crónica miscelánea de la sancta Provincia de Xalisco.* Guadalajara: Font, 1942, 1945.

———. *Libro segundo de la Crónica miscelánea de la santa provincia de Xalisco.* Guadalajara: República Literaria, 1891–1898.

"Tepotzotlán," *Artes de México,* 62–63 (1965), 7–38.

Terán, Miguel. "Baja Andalucía," *Revista de Occidente,* p. 157.

Toor, Frances. *A Treasury of Mexican Folkways.* New York: Crown, 1947.

Torquemada, Juan de. *Monarquía indiana* (1615). México: S. Chávez Hayhoe, 1943–1944.

Torre, Josefina Muriel de la. "El convento de Corpus Christi," *Anales del Instituto de Investigaciones Estéticas,* 7 (1941), 10–57.

Torre, Josefina Muriel de la, and Manuel Romero de Terreros. *Retratos de monjas en Nueva España.* México: 1952.

Torre Revello, José. *El gremio de plateros en las Indias Occidentales.* Buenos Aires: Instituto de Investigaciones Históricas, Universidad Nacional, 1922.

Torres Balbás, Leopoldo. "El estilo mudéjar en la arquitectura mejicana," *Al-Andalus,* 6 (1941).

Torres Lanzas, Pedro. *Relación descriptiva de los mapas, planos, etc. de México y Florida existentes en el Archivo General de Indias.* Sevilla: Mercantil, 1900.

Toscano, Salvador. "Chiapas: su arte y su historia coloniales," *Anales del Instituto de Investigaciones Estéticas,* 8 (1942), 27–43.

———. "Testamento de Manuel Tolsá," *Anales del Instituto de Investigaciones Estéticas,* 1 (1937), 50–54.

Toussaint, Antonio. "Colegio de las Vizcaínas," *Artes de México,* 42 (1962), 1–5.

Toussaint, Manuel. *Acolman.* México: Ediciones de Arte, 1948.

———. *Acolman, guía oficial.* México: Instituto Nacional de Antropología e Historia, 1949.

———. "Angahuan," *Journal of the Society of Architectural Historians,* 5 (1945–1946), 24–26.

———. *Arte colonial en México.* 2 ed. México: Universidad Nacional Autónoma de México, 1962.

———. *El arte flamenco en Nueva España.* México: Aldina, 1949.

———. *Arte mudéjar en América.* México: Porrúa, 1946.

———. *La Catedral de México y el Sagrario Metropolitano; su historia, su tesoro, su arte.* México: Comisión Diocesana de Orden y Decoro, 1948.

———. "La catedral de México; sus cronistas mas recientes," *Anales del Instituto de Investigaciones Estéticas,* 3 (1938), 5–20.

———. *La catedral y el sagrario de México.* México: Dirección General de las Bellas Artes, 1917.

———. *La catedral y las iglesias de Puebla.* México: Porrúa, 1954.

———. "El convento de Cuitzeo," *Arquitectura,* 6 (julio 1940), 17–22.

———. "Cuadros desconocidos de Alonso López de Herrera," *Anales del Instituto de Investigaciones Estéticas,* 12 (1945), 9–14.

———. "La escultura funeraria en la Nueva España," *Anales del Instituto de Investigaciones Estéticas,* 11 (1944), 41–58.

———. "Fray Andrés de San Miguel, arquitecto de la Nueva España," *Anales del Instituto de Investigaciones Estéticas,* 13 (1945), 5–14.

————. *El grabado en madera en México del siglo XVI a nuestros días.* México: 1928.

———— "Una joya de arte desconocida: El Santuario de Tepalcingo," *Anales del Instituto de Investigaciones Estéticas,* 6 (1953), 39–44.

————. *La litografía en México en el siglo XIX.* 2 ed. México: Biblioteca Nacional, 1934.

————. "Mexican Colonial Paintings in Davenport," *Gazette des Beaux-Arts,* 24 (1943), 167–174.

————. *1525–1925 (Iglesias de México, 6).* México: Secretaría de Hacienda, 1927.

————. *Oaxaca.* México: Cultura, 1926.

————. *Paseos coloniales.* 2 ed. México: Instituto de Investigaciones Estéticas, Universidad Nacional Autónoma de México, 1962.

————. *Pátzcuaro.* México: Universidad Nacional Autónoma de México, 1942.

————. *Pintura colonial en México.* Ed. Xavier Moyssén. México: Instituto de Investigaciones Estéticas, Universidad Nacional Autónoma de México, 1965.

————. "Pintura colonial; notas sobre Andrés de la Concha," *Revista mexicana de estudios históricos,* 1 (1927), 26–39.

————. *La pintura en México durante el siglo XVI.* México: Mundial, 1936.

————. "La pintura mural en Nueva España," *Artes de México,* 4 (1954), 8–30.

————. *Pinturas europeas en México.* México: Sociedad de Arte Moderno, 1946.

————. "Pinturas mexicanas en Davenport," *Anales del Instituto de Investigaciones Estéticas,* 14 (1946), 25–32.

————. "Las pinturas murales de Atotonilco," *Historia mexicana, Colegio de México,* 1 (1951), 173–184.

————. *Pinturas murales en los conventos mexicanos del siglo XVI.* México: Ediciones de Arte, 1948.

————. Proceso y denuncias contra Simón Pereyns en la Inquisición de México. Supplement, *Anales del Instituto de Investigaciones Estéticas,* 2 (1938).

————. "La relación de Michoacán; su importancia artística," *Anales del Instituto de Investigaciones Estéticas,* 1 (1937), 3–14.

————. "Supervivencias góticas en la arquitectura mexicana del siglo XVI," *Archivo español de arte y arqueología,* 11 (1935), 47–66.

————. *Tasco; su historia, sus monumentos, características actuales.* México: Cultura, 1931.

————. "Tres pintores del siglo XVI; nuevos datos sobre Andrés de la Concha, Francisco de Zumaya y Simón Pereyns," *Anales del Instituto de Investigaciones Estéticas,* 9 (1942), 59–61.

Toussaint, Manuel, Federico Gómez de Orozco, and Jus-tino Fernández. *Planos de la ciudad de México, siglos XVI y XVII.* México: Cultura, 1938.

Tresguerras, Francisco Eduardo. *Ocios literarios.* Ed. Francisco de la Maza. México: Universidad Nacional Autónoma de México, 1962.

Twenty Centuries of Mexican Art. México: Museum of Modern Art, New York, and Instituto Nacional de Antropología e Historia de México, 1940.

Urquijo, Conde de. *Casa y linajes de Echave y Laurcáin.* San Sebastián: 1929.

Valadés, Diego de. *Rhetorica Christiana.* Perusiae: apud Petrumiacobum Petrutium, 1579.

Valbuena, Bernardo de. *Grandeza mexicana* (1604). México: Sociedad de Bibliófilos Mexicanos, 1927.

Valle, Rafael Heliodoro. *Santiago en América.* México: Editorial Santiago, 1946.

Valle-Arizpe, Artemio de. *Notas de platería.* 2 ed. México: Herrero Hnos., 1961.

Vargas Lugo, Elisa. "La vicaría de Aculco," *Anales del Instituto de Investigaciones Estéticas,* 22 (1954), 103–114.

Velasco, Alfonso Alberto de. *Renovación por si mismo de la soberana imagen de Christo Señor Nuestro crucificado, que llamas de Ytzimiquilpan . . .* México: F. R. Lupercio, 1688.

Velásquez Chávez, Agustín. *Tres siglos de pintura colonial mexicana.* México: Polis, 1939.

Velde, Paul van de, and Henriette Romeike. *The Black Pottery of Coyotepec, Oaxaca, Mexico.* Los Angeles: Southwest Museum, 1939.

————. *Guide to Oaxaca, Monte Alban, Cuilapam, etc.* Oaxaca: 1933.

Vetancurt, Agustín de. *Chrónica de la provincia del Santo Evangelio de México.* México: Maria de Benavides, vda. Juan de Ribera, 1697.

————. *Teatro mexicano* (1698). México: I. Escalante, 1870–1871.

Veytia, Mariano. *Historia de la fundación de la ciudad de la Puebla de los Ángeles en la Nueva España.* Puebla: Labor, 1931.

Villalobos, Arias de. *México en 1623.* Ed. Genaro García. México: Vda. de Ch. Bouret, 1907.

————. *Obediencia que México, cabeza de la Nueva España dió a la Majestad Católica del rey D. Felipe . . . con un discurso en verso del estado de la misma ciudad . . .* México: Diego Garrido, 1623.

Villegas, Víctor Manuel. "La casa colonial popular de Toluca," *Anales del Instituto de Investigaciones Estéticas,* 26 (1957), 55–56.

————. *El gran signo formal del barroco; ensayo histórico del apoyo estípite.* México: Universidad Nacional Autónoma de México, 1956.

————. *Hierros coloniales en Toluca.* Toluca: 1936.

———. *Hierros coloniales en Zacatecas.* México: Universidad Nacional Autónoma de México, 1955.

Viñaza, Cipriano Múñoz y Manzana, Conde de. *Adiciones al Diccionario histórico de D. Juan Agustín Ceán Bermúdez.* Madrid: Huerfanos, 1889–1894.

Wagner, Max Leopold. "Die spanische Kolonialarchitektur in Mexiko," in *Zeitschrift für bildende Kunst,* 26 (1914–1915).

Weisbach, Werner. *Arte barroco en Italia, Francia, Alemania y España.* Trans. Ramón Iglesia. Barcelona: Labor, 1934.

Weismann, Elizabeth Wilder. *Mexico in Sculpture; 1521–1821.* Cambridge: Harvard University Press, 1950.

———. "Stone Sculpture of Colonial Mexico," *Magazine of Art,* 43 (March 1950), 106–110.

Wethey, Harold E. "The Problem of Toribio de Alcaraz," *Gazette des Beaux-Arts,* Ser. 6, Vol. 31, no. 963–967 (1947), 165–174.

Wilder, Mitchell, and Edgar Breitenbach. *Santos.* Colorado Springs: Taylor Museum, 1943.

Wuthenau, Alexander von. "The Spanish Military Chapels in Santa Fe and the Reredos of Our Lady of Light," *New Mexico Historical Review,* 10 (1935), 175–195.

———. *Tepotzotlán.* México: Von Stetten, 1941.

Zaldívar G., Sergio. *Arquitectura; barroco popular.* Guadalajara: Planeación y Promoción, 1960.

———. *Arquitectura; Jalisco en el arte, 8.* Guadalajara-México: Ediapsa, 1960.

Zamaçois, Niceto de. *Los misterios de México.* México: V. G. Torres, 1850.

Zavala, Silvio. *Fuentes para la historia del trabajo en Nueva España.* México: Fondo de Cultura Económica, 1939–1945.

———. *Ordenanzas del trabajo, siglos XVI y XVII.* México: Instituto de Historia de la Universidad Nacional Autónoma de México, 1947.

———. *Sir Thomas More in New Spain: A Utopian Adventure of the Renaissance.* London: Hispanic and Luso-Brazilian Council, 1955.

———. *La "Utopia" de Tomás Moro en la Nueva España.* México: Antigua Librería Robredo de J. Porrúa, 1937.

Zuno, José Guadalupe. *Las artes populares en Jalisco.* Guadalajara: Ediciones Centro Bohemio, 1957.

———. "Los enigmas del Museo de Guadalajara," *Gaceta municipal, XXIII,* 7 (julio 1954).

———. *Las llamadas lacas michoacanas de Uruapan no proceden de las orientales.* Guadalajara: Instituto Tecnológico de Guadalajara, 1953.

INDEX

Abel, Lorenzo: 194
Academia de San Carlos. SEE Academy of San Carlos
Academia Nacional de Bellas Artes. SEE Academy of San Carlos
académico de mérito: 405, 422, 429
Academies of Fine Arts: ideology, 401; outside Mexico City, 445, 446
Academy of San Carlos: locations, 307, 403, 419; ideology, 401, 430–431; history, 402–404, 455; directors general, 402, 432, 441, 444, 436; use of Baroque artists, 404, 440; directors of architecture, 404, 415, 419, 432; directors of engraving, 404, 418, 456; directors of sculpture, 404, 431, 435; directors of painting, 404, 440, 441; control of architecture, 405, 428; and Tresguerras, 422; director of plaster casting, 432; scholarships, 435, 436, 444–445; medals commemorating, 455
Acámbaro, Gto.: hospital chapel portal, 20, 116; Franciscan monastery, 89–90; fountain, 332, 420
Acapulco, Gro.: fortifications, 10
Acatepec, Pue.: church of San Francisco, 206, 262–263, 266, 370
Acatzingo, Pue.: font, Franciscan monastery, 58–59; sanctuary of the Virgen de los Dolores, 343–344
Acolman, Mex.: Augustinian monastery, 41–42, 50, 58, 59, 92, 115, 116, 267, 391
Actopan, Hgo.: Augustinian monastery, 29, 42–44, 92–93, 115, 118, 129
Acuitlapán, Gro.: monastery of San Diego, 193
Acuña,———(sculptor): 450
Acuña, Cosme de: 404, 441, 444, 454
Aguascalientes, Ags.: Cabildo, 304; church of El Señor del Encino, 340; pottery of, 388; sarapes of, 388
Agüero, Juan Miguel de: 110, 111
Aguiar y Seijas, Francisco: 160, 312
Águila, José Mariano del: 444, 450, 454, 456
Aguilar, José: 257
Aguilar, Pedro: 373
Aguilar y Cabello, José Manuel: 344
Aguilera, Juan: 244
Aguillón, Toribio: 357
Aguirre, Francisco de: 150

Aguirre, Ginés Andrés de: 404, 441
Alameda, Juan de: 84
Alarcón, Francisco de: 172
alarife: 13, 89, 185
Albuquerque, Francisco Fernández de la Cueva, Duque de: 239, 269
Alcántara, Gabriel de: 378
Alcántara, Juan de: 109
Alcaraz, Toribio de: 77, 84, 85, 111
Alcázar, Gabriel de: 378
Alcíbar, José de: 339, 404, 440–441
Alconedo, José. SEE Rodríguez de Alconedo, José Luis
Alemán, Bernardino: 456
Alemán, Juan. SEE Morales, Andrés
alfarjes. SEE Mudejar style, in architecture
Alfaro, Juan Antonio: 378
alfiz, alfices: 86–89, 104, 116–118
Allende, Ignacio: house of, 330
Allende, Narciso: 369
Almanza, Diego de: 378
Almoloya, Mex.: pottery of, 388
Alonso, Antonio: 194
altar fronts: 259, 366, 367
altarpieces. SEE retables
Álvarez, Bernardino: 19, 312
Alvarado, Antonio de: 231, 233
Alvarado, Juan de: 380
Alvarado, Pedro de: "House of Alvarado," Coyoacán, 16
Amado,———(engraver): 456
Amador, Francisco: 456
amantécatl: 70, 72. SEE feather work
Amarillas, Agustín de Ahumada y Villalón, Marqués de: portrait of, 338
Amaya,———(embroiderer): 169
ambones: 363
Ambrosio, Juan: 454
Amozoc, Pue.: ironwork in church, 173, 370; pottery of, 388
Analco, Pue.: church of El Santo Ángel, 263, 369
Andrade,———(engraver): 456
Angahua, Mich.: parish church, 57
Ángel, Luis: 167
Angulo, Francisco de: 231
Angulo, Nicolás de: 231
Antequera. SEE Oaxaca, Oax.
Antigua, Guatemala: Cabildo of, 16; Villalpando paintings in, 241
Antonelli, Bautista: 11
Alonso, Antonio: 194

Antonio, Nicolás: 261
Anunciación, Domingo de la: 102
Apan, Hgo.: retable, parish church, 293
Apartado, Marqués de: house of, 326
aqueducts: 32–33, 420
Aquino, Marcos de. SEE Cípac, Marcos
arabesque decoration. SEE *de romano*
Aráoz, Manuel: 454, 456
arca. SEE chests
arcades. SEE *portales*
Arce, Mariano: 437, 438–439
architects: military, 9–12, 111; 16th-cent., 14, 15, 18, 21, 23, 62, 77, 84, 88, 99, 102, 109, 110, 111, 115; friars and priests as, 84, 86, 90, 91, 92, 101, 186, 191; guild of, 277–278; control by Academy, 405–406, 422
architecture: European, 16th-cent., 3; pre-conquest, 4, 384; military, 9–12; domestic, 14–16, 123–125, 189–190, 314–331, 406, 413–414, 416, 420, 425; governmental, 16–17, 120–121, 186, 303–305; of hospitals, 17–20, 311–313; of schools, 20–23, 121–123, 186–189, 194, 307–311, 412–413; of churches, 23–24, 181, 191, 194–210, 279–302, 418–419, 420, 423–425; monastic, 23–32, 77–109, 180–181, 191–193, 201–202, 407, 414; influence of pre-conquest forms, 29, 31, 57, 79; popular, 98–99, 105, 116, 201, 205, 206, 329, 386, 390–391; of cathedrals, 109–115, 181–186, 202–203, 210, 409–412, 426
Arciniega, Claudio de: 23, 110, 115, 120, 123
Arciniega, Luis de: 136, 159
arcón. SEE chests
Arellano, Diego de: 380
Arenas, Bartolomé de: 231
Arenas, Luis de: 269
Arfe y Villafañe, Juan de: 449
Arias, José: 404, 431
armchairs, ecclesiastical. SEE chairs, *sillones*
Armenta, Antonio de: 170
armor: 371
arqueta. SEE chests
arquilla. SEE chests
Arreguín, José: 357
Arrieta, Agustín: 437, 446
Arrieta, Domingo: 353
Arrieta, José Manuel: 331

477

Arrieta, Pedro de: 196, 277, 307
Arrúe, Juan de: 62
Arrúe, Juan de, II: life and work, 87, 135, 136–137, 255; mentioned, 62, 134, 139
Arrúe, Juan de, III: 141
art: colonial, 4–6, 457
—, control of: legal, 64, 67, 162, 169, 270; ecclesiastical, 131–132; by the Academy, 405. SEE ALSO guilds
—, Indian: stylistic influence of, 4, 41, 49, 55, 57, 61–62, 84, 92, 99–101, 104, 121; influence of materials and techniques from, 44, 52, 69, 72–74, 84, 102; influence of motifs from, 29, 31, 42, 44–47, 48–52, 53, 55–59, 61, 79, 87, 89, 105, 267
—, popular: architecture, 98–99, 105, 116, 201, 205, 206, 298, 329, 386, 390–391; painting, 341, 386, 392–395, 446; sculpture, 347–350, 357, 384, 386, 395–397; minor arts, 371, 380, 386–390, 392; imitation of Fine Arts, 372, 384, 390–397; defined, 382–384; true types of, 385–390; graphic, 453, 455
—, pre-conquest: architecture, 3–4, 29, 78–79, 384; painting, 4, 38, 44–47; sculpture, 4, 48, 58, 59, 61, 384; minor arts, 4, 38, 63, 67, 69, 72–73, 173, 384, 389; described by Sahagún, 46; survival in popular art, 370, 384–385; as anthropology, 383–384
Arteaga, Sebastián. SEE López de Arteaga, Sebastián
Asia: art from, 318
las Atarazanas. SEE fortifications
Atitalaquia, Hgo.: parish church, 293
Atlatláuhcan, Mor.: Augustinian monastery, 42, 98
Atlihuetzía, Tlax.: Franciscan monastery, 88
Atlixco, Pue.: Franciscan monastery, 89; church of El Carmen, 191; church of La Merced, 202; hospital de San Juan de Dios, 312
Atotonilco, Gto.: Sanctuary, 249
Atoyac, D.F.: stone cross, 57; church of Santa Cruz, 118
atrio. SEE churchyard
Atzala, Gro.: custodia, 164
Atzayácatl: palace of, 4
Atzcapotzalco, D.F.: Dominican monastery, 44, 104; retables, 237, 241
Augustinian order: arrival, 23; typical monastery, 77–80, 90–91
—, establishments: Acolman, 41–92; Actopan, 29, 92–93; Atlatláuhcan, 41–98; Charo, 101; Cuitzeo, 99–101; Culhuacán, 42; Epazoyucan, 91; Ixmiquilpan, 93; Jonacátepec, 98; Malinalco, 42, 92; Metztitlán, 92; Mexico City, 91; Mixquic, 134; Molango, 115; Morelia, 254; Ocuilan, 91–92; Ocuituco, 41, 91; Tiripitío, 73, 98; Tlamaco, 116–118; Tlayacapan, 93–98; Totolapan, 91; Ucareo, 101; Valladolid, 98; Yecapixtla, 91;

Yuriria, 98–99; Zacualpan de Amilpas, 91
—, provinces: Dulce Nombre de Jesús de México, 91–98; San Nicolás de Tolentino de Michoacán, 98–100
Aulestia, Pedro de: 111
Austria: Mexican art in, 74
Avecilla, Joseph de: 269
Ávila, Alonso de: 57
Ávila, Jorge de: 91
Ávila y Rojana, José: 429
Aya, Joseph de la: 67
azulejos. SEE ceramics, azulejos in architecture

Bacerot, Juan Ignacio: 456
Báez, Enrique: 67
Báez, Francisco: 344
Bagally, Santiago: 456
Balbás,———(engraver): 456
Balbás, Isidro Vicente de: 296, 352, 409
Balbás, Jerónimo de: installs choir screen, Cathedral of Mexico, 268; high altar, 277, 366; Altar de los Reyes, 277, 350; portal, Hospital Real de Indias (?), 311; life and work, 350–352
balconies: 67, 329, 369, 377
Ballejo y Mandirano, Miguel: 344
Barba, Manuel: 378
Barbosa, Antonio de: 107
Barefoot Franciscans of San Diego. SEE Order of Barefoot Franciscans of San Diego
bargueños. SEE desks
Baroque style: causes and evolution in Mexico, 180; subordination to ensemble, 248; compared to Churrigueresque, 277; mentioned, 5, 457
—, in architecture: character and categories, 190; sober, 190–195; rich, 190, 195–203; exuberant, 190, 203–210; popular, 201, 205–206; façades, 214; use of tile, 266; interest in space, 279, 282; public buildings, 303–307; schools, 307–310; hospitals, 311–313; Palafoxian Library, 314; noble residences in Mexico City, 314–326; houses outside Mexico City, 327–331; Neoclassic opinion of, 406
—, in painting: subordination to ensemble, 225; the two styles, 227, 235, 238, 241, 242, 244; examples, 234–244; primarily decorative, 235; Correa as typical, 238
—, in sculpture: relation to architecture, 213; Baroque retable defined, 213; examples and artists, 213–224; estofado, encarnación, 222–223
—, in minor arts: silverwork, 258–262, 364–367; furniture, 262–263, 359–364; ironwork, 263–264, 370–371; bronzework, 268, 367–368; embroidery, 269
Barreda, Ignacio María: 340, 395
Barrientos, Nicolás de: 269
Barroso Escaloya, Vicencio: 184, 186

barracks: Cuartel de los Gallos, Mexico City, 305
Bartolache, Ignacio: 402, 444
Bartolico,———(sculptor): 356
Basacio, Arnaldo de: 20
basilicas: in 16th cent., 23; San Sebastián, Mexico City, 24; old cathedral, Puebla, 109
Bassoco, Antonio, Conde de: 326, 402, 418–419
Batán, Eugenio: 366
batihoja. SEE goldbeaters
Bautista, Juan: 170
Bazaine, Aquille, Marshal of France: house of, 414
Becerra, Diego: 270
Becerra, Diego de: 139, 231
Becerra, Francisco: 102, 109, 183–184
Becerra, Juan: 231
Becerra, Nicolás: 231
Bedolla, Miguel Lucas de. SEE Vedolla, Miguel Lucas de
beds: 69, 168, 263, 361
Beira, Manuel de: 160
bells: 267, 268, 269
Benavides,———(engraver): 456
Benevente, Toribio de. SEE Motolinía
Benites, Joseph Joachim: 357
Bergara, Antonio: 378
Bergara, José: 378
Bernal, Manuel: 374
Berrueco, Diego: 342
Berrueco, José Mariano: 342
Berrueco, Luis: 342
Berrueco, Miguel: 342
Berrueco, Nicolás: 342
Berrueco, Pablo José: 342
Betanzos, Domingo de: 39, 107
Bienvenida, Lorenzo de: 90
Biera, Manuel de: 160
bishoprics: 109, 111, 115, 184
blacksmiths. SEE guild of blacksmiths; ironwork
bodegones: 339–340, 446
Bogotá, Colombia: alfajes in, 127
Bolívar, Simón: 319, 323
Borda, José de la: proverb about, 277; builds Santa Prisca, Taxco, 296; houses, 319, 330; sells treasure of Santa Prisca to Cathedral of Mexico, 365–366
Borda, Manuel de la: 331
Borgraf, Diego de: 251–252
Borromino, Pietro: 355
Branciforte, Miguel de la Guía Talamanca, Conde de: 434
brass work: 367–368
Bravo, Antonio: 378
Bravo, Juan: 66
Briseño, Pedro: 191
Brizuela, Pedro de: 159
bronze work: in 16th, 17th cents., 267–269; in 18th cent., 367–368; Neoclassic, 451–452
bronze-gilt: 451–452

Brothers of Our Lady of Mt. Carmel. See Carmelite Order

Bucareli y Urzúa, Antonio María de: portraits of, 339, 340; eulogy (bronze), 367–368; mentioned, 275

Buenaventura, Juan: 268

Buenaventura, Simón: 268

Bueno Basorí, Pedro: 309

Buenos Aires, Argentine Republic: Cabildo of, 16

Buitrago, José: 289

Buitrón y Velasco, José: 429

Bustos, Hermenegildo: 395

Byzantine style: 44

Caamaño, Antonio: 452

Caamaño, Manuel: 415

Caballero, Juan: 296

Caballero, Marcos: 378

El Cabejón, Jal.: hacienda of, 425–426

Cabildos: of Mexico City, 10, 16, 166; of Veracruz, 16

cabinet-makers. See carpenters

Cabrera, Francisco de: 170

Cabrera, Miguel: 334–338, 341, 395

cacique: 14, 357

Cadena, Francisco: 374

Cadena, Juan: 372

Cadereyta, Lopé Díez de Aux de Armendáriz, Marqués de: 162

Cajigal de la Vega, Francisco Antonio: portrait of, 338

cajonera. See cupboards, sacristy

calain: 268

Calderón, Pedro: 244–246

California, U.S.A.: Costanso maps coast of, 407

Calkini, Yuc.: Franciscan monastery, 90

Calleja, Felix María del Rey, Conde de Calderón: portrait of, 446

Calpan, Pue.: Franciscan monastery, 86, 88, 118; posas, 55

Camacho,———(painter): 257

Camacho, Francisco: 374

camarines: at Tepotzotlán, 127, 215; at San Miguel de Allende, 127; at Ocotlán, 215

Campeche, Camp.: fortifications of, 10; Franciscan monastery, 90; desks made in, 168; hermitage of San Román, 357; customs house, 409

Campos Herrera, Antonio: 269

Canal, Conde de la: house of, 425

candleholders: 16th-cent., 65–66, 164–165; 17th-cent., 262; 18th-cent., 366, 367, 368, 370; of tortoiseshell, 380; Neoclassic, 449, 450, 451

cantero: 53

caña de maíz. See corn pith

capillas de indios. See chapels, open

Capuchin Order: convent of Las Capuchinas, Morelia, 195

Capuchinas. See Capuchin Order

Cárcamo, Diego de: 214, 224

Carcanio, Manuel: 340

Cárdenas, José de: 175

Cárdenas, Lázaro: 282

Cardona, Ramón de: 67

Cariaga, Joseph (José): 378

Carmelite Order: no 16th-cent. buildings, 109; typical monastery, 191; Andrés de San Miguel, architect, 191, 332

—, establishments: 191, 423

Caro, Antonio: 256, 345

Caro, Manuel (painter): 256, 345–346

Caro, Manuel (potter): 378

Caro, Mariano: 256, 345–346

Caro de Ayala, José: 256, 345

carpenters: 53, 158

Carranza, Miguel: 446

Carrillo, Antonio: 268

Carrillo, Bartolomé: 268

Casa de Ejercicios: in Puebla, 381; in Mexico City, 417

Casa de Fundición: 64, 162

casa sola: 189, 329

casa de vecindad: 189–190, 329, 386

casa de viviendas: 329

Casa Rul, Conde de: house of, 425

Casafuerte, Marqués de: portrait of, 244

Casanova, Francisco: 456

Casas, Bartolomé de las: 72–73, 107, 115

Casas, Ignacio Mariano de las: 287, 355

Casas, Mariano de las. See Casas, Ignacio Mariano de las

Casillas, Martín: 115

Castañiza, Marqués de: house of, 324

Castellanos, José: 374

Castellanos, Juan: 372–374

Castellanos, Juan de Dios: 374

Castera, Ignacio: 406, 416–419, 429

Castilla, Luis de: 167

Castillo, Diego del: 191

Castillo, José del: 231

Castillo, José Antonio del: 365

Castillo, José María del: 437

Castillo, Juan del: 374

Castillo, Juan Esteban del: 374

Castillo, Manuel del: 268

Castillo, Nicolás de: 175

castizo: defined, 435

Castro, Alberto de: 456

Castro, Antonio de: 456

Castro, Isidro de: 346

Castro, José Antonio: 445

Castro, José Damián. See Ortiz de Castro, José Damián

Castro, Simón de: 120

casts, classical: coins, 402; sculpture (plaster), 432

catafalques. See ceremonies, memorial

cathedrals: Chiapas, 109; Chihuahua, 202–203; Compostela, 109; Durango, 222; Guadalajara, 109, 115; Mérida, 109, 111–112; Mexico City, 23, 109–111, 181–183, 409–412; Michoacán, 109; Morelia, 184–186; Nueva Galicia, 115; Oaxaca, 109; Pátzcuaro, 111; Puebla, 23, 109, 183–184, 426; Saltillo, 293; San Cristóbal de las Casas, 109, 115, 186; San Luis Potosí, Tulancingo, Zacatecas, 210

Cayetano,———(wood carver): 224

Cebollos, Pedro: 166

Celada, Juan de: 66

Celaya, Gto.: church of El Carmen, 423–424; tomb of Tresguerras, bridge, obelisk, 423; theater, 424

Celis, Juan de: 175

Cempoala, Hgo.: aqueduct of, 33

censers: 66

census lists: Padrón de la ciudad de México (1753), 247, 365, 367; Padrón general de la Nueva España (1791), 356

ceramics: pre-conquest, 173, 385; establishment in Mexico, 173–174; 16th-cent., 174–176; talavera, 174, 264; from China, 176; guilds, 264–265; categories of pottery, 264, 265; 17th-cent., 265–267; 18th-cent., 374–378; popular, 385, 386–388

—, azulejos in architecture: 102, 194, 264, 266, 312, 317–318, 326, 374–378

Cerda,———(die cutter): 456

Cerda, Juan: 445

Cerda, Juan de la: 345

Cerda, Luis de la: 167

Cerda, Manuel de la: 345

Cerda, Mateo de la: 160

Cerda, Matías de la: 224

Cerecedo, Matías de: 170

ceremonies: of canonization, 246; memorial, 31, 36, 115, 135, 136, 137, 416, 429, 446; of royal homage, 36, 243, 247, 310, 416, 425, 455; of welcome, 36, 135, 137, 141, 145, 231, 233, 239, 253, 339

Cerezo, Augusto: 444

Cervantes, José: 456

Cervantes de Salazar, Francisco: 21, 91

Chachalaca, Pedro: 40

chairs: 16th-cent., 46, 69; icpalli (equipales), 69, 384; 17th-cent., 168; sillones, 263, 269, 360, 363; 18th-cent., 359, 360–361; popular, 384, 389

chalchihuite. See jade, jadeite

Chalco, Mex.: church of Santiago, 194–195

chalices: 65, 66, 166, 259, 366, 450

Chalma, Pue.: sanctuary of El Señor de Chalma, 365

chandeliers: 366

Chango, Juan Manuel: 429

chapels, open: examples of, 26–31, 42, 85, 87–90, 105, 119, 256; Indian influence in, 29; classified, 29–31; in other American countries, 31; position in churchyard, 78; Mudejar influence in, 125

Charles V: 45, 53, 62–63, 74, 151

Charles III: 402, 416

Charles IV: 416, 425, 434–435, 452

Charo, Mich.: Augustinian monastery, 101

chasubles: 169
Chavarría, Juan de: house of, 326
Chávez,——(painter): 346
Chávez, Diego de: 99
chests: 69, 168, 380, 389
chests of drawers: 362, 363
Chiapa de Corzo, Chis.: fountain, 34; *Descent from the Cross*, 53; Dominican monastery, 109; lacquer, 389
Chihuahua, Chih.: cathedral, 202–203
Chimalhuacán Chalco, Mex.: Dominican monastery, 58, 104, 116
China: art from, 167, 168, 176, 264, 364, 371, 378–380; influence from, 265, 374, 389
Chippendale style: 359, 360, 395
choir books: illumination of, 249–250
choir screens. SEE grilles
choir stalls: 159, 202, 218–222, 380
Cholula, Pue.: Capilla Real, 29–31; Franciscan monastery, 41, 55, 59, 65, 85, 118; portal of house, 50
chozas: 384
churches: 16th-cent., 23–26; typical monastic, 79–80; parish, 179–180, 181; typical convent, 180; Baroque, 191–193, 194–202, 205–210, 279–282; popular Baroque, 206, 391; Churrigueresque, 282–295, 296–302; Neoclassic, 418–419, 423–425. SEE ALSO under place names
churchyard: compared to temple precinct, 78–79; gates, 78, 104; arcaded, 90. SEE ALSO *posas*; chapels, open
Churriguera, José de: 275
Churrigueresque style: social background of, 275, 315; compared to Baroque, 277; showing Indian taste, 277; in embroidery, 371
——, in architecture: use of tile, 266, 288, 317, 327, 329, 375–378; Mexico City churches, 282–286; Querétaro churches, 286–288; Puebla churches, 288–292; Guanajuato churches, 292–293; churches elsewhere, 293–296; Santa Prisca y San Sebastián, Taxco, 296, 352; sanctuary of Ocotlán, 296–298; Seminary, Tepotzotlán, 298–302, 353; schools, 309–310
——, in sculpture: retables, 213, 289–293, 295–296; introduced by Balbás, 272, 350; pre-eminently sculptural style, 282, 347; Querétaro interiors, 286–287; Santa Prisca, Taxco, 296, 352–353; Seminary, Tepotzotlán, 299–302, 353; sculptors, 350–357
Churubusco, D.F.: aqueduct, 33; monastery of San Diego (Museo de Churubusco), 191, 310
Cíbola: 47
ciboria: 450
Cifuentes, Rodrigo de: 47
Cípac, Marcos: 40
ciprés. SEE high altars

Ciria, Marqués de, Mariscal de Castilla: house of, 317
Cisneros, Luis de: 137
city planning: 12–13, 16, 330
Ciudad Hidalgo (Tajimaroa), Mich.: Franciscan monastery, 58
Clapera, Francisco: 404, 440–441, 445
Clavé, Pelegrín: 443
cloisters: primitive, 32, 86, 89; typical, 82; Franciscan, 86, 89, 90; Augustinian, 91–99, 101; Dominican, 102, 107
coa: 370
Coatlatlauhcan, Oax.: *petates* of, 384
Coatlícue: 48
Cocupao. SEE Quiroga, Mich.
codices: pre-conquest, 4; post-conquest, 44–47
——, titles of: Aubin Codex 40; Codex of the Tecpan de Tlatelolco, 16; Codex of Tepetlaóztoc (Kingsborough Codex), 14, 46, 64, 73; Durán Codex, 46; Florentine Codex, 46, 64, 72, 166; Introducción de la justicia español en Tlaxcala, 46, 136; Lienzo de Jucutácato, 46; Lienzo de Tlaxcala, 44; Mendocino Codex, 45; Relación de Michoacán, 45–46; Osuna Codex, 46, 110; Sierra Codex, 46, 65; Tira de Tlatelolco, 44; Yanhuitlán Codex, 47
coins: 454–455
Coixtlahuaca, Oax.: Dominican monastery, 29, 57, 70, 104–105, 106
Colina, Marqués de la: house of, 319
Colli, Fernando: 40
Colón, Diego: palace in Santo Domingo, 15
colorín: sculpture of, 52
columnaria: 454
comales: 385
commodes: 362
Company of Jesus. SEE Jesuit Order
Compostela, Jal.: Cathedral of Nueva Galicia, 115. SEE ALSO Guadalajara, Cathedral of
confessionals: 363
Concha, Andrés de la: at Yanhuitlán, 107, 255; life and work, 135, 136, 141, 159
Congregation of the Divine Savior: 312
Congregation for the Propagation of the Faith: San Fernando, Mexico City, 222, 279–280; Orizaba, 414
Congregation of St. Philip Neri: Mexico City, 193, 414; Puebla (La Concordia), 193; San Miguel de Allende, 193; Oaxaca, 193
Conique, José: 303
Conkal, Yuc.: Franciscan monastery, 90
conquest of Mexico: 3, 44
Conrado, Gaspar: 252–253
Conrado, Tomás: 231–233
Contreras, José: 268
convents: 109, 181–182, 196
copper work: 368
Cora, José Villegas. SEE Villegas Cora, José

Cora, José Zacarías: life and work in Puebla, 354–355; saints for towers, Cathedral of Mexico, 412, 436–437; mentioned, 415, 426
corn pith: 52
Coronado, Bartolomé: 62
Coronado, Francisco. SEE Vásquez de Coronado, Francisco
Correa, Juan: influence on Rodríguez brothers, 233; typical Baroque painter, 234–235; oeuvre and style, 236–238, 241; paintings in sacristy, Cathedral of Mexico, 237, 239n; mentioned, 149, 152, 247, 333, 335, 342
Cortés, Juan: 172
Cortés, Hernán (Hernando), Marqués del Valle de Oaxaca: works on fort, 9; lives in Coyoacán, 14; takes over Casas Viejas and Casas Nuevas of Moctezuma, 14; house in Oaxaca, 15; founds hospitals, 17; shown in Lienzo de Tlaxcala, 44; golden lizard ex-voto, 63; gifts to Charles V, 63–64, 74; establishes silk culture, 70; tapestries, *guadameciles* in Cuernavaca house, 71–72; prospects for tin, 267; tomb, church of Hospital de Jesús, Mexico City, 452
Cortés, Manuel: 357
Cortina, Conde de la: house of, 324
Coscomatepec, Mex.: pottery of, 388
Costansó, Miguel: 406, 407–409, 429
Covarrubias, Melchor de: 218
Coyoacán, D.F.: Cabildo of Mexico first convenes in, 10; "Casa de Cortés," 14; houses, 16; Dominican monastery, 24, 57, 102–104; chapel of La Concepción, 128
Coyotepec, Oax.: pottery of, 387–388
credenzas: 363
Cremona, Francisco: 449
creole: 5, 179, 278, 315
criollo. SEE creole
Croix, Carlos Francisco, Marqués de: portrait of, 338
crosiers: 65, 166
crosses: churchyard, 57–58, 78, 89; crossroads, 57; silver, 65, 259; on roofs, 369–370, 410
crucifixes: corn pith, 52; stone, 61; silver, 66, 259; bronze, 368; ivory, 379–380; wood, 395; Neoclassic, 451
cruets, ecclesiastical: 66, 450
Cruz, Cristóbal de la: 160
Cruz, Jerónimo de la: 184
Cruz, Juan de la: 435
Cruz, Juana Inés de la: portrait of, 337
Cruz, Mateo de la: 263
Cruz, Pascual de la: 269
Cuadra, Gro: hacienda of, 332
Cuadros, Francisco Manuel. SEE Enríquez, Alberto
cuauhxicalli: 59
Cuautinchán, Pue.: Franciscan monastery, 87; retables, 136, 137, 153

Cuautitlán, Mex.: churchyard cross, 57; pottery of, 388

Cuéllar, Lázaro de: 170

Cuentas, Diego de: 257

Cuernavaca, Mor.: house of Cortés, 15; Franciscan monastery, 29, 41, 85; Borda gardens, 331; church of the Tercer Orden, 391

Cuevas, Miguel Hipólito de: 261

Cuevas y Sandoval, Domingo de: 261

Cuilapan, Oax.: basilica (open chapel), 26, 31, 115; Dominican monastery, 107

Cuitzeo, Mich.: Augustinian monastery, 99–100, 101, 116

Culhuacan, Mex.: Augustinian monastery, 42

cupboards: sacristy, 69, 262–263, 361, 362–363; domestic, 168–169, 359, 361, 389

cupolas: 89, 181, 184, 196, 203, 282, 411–412, 419, 423

custodias: 163–166, 258, 365–367

Custodio Durán, Miguel: 277, 296

Cuzco, Peru: Cathedral, 183–184

Daniel (embroiderer): 70

Davenport, Iowa, U.S.A.: Municipal Art Gallery, 149, 443

Dávila, Melchor (architect): 23, 122

Dávila, Melchor (locksmith): 173

Dávila, Rodrigo: 23, 123

Delgadillo, José (Joseph) Eligio: 429

Delgado, Sebastián: 378

de romano: 41, 132

Desierto de los Leones, D.F.: Carmelite retreat, 191; gardens, 332

Desierto de Tenancingo, Mex.: Carmelite retreat, 191; gardens, 332

desks: 168, 361–362

Díaz, Ignacio: 368

Díaz, Martín: 71

Díaz, Porfirio: 323

Díaz de Aguilera, Rodrigo: 183

Díaz de la Barrera, Pedro: 167

Díaz de Lisbona, Diego: 18, 62

Díaz de Rivera, Joseph: 380

Díaz del Castillo, Bernal: 9, 11, 14, 40

diecutting: 454

Dieguinos. SEE Order of Barefoot Franciscans of San Diego

Domínguez, Diego: 173

Dolores, José: 437

Dolores Hidalgo, Gto.: talavera ceramics, 175, 388; parish church, 292–293

domes: Baroque, 89, 196, 205, 266, 282, 376; of San Pedro y San Pablo, 120; of convent, parish churches, 181; of Cathedral of Mexico, 183–184, 411–412; of Cathedral of Puebla, 183–184; media naranja, 376; Neoclassic, 414, 419, 424

Dominican Order: arrival in Mexico, 23; typical monastery, 78, 101

—, establishments: Atzcapotzalco, 44, 104; Chiapa de Corzo, 109; Chimalhuacán Chalco, 58, 104; Coixtlahuaca, 29, 104–105; Cuilapan, 26, 107; Etla, 137; Huitzo, 137; Mexico City, 101–102; Oaxaca, 105–106; Oaxtepec, 44, 102; Puebla, 102, San Cristóbal de las Casas, 109; Tecpatán, 109; Tepetlaóztoc, 44; Teposcolula, 29, 105; Tepoztlán, 102; Texupan, 46; Tlacochahuayo, 137; Tlacolula, 171; Tláhuac, 128; Tlaquiltenango, 104; Tlaxiaco, 106; Yanhuitlán, 106; Yautepec, 29, 102; Zacatecas, 247

—, provinces: San Hipólito de Oaxaca, 105–107; San Vicente de Chiapas y Guatemala, 107–109; Santiago de México, 101–105

door knockers: 67, 172–173, 371

doors: 279

dorador. SEE gilder

Durán, Diego: 46

Durán Cornejo, Francisco: 71

Durán y Villasenor, José Alejandro: 428

Durango, Dgo.: Cathedral, 202, 222

Dzemel, Yuc.: parish church, 295

Echave Ibía, Baltasar de: 141, 143–145, 166

Echave Ibía, Manuel de: 141, 143–145

Echave Orio, Baltasar de (the Elder): 135, 141–143

Echave y Rioja, Baltasar de (the Younger): 141, 230–231, 238

Echavira, Antonio de: 186

Echeandía, José M.: 419, 429

Echeverría, Atanasio: 441, 445, 454, 456

Echeverría, Manuel: 378

El Cardonal, Hgo.: churchyard cross, 58

El Rosario, Jal.: pottery of, 387

embroiderers: Indians as, 70, 71, 372; guild ordinances for, 71; 16th-cent., 71; 17th-cent., 170, 269; 18th-cent., 371–374

embroidery: taught by friars, 70; feather work as substitute for, 73; Renaissance, 169–170; Baroque, 269; 18th-cent., 371–372; Indian mood in, 372. SEE ALSO textiles

Ena, Francisco de: 166

en blanco: defined, 222; retables, 293, 295

encarnación, encarnado: 223, 347

encerados: 269

Encian, Salvador de: 175

Encinas, Gaspar de: 174

encomienda: defined, 5

England: influence of art, on furniture, 359

engravers: listed, 456

engraving: wood, 452–453; metal, 453–454, 455–456

engravings: as models for Indians, 38; for paintings, 41, 46, 129, 130, 230–231; for sculpture, 53, 55, 87–88; Klauber's, 180, 355; for architecture, 196; in minor arts, 214, 449

Eno, Francisco de: 166

Enríquez, Alberto: 255

Enríquez, Antonio (painter): 345

Enríquez, Antonio (potter): 378

Enríquez, Martín: 110

Enríquez, Nicolás: 345

Enríquez del Castillo, Nicolás: 303

ensamblador. SEE carpenters

entallador. SEE wood carvers

Entrambas Aguas, Juan de: 33, 62

Epazoyucan, Hgo.: Augustinian monastery, 92, 129, 134

equipales. SEE chairs

Erongarícuaro, Mich.: Franciscan monastery, 89, 118

Escalona, Phelipe: 372

Escandón, Antonio, Conde de Valencia: 292

Escobar, Francisco: 356, 437

Escobar, Joseph: 247

Escobar y Llamas, Cristóbal de: 309

Escovar, Bartolomé: 357

Escovar, Mariano: 357

escribanía: 362

escritorio. SEE desks

Escuela Nacional de Artes Plásticas. SEE Academy of San Carlos

escultor. SEE wood carvers

eslabón: 371

espadañas: 90, 92, 94, 191

Espejo, Vicente: 456

Espina, Pedro de: 66

Espinosa, Antonio de (printer): 20

Espinosa, Antonio de (painter): 251

Espinosa, Bartolomé: 268, 368

Espinosa, Juan de: 247

Espinosa, Marcos de: 379

Espinosa, Rodrigo de: 270

Espinoza, Antonio de: 251

Espinoza, Diego de: 251

Esquivel, José Joaquín: 340

Esteban, Francisco: 66

Esteve, José: 402, 456

estípite: 213, 277, 286, 372

estofado: 222–223, 247, 347

Estrada, José María: 395

Estrada, Joseph: 261

Estrada, Mariano de: 247

etching: 453

Etla, Oax.: Dominican monastery, 137

Etzatlán, Jal.: open chapel of hospital, 31; sarapes of, 388

Europe: art from, 52–53, 71–72, 151–152, 161; Mexican art in, 52, 63, 74, 379

ex-votos: retablos, 386; milagros, 389

Fabregat, José Joaquín: first director of engraving, Academy, 404, 454; engraving of Charles IV's ceremony, 417–418; life and work, 456

Fabrís, Felipe: 445

facistoles: 363

factories: 407

Farfán, Jerónimo: 249

feather work: 4, 38, 65–66, 72–74

felipenses. SEE Congregation of St. Philip Neri

Feria, Juan de la: 175
Fernández, Antonio: 367
Fernández, Diego: 170
Fernández, Francisco: 357
Fernández, Juan: 159
Fernández, Marcos: 345
Fernández de Lizardi, José Joaquín (*El Pensador Mexicano*): 430–431
Fernández de Sandrea (Sandreda),———: 224
Ferra, Baltasar: 268
fire gilding. SEE gilding, fire
Flanders: artists from, 67, 134, 159, 172, 251; paintings from, 151–152, 255
Flora Mexicana: 445
Flores, Francisco: 257
Focher, Juan de: 20
Folco, Diego de: 214
folk art. SEE art, popular
fonts: baptismal, 58–59, 84, 104, 174; holy water, 59, 260, 262
forgery: 47, 149
fortifications: Villa Rica de la Veracruz, 9; San Juan de Ulúa, 11; Pánuco, 9; las Atarazanas, Mexico City, 9–10
———, monasteries as: 78; Tepeaca, 82; Yuriria, 99
fountains: in monasteries, 34, 61, 91, 98, 420; in towns, 33–34, 420, 425; in Mexico City, 33, 416, 419, 420
frames: Neoclassic, 450
France: artists from, 453
———, influence on art: in 19th cent., 5–6; in architectural sculpture, 322; on furniture, 360–361, 362, 363; in School of Mines, 413; in church of Loreto, 419; Salto del Agua fountain, 420; side door, El Carmen, Celaya, 424; ideology, 430–431; of Girardon on Tolsá, 434–435. SEE ALSO Rococo style; Louis XIV, Louis XV, Louis XVI styles
Franciscan Order: first missionaries, 23; Convento Grande de México, 23; early specifications for cloister, 31–32; school of art, San José de los Naturales, 38; typical monastery, 77–82
———, establishments: Acámbaro, 89; Acatzingo, 58; Atlihuetzía, 88; Atlixco, 89; Calkiní, 90; Calpan, 88; Campeche, 90; Chalco, 195; Cholula, 29, 41, 85; Ciudad Hidalgo (Tajimaroa), 58; Conkal, 90; Cuautinchán, 87; Cuautitlán, 57; Cuernavaca, 85; Erongarícuaro, 89; Etzatlán, 31; Guadalajara, 256; Huaquechula, 86–87; Huejotzingo, 41, 84; Huexotla, 32; Huichapan, 57, 89; Izamal, 90; Jacona, 119; Jilótepec, 57; Maní, 61, 90; Mérida, 90; Mexico City (Convento Grande de México), 23, 83–84; Milpa Alta, 157; Morelia (Valladolid), 89; Motul, 90; Otumba, 29; Pátzcuaro, 89; Puebla, 84; Quecholac, 26; Santa Fe de México, 53; Tecali, 87, 116; Tecamachalco, 49; Tecómitl, 32; Tehuacán, 137; Tepeapulco, 89; Tepeji del Río,

88–89; Tepepan, 174; Tepeyanco (de las Flores), 88; Texcoco, 55, 84; Ticul, 90; Tizatlán, 256; Tizimín, 90; Tlahuelilpa, 29; Tlalmanalco, 29, 84; Tlalnepantla, 86; Tlaxcala, 23; 84–85; Tochimilco, 86; Totimehuacán, 88; Tula, 85–86; Tulancingo, 127; Tzintzuntzan, 89; Uruapan, 89; Valladolid, Yuc., 90; Xochimilco, 89; Zacapu, 89; Zacatlán (de las Manzanas), 24, 86; Zinacantepec, 58; Zizantum, 90
———, provinces: Santo Evangelio de México, 82–89; San Pedro y San Pablo de Michoacán, 89–90; San José de Yucatán, 90
Franco, Alonso: 141, 145
Franco, Juan: 67
fresco painting: 40–44, 132, 235, 257
Frías, Bartolomé de: 21
Fuenclara, Pedro Cebrián y Agustín, Conde de: 162
Fuen-Labrada, Nicolás de: 233
Fuensalida, Luis de: 111
Fuentes, Pedro de: 66
furniture: pre-conquest, 68; 16th-cent., 69–70; 17th-cent., 168–169; Baroque, 262–263, 359–362; ecclesiastical, 262–263, 362–364; from Paracho and Peribán, 385; Neoclassic, 452

gachupines: 5, 179
Gage, Thomas: 168, 179
Galán, Felipe: 257
García Conde, Diego: 454
Galindo, Juan: 170
Gallegos, Sebastián: 224
Gálvez, Matías, Conde de: 402, 406
Gamboa, Francisco de: 83
Gándara,———(sculptor): 160, 224
Gante, Pedro de: 20, 38, 201
Gaona, Juan de: 20
Garcés, Julián: 109
García, José: 344
García, José Trinidad: 357
García, Joseph: 344, 356
García, Juan (blacksmith): 67
García, Juan (priest): 21
García, Manuel: 444
García, Sebastián: 175
García Bravo, Alonso: 9, 10, 12–13
García Carrillo, Juan: 174
García Conde, Diego: 454
García Cornejo, Cayetano: 368
García de las Prietas, I.: 456
García de Salamanca,———(wood carver): 159
García de Torres, José Joaquín: 404, 429
García Ferrer, Mosén Pedro: finishes cathedral of Puebla, 183–184; portal, Colegio de San Pedro y San Pablo, 194; tabernacle, angels of pendentives, Cathedral of Puebla, 214; life and work, 250–251; mentioned, 224, 233
gardens: 331–332, 407
Garzón, Juan. SEE Gersón, Juan

Germany: artists from, 67; furniture from, 168
Gersón, Juan: identified as Flemish, 92; Epazoyucan murals attributed to, 129; Tecamachalco paintings documented by, 129–131, 134; identified as Indian, 131n; documented in Puebla, 249
tabernacle, angels of pendentives, Ca-
Gil, Jerónimo Antonio: founder and director general of Academy, 402, 404, 455; portrait of, 443; does fire gilding, 451–452; life and work, 454–455, 456
Gil, Bernardo: 445, 455, 456
Gil, Gabriel: 445, 455, 456
gilder: 132
gilding: in Old Cathedral, Mexico City, 135; technique, 222–223; in old church, Taxco, 224; irridescent, 286; in Cathedral of Mexico, 350
———, fire: in 17th cent., 171; not on wood, 222; in 18th cent., 367; in Neoclassic artifacts, 449, 451–452
Giordano, Luca: 152
Girardon, François: 435
glass: 135, 269–270, 270–271, 362
glyphs: hieroglyphs, ideograms, 4, 44; symbols of speech, 53, 57; symbols of place, 267; for dates, 29, 49, 58–59, 87
goldbeaters: 65, 162, 261
goldsmiths: 63–64, 65, 162–163. SEE ALSO silversmiths
goldwork: pre-conquest, 4, 63; 16th-cent., 63–66, 164, 166, 167; 17th-cent., 258–261; 18th-cent., 364–367; Neoclassic, 450–451. SEE ALSO silverwork
Gómez, Bruno: 456
Gómez, Gabriel: 380
Gómez, Juan: 186–189
Gómez Beltrán, Francisco: 176
Gómez de Mora, Juan: 110
Gómez de Trasmonte, Juan: 109
Gómez de Trasmonte, Luis: 183
Gómez de Valdés, Ginés: jewelry in estate, 261
González, Bartolomé: 67
González, Esteban: 429
González, Gonzalo: 176
González, Juan (potter, apprenticed 1630): 175
González, Juan (potter, fl. 1701): 378
González, Juan de Sole: 214, 224
González, Manuel Bonifacio: 374
González Grajeda, Francisco: 173
González Velásquez, Antonio. SEE González Velásquez, José Antonio
González Velásquez, José Antonio: director of architecture, Academy, 404; designs cigar factory (La Ciudadela), 407; work, 414–416; chapel of El Señor de Ixmiquilpan, 415, 443; mentioned, 423, 429
Gordillo, J. Ignacio: 456
Gothic style: in Spain (Isabelline), 3; in Augustinian monastery, Yecapixtla, 55, 91; in decorative sculpture, 55; in sil-

verwork, 65, 166; in wrought iron, 67; in linen-fold panelling, 69–70; in monastic churches, 79, 82, 85, 86, 87, 89, 91, 93, 101, 102, 107

Goya y Lucientes, Francisco de: 440, 447

granaries: 16, 384, 428

Granados, Ignacio: 344–345

Granados, Victoriano: 344

grilles: of wrought iron, 67, 171–173, 263, 368–369; 16th-cent., 171; imported, 83, 268; of convent churches, 182; 17th-cent., 263, 267–268; bronze, 267–268; from Macao, 268; 18th-cent., 368–369

grotesque decoration. SEE *de romano*

Guadalupe, D.F. SEE Villa Madero, D.F.

guadameciles: 71–72

Guadalajara, Jal.: Cathedral of, 115, 186, 365; portal from house, 125; painting in, 256–257, 345; chapel of Aránzazu, 295; Palace of the Audiencia de Nueva Galicia (Palacio de Gobierno), 303; seminary (Museo del Estado), 309; Hospital de Belén, 313; sarapes and rebozos of, 388, 389; Hospicio Cabañas, 414; Casa de Misericordia, 419; Casa de Moneda, 435

—, churches in: El Carmen, 191; Jesús María, 198; La Merced, 202; Sagrario, 419; San Antonio de Padua, 439; San Diego, 439; San Felipe Neri, 193; Santa María de Gracia, 198; Santa Mónica, 198, 218

Guadalcázar, Diego Fernández de Córdoba, Marqués de: 270

Guanajuato, Gto.: house of La Valenciana, 369; house, Conde de Casa Rul, 425; Alhóndiga de Granaditas, 428

—, churches in: Cata, 292; La Compañía, 292, 369; parish, 193; San Diego, San Juan de Rayas, La Valenciana, 292

Guarneros, José: 378

La Guatapera. SEE Uruapan

Guatemala: artists from, 258; influence of, on Mexican art, 186, 350, 356–357; Mexican art in, 236, 241, 270, 339n

Gudiño. SEE Martínez Gudiño, Francisco

Guerrero, Ignacio: 456

Guerrero, José María: 444

Guerrero, Manuel: 368

Guerrero, Mayorazgo de: houses of, 325

Guerrero, Miguel: 456

Guerrero y Torres, Francisco: designs chapel of El Pocito, Villa Madero, 282, 378; La Enseñanza, Mexico City, attributed to, 286; designs Caja Real, Zimapán, 305; house, Marqués de Jaral de Berrio, Mexico City, attributed to, 319; designs house, Marqueses de San Mateo de Valparaíso, Mexico City, 321; house, Conde de Santiago y Calimaya, attributed to, 321; houses, Mayorazgo de Guerrero, attributed to, 325; not draughtsman, 406; mentioned, 429

Guevara, Antonio: 357

Guiberti, Maturino: 20

guild of architects: 277–278

guild of blacksmiths: 170

guild of carpenters, wood carvers, joiners, and viol makers: 158–159

guild of embroiderers: 71

guild of gilders. SEE guild of painters and gilders

guild of goldbeaters: 162

guild of goldsmiths. SEE guild of silversmiths

guild of harnessmakers: 380–381

guild of ironworkers. SEE guild of blacksmiths; guild of locksmiths

guild of joiners. SEE guild of carpenters, wood carvers, joiners, and viol makers

guild of locksmiths: 170–171

guild of painters and gilders: 132, 235

guild of potters: Mexico City, 175, 265; Puebla, 175, 264–265

guild of sculptors: SEE ALSO guild of carpenters, wood carvers, joiners, and viol makers

guild of silk workers: 70, 169

guild of silversmiths: 162–163, 365

guild of swordmakers: 371

guild of weavers. SEE guild of silk workers

guild of wiredrawers. SEE guild of silversmiths

guild of wood carvers. SEE guild of carpenters, wood carvers, joiners, and viol makers

Gutiérrez, Francisco: 67

Gutiérrez, José: 404, 419, 429

Guzmán, Diego de: 89–90

Guzmán, Juan: 368

Guzmán, Nuño de: 10, 11, 17

haciendas: of Cuadra, Gro., 332; of El Cabejón, Jal., 425–426

harness irons: 370

Havana, Cuba: 11, 111, 168

Haro, Andrés de: 175, 176

Henríquez, Clara: 166, 170

Heras Soto, Conde de: house of, 321–322

Heredia, Alonso de: 170

Heredia, Antón de: 170

Heredia, Joaquín: plans converting Inquisition to Academy, 307, 404; estimates restoration, School of Mines, 413; life and work, 419; listed in Academy, 429

Heredia, Joaquín, II: 195, 419

hermitages: Desierto de los Leones, 199; Desierto de Tenancingo, 200

Hernández, Agustín: 184

Hernández, Antonio: 66

Hernández, Francisco: 66

Hernández, Gabriel: 174

Hernández, José Mariano: 378

Hernández, Juan: 269

Hernández, Mariano: 378

Hernández, Martín: 378

Hernández, Pedro: 67

Hernández, Vicente: 454

Hernando, Lázaro Alonso: 67

Herra, Joseph Vicente: 378

Herrera, Alonso de: 166–167, 168

Herrera, Andrés de: 172, 173

Herrera, Antonio de: 269

Herrera, José (Joseph) Eduardo de: 277, 353

Herrera, Juan de (Spanish architect): 119

Herrera, Juan de (painter): 233

Herrera, Juan de (potter): 175

Herrera, Luis: 368

Herrera, Manuel: 368

Herrera, Miguel de: 246

Herrerian style (of architect Juan de Herrera): 110–111, 116, 119–120

Herrera, Marqués de: house of, 323

Hidalga, Lorenzo de la: 166

Hidalgo y Costilla, Miguel: 388

hieroglyphs. SEE glyphs

high altars: of Cathedral of Mexico, 166, 350; of Cathedral of Puebla, 414–415, 432–433

hinges: 172, 173, 367, 371

Historia de las cosas de Nueva España. SEE Sahagún, Bernardino de

Hocabá, Yuc.: parish church, 296

Holy Office of the Inquisition. SEE Inquisition

Hospitaler Order of St. John of God: 312

hospitals: 16th-cent., 17–20; Hospital de Jesús, 17–18, 268, 452; of Vasco de Quiroga, 19; Tzintzuntzan, 29, 89; Etzatlán, 31; Acámbaro, 90; 18th-cent., 311–313; Hospitalers of St. John of God, 312

houses: pre-conquest, 3–4; 16th-cent., 14–16, 123–125; Casa de Montejo, Mérida, 123–124; *casa sola*, 189; *casa de vecindad*, 189–190; *casa de viviendas*, 329; *accesoria*, 190; 17th-cent., Baroque, 193–194; Neoclassic, 413–414, 416, 420, 425

—, noble: social background, 314–315; typical form, 315; listed, 316–327; use of tiles, 377

—, provincial: Puebla, 327–329, 377; Querétaro, 329; Morelia, 329–330; San Luis Potosí, Guanajuato, Taxco, San Miguel de Allende, 330; Veracruz, 330–331

Huajolotitlán, Oax.: Arrúe works there, 255

Huaquechula, Pue.: Franciscan monastery, 59, 86–87

Huejotzingo, Pue.: Indians build Casas Viejas for Cortés, 14; Franciscan monastery, 41, 59, 70, 78, 84, 118, 134, 153; church of San Diego, 127

Huerto, Salvador del: 426, 446

Huexotla, Mex.: Franciscan monastery, 31–32, 59

Huichapan, Hgo.: Franciscan monastery, 57, 89

Huipulco, D.F.: churchyard cross, 57

Huitzo, Oax.: Arrúe in Dominican monastery, 137
Humanism: 3, 19
Humboldt, Alexander von: 330, 425
Hurtado, Mariano: 368
Hurtado y Mendoza, Mariano: 368

Ibáñez, Juan: 257
Ibar, Francisco: 446
Ibarra, José de: praises Alonso Vásquez, 139; life and work, 333-334; compared to Cabrera, 334-335
Ibarra, Manuel Marco de: 332
Ibía, Francisco de. SEE Zumaya, Francisco de
ideographs. SEE glyphs
Iguala, Gro.: furniture of, 395
Illanes, Juan Manuel de: 44, 346
Illescas, Andrés: 369
Illescas, Ignacio: 378
Illescas, Juan de (potter): 132
Illescas, Juan de (blacksmith): 369
Illescas, Roque Jacinto de: 369
illumination of choir books: 249-250
images: European in Mexico, 52-53; examination by church for painters of, 132; sculpture of, not to be clothed, 158; paintings of, not to be auctioned, 235; clothed, in 18th-cent., 347, 354; clothed in native dress, 384, 395
imaginero: 53, 132
Incháurregui, Antonio de Santa María: 329
Indians: labor of, 5, 14, 19, 20, 23-24, 123; training of, 20, 24, 38, 62, 70, 255, 435, 444-445; as sculptors, 23-24, 48-50, 52, 53-59, 61-62, 158, 160, 261, 357, 435-436; as painters, 38-42, 44-47, 129-132, 235; as embroiderers, 71, 170; as silversmiths, 63-64, 365
inkwells: 367, 368, 450
Inocencia, Joaquín: 415
Inquisition: artists tried by, 67, 134, 159, 183, 249, 255, 445, 453; artists employed by, 134, 150, 169, 230-231, 262, 269, 272; surveillance of paintings ordered by, 256; building of, 307
intarsia. SEE marquetry
inventories: estate of Clara Henríquez, 166, 170; Alonso de Herrera, 166-167; Luis Juárez, 168; Joseph Estrada, 260-261; Domingo de Cuevas y Sandoval, 261; estate of Francisco de Izarrazábal, 264
—, Cathedral of Mexico: of sacristy, 66, 163-164, 166, 259; of treasure, 259; of bells, 268-269, 450
Irapuato, Gto.: La Enseñanza, 425
Ircio, Martín de: 36
ironwork: 16-cent., 67-69; imported, 67, 83; balconies, 67, 369; door knockers, 67, 172-173, 371; stirrups, 68-69; guilds, 170-171; locks, 171-173, 370-371; for Old Cathedral, 172-173; hinges, latches, 172-173, 371; railings,

173-369; 18th-cent., 368-371; crosses, weathervanes, 369-370; candlesticks, scales, tools, harness irons, 370. SEE ALSO grilles
Isabelline style: in Spain, 3; in 16th-cent. churches, 79-80. SEE ALSO Gothic style
Isarti, Antonio: 456
Islas, Andrés: 340, 395
Isunza, José de: 367
Italy: artists from, 445, 446; influence on painting, 130-131, 135, 139, 143, 444; Mexican art in, 46, 74; paintings from, 151, 152, 255
Iturrigaray, José de: 434
Iturbide, Agustín: house of, 318
ivory. SEE sculpture
Ixcabá, Yuc.: retable, parish church, 295
Ixcatlán, Oax.: parish church, 36
Ixmiquilpan, Hgo.: Augustinian monastery, 93, 118; chapel of El Carmen, 295
Izamal, Yuc.: Franciscan monastery, 90
Izguerra, Juan: 357
Izucar de Matamoros, Pue.: pottery of, 388

jacales, jacalli: 4, 384
jade, jadeite: 4, 67
Jacona, Mich.: portal, Franciscan monastery, 119
Jaral de Berrio, Marqués de: house of, 318-319
Jerónimo, Juan: 194
Jerónimo, Juan Antonio: 194
Jesuit Order: no 16th-cent. remains, 109; develops typical school building, 309; confiscation of property of, 366
—, establishments: Guanajuato, 292; Mexico City, 120, 186, 196, 309-313; Morelia, 309; Oaxaca, 196; Pátzcuaro, 309; Puebla, 186-189; Querétaro, 194; Tepotzotlán, 299
jewelry: 16th-cent., 55; 17th-cent., 166-167; Baroque, 274; 18th-cent., 367
Jijón, Pedro: 368
Jilótepec, Hgo.: crossroads cross, 57
Jiménez, Francisco: 456
Jiménez, Miguel: 214
Jiménez, Nicolás: 214
Jiménez, Pedro: 71
Jimeno y Planes, Rafael: second director of painting, director general of Academy, 441; portraits of Gil and Tolsá, 443; murals, 443-444; mentioned, 404
Joaquín Pérez, Antonio: 554
Jocotepec. SEE Xocotepec
Jonacatepec, Mor.: Augustinian monastery, 98
Jordán, Francisco: 454, 456
Juaninos. SEE Hospitaler Order of St. John of God
Juárez, José: 225-228, 241
Juárez, Luis: life and work, 145-146; inventory of furniture, 168; family, 225, 241; mentioned, 149
Juárez, Manuel M.: 277

Juárez (Xuárez), Matías: 223, 224
Juárez (Xuárez), Tomás: 222, 223, 224
Jucutácato, Mich.: Lienzo de Jucutácato, 46
Jujuy, Argentine Republic: Cabildo, 16
Jura, Antonio de: 366

kitchens: 374, 392
Klauber, Ignace: 355
knives: 261

lace: 170
lacquer: 389
Lagarto, Andrés: 250
Lagarto, Francisco: 250
Lagarto, Luis: 249-250
Lagarto, Luis de la Vega: 250
Lagos de Moreno, Jal.: parish church, 295
lamps: silver, 164, 366
Lanciego y Equiluz (Eguilaz), José de: portrait of, 243
lapidaries: 67. SEE ALSO silversmiths
Lara, Antonio de (potter): 378
Lara, Antonio de (painter): 346
Lara Priego, Gregorio: 346
Larios, Diego: 366
latten. SEE brass work
lavaboes: 65, 166, 167, 259
Lavandera,——(painter): 257
Leandro (embroiderer): 373
leatherwork: 380-381
lecterns: 16th-cent., 69; of Cathedral of Mexico, 166, 363, 366; facistoles, 363-364; Neoclassic, 451
Legaspi, José María: 415, 437
Lemus, José de: 268
León, Fradique de: 169
León, Francisco de: 246
León, Nicolás de: 175
León, Rodrigo de: 34
Leyva Pavón, Juan de: 263
Lezama, Pedro Pablo: 415
libraries: 82, 314
Linares, Duque de: portrait of, 244
lithography: 426, 457
litters: 170
locks and keys: 171-173, 370-371
locksmiths: 170-171, 371
Los Remedios, Mex.: Nuestra Señora de los Remedios, 52; sanctuary of Los Remedios, 137, 365
López, Andrés: 340
López, Antonio: 175
López, Carlos Clemente: 404, 407
López, Cristóbal: 340
López, Diego: 172
López, Francisco: 224
López, Manuel: 268
López Calderón, Pedro: 246. SEE ALSO Calderón, Pedro
López Bernal, Francisco: 175
López Dávalos, Sebastián: 233
López de Arbaiza, Diego: 120
López de Arteaga, Sebastián: life and

work, 146–151; followers of, 225–231; influence of, 235, 238, 257
López de Berlanga, Pedro: 173
López de Flandes, Diego: 172
López de Herrera, Alonso: 139, 166
López Guerrero, Manuel: 448
López López, Manuel: 456
Louis XIV style: in Querétaro, 286; in furniture, 360; in popular portraits, 395
Louis XV style: in Querétaro, 286; in Puebla, 292; in furniture, 360–362; in popular portraits, 395
Louis XVI style: in furniture, 360, 452; School of Mines, 413; in silverwork, 450
Lozano Cerón, Juan: 175
Lucas (potter): 378
Lucas (wood carver): 223, 224
Luna, Atanasio: 357
Luna, Vicente: 357
Luna, Cosmé: 357
Luna, José: 357
Luque, Gómez de: 67

Macao: art from, 268
Machorro, José: 368
macuquinas: 454
Madero, Alejo: 402, 454, 456
Maestre, Marcos: 170
Maestro Mateo: 124
Magón, José Joaquín: 342–343
majolica. SEE talavera
Malaspina, Alessandro (Alejandro): 456
Maldonado, Antonio: 454
Maldonado, Miguel: 270
Maldonado, Pedro: 223, 224
Malinalco, Mex.: Augustinian monastery, 42, 92; retable, 134
Malpartida y Zenteno, Diego: 269
Mame, Yuc.: parish church, 296
mampostería: 298
Man, Juan: 429
Mangino, Fernando José: 402
Maní, Yuc.: stone crucifix, 61; Franciscan monastery, 90; retables, 157, 296
Manuel, Padre: 246
Manueline style: 118, 121
Manzano, José María: 414
Manzo y Jaramillo, José: supervises high altar, Cathedral of Puebla, 415; life and work, 426–427; self-portrait (?), 448; mentioned, 437
maps: Lake of Pátzcuaro in feather work, 73; Gulf of Mexico (c.1765), 407; bay of La Paz, Puerto Cortés (1768), 407; bay of San Bernabé (1768), 407; Pacific Coast (1770), 407; Gran Parte de la Nueva España (1777), 407
—, of cities: Tenango del Valle (1582), 13; Plaza Mayor, Mexico City (c.1565), 22; Plaza Mayor, Mexico City (1596), 22; Veracruz (1800), 407; Mexico City, (1807), 454. SEE ALSO city planning
Maravilla americana: 337

Marchena, Julián: 454, 456
Marcos de Aquino. SEE Cípac, Marcos
Marenco, Luis: 454
Marfil, Gto.: portal of church, 292
Marimón,——(painter): 344
markets: 313–314
marks, artisans': silversmiths, 163; potters, 265, 266
marquetry: 361, 380, 384
Márquez, Francisco (bell caster): 269
Márquez, Francisco (engraver): 456
Márquez, José: 251
Márquez Bello, Diego: 269
Márquez de Santillana, Antonio: 175
Martín, Diego: 66
Martín, Hernando: 167
Martín, Juan: 175
Martín, Luis: 429
Martínez, Andrés: 258
Martínez, Antonio: 378
Martínez, Diego (silversmith): 66
Martínez, Diego (coiner): 454
Martínez, Francisco (sculptor): 160, 224
Martínez, Francisco (painter, gilder): life and work, 246–247; gilds retables, 350, 353
Martínez, Hernando: 170
Martínez, Rodrigo: 64
Martínez de Roxas,——: 346
Martínez Gudiño, Francisco: 287, 288, 355
Martínez Guerrero, Juan: 21
Martínez Montañés, Juan: 161, 214, 426
Mascaró, Manuel: 407, 409, 429
masks: 385
Mata, Andrés de: 92
Mauricio, Miguel: 160
Mayorga, Martín de: 402
Mazo y Avilés, José del: 414, 416, 429
medals: 454–455, 456
Medel, Francisco: 175
media annata: 365
media naranja: 376
Medina, Tomás Antonio de: 378
Medina Picazo, Buenaventura: portrait sculpture of, 218
Medina y Torres, Conde de: house of, 324
Melchor, Gentil: 67
Mena, Pedro de: 161
Méndez, Héctor: 66
Méndez, Lucas: 214
Mendoza, Antonio de: founds Colegio de Santa Cruz, and University, 20, 21; commissions Codex Mendoza, 45; develops model plan for monasteries, 77; mentioned, 5, 10, 11, 15, 91
Mendoza, Atanasio José: 378
Mendoza, Athanasio: 378
Mendoza, Diego: 238
Mendoza, José Mariano: 429
Mendoza, Luis: 368
Mendoza, Manuel: 368
Mendoza, Miguel de: 238, 346
Mendieta, Jerónimo de: 32
Mengs, Antonio Raphael: 422, 441, 443n

Mera,——(engraver): 456
Mercedarian Order; no 16th-cent. remains, 109
—, establishments: Guadalajara, 202; Mexico City, 145–201; 279; Morelia, 293; Puebla, 201; Quecholac (?), 202
Mérida, Juan de: 90
Mérida, Yuc.: Casa de las Monjas, 16; Franciscan monastery, 90; Cathedral of, 111, 186; Casa de Montejo, 123–124; House of Rivero Traba, 125; church of La Candelaria, 296
Merodio, Mateo: 159
mesa revuelta: 446
Mesa, Francisco de: 64
Mesa, Gabriel de: 269
mestizo: defined, 4
metates: 173, 385
Metepec, Mex.: pottery of, 388
Metl, Francisco Juan: 100, 116
metlapiles: 385
Metztitlán, Hgo.: Augustinian monastery, 92, 116
Mexico City, D.F.: prisons, 9–10, 32, 304; planned and laid out, 13; tecpans, 16–17; Cabildo (Casa de Ayuntamiento), 16, 121, 263, 303; Plaza Mayor (Zócalo), 21, 23, 33, 62, 121, 392, 404, 409, 416; aqueducts, 32, 33, 420; draining of, 33; Palace of the Viceroys (Palacio Nacional), 120, 121, 134, 139, 184–186, 303, 325; Inquisition, 184–186, 307, 404, 419; Casa de Moneda, 268, 304, 403, 407; Royal Customs House, 304; "El Apartado" (National Mint), 304; Cuartel de los Gallos, 305, 409,416; hospice de Santo Tomás de Villanueva, 311; markets, 313; Castle of Chapultepec, 392, 409; gunpowder factory, 407; La Ciudadela, 407, 415, 416, 419; bull ring, 414; Casa de Ejercicios, congregation of St. Philip Neri, 414; Alameda, 416. SEE ALSO Academy of San Carlos
—, Cathedral of: foundations of, 46, 109–110; treasure of, 66, 163–166; vestments, 70, 170, 269, 371–372; plans for, 109–110; compared to Spanish cathedrals, 111; Renaissance or Purist style in, 116; Herrerian style in, 119; paintings in, 134, 230, 231, 233, 237–238, 243, 350, 443; railings, 171, 268; dedicated, 182; architects, 183, 409–412; retables, 213; façade, 214, 434, 436, 451–452; choir, 218–222, 268, 350, 353, 363–364, 379; Altar de los Reyes, 243, 247, 350, 430; silverwork, 259–260, 365–366, 380, 450–451; cupboards, 262; chairs, 263; window glass, 269–270; high altar, 350, 352, 366, 426, 430; figures on towers, 355, 435, 436–437; confessional, 363; cross and weathervane, 369; ivory sculpture, 379–380; 19th-cent. opinion of, 430
—, Cathedral of, Old: 23, 53, 66, 70, 109, 134, 135, 159, 171–173

—, chapels: Cemetery of Campo Florido, 420; Balvanera, 191; La Concepción, 191; La Escala Santa (Balvanera), 191; San José de los Naturales, 29–31, 38, 40, 115; San Miguel Nonoalco, 231; of El Señor de Santa Teresa, 415, 443

—, churches: Balvanera, 191, 266; Belén, 191; Las Capuchinas, 214; La Compañía, 143; La Concepción, 191; Corpus Christi, 196; La Encarnación (Secretaría de Educación Pública), 191, 214, 266, 407; La Enseñanza, 286, 293, 338; Espíritu Santo, 278; Jesús María, 145, 191, 420, 430; Loreto, 326, 406, 418–419; La Merced, 145, 201, 340; La Profesa (San José el Real), 53, 127, 196, 247, 270, 434, 436; La Regina, 218, 378; Sagrario Metropolitano, 282, 369, 434, 436; Salto del Agua, 280; San Antonio Abad, 191; San Agustín, 36, 91; San Agustín (Biblioteca Nacional), 195, 214, 326; San Bernardo, 195, 214, 218; San Camilo, 309; San Diego, 193, 420; San Felipe Neri, 193; San Fernando, 222, 279–280; San Francisco, 23–24; 29–31, 38, 40, 83–84, 115, 145, 227, 241; San Francisco (rebuilt), 84, 201, 286, 353; San Hipólito, 279, 409; San Jerónimo, 191; San José (parish church), 420; San José de Gracia, 191; San José el Real (La Profesa), 53, 127, 196, 247, 270, 434, 436; San Juan de Dios, 196; San Lázaro, 52–53; San Lorenzo, 191, 218; San Miguel de Belén, 279; San Pablo el Nuevo, 415; San Pedro y San Pablo, 120, 366; San Sebastian, 24; Santa Brígida, 279; Santa Catalina de Siena, 161, 191; Santa Clara, 120, 191; Santa Inés, 279, 325, 337, 378; Santa Isabel, 191; Santa Teresa la Antigua, 195; Santa Teresa la Nueva, 182; Santa Veracruz, 265, 286; Santiago Tlatelolco, 143, 191; La Santísima Trinidad, 277, 282, 325, 378; Santo Domingo (1st), 23, 53; Santo Domingo (2nd), 36, 101, 102; Santo Domingo (3rd), 280, 340, 434, 436; La Soledad de Santa Cruz, 279, 420

—, fountains: of Plaza Mayor, 33, 416, 419; Salto del Agua, 33, 420; de la Aguilita, 419; Chapultepec, La Tlaxpana, 420

—, hospitals: Amor de Dios, 18, 372, 403; Béistegui, 378; Divino Salvador (Secretaría de la Asistencia Pública), 312; Jesús Nazareno (La Purísima Concepción), 17, 62, 268, 452; Real de Indias, 311; San Andrés, 372, 403; San Hipólito, 312; San Juan de Dios, 312; San Lázaro, 9; 52; Terceros de San Francisco, 311

—, houses: Archbishop's Palace, 123, 277, 305, 325; on Argentina and Guatemala streets, 128; Basco, Antonio, 326; Bazaine, Aquille (Pérez Gálvez), 413–

414; Borda, José de la, 319; Casa de los Azulejos (Conde del Valle de Orizaba), 266, 317–318; 377; Casa de los Mascarones (Conde del Valle de Orizaba, country house), 326–327; Casa del Judío, 127–128; Casas Nuevas of Cortés, Casas Viejas of Cortés, 14; Casas Viejas of Moctezuma, 14; Castera, Ignacio, 416; Chavarría, Juan de, 326; on Cinco de Febrero 18, 326, 377; Conde de Heras Soto, 321–323; Conde de la Cortina, 324; Conde de la Torre de Cosío, 324; Conde de Medina y Torres, 324; Conde de Miravalle, 316; Conde de Regla, 324–325; Conde de San Bartolomé de Xala, 324; Conde de San Mateo de Valparaíso, 319; Conde de Santiago de Calimaya, 277, 321; Conde del Valle de Orizaba (Casa de los Azulejos), 266, 317–318, 377; Conde del Valle de Orizaba, country house (Casa de los Mascarones), 326–327; López, Jerónimo, 128; Marqués de Castañiza, 324; Marqués de Ciria, 317; Marqués de Herrera, 323; Marqués de Jaral de Berrio (Hotel Iturbide), 318–319; Marqués de la Colina, 319; Marqués de Moncada, 318–319; Marqués de Prado Alegre, 319; Marqués de Rivas Cacho, 319; Marqués de Salvatierra, 323; Marqués de San Juan de Rayas, 325; Marqués de San Miguel de Aguayo, 324; Marqués de San Román, 321; Marqués de Santa Cruz de Inguanzo, 324; Marqués de Santa Fe de Guardiola, 317; Marqués de Selva Nevada, 325; Marqués de Uluapa, 319; Marqués del Apartado (Secretaría de la Economía Nacional), 326, 413; Marqueses de San Mateo de Valparaíso (Banco Nacional), 321; Mayorazgo de Guerrero, 123, 325; Mayorazgo del Valle de Oaxaca (Nacional Monte de Piedad), 321; on Palma 35, 323–324; Pérez Gálvez, Pinillos, 413–414; Tolsá, Manuel, 414; on Uruguay, 117, 326

—, monasteries: SEE Mexico City, D.F., churches

—, monuments: Noche Triste, 409; equestrian statue of Charles IV, 416, 434, 435, 455

—, schools: Colegio de las Vizcaínas, 161, 309–310, 416; Colegio de Niñas, 186, 277; Colegio de San Buenaventura, 20; Colegio de San Gregorio, 434; Colegio de San Ignacio, 161, 309–310, 416; Colegio de San Ildefonso (Escuela Nacional Preparatoria), 309, 338; Colegio de San Juan de Letrán, 20; Colegio de San Miguel de Belén, 279; Colegio de San Pedro y San Pablo, 120, 186, 310–311; Colegio de Santa Cruz de Tlatelolco, 20; Colegio del Cristo, 311; Colegio del Pilar, 286; School of Mines, 412–413; 443, 452; Seminary, 309;

University of Mexico, 20, 21–22; 23, 121–122, 131, 310–311, 416
Michoacán, state of: 19, 45–46, 168
Miguel, Francisco: 298
milagros: 389
Milpa Alta, D.F.: *Assumption of the Virgin,* Franciscan monastery, 157, 161
Minaya, Bernardino: 106
Miranda, Jerónimo de: 374
Miranda, Salvador: 370
Miravalle, Conde de: house of, 316
mirrors: 362
Mixquic, D.F.: Augustinian monastery, 134, 263
Mixteca Alta. SEE Oaxaca, state of
Mociño, José: 445
Moctezuma II: 14, 45, 74
Molango, Hgo.: Augustinian monastery, 115
molcajetes: 173, 385
Molina, Alonso de: 42
Molina, Damián: 378
Molina y Garrido, José: 456
Molina de Flores, Mex.: chapel, hacienda of, 201
monasteries: Franciscan specifications for, 31–32; model plan for, 77–82
Moncada, Marqués de: house of, 318
Moneda, Luis: 368
monstrances: 258; 449. SEE ALSO custodias
Montejo, Catalina de: 21
Montejo, Francisco de: house of, 123–124
Montenegro, Mariano: 356, 437, 439
Montes Claros, Marqués de: 137–139
Montiel, José Justo: 395
Montúfar, Alonso de: 92, 101, 109–110
monuments: of the Noche Triste, Mexico City, 409; equestrian statue of Charles IV, Mexico City, 416, 434–435; obelisk, Celaya, 423; Column of Independence, San Luis Potosí, 425; Liberty, Querétaro, 438
Moorish art. SEE Mudejar style
Mora, José de la: 247
Morales, —— (painter): 437
Morales, Andrés: 67
Morales, Francisco de: 136
Morales, José: 456
Morales, Rafael: 374
More, Thomas: 19
Morelia (Valladolid), Mich.; laid out by Juan Ponce, 13; prison for men, 293; seminary of Valladolid (Palacio de Gobierno) and Jesuit College, 309; Escuela de Derecho, 428
—, Cathedral of: 184, 186, 270, 356, 365
—, churches in: El Carmen, 191; La Merced, 293; sanctuary of Guadalupe, 193; Santa Teresa, 419
—, convents in: Las Capuchinas, 195; Las Monjas, 195, 345; Las Rosas, 195, 293
—, monasteries in: Franciscan, 89–119; Augustinian, 98, 119, 254, 345; of San Diego, 193

Morelos, José María: death mask by Patiño Ixtolinque, 436
Moreno, Agustín: 456
Moreno, Andrés: 173
Moreno, Antonio Onofre: 456
Moreno, Francisco: 378
Moreno, Luis. 173
Morlete Ruiz, Juan Patricio: 338
Morones, Pedro de: 21
Mota, ——— (engraver): 456
Mota, José de la: 247
Motolinía (Toribio de Benevente): 40, 66, 72
Motul, Yuc.: Franciscan monastery, 90
Moya de Contreras, Pedro: 164
Mudejar style: in city planning, 12; fountain, Chiapa de Corzo, 34; arabesque decoration, 41; survivals of, 125–128; mentioned, 3, 5
—, in architecture: façade design, 19, 57, 118, 121; octagonal columns, 23; basilica church, 23; open chapel influenced by mosque, 29–31, 125; alfarjes, 84, 91, 98, 101, 126–127; painted decoration, 87, 98, 102; house plan, 126; vault on crossing arches, 127, 210. SEE ALSO alfiz; ceramics, azulejos in architecture
—, in minor arts: wrought-iron stirrups, 68–69; furniture, 69, 70; ceramics, 175, 266, 377; marquetry, 222, 380
—, Portuguese. SEE Manueline style
Muerte política de la República Mexicana: 446
Muñoz, Alonso: 71
Muñoz, Diego: 173
Muñoz, Pedro: 222
mural painting: pre-conquest, 4, 44; in fresco, 40–44; in the prison, Mexico City, 40; academic, 443
—, religious: 40–42, 87, 89, 91, 92, 98, 102, 104, 129–131, 134, 137, 166, 254, 255, 256, 392
—, secular: 16, 40, 134, 137
Murguía, Ignacio: 374
Murillo, Bartolomé Esteban: 152

Naranjo, Simón: 378
Narciso (blacksmith): 369
Nava, Sebastián de: 378
Nava, Tosian: 378
Navarro, Francisco: 90
Navarro, José Mariano: 456
Navarijo, ——— (maestraescuelas): 450
Náxera, J. de: 456
Nazari, Andrés: 170
Negroes: 265
Neoclassic style: history and ideology, 401; in architecture, 405–406, 430–431; destruction of older monuments, 434; in painting, 440–448; in minor arts, 449–452; in graphic arts, 454; mentioned, 5, 457
Netherlands. SEE Flanders
New Mexico, U.S.A.: Coronado's expe-

dition to, 47; popular religious sculpture, 396
Nieto, Agustín: 374
Nieto, Francisco: 374
Nieto, Manuel: 372
Nieva, Sebastián de: 173
Nolasco de Reina, Pedro: 223, 357
Nonoalco, D.F.: chapel of San Miguel, 237
Noriega, ——— (painter): 345
Núñez, Ignacio: 357
Núñez de Haro y Peralta, Alonso: 305, 340, 371, 450

Oaxaca (Antequera), Oax.: city plan, 13; house of Cortés, 15; 17th-cent. Baroque architecture, 194; painting in, 255, 356; archbishop's palace, 305; Palacio de Gobierno, 428; pottery of, 387–388; textiles of, 388; milagros, 389
—, Cathedral of: 109, 111, 365
—, churches in: El Carmen Alto, El Carmen Bajo, 191; La Compañía de Jesús, 196; La Defensa, 194; El Marquesado, 428; San Agustín, 196–198; 213, 214; San Felipe Neri, 193, 196; San Francisco, 295; San José, 194; Santo Domingo, 105–106, 115, 205; Los Siete Príncipes, 194; La Soledad, 198, 214, 365
Oaxtepec, Mor.: Dominican monastery, 44, 102
obsidian: 58, 67
Ocampo, Salvador de: 218, 223, 357
Ochoa, Juan: 256
Ocotlán. SEE Tlaxcala, Sanctuary of Ocotlán
Ocuilan, Mex.: Augustinian monastery, 91–92, 134
Ocuituco, Mor.: Augustinian monastery, 41, 91
Ocumicho, Mich.: pottery of, 388
Ojeda, José Mariano: 378
olambrilla: 266
Olinalá, Gro.: lacquer made in, 389
Olivares, Cristóbal de: 174
Olivares, José María: 437
Ontiveros, Francisco Javier: 372, 374
open chapels. SEE chapels, open
Oratory of St. Philip Neri. SEE Congregation of St. Philip Neri
Ordaz, Diego de: "House of Ordaz," Coyoacán, 16
Order of Barefoot Franciscans of San Diego: no 16th-cent. buildings, 109
—, establishments: Acuitlapan, 193; Churubusco, 191; Mexico City, 193; Morelia, 193; Querétaro (San Antonio), 194; Texmelucan (San Martín), 191–193
Order of Friars Minor. SEE Franciscan Order
Order of Friars Minor Capuchins. SEE Capuchin Order

Order of Our Lady of Mercy. SEE Mercedarian Order
Order of Preachers. SEE Dominican Order
Order of St. Augustine. SEE Augustinian Order
Order of St. Philip Neri. SEE Congregation of St. Philip Neri
Order of San Juan de Dios. SEE Hospitaler Order of St. John of God
Order of San Felipe Neri. SEE Congregation of St. Philip Neri
Ordóñez, José Julián: 437, 446
Orduña, Bernardino de: 305
Orizaba, Ver.: Colegio de la Propaganda Fide, 414, 416, 419
Orona, Mariano José de: 374
Orozco, José Clemente: 318, 414
Ortega, Cristóbal de: 368
Ortega, Juan de: 175
Orrego, Nicolás: 259
Ortiz, ——— (architect, sculptor): 288, 356
Ortiz, Juan: 453
Ortiz de Castro, José Damián: Noche Triste monument by, 279; mentioned by Tresguerras (?), 356; life and work, 409–411; convent of Santa Teresa, Querétaro (?), 425; mentioned, 429, 436
Ortiz de Castro, Francisco: 411, 429
Ortuño, Gaspar: 374
Ortuño, José Benito: 456
Ortuño, Ramón: 374
Ortúzar, Francisco: 367–368
Ossorio, Manuel de: 338
Osio, Gaspar: 258
Otálora, Pedro: 255
Otumba, Mex.: Casas Viejas built by Indians from, 14; Franciscan monastery, 29; Arcos de Cempoala near, 33
Oviedo, Martín de: 159
Oyanguren y Espínola, Mariano: 378
Ozumba, Mex.: Franciscan monastery, 131, 213

Pachuca, Hgo.: Caja Real, 305, 330
Padilla, Alonso de: 67
Padilla, José: 341, 392
padrón. SEE census lists
Páez, José de: 339
painters: Indians in 16th cent., 38–47; of fresco, 40–44, 132; of sargas, 132; guild of, 132, 235; as notaries, 149, 246–247; of popular art, 386, 392–395, 446. SEE ALSO gilders
painting: pre-conquest, 4, 38; in Puebla, 249–254, 342–344, 446–448; in Michoacán, 254–255, 345; in Yucatán 255–256; in Oaxaca, 255, 346; in Nueva Galicia, 256–257, 345; in Tlaxcala, 256, 345–346; in Querétaro, 257, 344–345; popular, 386, 392–395. SEE ALSO mural painting
Palacios, Doctor: 11
Palacios, José: 346

palabreros: 366

Palafox y Mendoza, Juan de: secularizes parishes, 180n.; completes cathedral of Puebla, 183–184; portraits of, 340; mentioned, 455

palmatoria: 368

Palomino, Juan: 368

Pan y Agua, Francisco Xavier: 380

Pánuco: fortifications, 9

Papalotla, Mex.: parish church, 128, 201

Paracho, Mich.: furniture of, 380

Paredes, Conde de: 175

Paredes, Tomás Antonio de la Cerda, Conde de: 231, 253, 264

Pardo, Alonso: 270

Pardo, Antonio (painter): 247

Pardo, Antonio (glass-blower): 270

Pardo, José Mariano: 270

parián. SEE markets

Paris, France: custodia of Borda in Cathedral of Notre Dame (?), 365

Parra, —— (bell-caster): 268

Parra, —— (engraver): 456

Parra, Joseph: 368

Parra, Manuel: 247

pastel: 448

patens: 66

Patiño Ixtolinque, Pedro: 415, 434, 435–436

patrones de platero: 364, 365

Pátzcuaro, Mich.: *Our Lady of Good Health,* 52; stone crucifix, chapel of El Humilladero, 61; map of in featherwork, 73; Cathedral of Michoacán in, 109, 111; Jesuit college, 309; silver *milagros* from, 389

——, churches in: La Salud, 111; San Agustín, 115, 119, 345; San Francisco, 89, 255; San Juan de Dios, 345

Pavedilla, Manuel: 429

Pavía, —— (engraver): 456

Paz, José: 378

Paz, José Agustín: associated with Castera in Loreto, 418–419; works by, 419, 420; mentioned, 413, 429

Paz, Mariano: 288, 356, 436

pearls: grading of, 260n, 261

pedestals: for images, 367

Peña, Damián de la: 378

Peña, Juan de la: 378

Peña, Pedro de la: 21

Peralta, —— (painter): 257

Peralta, Gastón de: 134

Peralta, José: 345

Perea, Francisco: 224

Peregrina, Mateo: 269

Pereyns, Simón: retable of Huejotzingo documented, 84, 153; side altar at Cuautinchán attributed, 87, 153; retables, Malinalco, Ocuilan, 92; life and work, 134–135; teacher of Juan de Arrúe (?), 137; at Coixtlahuaca, 255

Pérez, Alonso Martín (*el Partidor*): 13

Pérez, Cristóbal: 170

Pérez, Gaspar: 66

Pérez, Pascual: 254

Pérez, Pedro: 170

Pérez de Aguilar, Antonio: 339

Pérez de Espinosa, Juan: 175

Pérez de Rivera, Gaspar: 132

Pérez de Soto, Melchor: 183

Pérez Martínez, Antonio Joaquín: 354, 415, 426

Periam, Jorge: 456

Peribán, Mich.: crafts in wood, 380

Perines, Simón: SEE Pereyns, Simón

Perovani, José: 446

Peru: Alberto Enríquez from, 255

Perusquía, Mariano: 356, 437–438

Pesquera, Diego de: 141

petaca: 69

petate, petatl: 38, 384

Philadelphia Museum of Art: 237, 246

Philip II: 11, 115

Philip III: 110, 317

Philip V: 268

Philippines: art from, 363–364, 379

pie de gallo: 369

Piedra, Rodrigo de la: 252–253

Pila, Pedro de: 89

Pinto, Francisco: 224

Plateresque style: in hospital chapel, Uruapan, 89, 118; at Yecapixtla, 91; at Acolman, 92, 116; at Cuitzeo, 100–101, 116; examples, 116–119, 122–125; Casa de Montejo, 123–124; mentioned, 5

plates: silver, 261

platero de mazonería: 65

platero de oro: 65

platero de plata: 65

Polo, Bernardino: 254

Polo, José Aniceto: 254

Polo, José (Joseph) Patricio: 254

Pombo, Baltasar: 432

Ponce, —— (engraver): 456

Ponce, Alonso: 84, 89

Ponce, Juan: 13

Pons, Jaime: 374

Pontecillas, Rodrigo de: 14

Porras, Esteban de: 71

portales: 16

portería: 78

Portugal: artists from, 18, 67. SEE ALSO Manueline style

Posada, Ramón de: 402–403

posas: at Tlaxcala, 24, 53; defined, 78; at Huejotzingo, 84; at Calpan, 88; at Izamal, 90; at Tlaquiltenango, 104

Prado, José: 357

Prado, Tomás de: 141

Prado Alegre, Marqués de: house of, 319

Prieto, Francisco: 454

printing: 452–453

Priseño, Diego: 173

prisons: 10, 16, 40

Propaganda Fide. SEE Congregation for the Propagation of the Faith

Provinces: Dulce Nombre de Jesús de México (Augustinian), 91–98; San Diego de México (Barefoot Franciscan), 191–193; San Hipólito de Oaxaca (Dominican), 105–107; San José de Yucatán (Franciscan), 90; San Nicolás de Tolentino de Michoacán (Augustinian), 98–101; San Pedro y San Pablo de Michoacán (Franciscan), 89–90; San Vicente de Chiapas y Guatemala (Dominican), 107–109; Santiago de México Dominican), 101–105; Santo Evangelio de México (Franciscan), 82–89

Puebla (de los Ángeles), Pue.: laid out, 13; Alhóndiga, 125; Baroque architecture of, 193–194; sculpture in, 214, 218, 223–224, 354–355, 432–433, 436–437; painting in, 249–254, 342–344, 446–448; Hospital de San Pedro, 312–313; Parián, 314; Palafoxian Library, 314; popular pottery of, 388; silverwork of, 389; fountain of San Miguel, 420

——, Cathedral of: 16th-cent. campaign, 109; Renaissance style in, 116; north door, 118; Herrerian elements, 120; treasure, 163, 365, 366; finished, 183–184, 251; choir stalls, 222; paintings, 231, 239, 240, 334; choir books, 250–251; Altar de los Reyes, 251, 426; furniture, 262, 363; grilles, railings, 263, 369; tile, 266; high altar, 414–415, 432–434, 436, 452; redecorating of interior, 426

——, Cathedral of, Old: 23, 52, 109, 137

——, churches in: El Carmen, 375; La Compañía, 369, 376; La Concepción, 194, 253; Guadalupe, 376; La Luz, 376; Oratory of the Congregation of St. Philip Neri, 193, 375, 384; San Agustín, 194; San Bernardino, 137; San Cristóbal, 196, 203, 214; San Francisco, 289, 375; San Ildefonso, 120, 194, 196, 203; San José, 289, 369; San Marcos, 376; San Matías, 354; San Pablo, 354; Santa Catalina, 289, 376; Santa Mónica, 218; Santa Teresa, 355; La Santísima Trinidad, 194; Santo Domingo, 102, 120, 196, 203–205, 224, 233, 266, 292, 365, 426; La Soledad, 266, 376

——, convents in: Santa Rosa, 193, 374, 376; Santa Mónica, 376

——, houses in: Casa del Deán, 115; *del que mató el animal,* 124; archbishop's palace, 171, 305, 376; Baroque, 327–329, 377; del Alfeñique, 329, 369, 377; *de los gigantes,* 377

——, monasteries in: Dominican, 201; Franciscan, 84; Mercedarian, 201

——, schools in: Colegio de San Juan, 314; Colegio de San Pedro y San Pablo (Colegio del Estado, Universidad de Puebla), 186–189, 194, 214, 218

pulley: 369

pulpits: 59, 84, 363

Purist style: at Zacatlán, 24, 115; at Cuilapan, 26, 31, 115; at Tecali, 26, 87, 116; at Quecholac, 26, 115; at

Teposcolula, 29, 115; in Cathedral of Mexico, 110, 116, 119; defined, 115; Túmulo Imperial, 115; examples, 115–116

pyxes: 65, 66, 164, 259, 366

Quartas, Julián de: 255
Quauhtli, Pedro: 40
Quecholac, Pue.: Franciscan monastery, 26, 87, 115; church of La Merced (?), 202
Queen Anne style: in furniture, 359, 360
Querétaro, Que.: laid out, 13; Colegio de la Compañía, 194; Baroque architecture, 194, 286–288; Baroque sculpture, 218; painting in, 257, 344–345; domestic architecture, 329; 18th-cent. sculpture, 355–356; 1791 *padrón general*, 356; fountain of Neptune, 425
—, chapels in: El Rosario, 287–288; La Santa Escala, 439
—, churches in: Las Capuchinas, 194; La Compañía de Jesús, 194; La Congregación, 440; Guadalupe, 194; Hermanos del Cordón de San Francisco, 361; Sagrario, 354; San Agustín, 218, 288, 355; San Antonio de Padua, 195; San Francisco, 218, 244, 368; Santa Clara, 194, 287, 355, 368, 422; Santa Rosa, 194, 287, 355, 368, 380, 422, 563; Santa Teresa, 414, 424–425; Santo Domingo, 167, 287
—, houses in: Casa de los Perros, 329; Casa del Faldón, 329; Fernández de Jáuregui, 369; López de Cala, 269; Marqués de la Villa del Villar del Águila, 329; Rivera, Rosendo, 329
—, monasteries in: Augustinian (Palacio Municipal), 218, 288, 355
Quesada, Cristóbal: 47
Quiauló: 268
Quiera, Miguel José de: 309
Quintana, Pedro: 341
quinto real: 162
Quiñones, Antonio de: 270
Quiñones, Mathias de: 374
Quiroga, Vasco de: founds Utopian communities, 19–20; commissions *Our Lady of Good Health*, 52; commissions stone crucifix, 61; rings for weddings, 66; map of Pátzcuaro in feather work, 73; takes bishopric, 89; plans five-naved cathedral, 111
Quiroga (Cocupao), Mich.: lacquer of, 389
Quivira: 47
Quito, Ecuador: *alfarjes*, 127

railings: 367, 369
Ramírez, José: 415
Ramírez, Laureano: 224
Ramírez, Nicolás: 378
Ramírez, Pedro: 228–230
Ramírez de la Torre, Teresa: jewelry in estate of, 261

Rangel, Alonso: 85
Rangel, Antonio: 269
Real Academia de San Carlos. SEE Academy of San Carlos
Real del Monte, Hgo.: parish church, 340
Real y Pontificia Universidad de México. SEE University of Mexico
rebozos: 388–389
Regla, Conde de: house of, 324; portrait of, 340
reliquaries: 261, 380
Renaissance style: in Spain, 3; mentioned, 457. SEE ALSO Plateresque style; Purist style; Herrerian style
—, in architecture: 24, 29, 82, 85, 86, 87, 91, 92, 99, 102
—, in painting: 115 n, 129–131, 137
—, in sculpture: 84, 89, 153–158, 213
—, in minor arts: silver work, 65, 164–166; wrought iron, 67, 68, 171; furniture, 167; tile, 266
Rendón, Joaquín: 222
repartimiento (fiduciary assignment of labor): 20
Requena, Vicente, painter: active seventeenth century, 141
retables: 16th-cent., 40, 79, 84, 87, 89, 92, 153–158, 161, 213; Baroque, 213, 223–224; Churrigueresque, 213, 277, 287, 292–293, 295, 296, 299–302, 350, 352, 353, 355, 422; Neoclassic: 426, 430, 434, 436
retablos. SEE ex-votos
Revillagigedo, Juan Vicente de Güemas y Pacheco, Conde de, II: orders census of 1791, 356; rebuilding Mexico City, 406, 409, 416, 418; portrait of, 445; mentioned, 275
Reyes, Francisco de los: 132
Reyes, Gaspar de los: 172
Reyes, José de: 406, 418
Reyes Católicos, style of. SEE Gothic style (Isabelline)
Rhetorica Christiana: 38
Riaño, ——— (builder): 425
Ribera, José de: 149
Ríos, Antonio de los: 171
Rivas, Joseph: 378
Rivas Cacho, Marqués de: house of, 321
Rivera, Miguel José: 277
Roa y Velasco, Antonio de: 223, 357
Robles, Hernando de: 71
Robles, Pedro de: 132
Rococo style: in wrought-iron stirrups, 68; in Querétaro, 286, 353; in Puebla, 292, 353; in silver work, 365. SEE ALSO Louis XV style
Rodallega, José María: 450–451
Rodas, José: 357
Rodríguez, Antonio (painter): 225, 233, 235, 241
Rodríguez, Antonio (brazier): 368
Rodríguez, Francisco (locksmith): 173
Rodríguez, Francisco (engraver): 456
Rodríguez, Gonzalo: 67

Rodríguez, José: 378
Rodríguez, Joseph: 383
Rodríguez, Juan (architect): 14–15
Rodríguez, Juan (wood carver): 159
Rodríguez, Juan (potter): 175, 176
Rodríguez, Lorenzo: Sagrario, Santísima Trinidad, Mexico City, 282; chapel of the Tercer Orden, Santo Domingo, 282; "La Acordada," 304; portal, Colegio de las Vizcaínas, 310; house of the Conde de San Bartolomé de Xala, 324; mentioned, 292, 406
Rodríguez, Luis: 67
Rodríguez, Pedro (painter): 132
Rodríguez, Pedro (engraver): 456
Rodríguez, Pedro Vicente: 454, 456
Rodríguez de Alconedo, José Luis: designs catafalque, 429; life, 446–447; painting, 447–448; as silversmith, 452
Rodríguez de Borges, Juan: 176
Rodríguez de Carnero, Domingo: 233
Rodríguez de Carnero, José: 231, 233, 235
Rodríguez de Carnero, Nicolás: 233
Rodríguez de Herrera, Diego: 175
Rodríguez de Miranda, Juan: 175
Rodríguez de Quesada, Antonio de: 21
Rodríguez Juárez, Juan: family, 225, 233, 241; life and work, 243–244; mentioned, 333, 334, 335
Rodríguez Juárez, Nicolás: family, 225, 233; life and work, 241–243, 268; mentioned, 333, 335
Rojas, Juan de: 218–222, 223, 224, 357
Rojo, Manuel: 363–364
rollos: 13, 36, 46
Román, Miguel: 378
Romero, José Antonio: 378
Romero, Nícolás: 175
roofs: timber, 23–26, 83, 89, 109. SEE ALSO *alfarjes*; vaults
Rosillo, C.: 456
Rúa, Juan de la. SEE Arrúe, Juan de
Rubí de Marimón, Juan: 253
Rubio y Salinas, Manuel: 335–337, 450
Ruiz, Bartolomé: 66
Ruiz, Francisco: 66
Ruiz, Nicolás: 262
Ruiz de Ahumada, Pedro: portrait in sculpture, 218

S.T.M. (engraver): 456
Saavedra, Hernando de: 13, 46
Sacalcen, Yuc.: retable, parish church, 295
saddlery: 68–69, 370, 380–381
Sáenz, Juan de: 404, 443, 445
Sáenz de Mañozca, Juan: portrait of, 233
Sahagún, Bernardino de: teaches in Santa Cruz de Tlatelolco, 20; prepares *Historia de las cosas de Nueva España*, 46, 64, 72, 166
sala de profundis: 78
Salamanca, Gto.: Augustinian monastery, 292; parish church, 292
salamonic column: defined, 213
Salas, Alonso: 173

Salazar, Basilio: 83
Salazar, Gonzalo de: 14
Salcedo, —— (engraver): 456
Salcedo, Juan de: 166,259
Salcedo, Pedro de: 66
Saldaña, Joseph: 368
Saldaña, Juan de: 368
Salgador, Andrés: 378
Salguero, Juan: 233
Salguero, Pedro: 254–255
Salguero, Simón: 255
Salinas, Andrés de: 171
Sállago, Antonio. SEE Sáyago, Antonio
Salmón, Simón: 415, 452
Salta, Argentine Republic: Cabildo, 16
saltcellars: silver, 261
Saltillo, Coah.: Cathedral of, 293; sarapes of, 388
Salvatierra, Marqués de: house of, 323
Salvatierra, Gto.: Carmelite monastery, 191; parish church, 425
sambenito: 67
San Ángel, D.F.: SEE Villa Obregón, D.F.
San Antón, Mor.: pottery of, 388
San Bartolomé de Xala, Conde de: house of, 324
San Bartolo Naucalpan: quarries, 434
San Cristóbal de las Casas, Chis.: Dominican monastery, 109; Cathedral of Chiapas, 115, 186; house of Luis de Mazariegos, 125; *Juan Diego,* church of Guadalupe, 357
San Felipe Torres Mochas, Gto.: pottery of, 388
San Juan, Antonio de: 86
San Juan de los Lagos, Jal.: sarapes, 388
San Juan de Rayas, Marqués de: church at mine of, 292; house of, 325
San Juan de Ulúa, Ver.: fortifications, 11
San Luis Potosí, S.L.P.: Cathedral of, 194; sarapes of, 380; theatre, 425
San Marcos, Mex.: pottery of, 388
San Mateo de Valparaíso, Conde de: houses of, 318, 319, 321
San Miguel, Andrés de: 191, 332
San Miguel, Juan de: 19, 39, 57
San Miguel de Aguagyo, Marqués de: house of, 324
San Miguel de Allende, Gto.: *camarín* of the Santa Casa de Loreto, 127; Oratory of San Felipe Neri, 193, 210; San Francisco, 292, 425; Santa Clara, 292; Casa de Allende, 330, 369; pottery of, 388; house of the Conde de la Canal, 425
San Miguel el Grande. SEE San Miguel de Allende
San Román, Marqués de: house of, 321
San Nicolás, Pedro de: 40
Sanabria, Juan N.: 425
Sánchez, Bartolomé: 132
Sánchez, Bernabé: 233–234
Sánchez, Francisco: 368
Sánchez, Hernán: 268
Sánchez, Hernán, The Younger: 268
Sánchez, José: 378

Sánchez, Juan: 173
Sánchez, Juan de Dios: 378
Sánchez, Lázaro: 173
Sánchez, Mariano: 429
Sánchez, Nicolás: 378
Sánchez, Tadeo: 372
Sánchez Coello, Alonso: 152
Sánchez de Alanís, Juan: 13
Sánchez de Herrera, Cristóbal: 67
Sánchez de Muñón, Sancho: 110
Sánchez Salmerón, Juan: 234
Sánchez Talaya, Ginés: 12
Sancho, Dionisio: 435
Sandoval,——(engraver): 456
Sandoval, Ignacio: 412, 435
Sandoval, José Joaquín: 378
Sandoval, Pedro: 341
Sandoval, Santiago Cristóbal: 404, 412, 435
Santa Ana Chiautempan, Tlax.: weaving of, 388
Santa Anita, Jal.: parish church, 201
Santa Cruz, Marqués de: portrait of, 243
Santa Cruz, Alonso de: 18–19
Santa Cruz, Manuel: portrait sculpture of, 218; portrait of, 254; mentioned, 253, 305, 375
Santa Cruz, Jal.: pottery of, 387
Santa Cruz de las Flores, Jal.: ruins of church, 201
Santa Fe (de México), D.F.: hospital, 19; aqueduct, 33; Franciscan church, 53; gunpowder factory, 407
Santa Fe, New Mexico, U.S.A.: stone retable, church of Cristo Rey, 396–397
Santa Fe de Guardiola, Marqués de: house of, 317
Santa Fe de la Laguna, Mich.: hospital, 20
Santa María, García de: 135, 141
Santa María, J.M. de: 376
Santa María Atzompa, Oax.: pottery of, 387
Santa María del Río, S.L.P.: inlaid chests of, 380; rebozos of, 389
Santa Marta, Pue.: pottery of, 388
Santaella, Marcial de: 255
Santander, Antonio de: 252–253
Santander, Antonio de, The Younger: 252
Santander, José de: 252
Santiago,——(sculptor): 437
Santiago de Calimaya, Conde de: house of, 321
Santillán,——(engraver): 456
Santillana, Gómez de: 21
Santos, José de los: 175
Santos Castillo, José: 436
Santo Domingo, Dominican Republic: house of Diego Colón in, 15
sarapes: 388
sargueros: 132
Sayabedra, Bartolomé de: 175
Sáyago (Sállago), Antonio: 357
Sáyago, José de: 312
Sáyago, Juan de: 353
schools: 16th-cent., 20–23, 38, 90, 194;

Baroque, 186–187, 194, 307–311; typical Jesuit, 309; of engraving, 402; of the Academy of San Carlos, 402–404, 455; for Indian girls, projected, 419. SEE ALSO seminaries
screens: 120, 392
sculptors: Indian, in 16th cent., 23–24, 48–52; 53–59, 61–62, 158, 160; guild of, 53, 158–159; in 18th cent., 347
sculpture: pre-conquest, 4, 48, 50–52; 16th-cent., 48–62, 153–161; European in Mexico, 52–53; decorative, 53–59, 210, 347; in stone, 57–59, 61–62, 105, 160–161, 214; *tequitqui*, 61–62; in wood, 153–159, 213, 218–223, 347–353; popular, 347–350, 384, 386, 395–397; influence of Guatemaltecan, 350; in ivory, 363–364, 378, 379–380
——, provincial: Campeche, 357; Chiapas, 356–357; Oaxaca, 214; Puebla, 214, 218, 223–224, 354–355, 432–433, 436–437; Taxco, 160; Yucatán, 357
Secretaría de Educación Pública. SEE Mexico City, churches: La Encarnación
secular clergy: 109, 179–180
Segura, Andrés de. SEE San Miguel, Andrés de
Segura de la Frontera. SEE Tepeaca
Selma, Fernando: 404, 454
Selva Nevada, Marqués de: house of, 325
seminaries: 305, 309. SEE ALSO Tepotzotlán
Senteno, Joseph Francisco: 378
Sepúlveda, Martín de: 23
Serlio, Sebastiano: 361, 422
Serrano, Pedro: 159
Serrano, Roque: 173
Serrano y Peña, Diego: 175
Sessé, Martín de: 445, 454
Sevilla, José de: 175
Sevilla Olmedo, Juan de: 175
Sevillano, Alonso: 175
silk: 380, 381
silk industry: Cortés establishes silk culture, 70; ordinances, 70, 71; silk exchange established, 313; decline in 17th cent., 371. SEE ALSO textiles
sillones. SEE chairs
Silverio, Francisco: 456
silversmiths: Indian, European craftsmen, 63–64; division of guild, 65; lists of artisans, 66–67, 261, 367; guild ordinances, 162–163; chapel of silversmiths, Cathedral of Mexico, 163
silverwork: pre-conquest, 4, 63; 16th-cent., 46, 63–67; 163–167; lost-wax techniques, 64; prohibited in New Spain, 64; tax on, 162; 18th-cent., 364–367; popular, 389; Neoclassic, 449–451, 452; medals, 454–455
Simón, Antonio: 89
sisa: 222
solares: 14, 16
Soriano, Juan: 268
Sotomayor, Joaquín: 456

Sotuta, Yuc.: retable, parish church, 295

Spain: Mexican art in, 63, 74, 250, 258, 338n

spoons: 262

Spratling, William: 389

steel work: 264, 371

stools: 69, 168

Stradanus, Samuel: 456

stucco work: in Puebla, 106, 196, 203–205; Mudejar decoration, 127–128; around Texcoco, 128–201; in Oaxaca, 196–198, 205; in Jalisco, 199; San Francisco Acatepec, 206; Santa María Tonantzintla, 206; Sanctuary of Ocotlán, Tlaxcala, 206

Suárez,———(embroiderer): 372

Suárez, Josef: 374

Suárez, Juan José: 346

Suárez Calderón, Juan: 236

Sucre, Bolivia: *alfarje* ceilings in, 127

Suría, Tomás: with Gil, 402; engravings, 416, 454; friend of Fabris, 445; with Malaspina expedition, 455–456; life and work, 456

Suster, Adrián: 159

swords: 371

tabernacles: 214, 367

tables: 46, 69, 361, 363, 389

Tacuba, D.F.: coat of arms, 48–49; Pensil Mexicano, 331–332

Tajimaroa. SEE Ciudad Hidalgo

talavera: introduced, 173–176; 17th-cent., 264–267; as popular art, 387, 388

—, in architecture. SEE ceramics, *azulejos* in architecture

Talavera, Cristóbal de: 254

Talavera, Joseph de: 378

Talavera, Pablo José: 344

tapestry: 71, 72, 124

Tapia, Manuel Xavier: 345

Tapia, Miguel de: 378

Tapia, Pablo de: 71

Tarancón, Antonio de: 90

Tarralba, Leandro: 451

Taxco, Gro.: monastery (San Diego), 193; church of Santa Prisca y San Sebastián, 277, 296, 337, 352, 353, 363, 365–366, 368–369; houses, 330; silver work, 389

Tecali, Pue.: Franciscan monastery, 26, 87, 115, 116, 153–157; source of translucent stone, 214, 270

tecali: 214, 270, 426

Tecamachalco, Pue.: Franciscan monastery, 49, 118–119

Tecaxic, Mex.: pottery of, 388

Tecómitl, D.F.: Franciscan monastery, 32

tecpans: 16–17

Tecpatán, Chis.: Dominican monastery remains, 109

Tehuacán, Pue.: retable for Franciscan monastery, 137, 153; Calvario, 196; Hospital de San Juan de Dios, 312

Tehuantepec, Oax.: pottery of, 387

Tejada, Nicolás de: 132, 249

tejolotes: 385

Tejupan, Oax.: Sierra Codex, 46

Telchac, Yuc.: retable, parish church, 295

Temascalcingo, Mex.: pottery of, 388; rebozos of, 389

temascales, temaxcalli: 17, 384

Tembleque, Francisco de: 33

Tenancingo, Mex.: popular furniture of, 389; rebozos of, 389

Tenango del Valle (Teutenango), Mex.: plan of, 13

Tenochtitlán. SEE Mexico City

teocali: 3, 29

Teotihuacán, Mex.: window from, 50

Teotitlán del Valle, Oax.: sarapes of, 388

Tepalcingo, Mor.: murals, 445

Tepeaca (Segura de la Frontera), Pue.: *rollo,* 36; Franciscan monastery, 61, 82–83, 134, 157

Tepeapulco, Hgo.: Casas Viejas built by Indians from, 14; Franciscan monastery, 89

Tepeji del Río, Hgo.: Franciscan monastery, 88–89; pottery of, 388

Tepepan, D.F.: ceramic font, Franciscan monastery, 174

Tepetlaóztoc, Mex.: house of Gonzalo de Salazar built by Indians from, 14; Dominican monastery, 39, 44; Kingsborough Codex from, 46, 73

Tepeyanco (de las Flores), Tlax.: Franciscan monastery, parish church, 88

Teposcolula, Oax.: Dominican monastery, 29, 61, 105, 134, 363, 395

Tepotzotlán, Mex.: old church, 193; Seminary of San Martín (Museo Nacional del Virreinato), 127, 128, 210, 218, 277, 298–302, 334, 341, 353, 366, 369

Tepoztlán, Mor.: Dominican monastery, 29, 36–37, 44, 102

tequitqui: 61–62, 384

Terrazas, Pedro de: 175

Teutenango. SEE Tenango del Valle

Texcoco, Mex.: fountain, 34; Franciscan monastery, 55, 84; retable fragments, church of the Tercer Orden, 157; chapel of San Antonio de Padua, 201; chapel of the Molina de Flores, 201; church of La Concepción, 201; pottery of, 388; sarapes of, 388; rebozos of, 389

Texmelucan, Pue.: monastery of San Martín, 191–193; 370

textiles: pre–conquest, 4; 16th-cent., 70–72; Renaissance, 169–170; Baroque, 269; 18th-cent., 371–374; popular art, 371, 388–389. SEE ALSO silk industry; tapestry

Texupan. SEE Tejupan

tezontle: 118, 183, 193, 194, 266, 278, 282, 309, 310, 411

thuribles: 166

tianguis. SEE markets

Ticul, Yuc.: Franciscan monastery, 90

Tiepolo, Giambattista: 440, 443

Tilantongo, Oax.: coat-of-arms from, 49

tile, glazed. SEE ceramics, *azulejos* in architecture

Tinoco, Juan: 253

Tira de Tlatelolco. SEE codices

tirador d'oro: 65

Tiripitío, Mich.: Augustinian monastery, 73, 98

Titian (Tiziano Vecelli): 151, 254

Tizatlán, Tlax.: Franciscan monastery, 256

Tizimín, Yuc.: Franciscan monastery, 90

Tlacochahuaya, Oax.: retable by Arrúe, Dominican monastery, 137

Tlacolula, Oax.: Capilla del Santo Cristo, 171, 205

Tlahuac, D.F.: Dominican monastery, 128, 416

Tlahuelilpa, Hgo.: Franciscan monastery, 29

Tlaichiapan, Mex.: chapel, 201

Tlalmanalco, Mex.: Franciscan monastery, 29, 41, 55–57, 84, 116, 157, 213

Tlalnepantla, Mex.: Franciscan monastery, 86

Tlalpan, D.F.: garden in, 332

Tlalpujahua, Mich.: parish church, 295; houses, 330

Tlaltelolco. SEE Tlatelolco

Tlamaco, Hgo.: Augustinian monastery, 118

Tlapa, Gro.: pottery of, 388

Tlaquepaque, Jal.: parish church, 201; pottery of, 387

Tlaquiltenango, Mor.: *rollo de Cortés,* 36; Dominican monastery, 104

Tlatelolco: codex of the Tecpan de Tlatelolco, 16; Tira de Tlatelolco, 44

Tlaxcala, Tlax.: Hospital de San Lázaro, 17; Franciscan monastery, 23, 40, 53, 84–85, 127, 213; *rollo,* 36; *Introducción de la justicia española en Tlaxcala* (codex), 36, 46; Lienzo de Tlaxcala (codex), 44; Palacio de Gobierno, 121; Sanctuary of Ocotlán, 210, 254, 297–298, 346, 363, 366–367, 370, 391; parish church, 298; painting in, 345–346

Tlaxiaco, Oax.: Dominican monastery, 97, 106

Tlayacapan, Mor.: Augustinian monastery, 42, 93–98, 152

Tochimilco, Pue.: fountain, 34; Franciscan monastery, 86; panel from retable, 161

Tola y Salcedo, Luis: 429

Tolimán, Gro.: pottery of, 288

Tolsá, Manuel: life, 431–433; portrait of, 443; style in minor arts, 449

—, as architect: completes Cathedral of Mexico, 411–412; School of Mines, 412–413; houses, 413–414; Hospicio Cabañas, Guadalajara, 414; high altar, Cathedral of Puebla, 415; projects church of Loreto, 418

—, as sculptor: director of sculpture, Academy, 404, 432; equestrian statue of

Charles IV, 404, 416, 434–435; work, 433–435; *Virtues,* Cathedral of Mexico, 434; drawings for statues (?), 437
Toluca, Mex.: church of San Francisco, 353; pottery of, 388; popular furniture of, 389
tombac: 268
tombs: 36–37, 91, 102, 326, 409, 452
Tonalá, Jal.: pottery of, 387
tonalámatl: 87
Tonantzintla, Pue.: church of Santa María, 206, 372
Topoyanco de las Flores. SEE Tepeyanco
Toral, Francisco de: 111
Torino, José: 374
Toro, Pedro del: 99
Torquemada, Bartolomé de: 132
Torre, Diego de la: 175–176
Torre, Francisco de la: 90
Torre, Juan de la: 175
Torre, Nicolás de: 175
Torre de Cosio, Conde de la: house of, 324
Torrejón, Pedro de: 160, 224
Torres, Antonio de: 243
Torres, Francisco de: 456
Torres, Ignacio: 368
Torres, José Joaquín de: 305, 409
Torres, Vicente: 368
tortoise shell: 380, 451
Totimehuacán, Pue.: Franciscan monastery, 88; presbytery chairs, parish church, 363
Totolapan, Mor.: Augustinian monastery, 42, 55, 91
Toxoxhícuic, Miguel: 40
toys: as popular art, 389
Tresguerras, Francisco Eduardo de: opinions on Baroque sculpture, 355–356, 420; convent of Santa Teresa, Querétaro (?), 414, 424–425; life and work, 422–426; in Celaya, 423–424; in Querétaro, 424–425; in Guanajuato, 425; in San Luis Potosí, 425; in San Miguel de Allende, 425; documented as engraver, 456; mentioned, 354, 428, 429
triumphal arches. SEE ceremonies, of welcome
Troncoso, Baltasar: 456
Trujillo, Nicolás de: 173
trunks: 381
Tufino, Esteban: 169
Tula, Hgo.: Franciscan monastery, 69, 85–86, 134, 159
Tulancingo, Hgo.: *alfarje,* chapel of the Tercer Orden, 409; project to restore Franciscan church, 409
tule: 384, 389
Túmulo Imperial: 29–31, 115
Tunja, Colombia: *alfarjes* in, 127
Turkey: carpet from, 168
turquoise: pre-conquest use of, 4, 67
Tuxtla Gutiérrez, Chis.: stone lion in, 61, 384
Tzintzuntzan, Mich.: Franciscan monas-

tery, 29, 89, 119, 127; church of the Tercer Orden, 119; open chapel of hospital, 119; pottery of, 388
tzompantle: 52

Ucareo, Mich.: pre-fabrication of Augustinian monastery, 101
Ultra-Baroque style: 275. SEE ALSO Churrigueresque style
Uluapa, Marqués de: houses of, 319
Ureña brothers (wood carvers): 353
Uriarte, José María de: 446
urns: Neoclassic silver, 451
Urrola (Urriola), Gregorio de: 378
Urrutia, Antonio de: 429
Urrutia, José de: 407
Uruapan, Mich.: Franciscan monastery, 89; hospital chapel (La Guatapera), 89, 118, 119; lacquer of, 389
Utopia: 12
Utrera, Juan de: 101

Valadés, Diego de: 38
Valbás, Antonio: 378
Valderrama, Jerónimo: 46
Valdés Pérez, José: 368
Valencia, Juan de: 175
Valencia, Martín de: mural portrait of, 41
Valenciana, La. SEE Guanajuato, churches in
Valladolid, Mich. SEE Morelia
Valladolid, Yuc.: Franciscan monastery, 90, 295
Vallarta, Sebastián: 373–374
Vallarta, Vicente: 373–374
Valle de Bravo, Mex.: pottery of, 388
Valle de Oaxaca, Marqués del. SEE Cortés, Hernán
Valle de Orizaba, Conde del: houses of, 317, 326–327
Vallejo, Francisco Antonio: 338–339
Vanegas, Melchor: 172
Varela, Francisco: 175
Vargas, Luis de: 166
Vargas, Mariano: 415
Vargas, Miguel de: 175
Varia conmesuración: 449
vases: Neoclassic silver, 451
Vásquez, Alonso: 139, 143
Vásquez, José María: 404, 444
Vásquez, Mariano: 341
Vásquez de Coronado, Francisco: 47
vaults: earliest, 23; ribbed, 86, 89, 92, 102, 107, 115, 183; in Yucatán, 90; coffered, 91, 112; barrel, 92, 101, 102, 181; on crossing arches, 127, 210; groin, 181, 183; terrace, 183–184
Vayarta. SEE Vallarta
Vázquez, Nuño: 132
Vázquez, Pedro: 18, 62
Vecerra, Miguel: 378
Vedolla, Miguel Lucas: 256, 345
Vega, Antonio de: 170
Vega, Feliciano de la: 259, 269

Vega, Francisco de la: 444–445
Vega, Juan Cirilo de la: 368
Vega, Pedro de la: 444
Vega, Salvador de la: 268, 269, 368, 434
Vega Lagarto, Luis de la. SEE Lagarto, Luis de la Vega
Vega y Córdoba, Antonio de: 174
Velasco, Luis de: founds University of Mexico, 21; tomb in Santo Domingo, 36; mentioned, 5, 20, 132, 256
Velasco y Buitrón, José: 429
Velásquez, Antonio. SEE González Velásquez, José Antonio
Velásquez, Benito: 344
Velásquez, Diego: 378
Velásquez de la Cadena, Francisco: 374
velón: of brass, 368
velvet: 71, 170, 269
Venadita, Juan Ruiz de Apodaca: portrait of, 446
Ventura Arnáez, José: 339
Veracruz, Alonso de la: 21
Veracruz, Ver.: laid out by García Bravo, 9, 13; Cabildo, 16; houses, 330–331; map of (1800), 407
verges: silver, 66, 164
Vertavillo, Diego de: 91
vestments: gremial of Bishop Zumárraga, 70, 371; Renaissance, 170; for images, 258–259, 269; 17th-cent., 269; 18th-cent., 371–372
Vicente (embroiderer): 373
Vidales, Francisco: 170
Vielma, Juan Ignacio: 369
Vigas, Francisco de: 175
Vignola, Jacopo Barozzio: 422
Villa de Guadalupe. SEE Villa Madero
Villa Madero (de Guadalupe), D.F.: chapel of El Pocito, 282, 369, 378; treasure, sanctuary of Guadalupe, 365, 367; popular furniture of, 389; popular painting of, 392
Villa Obregón (San Ángel), D.F.: Carmelite monastery, 191, 378; portal from Hospital Real de Indias, 311n; Casa del Risco, 332
Villa Rica de la Veracruz. SEE Veracruz
Villafaña, Antonio: 426
Villafañe, Alonso de: 250
Villalobos, Juan de: 254, 256
Villalpando, Cristóbal de: life and work, 235, 238–241; influence on Rodríguez brothers, 333; mentioned, 335
Villalpando, Francisco de (painter): 241
Villalpando, Francisco de (Franciscan): 90
Villalpando, Luis de: 90
Villamanrique, Álvaro Manrique de Zúñiga, Marqués de: 158, 249
Villanueva, Diego de la Cruz: 176
Villard, Antoine: 413
Villardel, Damián de: 175
Villardel, Sebastián de: 175
Villasana, Alonso de: 137
Villasana, Gregorio de: 249

Villavicencio, Manuel: 456
Villegas, —— (engraver): 456
Villegas, José de: 234
Villegas Cora, José, The Elder: 354, 437
Villegas Cora, José, The Younger: 355, 437
Vitruvius: cited by Tresguerras, 355, 422
Vivero, Rodrigo de, Conde del Valle de Orizaba: 317
Vizarrón y Eguiarreta, Juan Antonio de: 305, 366
Vos, Martín de: 143, 152

wafer irons: 370
wall belfries: SEE *espadañas*
wardrobes: 361
wash basins: 367
weapons: 371
weathervanes: 202, 369–370
weavers: 70, 71, 170, 269, 371
weaving: 4, 71, 170, 371, 388–389. SEE ALSO textiles
wiredrawers: 65, 261
wood carvers: 158
wood cuts: 452–453
writing cases: 168, 262

Xicoténcatl, palace of: 256

Ximénez (sculptors): 224
Ximénez, Vicente: 357
Xinmámal, Francisco: 40
Xirón, Nicolás: 436
Xochimilco, D.F.: chapel of El Rosario, 128; Franciscan monastery, 89, 118, 153, 222
Xochitótotl, Luis: 40
Xóchmitl, Pedro: 40
Xocotepec, Jal.: sarapes of, 388
Xuárez, Matías. SEE Juárez, Matías
Xuárez, Tomás. SEE Juárez, Tomás

Yamas, Pedro: 357
Yanhuitlán, Oax.: Dominican monastery, 36, 44, 55, 106–107, 135, 218; Yanhuitlán Codex, 47
Yautepec, Mor.: open chapel, Dominican monastery, 29, 102
Yecapixtla, Mor.: Augustinian monastery, 42, 55, 59, 61, 91, 118
Yohualahuach, Miguel: 40
Yuriria (Yuririapúndaro), Gto.: Augustinian monastery, 42, 98–99, 116, 391

Zacapu, Mich.: Franciscan monastery, 89, 119

Zacatecas, Zac.: Colegio de Guadalupe (Museo de Guadalupe), 74, 247; Cathedral of, 210, 370; church of Santo Domingo, 247; houses, 330
Zacatlán (de las Manzanas), Pue.: Franciscan monastery, 24, 86, 115
Zacualpan de Amilpas, Mor.: Augustinian monastery, 42, 91
zaguán: 189, 315
Zamora, José: 374
Zápori, —— (architect, wood carver): 288, 356
Zapata, Cerón: portrait sculpture of, 218
Zárate, Antonio Alonso de: 234
Zavala, Miguel de: 374
Zendejas, Lorenzo: 446
Zendejas, Miguel Jerónimo: 343–344, 346
Zenón, Roque: 269, 372
Zepeda, Juan de: 195
Zimapán, Hgo.: Caja Real, 305
Zinacantepec, Mex.: baptismal font, Franciscan monastery, 58
Zizantum, Yuc.: Franciscan monastery, 90
Zumárraga, Juan de: 18, 70
Zumaya, Francisco de: 135–136, 141
Zumaya, Martín de: 141